BRITAIN BEGINS

BRITAIN BEGINS

BARRY CUNLIFFE

OXFORD
UNIVERSITY PRESS

OXFORD
UNIVERSITY PRESS

Great Clarendon Street, Oxford OX2 6DP

Oxford University Press is a department of the University of Oxford.
It furthers the University's objective of excellence in research, scholarship,
and education by publishing worldwide. Oxford is a registered trade mark of
Oxford University Press in the UK and in certain other countries

First Edition published in 2013

Impression: 2

British Library Cataloguing in Publication Data

Data available

Library of Congress Cataloging in Publication Data

Data available

ISBN 978–0–19–960933–8

Typeset by Sparks—www.sparkspublishing.com
Printed in Italy by L.E.G.O. S.p.A.

PREFACE

I T is part of the human condition that we feel the need to visualize a past. The enormous popularity of family history is a reflection of this. Centuries ago, before parish records, census returns, and computerized databases, it was the family Bible, passed from one generation to the next, accreting the family names as it travelled through time, that served as a record of the passing generations. For those who could afford it, family tombs provided a more visible way of proclaiming ancestry. Go back even further, into the early second millennium BC, and the time-marks recording the generations were visible for all to see in the sinuous rows of tumuli standing sombre against the skyline. An elder at the time would have been able to use the different shapes, sizes, and positions of these burial mounds to instruct the young about the succession of tribal ancestors and their heroic deeds.

We root ourselves in ancestors and we are curious about our origins. So it has always been. If hard information is lacking, imagination takes over and myths are created. All societies relish a good origin myth. For the early Greeks living between mountains and the Aegean like 'frogs around a pond', Ocean featured large in their imaginings. One particularly satisfying myth presented the beginning of the world in terms of the coupling of Thetis, goddess of freshwater rivers, with the salty Oceanus. From their union all things flowed. The barbarian Celts had different ideas. They believed they were descended from Father Dis (Dis Pater), a god of the dead who resided in the west, where the sun set. In the Irish tradition he is Donn, 'the Dark One', who lives on a rocky island off the south-west coast of Ireland, where all his descendants are made welcome when they die. For the Christians, whose early myths were those of desert peoples, perfection and happiness lay in a lush, well-watered garden—so it was that the imagery of the Garden of Eden became the dominant myth.

Origin myths are the product of lively imaginations vividly conscious of the world around them but unrestrained by anything as dull as reality. Passed down from generation to generation, they provide reassurance—fixed points in the flux and seeming chaos of everyday life—offering values and constraints to guide moral behaviour. But they also have a flexibility in the retelling, shifting shape as society changes and becoming more sophisticated in emphasis the better to serve the political imperatives of the changing times.

As knowledge increases, and accurate observation of the real world takes hold, a dialogue begins and confrontation inevitably results. Old myths recede and new myths are created embracing the new-found evidence. These in turn are modified and replaced as more data become available, and so the process begins to take on the mantle of scientific investigation, with observations leading to hypotheses that can be tested, to be accepted, modified, or rejected. In this way we progress from myth towards an understanding of the past as it really was. But the emphasis here must be on the word 'towards' since our vision of the past is always changing. The cherished beliefs of today, so painstakingly constructed and rigorously checked, will inevitably have to be modified tomorrow.

This book attempts to do two things: first, to give an account of how past writers have tried to understand the peoples of these islands and where they have come from, and then to offer a narrative of the first 12,000 years or so of the British and Irish based on current understandings. Any such narrative must, of course, be highly selective. This is not an archaeology of early Britain and Ireland. Others have given excellent up-to-date accounts, and no doubt more will follow in the years to come, attempting to keep up with the increasing flood of new data. The detritus of the past is eternally fascinating (and I have spent long years digging it up and trying to make some sense of it). But in this narrative the artefacts and, to some extent, the monuments are made to recede into the background so that we can better focus on the people who fashioned and used them. These people were driven by their inner chemistry to behave in particular ways: they were inquisitive, acquisitive, and aggressive, and they created behavioural systems to maintain an equilibrium, albeit unstable, so that different societies could live in comparative harmony. They were also conditioned by the environment in which they lived—an archipelago of islands dominated by the sea on the fringes of the European continent. The restless nature of humankind and the ever-present sea created a population for which mobility was a defining characteristic. Mobility, connectivity, and the sea are the themes that thread through this narrative.

An archaeologist writing of the past must be constantly aware that the past is, in truth, unknowable. The best we can do is to offer approximations based on the fragments of hard evidence that we have to hand, ever conscious that we are interpreters. Like the myth-makers of the distant past, we are creating stories about our origins and ancestors conditioned by the world in which we live.

For an archaeologist these are exciting times. The amount of new data coming daily from excavations is huge, while the analytical techniques used to study them are constantly being improved. Add to this stable isotope studies of human remains and input from geneticists and our understanding of the human past changes exponentially. What is offered here is a single perspective crystallized at a particular moment—next year the story will have changed. Herein lies the excitement of the subject.

B.C.
Oxford
December 2011

CONTENTS

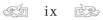

LIST OF ABBREVIATIONS
OF CLASSICAL WORKS

Caesar, *B Civ.*	Caesar, *Bellum Civile*
Caesar, *B Gall.*	Caesar, *Bellum Gallicum*
Pliny, *HN*	Pliny, *Naturalis Historia*

1

In the Beginning

MYTHS AND ANCESTORS

To the early classical authors trying to conceptualize the fringes of the world from the comforts of the Mediterranean, the distant offshore islands of Britain were places of mystery and of promise. Set far out into the surrounding ocean, they were liminal places—places where normal rules held no sway, places where anything could happen.

By the fifth century BC rumours of the far west had begun to circulate in the Mediterranean. The Greek historian Herodotus, writing at this time, had heard tell of Atlantic islands known as the Cassiterides where the all-important tin was to be had. But Herodotus was a careful scholar and felt bound to tell us that he had no supporting evidence—it was merely hearsay that he was reporting. Yet the stories persisted and it became widely held that the Cassiterides were part of the Britannic Isles. Such a view may well have lain behind the Roman belief that Britain was rich in metals and was thus worthy of conquest. But in the popular imagination Britain was always seen as a place of mysteries—of mists with creatures half-man and half-beast emerging from the gloom to strike fear into the hearts of civilized beings. To Julius Caesar, who had spent some months on the main island, it was the place where Druidism was believed to have originated, and he advised that those who wanted to study the religion should make a journey to seek out the ancient wisdoms of the isles.

Caesar's brief expeditions to the south-east of Britain in 55 and 54 BC, and the conquest initiated in AD 43 by Claudius, brought Britain firmly into the realms of the known world. The indigenous people could be observed first hand, their customs described, and their origins speculated about. The Roman historian Cornelius Tacitus, writing at the end of the first century AD, had the great advantage that his father-in-law, Julius Agricola, had served in Britain in the early 60s and had been governor of the island from AD 78 to AD 84, during which time he had campaigned widely in the north, his troops exploring as far into the unknown as the Orkney Islands. Tacitus was, no doubt, well informed by the retired governor when he came to write his famous book *Agricola*, and gave a glowing account of the general's activities in the island.

Early on in his narrative Tacitus presents an account of the land and the people, prefacing it, a little immodestly perhaps, 'Where my predecessors relied on graces and style to make their guesswork sound attractive, I shall offer ascertained fact.' In a brief introduction to the nature of the island, he shows a fascination with the ocean: 'nowhere does the sea hold wider sway: it carries to and fro in its motion a mass of tidal currents and in its ebb and flow it does not stop at the coast but penetrates deep inland' (*Agricola* 10). He then moves on to consider the local population: 'Who the first inhabitants of Britain were, whether natives or immigrants, is open to question: one must remember we are dealing with barbarians.' After this brilliant one-liner so typical of the man he cannot resist offering a few speculations of his own:

> But their physical characteristics vary, and the variation is suggestive. The reddish hair and large limbs of the Caledonians proclaim a German origin; the swarthy faces of the Silures, the tendency of the hair to curl and the fact that Spain lies opposite, all lead one to believe that Spaniards crossed in ancient times and occupied that part of the country. The people nearest to the Gauls likewise resemble them. It may be that they still show the effect of a common origin; or perhaps it is climatic conditions that have produced this physical type in lands that converge so closely from north to south. On the whole, however, it seems likely that Gauls settled on the island lying so close to their shores. In both countries you find the same ritual and religious beliefs. There is no great difference in their language ...
>
> (*Agricola* 11)

It is a remarkable piece of writing, rigorous in its presentation but full of insights. Here he is putting forward hypotheses based on observation and in doing so is providing a vision that was to be reiterated from time to time until the nineteenth century. Yet after this burst of objectivity he cannot resist the temptation to moralize, ending the paragraph with a comparison of the hardy, spirited Britons and the neighbouring Gauls, for many generations under Roman rule, 'enervated by protracted peace'. The idea of the noble savage and the decadent Roman world is never far from his critical gaze.

Ninety years before Claudius set in train the conquest of the island, Caesar had made two brief incursions into the south-east of the country, fighting his way through Kent and into Essex and Hertfordshire, accepting the submission of a number of local tribes as he went. His war commentaries *Bellum Gallicum* ('The Gallic War') are enlivened with brief accounts of the peoples he encountered. He is less concerned with origins than Tacitus but offers one piece of information:

> The interior of Britain is inhabited by people who claim, on the strength of their own tradition, to be indigenous. The coastal areas are inhabited by invaders who crossed from Belgium for the sake of plunder and then, when the fighting was over, settled there and began to work the land; these people have almost all kept the names of the tribes from which they originated. The population is extremely large.
>
> (*B Gall.* 5.12)

After describing the shape and size of the island, Caesar goes on to say that the most civilized of the Britons live in Kent and follow a lifestyle much like that of the Gauls, adding that

> All the Britons dye their bodies with woad, which produces a blue colour and gives them a wild appearance in battle. They wear their hair long; every other part of their body, except for the upper lip, they shave.
>
> (*B Gall.* 5.14)

This single account was avidly seized upon by commentators in the sixteenth century, at a time when the ancient Britons were coming in for renewed attention, to provide the first visual representations of imagined Britons (p.16).

Much of what Caesar and Tacitus had to say of the Britons was based on contemporary observation, in Caesar's case first hand, but the classical world already had some knowledge of these remote offshore islands. The earliest account comes from an ancient source quoted in the *Ora Maritima* ('Sea-Coasts'), a Roman poem of the fourth century AD which, in rather florid language, describes the sea-route from Massalia (Marseille) along the coast of Iberia and through the Strait of Gibraltar into the Atlantic seaways. The individual sources used in the poem are not properly attributed, but some scholars believe that the author, Avienus, made use of a Greek periplus (a navigation manual) from as early as the sixth century BC. There is much confusion and contortion in the way that the sources are spliced together, but the line relevant to our discussion is clear enough: 'There is a two-day journey for a ship to the Holy Island—thus the ancients called it. This island, large in extent of the land, lies between the waves. The race of the Hierni inhabits it far and wide. Again, the island of the Albiones lies near . . .' (*Ora Maritima*, line 108). The name Holy Island is probably the creation of a scribe confusing the native name of Ireland, Hiweros, with the Greek *hieros*, meaning 'sacred'. In the Celtic language 'Iweros' means the 'fat', or fertile, land. The neighbouring island of Albion, in the context used here, is Britain. Why Britain has two names is explained by the Elder Pliny in the first century BC when he refers to 'Britannia Island, famed in Greek and in our own records . . . Albion was its own name when all were called the Britannias.' The implication would seem to be that Pliny knew the whole cluster of islands as the Britannias, while the main island was known by the locals as Albion: he writes in the past tense, suggesting that the name was ancient.

While Avienus certainly made use of an ancient periplus to describe the journey from Massalia to the Tagus estuary, it remains a possibility that the more northerly references to Britain and Ireland come from another source. One contender for this is the work of the Greek explorer Pytheas, who about 320 BC journeyed overland from his native Massalia to the Atlantic and then by sea northward to Armorica (Brittany) and to Britain, which he appears to have circumnavigated before returning home to record his observations in a written text, *On the Ocean*. The book no longer survives, but it was widely read at the time and was used by later writers as a source for their own accounts of the Outer Ocean and its peoples.

It is quite probable that the description of Britain given by the Greek writer Diodorus Siculus in the first century BC derives wholly or largely from Pytheas. What is of particular interest is that he calls the island 'Pretannia' (Greek 'Prettanikē'), that is 'the island of the Pretani, or Priteni'. 'Pretani' is a Celtic word that probably means 'the painted ones' or 'the tattooed folk', referring to body decoration—a reminder of Caesar's observations of woad-painted barbarians. In all probability the word 'Pretani' is an ethnonym (the name by which the people knew themselves), but it remains an outside possibility that it was their continental neighbours who described them thus to the Greek explorers.

If we are correct in ascribing the information in Diodorus' description to Pytheas, then the inhabitants of Albion were known as Pretani as early as the fourth century BC. The name Pretannia features in the writings of Strabo at the beginning of the first century AD, but now the alternative spelling 'Britannia' makes an appearance as well. It was as Britannia that the island was known to the Romans throughout the period of occupation, and so it has remained. The P-spelling, however, continued in parts of

Celtic-speaking Britain, appearing in the name Picti, used for the indigenous people north of the Antonine Wall. The Celtic spelling is still used in Welsh, where the name for Britain is Prydain.

After the period of initial contact in the first century AD, the classical authors paid little attention to the ethnicity of the British other than mentioning, with evident distaste, the behaviour of some of the remote tribes they encountered in the north—the indigenous Picti, or the Scotti and Attacotti who came as raiders from Ireland. After all, the bulk of the population had settled down as Roman subjects and citizens; the rest were simply barbarians.

A View from Within

With the spread of Christianity, with its own very explicit set of origin myths, the educated elite of Britain needed to exercise an imaginative agility to blend the traditions surrounding their own origins with the biblical stories of the Creation and the Flood. In Genesis the Bible presented a strong narrative, complete with vividly drawn characters, covering the first chapter of human existence up to the time of the Flood. The precise ages given for the leading individual enabled the numerate clergy to calculate that this—the First Age of the World, as they called it—lasted 2,242 years. With the Flood the population was reduced to Noah and his family, and so the Second Age began. Noah, we are told, had three sons, who, after the waters had subsided, set out with their wives to populate the world, Shem to Asia, Ham to Africa, and Japheth to Europe. Leaving aside the slight difficulties of how all this was achieved, the story had a comforting simplicity and provided a vivid first act for the history of the world, its authority guaranteed. All that the British scholars had to do was to link Japheth with their own local origin myth.

The other good story that was widely known among the educated classes was the saga of the Trojan War and the flight of Aeneas to the west. In the story told by Virgil, Aeneas, son of Anchises and the goddess Venus, fled from the flames of Troy and, after a brief dalliance in Carthage, landed on the Italian coast in Latinum, where he married the king's daughter Lavinia and founded the town of Lavinium. Several generations later, after the paternal intervention of the god Mars, the twins Romulus and Remus were born. An act of fratricide left Romulus triumphant and he proceeded to found Rome. The legend, redolent with love, rape, treachery, and murder, appealed to the Roman audience, the more so after it was retold in the elegant verses of Virgil. It provided Rome with a 'history' rooted deep in the classical tradition, legitimizing Rome's claim to world leadership. Moreover, it was a history told in human terms with which it was easy for the citizen in the street to empathize.

For the Christian clergy who emerged as the intellectual elite in Britain after the collapse of Roman rule early in the fifth century, the challenge was to create a historical narrative that brought local beliefs about the origin of the British into line with the biblical tradition while at the same time endowing British history with a nobility that could compete with other emerging European states. An added challenge was to build into that history the events of the recent past that had seen the Picti of the far north join with the Scotti of Ireland in a series of raids on the province of Britannia in the late fourth century. Later, in the fifth century, Germanic peoples from the Continent had crossed the North Sea to settle in the south of the island, while the Scotti had begun to extend into the north-west of the island—the region that later became known as Scotland. To a historian looking back on these two centuries the mobility of populations was an ever-present reality: it provided a model for constructing a more distant past.

Two Christian scholars rose to the occasion: Bede, whose famous *Ecclesiastical History of the English People* (*Historia Ecclesiastica Gentis Anglorum*) was completed in AD 731, and Nennius, who created a compendium of texts relating to British history around AD 800 or soon after. The two works could not have been more different.

Bede had been sent by his parents at the age of 7 to the monastery of St Peter at Wearmouth in Northumbria, later transferring to the monastery of St Paul at Jarrow, where he spent the rest of his life in devotion and scholarship. His *History* was, as its full title implies, focused on the English Church, but the story is framed within the broader narrative of English history, written in a clear and vigorous style, colourful in its detail. On the origins of the British he is all too brief. There are presently, he says, four nations living on the island, English, British, Scots, and Picts. The indigenous people were the Britons, 'who, according to tradition, crossed into Britain from Armorica'. Later, Picti from Scythia (probably meaning north-western Europe) sailed first to Ireland and then were directed by the locals to continue to Britain to settle in the north of the island. Later still, the Scotti from northern Ireland settled in the western parts of northern Britain; and finally the Angles, Saxons, and Jutes from across the North Sea colonized the south of the country. What is remarkable in Bede's neat and succinct narrative is that there is no attempt to engage with origin myths. He is content to present a brief overview, largely free from speculation, and then move on to firmer ground.

The work of Nennius, *Historia Brittonum*, written in the early ninth century, was a more eclectic composition. Nennius was a Welsh monk working in north Wales. His method was highly original. Instead of attempting to compose a continuous narrative, he presented a compilation of extracts culled from all the sources at his disposal: in his own words, 'I have . . . made a heap of all that I have found, both from the

Annals of the Romans and from the Chronicles of the Holy Fathers and from the writings of the Irish and the English, and out of the tradition of our elders.' These extracts are laid out in broadly defined themes, allowing us to compare the different sources and to see for the first time the early Christian scholars grappling with the problem of British origins.

Three traditions are presented. The first is the Roman tradition, which begins with Aeneas fleeing from Troy. The novel element introduced here is the creation of a new character, Britto, a grandson to Aeneas, who accidentally killed his father and was driven from Italy. After spending time in Gaul, he eventually came to Britain, which was of course named after him, and 'filled it with his race'. By this neat addition, the British are provided with a respectable pedigree equal to that of the Romans themselves.

The second tradition is more elaborate. It comes, says Nennius, 'from old books of our elders'. It begins with Alanus 'of the race of Japheth', who was the first man to enter Europe. He had three sons, who between them produced twelve sons, each of whom founded one of the nations of Europe. One of these sons was Britto. Thus, in this pleasingly simple model, the British can be traced back directly to Noah and then to Adam.

The third tradition is an elaboration offering a direct line of descent from Japheth, through Aeneas, to a new character, Brutus, the founder of the British nation. This ingenious conflation, no doubt the product of the lively imagination of an unnamed British cleric, offers all things to all men: the British are now firmly placed in the European family that springs from Noah while being of the same stock as the founder of Rome and thus directly connected to a major event in world history, the fall of Troy. The tradition of Brutus as the father of the British people was compellingly satisfying. It was a story that was to be told and retold with many embellishments for almost a millennium. Even as late as the sixteenth century, as we shall see, it was still being vigorously championed, though in an academic world becoming increasingly sceptical. We shall return to Brutus again in a moment.

Nennius also had access to several traditions relating to the peopling of Ireland. The most extensive tells of repeated incursions from Spain. The first group was wiped out by plague. The second remained many years but eventually returned home. Of the third group, after various mishaps, only one ship-load survived and it was their descendants who peopled the island. A separate tradition—ascribed by Nennius specifically to Irish scholars—traces the ancestry of the Spaniards who came to Ireland back to the Egyptians. A helpful gloss added by a later scribe reminds the reader that 'there is . . . nothing certain about the history of the origins of the Irish'. Clearly, he was not impressed by what he was copying!

The 'Irish scholars' whom Nennius mentions would have had at their disposal oral traditions of some antiquity, dating from long before the Christian era. These they would have transcribed and edited, making them fit for a Christian readership. The earliest extant text is the *Lebor Gabála Érenn*, or *Book of Invasions of Ireland*, compiled in the eleventh century from a collection of earlier poems of the kind that would have been available to Nennius. The result is a confusing confection of myths, traditions, and inventions, wildly anachronistic but designed to give comfort and reassurance by linking Irish origins to the biblical story, so distancing it from its pagan reality. Simply summarized, Ireland was believed to have been colonized in a series of invasions by the descendants of Japheth. 'From Magog, son of Japheth are descended the people who came to Ireland before the Gaels.' And thus they are listed: Partholón, Nemed, and Nemed's descendants—'Gáileóin and Fir Domnann and Fir Bolg and Tuatha de Danann'. The Fir Bolg were defeated and driven into the west by the Tuatha de Danann ('the People of the Goddess Danu'). Then come the sons of Míl from Spain, whose descendants the Gaels thereafter became the dominant race on the island.

The recurring reference to Spain as the origin of the Irish invaders may simply be a mistaken belief on the part of the monks who composed the text that the Latin name for Ireland, Hibernia, was derived from 'Iberia'. However, given the archaeological evidence, which demonstrates long-term contacts along the Atlantic seaways in the prehistoric period, it may just be that the early oral traditions used by the monks preserved echoes of folk memories going back far in time. While folk traditions cannot be taken as evidence for past events, they should not be dismissed as entirely irrelevant.

The Story of Brutus Retold

The sketchy story of Brutus and his journey to Britain continued to be told, but it was bereft of detail and a yawning gap remained in the history of the country from the arrival of Brutus until the classical sources began to take up the narrative around the time of Julius Caesar's intervention. When Henry of Huntingdon wrote his history of Britain in the early twelfth century, he could find nothing about the early inhabitants and was forced to begin this story with the Romans. Imagine, then, the surprise and delight of the small educated elite when, around 1135, a cleric living in Oxford published a complete history of the British ruling dynasty from Brutus, grandson of Aeneas, to Cadwallader, the last historically attested British king, who abandoned Britain to the Saxons in the seventh century. The cleric was Geoffrey of Monmouth and his book, *Historia Regnum Britanniae* (translated as *History of the Kings of Britain*).

Geoffrey was of Welsh birth and may have come from Caerleon-on-Usk, which he refers to frequently and evidently knew well. By the 1120s he was resident in Oxford, quite possibly serving as a canon at the secular college of St George, run by Augustinian canons on the island of Osney just west of the city. It was here that he wrote his *Historia*. Later, in 1151, he became bishop elect of St Asaph in Flintshire, though he seems not to have taken up residence, spending his last four years in London, where he died in 1155.

Historia Regnum Britanniae is a detailed account of British 'history' packed with stories that had never before been heard. How did Geoffrey learn all of this? His answer was simply that his friend Walter, the archdeacon of Oxford, gave him 'a certain very ancient book written in the British language' which he had brought from 'outside the country' (*ex Britannia*). Geoffrey claims that he translated this text into straightforward Latin, making a précis of it and adding sections of his own, to create the *Historia*. Where the ancient book is supposed to have come from is not entirely clear. While it could have been Wales, Brittany is a more likely place of origin. But the outstanding, and unanswerable, question is, did such a book ever exist? There is no trace of it either physically or as a source used by others. It could be, as many have suggested, that Geoffrey simply made up the entire history, embroidering around the tales and speculations contained in texts such as Gildas and Nennius (sources which he did have to hand) a complete fabrication of his own. That said, there will always be the sneaking possibility that an old Breton text really did sit on Geoffrey's desk as he wrote—we shall never know for sure.

Geoffrey was not without his critics. The great Welsh historian Giraldus Cambrensis (1146–1220), although he wanted to believe the British history, wondered why there was no corroboration from other sources. William of Newburgh, writing about 1190 in his *Historia Rerum Anglicarum*, was more forthright: 'It is quite clear that everything this man wrote about Arthur and his successors, or indeed about his predecessors from Vortigern onwards, was made up, partly by himself and partly by others either from an inordinate love of lying or for the sake of pleasing the Britons.' But these were lone voices. Geoffrey's *Historia* conveniently filled a great gap in British history. It told stories about times past that were vivid and compelling, and it provided a continuous narrative peopled with characters that were both human in their behaviour and noble in their aspirations—characters one could be proud to claim as ancestors. In other words, Geoffrey had provided a British history that everyone wanted to believe in. It is hardly surprising that the *Historia* was still being championed 400 years later.

Geoffrey begins with a greatly embellished version of the Brutus myth, already outlined 300 years earlier by Nennius. After spending time in Gaul sacking

Aquitaine and fighting a major battle at Tours, Brutus decides to sail to the island of Albion, eventually landing at Totnes at the time when Eli was high priest (*c*.1170 BC). He found the island uninhabited 'except for a few giants'. 'Brutus then called the island Britain from his own name, and his companions he called Britons . . . A little later the language of the people, which had up to then been known as Trojan or Crooked Greek, was called British . . .'. After killing all the giants Brutus divided up his kingdom and built his capital, Troia Nova, on the River Thames. This soon became known as Trinovantum but was later renamed Kaerlud by King Lud: thus it became London.

And so the story continues with a succession of kings and other colourful characters: Bladud, who built Bath; King Lear and his three daughters; Brennus, who campaigned through Gaul and besieged Rome; and King Lud and his brother Cassivellaunus, bringing us up to the time of the invasion of Julius Caesar. The Roman interlude is covered in some detail, mentioning a number of real historical figures, before the narrative returns again to a more shadowy pseudo-history with King Coel of Colchester.

The coming of the Saxons and the British resistance provide the structure of the latter part of the book, featuring the story of King Arthur, told in extravagant and loving detail. The story ends with the Britons being driven into Wales, some fleeing across the seas to Armorica (which becomes Brittany). The Saxons take possession of much of the island, but a mysterious voice tells Cadwallader, the last of the British kings, that one day the Britons will return to reclaim their lost kingdom.

It is evident that, leaving aside the 'very ancient book', Geoffrey had access to a wide range of sources. His Roman episodes are informed by a number of classical texts, while for the post-Roman period he was heavily reliant on Gildas, Bede, and Nennius, but even in these sections there is much in his extended presentation that is original and must have come either from sources now lost or from his own creative imagination. For the pre-Roman period he uses the sketch of the Brutus story provided by Nennius, again filling out the narrative, but the succession of personalities and events covering the thousand years between Brutus and Cassivellaunus (who appears in Caesar's *Commentaries*) is entirely novel. Again we are forced back to the question, how much did he invent? For our purposes it does not much matter. What is important is that in the early twelfth century Britain had been provided with a highly readable, even racy, narrative 'history'. It was a strong story, vividly told, with comforting authority and assurance. Britain now had a noble past—a past which the emerging nation would find inspiring. The popularity of the *Historia* is reflected in the fact that nearly 200 manuscript copies survive today.

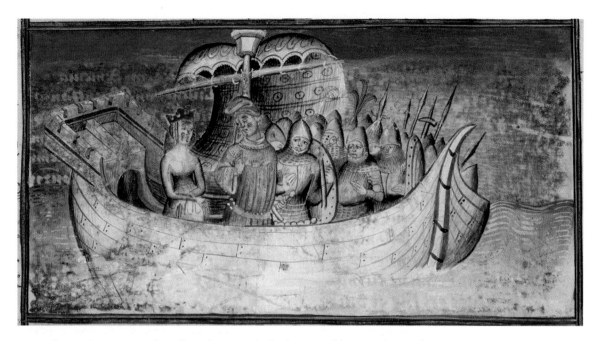

1.1 An illustrated manuscript of Geoffrey of Monmouth's book *History of the Kings of Britain* showing Brutus the founder of the British setting sail for the island

The *Historia* was more than just a good story—it was a text that had a strong emotional and political appeal. King Arthur had battled to protect the Britons of Britain and Brittany from oppression and had promised to return to save them. It was hardly surprising, then, that the Bretons should successfully petition that the heir to the Angevin empire, Henry II's grandson, should be called Arthur. Enthusiasm for the Arthurian romance grew apace. A few years later what were claimed to be the bodies of Arthur and Guinevere were exhumed at Glastonbury and Richard I could present what purported to be Arthur's sword, Excalibur, to Tancred of Sicily. Throughout the Middle Ages the *Historia Regnum Britanniae* continued to be regarded as a standard work of reference even though doubts were occasionally expressed about the earlier sections. John Rous, writing in the early fifteenth century, felt the need for an explanation of how there could have been giants in Albion before the arrival of Brutus, but, at about the same time, John Whethamstede, abbot of St Albans, rejected the story of Brutus altogether. Whethamstede's criticisms were probably shared by a growing number of scholars, but the accession of Henry Tudor to the British throne in 1485 gave the *Historia* a new lease of life. Henry was a Welshman and, as his supporters were keen to point out, his 'conquest' of England fulfilled the prophecy made to the last king of the Britons, Cadwallader, that his successor would once again rule the whole of Britain. A year after the battle of Bosworth (1485) the new king, Henry VII, named his son and heir Arthur, much to the delight of the Welsh.

The popularity of the *Historia* among the Tudors and their supporters made scholars think twice about offering criticism of its validity. Indeed, some decided to embellish the story still further. One such was Hector Boece (Boethius; 1465–1536), a Scotsman whose *Scotorum Historiae a Prima Gentis Origine* was published in 1527. His contribution was to introduce Scota, daughter of a pharaoh and a Greek prince, as the founder of the Scots, expanding on a story recorded by Nennius. He also revised the exploits of Arthur to the benefit of the Scots. But it was the Englishman John Bale (1495–1563), bishop of Ossory, who was to offer the most far-reaching amplification of Geoffrey's work in his book *Illustrium Maioris Britanniae*, published in 1548. While accepting the Brutus story and what followed, Bale was concerned to give Britain a pre-Brutus history, which he did by constructing two family trees, beginning with Noah. The first began with Noah's son Japheth, whose son Samothes became the first king of the Gauls and of Britain a thousand years before Brutus. It was the successors of Samothes who were responsible for introducing a range of skills into the island: astronomy, political science, urban design, philosophy, Druidism, music, and poetry. A second, and separate, dynasty sprang from Noah's evil son, Ham: it included Osiris and, eventually, Neptune, whose liaison with Amphitrite produced the giant Albion. Albion took over the island, giving it his own name and instigating a terrible age of increasing barbarism which lasted for five centuries, ending only with the landing of Brutus. Bale's imaginative creations satisfied the concerns of those who were expressing doubts about the giants; it also neatly linked the British narrative more firmly to the familiar biblical tradition.

But the critics of the *Historia* were by now becoming vocal. The most devastating attack came in 1521 from the pen of the clergyman–scholar John Major (1489–1550). In his modest and good-humoured book *Historia Maioris Britanniae* he demolished the entire edifice of Brutus, Scotia, and the like, though he was entirely happy to support the Arthurian stories—perhaps a wise precaution during the reign of Henry VIII. The title of Major's book is interesting; it is probably a pun on the author's name but it is usually translated as *The History of Great Britain*—the first time that Britain was called Great!

Another key figure in the debate about the *Historia* was Polydore Vergil (*c*.1470–*c*.1555), an Italian who arrived in England in 1502 and stayed under the patronage of Henry VII to write *Anglica Historia*. In it he presented a thorough and convincing demolition of Geoffrey's *Historia*. Geoffrey had enhanced his stories 'with most impudent lyeing', he wrote: the entire tissue of myth should be discarded. Other critics were to follow. A conservative rearguard mounted a staunch defence and the battle raged throughout the sixteenth century, but by the end of the century Renaissance scholarship had triumphed and Brutus was barely heard of again.

Topography and Anthropology in Renaissance Thought

The debate about British origins, which raged during the sixteenth century and trickled over into the next, represents the demise of the medieval clerical tradition with its emphasis on 'old documents', whether real or imagined, and its desire for a simple narrative. An awareness of the real world of tangible evidence was beginning to take hold. One of the earliest protagonists of this new curiosity was John Leland (1503–52). Leland was educated at St Paul's School, Oxford, and in Paris, returning to England in 1529 to be ordained as a royal chaplain. He soon became one of the librarians to the king, Henry VIII, and in 1533 was given a royal commission to travel the country 'to serche al the libraries of monasteries and collegies' for ancient texts. So enthused was he by what he saw that he extended his operations, travelling to all parts of England and Wales, observing and recording countryside and monuments alike in preparation for writing the first detailed topographical description of the country. His plan was to present his findings in a great book, *De Antiquitate Britannica*. For the next twelve years his travels took him to all corners of the country—no mean achievement given the state of the roads—but in 1550 he lapsed into insanity and died two years later. Fortunately he had compiled copious notes, which were extensively used by later topographers and subsequently published in 1710–12 as *The Itinerary of John Leland* under the editorship of Thomas Hearne.

Leland's great contribution was that he saw for himself the physical remnants of Britain's past scattered about the countryside and realized that here was tangible evidence of the country's history and prehistory. He was able to identify monuments of different dates, distinguishing between Roman structures and Iron Age hill-forts, which he interpreted correctly as pre-Roman. But for all the new evidence that he amassed, he remained an ardent supporter of the Brutus myth. His deep admiration for the Tudor monarchy made it impossible for him to question the narrative that led from Brutus to his beloved patron, Henry.

Although other scholars attempted to produce topographical accounts in the latter part of the sixteenth century, there was nothing to compare with the standards set by Leland until William Camden (1551–1623) published his remarkable *Britannia* in 1586. Camden was a young man at the time of publication. After studying at Oxford he spent time visiting antiquities throughout the country before becoming a master at Westminster School at the age of 24. He continued his travels in school

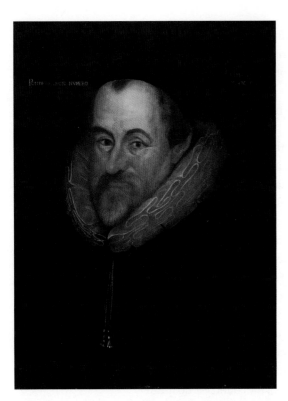

I.2 William Camden (1551–1623)

holidays—an arduous regime that was to last for eleven years—before his researches were ready for publication. His scope was ambitious: all of the British Isles were covered, including Ireland and outlying islands from Shetland to the Channel Islands. His intention, he said, was 'in each county . . . to describe its ancient inhabitants, etymology of its name, its limits, soil, remarkable places both ancient and modern'. This he achieved in full measure. The work was an immediate success and won Camden the reputation of being the foremost antiquary of the day. By 1600 five editions of *Britannia* had been published, and in 1610 the first edition in English appeared. It continued to serve as a model for antiquaries throughout the seventeenth and eighteenth centuries, with subsequent revised editions appearing in 1695, 1789, and 1806.

Camden had no time for the Brutus myth, though he was discreet about dismissing it, referring instead simply to the weight of contrary opinion amassed by both British and continental writers. He was of the view that the British were a branch of the Gauls—a view based on a careful comparison of the language, customs, and religion of the Gauls and Britons. In this he was following the observations recorded by Julius Caesar. The name Britannia, he said, had nothing to do with Brutus but was derived from a Greek word meaning 'land of the painted people'. What led him to such a view is not immediately clear, but it suggests that he had knowledge of the texts of Diodorus Siculus and Strabo, where 'Prettanikē' is used as the name for Britain (p. 4 above). His one concession to the old myth was that the Gauls could claim Gomer, son of Japheth, as their ancestor. The Gomerians were later to be known as Cimbri, from which the name Cymry (Wales) derived.

The publication of Camden's *Britannia* marked a turning point. Here was a Renaissance scholar sweeping away old nonsenses about the past and demonstrating that the early history of Britain had to be built on a sound factual basis—on the evidence of monuments and artefacts, and on a critical appreciation of the classical texts. He was, however, of an age when casting free of the biblical myths was too anarchic to be contemplated.

Camden was writing at a time when visions of the world were expanding at an astonishing rate: the discovery of the New World had, quite literally, opened up new

1.3 In William Camden's book *Britannia*, first published in Latin in 1586, he realized that some of the pre-Roman coins of Britain listed the names of British kings, like Cunobelinus and Tascovanus, and places such as the early towns of Verulamium and Camulodunum. The illustration comes from the 1600 edition of his book

horizons. From the early sixteenth century, accounts of the native inhabitants of America were beginning to be published and some scholars, like the French philosopher Montaigne, could wonder whether the Native Americans were not a purer representation of humanity than the Europeans. More enterprising explorers brought native peoples back to Europe as specimens to be wondered at. In 1532 William Hawkins presented a Brazilian 'king' to Henry VIII, 'at the sight of whom the King and all the nobilitie did not a little marvelle'. Knowledge of groups of Inuit abducted by Frobisher and brought to Bristol in 1576 and 1577 was widely disseminated through drawings made by John White. These were seen by William Camden, who commented on 'the women painted about the eyes and balls of the cheek with a blue colour like the ancient Britons'. White also accompanied Walter Ralegh's expedition to Virginia in 1585 and made a series of drawings there of the Algonquian Indians, as well as illustrating the local fauna and flora. White's depictions of natives were given wide circulation through engravings published in the first part of Theodore de Bry's magnificent *America* in 1590. In the second part of his volume, beginning with a new title page, de Bry gives a further five illustrations introduced as 'som picture of the Pictes which in the olde tyme dyd habite one part of the great Bretainne'. He included these pictures 'for to showe how that the Inhabitants of the great Bretannie have bin in times past as sauvage as those of Virginia'. This must be the first example of ethnographical analogy being used to throw light on prehistoric Britain.

1.4 A seventeenth-century vision of an ancient Briton from John Speed's *The Historie of Great Britaine*, published in 1611

Versions of these images were given even wider prominence in John Speed's *Historie of Great Britaine*, published in 1611. In a chapter entitled 'The Portraiture of the Ancient Britaines' he offers four wood-block illustrations of Britons clearly modelled on de Bry's Picts. All the icons—familiar to a reader of the classical texts—are here: the billowing moustaches and naked body of the warrior, complete with neck torc, weapons, and the severed heads of enemies. The Briton has now taken on a vivid visual reality—barbarous but noble, an ancestor one might even wish to take pride in.

The Phoenicians and the Coming of the Celts

The publication, throughout the sixteenth and seventeenth centuries, of an increasing number of classical texts, first in Latin and Greek and later in English translation, introduced contemporary accounts of Britons and Gauls and of the classical world to the educated reader. Gradually this newly available information was integrated into models of British prehistory.

One particularly inventive writer was the antiquary Aylett Sammes (c.1636–c.1679), who published his *Britannia Antiqua Illustrata, or, The Antiquities of Ancient Britain, derived from the Phoenicians* in 1676. Sammes was content to accept Camden's account of the first Britons resulting from a flow of Cimbri from the Black Sea region but could not resist adding Phoenicians arriving via the Atlantic seaways, followed by Greek traders in search of tin, who introduced the idea of the Homeric chariot. The Greek tin trade was well attested by Diodorus Siculus and Pliny, and Caesar gave a vivid account of chariot warfare in Britain. All Sammes was doing was to link the two with what was to him a plausible explanation. The idea of a Phoenician influx had first been put forward by John Twyne (c.1505–1581) in his *De Rebus Albionicis, Britannicis, atque Anglicis* of 1590, but not much notice was taken of it until it was accepted by the French antiquary Samuel Bochart (1599–1667) and expanded in his *Geographia Sacra* (1646), a popular but extreme work which championed the Phoenicians as the founders of much of ancient Europe. In spite of a total lack of evidence, the myth has shown a curious resilience and continues to do so in popular imagination even today.

With a wider reading of the classical texts came a growing awareness of the Celts, who were believed to have occupied much of west central Europe from the middle of the first millennium BC. Their migratory movements and raids southwards into the Italian peninsula and eastwards into the Balkans, Greece, and Turkey brought them into direct confrontation with the Greeks and Romans, who offered vivid descriptions of these northern barbarians.

The Celts were given a new prominence by a Breton cleric, Paul-Yves Pezron (1639–1706), whose book *L'Antiquité de la nation et de la langue des Celtes*, published in 1703, was to become very influential. The English translation appeared three years later and brought it to an even wider audience. The essence of Pezron's argument was that the Celts, descendants of Noah, lived in Asia Minor and spread through Europe in prehistoric times. They attacked Rome and Greece and settled in western Europe, where they were known as Gauls, and their descendants survive today in Wales and Brittany, where their Celtic language is still spoken. This view was broadly in harmony with the sketch given by Camden more than a century earlier, but it more closely related the traditional story to the now more familiar classical sources and to Pezron's own interpretation of the linguistic evidence. More to the point, it presented the noble, warlike, drunken, and really rather likeable Celt as the direct ancestor of both the French and the British. Yet by arguing that their true descendants were the Bretons and the Welsh, Pezron was making a clear distinction between indigenous populations and the incoming Franks and Anglo-Saxons, the antecedents of the oppressive nation-states of England and France. It was an interpretation that appealed to his fellow Bretons.

One British scholar who was particularly impressed with Pezron's model was Edward Lhuyd (1660–1709), keeper of the Ashmolean Museum in Oxford and a Welshman. Lhuyd had been engaged in updating the Welsh section of the new edition of Camden's *Britannia*, published in 1695, and had turned his attention to the collection and preparation of material for an ambitious new project: a multi-volume account of the antiquity of Britain to be based on his own extensive fieldwork, as well as new manuscript sources and an extensive correspondence with fellow antiquaries. Between 1697 and 1701 Lhuyd travelled widely in Cornwall, Scotland, Ireland, and Brittany, paying close attention to the languages spoken there. In 1707 the first volume of his *Archaeologia Britannica* appeared. It was subtitled *Glossography* and contained a detailed account of 'the original languages of Britain and Ireland', exploring the affinity between Welsh, Irish, Scottish, Cornish, and Breton. These languages he called Celtic, clearly influenced by Pezron, whose work he much admired. Lhuyd died in 1709, leaving the *Glossography*—the only volume of the *Archaeologia* to be published— as a monument to his scholarship. How he would have used his huge collection of new data in the creation of an early history of Britain we shall never know, but there are hints of his thinking in letters to friends and in the preface to the Welsh editions of the *Archaeologia*. To explain the variations he observed in the Celtic languages, he visualized an initial movement of Celts coming from Spain and settling in Ireland and a later movement coming from Gaul and pushing through Britain. Both views had been expressed earlier in the seventeenth century, and indeed both go back, as we have seen, to the early documents gathered by Nennius. In restating them here as an explanation for the linguistic evidence he had so carefully observed, he was building a hypothesis that was to be highly influential for the next 250 years.

Lhuyd's ideas of successive Celtic invasions were further developed by the Celtic philologist Sir John Rhys (1840–1915) in an influential book, *Early Britain: Celtic Britain*, first published in 1882. It provided the basic model used by archaeologists to structure their data well into the second half of the twentieth century. This is an issue to be explored in more detail in Chapter 7.

1.5 *Britannia Antiqua Illustrata*, by Aylett Sammes, published in 1676, was a curious compilation, largely of fantasy. One of his beliefs was that the first inhabitants of Britain were Cimbri, seen here migrating from the Black Sea

Stagnation and Despair

Two enthusiasms spilled over into the early decades of the eighteenth century: the fascination for seeing monuments in their landscapes, and recourse to the classical texts to provide colour and substance for the ancient Britons half-hidden in the dim recesses of prehistory. William Stukeley (1687–1765) was an adept practitioner of both arts. Educated at Cambridge as a physician, Stukeley spent his earlier years travelling extensively in England and Wales, eventually publishing an illustrated

1.6 William Stukeley (1687–1765) at the age of 40

account of his journeys in *Itinerarium Curiosum, or, An Account of the Antiquitys and Remarkable Curiositys in Nature or Art, Observ'd in Travels thro' Great Brittan* in 1724. But already he was developing a fascination with the great stone circles of Avebury and Stonehenge tucked away in the remoteness of the Wiltshire chalklands. Both monuments were already known to antiquarians. John Aubrey (1626–97), a Wiltshire scholar, had described them in a manuscript he was preparing. Previous writers had suggested that they were Roman, Phoenician, or Danish, but Aubrey pointed out that they belonged to a class of monuments—stone circles—that were found in Ireland and Scotland, way beyond the reach of these peoples. He concluded: 'All these monuments are of the same fashion, and antique rudeness: wherefore I conclude, that they were erected by the Britons: and were Temples of the Druids.' Stukeley had been shown a transcript of Aubrey's unpublished manuscript and was inspired by it. Each year from 1719 to 1724 he spent the late spring and early summer studying the two monuments, making detailed and accurate plans of them, as well as perspective drawings. He was also concerned with their broader landscape settings and with the lesser monuments that clustered around the two giant circles. His study was far more detailed and perceptive than anything that had gone before.

In 1723 Stukeley settled down to prepare a book, *The History of the Temples of the Ancient Celts*, but his interests were beginning to become more diverse, and publication was delayed. It was not until much later in life, after he had given up his scientific rigour, had become ordained, and had increasingly indulged himself in a whimsy of invented Druidism that fast became an obsession, that two slim volumes appeared: *Stonehenge* in 1740 and *Avebury* in 1743. His earlier objectivity had been abandoned, and fact and fantasy were now inextricably mixed. In his early life Stukeley had been an astute observer, noting the siting of barrows, silhouetted on false summits when seen from the valley bottoms, and identifying the boundaries of prehistoric field systems. He had also made a thorough study of pre-Roman coinage, correctly reading their inscriptions and realizing that they referred to British kings and to towns. And yet in mid-life he succumbed increasingly to an overheated imagination dominated by visions of the Druids he had read about in the classical texts. Rationalism had given way to mania.

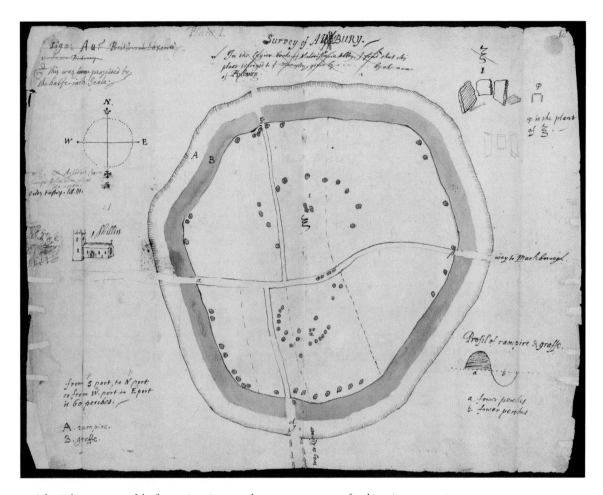

1.7 John Aubrey was one of the first antiquaries to produce accurate surveys of prehistoric monuments. His survey of Avebury was drawn at a scale of half an inch to a chain (66 feet) in 1663. It shows details of standing stones, many of which no longer survive

While Stukeley's critical decline may have been a feature of his own metabolism, it mirrored quite clearly what was happening more widely in Britain's intellectual life. After the excitement of the Renaissance had worked itself out, the country lapsed into a lazy Romanticism. Stukeley's later ramblings were symptomatic. In the world of the antiquary, some, undaunted by lack of evidence, simply invented the past they desired. In Scotland, James Macpherson (1736–96) published a group of poems ascribed to a semi-legendary bard, Ossian, son of Fingal. His sources, he claimed, were ancient manuscripts that had come into his possession. The 'Ossian' saga presented Scotland with an epic tradition worthy of Homer and became wildly popular,

THE HISTORY OF
THE TEMPLES
OF THE ANTIENT
CELTS.

O qui me gelidis in vallib Hæmi
Sistatq ingenti ramorum protegat umbra!
Fœlix qui potuit Rerum cognoscere caulas!

Atqȝ metus Omnes & inexorabile Fatum
Subjecit pedibus, strepitumq Acherontis
avari. Virg.

1.8 William Stukeley was intending to publish his studies of Stonehenge and Avebury in a book prepared in 1723, for which this was to be his title page. In the event, *Stonehenge* was published in 1740 and *Avebury* in 1743

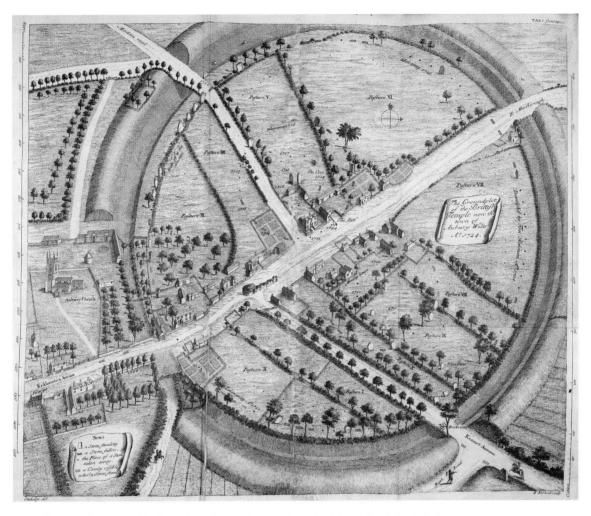

1.9 William Stukeley's plan of Avebury, drawn in 1724, is more schematized than Aubrey's but includes much of the same archaeological detail set among the modern topography

not only in Scotland but across Europe. But it was soon to be discredited as a fake—a construct of Macpherson's imagination, inspired by a few scraps of surviving folk tradition.

An equally impressive invention was that perpetrated in 1792 by a Welsh stone-mason, Edward Williams (1747–1826), who preferred to be known by his bardic name Iolo Morganwg. Iolo, deeply immersed in Welsh bardic mythology, created a 'bardic' ceremony known as Gorsedd, complete with a stone circle and Druidic altar, which was first enacted on Primrose Hill in London. It was pure invention, but by persuasive skill he managed to have it grafted onto the ancient ceremony of the Welsh Eisteddfod, of which it remains a part even today.

But alongside the wishful thinking of the Romantics there were men trying to understand the nature of humankind at a more philosophical level—men like Jean-Jacques Rousseau, whose *Discours sur l'origine et les fondements de l'inégalité parmi les hommes* was published in 1755, and Henry Home, Lord Kames, author of *Sketches of the History of Man* (1778). These ideas were particularly welcomed in Scotland, where links with French scholarship were strong. James Burnett, Lord Monboddo (1714–99), lord of session, speculated on the notion that the orang-utan was a type of human differentiated only by lack of speech. But such ideas were treated with derision by his contemporary Samuel Johnson: 'Sire, it is all conjecture about Things useless . . . conjecture, as to things useful, is good. But conjecture as to what would be useless to know, such as whether man went upon all fours, is very idle.'

One of the more interesting of the free-thinkers of the time was the colonial governor Thomas Pownall (1722–1805). Pownall had observed 'primitive' peoples during his service in New Jersey and Massachusetts between 1755 and 1760, and this informed a paper that he read to the Society of Antiquaries in 1770 (subsequently published in 1773) in which he speculated about the 'various species of mankind' being suited to the state of the earth at the time when they lived: 'The face of the earth being originally everywhere covered with wood, except where water prevailed, the first human beings of it were *Woodland-Men* living on the fruits, fish and game of the forest. To these the land-worker succeeded. He *settled* on the land, became a fixed inhabitant and increased and multiplied.' Here is a model offering a time-depth to prehistory based on a reasoned theory supported by ethnographic observations. It was a significant advance on biblical myths and Druidic nonsense.

The beginning of the nineteenth century saw the more energetic antiquaries, desperate to advance the understanding of the British past and tired of endless speculation, turn to excavation. This was not an entirely new pursuit. Stukeley and others before him had dug into monuments in the hope of enlightenment, but it was always on a very small scale and led to nothing. In 1800 all this changed when Sir Richard Colt Hoare (1758–1838), owner of the Stourhead estate in Wiltshire, joined forces with William Cunnington, a Wiltshire wool merchant, in a quest to explore the barrows of their native county. Over the next ten years their increasingly skilled team of labourers cut trenches through 350 monuments. Their results were published in two magnificent volumes, *The Ancient History of . . . Wiltshire* (1812–19). Colt Hoare introduces the work with a clarion call: '"We speak from facts, not theory". Such is the motto I adopt, and to this text I shall most strictly adhere. I shall not seek among the fanciful regions of romance an origin for our Wiltshire Britons.' It is a

1.10 Sir Richard Colt Hoare studying Bronze Age burial urns he had unearthed in his extensive barrow diggings. The picture is the frontispiece of his *Ancient History of . . . Wiltshire*, volume ii, published in 1821

1.11 Excavation in progress on Wiltshire barrows. The labourers dig while Sir Richard Colt Hoare and William Cunnington supervise. Watercolour by Philip Crocker, c.1807

worthy sentiment, but in the final reckoning he was forced to admit total 'ignorance of the authors of these sepulchral memorials . . . We have evidence of the very high antiquity of our Wiltshire barrows, but none respecting the tribes of whom they appertained, that can rest on solid foundations.' After ten years of persistent hard work it was a cry of despair. In a letter to his colleague William Cunnington, Colt Hoare had set out his ideas about the development of British prehistory. He recognized three eras. The first of these was of bone and stone 'belonging to the primeval inhabitants in the savage state': these were the Celts. The second was the era of brass, introduced by 'the more polished nations of Africa' (i.e. the Phoenicians) engaged in the tin trade; the recipients were the Belgae. The third was the era of iron, 'introduced but a little before the invasion of the Romans'. There is little new in all this that would not have been commonplace a century or more before, but in proposing eras of stone, brass, and iron Colt Hoare was venturing ahead of his time. Although the Roman writer Lucretius had talked in these terms in the first century BC, the Three Age System, as it became known, was not fully formulated until 1836 (p. 30).

The Antiquity of Man

Speculation about the chronology of Britain's past goes back to Nennius, who divided the history of the world into six ages based on time-lines related to the lives of the patriarchs set out in the Bible. The British, he said, came to Britain in the Third Age (from Abraham to David), while the Irish arrived in the Fourth Age (from David to Daniel). It was a chronology of sorts and survived well into the Renaissance.

Throughout the Middle Ages much effort was spent in attempting to work out the age of the world using the pedigrees listed in the Old Testament. Consensus was finally reached in 1650, when the archbishop of Armagh, James Ussher (1581–1656), arrived at the date as 4004 BC, which he published together with his proof in the *Annals* of the Old and New Testament. Even greater precision was added a little later by John Lightfoot, vice-chancellor of Cambridge University, whose calculations led him to the belief that 'man was created by the Trinity on October 23, 4004 BC at nine o'clock in the morning'. The archaeologist Glyn Daniel could not resist adding, 'we may perhaps see in these dates and time a prejudice of a Vice-Chancellor for the beginning of an academic year and the beginning of an academic morning'.

Acceptance of the date 4004 BC for the Creation meant, on Nennius' calculation, that the Flood should be dated to 1762 BC. This provided the time-frame that had to contain the whole of European prehistory. It was constraints like this that caused Colt Hoare, as late as the early nineteenth century, to date his Wiltshire barrows to between 500 and 1,000 years before Caesar's invasion. As the awareness of the complexity of the prehistoric record became gradually better understood, so the constriction of the biblical chronology became increasingly unacceptable.

The idea of an age of stone preceding an age of 'brass' was well established in British antiquarian writing. As early as 1650 William Dugdale was writing about stone tools as weapons used by the Britons before the art of making arms of brass or iron was known, and in 1766 Charles Lyttelton (1714–68), bishop of Carlisle, read a paper to the Society of Antiquaries describing some stone axes as 'coeval with the first inhabitants of this island', suggesting that they should be dated before the arrival of metals. So far there was no direct conflict with the Church's teaching, but thirty years later the society was to hear from a correspondent, John Frere, about a group of what we would now recognize as lower Palaeolithic hand-axes that were found at Hoxne in Suffolk at a depth of 12 feet. What was unnerving was that the undisturbed layer in which they were found also contained the bones of extinct animals. If the Bible was right, man and extinct animals could not have coexisted. In the printed version of his lecture, published in 1800, Frere carefully concluded that 'The situation in which these weapons were found may tempt us to refer them to a very remote period indeed, even beyond that of the present world.' Frere's momentous discovery seems to have passed unnoticed, or at least unremarked.

A generation later a Roman Catholic priest, Father John MacEnery (1796–1841), was excavating in the cave of Kent's Cavern at Torquay. He laboured there from 1824 until 1829, finding remains spanning the prehistoric period. Low in the sequence he came upon a thick, unbroken deposit of stalagmite, which he dug through, finding beneath it flint implements directly associated with bones of extinct animals. In some excitement he wrote to William Buckland (1784–1856), who had been professor of geology at Oxford but was now dean of Westminster. Buckland was recognized as one of the foremost scholars of his time and his *Reliquiae Diluvianae* (1823) was a standard textbook on, as its subtitle tells us, 'organic remains contained in caves, fissures, and diluvial gravel . . . attesting the action of an universal deluge'. He was, then, a scientist–clergyman who believed that scientific discoveries proved the Flood. Not unsurprisingly, when MacEnery presented his observations, Buckland was

1.12 One of the Palaeolithic hand-axes found in river gravels at Hoxne. It was illustrated and described by John Frere in a paper published in *Archaeologia* in 1797

1.13 William Buckland (1784–1856) dressed for fieldwork

entirely dismissive. The artefacts, he argued, must have got below the stalagmite floor as the result of pits being dug through it by later Celtic occupants, allowing more recent material to mix with the extinct animal remains below. MacEnery was insistent that this was not so, but in deference to the famous scholar he delayed publication. 'It is painful to dissent from so high an authority,' he wrote, 'and more particularly so from my concurrence generally in his views of the phenomena of these caves.' Intellectual torment combined with ill health and lack of money meant that his results remained unpublished until 1859—by which time the intellectual climate had changed out of all recognition.

William Buckland was a towering authority. Like other geologists of his time, he believed that the geological record could only be interpreted in terms of there having been a series of catastrophes in the remote past, each followed by a new act of creation. One school of French geologists identified twenty-seven such events. Although the number of catastrophes varied according to different authorities, the last act of creation, they all agreed, was the story told in Genesis, and the last catastrophe, the biblical Flood.

The catastrophists were not unchallenged. Since the end of the eighteenth century some geologists had been arguing that the geological record could only be interpreted in terms of processes observable today. 'No processes are to be employed', wrote James Hutton in 1785, 'that are not natural to the globe; no action to be admitted except those of which we know the principle': this was the doctrine of uniformitarianism. The foremost exponent of uniformitarianism was Charles Lyell (1797–1875), whose highly influential *Principles of Geology* was published in three volumes from 1830 to 1833 and was reprinted on many occasions throughout the nineteenth century. It was this work that was to have such a formative influence on the mind of the young Charles Darwin as he made his epic journey on the *Beagle*. The geological debate raged throughout the first half of the nineteenth century and formed the background to the fierce battle over the antiquity of man. Buckland believed passionately that there had been a succession of earlier creations and floods and that human remains could not be found in the last flood deposit, except of course in the vicinity of the Garden of Eden. But he was far from being a pure theoretician: he visited sites throughout the country, observing deposits in caves and gravels wherever the bones of extinct animals were found, and carried out lengthy observations on the eating habits of modern hyenas, one of which he kept as a pet. Since all his researches were made with the intention of proving the truth of the biblical Flood, it is understandable that when, in 1823, he exhumed, in a cave at Paviland in south Wales, the skeleton of what we now know to be a 30,000-year-old male, covered with red ochre and associated with artefacts of mammoth ivory and bones of extinct animals, he concluded that the 'Red Lady of Paviland' was a Roman burial dug into the earlier deposits on the cave floor: 'she was clearly not coeval with the antediluvian extinct species'. MacEnery's disconcerting discoveries in Kent's Cavern a year or two later did not cause him to reverse his views: the Flood was a fact; anything that suggested otherwise had to be explained away.

But the tide was turning against the diluvianists. Discoveries of human bones and artefacts in association with extinct animal remains were being reported from Germany, France, and Sicily and could not be ignored. In England attention turned once more to the Devon coast and Torquay. A local schoolmaster, William Pengelly, had continued the exploration of Kent's Cavern after MacEnery's death and had come to the conclusion that MacEnery had been correct. But the cave deposits were by now much disturbed, and what was needed to provide indisputable evidence was a new, untouched cave to use as a test before objective witnesses. A few years later just such a cave was found not far away in Brixham. Here, under the auspices of the British Association, Pengelly carried out a meticulously recorded excavation from the summer of 1858 to the summer of 1859. By the end, his work had demonstrated to everyone's satisfaction that flint implements associated with the remains of extinct animals were indeed sealed by a completely unbroken layer of stalagmite. MacEnery was vindicated, and his discoveries were fully published in 1859, eighteen years after his death.

It was in the same year that the archaeologist John Evans and the geologist John Prestwick visited gravel-pits in the valley of the Somme near Abbeville, where a French enthusiast, Boucher de Perthes, had for two decades been claiming to have found flint hand-axes mixed up with extinct animal bones deep down in the gravels. Both men were senior figures in their respective professions, and when they returned home to corroborate the finding in papers presented before the Royal Society and the Society of Antiquaries, the scientific world finally accepted the antiquity of man: it was three years after Dean Buckland's death. Something of the excitement of the time is captured by an entry in John Evans's diary:

BRIXHAM.

GREAT NATURAL CURIOSITY.

INTERESTING EXHIBITION ! !

THE

"Ossiferous Cavern"

Recently discovered on Windmill Rea Common, will be exhibited for a short time only, by Mr. PHILP, who has just disposed of it to a well-known scientific gentleman.

Those who delight in contemplating the mysterious and wonderful operations of nature, will not find their time, or money mis-spent, in exploring this remarkable Cavern, and as the fossils are about to be removed, persons desirous of seeing them had better apply early.

Many gentlemen of acknowledged scientific reputation, have affirmed that the stalactitic formations are of the most unique and interesting character, presenting the most fantastic and beautiful forms of crystallization, representing every variety of animal and vegetable structure.

Here too, may be seen the relics of animals that once roamed over the Earth before the post-tertiary period, or human epoch.

THE BONES AND TEETH, &c., OF

HYENAS, TIGERS, BEARS,

LARGE FOSSIL HORNS

of a Stag, all grouped and arranged by an eminent Geologist.

N.B. Strangers may obtain particulars of the locality, &c., of the Cavern, on application to Mr. BROWN, of the Bolton Hotel; or at the residence of the Proprietor, Spring Gardens.

THE CHARGE FOR ADMISSION TO THE "CAVERN," SIXPENCE.

Children will be admitted for FOURPENCE.

ated, Brixham, June 10th, 1858.

EDWARD FOX, PRINTER, &c., BRIXHAM.

1.14 The discovery of tools stratified with the bones of extinct animals in a cave at Brixham, Devon, in 1858 demonstrated once and for all the antiquity of humankind. The owner of the cave, John Philip, promoted the discovery widely in the interests of charging an admission fee

Think of their finding flint axes and arrowheads at Abbeville in conjunction with bones of Elephants and Rhinoceroses forty feet below the surface of a bed of drift. In this bone cave in Devonshire . . . They have found arrowheads among the bones and the same is reported of a cave in Sicily. I can hardly believe it. It will make my ancient Britons quite modern if Man is carried back in England to the days where Elephants, Rhinoceroses, Hippopotamuses and Tigers were also inhabitants of the country.

At the moment in which these revelations were stunning the academic community, Charles Darwin published his *On the Origin of Species*. The world would never be the same again.

Time-Lines

John Evans's expression of wonder at the antiquity of the human race was no doubt widely felt at the time, but people had been trying to bring some structure and some sense of chronology into their understanding of the past since Nennius had first offered his Ages of Man in the early ninth century. In the first decade of the nineteenth century Colt Hoare, as we have seen, was speculating about the successive ages of stone, brass, and iron, much as Lucretius had done 2,000 years before, but the dates he assigned were mere guesswork.

The simple concept of three ages was in the minds of many antiquaries throughout Europe, but it was not formally systematized until the curator of the National Museum of Copenhagen, C. J. Thomsen (1788–1865), reorganized the national collection into objects of stone, bronze, and iron in 1819. The publication of the museum's catalogue, in Danish in 1836, gave some publicity to the idea, but it was its translation into English in 1848 that brought the scheme fully to the notice of British archaeologists. Thomsen's successor, J. J. A. Worsaae (1821–85), was soon to demonstrate, through fieldwork and careful stratigraphic excavation, that the system worked in practice and was more than just a theory. His book, translated as *The Primeval Antiquities of Denmark*, was published in England in 1849. Among British archaeologists there was a general acceptance of the Three Age System, though some were still cautious and a few hostile.

When Sir John Lubbock (later Lord Avebury) came to publish his widely influential *Pre-Historic Times as Illustrated by Ancient Remains* in 1865, he added a refinement by dividing the Stone Age into two phases, the Palaeolithic and the Neolithic, while accepting the validity of the Bronze Age and the Early Iron Age ('Early' to distinguish it from the iron-using Romans and their successors). But chronology was still very much in debate, as he made clear in his opening words: 'The first appearance of man in Europe dates from a period so remote that neither history nor tradition can throw any light on his origin or mode of life': contemporary estimates for the age of Palaeolithic hand-axes found in the Somme gravels varied from 20,000 to 240,000 years. The very imprecision made this, as one writer said, 'a curious and interesting problem'.

While archaeological discoveries continued to be made in ever-increasing quantity during the latter part of the nineteenth century, the understanding of the peoples of Britain, rather than just their artefacts, remained static. The first textbook of the twentieth century, Thomas Rice Holmes's *Ancient Britain and the Invasions of Julius Caesar* (1907), presents the familiar picture of Palaeolithic man followed by a Neolithic invasion, a Bronze Age invasion, and an Iron Age invasion. No dates were suggested for the Neolithic, but the Bronze Age invasion was dated to around 1400 BC. The Belgae came later. It was not much of an advance on the scheme briefly sketched by Colt Hoare a century before.

The obsession with 'invaders' is easy to understand. British history as taught in schools spoke of successive waves of invaders from the Continent covering swaths of the British Isles: Normans, Danes, Saxons, Romans. It was not unreasonable to back-project this model into the depths of prehistory. Also taught were the glories of empire—of the Roman empire, and of the British empire following proudly in its wake. Primitive people were conquered by superior cultures introducing new religious beliefs, new technologies, and new forms of government, all producing beneficial change. In the mood of high Victorian imperialism, in which leaders like Lord Raglan could believe that 'natives don't invent things', it was not unnatural to interpret the changes identifiable in the archaeological record as the direct consequence of new people moving in to set up their ascendancy over indigenous populations.

In a post-colonial era, with a far more nuanced understanding of behavioural sciences, anthropology, and economics, these invasionist models may now seem crude and grotesquely over-simple, but they played an essential part in our striving to understand our history and prehistory. At best it is a warning that our views of the past will always be conditioned by current preconceptions: our understanding is circumscribed by our being.

2

Britain Emerges

THE STAGE IS SET

'BRITAIN, the best of the islands, is situated in the Western Ocean between France and Ireland . . . It provides in unfailing plenty everything that is suited to the use of human beings.' So wrote Geoffrey of Monmouth in the twelfth century. The richness of the British Isles is a theme that many of the early writers return to again and again. They were right. The British Isles are favoured by nature, and it is all due to two things, the Continental Shelf and the Gulf Stream, and it is with these fundamentals we must begin.

The British Isles are little more than the submerged uplands of an extensive plateau lying at the western extremity of the Eurasian land-mass. Their familiar form today is the result of distant geological forces modified by fluctuations in sea-level. The Continental Shelf comes to an abrupt end in a steep under-sea cliff, which separates the undulating surface of the plateau itself, now between 100 and 200 metres below the present sea-level, from the ocean depths at 2,000 metres and more. The satellite image and map show the extent of these shallow seas. To the south the North-East Atlantic basin comes in a deep bight close to the northern edge of Iberia, giving form to the Bay of Biscay. To the west the under-sea cliff is fronted by the Rockall Deep, beyond which is an ocean ridge represented now by the Rockall Bank and the Faeroe Islands. The Deep leads to the Norwegian Sea, and from there another deep channel,

2.1 This spectacular satellite photograph of western Europe shows, with great clarity, the extent of the Continental Shelf binding Britain and Ireland to mainland Europe. The sharp edge of the shelf where it plunges to the ocean deeps is particularly clear

the Norwegian Trench, extends, separating the Shelf from the ancient mountain range of southern Norway, creating the famous seaway the Skagerrak, which lies between Norway and Denmark and gives access to the Baltic. The Shelf, then, is a massive stretch of 'territory': it extends from latitude 46° north to 61° north and from the present continental coast to the longitude of 12° west. The unsubmerged pieces of land, Britain, Ireland, and the other islands, account for less than half of its area.

The reason why the Continental Shelf is so relevant to the very nature of Britain is that the shallow sea creates a special, and highly beneficial, environment. Rivers bring down nutrient-rich sediments, which blanket the Shelf, while the shallowness of the sea allows sunlight to penetrate the depths. The two factors in combination create ideal conditions for the growth of plankton, and the plankton provides food

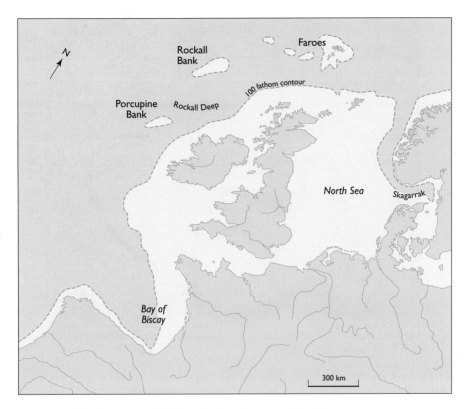

2.2 Britain and the Continental Shelf, showing the main topographical features

for the shoals of fish that thrive in the shallow seas. This rich maritime resource has been vital to the British and the Irish throughout their history.

But nature offers another benefit, the Gulf Stream, a flow of warm water that originates in the currents of the Caribbean and streams north-eastwards across the Atlantic to the ocean-facing shores of Europe before dissipating itself in the seas around Iceland and Greenland. The Gulf Stream brings two advantages: the warm waters greatly enhance plankton growth, thus boosting fish stocks still further, while at the same time ameliorating the climate of the islands and the neighbouring coastal zone. The British Isles are on the same latitude as Labrador and, without the comforting effects of the Gulf Stream, would suffer the same harsh climate. We shall see later something of the disastrous climatic deterioration that Britain experienced when changes in global temperature caused the Gulf Stream to cease to flow.

The British Isles, then, occupy a very favoured position in the world, allowing the land and the sea to provide, as Geoffrey said, 'in unfailing plenty' everything that humans could desire.

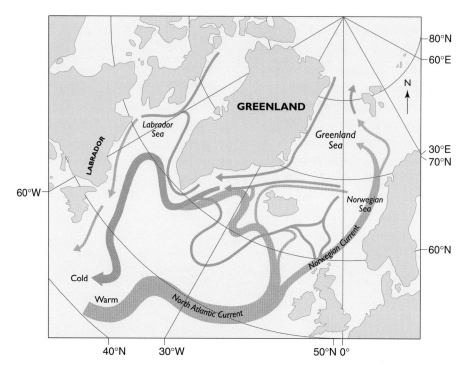

2.3 The ocean currents in the North Atlantic that bring warm water from the Caribbean and Gulf of Mexico region to the seas around Britain, giving north-western Europe its mild climate

Prelude: Charting the Deep Past

The story that we shall explore in this book starts around 10,000 BC, when the country was about to emerge from the last freezing downturn of the Last Glacial Maximum. In all probability so severe were the conditions that the hunter-gatherer groups who had been roaming the southern parts of Britain were driven southwards into what is now France. By about 9600 BC, however, the climate began suddenly to improve until around 8000 BC, when conditions became, if anything, a little warmer than they are today. It was in this brief period of climatic improvement that communities began once more to move in and colonize the empty landscape. These pioneers were the direct ancestors of the majority of the people living in the islands today.

Human groups, however, have lived in the land of proto-Britain on a number of occasions during the last 800,000 years. But during this time there were long periods when glacial conditions rendered huge areas uninhabitable and as parts of Europe and North America disappeared beneath thick ice-sheets. Traditionally there were believed to be four periods of glaciation with warm interglacials between, but this is something of an over-simplification. Recent scientific work has shown there to have been an altogether more complex pattern of twenty major climatic events when the temperature fluctuated from being very warm to being intensely cold.

The cause of these fluctuations lies in the complex relationship between the earth and the sun. We are all familiar with the fact that the earth orbits the sun and that it spins around its own axis, which is at an angle to the plane of its orbit. This causes some parts of the earth's surface to be nearer the sun for periods of time, accounting for the differences between summer and winter. If all parts of this system were stable, the earth's climate would remain constant, but this is not so: there are three factors that cause subtle variations in the distance between earth and sun. First, the earth's orbit is not circular but is slightly elliptical, causing a variation on a 100,000-year cycle. Secondly, the axis of the earth changes its tilt by a fraction over a 41,000-year cycle; and thirdly, the planet has a slight wobble about its axis as it spins, setting up changes over a cycle of 23,000 years. The combination of all these factors, creating very small changes in the sun–earth relationship, determines the expansion or contraction of the polar ice-cap and thus the sequence of fluctuating ice ages.

The complexity of these changes has taken some time to unravel. The earliest work was done on the Alpine region, and it was here that the four major stages of glaciation

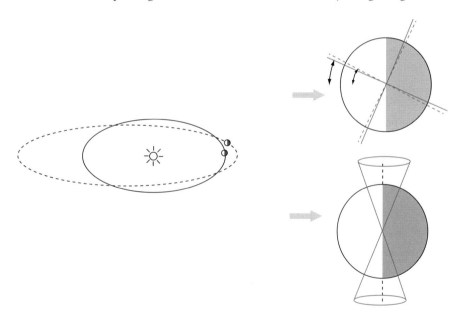

2.4 Cycles of climatic change, known as the Milankovitch cycles, are caused by cyclical changes in the earth's orbit. Left: A major eccentricity in orbit around the sun causes a 100,000-year cycle. Top right: Differences in tilt of the axis cause a 41,000-year cycle. Bottom right: Wobbles in the earth's spin give rise to a 23,000-year cycle

were identified, providing a useful regional sequence. More recently, over the last fifty years or so, work on deep-sea cores has pioneered a new way to study the phenomenon globally. The principle is quite simple. Deep-sea cores provide stratified sequences of calcareous accumulations derived from the shells of dead organisms. The calcium carbonate in these layers contains oxygen of two different atomic weights, ^{16}O and ^{18}O, which the organisms extract from the prevailing atmosphere. Since it can be shown that cold conditions favour ^{18}O over ^{16}O, then by assessing the ratio of the two it is possible to arrive at a direct measurement relating to the temperature of the ocean at the time of deposition. From these measurements a system of twenty phases, known as marine isotope stages, can be distinguished, reflecting changes in the earth's climate. The method was extremely valuable in providing a *relative* sequence, but it needed to be calibrated to give *absolute* dates.

The breakthrough came when, in one of the cores, it was possible to identify a point at which a major reversal had occurred in the earth's magnetic field, the time when the North and South poles took up their present positions. This same reversal has been recorded in rocks, where it could be dated to around 736,000 years ago using an abso-

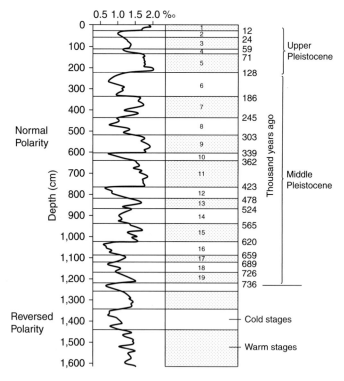

2.5 The major fluctuations in the earth's climate as reconstructed from deep-sea cores

lute dating method. With this one point securely established, and assuming that the deep-sea sediments had accumulated at a standard rate, it has been possible to assign dates to the entire sequence. Another valuable dating method, which has been developed over the last thirty years, is based on cores bored out of the Greenland ice-cap. The largest core is 3,000 metres deep and represents the build-up of the ice over a 110,000-year period. From the cores it is possible to measure *annual* increments, one year's winter ice being separated from the next year's by a fine dust layer formed during the summer melt. The temperatures prevailing at the time are estimated from the ^{16}O to ^{18}O ratios and from proportions of the wind-blown chemical particles. The cores provide a very precise dated sequence of climatic events extending back from the present.

The marine isotope stages provide a universal scale against which it is possible to compare and date local sequences. In Britain it was conventional to recognize three major phases of glaciation, the Anglian, Wolstonian, and Devensian, with warmer interglacials interspersed, the Cromerian preceding the Anglian glaciation, the Hoxnian between the Anglian and Wolstonian glaciations, the Ipswichian between the Wolstonian and Devensian glaciations, and the Flandrian (or Holocene, in the European nomenclature) following the Devensian and representing the period we are in now. These broad terms are still useful, but the marine isotope stages, together with recent work on the faunal remains found stratified in the glacial deposits, are beginning to show just how complex the true picture really was.

Conventional British stages		Oxygen isotope stage
Flandrian	Temperate	1
Devensian	Cold stage	5d+
Ipswichian	Temperate/interglacial stage	5e
	Cold stage	6
	Temperate/ interglacial stage	7
	Cold stage	8
	Hoxnian	9
Wolstonian	Cold stage	10
Hoxnian	Temperate/ interglacial stage	11
Anglian	Cold stage	12
Cromerian	Temperate/ interglacial stage	13

2.6 The major glacial and interglacial episodes correlated with the oxygen isotope stages

Enter the Early Humans

Human presence is demonstrated in a variety of ways, by tools, by tool marks preserved on animal bones, and by the skeletal remains of the people themselves. The earliest indications of human activity, in the area later to become Britain, belongs to the Cromerian interglacial and can be dated within the bracket 900,000–500,000 years ago, probably towards the earlier part of this range. Two sites are known, one in a cave at Westbury in the Mendips, the other on the muddy foreshore at Happisburgh in Norfolk. Both produced bones of extinct animals showing signs of butchery, together with a series of flint implements suitable for cutting up the carcasses.

It was not until around 500,000 years ago that the first physical trace of an actual British inhabitant was found. The site was a camp that had been set up at the base of what was then a sea-cliff but is now well inland in a gravel-pit at Boxgrove near Chichester. Alongside a scatter of flint debris, which represents waste from manufacturing hand-axes, two teeth and part of a tibia (shin-bone) were recovered. This remarkable find belongs to a species of human, *Homo heidelbergensis*, who was significantly different from modern man. He lived in Europe and became extinct about

2.7 Happisburgh on the Norfolk coast as it was in 2006, showing the rapid erosion of the sea-cliffs which exposed deposits that produced tools dating to the Anglian ice advance about half a million years ago

200,000 years ago. In the hominid family tree *Homo heidelbergensis* is probably ancestral to both the Neanderthals and modern man.

This first brief interlude of human activity was brought to an end with the onset of the Anglian glaciation around 470,000 years ago. For the next 60,000 years or so Britain was covered with an ice-sheet extending as far south as the Thames.

The Anglian glaciation was followed by the Hoxnian interglacial, lasting from about 410,000 to 380,000 years ago. This was a period of much milder climate, when herds of animals once more roamed Britain, attracting in their wake bands of human predators. It was at Hoxne (from which the interglacial was named) that John Frere made his momentous discovery of hand-axes and extinct animals found together deep in the gravels in 1797. An even more important discovery was made at Swanscombe in Kent in 1935 and 1936 when two large fragments of human skull were recovered. Twenty years later, by a remarkable chance, another skull-bone was found that joined to the other two. John Wymer, the young boy present on that historic occasion, went on to become the foremost Palaeolithic archaeologist in Britain. Understandably, the skull of Swanscombe Man has come under intense scrutiny, and it is now believed that, since he shows some of the characteristics of early Neanderthals, he may lie towards the beginning of the branch from which *Homo neanderthalensis* was to develop, well before modern man made an appearance.

2.8 Excavations in progress at Boxgrove quarry in West Sussex. The Palaeolithic surface is being carefully exposed to show hand-axes lying in position where they had been dropped by their makers

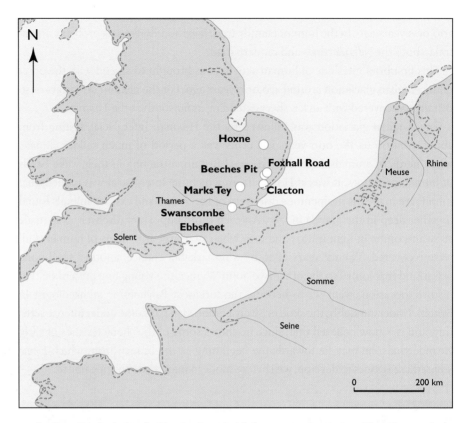

2.9 Southern Britain during the Hoxnian interglacial about 400,000 years ago. There is some doubt about whether or not there was a land bridge between Kent and Pas de Calais at this time

The northern latitude of Britain remained congenial for human hunting bands for only a comparatively short period of time, some 30,000 years, before glacial conditions returned again around 380,000 years ago and, with various fluctuations in temperature, lasted until 230,000 years ago. The retreat of the ice at this time encouraged the Neanderthals who now roamed Europe to spread northwards into proto-Britain. They are recognizable from their distinctive tools but are otherwise elusive in the fossil record. However, a small community occupied the cave of Pontnewydd near the north Welsh town of Rhyl, where eighteen teeth, representing at least five individuals, have been found.

The vicious cold episode to which the region of proto-Britain was subjected, characterized by sudden and violent swings of climate, meant that even in the warm periods the country lay at the extremity of the habitable world. It has been estimated that between 500,000 and 12,000 years ago humans were present in what is now Britain for only a fifth of that time, and between 180,000 and 70,000 years ago the land was entirely empty. No Neanderthals now ventured this far north, deterred perhaps by the nascent Channel. Around 70,000 years ago the temperature began slowly to cool again. This was the beginning of the Devensian cold stage—a period of fast-fluctuating temperatures getting progressively colder and culminating in the period of intense cold known as the Last Glacial Maximum, peaking around 27,000 years ago. At the beginning of this period falling sea-levels made the southern parts of Britain easily accessible once more, and groups of Neanderthals, recognizable from their distinctive Mousterian tools (named after the site in France where they were first found), began to return again. At one of their camp sites, at Lynford in Norfolk, remains of plants and animals showed that while temperatures were cooler than today, reaching a maximum of 13 °C in summer and falling to −10 °C in winter, this was well within the range acceptable for human habitation and the Neanderthals were a hardy breed.

How long Neanderthals continued to hunt in Britain it is difficult to say. Their tools have been found in cave sites in Derbyshire, the Mendips, Devon, and south Wales, but by about 40,000 years ago they were in rapid decline and were soon to become extinct. There has been much debate about the cause of their demise. One

2.10 A group of flint tools including hand-axes and curved-edged cutting tools characteristic of the tool-kit of the Neanderthals

factor may have been their inability to adapt to the increasing cold, but this is surely not the whole story. The primary cause probably lies in the competition they now faced from a new species, *Homo sapiens*, who first appeared in Europe about 50,000 years ago. The Neanderthals were no match for the twin onslaughts of clever rivals and bitter winters.

The First Modern Man

Homo sapiens emerged as a distinct species in Africa before 150,000 years ago and had spread to Europe, developing a tool-kit far more sophisticated than that of the Neanderthals, using bone, antler, and ivory as well as the ubiquitous flint which they now flaked with controlled delicacy. These early modern humans were first identified at the rock shelter of Cro-Magnon in France in 1868, a name that has often been used to identify them thereafter. Their presence in Britain is proclaimed by their tools from as early as 40,000 years ago, but the first physical remains of a Cro-Magnon, found in Goat's Hole Cave, Paviland, in south Wales, is 10,000 years or more younger. This is the burial already referred to above (p. 29), uncovered by Dean Buckland in 1823 and called by him the 'Red Lady of Paviland'. He was not only wrong about the sex of the burial but he dated it to the Roman period, unable to accept the association of human remains with extinct animals. There is a certain sadness in the fact that Buckland's fundamentalist Christian beliefs prevented him from being able to relish the true significance of his discovery: the first known Briton to have been buried with such care that his lineage must surely have believed in some kind of afterlife.

2.11 Section of Goat's Hole Cave, Paviland, on the Gower peninsula, excavated by William Buckland. It was here that he found the famous 'Red Lady of Paviland', the earliest remains of a modern human dating to about 40,000 years ago. Buckland believed that the 'Red Lady' was of Roman date

The first influx of Cro-Magnons into Britain was not long-lived. As the Devensian glaciation intensified and the ice-sheets spread, so the limit of human habitation was again pushed progressively southwards until, by about 25,000 years ago, the land of Britain was totally abandoned once more. And so it was to remain for 10,000 years.

The Last Glacial Maximum

The Last Glacial Maximum totally altered the face of north-western Europe. Scandinavia was covered by ice 2 kilometres thick, and much of Britain south to a line from the west midlands to the Wash disappeared between a 1.5-kilometre-thick sheet of ice that extended west to the Atlantic, blanketing the northern half of Ireland. So much water was tied up in these ice-caps that the sea-level sank to 150 kilometres below its present level, exposing considerable expanses of the previously submerged Continental Shelf. This in turn caused the many rivers to regrade to match the falling sea-levels, creating steep valleys cut into the earlier valley floors. There is some debate about whether the Scandinavian and British ice-caps coalesced, but the Shetland Islands were the focus of an ice-cap and it remains a distinct possibility that the ice was continuous along the North Atlantic fringe. What is certain is that the entire area in front of the ice, extending across what is now the North Sea, became land. The greatly lowered sea-level also meant that the sea receded from the English Channel zone, leaving only the Channel River, fed by its tributaries the Thames, the Rhine, and the Seine. The low-lying land between the British and Scandinavian ice-sheets became a polar desert largely devoid of life. Further south tundra spread for hundreds of miles—a desolate landscape supporting only mosses, lichens, and some herbaceous plants, in summer scoured by bitter winds blowing off the ice and carrying a fine dust of ice-ground rock particles, in winter blanketed with snow.

The intensification of glacial conditions drove human groups further and further south into the zone of park tundra to refuges in south-western France, northern Iberia, and further east into Ukraine. From these habitats hunting groups ventured into the northern tundra in summer, but at the height of the glaciation the ice-free parts of Britain remained well beyond the reach of humans. Not until about 15,000 years ago did the improvement in climate allow the southern parts of Britain to be populated again.

As the ice-caps retreated, leaving only a small ice-sheet in western Scotland, a huge expanse of land opened up, bounded on the north by the Norwegian Trench and on the west by the Rockall Deep. It was but a brief exposure. Meltwater from the fast-retreating glaciers poured into the sea, causing sea-levels to rise, progressively inundating low-lying areas of the northern lowlands. In this way the incipient North Sea

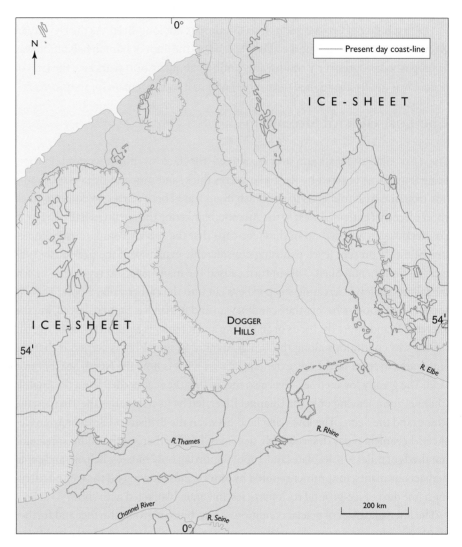

2.12 Reconstruction of the region later to become Britain and Ireland as it would have appeared during the height of the Devensian glaciation around 30,000 years ago when ice-sheets covered most of the country and the sea-level was very much lower

began to form. Soon the lower reaches of the Irish Sea River and the Channel River began to flood, creating wide inlets extending deep inland. Even so, the land-masses of Britain and Ireland were still very much part of continental Europe.

With the ameliorating climate the fauna and flora began to change. Large areas of the lowlands now supported woodlands of birch interspersed with stands of willow, poplar, and pine set in wide expanses of grassy parkland providing forage for mammoth, elk, red deer, aurochs, and horse, while predators like wolf, arctic fox,

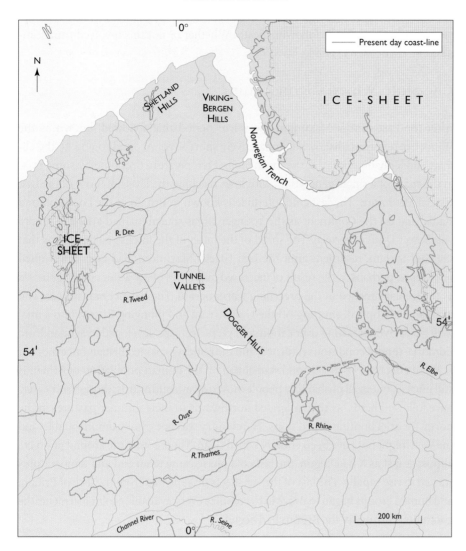

2.13 The region later to become Britain and Ireland during the Late Glacial (or Dimlington) stadial around 15,000 years ago. The ice-sheet covering Britain has now shrunk, but the sea-level is still low so that Britain and Ireland are one with continental Europe

and bear sought out their prey. There were periodic cold spells, but overall it was a highly congenial landscape for hunting bands to exploit. Optimum conditions for settlement lasted a comparatively short time—only some 4,000 years—but there is ample evidence for hunter-gatherer activity in Britain in the caves of Creswell Crags in Derbyshire, Kent's Cavern, Devon, and in the Mendips, especially at Gough's Cave in Cheddar Gorge, where the remains of at least three adults and two children were found. The bodies show evidence of having been cut up and defleshed, possibly as part of prescribed rituals following death. Whether or not this involved ritual cannibalism is a debatable issue.

Che Slate Wiped Clean Again?

After the Last Glacial Maximum the warm period that followed, known as the Windermere interstadial, was comparatively short-lived. Around 10,900 BC the climate suddenly deteriorated, the mean annual temperature dropping by some 15 °C in the space of a single generation, with lows reaching the levels of those of the Last Glacial Maximum. The last cold interlude is known in Britain as the Loch Lomond stadial and on the Continent as the Younger Dryas stadial (named after the tundra wildflower *Dryas octopetala*). The speed of the onset of the intense cold suggests that the Gulf Stream, resurgent after the Last Glacial Maximum, had been interrupted once more, perhaps as the result of increased quantities of icy water entering the sea as the ice-caps melted in the preceding warm period. The balance was delicate and was suddenly tipped, shutting off the Gulf Stream and plunging Britain into a final long glacial winter lasting over a thousand years. Ice-caps developed in Scotland and Cumbria, tundra conditions returned, and the reindeer roamed Britain once more.

What effect the Loch Lomond stadial had on the human population of Britain is still unclear, but in all probability people moved away southwards, though some may have followed herds, as they migrated northwards to their summer pastures in the north, for brief hunting expeditions. The country was not wholly uninhabitable, and the slate might not have been entirely wiped clean. Then, sometime around 9600 BC, almost as fast as it had begun, the last cold phase came to an end and temperatures started to rise rapidly. The last of the ice-sheets disappeared from the face of Britain, and human groups began to move in to colonize every available ecological niche: the continuous history of the Britons had begun.

Che Delicate Relationship between Land and Sea

To understand how the isles of Britain and Ireland gained their familiar shapes it is necessary to consider the very delicate relationship between the sea and the land—a relationship that is constantly evolving. For a region like Britain, located on a shallow continental shelf, it is evident that even a slight variation in the sea-level relative to the land will cause widespread changes to the topography of the low-lying regions. The ice ages were a particularly powerful force for change. The creation of permanent ice-caps several kilometres thick during the glacial maxima wrought massive transformations to the face of north-western Europe. The sheer weight of the ice distorted the earth's crust, depressing the land beneath and pushing up a forebulge around the edge, while the huge volumes of water bound up in the ice-caps caused significant falls in the sea-levels. With the retreating of the ice-caps two processes were set in motion. The first is called isostatic uplift. As the ice-cap melts and its weight decreases, so the distorted crust of the earth begins to readjust to its former contours, the readjustment being proportional to the thickness (and therefore weight) of the ice. This means that the rate at which the land rises is greatest where the ice was thickest. Isostatic uplift was rapid at first, becoming slower with time. It is still in progress today. Scandinavia, which supported a massive ice-cap, continues to rise, with the greatest rate, 9 millimetres per year, being in the Gulf of Bothnia. Even Scotland with its lesser ice-cap is rising at a rate of 3 millimetres per year.

But another factor has to be taken into account: the eustatic readjustment of global sea-levels resulting from the inflow of huge quantities of meltwater as the glaciers

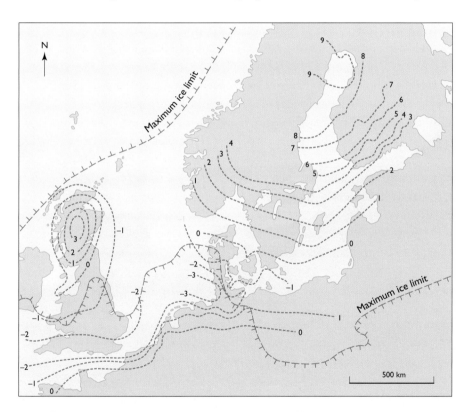

2.14 Following the retreat of the ice-sheet, the land once depressed by the heavy ice began to rise, but at the same time the sea-level also rose as ice became water. The land and sea are still readjusting in relation to each other. The map shows the rate of uplift and subsidence (the negative values) in millimetres per year at the present time

diminish. The eustatic rise in sea-levels affects all parts of the earth's surface, but in areas that have been glaciated, the isostatic rise in the land is in competition with the sea-level rise. The different rates of change relative to each other mean that the land–sea relationship will vary from place to place.

In areas like the British Isles and its region, the interplay between global glacio-eustatic sea-level rise and local isostatic uplift is complex since the transformation of the land depends entirely upon the rate of change of the two variables. To begin with, as the ice retreated, the north of Britain rose rapidly. This is evident from the raised beaches and fossil cliff lines still clearly dominating the landscapes of Jura in the Hebrides. And, as we have seen, the land in this region is still rising more rapidly than the sea. In the south, however, the glacio-eustatic rise in sea-level soon outstripped the rise in the land—a fact dramatically demonstrated by the 'fossil forests' that can still be seen at low tides around the coasts of Britain. Current estimates suggest that in the south relative sea-levels are rising at a rate of 2 millimetres per year,

2.15 Raised shore-lines on the north-east coast of the island of Islay in the Inner Hebrides. The old shore-line is now at a height of 30 metres OD as the result of isostatic uplift following the melting of the ice-sheets. In Scotland the uplift of the land has outpaced the rise in sea-level

but that is likely to increase as global warming caused by CO_2 emissions begins to take effect.

From detailed observations made in estuarine and coastal depositions the overall rise in mean sea-level in the coastal waters around Britain since the last glacial episode can be worked out. The figures for the Dutch coast suggest a rapid rise of some 7 metres from about 5500 BC to about 2000 BC with a slower rise of a metre and a half from 2000 BC to the present day. But there was much regional variation. As the isostatic and eustatic forces competed with each other, it is possible to identify

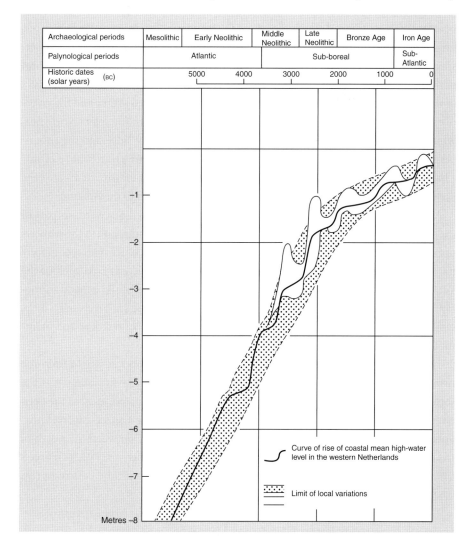

2.16 The gradual rise in sea-level from 5000 BC based on data from the Netherlands

periods of rapid sea-level rise interspersed with episodes of much slower change. There were also localized effects caused by changes in tidal amplitude and the prevalence of storm surges. Taken together these factors mean that each region needs to be assessed in its own right.

Britain Takes Shape

In the warm period between the end of the Last Glacial Maximum and the brief cold of the Younger Dryas–Loch Lomond stadial—a period known as the Bølling–Allerød interstadial in continental terminology and the Windermere interstadial in British terminology—proto-Britain was part of continental Europe. Viewed in the broader perspective the mountains of Scotland, the Pennines, and Wales lay at the western limit of the vast North European Plain, which stretched eastwards to the Urals. The rivers of the plain for the most part flowed northwards. The Elbe and Weser and the rivers of eastern Britain from the Ouse northwards all emptied into the incipient North Sea, which was beginning to form between the Shetland–Orkney ridge and the mountains of Norway. The Rhine, Seine, and Thames flowed south-westwards into a proto-Channel estuary, while a river flowing through what is now the Irish Sea drained the meltwater from the remaining Scottish ice-sheet southwards into the Atlantic.

Already proto-Britain was an in-between territory: it looked eastwards as part of the great continental plain and it looked westwards to the Atlantic and to the seaways of ocean-facing Europe. Irrespective of the transient effects of ice ages, geography had already begun to determine the character of Britain. The last cold spell of the Younger Dryas (10,900–9600 BC) probably saw little change to the general topography of proto-Britain. The ice-caps increased in size and the sea-levels fell a little, while the grassy plains and light woodlands with their herds of red deer and mammoth gave way to tundra, the home of reindeer.

The return to temperate conditions beginning around 9600 BC set in train the processes that created the British Isles familiar to us today. The first stage was the separation of Ireland from the mainland. This occurred around 9000 BC as the deep river valley, scoured out by the flow of meltwater from the Scottish ice-cap, was progressively flooded by the rising sea until the last land bridge between the north of Ireland and the Inner Hebrides was broken through. The deeper water of St George's Channel and the North Channel, now below 50 fathoms, mark the course of this original valley.

The separation of Britain from the Continent came later as the large expanse of lowlands, which archaeologists call Doggerland (after the Dogger Bank), became gradually submerged by what is now the North Sea. In parallel with this, the progressive

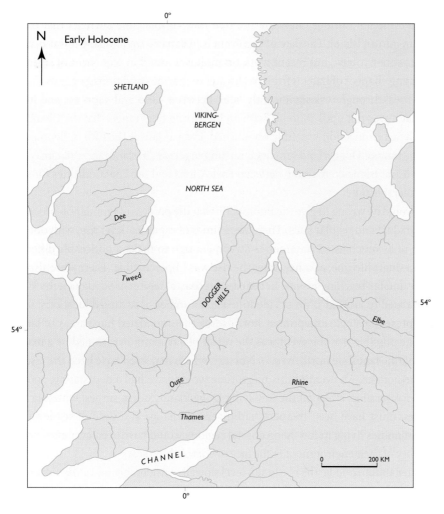

2.17 Britain in the early Holocene, *c.*9000 BC

flooding of the Channel River drove a widening wedge between southern Britain and what is now northern France. Since the Thames and the Rhine flowed southwards into the Channel estuary, the chalk ridge between Dover and Cap Gris Nez must already have been breached. The progressive rise in sea-level would have widened the gap still further, allowing the sea to penetrate further and further inland until all that remained to join Britain to the Continent was a band of lowland hills stretching from East Anglia to the Low Countries, representing the interfluve between the northern river system, of which the Ouse and Trent formed tributaries, and the southern system incorporating the Rhine and Thames. The continued rise in sea-level finally flooded the land bridge, allowing the free flow of maritime currents that turned Britain into an island. The date of this event is in debate. Traditionally it was believed to be 7500–6500 BC, but recent work on molluscs found in sequences of sediment, reflecting changes of habitat from freshwater to marine conditions, suggests that the final breakthrough was significantly later, between 5800 and 5400 BC, and it may be that it was not until 3800 BC, with an increasing tidal range, that the Channel to North Sea connection was fully established. Even as late as the fifth millennium BC a large tract of Doggerland remained unsubmerged as an island, and there may have been lesser islands remaining between East Anglia and the Low Countries for some considerable time.

It would be wrong to give the impression that the process of inundation proceeded at a gradual and regular pace. There were times of rapid sea-level rise, with one estimate of as much as 48 millimetres a year, enough to make a noticeable difference over a single lifetime; at other times the rise was imperceptible. There were also dramatic and far-reaching events. In the eastern coastal region of Scotland a thick sand layer dated to around 5800 BC, identified at a number of scattered locations, seems to represent a single exceptional storm surge that inundated huge areas of land. It is quite possible that the event was the result of a tsunami occasioned by a massive submarine landslide north-west of Norway, which may itself have been the result of an earthquake. An event of this magnitude would have had a devastating, and perhaps irreversible, effect on the low-lying Doggerland. Storm surges, whatever their causes, must have been frequent harbingers of change at a time of sea-level rise. Communities living in low-lying coastal regions would have been ever aware of the fragility of their environment in the face of encroaching sea.

After about 2000 BC the rise in sea-level slowed considerably, and although change to coastal regions continued, such changes as there were were more localized, and invariably more complex, as other factors, such as the creation of sand and gravel bars by long-shore drift, the growth of peatbogs, and alluviation, began to affect coastal topography. In some areas, like the Scilly Isles, large tracts of land were lost and the single island fragmented into many. In other regions, like Romney Marsh, the build-up of coastal bars led to the development of extensive tracts of new land as marshes formed behind their protective shield. Coastal topography continued to change, and still does. It is a reality with which over the next century we are all too likely to become increasingly familiar.

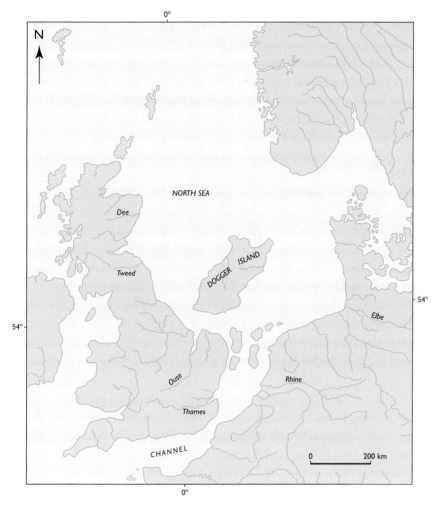

2.18 Britain *c.*5000 BC, just after the land bridge with the Continent had been breached

New Plants and Animals as the Climate Becomes Warmer

The sharp rise in temperature after the end of the last glacial episode brought with it a change in vegetation as tundra gave way to grassland and grass was replaced by woodland. So quickly did the tree cover seem to spread that it may be that some hardy specimens had managed to survive the cold of the preceding Younger Dryas. The regeneration seems to have followed a similar progression in most areas: first came the grasses and shrubs, to be followed rapidly by birch with some willow and aspen. Later, pine spread west and north but never as a dominant species. By 8000 BC hazel had begun to dominate, and within the millennium a mixed forest of oak, elm, alder, and hazel covered much of the land. There was, of course, local variation both in species mix and in density of tree cover. Pine seems to have been more common towards the south and east, but for the most part, over the 3,000 years or so following the last of the cold, Britain had become a land of mixed oak forest relieved only by lakes and marshes and by the sparse vegetation of the higher altitudes.

With a change in vegetation came a change in fauna. Reindeer seems to have retained a hold until the mid-tenth millennium, but it could not survive for long in the rising temperatures and the rapidly spreading birch woodlands. As the woodland canopy became denser and more varied, so new animals appeared: horse, aurochs, red deer, roe deer, elk, and wild pig, together with otter and beaver. Wolf, dog, and badger also make an appearance but may have arrived a little later. Contemporary sites in north Germany have also provided evidence of brown bear, lynx, and wild cat. The lakes and marshes teemed with a variety of waterfowl, while the sea offered fish in plenty, with seals and whales in the more northerly waters. For a hunter-gatherer prepared to follow the herds and to move with the seasons, there was no shortage of food.

As human groups began to move into the wildwoods and to manipulate them for their own needs, so the forest cover began to break up. Sometimes humans were the catalyst for widespread changes leading to the formation of heathlands on the thinner sandy soils or to blanket bogs in certain upland regions. After 4000 BC deliberate clearance began to provide land for the growing of crops and for the pasturing of domestic animals.

But alongside these anthropogenic impacts, minor fluctuations in climate brought their own changes. By 8000 BC the temperature had risen to levels higher than at present, but around 6200 BC there was a sudden cold spell lasting for a decade or two. Thereafter there was comparatively little variation except towards the beginning of the first millennium, when the previously warm, dry conditions gave way to a cooler, wetter phase. During the climatic optimum, c.1250–c.1000 BC, cultivation could take place up to 400 metres above sea-level, but as the weather became more stormy with mean temperatures falling by nearly 2 °C, the shortened growing season meant that many upland settlements above 250 metres had to be abandoned. Minor climatic fluctuations clearly affected communities living at the extremes, but for the vast majority of the population these will have had comparatively little effect. Human communities adapted quickly to the micro-environments offered by the islands and showed significant flexibility in adjusting their economic strategies to the changes they faced.

Cognitive Geographies

How the early Britons perceived the lands in which they lived is impossible to say with any degree of certainty. Until around 6000 BC hunter-gatherer groups will have had little conception of the major geomorphologic change going on around them, but thereafter the rate of inundation and the catastrophic effects of storm surges were on such a scale that coastal communities, particularly those around the fast-expanding North Sea, will have experienced irreversible change within a lifetime. The sense of the sea as a force for change and as an inundator would have become embedded within the folk memory. It might not be too fanciful to suggest that the many traditional stories of inundation told in the early medieval period derive from very distant memories passed from one generation to the next—legends that would remind communities of the fickle behaviour of the ocean and of the liminal nature of the interface between land and sea. In this way they will have built up a cognitive geography of their landscapes.

For those used to exploiting territories in the southern North Sea region, the eventual separation of Britain from continental Europe, probably in the fifth millennium BC, may have given some awareness of Britain's growing isolation but little sense of its true island nature. When the concept of island Britain first became understood, we can only speculate. In the east it may have only gradually come into consciousness as the last of the land between Essex and the Low Countries disappeared beneath the sea, but in the west the sense of separation between Britain and the adjacent continent was very real, especially for those attempting to make the sea journey. Perhaps the different geographies led to different concepts of space. In the east, the land was the dominant feature: it was a place of marshlands, inlets, and rivers that could be navigated on foot or by boat following watercourses and coast-lines. The west was entirely different. It was a land of promontories confronting the ocean. Movement over any distance meant taking to the sea and making journeys out of sight of land. The movement of hunter-gatherer communities into Ireland can only have been accomplished by taking long sea journeys across the dividing waters and, as we shall see later, there is evidence to suggest that even longer voyages were occasionally made. While the peoples of western Britain may not have conceived of their land as an island, they will have been all too aware of the sea as a dominant reality. The experience of different personal geographies led to very different perceptions of space and to different attitudes to mobility.

Britain as an Island

Strabo, Diodorus Siculus, and Caesar, writing in the first century BC, were well aware that Britain and Ireland were islands, but the origin of this knowledge is not immediately apparent. Herodotus, in the fifth century BC, had heard of offshore islands in this part of Europe, but his awareness was vague and was probably based on travellers' tales eventually reaching the Greek colony of Massalia (Marseille). A more likely source for the information used by first-century writers is Pytheas, himself a native of Massalia, who explored the north-western fringes of Europe in about 320 BC and probably circumnavigated Britain as part of his expedition. Pytheas' description of these remote regions was well known to later writers like Timaeus and Eratosthenes, and it was through them that his observations were made accessible to the first-century BC writers whose texts survive today. Indeed, Strabo acknowledges Pytheas as a source for some of his information about Britain, even though he is dismissive of much of what Pytheas says.

Pytheas' journey was, by any standards, a remarkable achievement. The simplest interpretation of the tantalizing scraps of information that survive is that he used local ships, reaching Cornwall from Brittany and then travelling northwards along the Irish Sea to the Shetlands. There is the possibility that he went on to Iceland, or at least talked to people who had been there, before sailing south along the east coast and then westwards along the south coast, returning home, presumably via Brittany, the way he had come. How long the journey took, and how many detours he made, we can only guess. His own claim that he 'traversed the whole of Prettanikē accessible by foot' suggests that it was a thorough exploration, while his detailed knowledge of the amber production on the coast of Jutland hints of at least one possible excursion.

The picture of Britain that Pytheas brought back to the Mediterranean world is probably most closely reported in the descriptions given by Diodorus Siculus more than two centuries later:

> Britain is triangular in shape, much as is Sicily, but its sides are not equal. The island stretches obliquely along the coast of Europe, and the point where it is least distant from the continent, we are told, is the promontory which men call Kantion [the Isle of Thanet] and this is about 100 stades [19 kilometres] from the mainland, at the place where the sea has its outlet, whereas the second promontory, known as Belerion [Land's End], is said to be a voyage of four days from the mainland, and the last, writers tell us, extends out into the open sea and is named Orcas [Orkney]. Of the sides of Britain, the shortest, which extends along Europe, is 7,500 stades [1,400 kilometres], the second from the Strait to the tip [at the north] is 15,000 stades [2,800 kilometres], and the last is 20,000 stades [3,700 kilometres], so the entire circuit of the island amounts to 42,500 stades [7,900 kilometres].
>
> (Diodorus Siculus 5.21–2)

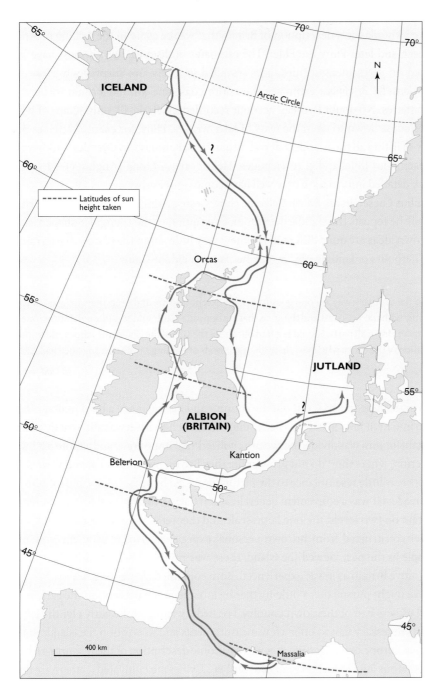

2.19 A reconstruction of the journey of Pytheas about 320 BC. The latitudes at which he measured sun heights are shown. Whether or not he journeyed to Iceland and Jutland or simply learned of these places from other travellers is uncertain

Here is the classical description of Britain that we see again in the writing of Strabo, Caesar, and later Pliny the Elder. The estimates of distance, which must have been based on assessments of distances travelled in a day, are surprisingly close. The *Encyclopaedia Britannica* estimates the entire coast-line around Britain to be 7,580 kilometres. No doubt Pytheas' account recorded much detail, only scraps of which have come down to us in the texts of later writers. Pliny, for example, makes great play of listing all the islands that constitute the Britannias: '40 Orcades [Orkneys] . . . 7 Haemodes [Shetland?], 30 Hebudes [Hebrides] . . . Mona [Anglesey]' (*HN* 4.103). Such detailed information may well have come from Pytheas.

Julius Caesar, in his *Bellum Gallicum*, shows a surprising uncertainty about Britain. While he repeats the standard textbook description of the triangular-shaped island, his own ideas are quite different. He knew very little about the people, the terrain, or the harbours or landing places. Nor, he claimed, did the Gauls.

In the ordinary way no one goes to Britain except traders, and even they are acquainted only with the sea-coast and the areas that are opposite Gaul. And so, although I summoned traders from all parts, I could not find out about the size of the island, the names and population of the tribes who lived there, their methods of fighting or the customs they had.

(*B Gall.* 4.20)

Having sent people to scout out the country and having made a brief military incursion into Kent in 55 BC, he was better informed, but his vision was still strictly limited. Britain for him was divided between a civilized 'maritime zone' and a more backward 'interior', where they 'do not grow grain: they live on milk and meat and wear skins'. This bears little resemblance to the picture provided by archaeology, but for him and his readers it was a convenient generalization. Caesar, then, was able to comprehend Britain on two levels: the one large-scale and theoretical, based on earlier texts; the other constructed from his own personal experience. This is probably how most people in the past viewed the island: there was mythical Britain as it was told and cognitive Britain as it was experienced. Both contained elements of reality.

We might pursue this a little further by looking at the perception the early medieval writers had of their own country. For Bede, writing in the early eighth century, it was necessary first to offer a few measurements and to position the islands in relation to Europe before getting down to a fulsome description of the resource-rich and prosperous land as 'rich in grain and timber . . . vines are cultivated . . . there are many land and sea birds . . . plentiful springs and rivers abounding in fish . . . salt and hot springs . . . rich veins of many metals', and so on. Bede's intent, as a pious churchman, was to praise God's bounty and to present Britain as a favoured land.

Nennius, nearly a century later, in selecting from the documents available to him, chose to put a particular emphasis on the sea, telling us that Britain had three large islands: one 'towards Armorica', called the Isle of Wight; the second between Britain and Ireland, called the Isle of Man; and the third at the extreme edge of the world, called Orkney. He continues:

> In Britain there are many rivers, that flow in all directions, to the east, west, south and north. But two rivers excel beyond the rest, the Thames and Severn, like the two arms of Britain, on which ships once travelled, carrying goods for the sake of commerce. The British once occupied it and ruled it all from sea to sea.
>
> (*Historia Brittonum*, 9)

Here is a different vision from Bede's: the sea takes prominence over the land. Bede views Britain from within, while Nennius looks on the island from without. Their cognitive geographies were diametrically opposed.

Sufficient has been said to show that the way people see geography is conditioned by many factors embedded in their own experience. It will be important for us, as we consider the successive generations of Britons, to attempt to put aside our geographies, based as they are on maps and Google Earth, and to enter into theirs, constrained by personal experience enhanced by travellers' tales.

The Various Faces of Britain

The discussion of cognitive geographies offers a warning against too great a reliance on geographical determinism; however, the physical diversity of the British Isles must have conditioned the way in which human communities responded to the varied constraints and opportunities offered by geomorphology and climate.

At a very simple level Britain can be divided into north and south and into east and west. The country extends across 11° of latitude from 50° north to 61° north, a distance of 1,200 kilometres. As a consequence, the average July day on the south coast will experience 6.5 hours of bright sunshine, while at the northern extremity of the island this is reduced to 4.5 hours. The east–west divide is created by the relief of the land, with the west dominated by its chains of mountains and uplands. These form a barrier to the predominantly Atlantic weather systems and cause the moist air to rise and precipitation to occur. As a result, western areas of the country receive over 1000 millimetres of rain a year, while eastern areas have less than 600 millimetres. Given these basic variables, it is inevitable that the crop-growing capacity of the north-west will differ significantly from that of the south-east. Such differences are bound to condition the subsistence regimes practised, and these, in turn, will limit the holding capacity of the landscape and thus affect the social system.

But against this overarching structure there are many variables. Local differences in relief, soils, and climate cause a palimpsest of micro-environments to which communities respond in varied ways, while in the *longue durée* (the deep rhythms of slow change that underlie long periods of the past) minor fluctuations in climate may significantly alter the crop-growing capacity of land, especially in the marginal areas. Add to this the power of human activity to bring about major and lasting change in the landscape, whether intentional or unintentional, and something of the complex dynamics of the human–environment interaction begins to become apparent. The archaeologist has constantly to change focus to move between the broad generalizing overviews and the more finely textured regional and local patterns. Both are essential to our understanding, as will become apparent, but here we shall consider only the broader picture.

Central to the theme of this book is an understanding of the networks of connectivity that bind Britain to the neighbouring continent. These are, to a large extent, conditioned by geographical proximity. We can distinguish a number of distinct but overlapping zones. Three provide the most direct links between Britain and the Continent, the Atlantic core zone, the Channel zone, and the southern North Sea zone. In each, a ship's master setting off from one shore, armed with a knowledge of local winds and tides and having some competence in seamanship, could reasonably expect to reach the adjacent coast within one, or two at the most, days of direct sailing. While the more experienced might have chosen to take the shortest distance, requiring him to be out of sight of land for some period, a more cautious seaman might have taken a longer route to keep land always in view. Thus, a practised ship's master setting out from the Rhine mouth bound for the estuary of the River Yare might have chosen to sail on the latitude across the southern North Sea direct to the British coast and then follow the coast northwards to his planned destination. A less confident sailor might have chosen to take the longer route south-westwards down the continental coast until Kent could be sighted and then across the straits to follow the British coast northwards to the point of destination. The choice of route may have depended on experience, but managing the winds and tides will have played a significant part. Those sailing between Armorica and south-west Britain had rather less choice since part of the journey would always be out of sight of land, but a crossing could be done at night steering on true north. If the journey had been planned in two stages, using Guernsey as a midway point, the open-sea journey would have been reduced.

Beyond the three core zones onward journeys could be made using the North Sea, the inner Atlantic, or the outer Atlantic coastal routes. Experienced seamen making long-distance journeys, knowing the sea-marks and with a good 'mental chart', would

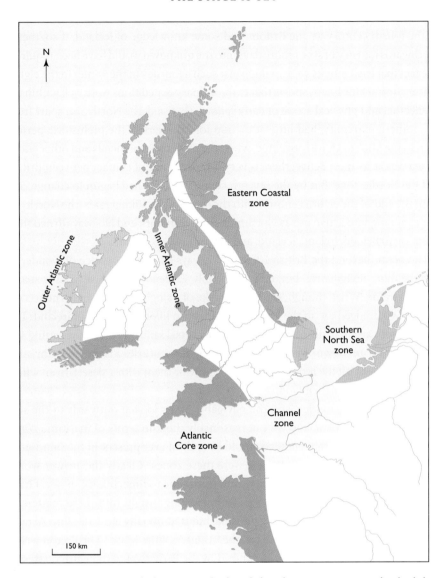

2.20 The major zones into which Britain, Ireland, and the adjacent continent can be divided are dependent largely upon ease of access by sea

have chosen to keep well out to sea, making landfall only where necessary to take on food and water, but there must always have been a lively pattern of local shipping engaged in short-haul cabotage (coastal trading). For communities living in the coastal zone, movement by sea would have been quicker and safer than movement by land.

The extent to which more adventurous long-distance voyages were made out of sight of land must remain largely unknown. There is circumstantial evidence that

65

by the fourth century BC the Britons had some knowledge of Iceland. If so, then a northwards journey of six or more days into the unknown would have been required. The fact that Irish monks were making just such a journey in the winter in the eighth century, using hide boats, shows that extraordinary expeditions were well within the intellectual and physical scope of early sailors. That said, the North Sea, apart from its southern extremity, had little attraction for travellers in the prehistoric period. Even in the Mid- to Late Bronze Age, when the movement of metals and other goods by sea was at its most active, there is very little evidence of contact between Britain and the Nordic zone. But by the seventh century AD this had begun to change, and from the end of the eighth century, with the onset of the Viking raids, the North Sea routes sprang into active use as Northmen from Denmark and Norway turned their attention to Britain, Ireland, Iceland, and eventually Greenland.

The ocean beyond the British Isles must always have been a place of wonder to lure the more imaginative, but, understandably, evidence of such voyages is sparse in the extreme. What, though, should we make of a single Roman pot of the second century AD dredged up off the Porcupine Bank, 250 kilometres west of Ireland? Did it come from a ship badly off-course or from a vessel sailing towards the setting sun to explore the unknown? In the seventh and eighth centuries AD the Irish Christian monks (*peregrini*) felt the lure of the ocean to provide them with a 'desert' from where better to contemplate their God.

The coasts, the estuaries, and the navigable rivers looked outwards to the sea-routes that bound them, and we can reasonably think in terms of maritime zones where the sea and all that entailed would have been ever present in the mindset of the communities. But how extensive were these zones? Clearly the answer would have varied from location to location, and from time to time, but it can never have extended deep inland. Brittany offers an interesting insight into these matters. It may be thought of as a maritime peninsula, but traditionally it divides into Armor, 'the country near the sea', and Argoat, the 'country of the wood'. The Breton writer Pêr-Jakez Helias, describing his childhood in the early twentieth century, stresses the very sharp divide that existed between the coastal communities, who were 'of the sea', and the landsmen only a few kilometres inland, who firmly turned their back on the maritime world. So it may have been for Britain. But the situation is a little more complex. Perhaps we should distinguish between a coastal interface and a maritime zone—the coastal interface being the region in which communities had a direct relationship to the sea and the estuaries, and the maritime zone being the territory behind it, where the influence of the sea was manifest in terms of social and economic interactions. The extent of this zone would be conditioned by ease of inland communication.

Standing back and viewing the British Isles from a distance, they fall not into the traditional north–south divide with which we are familiar today, but into two very different countries, east-facing and west-facing, both with extensive coastal interfaces and deep maritime hinterlands. Progressing further inland away from the sea, one enters a more uncertain land—a zone between—with its own distinctive characteristics. This is a generalization, of course, but it offers a model that may help us to structure our approach to understanding the Britons in all their variety.

People on the Move

One of the principal themes explored in this book is human mobility. The propensity for mobility in the human is a complex phenomenon involving such innate characteristics as instinctive behaviour, compulsion, and aspiration, as well as the capacity to create enabling technologies. The human animal is hard-wired to be mobile, and herein lies its success in colonizing virtually every ecological niche on earth. This has been achieved over a comparatively short period of time and has required rapid adjustment to a range of differing environments. No other animal has managed the like.

A genetically conditioned predisposition to be mobile is, however, balanced by a sense of territoriality which mitigates against wandering. The equilibrium between the two is delicate and unstable. Mobility can easily be triggered by external factors (compulsion) or by internal imperatives (aspiration). Thus, if the community grows to such a size that it can no longer sustain itself in the territory it controls, the natural response is to extend the borders of the territory or to disperse sectors of the population to colonize more distant ecological niches. If a society structured itself so that movement away from home to found a 'colony' was viewed as prestigious, then a process of constant forward movement would be set in train. An explanation of this kind would account for the very rapid spread of food-producing communities across Europe in the period 6000–5500 BC. In addition to population growth, other 'compulsions' might include climatic deterioration or aggressive pressures from neighbours or any combination of all three.

Aspiration as an imperative for mobility is more difficult to demonstrate, but in the example given above a young man aspiring to leadership would welcome the opportunity to set off on a colonial mission, thus enhancing his status in society. Similarly, status related to the acquiring and disposal of goods might encourage mobility in pursuit of the desired raw materials. A rather more esoteric form of aspiration is status attained by travel for the sake of having made a distant voyage and for gathering exotic artefacts and arcane knowledge. This might, at first sight, seem to be rather unlikely, but such systems are well known to anthropologists and provide the motivation behind the journeys described in Homer. The Viking who set out from northern France by ship to attack Rome was more interested in the prestige of the daring exploit than in any spoils he might come by. The fact that he mistakenly attacked the port of Luni thinking it to be Rome did not diminish his achievement. He could still come back and tell a good story.

Mobility, then, could enhance status through the acquisition of commodities or esoteric knowledge and by demonstrating qualities of leadership and daring. All these elements in equal measure motivated Caesar's conquest of Gaul and his expeditions to Britain, and, later, lay behind the many west European expeditions to the Americas. Today's passion for travel to exotic and out-of-the-way places, and the need for images and artefacts brought back to enhance our story-telling, are another manifestation of the deep-seated human desire for mobility.

In the hunter-gatherer period before Britain became an island, communities were habitually mobile. Their lifestyle required segments of the population to move in search of food as the seasons demanded. In the Upper Palaeolithic period, immediately following the last ice age, the movement of hunters following wild animals took place over considerable distances and would have required an ability to navigate using the stars. It must have been in this context that a detailed knowledge of the night sky was gained and passed on as an essential part of the communities' oral tradition. By the Mesolithic period, with the spread of forest and a new range of smaller animals, the hunting territories may have become more restricted in extent, but the need for navigation remained.

Evidence for fishing suggests that coastal communities had now begun to exploit the more open seas, following shoals as they changed their feeding grounds. The navigational skills learnt by hunters operating on land would have been essential to those taking to the sea. We know that by about 3000 BC the farming communities of the Atlantic zone had developed a sophisticated understanding of celestial events— an understanding that they celebrated in the construction of megalithic monuments. What we are seeing embedded in the great megalithic tombs of Newgrange in the Boyne valley and Maes Howe in Orkney is an awareness of the heavens, based on careful observation, developed and passed down from one generation to the next over the 6,000 years or so of hunter-gatherer activity. It is probably no exaggeration to say that knowledge gained and refined in this period provided the full range of skill sets used by navigators, largely unaugmented until the introduction of the magnetic compass in the twelfth century AD.

Sailing in the waters around the British Isles required a formidable array of skills. First and foremost was a knowledge of the tidal flows, especially their periodicity, their varying forces, and the moderating effects of winds. All this could be learnt only from experience transmitted orally in sea lore. Lack of that knowledge could lead to disaster, as Julius Caesar was to find out to his cost when, in 55 BC, he sent an expedition to Britain. Four days after the initial landing eighteen transport vessels set sail from the Gaulish coast:

> When they were getting close to Britain . . . suddenly such a sudden storm blew up that none of them could hold course. Some were carried back to where they had started from; others were swept down to the south-west part of the island, at great peril to themselves, but even so they dropped anchor. However, when they began to ship water, they were forced to put out to sea into the darkness of the night to make for the continent. That night there happened to be a full moon. This time of the month, though we did not realize it, regularly brings the highest tides in the Atlantic. So the warships I had used for transporting my army, and which had been hauled up on the beach, were engulfed by the tide, and at the same time the transports that were riding at anchor were battered by the storm . . . Several of the ships were smashed; the rest were unusable, having lost their cables, their anchors, and the rest of their gear.
>
> (*B Gall.* 6.289)

It was a hard-learnt lesson, but Caesar's force still lacked a detailed understanding of the Channel tides. The next year another expedition set out from Gaul:

> We set sail about sunset, carried along by a gentle south-west breeze, but about midnight the wind dropped and we could not maintain course. The tide carried us on too far and when dawn came we saw Britain far behind us on our left. Once again we followed the turn of the tide and used our oars to reach the part of the island that last summer's experience had shown to have been the best landing places.
>
> (*B Gall.* 5.8)

Having successfully landed and set in train the land operation, they were struck by disaster again:

> On the previous night there had been a great storm that had damaged almost all of our ships and cast them up on the shore; the anchors and cables had not held firm, and the sailors and pilots could not cope with the force of the gale; as a result a great deal of damage had been caused by ships colliding with each other.
>
> (*B Gall.* 6.10)

By the end of the British campaign of 54 BC Caesar was anxious to leave the island. When a second wave of transports sent from Gaul failed to arrive, having been 'driven back', presumably by weather, Caesar managed to put the remaining troops in the ships available to him, 'afraid that the approaching equinox would prevent us from sailing'. He must have been very relieved that he did not have to face the ocean again. This episode shows just how difficult Britain's waters could be to those unschooled in the vagaries of its winds and tides.

A ship's master working the seas around Britain needed two rather different skills, those of pilotage and of navigation. Since much of the sailing time would have been in sight of land, his skills as a pilot would have been of vital importance. Inshore sailing was dangerous. Winds could drive a ship onto a lee shore, while the massive tidal range experienced in these waters could expose shelving rocks far out to sea. He also needed to know the safest anchorages and landing beaches and how to approach them or take departure under different conditions of tide and wind. Since it is highly likely that most shipping movements were short-haul in restricted waters, knowledge could be accumulated and passed down from one generation to the next, building up a very detailed familiarity with the local conditions.

Navigation in open waters required the ship's master to have a mental map of his sphere of operations, knowing the relationship of places and the distances apart measured in sailing times in a fair wind. He needed to be able to estimate speed and direction of travel and to be able to compensate for leeway caused by winds. All navigators would have had to set a course requiring that they sailed in a preconceived direction. To maintain that direction was vital. This could most conveniently be done by sailing at night so that the stars could be used, but another valuable indicator of direction was swell, the movement of the sea set up by the prevailing wind. Swell persisted over long periods and was largely unaffected by currents or tides. A competent sailor could easily distinguish the direction of the 'mother wave' from other, more superficial movements of the sea. But however good a navigator's judgement was, the moment of truth arrived when land came into sight. This was the moment when a new set of decisions had to be made. The safety of the venture depended on assessing exactly where the vessel was in relation to its planned landfall. Misidentification of the approaching land could be disastrous. In good visibility a headland 300 metres high could be spotted from 35 nautical miles out to sea, while land 30 metres high only became visible from 11 nautical miles. The lower the land, the less time there is for corrections to be made to the course before the dangers of the coastal waters are reached. In the case of a ship setting out in the first century BC from a port on the north coast of Brittany making for the haven sheltered by Hengistbury Head, the shipmaster would aim to position himself at dawn so that he would catch sight of St Alban's Head to port and St Catherine's Head to starboard. After a few more nautical miles his position would be confirmed when the distinctive chalk headlands of

Durlston Head and the Needles came into view. He would then be able to adjust his course to make for Hengistbury Head and its sheltered anchorage on Christchurch Harbour. Failure to see the first pair of sea-marks at the expected time would warn him that he was off-course and in danger of having to face the perils of Portland Bill or the contrary tides of the eastern Solent.

Sailing in less familiar waters out of sight of land was a more dangerous pursuit, and some sense of the proximity and direction of the land was essential. There were many indicators that an experienced sailor would look out for. The orographic clouds that formed over land could be spotted long before the land itself came into view, while the direction of land might be indicated by the flight of birds such as the

2.21 Hengistbury Head, protecting the almost landlocked Christchurch Harbour, was an important point of entry in prehistoric times. The harbour was well shielded from excesses of weather and linked to the hinterland of Wessex by river valleys. The sea-marks on the approach helped sailors to navigate safely to the port

fulmar, which makes for land to roost as dusk sets in. Bird flight was an important indicator to the sailor, as the myth of Noah and the dove reminds us. There is also the story of the Viking explorers who were guided to Iceland by the flight of a bird released from the boat. It may have been the annual migration of the whooper swan, flying northwards up the west coast of Britain, that stirred the curiosity of sailors: encouraged to follow the flight, they could have reached Iceland. The circumstantial evidence recorded by Pytheas, as we have seen, hints strongly that Iceland may have been known as early as the fourth century BC.

Ships and Sails

That people took to the sea implied the existence of craft capable of giving the assurance of a safe return. While the physical evidence of such vessels in British waters is rather sparse, we can be sure of the existence of three kinds of boat: log boats, skin boats, and plank-built vessels. The log boat was a comparatively simple structure consisting, as its name implies, of a felled tree that had been hollowed out sufficiently to give it stability on water and a capacity for carrying people and cargo. The technology necessary to create such a vessel required little more than a stone axe or adze, aided by the use of fire. The earliest known log boats, dating to the Mesolithic period, are found in France, the Netherlands, and Denmark, but the general type continued in use well into the Middle Ages. In Britain the earliest known log boat dates to the fourth millennium BC. While craft of this sort were well suited to rivers and estuaries and could have been used safely in inshore waters, their capability on more open sea is less sure. However, some of the continental examples have had holes bored through their sides near the top edge, which may have been to attach wash-strakes. An alternative possibility is that they were to fasten stabilizers or outriggers, or to facilitate the lashing of two or more boats together. By widening the beam in this way the vessel would have been given the greater stability necessary for sea travel. The discovery of log boats containing hearths at the Danish Mesolithic site of Tybrind Vig might support the idea that these vessels were away from land for extended periods of time. Log boats would normally have been propelled by paddles, examples of which have been found, but in shallow waters they could well have been punted.

Alongside the log boats we may assume that boats of hide stretched on a light wood framework were also being used from the earliest times, at least from the Mesolithic period. Although no physical remains have been found, the technologies were certainly available. There is ample evidence for leather working, and considerable skill in fashioning small wood is demonstrated by elaborate fish traps found on a number of Mesolithic sites. A hide boat has many advantages: it can be built broad-beamed, giving it both seaworthiness and a bulk-carrying capacity, and it is light enough to be quickly beached and carried easily overland.

The earliest evidence we have of hide boats in Atlantic waters comes from the fourth-century AD poem *Ora Maritima* ('Sea-Coasts') by Avienus, which, as we have seen, incorporates an earlier account that goes back to at least the fourth century BC. It refers to 'skiffs of skin . . . [they] marvellously fit out boats with jointed skins and often run through the vast saltwater on leather' (lines 101–6).

It is possible that the original source may have been Pytheas, writing at the end of the fourth century BC. Pytheas is almost certainly the source from whom the third-century writer Timaeus learnt of six-day sea-crossings made by the Britons to the Continent in 'boats of osier covered with stitched skins'. On this Timaeus is quoted by Pliny the Elder (*HN* 4.104). Later, in the first century BC, Julius Caesar refers to boats used by the Britons that he had observed in 55 or 54 BC: 'The keels and ribs were made of light wood; the rest of the hulk was made of woven withies covered with hides' (*B Civ.* 1.54). And a little later Strabo mentions 'boats of tanned leather' sailing on the 'flood tides and the shoal water' off the coast of north-western Iberia (Strabo 3.37). Taken together, the literary evidence leaves little doubt that the skin boat played a prominent role in Atlantic seamanship in the last half of the first millennium BC. The vessel type with its high freeboard was well suited to Atlantic conditions, its buoyancy enabling it to ride the waves with ease. The tradition continued in Ireland into the early medieval period, as we learn from the vivid account of the hide boat built by St Brendan for his voyage into the Atlantic in the sixth century, and continues today in the currachs of the Aran Islands, though now the hides have been replaced by tarred canvas.

The only physical evidence we have of a hide boat is a remarkable gold model of the first century BC found at Broighter in County Derry. It represents a wide-bodied vessel kept rigid by eight thwarts providing seats for the rowers. The model is provided with eight pairs of rowing oars and a steering oar, and has a centrally placed cross-rigged mast showing that the vessel depicted was also powered by sail. A vessel of this kind with its crew of nine could with ease have carried bulky cargoes across the open seas.

The sail is an interesting addition. The Broighter boat model dates to about the time of Julius Caesar, and it is from Caesar, writing about the Venetic plank-built ships that he encountered off the southern coast of Brittany, that we learn of sails of rawhide suitable in toughness to contend with Atlantic gales. At what stage the sail was developed along the Atlantic seaboard it is difficult to say, but in the eighth century BC square-rigged Phoenician sailing vessels were making their way from the Mediterranean into the Atlantic and were exploring the seaways at least as far north

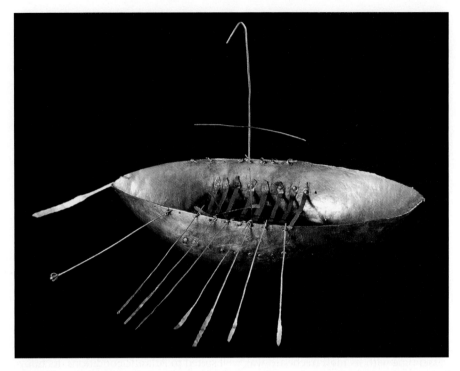

2.22 Gold model of a skin boat found at Broighter in County Derry dating to the first century BC. It had provision for eight rowers, a sail, and a steering oar, and clearly depicted a large vessel with considerable capacity

as Galicia (north-western Iberia). It is quite possible that Atlantic shipbuilders learnt the advantages of the sail from them, though the possibility that they may already have invented the concept should not be entirely rejected.

Log boats and hide boats were simple constructions requiring a limited tool-kit to produce. Given its versatility, the hide boat is likely to have been far more widely used for open-sea sailing than the log boats, whether or not they had been modified with outriggers. It remains a possibility, however, that the log boat, given greater capacity by the addition of wash-strakes to the sides, may lie at the beginning of a tradition that was to flourish in the second millennium BC: the tradition of the sewn-plank boat. Fragments of ten of these are known in British waters, five from the Humber estuary with another coming from the nearby coast, two from the Severn estuary, one from Dover, and one from the River Test. We shall consider the form and context of these remarkable vessels later (p. 227). What is relevant here is their position in the British shipbuilding tradition. They appear, fully developed, around 1900 BC, suggesting that they were the evolved product of a tradition going back presumably to the log boat. What is remarkable about them is their sophisticated carpentry, involving the fashioning of complex cleats, integral with the planks, to provide sockets for cross-strengthening timbers. This would have required the use of tools of copper or copper alloy. That metal tools were, indeed, used is shown by adze marks on the timbers. Since the earliest copper axes in Britain, of Irish manufacture, came into use around 2400 BC, with full bronze two centuries later, it is tempting to suggest that the development of copper and bronze technology empowered the carpenters, leading to these spectacular advances in shipbuilding. The improved vessels contributed to a surge in maritime traffic.

2.23 Large skin boats known as umiaks are still in use in Greenland. The technology used to build them has changed little since the Mesolithic period, and vessels like these would have been common in the prehistoric period in Atlantic waters

There is little evidence yet to show how the skills of the shipwright developed over the next millennium, but by the first century BC the Venetic sailors of southern Brittany were building sturdy plank-built vessels with keels and high bows and sterns, powered by sails set just in advance of midships. These are the vessels that so impressed Julius Caesar when he confronted them in a sea battle off Quiberon in 56 BC. He describes their massive frames constructed of timbers a foot thick fastened with nails 'as thick as a man's thumb'. Vessels of this kind continued in use in the Channel and southern North Sea throughout the Roman period and are well known from wrecks discovered at St Peter Port in Guernsey and at Blackfriars in the Thames. What inspired their development is uncertain. It may have been the Phoenician craft plying the coasts of Iberia from the eighth century, but without a ready supply of iron, needed in quantity to make the nails that held the timbers, such vessels could not have been constructed. In Britain the use of iron only began to become common in the third century BC. Once more, it seems, it was the appearance of a new metal that facilitated a major advance in shipbuilding. These new vessels were able to carry bulk cargoes on an unprecedented scale.

Sufficient will have been said to show that the sea, far from being a barrier to connectivity between Britain and the Continent, facilitated the movement of people, commodities and ideas. In the prehistoric period those with the resources to build sea-going vessels and the skills to sail them must have been revered as an elite—men with exceptional powers. In the exotic materials they were able to command and the esoteric knowledge they acquired, their power over land-based farmers was assured. They were a separate maritime caste.

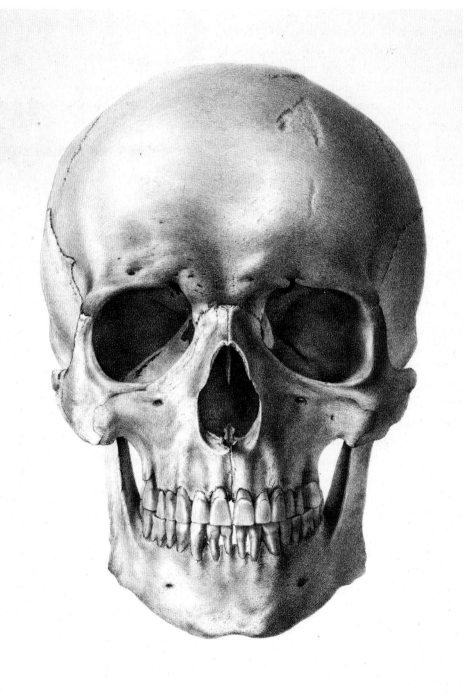

3

Interlude

ENTER THE ACTORS

WHEN Tacitus noted physical differences in the British population, suggesting that the red-haired, long-limbed Caledonians were of German origin while the swarthy faces and curly hair of the Silures in south Wales proclaimed a distant ancestry in Spain, he was engaging in the age-old practice of race recognition—a practice deeply rooted in our humanity. The human animal has always felt the need to distinguish 'us' from 'the others', and physical characteristics provide a ready method of doing so. Tacitus' observations on the Britons were made to give his readers some sense of historical depth where there was no real history to call on: he was using racial stereotypes, but in this instance he was not making value judgements.

In all populations there is visible variation. These variations are the result of genetic differences that are inherited. Thus, our appearance is to a large degree conditioned by our ancestry. This much has been understood for centuries, but only since the middle of the twentieth century, with the unravelling of the complexities of chromosomes and DNA, have the precise mechanisms of inheritance begun to be more fully understood. Before that breakthrough the only way in which scientists could attempt to separate out the different racial components in a population was by observing, measuring, and interpreting physical differences, an inexact and limited procedure prone to prejudice. The study of DNA has changed all that since we can now objectively study the genetic codes that determine physical appearance. By sampling the DNA of modern populations it is possible to identify the multiple lineages present and, knowing something of lineage formation, to begin to reconstruct the history of that population: it is a massively powerful tool, as we shall see. Another potentially valuable approach to charting ancestry is to study ancient DNA extracted from human skeletons or surviving tissue. Work has begun on this, but there are many difficulties to be overcome before a significant body of results can be obtained.

Characterizing the Britons by whatever methods were in favour at the time has been the pursuit of many ethnologists, archaeologists, and geneticists over the last two centuries.

Human Skulls

The work of the early barrow diggers like Cunnington and Colt Hoare in the early decades of the nineteenth century unearthed bones of 'ancient Britons' in quantity, but, partly because they were considered to be uninformative and partly because of the mores of the time, human remains were usually left in place unstudied. In Scandinavia, however, scientists were beginning to develop an interest in ethnology through the study of the physical remains of past populations, in particular skulls, which, they believed, allowed racial differences to be categorized. A breakthrough came in 1842, when the Swedish anatomist Anders Retzius (1796–1860) published a technique for measuring the cephalic index, providing a relative method for defining head form, dividing brachycephalic (short-headed) from dolichocephalic (long-headed) types. His results, presented to the British Association for the Advancement of Science in Southampton in 1846 in a paper entitled 'On the Ethnographical Distribution of Round and Elongated Crania', inspired an enthusiasm among British antiquaries for the new scientific study of craniology: here was a way to begin to tease out the racial component of early British populations.

One of the earliest British proponents of the Scandinavian approach to craniology was the Bristol physician James Cowles Prichard (1786–1848), and it was through him that William Wilde (1815–76), an Irish ethnologist and doctor (who is invariably introduced in books of this kind with the irrelevance that he was the father of Oscar), developed an interest in the subject. By studying Irish skulls Wilde believed he could pinpoint successive waves of immigrants: first, the 'simple pastoral' Firbolgs, and then the 'globular-headed, light-eyed, fair-headed Celtic people', whom he equated with the incoming Tuatha Dé Dannan, and finally the arrival of northern races coming from Scandinavia in the ninth century AD. The significance of Wilde's work was that not only was he using his collection of ancient skulls to enliven Irish prehistory, thus

3.1 Nineteenth-century excavations in progress at a Bronze Age barrow on Shapworth Heath, Dorset. From C. Woolls, *The Barrow Diggers*, published in 1839

demonstrating the importance of physical anthropology, he was also arguing that the 'Celtic race' was not the first to inhabit Ireland, which was a significant innovation at the time. A little later the Scottish antiquary Daniel Wilson (1816–92) made much the same point about his home country, again with the aid of craniology, in his work *Inquiry into the Evidence for the Existence of Primitive Races in Scotland prior to the Celts* (1850). Wilson was also the first person to coin the word 'prehistory'.

Wilde and Wilson, using the comparatively limited collections of ancient skulls available to them, had amply demonstrated the potential of craniology. What was now required to advance the study was a larger sample. The man who rose to the challenge was the enthusiastic barrow digger Thomas Bateman (1821–61), who, unlike Cunnington and Colt Hoare, understood the value of skeletal material and amassed a considerable collection of skulls, which he published in his *Ten Years' Digging in Celtic and Saxon Grave Hills* (1861). It was seeing Bateman's collection displayed in his private museum that inspired another gentleman scholar, Joseph Barnard Davis (1801–81), to take up the study of craniology. Davis, together with the physician John Thurnam (1810–73), began work on a monumental study, *Crania Britannica*, which they published in six parts between 1856 and 1865, illustrating and describing in minute detail fifty-

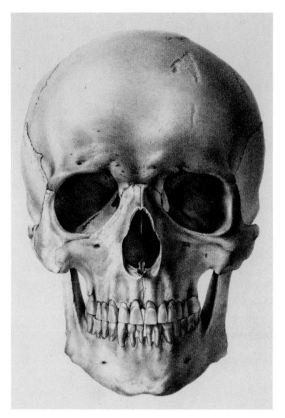

3.2 Skull of an 'ancient Briton' from Green Gate Hill, Yorkshire. From an illustration in *Crania Britannica* by Joseph Barnard Davis and John Thurnam, published between 1856 and 1865

six skulls. The work was a masterpiece of presentation, but the relatively small sample and significant variability among the skulls meant that the authors were reluctant to be too specific in their conclusions. However, in a paper read to the Anthropological Society of London in 1865, Thurnam was prepared to go so far as to distinguish between a dolichocephalic (long-headed) Stone Age race and an incoming brachycephalic (round-headed) Bronze Age population.

This broad division passed rapidly into the general literature on prehistory. Though Thurnam had been cautious in his conclusions, later writers, distanced from the reality of the limited data set, were prepared to be more expansive. Thomas Rice Holmes, in *Ancient Britain and the Invasions of Julius Caesar* (1907), describes the Neolithic inhabitants of the islands thus:

> All, or almost all, had long narrow skulls, their faces were commonly oval, their features regular, and their noses aquiline: most of them were of middle height and their limbs, as a rule, were rather delicate than robust.

He goes on to say that they shared the same physical characteristics with the Gauls and the Spanish. These indigenous inhabitants, he says, were replaced in the Bronze Age by men who

> were taller and much more powerfully built than the aborigines: their skulls were comparatively short and round; they had massive jaws, strongly marked features, enormously prominent brow ridges and retreating foreheads; and their countenances must have been stern, forbidding and sometimes almost brutal.

In the interests of painting a vivid picture of Britain and the Britons, Rice Holmes embroiders the tentative conclusions of Davis and Thurnam, pushing well beyond the limitations of the evidence. The truth is that the sample was too small and too varied to sustain such rigid classifications, a fact that has been increasingly acknowledged over the past hundred years. Craniology has passed out of fashion, but, as we shall see, in the context of modern population studies, it may yet have something to offer.

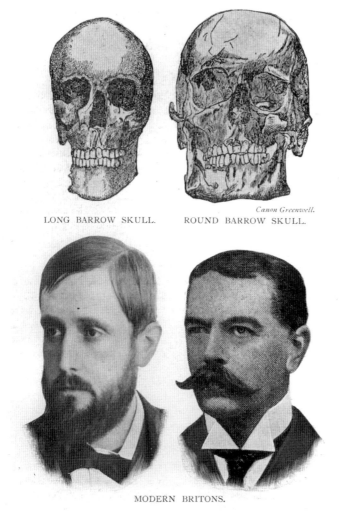

Canon Greenwell.

LONG BARROW SKULL.   ROUND BARROW SKULL.

MODERN BRITONS.

3.3 The two physical types of Britons as conceived by the Victorians

Faces, Eyes, and Hair

Many inherited characteristics, in addition to skull shape, create individual faces that can be recognized. Most societies understand this and have stereotypes that enable them to 'place' other people in relation to themselves. Casting an eye over fellow passengers in a tube train, most of us would be able to make a guess at the region of origin of our co-travellers with varying degrees of accuracy. It is the same reasoning, based on a mix of observation and preconception, that allowed Tacitus to speculate about the origins of the Caledonians and the southern Welsh. The desire and ability to 'place' others is innate to the human condition.

Characterizing physical differences among the British population became a consuming and lifelong passion for the Bristol physician John Beddoe (1826–1911). His position, first as a doctor in private practice and later as a consultant at Bristol Royal Infirmary, provided him with an ideal opportunity to observe his fellow beings at close hand. When possible he took skull measurements, but, realizing the difficulties in obtaining a large and varied enough sample to provide grounds for generalization, he decided to initiate a wide-ranging survey using only hair colour and eye colour, both of which could be observed quickly and without the need to engage personally with the specimen under study. To facilitate recording he devised three categories of eye colour based on degrees of lightness and darkness, and five classes of hair colour from red or auburn to jet black. At each of his sampling localities scattered throughout the country he stood unobserved and recorded everyone who passed within three yards. Then, using a formula, he worked out a score for each, which he called the 'Index of Nigrescence'.

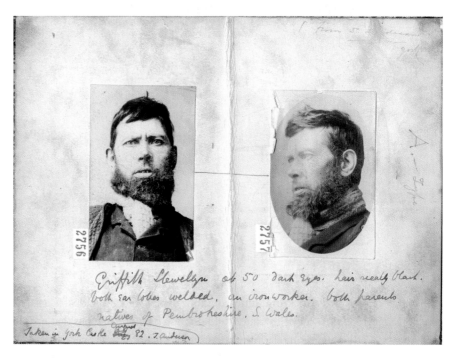

3.4 One of the pages from an album of photographs recording the physical types prevalent among the Britons compiled by John Beddoe in 1882

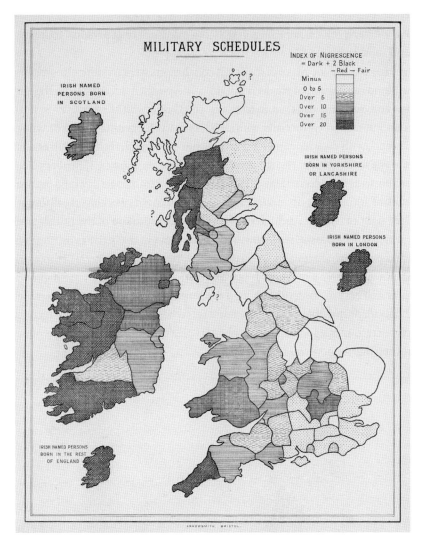

MILITARY SCHEDULES

INDEX OF NIGRESCENCE
= Dark + 2 Black
― Red ― Fair

Minus
0 to 5
Over 5
Over 10
Over 15
Over 20

IRISH NAMED
PERSONS BORN
IN SCOTLAND

IRISH NAMED PERSONS
BORN IN YORKSHIRE
OR LANCASHIRE

IRISH NAMED PERSONS
BORN IN LONDON

IRISH NAMED PERSONS
BORN IN THE REST
OF ENGLAND

3.5 Map from John Beddoe's *The Races of Britain*, published in 1885, showing his 'Index of Nigrescence' based on hair and eye colour

Beddoe's activity was prodigious. He visited 472 different localities throughout Britain and Ireland and made a total of 43,000 observations. To this he added details of 13,800 army deserters from lists compiled to facilitate their pursuit and 4,390 records of his own patients. By any standards it was a massive database. Though lacking in statistical rigour, it gave a detailed picture of the British population showing the situation to be far more complex than previous generalizations had allowed. His book *The Races of Britain*, published in 1885, is a masterpiece of personal industry and scientific observation.

But what did Beddoe make of it all? His conclusions were modest: 'the greater part of the blond population of modern Britain . . . derive their ancestry from the Anglo-Saxons and Scandinavians'. In Ireland and the Gaelic west the population resulted from an interaction of Iberians with a 'harsh-featured, red-haired race', while the 'Celtic type', with dark hair and light eyes, he thought, might be the result of adaptations to the local climate. He had gone as far as his data allowed. If further advances were to be made in understanding the origin of the British, he said, it would be through the work of anthropologists, antiquarians, and philologists working in collaboration.

In the light of current research on the genetic constitution of the British population, which will be considered below, it might be thought that reliance on the physical appearance of an individual is too crude an approach to characterize ethnic origin. Faces, however, offer a real possibility for further study since they are highly polymorphic and easy to observe. Although the genes governing facial variations are still to be fully identified, this is one of the few cases where the DNA sequence (genotype) directly determines appearance (the phenotype). The genetics of the face offers an interesting line for new research.

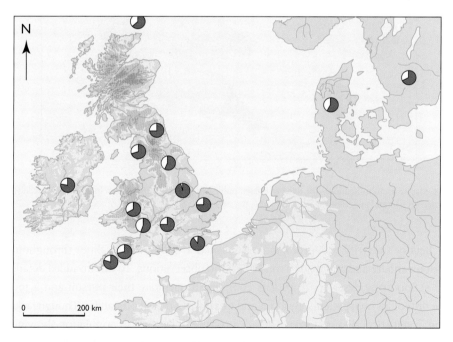

3.6 Map of the 'red hair' allele frequencies (MC1R). The white parts of the pie charts represent the percentage of carriers of red hair

Below the Skin

In the early decades of the twentieth century scientists came to appreciate that human blood could be divided into a number of sometimes incompatible groups. In 1900 the principal groups, A, B, and O, were defined, with AB identified two years later. As research progressed, new groups were discovered, but it was not until the end of the First World War that medical researchers attached to the army began to understand something of the geographical distribution of the different groups and to realize that blood groups must be inherited. This provided an entirely new tool for scientists to begin to consider the development of world populations—and one freed from the subjectivity of old methods of hair and eye colour recognition.

After the Second World War the task of compiling a corpus of all the extant blood group data fell to the molecular biologist Arthur Mourant. In 1976 Mourant published a magisterial volume, *The Distribution of the Human Blood Groups*, comprising nearly half a million individual readings. From such a large database, treated statistically it is possible to define a multitude of patterns reflecting the genetic history of the different populations. The patterns are, however, just that: they offer no explanation of population movements, nor do they take with them any chronological implications.

A few examples will illustrate the problem. In Ireland blood group O is dominant, particularly in the west of the country, where, in County Clare, it runs to 80 per cent of the population. If one takes the 70 per cent contour as a marker, a distinct Atlantic zone becomes apparent, including the whole of Ireland together with Scotland, north-west England, north Wales, much of the Breton peninsula, and north-eastern Iberia together with Aquitania. These regions, with a high percentage of blood group O, have a correspondingly lower percentage of blood group A (less than 25 per cent) when compared to the rest of western Europe. The simplest interpretation of these observations would be to

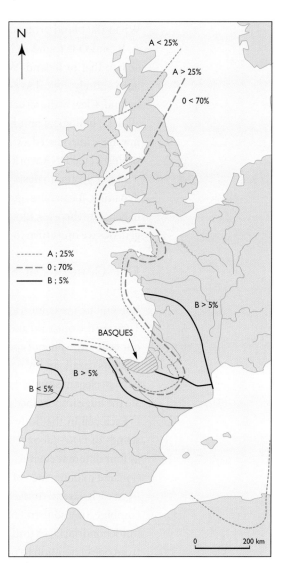

3.7 Selected blood group variations, showing the distinction between the Atlantic zone and continental Europe

suppose that this entire Atlantic zone may have shared a common ancestry, perhaps facilitated by movement by sea. If this is correct, it raises the question of how far back in time this contact goes: to this, blood group studies have no answer, though, as we shall see, DNA analysis is able to offer some suggestions.

Another intriguing example is the population of Iceland, which is known historically to have been settled by Norse communities arriving in the decade or two after AD 800. Before that the island was largely uninhabited apart from a few Irish monks. When the blood groups of the Icelandic population are studied, the percentage of A, B, and O is found to be very different from that of Norway but closely comparable to that of Ireland. Without the constraint of the historic record it would have been entirely logical to conclude that Iceland received an inflow of population from Ireland. Clearly the situation is complex, and to provide an explanation inclusive of all data, biological and historical, it is necessary to suppose that the Norse settlers may have introduced a strong Irish component, perhaps as wives or slaves. The more sophisticated DNA work suggests that this was indeed so.

Blood group analysis is, therefore, a limited tool for understanding population dynamics. It can raise questions and give hints, but of itself it does not have the power to generate theories. Blood groups are an ill-focused reflection of genetics, and it is to genetics we must turn for greater clarity.

The Genetics of Modern Populations

Hair colour, eye colour, and blood groups are all determined by our genetic make-up. They are the outward and visible signs of the genetic key encoded in the chemistry of our cells—the phenotype controlled by our genotype. Genetics is a complex subject in all its detail, and is becoming increasingly so by the day, but the basic concepts have an elegant simplicity and these, fortunately, are all we need to master to appreciate the huge importance of the subject to our understanding of the past.

Each cell in the body contains two sets of genetic information encoded in long strings of DNA (deoxyribonucleic acid). These codes are 'written' in combinations of four different chemicals. DNA provides the molecular blueprint for the construction and maintenance of the entire body, and this DNA we inherit in equal measure from each parent. At the time of conception, when strands of DNA from each parent combine, tiny adjustments are made in all but two areas: the Y chromosome and the mitochondrial DNA (mtDNA). In these regions the genetic information is transferred from one generation to the next unchanged.

The Y chromosome is one of forty-six chromosomes contained within the nucleus of the cell. Each parent contributes twenty-three chromosomes, which lie in strands side by side in a double helix. Twenty-two of the chromosomes are exactly paired. The remaining two, known as the X and Y chromosomes, are different and are not always inherited from each parent. A person with two X chromosomes is a female; one with X and Y is a male since the Y chromosome carries the active gene for maleness. In the reproductive process male sperms may carry either the X or the Y chromosome. If the egg is fertilized by a Y chromosome, then the progeny is a male. In other words, all males inherit their Y chromosome from their fathers and thus it has always been. Since the Y chromosome is not subject to recombination, as are the other chromosomes, it is ideal for the construction of family trees through the male line.

The mitochondrial DNA is quite different. It exists as a circular strand in small tubular packages in the cell wall and may have originated as a separate bacterium-like organism that invaded the cell. Its function is to control the cell's metabolism. It divides by simple binary fission and in this way reproduces its own DNA. Since males cannot pass on their mtDNA to their offspring, we all, whether male or female, inherit our mtDNA from our mothers.

So, Y chromosome DNA allows us to trace our male ancestry, while mtDNA charts our maternal inheritance. There is a pleasing simplicity in all this.

We must now introduce a second, crucial, factor: mutation. The creation and maintenance of a single human from a fertilized egg cell involves billions of cell divisions. Each cell division involves the copying of the cell's DNA and, although that division is achieved with a stunning accuracy, occasionally there is a minor error in copying which is then passed on in subsequent copying, causing a change—or mutation—in the organism; this leads to genetic variation within the species. The vast majority of these mutations have little or no effect. One example is the mutation that gave rise to the A, B, and O variation within the gene controlling blood corpuscles. A few mutations are detrimental, while fewer still are beneficial. Clearly, lineages inheriting mutations detrimental to their well-being will soon die out, while those with beneficial mutations will flourish. Mutation, then, is dynamic. That makes evolution possible.

Mitochondrial DNA mutates at the rate of about one mutation every thousand generations. In each of us our mtDNA embodies mutations that are a cumulative register of our maternal ancestry. A mutation occurring in the egg of a mother will be inherited by all her descendants down the female line, and at certain points in the line new mutations will be introduced to augment those already inherited. Thus, starting with females alive today, it should be possible to construct a family tree back to the distant past. Moreover, assuming a steady rate of mutation (and this is a big assumption), it ought to be possible to give absolute dates to the various points of divergence when a new mutation was introduced. On this basis it has been shown that the oldest mutation in mtDNA took place in Africa between 190,000 and 150,000 years ago, with new mutations appearing in Asia between 80,000 and 60,000 years ago. By about 50,000–40,000 years ago modern humans had reached Europe.

In the early 1990s work on the European population was sufficiently advanced for geneticists to be able to identify seven distinct groups as lineages based on their mtDNA. In total, 95 per cent of European females belong to one of these groups. Since all the females in any one group must at some distant point in time have had a common female ancestor, it follows that the female population of Europe must be descended from seven 'clan mothers'. We are looking, of course, at the successful lineages: there must have been many more that, for a wide variety of reasons, have died out leaving no successors in the present-day population. To give a feeling of reality to this remarkable phenomenon it has been conventional to give the 'clan mothers' specific female names. By noting the number of mutations and assuming an average rate of mutation, it has been possible to give broad assessments of the date of origin of each branch. Thus, the oldest is the 'Ursula' clan, originating 45,000 years ago, and the youngest, 'Jasmine's', appearing 10,000 years ago.

Attention then turned to the question of where, geographically, the clans originated. By calculating when the clan had accumulated the most additional mutations and where at present it has the highest concentration of these individuals, it was possible to arrive at likely regions of origin: thus, the Ursula clan appears to have originated in Greece, while the Jasmine clan began in Syria.

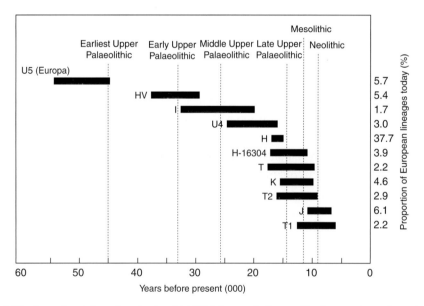

3.8 The figure shows the main mitochondrial DNA lineages in Europe. The bars represent the period within which the lineages are thought to have developed based on an assessment of mutation rates

The popular model of the seven 'clan mothers' of Europe, or the 'seven daughters of Eve' as they are sometimes called, is based on the detailed statistical treatment of large samples of DNA data and can be accepted as sound science. The dating of their origins is predicated on the assumption that the rate of mutation was regular and is capable of estimation. The reliability and accuracy of this assumption has yet to be demonstrated. The definition of the female lineages of Europe using mtDNA is one of the great breakthroughs in population studies. It opens up huge potential for modelling patterns of early human mobility across the continent.

As we have seen above, the Y chromosome also offers the potential for charting the emergence and dispersal of male clans, and although it presents more technical difficulties than working with mtDNA, not least in estimating time depth, major advances are being made. In deep prehistory Y chromosome studies generally support the mtDNA results in suggesting a shared ancestor in Africa for modern humans and a more recent shared ancestor in Asia for all other non-African humans. But men's contribution to the gene pool differs from that of women in that there is considerable variation in the number of offspring generated by males. Over a single lifetime the dominant male creates more children than his more timid rival, with the result that some male lines become extinct quite quickly while others flourish. This is in contrast to females, among whom there is much less variation, and may explain why Y chromosome DNA offers much greater geographical resolution compared with mtDNA. Males also show a tendency towards greater mobility. Eighteen genetic branches, or paternal clans, have been identified, and these are usually referred to by the letters A–R, though some writers have chosen to assign male names to them for ease of memory. Eleven of the paternal clans (or haplotypes) are relevant to Europe, and of these, ten are found in Britain. By further refining the analysis, more than forty subgroups or clusters have been defined. This larger number reflects the fact that the Y chromosome carries far more genetic information than mtDNA.

To sum up so far: by characterizing both mtDNA and the non-recombining section of the Y chromosome in present populations it is possible to identify a number of closely defined maternal or paternal clans (haplotypes), which can be further subdivided into gene clusters. The definition is based on the recognition of successive mutations which allow the individual samples to be arranged in a dendritic pattern. The simplest and most appropriate analogy is the tree. The present population represents the tips of the branches, all of which relate back through successive branchings to the original trunk. By studying the number of mutations, which are believed to have occurred randomly but at a constant rate, it is possible to offer an estimate of time before the present when a particular branch was initiated. Knowing the genetic

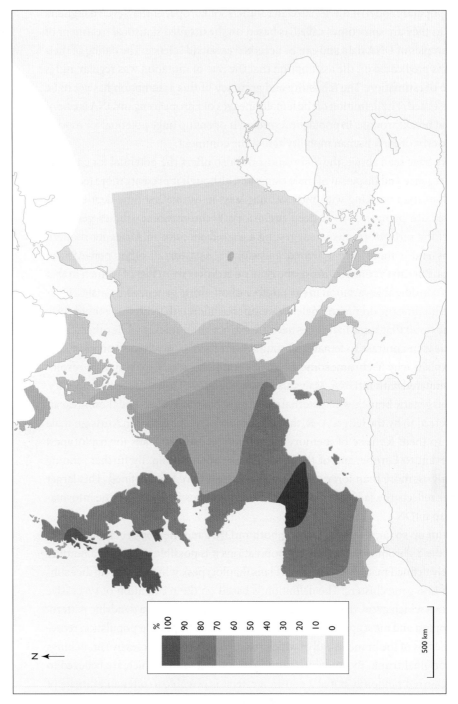

3.9 The frequency of the genetic haplogroup R1b in Europe, suggesting that it may have originated in a north Iberian refuge and spread along the Atlantic fringe of Europe at the end of the last ice age; after drawing by Martin Crampin, redrawn after S. Oppenheimer, *The Origins of the British* (London, 2006), Figure 3.6a

constitution of the present population and its geographical distribution, it is, in theory, possible to build up a history of population movement.

If one assumes that the scientific principles and statistical methods are correct and appropriate (and here a non-specialist simply has to be trusting), it remains only to acquire a sufficient data set constrained by the proper geographical controls and to present the results in a manner that is clear and directly addresses the question of population movement. All this is easier said than done.

A number of programmes have addressed the question of data sets. The Oxford Genetic Atlas Project, which began in 1996, has acquired a database of over 10,000 samples, while the more recent People of the British Isles, which is also an Oxford-based project, is still collecting data using sampling procedures that ensure a full coverage of the country. To address the possible distortions caused by very recent population movement, samples are only taken from individuals having all four grandparents living within 30–40 miles of each other. This rigour is necessary if the results of the analysis are to be reasonably representative of the localized population. The People of the British Isles programme is producing a high-density and high-resolution resource and will have much to offer to the population history of the isles when the sampling and analyses are complete.

The presentation and interpretation of the results of DNA studies require care if they are not to be misinterpreted. Two principal methods are used: principal components analysis and phylogeography. Principal components analysis synthesizes many hundreds of thousands of genetic variables to generate synthetic variables (principal components), which allow broad patterns to be recognized. It presents a picture of the present population that could have resulted from any number of 'histories'. Thus, while useful at a gross level, it has limited historical value. Phylogeography sets out to explain the geographical distributions of the different branches of the gene tree, in other words the descent of a single DNA segment. To be of real use to historical demographics it is necessary to use a wide choice of different markers to reflect the population better, rather than to rely on single lines, which may be at variance with population trees.

Sufficient (perhaps too much) has been said to show that the study of genetics, though of immense potential value in helping us to understand the way in which Britain and Ireland were peopled, has limitations. It can seldom, if ever, give direct and simple answers to questions posed by archaeologists about incoming populations, and there is always a danger that archaeological–historical preconceptions will be used by geneticists to explain observations noted in the genetic data, thus creating self-supporting circular arguments. That said, DNA studies have created an invaluable source of new data for population historians, and we shall be returning to these matters at various points in the chapters to follow.

Before leaving the subject, we should consider several issues that serve as a warning against the over-simple use of genetic data. If the British population was the result of successive, and time-limited, migrations of people from the Continent and genetic dating can be demonstrated to be accurate, then it ought to be possible to create a chronological narrative from genetic data that can be compared with the archaeological–historical narrative. But it is not that simple. A broadly agreed interpretation of the genetic data is that a post-glacial repopulation of western Europe from a Franco-Cantabrian refuge was responsible for introducing the bulk of the present gene pool to Ireland and western Britain. There is nothing in the archaeological record to disagree with this entirely reasonable interpretation. But can we really take this to mean that 70–90 per cent of the British and Irish population are descended from people who arrived in the *immediate* post-glacial period when the archaeological evidence shows *continual* movement along the Atlantic seaways, of ideas, technologies, beliefs, and peoples, over the *longue durée* of at least 5,000 years since the Mesolithic period? These long-term movements cannot fail to have influenced the gene pool over the millennia, enhancing its distinctiveness. Archaeology shows just how complex was the reality.

A similar issue is raised by contacts between continental Europe and southern Britain across the eastern Channel–southern North Sea axis. While geneticists seek to identify 'Germanic' populations arriving at the time of the Saxon influx in the fifth and sixth centuries AD, the reality of the archaeological evidence shows that the two regions have always been in close contact, involving the intermingling of peoples. To what extent, then, can a Germanic component in the British population be distinguished as Saxon rather than Roman, Iron Age, or Later Bronze Age when both regions can be shown to have had extensive social interaction over this extended period? If genetic dating was accurate enough to show that the Germanic component dated to the fifth–sixth century AD, this would tighten the argument, but genetic dating is not as precise a science as that, and a better explanation of the genetic patterning would be to see it as the result of progressive Germanization stretching over many hundreds of years. Only when geneticists and archaeologists engage at a level at which both understand the strengths and weaknesses of each other's data, and are prepared to move beyond over-simple and outdated historical interpretations, will we begin to realize the full potential of the methods for characterizing the Britons.

Ancient DNA

The comparative successes of modern DNA studies in attempting to understand population mobility inevitably raise the question of the use of ancient DNA preserved in human tissue or skeletal material. In theory it should be possible to extract DNA and to characterize it using presently available techniques. There are, however, difficulties to be overcome. The first is that DNA might not survive or, if it does, then it is usually only in small quantities and in a very fragmented state. But if DNA is present, it can be extracted and subjected to a process of amplification to facilitate identification. A more serious problem is that of contamination resulting from contact with modern humans—from the hands of the archaeologist who excavated the bone and from the specialist who subsequently studied it. Developing methods and standards to eliminate contamination and to give assurance that the DNA measured is really ancient DNA is an issue that has to be solved before the ancient DNA of *Homo sapiens* can be made to yield valuable results.

The one example where the method has proved its use is in characterizing Neanderthals. Ten individuals have now produced ancient mtDNA showing them to be distinct from modern humans. What facilitated this particular study was that the species were sufficiently different to allow contamination from modern humans to be quickly eliminated.

Once the protocols for extracting the DNA from ancient *Homo sapiens* are in place and thoroughly tested, it will be an arduous job to build a database of sufficient size to be statistically useful. Yet future prospects are good and we can look forward to a time when it may be possible to define family groups in cemeteries and to identify foreign individuals marrying into the community from the outside.

Man Is What He Eats

In recent years new methods of analysis have been developed to identify the chemical signatures left in our bodies by the different foods we eat. The principle is quite simple: the food and water we ingest is composed of chemical elements that are present in different isotopic states identifiable by their atomic weights; for example, carbon may be present as ^{13}C or ^{12}C and nitrogen as ^{15}N or ^{14}N. Once inside our bodies these isotopes are laid down in our tissues, including the collagen in our bones, which has the advantage of surviving in most archaeological contexts. Thus, given a skeleton, it is possible to measure the ratios of a number of stable isotopes that directly reflect our food and water intake.

This basic chemistry has led to the development of two main areas of study, one using carbon and nitrogen, which enables diet to be examined, the other using strontium and oxygen, which help to indicate the region in which the individual spent his or her childhood.

To take the carbon and nitrogen analysis first, one useful distinction that can be made, based on ^{13}C to ^{12}C ratios, is whether the plant food ingested came from a maritime or land environment. In an early study carried out in Denmark using this principle it was possible to show that Mesolithic hunter-gatherers living in coastal areas ate high percentages of maritime plants, while later Neolithic settlers in the same region preferred land-based plants, the implication being that, since the environment had remained largely unchanged, the preference for food was based on cultural rather than practical considerations. Nitrogen isotopes are also a useful indicator. The ratio of ^{15}N to ^{14}N increases as nitrogen passes up the food chain from plants to animals and reaches its highest levels in sea-fish and shell-fish. By considering both nitrogen and carbon ratios one can therefore arrive at an accurate assessment of the basic diet that an individual had enjoyed over the last five to fifteen years of his or her life. In one such study, of a hunter-gatherer community on the southern coast of Brittany, differences in male and female diet were defined, leading to the suggestion that some of the wives of the coastal community may have come from inland areas, thus implying exogamous marriages.

Strontium isotope ratios (^{87}Sr/^{86}Sr) vary according to geology and are transferred to living creatures through ground-water, eventually ending up in bones and teeth. Thus, the isotope ratios in bone and teeth must directly relate to the diet of the individual, which is assumed to mirror the strontium isotope ratios of the underlying local geology. Since bone tissue is constantly being replaced during life, the isotope ratios in bone reflect those of the locality where the individual spent the later years of life. Tooth enamel, however, is formed during childhood and remains little changed thereafter. Therefore, it follows that strontium isotope ratios in tooth enamel must match those of the area where the individual grew up: significant differences between ratios in bone and in tooth enamel would indicate that a person had migrated during his or her lifetime. The potential for studying the mobility of populations is obvious, but there are problems to be overcome. For example, since the strontium isotope ratios in bedrock and ground-water vary within the local area and also in any one population, there is always a range of values in bone and enamel isotope ratios, making the distinction between locals and immigrants in any group difficult to recognize.

Recent work has begun to address these issues. Clearly it is essential to be able to estimate accurately the amount of biologically available strontium isotopes present at any particular locality. This is best done by taking measurements from the tooth enamel of small mammals, preferably found in archaeological deposits contemporary with the human population, or, if this is not possible, from the living small-mammal population—the assumption being that small wild mammals better represent the local ratio levels than domestic animals, which may have been moved over distances. With a sufficiently large sample an accurate assessment can be made of the biologically available strontium to compare with that in the bones and tooth enamel of past human populations buried in the area. A further complication is that the variation of strontium ratios in humans is caused by several factors, notably diet, length of residence, and multiple movements. The problems this poses are best overcome by using rigorous statistical criteria to separate migrants from indigenous populations.

Strontium isotope analysis offers enormous scope for studying mobility in human populations: the technique is scientifically robust but needs to be tested and refined. It is most appropriately used when large samples are available for study. In one example, involving eighty-one individuals from later third-millennium BC Bell Beaker cemeteries extending from southern Germany to Hungary, it was possible to show that fifty-one had moved during their lifetime. This represents a significant level of mobility. We should, however, be more wary of claims made for individual skeletons given the limitations of the method. It is all too easy when a new technique comes on stream to rush at it enthusiastically and make generalizations that in retrospect, when the scientific constraints are better understood, seem less easy to justify. Stable isotope analysis offers exciting possibilities for studying the mobility of human populations and of the flocks and herds on which they depended.

The Nature of the Human Species

In common with all other animal species, humans are driven by the primary desires to feed themselves and to reproduce: without achieving these two basics the species would waste away and become extinct. Both imperatives require aggression and self-assertiveness, instincts that are hard-wired into animal biology but are constrained, to prevent them from being purely destructive, by the establishment and acceptance of hierarchies of status. Thus far, humans and other animals behave in much the same way. What sets humans apart is their capacity for symbolic behaviour, expressed in material culture such as artefacts and structures. As the human species developed, so symbolic behaviour, and its material expression, have become increasingly more complex and varied. Language developed early to help conceptualize ideas and to communicate them, and writing, when it came, provided a ready means of codifying behaviours and beliefs to make them more widely accessible.

While humans are by nature aggressive, they are also communal beasts. To balance these often antithetical traits humans have developed a social culture which moderates destructive excesses of behaviour and provides an agreed social hierarchy to contain and guide human interaction. But there remains a desire to aspire and to achieve—the two characteristics that drive human cultural development. Aspiration and achievement manifest themselves in different ways. One, which is comparatively easy to recognize in the archaeological record, is the acquisition of rare and desirable commodities that can be used for display or in cycles of conspicuous consumption such as feasting, gift-giving, or funerary rituals. A lineage that can bury a leading member with gold and other rare materials, in full view of others, is clearly demonstrating its supreme status.

The acquisition of such materials demands complex systems involving procurement, enhancement, and gift exchange. The desire to accumulate material wealth, therefore, gives rise to mechanisms for resource exploitation and distribution embedded within the differing social systems. The uneven occurrence of rare commodities requires there to be not only extensive networks of distribution but also a degree of mobility: commodities are moved by people and with them flow ideas and beliefs. Mobility itself, as we have seen (pp. 67–8), takes with it a high degree of status. The ship's master who maintained a craft and a crew and had the ability to sail it across the Channel in the second millennium BC would have been a man of some standing within his own society and among those with whom he engaged. The gifts given and exchanged in such encounters—items of gold, silver, amber, and jet—were items of considerable value conferring prestige. The desire for status through acquisition and mobility bound Britain and the Continent together in complex networks maintaining connectivity across the generations.

Alongside the many and various expressions of symbolic behaviour there must be placed the dynamics of demography. Simply stated, if left unchecked, the population would increase exponentially; but there are always checks, most notably the holding capacity of the particular ecological niche in which the community lives. A given territory exploited by a particular technology could support only so many people. Once the population density approached the holding capacity, society had to institute changes. They could raise the holding capacity of their land by introducing new food-producing technologies or by exploiting new resources, they could change social conventions to make them less demanding of local products, or they could colonize more territory. Alternatively they could control the rate of population replacement by infanticide, or by enforcing constraints on marriage, or by warfare. There may also have been external factors affecting demography. Climatic deterioration, sea-level rise, depletion of soil nutrients through overcropping will all have had their effects. For many, life would have been a delicate balance—a constant contest with nature.

Demographic factors are notoriously difficult for archaeologists to grasp given the kind of evidence that survives, but there can be no doubt that they are crucial in attempting to understand the development of human societies. In Britain and Ireland the population was never large. Starting with a few hunting bands moving into the territory as the ice receded, the population may have peaked at around 3 or 4 million by the second century AD before declining for a century or two and then rising again to a new peak of 7 to 8 million in the early fourteenth century before the Black Death caused another dramatic fall. But these are approximate and ill-focused estimates. In reality there would have been much regional variation, with each community experiencing its own population dynamics and being forced to respond appropriately.

Sufficient will have been said in this chapter to give some idea of the ways in which it is possible to begin to understand the complexity of the population of the British Isles and Ireland—of immigration, mobility, and demography. Until the 1980s our only resource was archaeology—rather cruelly characterized as the study of other people's rubbish. This constrained the narrative we were able to write. Now, with the study of DNA and stable isotopes, the opportunities to explore new narratives are fast opening up. No single approach will give the complete picture. Only by using archaeology, genetics, and bone chemistry together, to augment and constrain each other, shall we be able to begin to move to a new understanding of the people of these islands in their formative millennia.

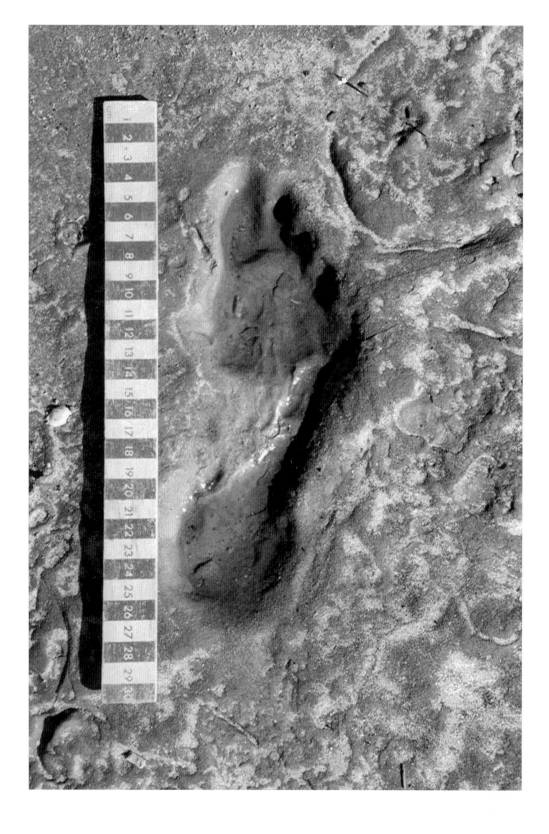

4

000

Settlement Begins,
10,000–4200 BC

A ROUND 10,000 BC the western extremity of the great North European Plain, later to become Britain and Ireland, was still in the grip of a bitterly cold period known as the Younger Dryas (or, in Britain, the Loch Lomond stadial). An ice-sheet covered central and western Scotland, and tundra, roamed by herds of reindeer, extended over much of the rest of the country. The bands of hunters, who in the preceding, milder interstadial (the Late Glacial, or Windermere, interstadial) had made their homes in the caves of the Peak District, the Mendips, south-west Wales, and Devon, and had ventured as far north as Edinburgh to camp at Howburn near Biggar in south Lanarkshire and Fairnington near Kelso, were driven south by the persistent severe weather to refuges in the south-west of France, northern Iberia, and other milder parts of Europe. Whether or not a few of the bands who ventured north-wards during the summer months following herds of reindeer strayed into the area later to become Britain is debatable. A few scraps of humanly worked bone and antler have been found in Suffolk and Staffordshire, apparently dating to the peak of the cold period. If the dating is reliable, then they indicate human presence, but it need have been little more than cursory visits made fleetingly in the few weeks of summer.

The last ice age came to a sudden end about 9600 BC with a rapid rise in tempera-tures exacerbated by the re-establishment of the Atlantic Ocean currents, bring-ing the warm waters of the Gulf Stream once more to the Atlantic-facing shores of

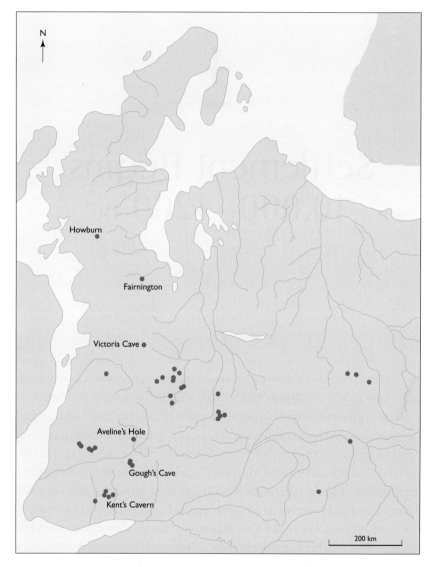

4.1 Britain and the adjacent continent in the early part of the Late Glacial Interstadial around 12,000 BC, showing the places where human activity has been identified

Europe. This marks the end of the period known as the Pleistocene and the beginning of the Holocene, the period in which we now live. Pollen sequences and ice core data have allowed climate scientists to model, in some detail, progressive changes in climate and vegetation throughout this period. They have identified three broad phases relevant to the time-span we are considering: the Preboreal (c. 9600–c. 8800 BC), a cold, dry period; the Boreal (c. 8800–c. 5800 BC), a warm, dry period; and the

Atlantic (*c.* 5800–*c.* 4000 BC), a warm, wet period. But alongside these general trends in the ameliorating climate there were surprises to be experienced. In the centuries around 6200 BC changes in the structure of the North American ice-sheet caused the temperatures to plunge to a sudden low for several centuries. In Norway the temperature dropped about 2 °C, while in Greenland the fall was about 5 °C. But the balance was soon adjusted and the climate remained reasonably stable until the advent of another cold snap around 4500 BC. For hunter-gatherer communities, often living at the extremes of environmental tolerances, sudden plunges in temperature, however small, will have had far-reaching effects, forcing lifestyles to change significantly over the space of a few generations. Such unpredictability made life difficult.

The gradually improving climate over the long term brought with it changes in vegetation, beginning with open scrub-land with occasional surviving trees and culminating in closed-canopy 'climax' woodland—the wildwood that was to clothe almost the entire country by the fifth millennium. While soils, altitude, and latitude all conditioned plant growth, the general progress of woodland advance can be traced across the country. In the Preboreal period the great expanses of grassland with shrubs were soon colonized by birch with some willow, aspen, alder, hazel, juniper, and pine, depending on local conditions. Trees were at first sparse but gradually increased in density, with hazel becoming the major component by about 8000 BC. A thousand years later the diversity had increased, with oak, elm, and alder, alongside hazel, now forming a significant part of the woodland canopy.

The spread of birch-woods in the Preboreal and the accompanying rise in temperature created an environment uncongenial to reindeer, which had been a major source of food for hunting communities at the end of the Younger Dryas across considerable swaths of Europe, but there were still reindeer in Britain as late as 9000 BC and they may have survived in the north for even longer. With the spread of woodland came a new range of woodland animals: red deer, roe deer, elk, aurochs, horse, and wild pig, together with brown bear, wolf, badger, wild cat, lynx, beaver, otter, and hare. The estuaries and coasts also attracted varieties of waterfowl and fish. The overall effect of the amelioration of climate was the replacement of the tundra and grassy steppe with an extraordinarily diverse mosaic of different environments ranging from dense wildwoods to open uplands and from wide meandering river valleys to broad estuaries and open coast-lines with rich and varied intertidal zones and the prolific seas beyond. Each ecological zone teemed with food for the taking, the resources now so varied that if one was to fail, others nearby could be exploited more intensively. The basis of subsistence was now much broader and much more reassuring than in past times, when survival depended on unmitigated reindeer eked out by horse-meat.

Return to Britain

Studies carried out in the cave refuges in Britain used intensively in the Later Glacial interstadial showed that the caves had been totally abandoned during the Younger Dryas cold spell, though, as we have seen, it is just possible that a few transient groups may have ventured as far north as southern Britain for brief summer expeditions. But with the beginning of the Holocene the land that was to become Britain and Ireland, still at this stage an integral part of the continent, grew increasingly attractive to hunter-gatherer communities, and so the settlement by pioneer communities began. These were the first Britons, the ancestors of a significant component of the present-day British population.

The first people who moved northwards as the tundra retreated came from refuges stretching from the Atlantic coast of France across to Germany. They were communities who had traditionally relied on hunting reindeer and wild horse and who, rather than modify their subsistence strategies to suit the changing vegetation, chose to move northwards to keep up with the march of the ecological zone with which they were familiar. Culturally these people were indistinguishable from those of the Ahrensburgian group known from a number of sites in Belgium, the Netherlands, Poland, and Germany, most particularly from the famous site of Stellmoor near Hamburg in northern Germany, one of the camps used by hunters to intercept migrating reindeer. Reindeer spent the winter widely scattered in small groups across the North European Plain but began to assemble in large herds at the beginning of spring to migrate southwards using traditional routes, often along river valleys. By targeting choke points along these routes the hunters could be sure of a kill in both the early spring and the autumn, when the beasts returned with their calves to the northern tundra.

Evidence for hunting groups in Britain at the end of the Younger Dryas and in the early Preboreal (c. 10,000–c. 9000 BC) rests on the discovery of some thirty sites in south-eastern Britain, mainly in East Anglia and the Thames valley, where distinctive flint tools have been found, the characteristic types being tanged points, serving as missile heads, and long blades with evidence of use along one edge (lames mâchurées), probably resulting from the working of bone and leather. Very little is known about the subsistence economy of these groups, but at one site, Three Ways Wharf in the valley of the River Colne, bones of reindeer and horse have been discovered and two others have produced horse bones. Although the evidence is at present slight, it might be that the British hunter-gatherers developed a specialization for hunting wild horse as the favoured reindeer became increasingly scarce.

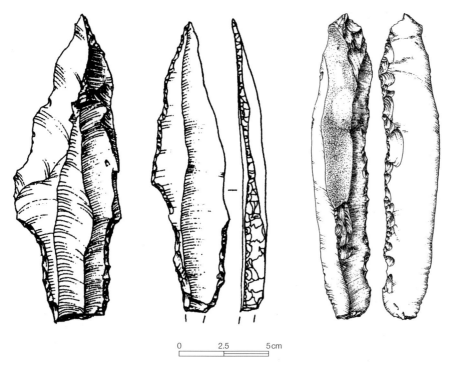

0   2.5   5 cm

4.2 Flint implements characteristic of the period 12,000–10,000 BC. The shouldered points are from Hengistbury Head, Dorset, and the long 'bruised' blade from Launde, Leicestershire

But the world was changing, and by about 9000 BC birch- and pinewoods were fast spreading across Britain, to be followed a few centuries later by the invasion of hazel, which is usually taken to mark the beginning of the Boreal. The changes were comparatively rapid and meant that hunter-gatherer bands had two options: either to continue to move north following their traditional prey animals or to adapt to the new conditions in the home territories by exploiting a different range of animals in the now predominantly forest conditions. Those who chose this second option had to face new challenges requiring quite significant changes in behaviour and organization. To begin with, the quantity of animal protein available was now much diminished: forested habitats support only 20–30 per cent of the total biomass of animals compared with more open landscapes. Moreover, forest animals are much less migratory in their habitats and are more widely dispersed in smaller groups than the herds of horse and reindeer. Adapting to these new conditions would have led to smaller hunting bands working more limited territories. It may also have encouraged the communities to explore more varied food resources, including plant foods,

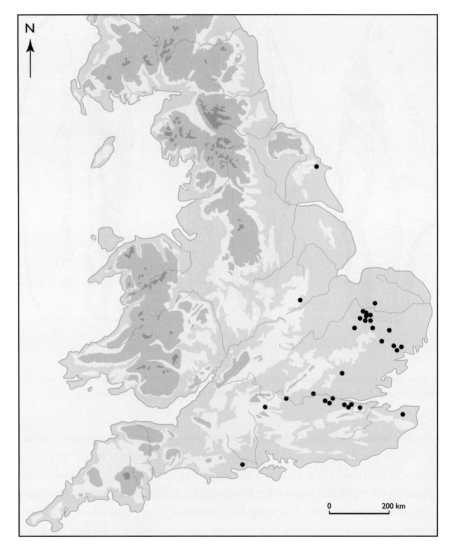

N

0   200 km

4.3 Distribution of 'bruised' blades of the period 12,000–10,000 BC gives an indication of the extent of human settlement in this period

waterfowl, and the rich haul of produce to be had from the shores and the sea. In other words, it forced greater diversification. To adjust to the new conditions, the hunter-gatherers of the North European Plain developed new tool-kits characterized by small tool components (microliths) snapped from large flint blades, designed to be set into wooden hafts, and larger axes and adzes useful in carpentry for cutting down or ring-barking trees and for grubbing up roots and rhizomes. Bone and antler

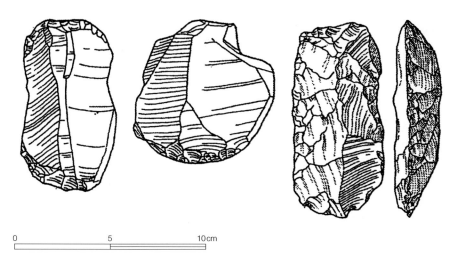

0   5   10 cm

4.4 A small flint axe and two flint scrapers from the ninth-millennium BC camp site of Star Carr, North Yorkshire

was also widely used to make barbed harpoon heads and bone points suitable for leather working. These tool-kits are characteristic of the Mesolithic period, which is coincident with the beginning of the Holocene. While there was much regional and temporal variation, a broad similarity in tool-kits across the face of north-western Europe offers clear evidence that populations were settling down to adapt to the palimpsest of forest environments, and that a degree of mobility ensured that contact was maintained over large areas.

In the eastern regions of Britain, still part of the North European Plain, the pioneer hunter-gatherers of the tenth millennium BC gradually adapted to the expanding forest environment, developing new lithic technologies to match the changed lifestyle, innocent of the fact that they were passing from the Upper Palaeolithic to the Mesolithic. On present evidence the earliest Mesolithic sites in Britain date to the ninth millennium BC, with Thatcham in the Kennet valley beginning around 9000 BC, Star Carr in Yorkshire spanning the period 8770–8460 BC, and Cramond near Edinburgh starting at around 8500 BC. There is no evidence yet to suggest that Ireland, now an island, was occupied at that time.

Strategies for Survival: The Great Forested Plain

The huge expanse of low rolling hills referred to by archaeologists as Doggerland, which joined the south-east of Britain to the adjacent continent from Pas de Calais to Denmark, was gradually becoming inundated as the sea-level rose in relation to the land. This process continued until sometime probably between 6500 and 5500 BC, when the tidal currents of the expanding North Sea and the Channel joined up, turning Britain into an island. Throughout this long period of perhaps as much as four millennia, hunter-gatherers could roam at will across the forested plain, with its rivers, lakes, and ever-expanding inlets providing a welcome variety of habitats for the human communities to exploit. Judging from artefact types and distributions, a broad similarity of culture existed across the entire plain from the Pennines to Poland, but within that, regional styles can be recognized, suggesting networks of contact covering more restricted territories. This is clearly demonstrated by the distribution of different versions of harpoon heads—a category of hunting weapon used throughout the broader area. A distinctive type links eastern Britain with northern France, Belgium, and the Netherlands, and no doubt there are more to be found scattered across drowned Doggerland. At best, distributions of this kind indicate regions of connectivity wherein mobile bands related one with another, the interaction leading to the sharing of ideas, technologies, and beliefs across wide territories.

The question of mobility in the Mesolithic period has been widely discussed by archaeologists, informed by ethnographic analogy. There has been the general assumption that sectors of the community moved between winter base camps in the more wooded areas and summer hunting camps in upland areas or on the coast, where particular resources available for limited periods were to be exploited. Base camps might have been occupied year-round, at least by the aged and very young, and were the places to which the active hunters and gatherers would return when the season's gleaning was over. At different camps selected activities might be undertaken: tasks such as the making and repairing of tools and the working of skins to make clothing and shelter. Some such simple system may well have been in operation, but the increasing body of archaeological evidence is suggesting that the picture may have been rather more complex, with much regional variation, yet seasonal mobility within a set territory was probably the norm and there may well have been times and places when larger groups assembled. A few examples will help to show something of the variety of behaviour preserved in the archaeological record.

One particularly favoured location was the valley of the River Kennet between Newbury and Thatcham, where a number of sites have been identified along a 5-kilometre stretch of the valley. At one location, excavated between 1958 and 1961, a settlement was found located on a gravel terrace overlooking a reed swamp with an extensive forest of birch and pine rising up behind. The faunal remains recovered

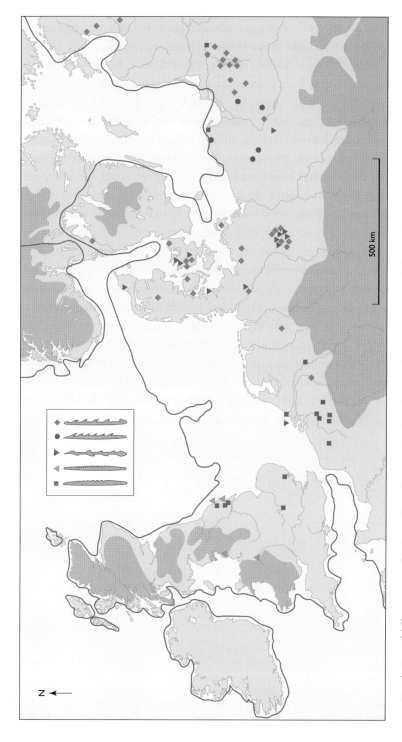

4.5 Distribution of different types of antler and bone harpoon heads in the period 10,000–7500 BC. The brown line shows the approximate coast-line at the time. Each type tends to be specific to a distinct territory but some types are more widely distributed, indicating interconnections between the various hunting groups

showed that red deer, roe deer, pig, aurochs, and elk were hunted in the neighbouring forests and were brought to the site for storage and consumption. The marsh provided a range of birds, including mallard, teal, and crane, but rather surprisingly the nearby river seems to have been under-exploited (unless fish-bones have failed to survive or be recognized). Among the vegetable foods to be gathered were hazelnuts, which were found in quantity. The extensive tool-kit shows that a wide range of activities were carried out at the site: the working of bone and antler, the repair of wooden equipment, and the preparation of skins. Taken together, the evidence suggests that the site may well have been the home camp occupied during the winter months before the group began to disperse for the spring and summer hunt.

Upstream from the Thatcham site a rather different kind of camp was identified at Faraday Road, Newbury, in 1997. Here a small, and probably quite short-lived, camp had been set up by a group of hunters whose prime interest was to kill young wild pigs. Analysis of the total assemblage of animal bones showed that more than 80 per cent were of wild pig, representing at least thirteen animals, with only a few bones of aurochs, red deer, roe deer, wild cat, and beaver. The pigs were predominantly young, captured when they were most vulnerable, and butchered on the site, some to be eaten there, the rest carried away for storage. That the tool types recovered were limited in range and entirely appropriate to pig hunting suggests that the camp was a base used by a specialized, and evidently successful, group of hunters who may have been there for only a few days before carrying their haul back to their base camp. It is highly likely that other sites in this part of the Kennet valley were also the bases for

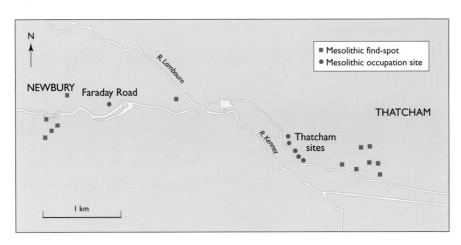

4.6 A number of Mesolithic sites are known in the valley of the River Kennet between Newbury and Thatcham, showing that the valley offered a rich environment which was heavily exploited by hunter-gatherer communities

specialized hunting or gathering expeditions, but whether they represent the activities of a single social group, and how extensive were their territories of exploration, is difficult to say from the evidence presently available.

A rather different environment, much favoured by Mesolithic hunter-gatherers, was the Greensand of the Weald. Many hundreds of sites are known, but the most extensively examined is Oakhanger to the south-east of Alton, where several discrete locations of activity have been identified. The local acid soil conditions have destroyed all trace of bone and antler, but pollen is well preserved, giving some insight into the local vegetation. One notable find was that the percentage of hazel pollen was exceptionally high. This suggests that there may have been deliberate felling of other trees such as alder, lime, and oak around the camp to allow hazel to flower more freely and thus to produce a greater yield of hazel-nuts. An unusually high percentage of ivy pollen is more difficult to explain, but one suggestion is that ivy was collected and brought to the periphery of the camp as fodder to attract deer during the winter months, when food was in short supply. Lulled by the piles of feed, the hungry beasts would be easy prey. The tool-kit found at the camp was dominated by processing tools, adding support to the idea that the site was occupied during the autumn and winter, when there was time to make and repair equipment.

Oakhanger is situated close to the edge of the Weald, where the varied geology would have given rise to a range of environments each with its own potential. A short 4-kilometre walk would have taken a hunter across a band of very heavy and densely wooded clay, followed by the lighter calcareous Upper Greensand, to the scarp of the chalk uplands. At different times of the year these landscapes would have yielded all the foods and other resources necessary to maintain the communities. If more variety was needed, the sea lay only a few days' travel to the south.

The best-known of Britain's Mesolithic sites is Star Carr, lying in the Vale of Pickering in north Yorkshire. The importance of the site, originally excavated in 1949–51, lies in the scale and quality of the excavation and the fact that waterlogged conditions have preserved animal bones and plant remains. More recent examination of sediment cores has clarified the nature of the contemporary environment and has provided a secure dating framework for the human activity.

The camp lay close to the edge of the former Lake Pickering in an area of reed swamp fringed by birch and poplar giving way to more open birch woodland on the drier land beyond. To provide stability for the settlement a platform of birch brushwood had been laid close to the lake edge. The rich haul of animal bones showed that red deer was the principal catch, followed by roe deer, elk, aurochs, and pig. Bear, badger, fox, and wolf were also caught, probably for their pelts, while domesticated dog was also present, no doubt serving as both a companion and a partner in the

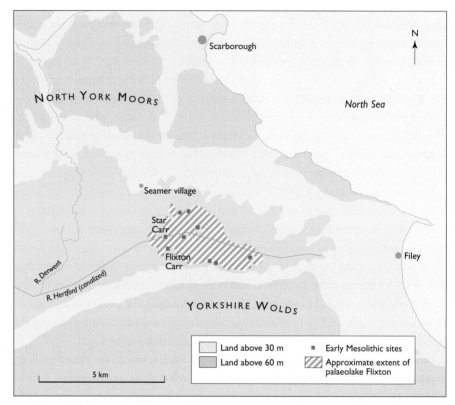

4.7 The palaeolake at Flixton in the Vale of Pickering was extensively used by hunter-gatherer communities and was close to a range of other ecological zones, including the sea, which could easily be reached. The famous site of Star Carr lay on the lake edge

chase. Waterfowl such as stork and crane were also captured, but fish, as at Thatcham, were noticeable by their absence, hinting that the eating of freshwater fish may have been taboo, at least to some communities.

The artefact assemblage from Star Carr is rich and varied and raises a number of interesting questions about the function of the site. The most notable find was of twenty-one frontlets of red deer skulls with antlers still attached. The skulls and antlers had been thinned to reduce their weight and had been perforated to allow them to be tied, quite possibly to human heads, to serve as a kind of headdress. Another unusual feature of the assemblage is a very high number of barbed points, 101 in all, most made from red deer antler. There is also evidence that antlers were being worked on the site to make the blanks from which the barbed points were crafted. When it is realized that on other sites, if found at all, barbed points occur in ones or twos, then the exceptional nature of Star Carr becomes apparent. What is clear is that those who used the birch bark platform on the lake edge had a special relation-

4.8 A tree felled in the Mesolithic period lying on the edge of the lake at Star Carr. The left-hand photograph shows the tree as excavated in the 1930s. The right-hand photograph shows the trench re-excavated in 2010 to check the rate of deterioration caused by the lowering of the water-table

ship with the red deer—the beast that provided the bulk of their food. The frontlet, perhaps used by those stalking the deer, brought man close to the animal and allowed him to triumph, while the barbed points made from deer antler were used in the kill. Clearly, a complex web of relations must have existed between humans and the deer. The deposition of the frontlets and barbed points in the lake together with the remains of carcasses may have been an act of respect for the beast carried out to propitiate the animal's spirit and in expectation that their close relationship would be fruitful in the season to come.

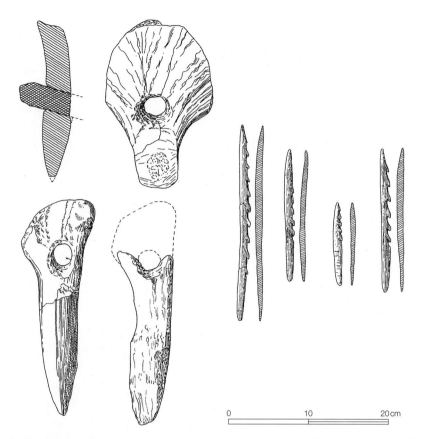

4.9 Antler mattock heads and antler barbed points from the ninth-millennium camp site of Star Carr, North Yorkshire

Other aspects of the Star Carr assemblage also point to the unusual nature of the site. A significant number of mattocks made of perforated elk antler were deposited in the lake, hinting at a special relationship with the elk—another animal captured in the hunt—while small beads of stone and amber and perforated bears' teeth occur in quantities unparalleled on other sites. Together the evidence strongly suggests that Star Carr may have played a significant role in the spiritual life of the community. It was a preferred location, a special place to which people returned over time and where they could mediate with the powers who controlled the natural world. A study of the lake cores suggests that activity began around 8770 BC and continued for about eighty years. After a century of inactivity the site was brought back into use and was visited on a regular basis for the next 130 years until around 8460 BC.

Star Carr is only one of a number of Mesolithic sites clustering around the old lake, but none compare with it and all show considerable variability both in location and in the intensity of activity. We shall probably never know how these different sites relate to the life systems of the larger community, but we can be sure that the pattern was complex, and for a good part of its duration Star Carr was the point of reference to which people habitually returned.

Standing back from all the detail, it is becoming clear that the patterns of annual movement were probably far more complex than is suggested by the simple model of spring dispersal to the hunting–gathering grounds and autumn return to the home base. While some such cycle may have broadly underlain the annual rhythm, the use of the landscape would have been opportunist, especially in the early millennia of the Mesolithic, when the vegetation was still adjusting to the ameliorating climate. The size of foraging groups would have varied, and their strategies and territories of exploitation would have changed, as over-exploitation, population pressure, and outbreaks of local hostility took effect. That said, the land and sea were productive, sufficient to provide the hunter-gatherer groups with a plentiful and varied diet and the leisure to enjoy it.

One of the fascinating questions to remain is, to what extent did the Mesolithic communities manipulate their environment? We have already mentioned the intensification of hazel growth and the stockpiling of ivy fodder at Oakhanger. There is also ample evidence of the use of fire to clear vegetation. This happened as a prelude to both phases of occupation at Star Carr and has been recognized in a number of pollen sequences in upland regions. The use of fire to clear dense woodland, particularly along forest margins, would have been a productive strategy. It would have encouraged new growth, attracting herds of ungulates to accumulate to browse on the young shoots. The burning of woodland can increase the ungulate biomass by up to a factor of ten. Thus, by using fire as a tool, Mesolithic communities invited the massing of browsing animals, which in the open landscape are an easy prey. Moreover, by such means, and by providing piles of feed, beasts like red deer could be made to become used to the human presence—the first stage in the process of domestication.

The Atlantic Façade

By the beginning of the Holocene the Atlantic seaboard of Europe was beginning to take on an appearance not altogether unlike that of today. The Cantabrian coast was close to its present line, but there was significantly more land along the western coast of France, low-lying and fragmented by the broad estuaries of the Garonne and the Loire. Armorica, too, was more extensive, with shelving rocky coasts. The English Channel was now a wide waterway up to 100 kilometres across, thrusting deep into the land to the east. Further north what was to become the Irish Sea was a channel around 50 kilometres wide, separating Ireland from Britain. The whole of the Atlantic façade, warmed by the Gulf Stream, was a highly congenial environment. The sea and the littoral zone produced an abundance of varied food resources. The many estuaries and coastal marshes offered a nutritious plant biomass as well as a plethora of migrating waterfowl, while just inland were the wildwoods, teem-

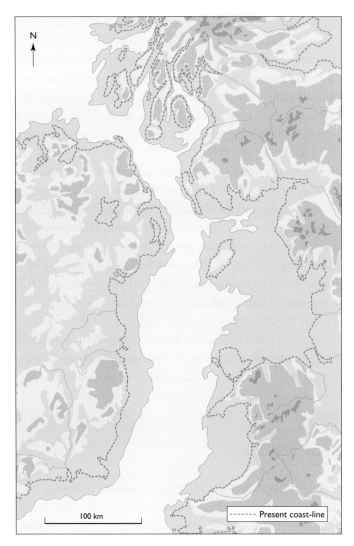

4.10 At the time when Ireland was beginning to be colonized by hunter-gatherer communities early in the seventh millennium the channel between Britain and Ireland was much narrower and would have presented little obstacle to movement

ing with ungulates and rich in berries and nuts. In a short walk of a few kilometres the entire range of ecozones could be accessed: nowhere else in Europe offered such varied food resources within so narrow a compass. There was also another advantage, which should not be underestimated: the littoral zone between low tide and the forest edge provided an easy passage, while for those with the necessary skills the sea itself was the fastest means of transit.

The extraordinary benefits of the Atlantic zone would not have been overlooked by hunter-gatherers, but our knowledge of their early settlement is limited, largely because the gradual rise in sea-level will have eroded away or inundated huge expanses of the early Holocene coast-line, destroying, or at least obscuring, all trace of earlier settlements. Only in rare cases has evidence survived, for example around the south coast of Brittany on unsubmerged islands and peninsulas, and, more impressively, in western Scotland, where isostatic uplift has outstripped the rise in sea-level, leaving coastal middens now some distance inland.

We have already seen how, as the climate improved after the Younger Dryas, hunter-gatherer communities spread into the eastern areas of Britain across the Doggerland plain from the more eastern and southern parts of the North European Plain. We can be equally sure that a similar spread of settlers emanating from the Late Glacial refuges in Cantabria and south-western France spread northwards along the Atlantic coastal zone. Early in the last century this was frequently discussed in the archaeological literature but for some reason has been lost sight of in more recent discussions, which have tended to focus exclusively on movements from the east through the forests of the Doggerland plain. Here we must attempt to redress the balance.

The importance of the Atlantic coastal corridor was admirably summed up by the great European prehistorian V. Gordon Childe in 1935 and deserves to be quoted in full:

> the colonists who had settled near Oban and on Oronsay in Atlantic times must have arrived by sea, ultimately from northern Spain or south-western France. It sounds fantastic to bring primitive fishers and hunters who did not even possess an axe from so far afield, especially when intermediate finds are lacking. But we do not envisage a single direct voyage from the mouth of the Garonne to Galloway. On the contrary, the fishers would have progressed very slowly, halting at many points on the way, perhaps for several generations at each . . . In south France the Azilians seem to belong to the Boreal period so that ample time was available for them to reach Scotland in the Atlantic epoch. The apparent absence of intermediate sites may be due to land-sinking. The Azilians, not being equipped for dealing with forest, had to keep to the shore.
>
> (*The Prehistory of Scotland*, 17)

115

Childe's main concern was to explain the origins of the Mesolithic communities of western Scotland, which were then known as Obanian: this he did by seeing them as the direct, if distant, descendants of the early Mesolithic Azilian culture of Cantabria and south-western France, which had evolved locally out of the late Upper Palaeolithic Magdalenian culture. One of the reasons that Childe and others believed in the Atlantic link was the close similarity of bone barbed fish spears found in both regions.

The general hypothesis is not at all unreasonable. It makes good geographical sense and there are broad cultural similarities discernible along the Atlantic seaways at the time. In south-west France the Azilian dates to the tenth and ninth millennia.

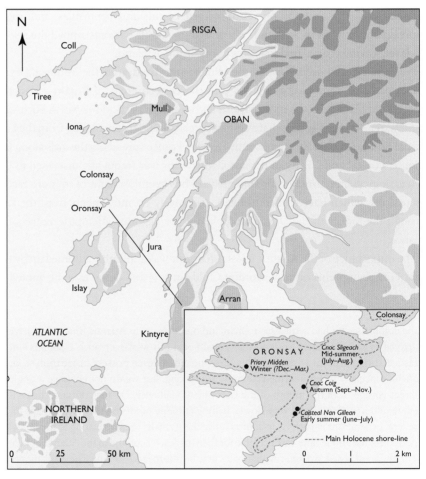

4.11 The island of Oronsay, one of the Inner Hebrides off the west coast of Scotland, showing the locations of the four Mesolithic fishing camps in relation to the contemporary shore-line

The earliest dates at present for the Atlantic Scottish Mesolithic lie in the seventh millennium, so a gradual migration northwards along the Atlantic littoral is a distinct possibility. As we shall see (pp.128–30), recent work on DNA has much of direct relevance to contribute to the debate.

Whatever their ultimate ancestry, the Mesolithic cultures of the Atlantic zone show a degree of regionalization that may, at least in some areas, have resulted from interaction with other communities coming from the east of the country. One striking characteristic of these groups is their reliance on the sea, which is often manifest in the creation of large shell middens. The west coast of Scotland and the Inner Hebrides are particularly rich in sites of this kind. The best-known lie on the little island of Oronsay, barely 4 square kilometres in extent. Here five shell middens were created at different points along the coast. The contents show that the community was exploiting limpet, periwinkle, whelk, oyster, cockle, scallop, and razor-shell, as well as fishing in the shallow waters for wrasse, saithe, and ling. A detailed study of the ear-bones (otoliths) of the saithe (bones that grow at such a rapid rate as the year progresses that the season of kill can be estimated) showed that the middens were occupied at different times during the year. The implication is that either foragers from the mainland camped on the island at intervals during the year, changing their camp site to provide the best protection from the prevailing weather; or, less likely, a single community occupied the island throughout the year, changing camp sites with the seasons.

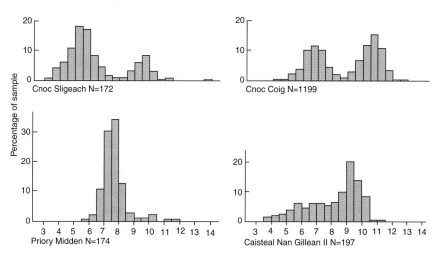

4.12 Histograms to show the different sizes of the otoliths (ear-bones) of saithe. Since the otoliths grow very quickly, the length of the bone can give a close indication of the season in which the fish were caught. The histograms compare the bones from four midden sites, demonstrating that the different locations were used at different times of year

Among the mammal remains from the island middens were grey seal, probably from a local breeding colony, and red deer, reindeer, and wild pig, which were probably brought in as meat from the mainland or one of the larger islands. That a significant number of red deer were small suggests an island source. A wide variety of sea-birds were also exploited, including cormorant, shag, goose, tern, gull, razorbill, great auk, guillemot, and gannet. While lengthy species lists may be tedious to recount, they do show something of the abundance of food available and the resourcefulness of the foraging communities. It remains unclear, however, whether the available edible bio-mass from this tiny island could have sustained a community of any size. It is worth remembering that it takes several tens of thousands of limpets to match the food value of a single deer. The coastal resources can only have been one component of the diet.

The survival of shell middens in Scotland is a feature of isostatic forces raising the old beach-lines above the destructive effects of coastal erosion. Elsewhere shell middens are rare, but examples have been recorded on the coasts of Dorset, north Devon, and south-west Wales. These can only be a pale reflection of what must once have existed before the rise in sea-level.

The date of arrival of the coastal hunter-gatherer communities in the western parts of Scotland has not yet been determined with any certainty. Among the earliest radiocarbon dates are assessments of *c.* 6700–*c.* 6500 BC for a bone barbed point from Druimvargie rock shelter in Oban and *c.* 6500–*c.* 6400 BC for the basal levels of a midden in Ulva Cave. Together these dates suggest that settlement was well under way in the early seventh millennium. The main cluster of Obanian dates comes in the sixth millennium, by which time the population had expanded to exploit much of the extensive coastal zone offered by the long inlets, peninsulas, and islands. The predominantly maritime distribution leaves little doubt that the early foragers were competent sailors well used to coastal waters.

The Peopling of Ireland

The initial colonization of Ireland, now an island in its own right, seems to have begun at about the same time as that of the west coast of Scotland, with the earliest dates appearing at the beginning of the seventh millennium. Early Mesolithic sites are most common in the north-east, favouring coastal locations and clustering in some number in the valley of the River Bann. Another cluster of early sites is to be found in the Blackwater valley in the south. It is difficult to say to what extent this is a true representation of the distribution of the early population: distribution of archaeological sites is often a reflection of the distribution of active archaeologists. However, the concentration of early settlement in the north-east is real, and it was

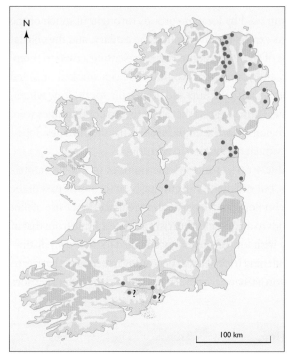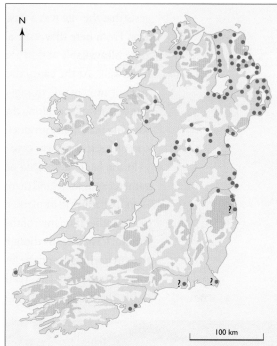

4.13 The distribution of Mesolithic sites in Ireland (mapped in 1989). The left-hand map shows early Mesolithic sites, the right-hand map those of the later Mesolithic. More recent work is filling the gaps, but the relative percentages are much the same

probably in this region, on the shores of Antrim and Down, that the pioneer foragers made their landfalls. Studies of the earliest known tool-kits give few clues to origins, though there are similarities with assemblages from eastern Britain and western France. All that can safely be said is that the settlement of eastern Ireland was part of the expansion of earlier hunter-gatherers along the Atlantic seaways. Colonization was probably by a small group of related peoples entering Ireland over a period of time in sufficient numbers to establish a stable breeding population.

The most extensively examined of the early forager settlements is Mount Sandel, situated on a bluff overlooking the River Bann. The site is unusual in providing clear evidence of structures in the form of circular settings of stake-holes, representing shelters up to 6 metres in diameter built of light timber framework and probably covered with skins. There were also pits, probably used for food storage. The excavations were important in providing extensive evidence of the foraging economy. The diet was based on young wild boar and fish, most notably salmon and trout augmented by eel and sea-bass. The long list of hunted birds was dominated by mallard and wood-pigeon, while plants gathered for storage included hazel-nuts, water-lily seeds, wild pear, and crab-apple. The different seasons at which these various foods became available suggests that the site was a base camp used by foraging groups throughout much of the year. From here they were able to exploit the river valley, the estuary, and the coastal zone, all available within a radius of about 10 kilometres, representing a two- to three-hour walk. At the camp the fish and young boar would have been smoked or salted and put away in safe storage, together with the nuts and dried fruit, for the long winter. The density of sites along the River Bann suggests that a number of communities were working this highly productive region. If so, the implication is that they had developed complex social networks to allow them to function in harmony.

In the later Mesolithic period (*c.* 5500–*c.* 4000 BC) the number of known hunter-gatherer sites in Ireland increases, but still there is an emphasis on the north-east of the island. Changes in implement technology, and in particular a reliance on the use of flint blades rather than microliths, tends to distinguish the Irish later Mesolithic from that of Britain. It is rather as though the Irish foragers had now adjusted to their own distinctive environment, and the fast-widening Irish Sea was beginning to become a barrier to long-distance contacts. Yet the North Channel between Ireland and the Inner Hebrides

4.14 Excavation in progress on the early Mesolithic house found at Mount Sandel overlooking the River Bann in Northern Ireland, showing the holes for the wall timbers cut into the bedrock

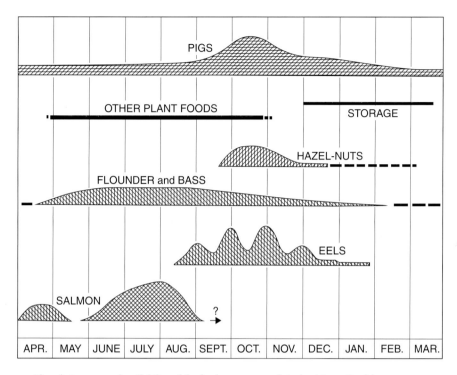

4.15 The relative seasonal availability of the food resources exploited at Mount Sandel

was barely 30 kilometres wide, and it is inconceivable that the two communities within sight of each other should not have indulged in some kind of social engagement.

Patterns of Connectivity

The question of how mobile the Mesolithic hunter-gatherer communities really were needs to be considered. The fact that the group using Mount Sandel as a base could have gathered all its necessary resources within a 10-kilometre radius does not necessarily mean that the community restricted itself to this comparatively limited territory. There may well have been times when bands ventured much further afield, for a variety of reasons, to acquire rarer resources, to engage in social intercourse with other communities, or simply to explore: one should never forget the innate drive in humanity that makes us curious about what lies over the next hill. Among more recent hunter-gatherer groups it is quite common to find longer journeys being made, with distant communities meeting at prescribed times to reaffirm relationships, exchange gifts, and agree marriages. Among the Pacific Coast Indians of North America, coastal journeys of hundreds of kilometres were made every few years, culminating in cycles of feasting that lasted for days.

Tracing such journeys and encounters in the archaeological record is by no means easy, but occasionally this can be done through the surrogate of raw materials exchanged during such encounters. One very clear example is provided by a distinctive stone found at Bloodstone Hill on the western coast of the island of Rhum in the Inner Hebrides. Rhum blood-stone fractures easily in such a way as to be convenient for making tools. As might be expected, it is a major component of Mesolithic detritus scattered on the island itself, but it is also found at twenty-two other sites on neighbouring islands and peninsulas of the west coast of Scotland up to 70 kilometres from the source. The implication is that either the stone was extracted by locals and exchanged with neighbours, or people came to Bloodstone Hill to collect the material for themselves. Whichever was the case, it implies a degree of maritime connectivity extending over a considerable social territory. The blood-stone, of course, would not have been the only commodity changing hands within this network. One can imagine the exchange of a range of perishable materials that leave no archaeological trace: foodstuffs, furs, skins, feathers, and wives.

The Rhum network, if we can so call it, is one of three that can be distinguished in Atlantic Scotland. A second is represented by the distribution of a distinctive mudstone from the island of Skye, which was used extensively in the Outer Hebrides as well as on the island itself and the adjacent Scottish mainland. The third network, involving the distribution of a pitchstone from Arran, encompassed much of the west coast and the islands from Rhum in the north to almost as far south as the English border. The three networks overlap to some extent, as might be expected. What is clearly evident is the importance of the sea as a means of communication. The sea provided the connective tissue that bound the coastal settlements together. Although we know nothing of boat-building or navigation skills at this time, we can be sure that the communities were highly competent sailors since life depended on mastery of the sea.

Another area in which connectivity can be traced through scatters of stone artefacts is southern Britain. Chert, a silicious stone from the Isle of Portland in Dorset, useful for tool-making, has been found on a number of sites across central southern Britain, including the Isle of Wight. This distribution is also reflected by artefacts of slate and distinctive pebbles drawn from sources lying in coastal regions of Cornwall and Devon. The implication must be that these items were being transmitted socially through contacts between different hunting bands, perhaps at annual gatherings when distant groups came together to enjoy each other's hospitality. Small useful items could be passed from group to group, changing hands many times before eventually being deposited, discarded, or lost for archaeologists to find.

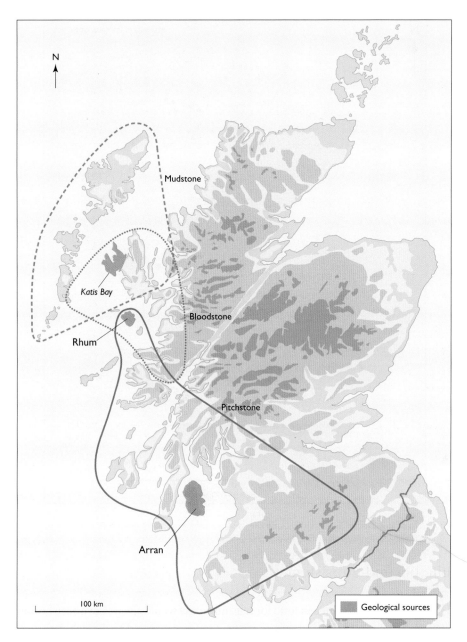

4.16 Distinctive stone from restricted locations exploited in the Mesolithic period was distributed quite widely in Atlantic Scotland, clearly showing the importance of the sea as a corridor of communication

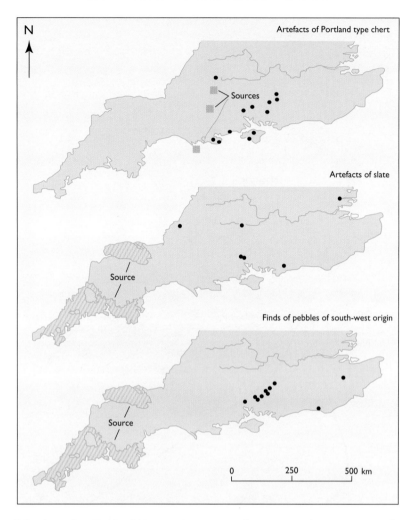

4.17 Utilized stone found in Mesolithic camp sites may come from a variety of sources some way from the camps. These distributions show the considerable distances over which stone was carried and exchanged

Life beyond Subsistence

The drive to acquire sufficient food for self and family would always have been bound up with beliefs that helped people to understand and respond to the world around them and the realms that they perceived to lie beyond, inhabited by spirits and the gods. No sharp distinctions would have existed between 'secular' and 'religious', between the physical world as observed and the spirit world as conceived: the one elided into the other. Just as the pangs of hunger had to be addressed, so too did the ever-present demands of the supernatural.

We have already seen how the archaeological evidence surviving at Star Carr strongly implies complex patterns of behaviour associated with man's very close relationship with the red deer, and probably the elk, which were the mainstay of his hunting activities. It is not unlikely that the spirit of the beast was revered and had to be placated to ensure the continued success of the hunt, and that the camp at Star Carr at the water's edge was the place where the rituals underpinning these beliefs were enacted. It is also possible that the shell middens, especially those like the Oronsay middens that lay on the original shore-line, were sited to be in the liminal zone between land and sea. Indeed, they may have been deliberately built to be dominant, serving to express the community's control of resource and territory through the construction of 'monuments'. That shell middens were places of social enactment is suggested by the discovery of human bones in one of the Oronsay middens. While there is nothing unusual in finding isolated fragments of human bone in Mesolithic deposits, the find at Oronsay was rather out of the ordinary, in that, of the forty or so bone fragments recovered, thirty were small bones from the hands and feet, and one of the groups of human finger bones was found to lie on a cluster of bones from a seal's flipper. It is possible that the prevalence of toe and finger bones may have resulted from the practice of excarnation, involving the exposure of the body at the midden site and the subsequent removal of the larger bones, leaving only those too small to collect. This does not, however, explain their juxtaposition with seal flipper bones, which would appear to be a deliberate act of association.

Excarnation was very probably a widely practised rite of disposal and accounts for the rarity of complete inhumations. Inhumation may only have been practised in exceptional cases, for example when the deceased was considered dangerous or in some way malign. One of the few complete skeletons known—that of a young adult male—was found in Gough's Cave, Cheddar, and dated to the eighth millennium BC. Why he was chosen for disposal entire in the cave we shall never know, but a suppurating lesion above his right eye, which has left a scar on the skull, may have singled him out as someone unclean. Even more enigmatic is the large deposit of human bones placed in Aveline's Hole, another of the caves of the Cheddar region. Records are poor and much of the collection is lost, but more than fifty individuals were represented. Most of them were disarticulated, but at least two were deposited entire. Near the head of one had been placed seven pieces of fossil ammonite. Other finds included red ochre and perforated animal teeth, suggesting that some at least of the bodies may have been adorned. Radiocarbon dates show that the entire population buried here—men, women, and children—died within a comparatively short period of time between 8400 and 8200 BC. What the Aveline's Hole funerary deposit means is beyond recovery, but it gives some idea of the complexity of the belief systems that guided the community when faced with death.

It is a reasonable assumption that certain places in the landscape were revered by the community, and it may be that structural modifications were made to define the special quality of the place. At its simplest, it might be a simple clearing in a forest, or a cleared area isolating a sacred tree or rock. In the case of Star Carr it was a brush-wood platform along the marsh edge, but this could hardly be called monumental architecture. There is, however, one example of a Mesolithic structure that can fairly claim to be a monument. Archaeologists monitoring the construction of the car park at Stonehenge discovered a row of three (possibly four) very large holes spaced at intervals of between 10 and 14 metres that once held vertical timbers of pine up to 0.8 metre in diameter. Since the holes were over a metre deep, the timbers are likely to have stood many metres in height. Pollen analysis shows that the structure had been put up in a clearing in the mixed pine and hazel woodland. Simple description does scant justice to this remarkable monument. Were the timbers carved to communicate society's myths, as were the totem poles of the North American Pacific Coast Indians? Were the images coloured, and what kinds of ceremony took place around them? We shall never know. These mute holes in the chalk are all that remains of a very special place where people would have congregated in awe and wonder nearly 10,000 years ago to communicate with the spirits, their ancestors, and their inner selves. How many similar places are there still to be found?

And What of the People?

We know so little about our ancestral first inhabitants since only one skeleton, Cheddar man, survives in tolerable condition. He was lightly muscled, short by modern standards, 1.66 metres in height, though with comparatively long arms and legs. As we have seen, he suffered from a debilitating bone infection above his right eye. The less complete skeletal remains from nearby Aveline's Hole were also from lightly built individuals. Some showed signs of growth stress in the bones and teeth, which might have been the result of poor nutrition or ill health in childhood. The arm-bone of one adult displayed the kind of distortion that would have resulted from repetitive activity such as missile throwing or paddling a canoe. This is not much to go on but enough to begin to visualize real people living real lives.

But nothing brings us closer to the people than the remarkable trails of human footprints preserved in successive mud surfaces in the Severn estuary near Goldcliff in south Wales and the Mersey estuary close to Formby Point. In these estuaries, as sea-levels rose, gradually encroaching on the forest edges, high tides swept in deposits of fresh mud, blanketing earlier surfaces. Across these open expanses hunters and foragers walked, as did their prey, leaving trails of footprints; crane, rail, and oystercatchers, as well as deer, aurochs, horse, dog or wolf, and wild boar, shared the mudflat with humans. A careful study of the footprints near Formby Point suggested that the women and children had stayed close to the water's edge to collect razor-shells and shrimp, while the men travelled faster, closer to the forest edge, following red deer and roe deer. So well preserved were some of the human footprints that it was possible to estimate heights, with the tallest in the range of 1.65 metres and the shortest around 1.45 metres. It is tempting to think that this is a dichotomy that may represent the difference between men and women.

What the total population of Britain and Ireland was in the Mesolithic period it is impossible to say with any degree of assurance. One estimate, based on population densities among recent hunter-gatherer groups, suggested that the number could be anywhere between 3,000 and 20,000 people at any one time, but this is surely a considerable underestimate given the rich and varied resources which the isles had to offer. The Mesolithic period covers nearly 5,000 years: no doubt, during this time the population densities would have varied. We can envisage small groups arriving along the Atlantic seaways and across Doggerland, gradually establishing themselves in the wild and unpeopled landscape. Populations grew and new people arrived, requiring further movement into hitherto unsettled areas. There would have been disputes and sometimes warfare as people jostled to reserve sustainable niches for themselves: in remote areas small groups may not have been able to maintain population levels sufficient to reproduce themselves. Over 5,000 years the turbulence of the early pioneering centuries will have given way to times of greater stability as the hunting communities carved out regular territories and developed social systems to manage relationships with neighbours. By the end of the period so much of the varied landscape of the isles was being utilized that the popu-

4.18 Formby Point in the Mersey estuary. A trail of Mesolithic footprints exposed when the overlying deposits were eroded

4.19 Footprint of a teenager or young woman preserved in the mud at Formby Point at the mouth of the Mersey estuary. The footprint dates to the Mesolithic period

lation may have reached several hundred thousand. These are the ancestors from which a majority of modern British and Irish are descended.

The Story Told by DNA

The archaeological evidence suggests that Britain and Ireland were largely or totally bereft of population during the last cold downturn of the Younger Dryas and that, with the beginning of the Holocene around 9600 BC, hunter-gatherer groups began to colonize the country, moving in from the south along the Atlantic seaways and from the east across Doggerland. The study of the DNA of the present-day population gives strong support to this view. There is broad agreement among geneticists that a high percentage of the modern population can trace its ancestry back to the period of recolonization between the end of the Last Glacial Maximum and the beginning of the Neolithic period. One study offers quite startling figures for the percentages of the present population whose ancestry pre-dates c.4000 BC: 88 per cent of the Irish, 81 per cent of the Welsh, 79 per cent of the Cornish, 70 per cent of the Scots, and 68 per cent of the English. If these figures are accepted on their face value, then immigration over the more recent 6,000 years must have been comparatively slight.

There are two issues to be considered: from which direction did the immigrants come, and over what time-scale?

Taking the maternal gene lines first, identified through mitochondrial DNA, the dominant haplotype is H, which appears to have had its origins in a north Iberian refuge and to have expanded from there after the Last Glacial Maximum largely along the Atlantic seaboard, though extending to much of Europe. Five different branches can be identified that emerged during the period of expansion. On the evidence presented it would seem that the majority of British H genes are likely to have arrived along the direct Atlantic route, but some could have come by a more circuitous route from the North European Plain across Doggerland. The paternal gene lines, recognized through Y chromosome DNA, are more complex. Once again a northern Iberian origin seems to dominate, with R1b-9 being the ancestral haplotype concentrated in the Basque region, from which a number of the gene clusters found in Britain arise. An eastern component can also be recognized, originating in Balkan and Ukrainian refuges, bringing the I1a and I1c gene lines to Britain, but its contribution to the British gene pool was small compared to that of the northern Iberian refuge.

Thus far the genetic data are in broad agreement with the archaeological evidence. After the Last Glacial Maximum north-western Europe was gradually colonized from refuges in the south. That the principal source of population should have been in the northern Iberian zone and in southern France should occasion no surprise. The suc-

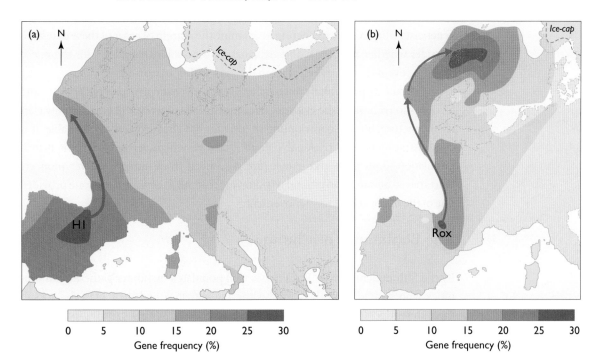

4.20 Two maps to illustrate the possible spread of gene clusters from a north Iberian refuge at the end of the ice age. Map (a) plots the female subgroup H1; map (b) plots the male cluster Rox (R1b-9); after S. Oppenheimer, *The Origins of the British* (London, 2006), Figures 3.5 and 3.6b

cessors of communities emanating from these regions could have reached Britain and Ireland either along the Atlantic littoral zone or through the inland forests, arriving along a broad front. The prominence that the genetic evidence seems to be placing on the Atlantic route is particularly interesting in that it does seem to challenge archaeological preconceptions, which have tended to emphasize inward migration across Doggerland.

Where a more serious problem arises is with the genetic dating. While the currently preferred method for assessing dates, based on mutation rates, suggests that several of the gene lines arrived in the Mesolithic period, some of the patriarchal and matriarchal lines are said to have reached Britain in a period before the Younger Dryas. In the case of the male haplotype R1b-9 it is argued that it gave rise to six male founding clusters in Britain before the onset of the Younger Dryas, accounting now for some 27 per cent of modern man. If so, it requires us to accept that a significant population remained in Britain throughout the last intensely cold period. While this is not impossible, it seems more likely, on present archaeological evidence, that much of the land remained empty during the Younger Dryas, with only a few bands of hunters straying this far north during the summers. Here the challenge is to those geneticists who favour early dating to examine the margin of error of these dates and consider whether a more flexible explanation is possible that allows for the major founding events to have taken place in the period after 10,000 BC.

The debate is particularly interesting in that it challenges preconceptions and forces us to reconsider the evidence. Another decade of work will undoubtedly clarify the picture, but the contribution of genetics has already been considerable. It is demonstrating beyond reasonable doubt that a very high percentage of the British population, both male and female, are descended from hunter-gatherer pioneers who arrived before 4000 BC, and it is showing that the Atlantic littoral zone provided one of the major corridors of movement.

The Beginnings of Change

By the fifth millennium BC Britain was well populated by hunter-gatherer communities who had adapted their food-gathering activities and their lifestyles to suit the different ecological niches they chose to occupy. With a growing population came increasing complexity both in subsistence strategies and in the social systems that governed the relationship between neighbours. Some of the evidence for gift exchange that reflected networks of connectivity between communities extending over quite considerable distances has been presented above. That even more extensive networks were in operation along the Atlantic seaways is suggested by discoveries at the hunter-gatherer site of Ferriter's Cove on the Dingle peninsula in the extreme south-west of Ireland. Here, close to the sea-shore, lived a small community basing its subsistence on wild pig, sea-fish, and molluscs, mainly limpets. That they were, however, part of a much wider network is shown by a cache of fine polished stone axes and bones of domesticated cow. Clearly the community was able to acquire items from distant people who were now practising farming. Since the settlement is dated to c.4350 BC—before Neolithic communities had become established in Britain and Ireland—the possibility is that these gifts were acquired through Atlantic maritime networks extending as far south as Armorica and western France. Neolithic communities were by this time occupying the French coast between the Garonne and the Loire, and contemporary hunter-gatherers in southern Armorica were beginning to acquire domesticated animals from them. It is not unreasonable to suggest that maritime networks embracing Ireland carried exotic gifts from the south, including haunches of smoked or salted exotic meat. Ferriter's Cove is not alone: three other Mesolithic sites, on or close to the Irish coast, have yielded bones of domestic animals.

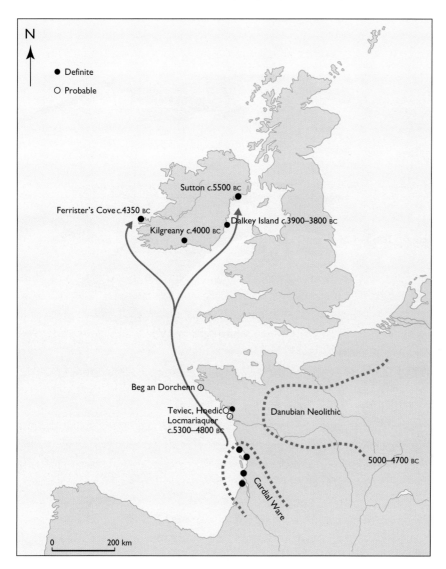

N

● Definite

○ Probable

Sutton c.5500 BC

Ferrister's Cove c.4350 BC

Dalkey Island c.3900–3800 BC

Kilgreany c.4000 BC

Beg an Dorchenn ○

Teviec, Hoedic ○●
Locmariaquer ○
c.5300–4800 BC

Danubian Neolithic

5000–4700 BC

Cardial Ware

0   200 km

4.21 By the end of the sixth millennium BC Neolithic lifestyles (the Danubian Neolithic and the Cardial Ware Neolithic) were reaching north-western France. The discovery of domesticated animals in Mesolithic contexts in Ireland suggests the existence of maritime routes between the Atlantic coast of France in the century before the Neolithic lifestyle spread to Britain and Ireland

The evidence, while comparatively slight, is sufficient to suggest that by the fifth millennium BC maritime networks may have linked the communities together along the length of the Atlantic façade. As we shall see in the next chapter, the Atlantic seaways were to become a major highway for the spread of beliefs and knowledge in the fourth millennium.

5

〰️

New People, New Ideas, 4200–3000 BC

I<small>N</small> four brief centuries, 4200–3800 BC, the landscape of Britain and Ireland was transformed by the arrival and spread of new practices and behaviours that together make up what may be called the Neolithic package. The transformations were fundamental and irreversible and set in motion dynamics of change that are still being played out today.

The most far-reaching of the innovations was the introduction of an already fully developed food-producing strategy based on the cultivation of barley and emmer wheat and the husbanding of domestic cattle, pigs, and sheep. All of these cultivates and domesticates had, in the first instance, to be carried to Britain and to Ireland by boat from the adjacent continent, and land had to be cleared to provide appropriate environments for their propagation and care. The new subsistence strategy rapidly reduced the dependence on hunting and gathering to such an extent that even in coastal regions there was a sudden abandonment of the maritime resource, the protein intake now coming from land-based animals. Such a dramatic change in diet must represent a major readjustment of behaviour and value systems—even perhaps the creation of taboos against food from the sea.

Alongside these major changes in food sourcing came a much-reduced mobility in everyday life. While flocks and herds would have been allowed to wander as they browsed, the need to tend them and to protect fields of grain meant that populations necessarily became more sedentary and the home base became increasingly important. It is no coincidence that large timber-built houses now began to appear for the first time.

A new range of material culture was also introduced. The first pottery—well-made carinated (sharp-shouldered) bowls—appear widely across the country in the first two centuries of the fourth millennium. This is the first artificial material to be made in the isles, the product of carefully controlled pyrotechnics. Another technical innovation was the grinding and polishing of stone to make symmetrical and aesthetically satisfying axe-heads, the more finely finished examples no doubt being highly valued. The flaked-stone repertoire also developed to include leaf-shaped arrow-heads and plano-convex knives.

As the new communities settled into their ecological niches, so their surplus energies were harnessed by the coercive powers within society and directed to the creation of communal works and monuments. The first were the flint mines of the Sussex Downs. Not long after, long barrows, long mortuary enclosures, and cursus monuments (parallel earthworks defining strips of land) were being built, with more-circular enclosures defined by discontinuous ditches, known as causewayed camps, first appearing at the end of the thirty-eighth century BC. These varied structures, whatever their functions, reflect a high degree of social cohesion and a desire by the community to impose itself upon the landscape.

Perhaps the most dramatic aspect of the introduction of the Neolithic package was the rapidity with which it was taken up and spread across the varied landscapes of Britain and Ireland in the period 4100–3800 BC, leading to the equally rapid demise of the indigenous hunter-gatherer lifestyle. In this brief episode the isles were transformed: it was a transformation brought about by a myriad of local acts and local decisions, of successive compromises and failures. Archaeology cannot hope to chart the detail, but it can begin to untangle the main threads of the story.

Crucial to producing a narrative is the ability to assign accurate dates to events. Until recently, even with radiocarbon dating, it has not been possible to do this with any kind of precision: at best the dates available allowed only a fuzzy prehistory to be constructed. But recent advances are changing all this. More precise scientific methods, the careful choice of sample to select only short-life material like seeds or nut shells or quick-growing trees, the use of more refined calibration methods, and the analysis of dated sequences using Bayesian statistics have all combined to provide a growing series of precise dates for events such as the building, use, and abandonment of monuments. We are at last reaching a position from where we can begin to write a real history, accurate to within a generation or two.

New People?

The nature of the Mesolithic–Neolithic transition in Britain has been a subject of energetic debate for several decades. Until the 1960s it was widely believed that the change came about as the result of an influx of new people from the adjacent continent, bringing with them the fully fledged Neolithic package and taking over the land from the Mesolithic hunter-gatherer groups. After this 'primary' Neolithic influx a degree of acculturation took place, with the remaining indigenous population accepting the new lifeways, giving rise to a hybrid, or 'secondary', Neolithic culture. This simple model neatly contained the known facts—and had the benefit of being a common-sense explanation.

But by the 1970s the 'invasion' model of prehistory had been largely rejected as too simplistic. It was embedded in a colonialist view of the past which, in a post-colonialist era, was widely held to be anachronistic when applied to prehistoric times. Moreover, in spite of decades of careful research, it was proving very difficult to identify the continental homeland of the supposed immigrants. Instead, an alternative hypothesis began to be put forward which argued that the indigenous late Mesolithic hunter-gatherer communities, in contact by sea with their continental neighbours, adopted new ways of living, adapting them to suit local conditions. These new subsistence strategies, and the technologies and belief systems that supported them, spread rapidly throughout the country through existing systems of social connectivity. In other words, by a process of acculturation the indigenous hunter-gatherer populations of Britain and Ireland became Neolithic.

More recently there has been a shift back towards allowing there to have been a significant element of immigration from the adjacent continent. The inspiration comes, in part, from the creation of an accurate radiocarbon chronology for the very earliest Neolithic. That a remarkably uniform new culture had spread over much of Britain and Ireland in as little as 300 years has been taken to imply a high degree of population influx and mobility. This, together with a more nuanced understanding of the complex processes of migration, has opened up the debate once more and, as we shall see, DNA evidence is now adding support for the view that new gene lines were entering Britain at about this time. The discussion has now turned to questions of where the new communities were coming from. Were there multiple points of entry into Britain from along the continental shore stretching from Brittany to Denmark? What factors inspired people to leave home to explore the offshore islands? And were contacts then maintained between the various homelands and immigrant communities?

One hypothesis, recently put forward, is that climatic changes taking place around 4100–3800 BC may have encouraged population mobility. Two factors combined to create quite significant changes: the temperature range increased, giving rise to colder winters and warmer summers, while decreased airflow over the north-west Atlantic caused a reduction in winter rainfall. The overall result was that, over considerable areas of north-western Europe, the season suitable for growing cereals was lengthened significantly, extending the territories in which the cultivation of wheat and barley could take place. These climatic factors, however, are more likely to have been a facilitating change rather than a prime cause of population movement.

The spread of Neolithic economies and culture to north-west Europe had been a complex process involving two principal axes of movement: one, characterized by the Linearbandkeramik culture, spreading from eastern Europe and reaching the Seine valley by 5500 BC; the other, typified by the Impressed Ware cultures, spreading northwards from the west Mediterranean coast to reach Atlantic France south of the Loire by much the same time. From these primary zones of settlement Neolithic lifeways extended rapidly to the Channel coast and into the southern Netherlands and the Armorican peninsula during the second half of the fifth millennium.

The communities living around the fringes of the North Sea from the Rhine mouth to southern Scandinavia stubbornly retained their hunter-gatherer lifestyles for some time. In the Netherlands the coastal foragers came gradually to embrace domesticated animals and cereal growing over the period 5000–3600 BC, while to the north the Ertebølle culture of southern Scandinavia remained essentially Mesolithic until around 4000–3900 BC, when traditional systems were quite suddenly replaced by food-producing strategies. It is not impossible that this dramatic change in subsistence was facilitated by the climatic changes mentioned above, causing increased salinity, which affected the fish stocks and shell-fish upon which the foragers depended. These environmental factors, together with a steady increase in population, will have created stresses, upsetting the social equilibrium. Perhaps the more ambitious leaders responded by embracing the benefits of Neolithic culture to gain an advantage over their competitors.

Around the end of the fifth millennium quite far-reaching cultural changes were becoming evident in Armorica. This is most dramatically demonstrated by the fact that a number of the large decorated menhirs of the early Neolithic were at this time pulled down and broken up to be reused as cap-stones in large passage graves. Some have argued that this reflects a period of social tension and perhaps outright conflict within the peninsula.

Standing back from the detail, then, it would seem that after a period of Neolithic 'colonization' in the sixth millennium, north-western Europe remained stable until

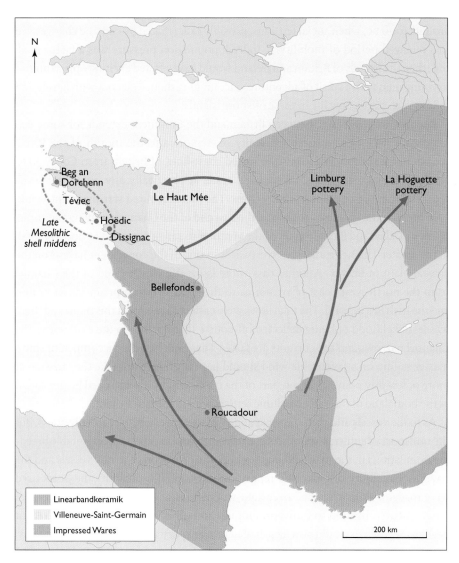

5.1 The Neolithic way of life initially spread into northern and western France by two routes, one through the centre of Europe into Normandy (the Danubian, or Linearbandkeramik), the other via the Mediterranean to the Atlantic coast (Impressed, or Cardial, Ware). Influences from the Impressed Ware groups of southern France may have filtered northwards to contribute to the Limburg and La Hoguette pottery styles. For a while late Mesolithic groups maintained their own way of life in southern Brittany around 4000 BC, when social tensions, possibly exacerbated by climatic changes, led to a renewed period of mobility. If, indeed, population pressure was a factor in all this, then the islands of Britain and Ireland would have offered exciting opportunities to young men with a spirit of adventure, encouraging them to set out with family and followers to start a new life in these offshore islands.

The maritime interface between Britain and the Continent extends for some 650 kilometres. From the western extremity of Armorica to the mouth of the Rhine the continental shore confronts the varied coast-lines of Britain from Cornwall to Norfolk. Sea-crossings could have been made at practically any point, but some routes were more convenient than others. The most favoured starting point would have been on the shortest crossing, at the east end of the Channel. Leaving the coasts of Pas de Calais and Picardy allowed the venturer to sail northwards to find a landfall in the greater Thames estuary, or westwards to one of the convenient havens on the coastal plain of Sussex. Another easy route lay at the western end of the Channel from the north-west coast of Armorica to the south-western peninsula of Britain and the Irish Sea beyond. The tidal flows were easier to manage at this point and there was less likelihood of being deflected off-course than further to the east, where the Channel narrows and the currents are faster. That said, however, a competent ship's master sailing on a favourable wind should have been able to make the crossing at more or less any point. Thus, no part of the continental seaboard need be precluded as the homeland of the early Neolithic settlers who set out for Britain.

As to the vessels and the sailing capability of the travellers, we can only guess, but the transport of sufficient numbers of cattle, pigs, and sheep to set up suitable breeding populations in the new land implies both the provision of sturdy vessels and the navigational ability to make and repeat journeys. In all probability the boats used were made of skins stretched over light wooden frameworks in much the style of the Irish currachs used to transport animals and other heavy loads in more recent periods. Seed-corn would also have had to be transported in bulk, as well as the pioneer farmers and their dependants. To set up a colony adequately stocked to succeed would have required a small flotilla of vessels, each making a number of journeys.

Where this array of maritime skills was to be found raises interesting questions. It is most unlikely that the Linearbandkeramik farmers moving through the centre of the European continent knew much, if anything, of maritime matters, but in the coastal regions they will have encountered hunter-gatherer communities whose livelihood depended on mastery of the sea. The complex processes of acculturation between the immigrant farming groups and the indigenous population over the period from c. 5500 to c. 4000 BC will have given rise to multi-skilled communities,

5.2 Currachs, boats made of a small wood frame covered by tarred canvas, in use on the Aran Islands in Galway Bay

now wholly Neolithic in their subsistence mode, along the entire north French and Belgian coasts. They, like their ancestors before them, may have been used to making cross-Channel journeys to maintain their traditional social networks. To transport pioneer settlers and their livestock and seed-corn would have been little challenge.

The archaeological evidence at present available suggests that the earliest Neolithic population in the eastern regions of Britain arose as the result of the arrival of different groups of settlers coming from north-east France, Belgium, and the southern Netherlands, where the middle Neolithic cultures of Northern Chassey and Michelsberg were already established. It was in these regions that people were using an assemblage of pottery characterized by elegant round-bottomed carinated bowls similar to the earliest Neolithic pottery found in Britain. It was here too that leaf-shaped arrow-heads were widely favoured and mines were being dug to acquire flint nodules suitable for tool-making. The earliest flint mines in Britain, dated to the forty-first or fortieth century BC, were found on the South Downs not far from some of the coastal landfalls that might have been used by the earliest settlers.

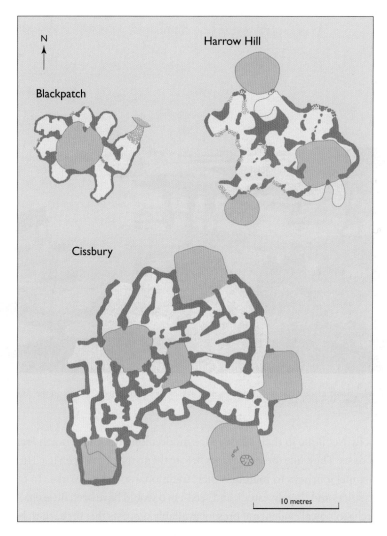

5.3 The plans of three different Neolithic flint mines on the Sussex Downs, where the earliest British flint mines are found. The large circular or sub-rectangular shafts were dug down to the required seam of flint, and galleries were dug out from the bottom of the shafts to allow the maximum amount of flint to be gained

That precise parallels between the cultural package widely used in Britain and that of the putative cultural homelands have yet to be identified need not be of too great a concern. Pioneering communities that arise from movements of small groups of people from varied homelands arriving over a period of several generations are unlikely to replicate a particular culture. Instead the innate knowledge and preferences of individuals will express themselves in different ways as groups fragment

5.4 Early Neolithic flint mines at Harrow Hill, West Sussex, during the excavation of 1925. The galleries running outwards from the shafts follow the seams of usable flint

and recombine in new social configurations and as the challenges of the new environment are met. Relationships with indigenous populations through, for example, exogamous marriages will also introduce change. In other words, the pioneer communities who succeed and become socially cohesive are likely, very soon, to develop their own character, distinct in many details from that of the mother country.

The success of the pioneer culture characterized by the distinctive carinated bowls is demonstrated by its very rapid spread throughout the south and east of Britain, reaching as far north as the southern fringes of the Grampian mountains within no more than two centuries. That the early carinated bowl culture is most prolific along the eastern seaboard of Britain from the Thames estuary to the Firth of Tay—a distance of some 600 kilometres—suggests that movement by sea may well have accelerated the rapid spread northwards. But there was also a westerly penetration across the island, with the early cultural package, including the characteristic carinated bowls, reaching Ireland by the thirty-eighth century.

It is probably fair to conclude that settlers from north-eastern areas of France and from Belgium had the greatest impact on the development of the Neolithic lifestyle of the British, but another distinctive contribution was made along the Atlantic sea-ways. We have already seen that Mesolithic coastal communities in Ireland were in receipt of domesticated animals (or joints thereof) from western France in the middle of the fifth millennium BC. These exotica probably arrived as the result of sporadic long-haul journeys made to set up or maintain social relationships between distant communities. At the very least, they offer a glimpse of the seaways as a functioning system.

A little later, within the bracket 4200–3800 BC, contact appears to intensify, quite possibly as the result of people moving from southern Armorica to settle in Ireland, the coast of Wales, western Scotland, and perhaps south-western Britain. The evidence put forward to support this view centres on the appearance of burial monuments in Britain and Ireland in the form of closed polygonal megalithic chambers and small, simple passage tombs of the type found in the Morbihan region of southern Brittany. One such tomb, excavated at Achnacreebeag on the west coast of Scotland, produced a pot decorated with arc motifs closely similar to pottery known as the late Castellic style found in simple passage tombs in the Morbihan region dating to *c.* 4300–*c.* 3900 BC.

While it must be admitted that the evidence is tenuous, the simplest explanation for the introduction of the earliest Neolithic in the west of Britain and Ireland is that it resulted from settlers from the Armorican peninsula arriving along the existing Atlantic networks embracing the Irish Sea and beyond. The simple megalithic structures introduced into the western regions at the end of the fifth millennium provided the inspiration from which the megalithic tombs of the fourth and third millennia were to develop—the portal tombs, the passage graves, and the court tombs—monuments that helped to give the Atlantic zone its very distinctive character. Further support for the view that there were active networks along the Atlantic seaways comes, somewhat unexpectedly, from recent studies in animal genetics. A distinctive species of vole known as the Orkney vole (*Microtus arvalis orcadensis*) was shown to have a genetic make-up that implied that it had been transported to the Orkneys from western France or Iberia in a single step. Since the vole is known to have been in the Orkneys at the end of the fourth millennium, it is tempting to suggest that the first immigrants arrived on ships in the Neolithic period. A similar study of the pygmy shrew (*Sorex minutus*) identified a genetic strain that was found only in the Pyrenees and Ireland. The

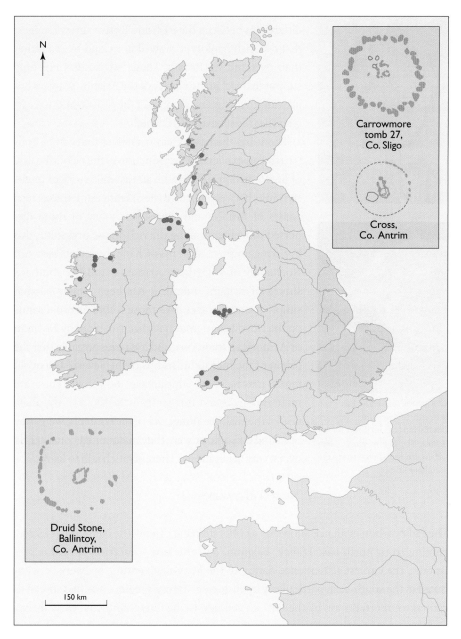

5.5 Distribution of closed chambers and simple passage tombs in Britain and Ireland with plans of selected Irish examples inset. The distribution suggests that the maritime routes were important to the spread of the tomb type which may have originated in southern Brittany

5.6 *Top*: The Orkney vole (*Microtus arvalis orcadensis*) has been on Orkney from the end of the fourth millennium. They are unknown in Britain and were probably introduced direct by sea from Atlantic France or Iberia. *Bottom*: The pigmy shrew (*Sorex minutus*) was probably introduced to Ireland direct from the Pyrenees. They are unknown in mainland Britain

differences between the Irish and British shrews suggest that the Irish haplotype arrived in Ireland by sea rather than overland via Britain. These two studies not only support a belief in the vitality of the Atlantic seaways but provide an intriguing glimpse of the rodent-infested cargoes that must have been carried.

There are, then, two clear narratives that can be constructed to explain the introduction of the Neolithic way of life to Britain and Ireland: an east-side story of intensive links between north-eastern France and the eastern coasts of Britain, and a west-side story of more dispersed movements along the Atlantic seaways. But this by no means precludes cross-Channel contacts between Normandy and northern Armorica and the southern shores of Britain. Indeed, it has been suggested that simple passage graves, like those found at Broadsands on the Devon coast, may have been inspired by Norman or Armorican traditions, and it is quite possible that the origin of the megalithic tombs of the Severn–Cotswold region may lie in the same area (p. 160 below). These are matters that deserve further study. So too does the question of the scale and longevity of the contacts: were they brief and episodic or were they maintained consistently over many generations? There is much still to learn.

New Lifeways

The radiocarbon evidence allows us to offer a sketch of how the Neolithic package, coming from north-east France, Belgium, and the Low Countries, spread across Britain. The earliest settlements, dating to the forty-first century BC, were concentrated in the south-east, particularly in the greater Thames region, and had spread to central southern Britain by the fortieth century. In the thirty-ninth and early thirty-eighth century BC there was a rapid expansion westwards into south-west Britain, northwards into Scotland south of the Great Glen, and across Britain to the Isle of Man and Ireland. South Wales and the Marches began to embrace the Neolithic in the later thirty-eighth century BC.

Perhaps the most striking characteristic of the early phase of settlement is the appearance of large rectangular timber-built houses, or halls, as they may more appropriately be called. They have been found across Britain from White Horse Stone in Kent and Yarnton near Oxford to a number of finely preserved structures in eastern Scotland. A comparable example has been excavated at Llandegai near Bangor in north Wales, while at least forty-six rectangular houses have so far been identified in Ireland. Although there is some variation in size and structural detail, all are imposing structures representing the concerted effort of the community working together to identify, cut, haul, trim, and erect the timbers. Many of the larger buildings show a marked similarity in plan, size, and internal layout, having partitioning dividing the large enclosed space into discrete areas for different functions. Clearly we are dealing with a *tradition* of building.

The halls represented the desire of the social group to make a mark on the landscape—to create a 'place'. Their very existence is symbolic of the community's willingness and ability to work together. Thus, they represent group cohesion, but how did they actually function? They could have housed extended families, the larger examples being capable of sheltering between twenty and twenty-five individuals, but they could equally well have been communal buildings used for assemblies or reserved for the performance of

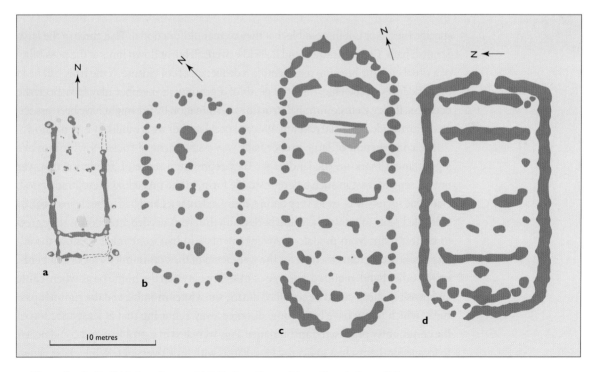

5.7 Plans of early Neolithic long-houses: (*a*) Ballyglass, County Mayo. Plans *b–d* are all from eastern Scotland: (*b*) Balfarg Riding School; (*c*) Claish Farm; (*d*) Balbridie

5.8 An early Neolithic timber hall under excavation at Warren Field, Crathes, Aberdeenshire

specific rites. Nor is it impossible that they were multifunctional. That three of the large Scottish halls, Claish, Crathes, and Balbridie, were all burnt down hints at the possibility of a ritual end, the burning representing a deliberate act of closure. If the halls had been the residences of the elite, then the death of a prominent member may have been the occasion. If they were communal structures, termination by fire might have been associated with the idea of social renewal. We can speculate, but we are unlikely ever to know.

The construction of large timber halls was a statement of society's wish to make a permanent mark on the landscape. They represent a sense of 'residence' that was not present, at least in such a demonstrable form, in the preceding Mesolithic period. Neolithic society was, by its very nature, more sedentary. Land had to be cleared to provide tilled plots to grow wheat and barley, and the crops needed attention as they grew to protect them from predators. Arrangements also had to be made to store the all-important seed-grain essential for the well-being of the community. Flocks and herds, on the other hand, required a degree of mobility between the home base, where cattle and possibly sheep could be corralled during the winter months, and the summer pastures, which might have been some distance away, requiring that at least a section of the community practised transhumance. Pigs were less of a problem and could be left to forage for themselves in nearby woodlands with little oversight. While these generalizations apply broadly across the country, differences in environment required there to be many different subsistence strategies. Changes were also observable over time.

Grain cultivation required the ground to be broken either by hand with the hoe or spade, or with the aid of an ox-drawn ard (a primitive plough), which scored the ground. Where the soil was particularly rocky, there would have been an advantage in moving the stones to the edges of the plots or piling them up in clearance cairns. An example of ard marks scoring the chalk subsoil was found beneath a Neolithic long barrow at South Street in Wiltshire. Here the ground had been worked in two directions at right angles, either in a single act to break up the soil thoroughly or on two separate occasions. How widespread was the practice is unknown, but it may be that the ox-drawn ard was used only in the initial act of breaking the land and that thereafter cultivation was by hoe or spade.

A spectacular example of early land clearance survives buried beneath a peatbog above Céide Cliffs on the coast of County Mayo on the west coast of Ireland. Here a series of low stone walls runs across the countryside for distances of up to 2 kilometres. The walls are set out roughly parallel with each other, 150 to 200 metres apart, forming

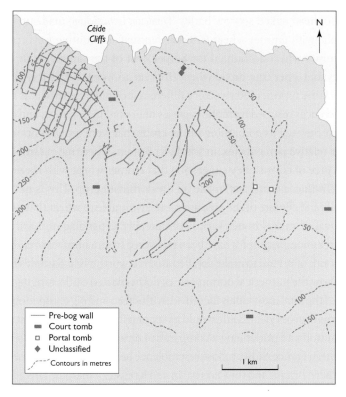

5.9 Plan showing the co-axial field system at Céide Fields, County Mayo, and the megalithic tombs in the neighbourhood. For the most part the field system was covered with blanket bog, which formed soon after their abandonment

long strips of land further divided by cross-walls into rectangular fields up to 7 hectares in area. Some 1,000 hectares had been cleared and divided in this way, a colossal area that would have required the coordinated effort of a sizeable community committing much time to the labour. The walls are low, seldom more than 0.8 metre high, and may reflect the desire to clear rubble from the land in an orderly manner, with the boundaries demonstrating ownership rather than the creation of significant barriers. Fields of this size would have been ideal for pasturing livestock, but pollen evidence shows that wheat and barley were also grown, though perhaps in the smaller plots using a system of rotation. The fields were in active use from about 3700 to 3200 BC, after which the spread of blanket bog brought farming activity to an end.

The discovery of carbonized grains in some Neolithic settlements provides direct evidence of the actual crops grown, but the data have to be used carefully since we can know little of how the surviving samples came to be selected. One example, based on evidence from two broadly contemporary Scottish sites dating to the early fourth millennium, Boghead in Moray and Balbridie in the Grampian region, will suffice. At Boghead naked six-row barley (*Hordeum hexastichon*) made up 88 per cent of the sample, with emmer wheat (*Triticum dicoccum*) accounting for 11 per cent. At Balbridie emmer wheat accounted for 80 per cent of the sample, with 18 per cent naked barley and 2 per cent bread wheat (*Triticum aestivum*). While it is possible that the samples fairly represented two very different cropping regimes, it is more likely that the differences resulted from the vagaries of processing, storage, and chance survival. At best they tell us something of the crops that were grown but nothing reliable of their relative percentages. In southern Britain, where more samples survive, there is a degree of consistency suggesting that emmer wheat with lesser quantities of einkorn (*Triticum monococcum*) made up the dominant crop. This is not surprising since the soils and climate of the area are more favourable to wheat than to barley.

The survival of animal bones varies considerably, depending on local soil conditions, but large enough samples have been recovered from a number of early Neolithic sites in the south of Britain to make detailed analysis worthwhile. Samples from across the region show the numerical dominance of domesticated cattle, ranging from 50 to 88 per cent of the total individuals identified, with sheep and pig competing for second place. In terms of gross yield, cattle would have contributed by far the most meat to the diet, with mutton and pork being a comparative rarity. Comparison with similar-age sites in northern France shows a close resemblance between the faunal assemblages of central southern Britain and the Paris basin and its eastern margin. This adds support to the view that it was from this broad region of north-eastern France that the early Neolithic migrants to Britain came, bringing their domesticated livestock with them. The similarity of the environments on each side of the Channel would have meant that it was comparatively easy to transfer the husbandry strategy, complete with its management practices and taboos, from one region to the other.

One of the outstanding questions concerning food-producing strategies is, what was the relative balance of pastoralism and agriculture in food production and how did it vary from one part of the country to another? There is no reliable way to approach this by quantifying animal bones and seed remains since their survival on archaeological sites is the result of a range of factors that cannot be assessed, but isotope analysis of human bone offers a way to approach the question. An array of analyses from various parts of the country show that there was a stark change in diet at the beginning of the Neolithic period, with the Neolithic population, even in coastal areas, obtaining their protein from terrestrial sources. The avoidance of sea-fish and shell-fish was clearly a deliberate choice conditioned by new social values and taboos. Recent work on Neolithic human skeletal remains from Hambledon Hill in Dorset have taken the study further, showing that while the protein intake reflected a wide range of diets, most of the adults obtained their protein from meat and milk. This tends to support the view that animal husbandry may have played a more significant part in the economy than the growing of cereal crops.

One study has shown that perhaps as much as 60–80 per cent of the protein intake may have come from animal sources, but care needs to be taken in interpreting figures of this kind. Even if they are correct (and slight changes in the working assumptions could reduce them considerably), they translate into a diet of two-thirds cereal and one-third meat when measured by bulk. That said, cattle are likely to have been important to the community, and the status of the group or the individual may well have been measured by the size of the herd.

Structuring the Land: Monuments to the Dead

The larger timber halls built throughout Britain and Ireland in the early centuries of the Neolithic are the first manifestation of monument building—the initial act of pioneering communities wishing to impose themselves on the alien landscape. Over the next 1,500 years the desire to monumentalize the landscape by creating 'places' continued with the construction of an impressive array of monuments, including timber funerary houses, long barrows and other long cairns, megalithic burial chambers, causewayed camps, cursus monuments, and henge monuments. Putting variety aside, what they all have in common is that they demonstrate the concerted effort of the community, working together to an agreed end. They proclaim the belief systems and values of the group, and the act of construction creates a point in time to which subsequent generations can refer. In other words, they identify the people in their landscape and provide visible and lasting references to their history.

The earliest monuments to be built in the south and east of Britain are mortuary enclosures and the long barrows and long cairns usually associated with the disposal of the dead. The structures were first built in the middle of the thirty-eighth century and continued to be erected until the thirty-fourth century. Their individual histories varied considerably, but generally in each there was a period during which human remains were gathered together in some kind of mortuary structure, and this was followed by an act of closure bringing the procedure to an end. In one system the mortuary structures were built of timber, and the act of closure involved burying them beneath mounds of soil and stones derived from two flanking ditches. Fussell's Lodge and Nutbane long barrows, both in Hampshire, provide well-excavated examples of such a practice. In another system the depositions took place in stone-built chambers set within a larger rubble mound but accessible from the outside. In such cases the act of closure might have involved blocking the entrance with large stone slabs, as happened at the West Kennet long barrow. The rather more complex structure at Wayland's Smithy on the Berkshire Downs combined both traditions. In the first phase the primary mortuary

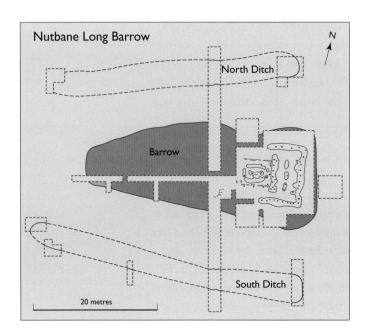

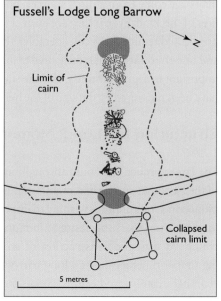

5.10 Two well-excavated long barrows in Hampshire. In both examples complex mortuary rituals were carried out involving the exposure of a number of bodies before the barrow mounds were finally built. In the case of Nutbane a mortuary house was built and modified on several occasions before the structures were finally sealed

5.11 The West Kennet Long Barrow viewed from the east with the entrance court in the foreground

building comprised a long wooden-roofed structure accessible for deposition, probably for a generation or so in the early thirty-sixth century. After a century a mound was constructed over it. Then, after another period of a generation, sometime between 3460 and 3400 BC, a long mound with a megalithic chamber was built and remained in use for burial until the middle of the thirty-fourth century.

Long barrows and mortuary structures are found as far north as southern and eastern Scotland in the early centuries of the fourth millennium and are thus broadly contemporary with developments in southern Britain, but the tradition is restricted largely to the eastern side of the island. In the western parts of Britain and in Ireland the rather different tradition of megalithic tomb building prevails.

151

We have already seen that there is some evidence to suggest that megalithic tomb building was introduced into the lands around the Irish Sea, probably from Armorica, at the end of the fifth or very beginning of the fourth millennium BC. These early monuments—closed megalithic chambers, simple passage tombs, and timber mortuary structures—lay at the beginning of several distinct traditions of tomb building in the west that continued to evolve for more than a millennium.

One of the more ubiquitous of the megalithic funerary monuments is the portal tomb, of which nearly 400 examples are known. Portal tombs are simple rectangular chambers covered by a single cap-stone with an entrance flanked by a pair of tall portal stones. The very simplicity of the type makes it difficult to place in a typological sequence with other megalithic monuments, but radiocarbon dated human bones from the Irish example at Poulnabrone in the Burren in County Clare date to between 3800 and 3200 BC, while the Welsh tomb of Dyffryn Ardudwy was blocked at a time when pottery of the early fourth millennium date was in use. The evidence,

5.12 The portal dolmen at Ballykeel, County Armagh

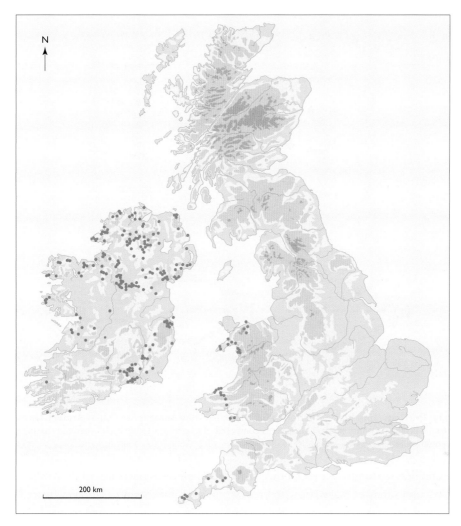

5.13 Distribution of portal dolmens in Britain and Ireland. These simple mortuary structures are among the earliest megalithic tombs in the islands

then, suggests that the portal tomb tradition began early in the Neolithic period. It may have developed from the very early small closed polygonal chambers or possibly from simple timber chambers.

The most common type of megalithic tomb found in the northern part of Ireland is the court tomb. Their characteristic feature is an oval or semicircular courtyard defined by wings extending from the main tomb mound. The court gives access to the tomb chamber, set beneath the mound. Given the large number of court tombs known (some 400), it is not surprising that there is much variation in plan. In some

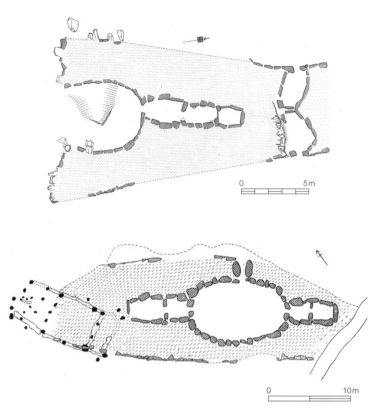

5.14 Two court cairns from the north-west of Ireland. *Top*: From Annaghmare, County Armagh; *bottom*: from Ballyglass, County Mayo. This latter is composed of two tombs facing each other and sharing a central court

examples two tombs face each other, sharing a single oval courtyard, while in others, two tombs may be placed back to back within the same mound. Dating evidence is limited, but the court tomb of Ballyglass in County Mayo was found to overlie an early timber hall associated with carinated bowl pottery, suggesting a comparatively late date. Such radiocarbon dates as there are would support this, indicating that court tombs saw their main use in the second half of the fourth millennium. The origin of the type remains obscure, but one possibility is that they developed as stone versions of earlier timber funerary monuments.

The court tombs of Ireland show a striking resemblance to the Clyde cairns concentrated along the west coast of Scotland, particularly around the Firth of Clyde. Given the similarity and proximity of the two groups, with only the narrow North Channel to separate them, it is highly likely that the two regions maintained active contacts with each other. That they did, indeed, enjoy social interaction is shown by

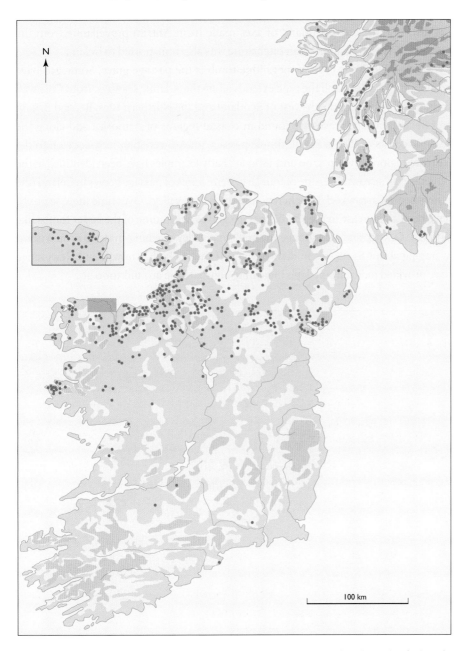

5.15 Distribution of Neolithic court cairns in Ireland and the closely related Clyde–Carlingford tombs in Scotland. Similarities in plan suggest that the communities in the two countries maintained contact with each other across the narrow sea-passage that separated them

the distribution across Scotland of axes made from Antrim porcellanite from the quarries at Tievebulliagh. Arran pitchstone was also transported to Ireland.

A more ubiquitous type of megalithic tomb is the passage grave. Some 230 have been found in Ireland and the type extends along the Atlantic seaways, from Cornwall through Wales, to the north-west of Scotland and the Northern Isles. Beyond Britain and Ireland passage graves are found in coastal regions of Armorica and along the Atlantic coasts of Iberia. Small, simple passage graves were first introduced into the Irish Sea region between 4200 and 3800 BC. Early examples have been identified in the cemetery of Carrowmore, one of four large cemeteries of passage graves in Ireland (the others being Carrowkeel, Loughcrew, and the Boyne valley). Over time there seems to have been an increase in the size of passage graves, with some of the larger tombs like Knowth, Dowth, and Newgrange in the Boyne valley reaching massive proportions, averaging about 85 metres in diameter and 11 metres high. Knowth and Newgrange have provided radiocarbon dates indicating construction around 3000 BC.

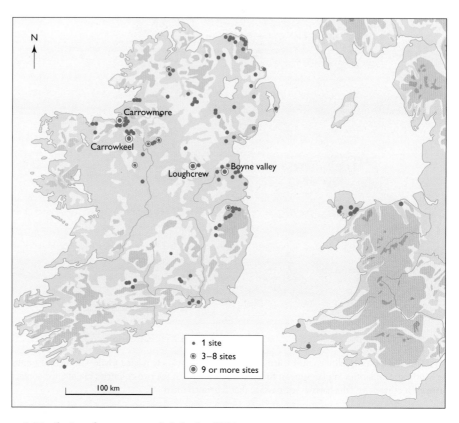

5.16 Distribution of passage graves in Ireland and Wales

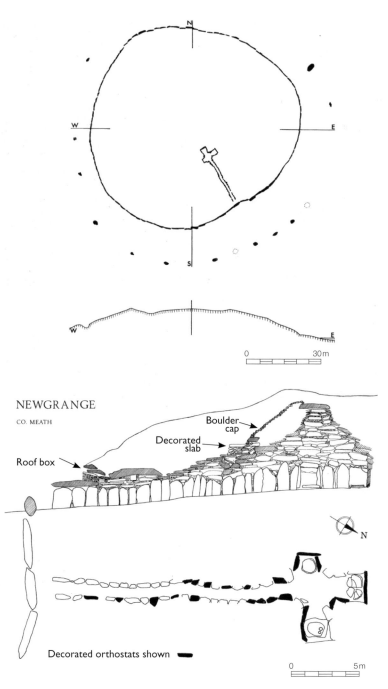

5.17 Details of the giant passage grave of Newgrange, Meath. The section, below, is taken along the passage and chamber. The 'roof box' marked is the slot through which the sun's rays pass at sunrise on the midsummer solstice

5.18 The interior of the passage grave of Newgrange in the Boyne valley. At the time when it was built, around 3000 BC, sunlight would have shone along the passage at sunrise in midsummer to light the stone with the triple spiral

Other substantial and elaborate passage graves are known along the western seaways. On the island of Anglesey, Barclodiad-y-Gawres and Bryn Celli Ddu share many similarities, in both form and decoration, to the Boyne valley tombs lying barely 130 kilometres away across the Irish Sea. Further to the north, in north-west Scotland, the passage graves are generally more modest, but there is a cluster of large and impressive structures on Orkney, most notably Maes Howe with its superbly built central chamber 4.6 metres square and a corbelled roof once 5 metres high.

The huge monumental tombs of the Boyne valley, Anglesey, and Orkney, all built at around 3000 BC, represent the culmination of a thousand-year tradition. They share the same architectural styles, the same artistic values represented in stone carving, and the same desire to capture major events in the solar calendar through the alignment of their passageways on the sunrise or sunset at the solstices. While there can be no reasonable doubt that the monuments were the result of local developments, the shared beliefs and values embodied in the structures imply that the disparate

5.19 *Left*: Inside the chamber of the eastern tomb at Knowth, in the Boyne valley, with a decorated stone basin in position in front of a decorated orthostat

5.20 *Below*: The mound of the great passage grave at Knowth with subsidiary tombs clustering around it

communities must have remained in contact with each other along the ever-convenient seaways. Their ancestors, who first settled the west at the end of the fifth millennium, set up social networks that were still being honoured a thousand years later. How these networks functioned, whether they were in regular use or were punctuated by long periods of abeyance, whether they were reciprocal or one-way, and how many people made the long sea journeys, we are unlikely ever to know, but we can be sure that robust systems of connectivity were now in place.

If the Irish Sea communities were bound by long-established social networks, it is worth considering what evidence there may be for more extensive links along the Atlantic seaboard. Similarity between motifs carved on passage graves in Ireland and the Morbihan region of Brittany are certainly close enough to suggest exchanges of ideas between the two regions, while several artefacts found in Irish passage graves— a carved stone mace-head from Knowth, carved bone pins from Four Knocks, and bone pendants from Carrowmore, Carrowkeel, and Loughcrew—all have close parallels in contemporary sites in Iberia, particularly in the Lisbon area. Taken together, the evidence is sufficient to suggest that long-distance journeys were, indeed, being made between the disparate passage grave builders of the Atlantic zone. As to the frequency of those journeys we must remain ignorant: it may be that maritime contacts were continuous throughout the fourth millennium, but equally they could have been episodic, energized by particular events or charismatic individuals, with long periods of quiescence between.

One final group of megalithic burial monuments needs to be considered: the tombs of the Severn–Cotswold group, which are found on either side of the Severn estuary extending into south Wales but with a particular concentration in the Cotswolds. In all, some 175 examples have been found. In all cases the megalithic burial chambers lie within the body of a long burial mound usually trapezoidal in shape. The arrangements vary, the norm being for the chamber to open through a portal at the end of the mound. Some had simple terminal chambers, others were provided with transepts. In other cases the portal was false, the chambers opening separately from the sides of the mound. Dating evidence is not readily forthcoming, but the few that provide dates indicate construction in the first half of the fourth millennium. The structure of some of the monuments suggests that they may have developed over time. At Ty Isaf in the Black Mountains, for example, an earlier circular mound with transepted burial chambers was incorporated into a larger trapezoidal mound with lateral chambers, while at Notgrove in the Cotswolds the later long mound encapsulated a closed cist set in a circular cairn.

5.21 (*opposite*) Three excavated long barrows of Severn–Cotswold type. *Top*: Ascott-under-Wychwood; *middle*: West Kennet long barrow; *bottom*: Wayland's Smithy. In the last, a small long barrow was replaced by the much longer tomb with a megalithic chamber

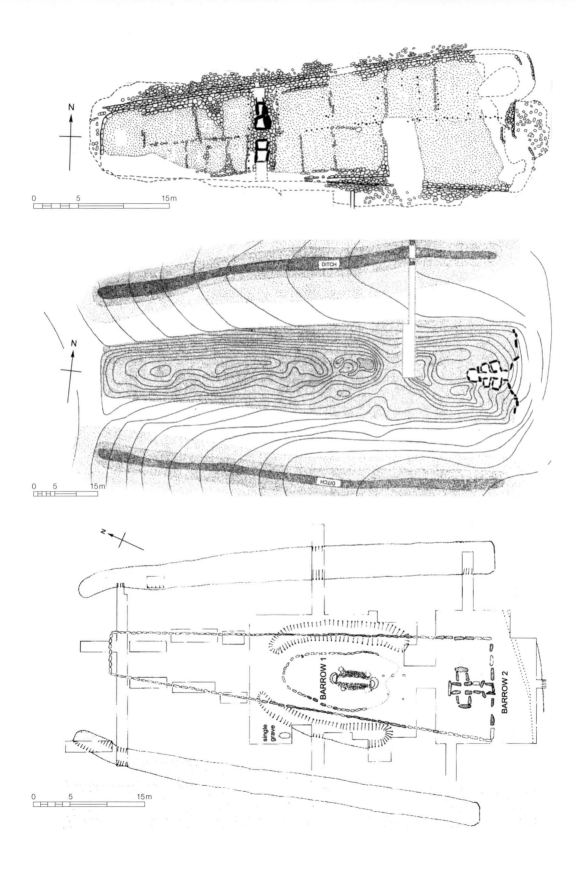

0   5   15m

0 5   15m

DITCH

DITCH

0   5   15m

BARROW 1

BARROW 2

single grave

N

N

N

The monuments would appear to be a combination of the megalithic tomb traditions and the concept of the long barrow so prominent on the Wessex uplands. The simplest explanation, therefore, would be to see them as a British hybrid, the megalithic idea being introduced along the Atlantic seaways or across the Channel with the long barrow tradition coming from the east.

Enclosing Spaces

Another way of creating a 'place' that became popular in the south-east of Britain in the fourth millennium was the construction of what archaeologists refer to as causewayed enclosures. These are essentially ditched enclosures, roughly circular or oval in plan, with the ditch dug in lengths separated by undug sections. Spoil from the ditches was piled up along the ditch lip on the inside of the enclosure, sometimes, but not always, forming a continuous bank. In some cases the bank was strengthened by a palisade, creating a significant barrier. Where the topography of the land allowed, causewayed camps were usually sited on hill-tops, but they are also found in river valleys and in other low-lying regions. Some enclosures have more than one circuit of ditches, usually widely spaced. The three circuits at the famous Windmill Hill in Wiltshire are thought to be of different dates, the innermost being the first, the outermost the second, with the median circuit coming last in the sequence.

Radiocarbon dating shows that in the south and east of Britain causewayed enclosures began to be built in the mid-thirty-eighth century BC and continued to be maintained for four centuries or so. The tradition was already well established in continental Europe at this time. Close parallels in the Paris basin suggest that it was probably from this region that the concept came, but since it was not apparent in Britain until several centuries after the first Neolithic arrivals in the south, the implication is that either contact was maintained between British communities and their continental homeland throughout the early fourth millennium or the thirty-eighth century saw further new arrivals.

Causewayed enclosures are concentrated in the south-east of Britain south of the Wash–Severn axis, with a few isolated examples spreading up the east coast as far as the Firth of Tay. A scattering appear in the west in Wales, the Isle of Man, and the extreme north-east of Ireland. One particularly interesting anomaly is the enclosure found at Magheraboy in the west of Ireland dating to around 4000 BC, significantly earlier than the earliest southern British example. If the dating evidence is accepted as reliable, Magheraboy could be most simply explained as the inspiration of an unusually adventurous band of immigrants, perhaps from the Paris basin region, joining with the Atlantic pioneers who were on the move at the time.

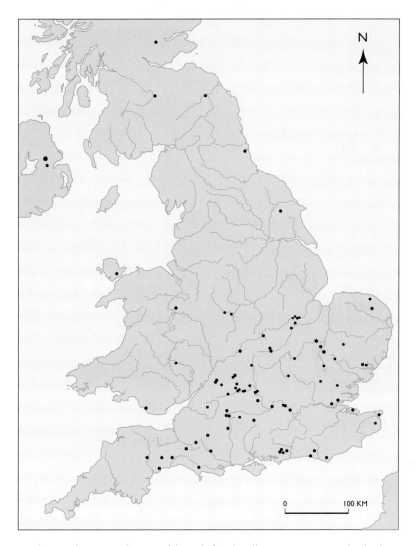

5.22 Distribution of causewayed camps of the early fourth millennium in Britain and Ireland

The function of the causewayed enclosures has been energetically discussed over the last few decades, with a variety of ideas being put forward, but the broad consensus is that they were places where the wider community could assemble from time to time to carry out the many tasks that were necessary to maintain social cohesion: communal worship, feasting, competitions, agreements over boundaries, exchanges of gifts including wives, homage to ancestors, and so on. In other words, they were the areas where the community could renegotiate and publicly affirm its social

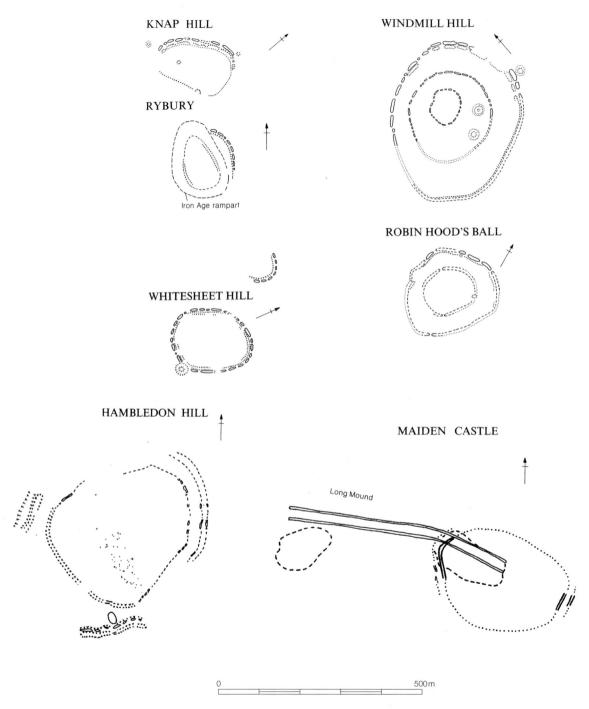

KNAP HILL

WINDMILL HILL

RYBURY

Iron Age rampart

ROBIN HOOD'S BALL

WHITESHEET HILL

HAMBLEDON HILL

MAIDEN CASTLE

Long Mound

0   500 m

5.23 Plans of a selection of causewayed camps from southern Britain

5.24 The Iron Age hill-fort on Hambledon Hill, Dorset, overlooks an earlier Neolithic causewayed camp sited on a ridge commanding three corries. Less than half of the Neolithic enclosure is visible; the rest has been obliterated by ploughing in the field to the right. The double dykes to the left have since been damaged by ploughing

obligations, allegiances, and hierarchies. They were neutral territory, perhaps even liminal places between the secular, outer world and the realm of the deities. In such places the rules of society might be guaranteed by the authority of the gods, creating sanctuaries of safety for all.

Causewayed enclosures probably came to represent the wider community who created them and used them. In times of conflict they could have become places of refuge and the targets of enemies. At four sites, Carn Brae in Cornwall, Hembury in Devon, Crickley Hill in Gloucestershire, and Hambledon Hill in Dorset, there is evidence of attack and destruction. The entrance at Crickley Hill was littered with arrow-heads, and large numbers of arrow-heads were found at the other sites—as many as 800 at Carn Brae. All four enclosures showed signs of extensive burning, but at only one, Carn Brae, was the destruction final. Evidently the south-west was a

5.25 The Stonehenge landscape, showing the Neolithic cursus monument that straddles the chalk downs to the north of Stonehenge. Later a small Bronze Age barrow cemetery grew up alongside

place where warfare—probably endemic in society—could burst into open conflict. We shall see later other evidence of this.

The *floruit* of causewayed enclosure briefly came to an end in the thirty-sixth century at about the time when a new type of monument, the cursus, was being constructed throughout southern and eastern Britain. Cursus monuments are very long, narrow enclosures defined by parallel ditches and banks or by rows of vertical timbers. One of the largest, the Dorset Cursus on Cranborne Chase, was 5 kilometres in length as initially laid out, but was later extended by a further 4.5 kilometres. The cursus lying to the north of Stonehenge was 2.7 kilometres long: close by was another, known as the Lesser Cursus, which was only 400 metres in length. The function of these monuments is obscure. The antiquaries of the eighteenth century compared them to the running tracks of the classical Mediterranean world—hence the name— but this was pure guesswork. Yet the very form suggests that they were associated with some kind of procession through the landscape: in this way they contrasted with the causewayed enclosures, which reflected static assembly at a defined place. Cursus monuments are found in the same regions as the enclosures, often quite close to them, but at several sites, for example at Fornham All Saints in Suffolk and Etton in Cambridgeshire, cursus monuments were laid out over earlier causewayed enclosures, suggesting the replacement of one by the other.

While the long barrows and causewayed enclosures were constructions with a clear ancestry in continental Europe, the cursus monuments would appear to be a British invention and may indeed have first developed in the north-east, in Scotland, where those with the earliest radiocarbon date can be found. They represent, then, an innovation reflecting new beliefs and practices that are truly British in origin.

The cursus monuments lie at the beginning of the development of a series of communal structures, usually classified under the portmanteau term 'henge monuments', that began to be built in the thirty-first century and reached their *floruit* in the middle of the third millennium. These structures were mainly enclosures defined by continuous ditches with banks on the outside, and many reach considerable proportions, as at Durrington Walls, Avebury, Mount Pleasant, Marden, and Knowlton, all in Wessex. A number of these henge enclosures contain massive circular timber constructions composed of concentric rings of posts. Others, like the early henge enclosure at Stonehenge, had a circular setting of pits, containing cremated human remains, set around its perimeter. The variety among henge monuments is considerable and must reflect diversity of practice across the country, intensifying with time. We shall return to the question of henges in Chapter 6.

Standing back from the detail, all too briefly outlined here, we might then discern two broad periods: an initial Neolithic, *c.* 4200–*c.* 3700 BC, represented by an inflow of new people bringing new technologies and belief systems into Britain and Ireland by a variety of routes from the long continental interface; and a developed Neolithic, c. 3700–c. 2500 BC, when local inventiveness took over, leading to a variety of distinctive regional cultures. This raises the interesting question of what this means in terms of mobility of population. While there can be no doubt that the period 4200–3700 BC saw people on the move, evidence for communication between Britain and the Continent after that is harder to discern in the eastern part of the island, though the developed passage graves of the western zone suggest a continued lively exchange of ideas along the Atlantic seaways. Here, then, we are beginning to see the consolidation of an east–west divide that is to characterize the history of the isles thereafter.

Connectivity and Commodities

The most direct way to study the close links that communities established is by tracing the distribution of artefacts made from materials that are only found in very specific locations, the not unreasonable assumption being that artefacts can only move through human agency. In the Neolithic period the one artefact that was particularly susceptible to movement away from its immediate region of origin was the polished stone axe, an item that embodied much human effort through the laborious tasks of mining or quarrying, chipping or pecking, and finally polishing. While axes were an everyday tool necessary for clearing land and for basic construction tasks, and were made in their hundreds of thousands, some seem to have been valued more than others, probably by virtue of the quality of the craftsmanship and fineness of the stone, but also, perhaps, because of their particular histories. A venerable axe passing in cycles of gift exchange from one member of the elite to another will have grown in value as it travelled, its biography enhanced with every move. The type of stone used also seems to have been a factor affecting worth and therefore volume of production and extent of distribution. It may be that specific production sites were believed to be endowed with special powers that could be transferred with the axe: such items would have had enhanced value. They might have been acquired through gift exchange or perhaps through pilgrimage to the source itself.

One of the most spectacular of the stones used for axe manufacture was a greenish-grey metamorphic rock generally known as jadeite, found in the western Alps, in the Italian Piedmont and Liguria, where specific quarries have been identified in the high mountain valleys. The axes were made throughout the fifth millennium and into the beginning of the fourth and were distributed across western Europe from north-eastern Iberia to Scotland and from the west coast of Ireland to the middle

Danube valley, travelling along a series of well-defined routes, usually along river arteries.

In total, some 140 jadeite axes are known in Britain and Ireland. Of those that have been assigned exactly to source by spectroradiometry and ascribed to type, the majority probably arrived via Channel crossings along the interface stretching from Normandy to Pas de Calais. They belong to types that were being made in the Alpine quarries from the middle of the fifth millennium and were in circulation in northern France around 4300–4200 BC. The latest type to reach Britain, though in small numbers, was current on the Continent between 4000 and 3900 BC. Thus, we can be reasonably confident that jadeite axes were brought to Britain via the eastern Channel routes around the fortieth century BC or perhaps a little earlier. This fits nicely with the date of the earliest Neolithic colonization of eastern Britain and is consistent with its being a comparatively short-lived episode. That the axes concentrate predominantly on the eastern side of Britain and are found as far north as the Great Glen suggests that they were part of the early Neolithic package characterized by carinated bowls. It is tempting to see them as tokens of group identity recalling ancestral origins and evoking a distant memory of the great mountain from which they originated. Their value must have been immense. One of the pioneer communities, settling on the fringes of the Somerset marshes, built a remarkable wooden track, known as Sweet Track, across the marsh from the Polden Hills to the island of Westhay: it was dated by dendrochronology to precisely 3807–3806 BC. Beside the track someone had carefully placed a perfect jadeite axe, perhaps as an offering to the deities to ensure the safety of travellers or as propitiation for having invaded the realm of the gods. To have deposited such a valuable item must have been an act of great moment that may have continued to feature large in the oral history of the community for generations to come.

Three of the axes found in Britain (in Devon, Hampshire, and Nottinghamshire) belong to types that were reshaped in southern Armorica, where they are found in considerable quantity. It is conceivable that they were transported across the western Channel routes. Some support for this comes from another discovery, of four axes found in central southern Britain made of dolerite from Plussulien in central Armorica. The quarry began production at the end of the fifth millennium and continued in use to the third millennium. The British finds show that cross-Channel exchange, which may have begun around 4000 BC with the jadeite axes, probably continued for some generations with the importation of Armorican axes. That said, given the massive popularity of Plussulien axes in western France and the length of time over which they were manufactured, the meagre distribution in southern

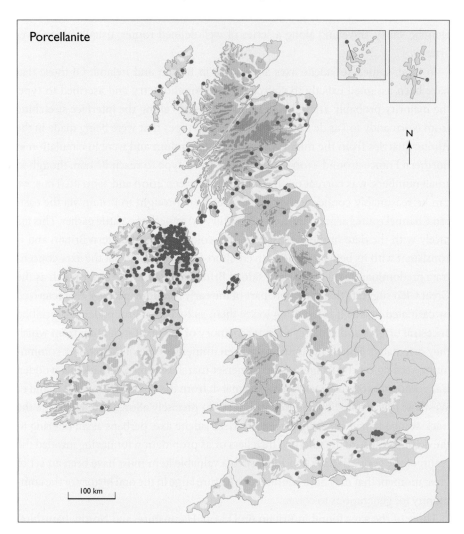

5.26 Three maps illustrating the distribution of polished stone axes derived from specific source locations. Together they reflect mobility of axes in Neolithic society, suggesting that axes were used in cycles of gift exchange: porcellanite from Tievebulliagh, County Antrim; gabbro from the Lizard peninsula, Cornwall; greenstone from Langdale, Cumberland

Britain suggests that after around 4000 BC the western cross-Channel route may have remained largely dormant for some time.

Very soon after the Neolithic lifestyle was established in Britain and Ireland, local stone sources began to be exploited. Some produced axes for local or regional use; others were more popular, with their products extending across very considerable areas. One of the more prolific of the production sites lay on the slopes of Tievebulliagh in County Antrim, where a hard blue-grey porcellanite outcrops. It was

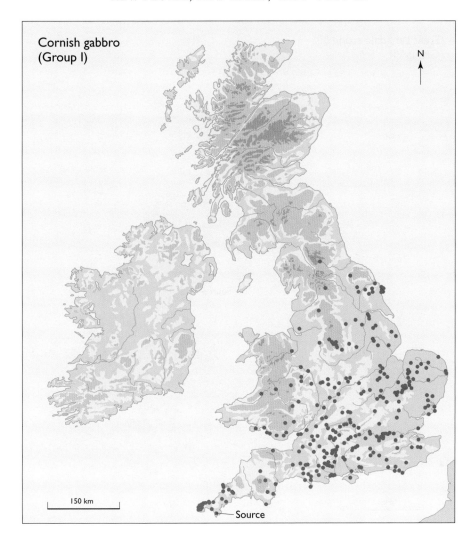

Cornish gabbro
(Group I)

N

150 km

Source

exploited, largely for the production of polished stone axes, from the early fourth millennium until well into the third millennium, during which time it supplied nearly 54 per cent of all the stone axes found in Ireland. The distribution also extends across the North Channel into Scotland and throughout Britain to as far away as Kent. Another very productive centre was Great Langdale in the Lake District, with products reaching north to the Outer Hebrides and south to the Land's End peninsula. The distribution pattern is, however, not what one might expect, with products becoming rarer the further one gets from the source. Instead, there was very considerable concentration in Yorkshire and the valleys of the Trent and other eastern-flowing rivers, but surprising sparseness in Wales and Northern Ireland, which were within easy reach

Great Langdale stone
(Group VI)

Source

150 km

by sea. Clearly there were distorting factors at work here. One possible explanation is that a special relationship existed between the Langdale production centre and the communities of coastal Yorkshire and it was from Yorkshire that axes were distributed by sea along the eastern seaboard of Britain, having been moved in bulk from the quarry site.

Another somewhat skewed distribution is that of axes made of gabbro from the Lizard peninsula in Cornwall. The relative paucity of these axes in Devon but fairly even scatter over much of south-eastern Britain hints that movement by sea might have been a factor in their distribution. This is neatly supported by another distributional study focusing on early Neolithic pottery also made in the Lizard peninsula,

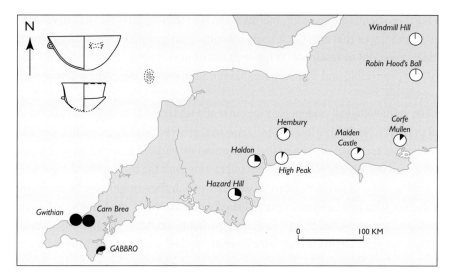

5.27 Neolithic round-bottomed bowls made in a distinctive fabric incorporating crushed gabbro from the Lizard peninsula in Cornwall are found across south-western and central southern Britain. The pie charts show that they dominate the pottery assemblages in Cornwall but the percentages diminish with distance from the source

recognizable from the gabbro grit mixed with clay to give the vessels greater resilience when used for cooking. Gabbroic pottery has been found on a number of early Neolithic sites in south-western and central southern Britain, though, as one might expect, it becomes more scarce as one moves away from its Cornish origin. At nearby sites, like Gwithian and Carn Brae, all the pottery is gabbroic, while at Windmill Hill in Wiltshire, 270 kilometres away, only 0.2 per cent of the total found was of Cornish origin. What is particularly revealing, however, is that distance from source is not the only factor affecting quantity. Sites near the south coast have significantly more gabbroic pottery than those inland, adding strength to the suggestion that the transport of commodities by sea played a role in the systems of connectivity that bound disparate societies together.

Regionality

The distribution of commodities like polished axes from identifiable rock outcrops, often extending over wide territories, at best gives an indication of the extent of the complex networks of gift exchange that must have developed during the fourth and third millennia BC. That one axe made in the western Alps could eventually end up in northern Scotland, 1,700 kilometres away, is a sobering fact. We shall never know the biography of that axe, but it must have involved a number of journeys punctuated by episodes of residence. What such distribution tells us is that Neolithic society was permeable and that favoured commodities were able to flow across social boundaries.

The archaeological evidence, as we currently understand it, suggests that the initial period of Neolithization, from c. 4200 to c. 3800 BC, was a time of intense social mobility as tranches of continental communities trickled into Britain and Ireland and spread out rapidly across the isles, interacting with the resident hunter-gatherers to evolve cultures different from those from which they originated. In this period of mobility, material culture—the polished stone axe-head, the leaf-shaped arrowhead, and the carinated bowl—looked remarkably similar throughout Britain and Ireland, but once territories had been created, marked out by ancestral burial monuments and community-built enclosures, distinct identities began to be defined. While friendly relationships with neighbours, maintained through gift exchange and other social mechanisms, were an imperative, so too was the desire to distinguish self from other. The new regional identities that began to crystallize are reflected in the archaeological record by preferences for particular tomb types, styles of pottery, and favoured sets of artefacts.

We have already considered some aspects of the origins of mortuary architecture in Britain and Ireland. What stands out quite starkly is the distinct regionality in material culture that must represent local variations in belief systems and practices. The distribution of court tombs in the northern part of Ireland and the broadly similar Clyde tombs in western Scotland reflect a broad zone composed of a cluster of regional territories wherein people would have recognized a degree of shared identity. Yet within much the same region of Ireland broadly contemporary portal tombs and passage graves are also found in some number. Although chronologies are still somewhat imprecise, it is clear that during the fourth millennium all three tomb types were in active use. What does this mean? The simplest explanation would seem to be that local lineages favoured particular ways of disposing of the dead based, perhaps, on ancestral traditions, and that in any larger community, made up of a number of lineages, different burial practices were tolerated. In other words, there are many different levels of identity and different degrees of social coherence. The comparative simplicity of the archaeological evidence should not be allowed to obscure the kaleidoscopic variety within the social fabric.

Pottery provided a convenient medium for groups to display their identities. The earliest Neolithic pottery was comparatively simple, comprising round-bottomed vessels, either in simple bowl form or carinated. At first there was a broad similarity across much of Britain and Ireland, but, as time passed, regional variation appeared, and increasingly the surfaces of the vessels were decorated before firing, with impressions made by fingers, sticks, bird bones, and twisted cords. Different regional styles can begin to be identified by the middle of the fourth millennium, each given a name usually based on a site where the style was first, or most clearly, identified. Pottery decoration is a powerful way to express identity and to distinguish self from other. The appearance of distinctive decorative styles is, then, a direct reflection of the increasing desire of the different social groups to define themselves. It is what might be expected to happen at a time when the population was growing and the landscape was filling up.

The Living and the Dead

The practice of careful burial in structures designed for the purpose, introduced at the beginning of the process of Neolithization across Britain and Ireland, has ensured that a large sample of human skeletal material has survived for study. The majority of the burials were collective; that is, they comprise human remains brought together at one location for the purpose of eventual interment. In theory the deposits might comprise fresh bodies still completely articulated, mummified bodies wrapped in bundles, old bodies or parts thereof collected from excarnation sites, or even stray bones or body parts brought in from elsewhere. The assembly of the final deposit could involve the movement of old bodies, causing disintegration, the removal of bones for use at other locations, or the placing together of disparate body parts to make up a complete body. Untangling the processes of deposition clearly requires forensic skills that have rarely, until comparatively recently, been brought to bear on the problem.

A number of burial deposits have, however, received thorough study. One undisturbed and well-excavated example was the deposit found beneath the long barrow at Fussell's Lodge in Hampshire. Here the minimum number of individuals buried was thirty-four, of whom eight were children or adolescents. Careful analysis identified several main groups of bones. One was a single individual, while a second appeared to be a single individual but was in fact made up from parts of two people. There were also clusters of disarticulated bone, some already dry, brittle, and broken at the time the cluster was assembled, suggesting that the bones came from a body that was at least 10 years old before final deposition. A further point of interest is that some of the bones in the different groups were from the same individuals. Clearly, the process of deposition took place over a long period and involved assembling some 'old' material. Radiocarbon dating allows several possible scenarios to be offered. In one it is suggested that two distinct phases were represented, spanning between four and six generations. An alternative is that the first phase represents one to three generations, the second one or two. In any event, the process of deposition was long and complex; it was eventually brought to completion when the covering barrow was constructed.

Another well-excavated funerary deposit was found beneath the primary barrow at Wayland's Smithy. Here some fourteen individuals were represented: eleven males, two females, and a child. At least four, and probably more, were deposited as fresh or only partially decomposed bodies. Radiocarbon dating suggests that deposition took place within a single generation. The fact that arrow-heads were found associated with three bodies, one embedded in a pelvis, having entered the body through the abdomen, taken together with the disproportionate number of men in the burial, suggests that at least some of the bodies may have been victims of human aggression, and indeed the entire deposit might be the result of a single massacre. Similar evidence of death from arrow wounds has been found at Ascott-under-Wychwood and West Kennet long barrows, and we have already seen that the enclosures of Hambledon Hill, Hembury, Carn Brae, and Crickley Hill suffered attacks from bands of archers. Interpersonal violence seems to have been an ever-present reality, particularly in the period from the thirty-seventh to the thirty-fifth century in the west of Britain, from where much of the evidence comes. In all probability warfare was widespread and endemic. Neolithic society was in a state of unstable equilibrium: an uneasy peace could be maintained through systems of social interaction such as gift exchange, feasting, and intermarriage, often for long periods, but tensions could spark at any moment into acts of aggression, quickly to escalate into all-out warfare.

The comparatively large sample of human skeletal material recovered over the years allows certain broad generalizations to be made about the Neolithic population. The average height of males was 1.68 metres, with females generally shorter, and the cranial indices, where they can be measured, conform to the dolichocephalic (long-headed) type. Among the diseases noted, osteoarthritis was prevalent among those over 30 years old, and tooth loss and abscesses were not uncommon. Of more interest is the comparatively high incidence of morphological variation caused by genetic factors, such as shovel-shaped incisors and the occurrence of wormian bones in the skull. This might suggest that the individuals buried in the collective tombs came from families that were closely interbreeding. There is potential here for ancient DNA studies, but little work has yet been attempted.

The Contribution of Modern DNA

The archaeological evidence strongly suggests that there was a significant influx of population into Britain and Ireland in the century or two around 4000 BC, one stream, probably the most numerous, coming from north-eastern France and Belgium across the eastern Channel–south North Sea, the other from Armorica or western France along the Atlantic seaways. These two movements might be seen as the final thrust of the European-wide movements, beginning three millennia earlier with the spread of Neolithic lifestyles from the Near East and Anatolia, one wave (the Linearbandkeramik) spreading through central Europe, the other (Cardial Ware) via the Mediterranean, bringing the Neolithic package to northern and western France by the middle of the fifth millennium. Human mobility on this scale was a complex process. However large was the component of eastern genes at the initial stages of the spread of the Neolithic practices into eastern Europe, one can be reasonably sure that the pioneer communities absorbed indigenous European genes through acculturation as the Neolithic spread. Thus, the Neolithic people of northern and western France, whence came the pioneers who settled in Britain and Ireland, may well have had a comparatively limited genetic inheritance from the east. These are just some of the complicating issues that have to be faced by geneticists attempting to model past population movements from the DNA of modern populations.

While it must be admitted that there are considerable areas of doubt, not least caused by attempting to date the origins of distinctive gene lines, there is broad agreement that three maternal gene groups (J, T1, and U3), arriving from the Near East at about the onset of the Neolithic, can be identified among the European population. Of these, J is the most prolific and can be divided into a number of sub-branches. J1a represents a haplotype characteristic of the central European spread, while J2 seems to reflect the Mediterranean and Atlantic spread. Both occur in significant percentages in Britain and Ireland. More difficult to accommodate in the archaeological model is the suggestion that another strand, J1b1, arrived in Scotland from Norway. In the total absence of archaeological evidence for such contact at this time, it must remain a possibility that the genetic signature has been misdated and belongs to a later event, perhaps related to Viking settlements.

The paternal lines are even more complex and difficult to interpret, but it does seem possible to identify a central European genetic stream, I1a, coming ultimately from the Near East, and several haplotypes, I1b-2, E3b, and J2, which may have originated in the Mediterranean, echoing the evidence of the maternal lines.

Assessing the evidence overall, it has been suggested that between 10 and 30 per cent of the present population of Britain and Ireland may have genes ultimately of

Near Eastern origin that arrived in the isles with the pioneering Neolithic settlers. But here again it must be stressed how uncertain the dating evidence for genetic inflows is. Britain and Ireland remained in active contact with the Continent after the initial early Neolithic incomings, and people from the Continent bearing Near Eastern gene signatures would have continued to arrive throughout the prehistoric period.

The Transformation in Summary

The appearance of Britain was transformed in the brief period 4200–3800 BC. Large areas of woodland had been cleared, settlements created, and permanent monuments, symbolic of social cohesion, created. New people had arrived by sea, bringing their domestic livestock and seed-grain with them. Those of the indigenous population who were prepared to embrace the new lifestyle soon became indistinguishable from the immigrant population through intermarriage and emulation. Those who found it alien died out. By the thirty-eighth and thirty-seventh centuries BC the successful farming communities were hybrids, inheriting most of their genes from the indigenous peoples of the islands.

The transformation had taken place over little more than ten generations. For the next forty generations, covering twelve centuries, the Neolithic communities settled into their landscape, developing regional distinctions as they became better adapted to their environments and felt the increasing need to distinguish themselves from their neighbours. A gradual increase in population over most of the country probably added to the imperative of defining identity, thus encouraging social cohesion in the face of endemic hostility between groups.

The initial phase of colonization would have involved the influx of pioneer farmers spread over a number of generations and a high degree of mobility within the country, but thereafter the archaeological evidence suggests that contact with the Continent decreased, while a distinctly British and Irish Neolithic culture developed in all its regional variety. No doubt the sea-lanes continued to be active, with people maintaining traditional social links, but there is little in the archaeological record to indicate this. The one exception is the Atlantic seaways, where around 3000 BC the communities building passage graves in Ireland, north Wales, and the Orkney Islands were sharing knowledge, values, and behaviours with neighbours to the south in Armorica and Atlantic-facing Iberia. This may have resulted from a brief interlude of contact, but it could equally have reflected connections over a long period of time, maintaining the network of interaction that can be traced back to the fifth millennium. Although the evidence is not decisive, one is left with the impression that the Atlantic seaways remained active throughout.

6

Mobilizing Materials

A NEW CONNECTIVITY, 3000–1500 BC

THE coming of migrants who brought with them food-producing strategies, new belief systems, and a package of material culture transformed Britain and Ireland over the surprisingly brief period of 4200–3800 BC. They created a changed landscape and a network of communities increasingly bound by social systems evolving fast to hold the competing interests of the growing population in some sort of equilibrium. Through monumental structures like long barrows, megalithic tombs, causewayed enclosures, and cursus monuments, lineage groups demonstrated a degree of cohesion by their ability to work together for a common purpose, while, through the exchange of rare commodities such as polished stone axes, broader social networks were maintained. Once established, the different communities followed their own individual trajectories of development. The long period from 3800 to 2500 BC, which followed the formative centuries, saw indigenous development intensify, but while regional differences can be identified, what stands out is the remarkable degree of cultural similarity across the whole of Britain and Ireland. It was as though ideas flowed freely and were eagerly taken up. This was the period when a large number of ritual monuments, among them Stonehenge and Avebury, began to dominate the landscape.

Then, around 2500 BC, things began to change as Britain and Ireland were caught up in a new pan-European spate of mobility associated with the Beaker phenomenon, an issue we shall explore in some detail later. Suffice it to say that this involved a degree of renewed immigration from the Continent and the wide acceptance of new value systems involving the social use of a greatly extended range of exotic raw materials such as metals, amber, jet, and faience. This movement of commodities on a much larger scale than before implies even greater contact between communities, and with it ideas and value systems travelled over great distances.

Here, then, is the agenda for this chapter. In terms of the old technological model of the past, the period from 3800 to 2500 BC represents the middle and late Neolithic. With the introduction of copper technology around 2500 BC, we enter the Chalcolithic period, with the full Bronze Age starting about 2100 BC. These broad characterizations are still useful as a convenient shorthand.

Inward-Looking Britons

The passion for monument building, already evident in the early centuries of the fourth millennium, picks up a new momentum in the thirty-first century BC with the development of 'henge monuments'—a general portmanteau term embracing a range of non-domestic structures thought to reflect the ritual life of the community. In broad terms, henge monuments consist of an enclosing earthwork comprising a ditch with a bank piled up on the outside. They are usually circular, or nearly so, and may be provided with one or a pair of entrances. Within the enclosure there may be settings of posts, stones, pits, or one or more burials. Size varies considerably from the little Coneybury henge south of Stonehenge, some 2 hectares in extent, to massive structures like Durrington Walls, 2.5 kilometres to the north-east, where the enclosed area is 12 hectares. Henge monuments are found throughout the British Isles from Cornwall to Orkney, and a number are known in Ireland.

Another manifestation of broadly the same idea is the stone circle—a type of monument particularly prevalent in the west of Britain, and in parts of Ireland, where suitable stone is readily to hand. Some stone circles conform to the henge type in that they have the enclosing ditch, while others are without the ditch element. A number of examples are known of typical henges later being enhanced with stone circles. The classic example is Stonehenge, which began its life around 3000 BC as a circular earthwork enclosure with a circle of pits, possibly once taking bluestone uprights, set just inside the ditch. Several centuries later an arc of bluestones was set up in the centre, eventually to be remodelled when the sarsen trilithons were erected in about 2500 BC. Avebury is another case. Here the first phase of the henge, dating to around 3000 BC, consisted of a circular enclosure defined by a ditch and bank with four entrances. The earthwork was reconstructed a century or two later, and it was later still, probably between 2400 and 2200 BC, that the massive sarsen stones were set up around the inner lip of the ditch. The erection of stone circles at existing henge monuments raises the possibility that stone circles may have been a later phenomenon following the inception of henge monuments in about the thirty-first century.

It is difficult to say with any degree of certainty what concepts and beliefs lie embedded within the structure of henge monuments. Circularity was clearly significant. The circle is the simplest geometric shape to lay out. It can be accomplished using a stake and rope, and it may have been its very simplicity and the perfection of the shape that commended it as the appropriate form for a ritual space where humans and the deities could communicate. Settings of vertical timbers or standing stones are another recurrent feature, evidently having deep significance. Perhaps the structure that they together created had meaning as a 'house' occupied by the gods or as an appropriate place to enact rituals and to keep religious regalia. Another possibility is that the individual uprights had a meaning of their own, representing perhaps the members of a lineage or even individual personages or deities. The possibilities for speculation are endless.

The placing of the ditch inside the line of the bank is a revival of the arrangement used at the earlier causewayed enclosure and makes little sense as a defence. In the case of the henges it may be that, while the ditch separated secular from religious, the outer bank provided a place for spectators to observe the ceremonies going on inside. Some of the monuments were set out so that their main axes were aligned with major events in the solar calendar. The best-known example is Stonehenge, where the axis focused on sunrise on the midsummer solstice and sunset on the midwinter solstice. The implication here, and in many other examples, is that the monument 'captured' the event, making it accessible to man. While we can only speculate about the many levels of meaning embedded within the structure of the henge monuments, that they provided special places where humans could relate to their gods seems reasonably sure. Such places would have been essential to the well-being of society. Henges and related monuments are found extensively across Britain and Ireland, implying that a remarkable degree of homogeneity in religious practice was developing throughout the isles during the third millennium.

At present the earliest henge monuments known are in Orkney, where they are dated to the end of the fourth millennium. It seems that it was not until about 3000 BC that henges were being built in the south of the country: flagstones near Dorchester in Dorset, the first phase of Stonehenge, and the first phase of Avebury all belong to this initial period. Given that comparatively few sites have yet provided reliable dating evidence, however, it is best at present to leave open the question of origins. By 3000 BC, then, henges were being constructed throughout Britain, and monuments of this kind with regional variations and different styles of elaboration continued to be created and used for much of the third millennium.

Over this long period of development certain landscapes became particularly favoured for the building of ritual monuments. These preferred locations occur throughout Britain and Ireland. One of the most spectacular concentrations is to be found on the chalklands of central southern Britain, where five monument clusters are known, each dominated by a massive henge monument: Mount Pleasant, Knowlton, Durrington Walls, Marden, and Avebury. But in each case the megahenge is simply one element in a far more complex ritual landscape. The immediate landscape of Durrington Walls includes the massive circular timber building known as Woodhenge, and not far away is Stonehenge, with its avenue leading to the River Avon, Coneybury henge, and two earlier monuments, the Cursus and the

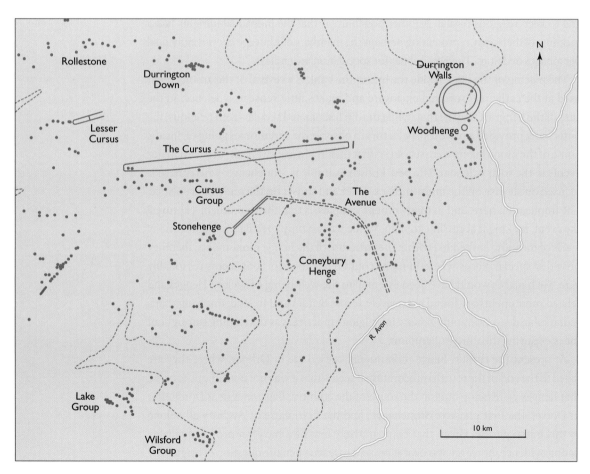

6.1 The dense distribution of late Neolithic and Early Bronze Age monuments to the west of the Wiltshire Avon in the vicinity of Stonehenge. The major Neolithic monuments (in orange) formed the focus around which the Late Bronze Age barrow cemeteries (purple circles) developed

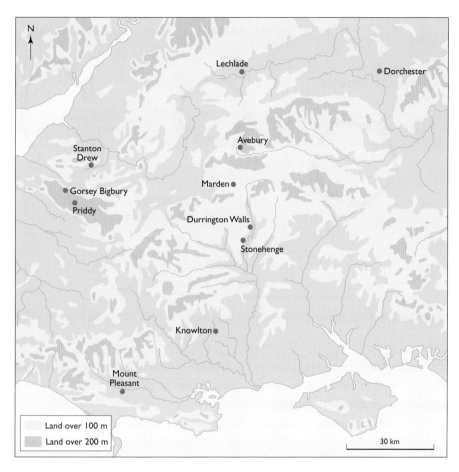

6.2 The major ritual locations of the late Neolithic period in Wessex. Each site comprises a number of individual monuments

Lesser Cursus. It is inconceivable that this remarkable group of structures was not in some way functionally linked throughout the course of the third millennium as old monuments were modified and new structures built.

Avebury presents another palimpsest. There is the great henge itself, the Sanctuary on Overton Hill, comprising a massive timber building surrounded by a henge enclosure, the West Kennet enclosures, Silbury Hill, and the Longstones enclosure, as well as the remarkable avenues delineated by standing stones that linked the Longstones enclosure to Avebury and Avebury to the Sanctuary. These monuments were built in a landscape already redolent with ancestral memories embodied in a number of long barrows, including the West Kennet long barrow, and the entire region was overlooked by the causewayed enclosure on Windmill Hill. Indeed, it is a character-

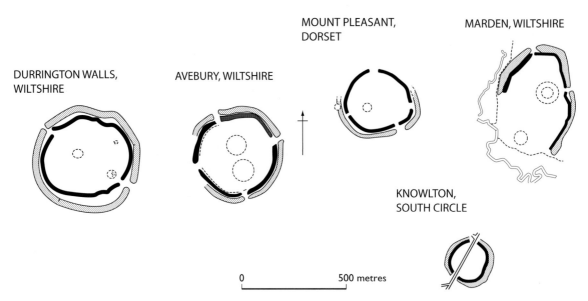

6.3 The five large henge monuments of Wessex constructed in the middle of the third millennium BC

istic of many of the preferred locations with henge monuments that they developed where clusters of earlier monuments—causewayed enclosures, cursuses, and long barrows—were already in existence.

Clusters of monuments, including henges, occur widely across the country. Among the better known are the Priddy Circles on the Mendips, the stone circles and great circular timber monument at Stanton Drew in north Somerset, the row of massive henges at Thornborough in North Yorkshire, the Millfield complex in Northumberland, and the cluster of remarkable structures on Orkney stretching along peninsulas between the Loch of Harray and the Loch of Stenness, and the great passage grave of Maes Howe. Maes Howe is particularly interesting in that the passage grave was set within a circular enclosure consisting of a wide, flat-bottomed ditch with the bank built along the outer lip in the style of a henge enclosure. This is one of the earliest henges known and hints at a possible origin for the type.

Another preferred location where passage graves are associated with henge monuments is the Boyne valley in County Meath, Ireland. Here the three great passage graves of Dowth, Knowth, and Newgrange are set within a ritual landscape provided with standing stones, long mounds, and henge enclosures. The exact chronological relationships of the various components have not been defined, but at Knowth a timber circle close to the entrance to the east passage has provided dates ranging from the twenty-eighth to twenty-fifth centuries.

6.4 The great henge monument of Durrington Walls to the north of Stonehenge can be traced by the remnants of its enclosing bank and ditch, which can still be made out in the ploughed fields. The smaller monument of Woodhenge can be seen in the corner of the field (*top left*)

While the earliest henges date to the last centuries of the fourth millennium, henge-related structures continued to be added to the ritual landscapes for centuries afterwards. At the complex around Dorchester in Dorset, following the demise of the causewayed enclosure and long mound on the hill of Maiden Castle, an early henge was built at Flagstones around 3000 BC. Beneath Dorchester itself, at Greyhound Yard, a massive monument built of standing timbers a metre in diameter is dated to *c.* 2700 BC, while the great henge at Mount Pleasant, 2 kilometres away, and the circular timber building inside it belong to around 2500 BC and are broadly contemporary with the henge at Maumbury Rings on the southern outskirts of Dorchester. Once built, the Mount Pleasant henge remained the focus of activity for centuries to follow. Its western entrance was remodelled about 2100 BC. A century later the great circular timber building was replaced by a circle of standing stones, and the entire hill-top

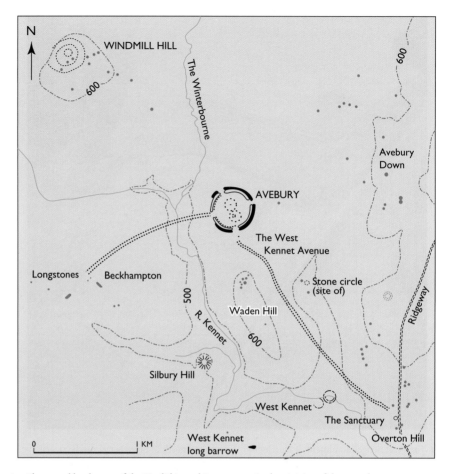

6.5 The sacred landscape of the Neolithic and Bronze ages in the vicinity of the great henge monument of Avebury on the north Wiltshire Downs

within the ditch was enclosed by a substantial palisade of closely spaced timbers, possibly standing to a height of as much as 6 metres. The palisade was later burnt and partially removed, but the hill-top continued to be used until it was finally abandoned in the twelfth century BC.

The long periods of time during which these monuments were in use are vividly demonstrated by recent research at Stonehenge, which has suggested an eight-stage model for the monument's development. While contentious in part, it probably fairly reflects the continuous series of changes to which the monument was subjected. It begins in *c.* 3000 BC with the construction of the henge bank and ditch and the digging of the Aubrey Holes (named after the antiquary who first noted them) within the ditch line. It is suggested that these holes might have taken a circle of bluestones

6.6 The henge monument of Avebury on the north Wiltshire chalkland. The great enclosing bank and ditch survive remarkably intact. A number of the standing stones that can be seen were re-erected in the 1930s. The village spreading into the monument dates from the late Saxon period

brought from the Preseli Mountains in south-west Wales. In stage 2, *c.* 2900–*c.* 2600 BC, the bluestones were rearranged and a large timber structure was built. Sometime around 2500 BC (stage 3) the sarsen circle and trilithons were erected and the bluestones rearranged again. Stage 4 (*c.* 2450–*c.* 2210 BC) sees the digging of a large pit in the centre of the monument. There follow two stages in the further rearrangement

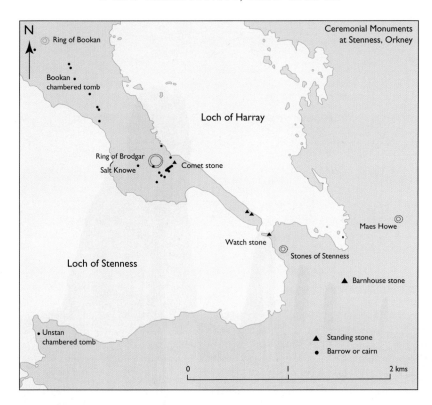

6.8 The ceremonial monuments in the sacred landscape at Stenness, Orkney

of the bluestones, first in a central oval and later in the central horseshoe we see now, between the twenty-second and nineteenth centuries, and finally, in stages 7 and 8, circles of holes were dug around the standing stones between the nineteenth and sixteenth centuries. Further research may change the detail of the interpretation, but the fact remains that the narrative of Stonehenge was one of sequential remodellings over a period of a millennium and a half. While all this was in progress, other sites within the surrounding ritual landscape were being built, remodelled, and abandoned.

The henge phenomenon of the third millennium is remarkable for its ubiquity throughout the islands and for the intensity of the sustained effort that went into its maintenance. You could not travel far without confronting a sacred location: the entire landscape seemed to belong to the gods.

6.7 (*opposite*) The three henge monuments at Thornborough in the Vale of Mowbray in North Yorkshire are arranged in an almost straight line equidistant from each other. The land around has been extensively quarried for gravel, at one time threatening the survival of the monuments

6.9 The Ring of Brodgar on Orkney mainland is a massive stone circle 104 metres in diameter set on the lip of a circular ditched enclosure. It is one of a number of Neolithic monuments occupying a neck of land between the lochs of Harray and Stenness just north of the great passage grave of Maes Howe

It is against this background that we must consider another phenomenon: the appearance throughout Britain and Ireland of a highly distinctive type of pottery given the somewhat mundane name of Grooved Ware. Grooved Ware vessels are flat-bottomed with straight, often slightly flaring, sides—rather saucepan-shaped in appearance. They are characteristically decorated with patterns composed of lines and stabs imposed on the surface when the vessel was leather-hard before firing. What is particularly remarkable about this class of pottery is that it remained in fashion for about a thousand years from its origins in the thirty-second or thirty-first century, and it is to be found, with some local variations, throughout Britain and

6.10 The archetypical henge monument, and the one from which the type name derived, is Stonehenge, dominating the rolling chalk landscape of Wiltshire. The stone circles occupy the centre of a much larger circular enclosure constructed around 3000 BC

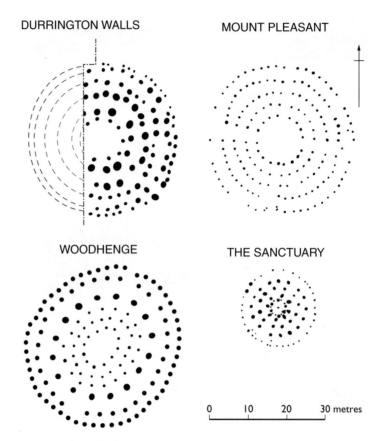

6.11 Plans of the massive timber building associated with the henge monuments of Wessex

Ireland contemporary with other, mainly round-bottomed, Neolithic wares, which had developed from earlier traditions. That Grooved Ware has invariably been found in association with henge monuments has led to the suggestion that it was an elite ceramic set used only by those who had access to ritual sites. But care is needed here. Since so few non-ritual third-millennium sites have been excavated, statistically valid comparisons cannot yet be made. Even so, the close association of henge monuments and related structures and Grooved Ware is not in doubt.

What does it all mean? Some writers, noting that the earliest dates of both henges and Grooved Ware appear to be in the Orkneys, have suggested that the belief systems that they represent may have begun here in the north and spread to the rest of Britain down the east coast routes and to Ireland via the Atlantic seaways at just the time when the passage graves had reached their most elaborate forms. This may

(a)

(b)

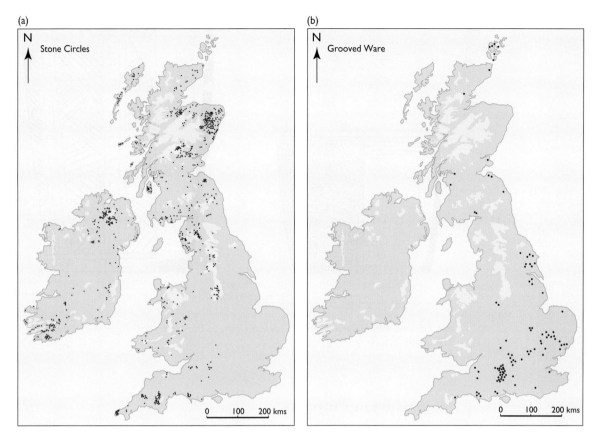

6.12 The two maps display contrasting distributions. The left-hand map shows the distribution of stone circles, while the right-hand map shows the distribution of the highly distinctive Grooved Ware. The two are broadly contemporary and suggest an east–west divide in Britain at this time

be so, but a more precise chronology is needed before the matter can be resolved with any degree of certainty. At the very least, however, it is clear that Britain and Ireland shared a belief system that presented itself in the form of highly distinctive monuments and ceramics. Where that belief system developed and by what means it spread so rapidly we may never know. What it does show is that a remarkable degree of social interaction existed throughout the third millennium: ideas and beliefs could spread like wildfire. This was, after all, the society that conceived of the notion of bringing massive bluestones, possibly an existing stone circle, from the Preseli Mountains in the extreme south-west of Wales to Stonehenge in the centre of the Wessex chalkland. Even more astonishing is the fact that they succeeded in doing so.

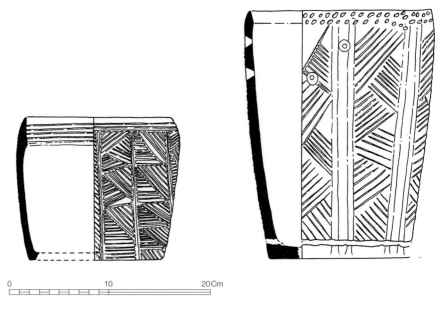

0   10   20 Cm

6.13 Grooved Ware of the later Neolithic period. *Left*: From Durrington Walls; *right*: from Wilsford, both in Wiltshire

Meanwhile in Europe

It is necessary now to broaden our horizons briefly to explore two of the dramatic changes that were under way in Europe in the first few centuries of the third millennium while the Britons were developing their own highly distinctive late Neolithic culture in relative isolation. The first was the movement of a nomadic people, known archaeologically as the Late Yamnaya culture, from their homeland on the Eurasian Steppe westwards along the lower Danube and into the Carpathian basin (now Hungary). The second was the emergence of a highly innovative Chalcolithic culture on the Atlantic coast of Iberia, in the vicinity of the Tagus valley, giving rise to what has been called the Beaker phenomenon, which spread rapidly in the west.

The Late Yamnaya culture of the Pontic Steppe represented a largely semi-nomadic pastoral society whose mobility lay in ox-drawn wooden wagons and the domesticated horse for riding. They relied heavily on herds of cattle and to a lesser extent on sheep deliberately bred to develop their wool. Burial was by individual inhumation beneath round barrows, while their distinctive material culture included shaft-hole axes of copper and stone and pottery decorated with cord impressions. The

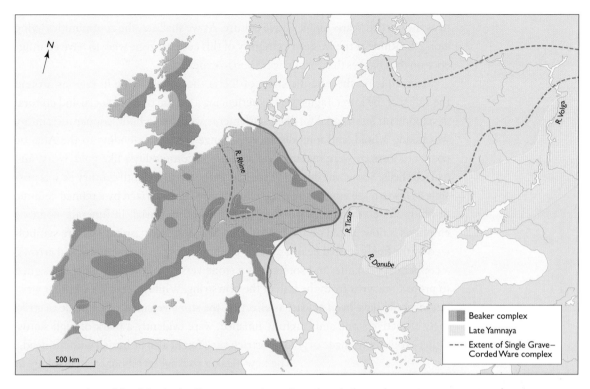

6.14 Europe in the middle of the third millennium BC. The Beaker culture had spread to cover most of western Europe and was particularly prevalent in the areas indicated in the darker tone. The Late Yamnaya culture from the steppe had spread as far west as the Great Hungarian Plain. To the north, and overlapping with the Beaker spread, was the Corded Ware–Single Grave complex. Where this complex overlapped with the Beaker zone there was much interaction, especially in the Rhine valley region

migration of these steppe communities into eastern and east central Europe took place around 2900–2700 BC, when they were seeking out environments similar to the grassy steppe of their homeland. Thus it was that they passed along the Danube corridor and into the Carpathian basin, settling along the River Tisza, which ran through the Great Hungarian Plain, Europe's westernmost area of steppe land.

The presence of the Late Yamnaya communities in a great swath from the Volga to the middle Danube influenced the development of the many varied communities lying in the vast North European Plain eastwards of the Rhine. During the opening centuries of the third millennium these people adopted many of the values and technologies of the steppe communities, most notably the rite of single burial beneath a round barrow, the burial usually accompanied by grave goods, including the cord-decorated beaker and the shaft-hole battle-axe. Collectively these groups are referred to as the Corded Ware–Single Grave culture. As we shall see, the communities living along the Rhine at the western extremity of this cultural zone were to have an influence on the changes that Britain was soon to experience.

Meanwhile, on the Atlantic coast of Iberia the people living in regions around the valley of the lower Tagus were experiencing a period of rapid social and cultural development. Substantial fortified settlements were being built, copper metallurgy was taking a hold, and long-distance exchange systems extending to the Atlantic coast of Morocco were making available exotic commodities like gold, ivory, and ostrich shells. Sometime during or soon after the twenty-eighth century BC it is possible to discern the emergence of an elite culture characterized by a refined ceramic drinking vessel, the beaker, used in daily life and in burial. In funerary contexts emphasis is now placed on the individual whose status, or aspirations, are symbolized by the finely crafted beaker and the equipment of the hunter: bows and arrows, a copper dagger-knife, and sometimes a stone version of the wrist guard designed to protect the wrist from the lash of the bowstring. While in practice a leather wrist guard would have been at least as effective, the stone versions, often made of strikingly attractive stone and carefully finished, were evidently a mark of high status. Other exotic items made of gold or ostrich shell might also be buried with the dead.

6.15 A classic Maritime Bell Beaker of the later third millennium BC from a burial at Barrow Hills, Radley, in Oxfordshire

The new 'Beaker package' symbolized an ideology in which power, knowledge, status, heraldry, and religious belief were all embodied. The knowledge, which underpinned status and belief, may have been acquired from personal journeys. It would have included an understanding of pyrotechnology, which allowed metallic copper to flow from stony ore, and perhaps even the command of mind-altering alcoholic beverages shared from the ubiquitous beaker.

It was in the twenty-seventh and twenty-sixth centuries that this new package spread widely into western Europe, where it is characterized by the distribution of a particular form of beaker known as the Maritime Bell Beaker. The spread took place over a wide front, overland through the centre of Iberia, by sea into the Mediterranean to southern France and beyond, and via the Atlantic northwards to southern Armorica. Just what this archaeological signature means in real terms is a matter of debate. It may be that the attraction of the ideology and its symbolism was such that it caught on

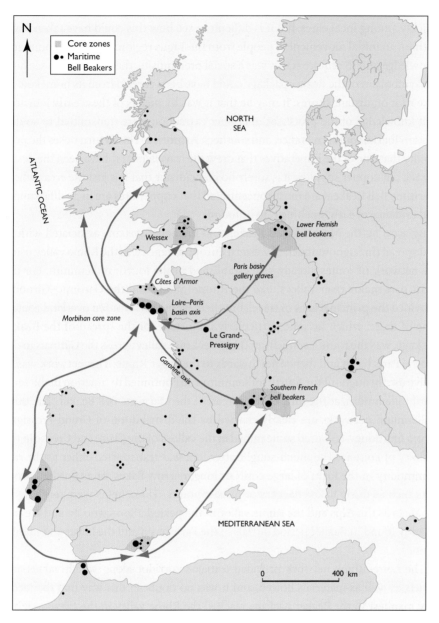

6.16 The Maritime Bell Beaker developed in the Tagus region of Portugal in the first half of the third millennium BC and the idea spread from there to many parts of western Europe, including Britain and Ireland. The distribution of the distinctive type of beaker gives an indication of the routes in use at the time. The sea played an important role

quickly among local elites, but it is difficult to see how this could have taken place without an initial movement of people from the Tagus region. If travel to command knowledge and to acquire status was a social prerequisite, then it is easy to see how the symbolism of the Beaker package could have been carried from its homeland to take root on distant shores. It may be that it was by means of these early journeys that knowledge of the processes of copper extraction were transmitted to south-eastern Iberia, southern France, and southern Armorica. This in turn raises the possibility that one of the imperatives that drew the travellers may have been the desire to seek out copper supplies: it is surely no coincidence that it is just the areas where Maritime Bell Beakers are most concentrated that copper ores are in prolific supply and evidence of early smelting is to be found.

By 2500 BC the Maritime Bell Beaker, and the belief systems associated with it, had spread throughout much of western Europe as far east as the Rhine valley using the network of routes already well established in the fourth millennium. For the most part major river valleys, like the Rhône–Saône and the Garonne–Gironde, provided the principal axes of travel, but there were also favoured overland routes. One of these, which became particularly important for the spread of the Beaker package, was the route leading from the lower Loire valley across the Gâtinais to the central Paris basin and thence northwards to the lower Rhine. This network was in active use throughout the fourth millennium and continued to function in the early third millennium, at the time of the spread of the Maritime Bell Beaker. The third millennium networks are clearly charted by the distribution of Grand-Pressigny flint, a fine honey-coloured stone mined in the valleys of the Claise and Creuse in the vicinity of Poitiers. The much-sought-after flint was transported either as the raw commodity in the form of large cores or long, narrow flakes, or as finished products such as finely flaked daggers or missile points. These items were reaching as far afield as the Alps and the Rhine valley in the period 2800–2500 BC and are frequently found in Beaker period burials in the Paris basin and the lower and middle Rhine.

The Loire–Rhine network provided a major corridor along which values and beliefs as well as materials flowed, and it was no doubt in this way that the ideology manifest in the Beaker package reached the Rhine valley in the twenty-eighth and twenty-seventh centuries, where it encountered communities who had already adopted the Corded Ware–Single Grave culture. What emerged in this vital contact zone was a hybrid culture characterized, in its initial stages, by a distinctive beaker type (the All-Over Ornamented Beaker), frequently found in single graves accompanied by items of Grand-Pressigny flint. From this contact zonc ideas and values of the Corded Ware–Single Grave culture flowed westwards along the lower Rhine–

lower Loire axis, merging with Bell Beaker concepts spreading eastwards from the Atlantic coast. The result was a heterogeneous and highly innovative culture with many regional variants extending in a broad arc from Armorica across northern France to the Low Countries. It was from this zone, in the period 2500–2200 BC, that Britain was to receive its Beaker culture.

The Metal-Rich Atlantic

We have suggested that one of the motives behind the movement of the beaker-using elites of the Lisbon region in the early third millennium was to explore the sources of rare raw materials, among them copper. It is hardly surprising, therefore, that we should find the signature artefact associated with this phase of mobility, the Maritime Bell Beaker, concentrated in the three regions where copper ores of the kinds they were used to smelting are found in abundance: south-eastern Iberia, southern France, and southern Armorica.

It was probably from Armorica that the people with the technical ability to smelt copper ores travelled to the south-west of Ireland in the twenty-fourth century BC to work the rich copper deposits found at Ross Island on Lough Leane in County Kerry. The absence of any earlier trace of copper-working in Ireland and the presence of Beaker pottery at the mining camp strongly suggest that the new technology was introduced by experts from abroad. While it is quite conceivable that their journeys were driven by the desire to find sources of rare commodities, it is equally possible that, through the maritime links that existed between Armorica and southern Ireland, knowledge of Ireland's mineral resources became known and was shared in the social exchanges that took place. In any event, that the first copper workers were immigrants is difficult to refute.

At Ross Island an extensive programme of archaeological research has shown that mining actively focused on surface deposits, extending to 13–18 metres in maximum depth, and involved the digging of shafts and galleries. Nearby was the mining camp where the ore was crushed and sorted and then smelted. The ore being processed was tennantite-rich (fahlerz) and chalcopyrite–arsenopyrite mineralization, which together produced an arsenic-rich copper containing traces of antimony and silver. This distinctive composition, called Group A metal by archaeometal-lurgists, allows the output of the Ross Island mines to be identified and its distribution traced. The principal finished product was a thick-butted trapezoidal axe, but copper was also used to make halberds and daggers. Over 95 per cent of these weapon types found in Ireland were made of arsenical copper, much, if not most, of which must have come from Ross Island. The mines provided for Ireland's metal

6.17 On Ross Island in Lough Leane near Killarney evidence has been uncovered for the earliest copper working in Britain and Ireland, dating to around 2400 BC. The photograph shows the mouth of a mine dug at this time to extract the tennantite ore for smelting

needs for 500 years, but by the end of that period production had decreased and in the end the mines had to be abandoned because of flooding long before the lode was exhausted. By this time other sources of supply had begun to take over. One source, soon to be prolific, was Mount Gabriel in County Cork, where mines were in production from 1700 to 1500 BC. Ross Island metal was also exported to Britain in some quantity. It was used to make the first copper items in use in western and northern Britain: about 80 per cent of the early copper axes circulating in western Britain were of Irish origin.

The impact of the Ross Island mines was, clearly, considerable, but this does not necessarily mean that there was a significant inflow of new settlers to south-western Ireland during the Beaker period. A few specialists with metalworking skills would have been all that was required. Beaker pottery is not particularly prolific in Ireland, and when it occurs it is usually found in settlement sites alongside indigenous pot-

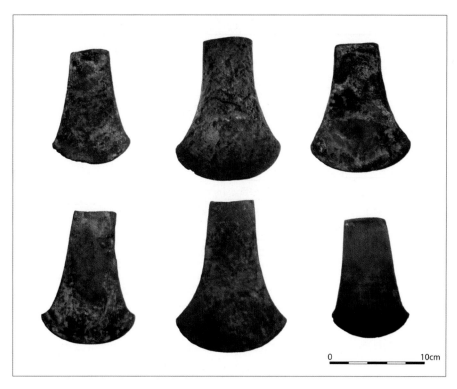

6.18 Early Irish copper axes from a hoard found at Cappeen, County Cork. These flat axes were the earliest metal axes to be made and were circulated widely in Ireland and also in Britain

tery, or with burials made in pre-existing tombs. This is very similar to the situation in which beakers are found in Armorica and western France, and in stark contrast with Britain, where Beaker pottery is commonly found with single burials accompanied by other grave goods set beneath round barrows in a manner similar to the burials of the adjacent continent. Ireland, then, evidently shares the Atlantic tradition, which is quite separate from that of Britain. That there is little significant change in culture evident in Ireland at this time, except for the introduction of copper metallurgy, suggests that the number of people involved in introducing the new concepts to the indigenous population may have been comparatively small.

The skills necessary for copper production soon spread to Wales, where several rich sources were readily accessible. At Copa Hill near Aberystwyth a copper lode was being exploited from 2100 to 1500 BC in an open-cast mining operation, but far more elaborate was a massive mining undertaking on Great Orme above Llandudno in north-west Wales, which was in operation by 1800 BC. Mining here seems to have begun with open trenches running from exposed cliff faces but soon developed into

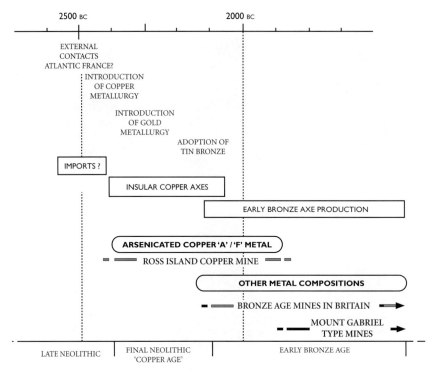

6.19 The early development of gold extraction and copper mining and metallurgy in Ireland began together in a short period at the end of the third millennium

a huge complex of linked galleries and shafts extending to depths of more than 70 metres, making it one of the largest mining operations in prehistoric Europe. The Welsh sources, together with mines at Ecton in Staffordshire and Alderley Edge in Cheshire, began to provide for British needs after the output of the Ross Island mines had started to decline.

With copper working under way in Armorica and south-western Ireland around the middle of the third millennium, it was only a matter of time before the mineral wealth of the Atlantic west began to be exploited to the full. The peninsulas of old, hard rock that thrust into the Atlantic—Armorica, south-west Britain, Wales, and southern Ireland—were prolific with metal. Besides copper, there was gold in the Wicklow Mountains of southern Ireland, and more gold was to be had in the north. Wales had gold and copper to offer, Devon and Cornwall were a major source of tin as well as producing copper and some gold, while Armorica was well known for its tin as well as having sources of copper and a little gold. By the end of the third millennium all these metals were being widely exploited.

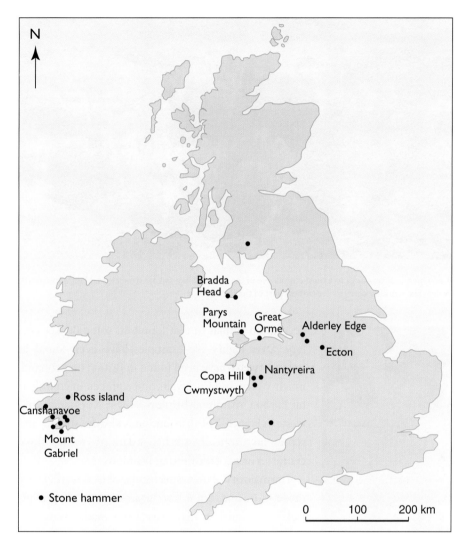

6.20 The copper-mining sites of Britain and Ireland in use during the Chalcolithic and Early Bronze Age. Some are known from extensive workings, others from the occurrence of distinctive hammer stones

The principal source of gold in use at this time was Irish and probably lay in the Wicklow Mountains, though gold sources have also been claimed in the north. Among a range of gold artefacts the most spectacular were lunulae—crescent-shaped sheets of gold designed to be worn around the neck and to cover the upper chest. They were usually decorated towards the terminals with inscribed geometric

6.21 Open-cast workings to extant copper ore in the Pyllau valley, Great Orme Head, Llandudno, north Wales. The working dates to the earliest part of the Bronze Age

6.22 An alder-wood launder, to drain away water, from the Bronze Age copper mines on Copa Hill, Cwmystwyth, in central Wales

decoration similar to that found on some Beaker pottery. Over eighty-five examples have been found in Ireland, twelve have been found in Britain (in Scotland, north Wales, and Cornwall), and eighteen in continental Europe, mainly in Brittany, Lower Normandy, and western France. The distribution is clearly Atlantic and represents a zone of interchange dating to the last three centuries or so of the third millennium.

The majority of these spectacular objects were clearly made in Ireland, but a few, regarded to be of 'provincial' workmanship, may have been made elsewhere. One such provincial piece was found at Harlyn Bay in Cornwall along with one of Irish origin, suggesting that a local craftsman may have been inspired by the Irish-made imports to try his own hand. A provincial lunula found at Kerivora in northern Brittany was so similar to the Harlyn Bay example that it probably came from the Cornish school. The distribution of lunulae, both Irish and provincial, reflects a system of exchange that echoes the networks along which the first copper metallurgy was introduced to the north-western Atlantic zone a century or two earlier.

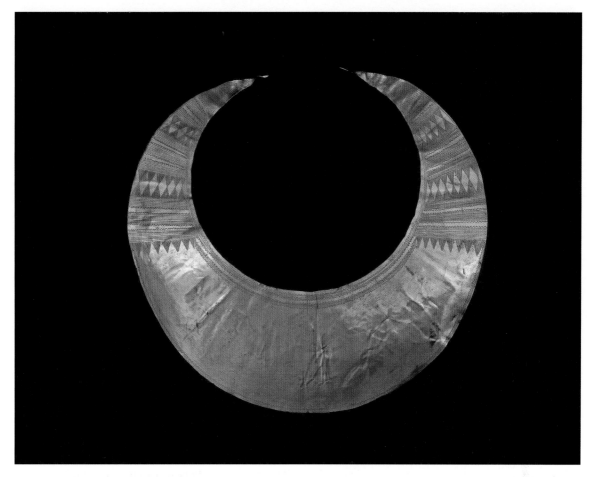

6.23 Gold lunula from Harlyn Bay, Cornwall

The other metal of great importance was tin, which, while rare, was to be found in quantity in Cornwall and western Armorica. Tin alloyed with copper produced bronze, a tougher and more serviceable metal. In Ireland and in Britain the change from arsenical copper to tin bronze took place over a short period of time around 2200–2000 BC. After this virtually all metal in use contained more than 5 per cent tin, with over half having between 8 and 14 per cent. Since the optimal ratio to give a strong alloy was around 10 per cent tin to 90 per cent copper, this can only mean that the two metals were being deliberately alloyed and that, by experiment, the bronze-smiths had already discovered the best ratio to provide a metal with the required qualities.

Bronze alloys were being experimented with in eastern Europe, the Troad in Anatolia, and the Aegean before 2200 BC, but the transition to full bronze use began in Britain and Ireland: it was not adopted in western and central Europe for at least another two centuries. This precocious behaviour is in part explained by the rarity of tin in the rest of Europe, but it must also reflect the innovative skill of the British and Irish metalworkers. Tools made from arsenical copper of the kind produced at Ross Island were tough. As Ross Island metal decreased in supply and other sources of copper, without arsenic, came on stream, it may be that the metalworkers began to experiment with alloys of copper and tin in order to produce a suitable replacement. However it was done, the production of a regular tin bronze can fairly be regarded as one of the great achievements of the Hiberno-British craftsmen. These skills, together with a command of the Cornish tin supplies, will have assured the supremacy of British metalworkers in the west European networks at this time.

The Beakers Come to Britain

The distinctiveness of Beaker pottery has continued to impress antiquarians and archaeologists over the last two centuries. In Britain the appearance of Beaker burials, with their characteristic array of grave goods, marks a sudden change in culture: not unreasonably early antiquarians interpreted this as an influx of new people from the Continent. Cranial measurements added some support to this by suggesting that the Beaker people were more round-headed than the indigenous people buried in the Neolithic long barrows. So it was that the invasion of round-headed Beaker folk became a 'fact' of prehistory. But by the 1970s invasion hypotheses were being rejected as too simplistic, and more nuanced explanations were being sought for the culture change. After all, it was pointed out, single burial and round barrows were already in common use in Britain. Could it not be that the Beaker package was simply adopted by the indigenous British elite as a means of emphasizing their status? Admittedly this implied social contacts with the Continent and a degree of mobility, but there was no need to conjure up large-scale influxes of new people to explain the uptake of Beaker culture. More recently this 'extreme' non-invasionist view has given way to the acceptance that there may have been more mobility of population than previously supposed, at least in the initial stages—a view that is rapidly gaining increasing support from stable isotope studies, as we shall see (p. 214). The debate now revolves around trying to distinguish between the arrival of new people and the response of local populations to new systems of belief.

In Britain and Ireland in excess of 2,100 sites have produced Beaker pottery, and of these more than 800 are complete pots from burials. The database is therefore substantial, but its sheer size and the variations within it render simple interpretation difficult. The social and cultural situation was evidently one of considerable com-

6.24 A Beaker period grave group from a burial at Garton Slack, Yorkshire. The shaft-hole axe, flint knife, jet button, and beaker (possibly once containing an alcoholic drink) accompanied the dead person in the grave

plexity; however, it is possible to begin to distinguish the main threads of the broader narrative.

The distribution of beakers is by no means even. They concentrate in Wessex and the upper Thames valley and along the entire eastern seaboard from the Thames estuary to the Great Glen. The south-west peninsula, Wales, the west midlands, Ireland, and western Scotland and the Western Isles are all sparsely served. The beakers, then, concentrate in those regions that are accessible from the eastern Channel and the North Sea: the regions of Britain that face the long continental interface stretching from Lower Normandy to the Low Countries, where, as we have already seen, cultural elements emanating from the Loire estuary zone (the classic Maritime Bell

Beaker package) and the Rhine valley (the Corded Ware–Single Grave complex) were interacting with each other. It is no surprise, then, that the cultural preferences of the continental interface are reflected in the neighbouring British regions. This simple observation suggests that Beaker influences, both people and ideas, were probably entering Britain at many points along its long southern and eastern coast-line.

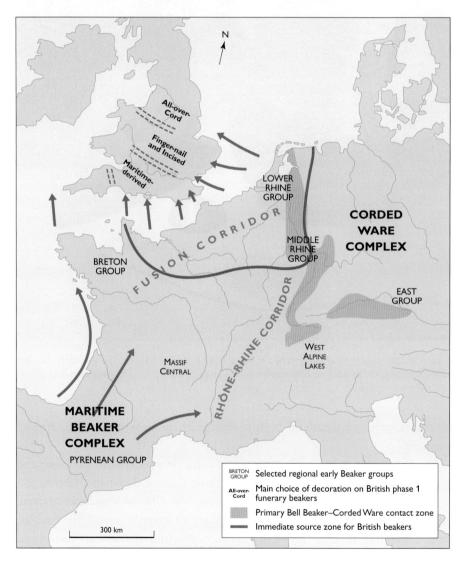

6.25 The spread of the Beaker package to Britain and Ireland was a complex process involving transmission along the Atlantic seaways and from the long continental interface between the Cherbourg peninsula to the Rhine

With the advent of more and accurate radiocarbon dates it is becoming possible to distinguish a progression in the uptake of Beaker culture in Britain. A recent study suggests that three major phases can be distinguished. Phase 1, *c.* 2500–*c.* 2250, was the time when Beaker culture and funerary rites were fast being adopted in Britain. The new culture was, at this stage, spread thinly among the existing indigenous final Neolithic culture, characterized principally by Grooved Ware. The new graves are comparatively rare, but where they occur, they share certain characteristics. The beakers have an easily identifiable form, either with a low carination or, in the case of taller beakers, with a mid-carination, and the burials may be accompanied with gold ornaments, copper daggers, stone wrist guards, and spatulas of antler or bone. The decoration of the low-carinated beaker favoured three particular styles: the Maritime-derived style, the All-over-Cord style, and the All-over-Comb style. Each has a distinctive distribution. The Maritime-derived Beakers are concentrated in central southern Britain, while the All-over-Cord zone beakers are mostly found north of the Humber. The All-over-Comb group has a central southern British bias similar to the Maritime-derived type.

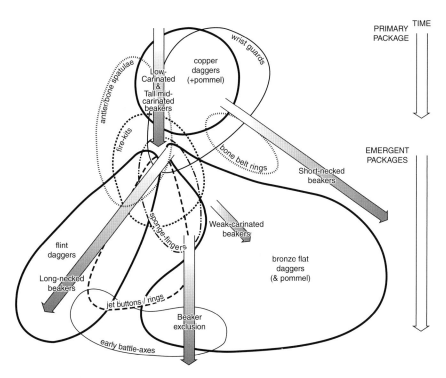

6.26 The development of Beaker grave assemblages involved a number of interactions. The diagram explains the way in which diversity developed from a comparatively simple primary package

The simplest way to explain the observed facts is to accept that there was an inflow of population into Britain over this period, with people arriving perhaps in family groups, bringing with them a new ideology that embodied religious belief, new restricted knowledge, and the symbols of enhanced status. They settled among existing communities and were presumably accepted as individuals of value. Their knowledge and their social networks, linking them to continental homelands, brought benefits to all, not least in opening up the flow of commodities, in which all could share.

Support for the view that there was a degree of social mobility at this time is provided by the study of stable isotopes preserved in human teeth. One of the most informative of the recent discoveries is that of a Beaker burial found on Boscombe Down near Amesbury, Wiltshire. The burial, popularly known as the Amesbury Archer, dates to the twenty-fourth or twenty-third century BC and was of a man 35–50 years old. He was buried in a timber-lined grave pit accompanied by an unparalleled range of artefacts including five beakers, three copper knives, two wrist guards, fifteen arrow-heads, a shale belt ring, two gold basket 'earrings' (probably for decorating hair), an antler spatula, a bone pin, a strike-alight, boars' tusks, flint tools, and a cushion-stone, the last suggesting that he was a coppersmith. It may be that it was his high status as a craftsman able to manipulate metal that explains his exceptional treatment in death.

Examination of the Amesbury Archer's skeleton showed that he had suffered a severe knee injury, causing his left leg to wither and leaving him with a pronounced limp. We shall never know how he sustained the injury, but in some traditional societies it was not unknown for the smith to be deliberately maimed to discourage such a skilled and valued person from moving away from his community. The Amesbury Archer was, however, a migrant. A study of the oxygen isotopes in his teeth showed that he grew up in a colder climate than prevailed in Wessex, and when the strontium isotopes are considered, the best-fit location for his childhood home can be narrowed down to southern Germany or the Alpine region. There is a further twist to the story. Another burial was found nearby—that of a young man of 20 to 25 years old. He, too, had been provided with two gold tress rings. A study of his skeleton showed that he shared with the Amesbury Archer an inherited anomaly in his feet. That this anomaly is very rare strongly suggests that they were related either as brothers or as father and son. When the teeth of the second burial were examined, the oxygen and strontium isotope ratios identified showed that he had probably grown up locally. Thus, while the Amesbury Archer was a migrant from middle Europe, his son (or brother) was Wessex-born.

Strontium isotope studies carried out on Beaker period skeletons found along the upper Danube valley have shown that out of a total of eighty-one individuals sampled, fifty-one had grown up in regions some distance from where they were buried. This represents a high degree of mobility among the population but tells us little yet about the nature or magnitude of the movements. Some could have been the result of long-distance migration by lineage groups, but equally the results could reflect the exchange of marriage partners within dispersed Beaker communities. The method has considerable potential in elucidating the question of Beaker period migrations and further analyses are eagerly awaited.

The second phase in the Beaker narrative in Britain dates to the period 2250–1950 BC. This is marked, particularly at the beginning of the period, by great diversification both in beaker forms and decoration and in material culture. The dagger-knife now becomes an important symbol, whether made in flint or in bronze, and carefully perforated stone battle-axes make an appearance. Beaker burial rite is now far more widely adopted, suggesting that what had been the privilege of a few was fast becoming the culture of the many: Beaker culture was now becoming democratized. But there is still evidence of continuing mobility. Beaker pot forms and decoration share in continental developments, particularly those of the Low Countries, and the adoption of the perforated stone battle-axe as a preferred symbol of status in some burials was probably also inspired by the value systems of the Low Countries. Whether this implies continued settlement from the Continent remains unclear, but, at the very least, trans-maritime social networks were still flourishing and this implies a degree of human mobility.

The final phase, phase 3, lasting from 1950 to 1700–1600 BC, is something of an epilogue. While some communities were still making pots in the Beaker tradition, others had begun to use heavier vessels—food vessels and collared urns—which owe much to indigenous pottery traditions. It was as though the special status symbolized by the Beaker was fast waning and in places had been forgotten. The burials, too, became generally poorer across much of the country, though in a few places like the Wessex heartlands the elite managed to maintain a tradition that saw the conspicuous consumption of a wide range of rare and valuable materials buried with the dead, often beneath massive burrows. These are matters to which we shall return.

If we are correct in assuming that the Beaker phenomenon in Britain was instigated by new people, however few, who introduced a new ideology embodying rare knowledge, underpinned by social networks providing access to a range of valuable commodities, it is worth considering what effect they may have had on the world of the indigenous monument builders, whose unity was symbolized by a preference for Grooved Ware pottery. The appearance of Beaker pottery at a number of the traditional monuments implies some degree of involvement, but this need mean nothing more than a continuation of behaviour and practice largely unchanged. There are, however, some building works that suggest that something new was happening. The massive palisaded enclosures that were constructed at West Kennet Farm and around the monument at Mount Pleasant belong to around the twenty-third and twenty-second centuries, while the construction of the astonishing Silbury Hill took place during the twenty-fourth century. The great stone circle at Avebury and the stone-defined avenues are also best dated to the Beaker period. And what of Stonehenge? If the date of *c.* 2500 for the erection of the sarsen circle and trilithons is correct, this would be a little early for Beaker involvement. There were, however, several stages of rearrangement of the bluestones in the centuries to follow. All these developments could, of course, have been the result of indigenous compulsions and energies, but it is tempting to think that the new elite and those who adopted the new ideologies may have taken a constructive interest in the vibrant religious life of the community.

The Mobilization of Commodities

The desire to acquire rare commodities is probably as old as humanity. We have seen it in the Mesolithic period with the spread of Portland chert and Rhum blood-stone far from their places of origin, while the distribution of jadeite axes from the western Alps, scattered over distances of more than 1,500 kilometres, offers a spectacular demonstration of the phenomenon in the fourth millennium. The movement of these commodities would have been conditioned and controlled by the social system prevalent at the time, but the imperative to acquire was hard-wired into the genetics of humans. This 'instinct' was ultimately the force behind the creation of the complex webs of connectivity that bound human societies together: commodities provided a means by which communities articulated their social engagements.

The spread of copper and, soon after it, bronze technology gave a new impetus to the movement of materials. Metal objects became highly desirable—things to be acquired and displayed. To begin with, it is probable that metal passed through existing social networks. The thick-butted copper axes made of Ross Island metal that found their way into Scotland most likely used systems of exchange that had earlier governed the distribution of porcellanite axes from Tievebulliagh. In both cases it was the materials that were desirable, not the tool or weapon into which they were fashioned. Suddenly the new, shiny, malleable substance was in great demand, and it was soon used to fashion other items of authority like daggers and halberds. Once awareness of the magic qualities of metal became known—its ability to metamorphose through the use of heat—the search was on for more varieties, and it was not long before gold was discovered in Ireland and probably in Armorica. It may have been the search for alluvial gold in Cornwall that led to the discovery of tin. In a brief half-millennium, *c.* 2500–*c.* 2000 BC, the world of the Britons and the Irish had been transformed. Pyrotechnical knowledge had introduced an entirely new range of desirable acquisitions, while the control of metal supply irrevocably changed the political geography. The movement of commodities escalated, and with it came an increased mobility bound up with the spread of new ideologies.

New commodities were soon added to the list of desirables, among them amber and jet. Both were resinous and shiny, and warmed quickly to the touch, while their unusual lightness and their electrostatic properties endowed them with an irresistible magic. Jet was a very rare substance, occurring in reasonable quantity only on the east coast of North Yorkshire in the vicinity of Whitby, where raw lumps could be gathered from cliff exposures. Similar-looking materials such as lignite from Brora in Sutherland and shale from Kimmeridge in Dorset were also used, but as inferior substitutes. Amber, a fossil resin, occurs naturally in the eastern Baltic and also on the northern and western coasts of Jutland, the nearest and most convenient source for Britain. Lumps eroded from these Danish exposures were also carried by currents across the North Sea to be deposited on the Norfolk coasts, where they could be found in pieces of usable size. How much of the amber used in prehistoric Britain came from the primary Jutish sources and how much was picked up on the east coast is not easy to decide.

Jet and amber were used to make much the same range of objects designed for personal adornment. These included buttons, pulley ring fastenings, and simple decorative plaques, but, most spectacularly, elaborate necklaces composed of multiple strings of beads held apart by decorated spacer plates. These necklaces, whether of jet or amber, were similar in general form to the gold lunulae, and it may be that the inscribed decoration on some of the lunulae was meant to reflect the arrangement of the spacer plates. The real skills in manufacturing the buttons and the beads lay in drilling the perforations for the strings. The buttons usually required the perforation to be V-shaped, while some of the spacer plate terminals involved a more complex Y-shaped drilling. These craft techniques distinguished the British manufacturers. The elaborately perforated amber spacer plates found in Wessex, and quite possibly manufactured there, are paralleled only by items from the shaft graves of Mycenae. We can only guess what this startling distribution implies: could it have resulted from the journey of someone carrying or wearing the necklace, perhaps a British wife for a Mycenaean lord?

The distribution of jet and amber artefacts in Britain and Ireland is a reflection both of the networks of exchange in operation and of the desire of individuals to

6.27 A collection of jet buttons and a pulley ring deposited together at Harehope in Peeblesshire. The jet probably came from the Yorkshire coast near Whitby

acquire. As one might expect, the networks spread wide. A button of Whitby jet has been found in an Armorican grave, and it is a distinct possibility that the amber items found in Armorica at the time arrived via Wessex. One notable aspect of the distribution of Whitby jet is the way it spread up the east coast of Britain as far as the Orkney Islands, demonstrating the vitality of east coast cabotage. There is also a significant cluster of finds on the west coast, which presumably travelled cross-country via the Clyde–Forth axis.

Another substance avidly acquired during this period was faience, used to make beads or sometimes pendants. Faience is an artificial material with a striking bright-blue glassy surface. It is made by moulding a core compound of crushed quartz grains mixed with lime to the required shape. In the case of beads, this was probably done around a straw to provide the central perforation. The core was then coated with a glaze made up of a soda–lime–quartz mix to which copper compounds were added

6.28 A jet necklace with spacer plates from a Bronze Age burial at Inchmarnock, Argyll and Bute

to give the bright-blue colour. The whole was then fired to a high temperature. There has been much debate about the origin of the faience beads found in Britain, but it is now accepted that they are British products made at more than one site. While the necessary knowledge may have derived ultimately from Europe, it remains a possibility that British metalworkers developed the technique for themselves. The glassy blueness of the beads, quite unlike anything that appears in nature, apart from certain copper ores, would have endowed the beads with a special, magical value. Beads of varying type are found throughout Britain and along the entire seaboard of Ireland. A scattering found in the Channel Islands, in Armorica, and in the Netherlands are likely to have been exported from Britain.

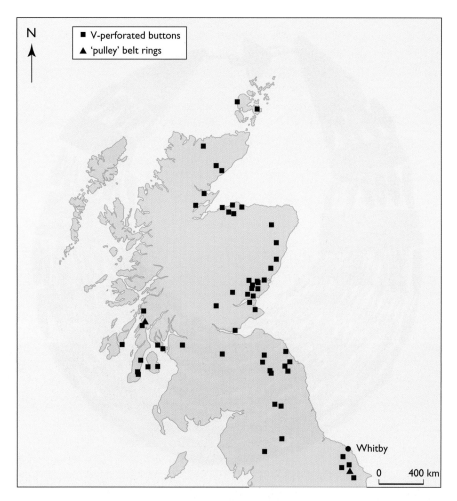

N

■ V-perforated buttons
▲ 'pulley' belt rings

Whitby

0   400 km

6.29 Jet, a fine black shale acquired from the cliffs at Whitby, was widely used to make a variety of ornaments in the prehistoric and Roman periods. The map shows an early phase in the exploitation of the stone in the Early Bronze Age, when it was used to make a limited range of luxury items. The distribution suggests that the eastern coastal route was widely used

Several beads of real glass have also been found in second-millennium contexts in Britain and Ireland. Though comparatively few in number, they concentrate on the west side of Britain and in Ireland, which suggests that they may have arrived from the Mediterranean, along the Atlantic seaways. A bead like the 'sealing wax' red example found in a burial at Wilsford, Wiltshire, must have been a source of wonder to all who saw it. What it meant to its owner and what influence he used to acquire it we can only guess.

Rare raw materials, often spectacular in colour and crafted with huge skill into unusual shapes, flooded into circulation in the early second millennium. Some have been mentioned, but there was much more beside, like the elegant mace-heads and battle-axes made from stone frequently chosen for its striking crystalline texture. There would also have been fine linen fabrics coloured with vivid vegetable dyes, only tiny fragments of which survive, and no doubt other items no longer visible in the archaeological record, like colourful feathers, fine leather-work, and carpentry, as well as rare herbs and essences. Those with the facility to acquire exotic things, and to take ownership of the power embedded in them, inhabited an extraordinary world where ever-expanding networks opened up new ways of obtaining power and knowledge: it was a restless world where people were always on the move.

6.30 A selection of finely fashioned battle-axes from Scotland. *Left*: Broomend of Crichie, Aberdeenshire; *back*: Chapelton, Lanarkshire; *front*: Longniddry, East Lothian

Centres of Power

While artefacts made in a variety of materials were dispersed widely across Britain, Ireland, and the adjacent continent, preferences for a mode of burial or for a particular style of pottery decoration marked out, often quite starkly, regional differences. Some regions were highly conservative, holding onto traditional burial rites and even reinventing them, while others were innovative, able to absorb what was new and to make it their own. Many factors would have combined to create this regionalism, but among them geographical location was paramount. While some communities occupied remote places with limited resources, others commanded sought-after commodities or controlled communication routes.

One of the more spectacular examples of a region controlling a nexus of routes is Wessex, or more particularly the arc of chalk uplands stretching from the coast of Dorset to the middle Thames valley. This was the region that throughout the third millennium had developed a series of prominent ritual landscapes characterized by mega-henges, including the great complexes at Avebury and Stonehenge. The monuments would have been foci of attraction, and it is likely that the extraordinary developments of Stonehenge drew in people from far and wide. But the region had other attractions: it was, in effect, a major route node. The southern flanks were served by a number of rivers reaching the sea at convenient harbours like those of Poole and Christchurch, which in turn linked to the cross-Channel sea-routes and to the cabotage routes westwards along the southern British coast. The west flank of the chalk was similarly served by rivers flowing into the Severn estuary, giving access to the sea-routes to south Wales and Ireland, while along the whole western flank ran the ridge of Jurassic limestone providing a major upland route to the midlands and the north beyond. And to the east lay the Thames, with its tributary the Kennet, leading to the estuary and the southern North Sea. At a time of increased mobility and commodity flow Wessex could not have failed to benefit.

The first half of the second millennium is characterized by the appearance of about a hundred or so very rich burials clustering on the Wessex chalkland. When the group was first described in the 1930s, the burials were considered to belong to a distinct culture, called at the time the Wessex culture, set up by an intrusive elite arriving from Armorica. It is now accepted that they were simply the more elaborately furnished graves of indigenous communities, the less exalted members of which occupy the many hundreds of more modestly equipped burials scattered throughout the region.

The rich Wessex burials can be divided into two phases based on the dagger type in use: an 'early' group known as Wessex I, or the Bush Barrow phase, and a 'late'

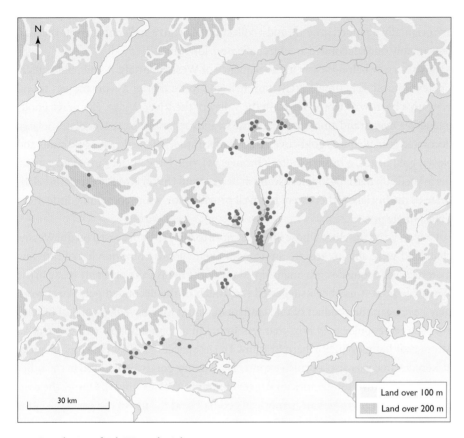

6.31 Distribution of rich Wessex burials

group, Wessex II, usually called after the Camerton–Snowshill dagger type. Wessex I begins around 2000 BC, with Wessex II taking over about 1700 BC and lasting until 1500 BC. The division is simply a classificatory convenience since the phenomenon is continuous, but the Wessex I burials tend to be richer than those of the later period, 'richness' being measured by the quantity of rare goods—gold, amber, jet, shale, and bronze—accompanying the body in the grave. There is also a change from inhumation to cremation over time.

The most famous of all the Wessex burials is that found beneath Bush Barrow—a massive round barrow that dominates the sky-line south of Stonehenge. The burial was of a male whose body had been laid directly on the surface of the ground. He had been provided with three bronze daggers, the hilt of one of which had been decorated with tiny studs of gold. Nearby were two lozenges of sheet gold and a gold plaque with hook attached, all three decorated with incised patterns. Other finds include a stone mace-head, decorative bone fittings from a wooden staff, a flat bronze axe originally wrapped in cloth, and a collection of bronze and copper rivets that had presumably once decorated an object of wood, long since decayed.

Bush Barrow belongs early in the sequence of Wessex burials. A later, but equally opulent, burial, this time a cremation believed to be that of a woman, was found beneath a barrow at Upton Lovell in the valley of the River Wylye. Her grave goods included a five-strand amber necklace, the strands separated by spacer plates, a large decorated gold plaque, a gold-covered cone of Kimmeridge shale, two gold studs and eleven gold beads, a bronze knife, a bronze awl, one large pottery urn, and a small perforated cup perhaps for incense. Bush Barrow and Upton Lovell are the most elaborate of the burials. Others were less well provided for, some containing little more than a single pot.

For 500 years the elites whose lineages chose to bury their deceased on the Wessex chalkland were able to acquire an array of exotic goods compounded of rare raw materials and exquisite craftsmanship. Many of the items were probably made in the Wessex region. It has been suggested that much of the decorated gold-sheet work may have been the product of one craftsman, and it may have been one of his creations, a rectangular gold box, that was found in a contemporary rich grave at La Motta near Lannion in northern Brittany. The jet spacer bead from the Breton burial at Kerguévarec was also a British export. That luxury goods also moved in the other direction is shown by Armorican daggers found in Wessex graves. One of the daggers from Bush Barrow is an Armorican product, and the use of the small gold pins to decorate the handle is typical of Armorican workmanship. After about 1700 BC the sphere of contact broadens to include the eastern end of the Channel, particularly Normandy and Picardy and the Rhine mouth, whence came inspiration for the later types of dagger as well as dress pins.

The movement of pottery vessels provides another way of tracing networks of interaction alongside the exchange of rare commodities and elite metalwork, and the sharing of ideas and fashions. Distinctive vessels, named after the type site of Trevisker in north Cornwall, are found at several locations in central Wessex and on the Solent coast and the Isle of Wight, while handled vessels known as *vases à anse*, common in Armorica, are found on the Channel Islands, the Isle of Wight, and Wessex, again with an emphasis on the coast. The distribution pattern of both pottery types implies that they were transported by sea. The social context for the movements is more difficult to ascertain: while the vessels may simply have been containers for some desirable commodity, they could have accompanied women, who in traditional societies often had control of making pottery, reflecting perhaps marriage arrangements between the disparate communities. We shall see later (Chapter 8) that

BUSH BARROW

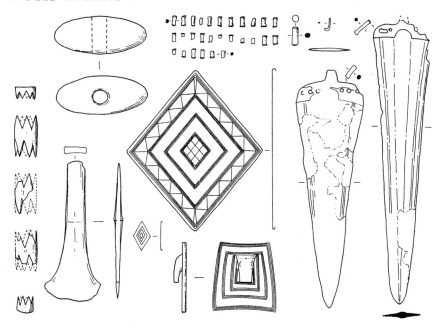

UPTON LOVELL

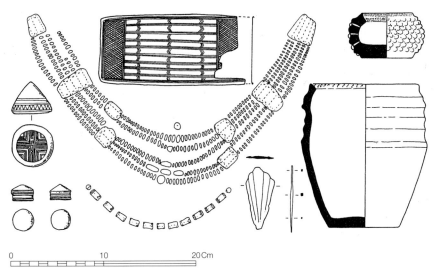

0   10   20 Cm

6.32 Two sets of grave goods from the Wessex barrows found in Wiltshire. The Bush Barrow burial was of a male, the Upton Lovell burial was of a female. Both were well furnished with gold

there was soon to be a high degree of convergence between pottery traditions on both sides of the Channel and the southern North Sea. This can best be explained by intensified social relationships growing from social networks developing in the earlier second millennium.

There is much archaeological detail reflecting on maritime links in the early second millennium. The overall impression is that the networks bound Wessex, the south-west of Britain, and Armorica closely together in the period *c.* 2000–*c.* 1700 BC but that after that interactions extended eastwards up-Channel to encompass the southern North Sea, drawing on influences from the Rhine valley and beyond. From the broader perspective this is hardly surprising. We have already seen that in the Beaker period, *c.* 2500–*c.* 2000 BC, the entire Channel–southern North Sea zone provided the long interface across which the Beaker ideology and its accompanying cultural package was introduced to Britain. No doubt these contacts, once established, were maintained. The intensification and expansion of connectivity in the second millennium is simply a development of what had gone before.

Our emphasis on Wessex and the southern seas should not be allowed to detract from the significance of the other sea-routes. The overall distribution of intensive Beaker activity, and later the spread of elite commodities, is a direct reflection of the importance of the cabotage routes along the east coast leading to northern Britain. While coastal trafficking was surely the norm, there is no reason why open-sea journeys should not have been made occasionally to the shores of Jutland and the estuaries of the Elbe and Weser. Nor should we forget the continued vitality of the western routes that criss-crossed the Irish Sea. Ireland was still the main provider of gold, and its elites continued to find amber and faience from Britain acceptable acquisitions.

Commanding the Seas

The distribution of archaeological materials leaves little doubt that sea travel played an essential part in the increasing complexity of life in the period *c.*2500–*c.*1500 BC, and it is a reasonable assumption that those who had the skills to build sea-going vessels and to sail them successfully would have been held in high esteem in society. Indeed, command of the sea, and of the knowledge of rare commodities that naturally flowed from it, would have been a highly prestigious occupation appropriate to the elite. Successful maritime enterprise would have become socially competitive, and competition would have led to the kind of intensification and expansion of the networks that were being formed in the first half of the second millennium.

The normal mode of sea transport until the end of the third millennium was prob-ably the hide boat, a structure easy to build and highly flexible both on open water and in shallows. It was also light enough to be carried on overland portages. The development of copper and bronze axes after the middle of the third millennium opened up entirely new possibilities for shipbuilders in that the new metal greatly facilitated complex carpentry, enabling the craftsmen to manipulate heavy wood in precise ways to create components that could be joined to make composite struc-tures. Given the increasing mobility of the period, these skills would soon have been turned to boat-building, with the result that by about 2000 BC a highly sophisticated tradition of sewn-plank vessels had evolved.

Remains of seven such structures dating to the period c. 2000–c. 1500 BC have been found along the British coasts: three in the Humber estuary with one from the coast nearby, one at Dover, one in Southampton Water, and one in the Severn estuary. All share the same construction traditions in that they were composed of planks sewn together with twisted yew withies and given a degree of rigidity with cross-strengtheners passing through cleats integral with the planks. The two best-preserved examples are the Ferriby boat 1 from the Humber and the Dover boat, the first measuring about 13 metres in length, the second estimated to be about 11 metres. Both vessels were flat-bottomed and without a keel, though in the Ferriby boat the central plank was thicker than the adjacent planks. The sides were built up, with separate strakes attached in the same way as the base timbers. The bound joints were made watertight with caulking of moss held in place with laths, but the Dover boat had the added refinement of using a stopping compound made of animal fat and beeswax.

There has been much debate about the seaworthiness of these vessels, but it is now generally agreed that the sewn boats could safely have taken to the open sea so long as the conditions of sailing were carefully chosen: the vessels were not designed for rough-weather sailing. Propulsion would have been by paddle, but it is not impos-sible that sails were rigged, a suggestion based on there being projections on the base plank of the Ferriby 1 vessel that could have provided seating for a light temporary mast. Sea trials using a half-size replica showed that it could perform effectively and safely with a sail in open waters.

The sewn boats of the Early Bronze Age were sophisticated structures. In challen-ging the realms of the sea—a liminal and dangerous place—they would have acquired supernatural powers, and those who sailed in them would have embraced the mys-teries, sharing an exclusive elite status. One interesting suggestion that has recently been put forward is that this maritime fraternity used cups made of precious materials

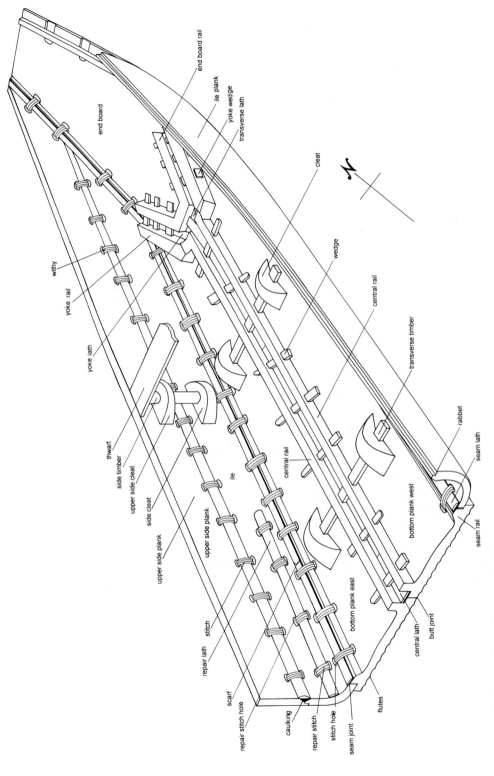

end board rail

ile plank

yoke wedge

transverse lath

end board

cleat

withy

yoke rail

wedge

central rail

yoke lath

transverse timber

thwart

side timber

upper side cleat

side cleat

central rail

ile

rabbet

seam lath

upper side plank

bottom plank west

central rail

seam rail

upper side plank

bottom plank east

repair lath

stitch

scarf

central lath

butt joint

repair stitch hole

caulking

flutes

repair stitch

stitch hole

seam joint

6.33 The diagram shows the way in which the Dover Bronze Age boat was constructed. It is not clear whether the end recovered was the fore or aft

6.34 The Dover boat at the time of its excavation

in their bonding rituals. In all, some sixteen cups are known: nine from southern Britain, mostly from coastal locations, three from Armorica, and the remainder from Germany. The cups are spectacular pieces of craftsmanship. Of the British examples, two are gold, from Rillaton in Cornwall and Ringlemere in Kent; two are amber, from Clandon in Dorset and Hove in West Sussex; and four, from Dorset, Devon, and probably Wiltshire, are of Kimmeridge shale. The Armorican examples included one of

6.35 Three Early Bronze Age cups: (*a*) in gold from Rillaton, Cornwall; (*b*) in amber from Hove in West Sussex; (*c*) in Kimmeridge shale from Farway in Dorset

gold and two of silver. By virtue of their materials and construction techniques the cups very probably represent the products of different craftsmen working at different times during the first half of the second millennium. Their largely maritime distribution and their extreme value does, however, suggest that they were in some way associated with an elite with links to the sea.

Another artefact type with a marked coastal distribution is that of the so-called slotted incense cups, small ceramic vessels with elongated vents in the sides, which are usually found with burials. While a few are known in the Wessex heartland, most are found on or close to the coast stretching from Dorset to Kent, with two others on the North Yorkshire coast. It is tempting to think that they, too, were attributes of the maritime elite, to be used in the rituals exclusive to their special status. However, the dangers of reading too much into sparsely distributed artefacts will be all too self-evident.

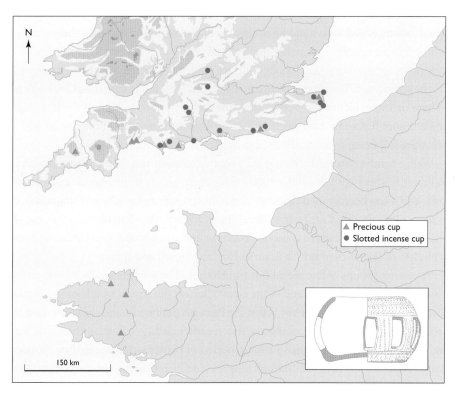

6.36 Around 2000 BC cups made of precious materials (gold, silver, amber, and shale) became evident on both sides of the Channel. These may reflect the behaviour patterns of an elite who commanded the seaways. The highly distinctive slotted incense cups found with burials of this period also have a coastal distribution and may in some way be connected with the belief systems of the same elite

Some Peripheries

Our discussion has tended to focus on regions that, because of the richness of the archaeological record, appear to be centres of power commanding access to rare raw materials, and upon the networks that bind them. Yet in the rest of Britain and Ireland life continued, often giving rise to quite distinct regional cultures. To review the entire scene is not possible, but a few examples will give a sense of the rich variety of regional British and Irish culture.

In some areas of the west and the north the burial rites of the period *c.* 2500–*c.* 1500 BC adhered to ancestral traditions favouring deposition in megalithic chambers set in barrows or cairns. The most extreme examples of this are the wedge tombs covered by elongated 'mounds' of northern and western Ireland, of which over 500 examples have been identified. Wedge tombs are characterized by having a single rectangular chamber that decreases in width and height from front to back. The chamber is built of orthostats supporting a roof of cap-stones, and the whole is covered with an elongated mound edged with standing stones. Various elaborations occur at the entrance, while in some examples there is a small closed chamber at the rear. One notable feature of the tombs is that the chambers all face west, with the majority of them aligned on the setting sun. The burials were usually cremations, but inhumations are known. Where dating evidence has been found, the earliest tombs belong to the late third millennium, but some continued in use throughout the second millennium and a few were still being sporadically used in the first millennium.

Wedge tombs covered by elongated 'mounds' concentrate in the west of Ireland. While they show certain similarities to the gallery graves of the Armorican peninsula, and it has been argued that they derive from there as the result of migration, it is more likely that they are an Irish development. They represent the strong desire of the community to adhere to ancestral means of burial in a broad Atlantic-facing zone well clear of the reach of British luxuries like faience, jet, and amber.

Two other groups of late megalithic tombs should be mentioned: the Clava tombs clustering at the north-east end of the Great Glen on the southern side of the Moray Firth and the entrance graves of Scilly, the Penwith peninsula, and the south-east of Ireland. The Clava tombs resemble the much earlier passage graves of the north, but radiocarbon dates suggest that the main period of construction lies in the centuries 2200–2000 BC. It is almost as though they are a deliberate archaism, the community searching back into its ancestral past to find a burial made to proclaim its deep identity. The entrance graves of Scilly and western Cornwall are simple elongated galleries or passages set within circular mounds. On Scilly they are particularly numerous,

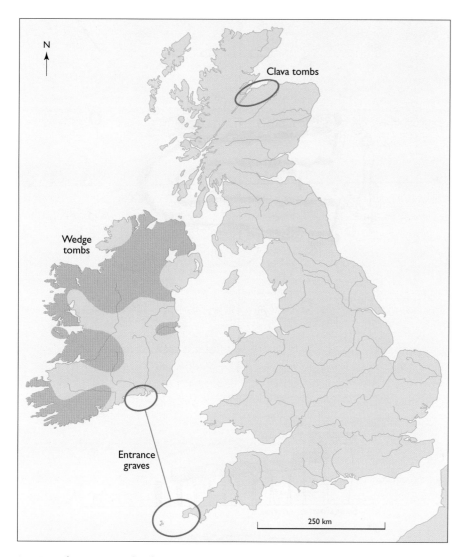

6.37 Some distinctive peripheral groups

but finds are sparse. Such material as there is suggests that they were in use during the second millennium, and indeed it is possible that the islands were not settled until then. In spite of the remoteness of Scilly, the discovery, at Knackyboy Cairn, of eight beads of glass and one of star-form faience shows that the island communities were sufficiently connected to acquire at least a sample of the luxury goods circulating in the more cosmopolitan centres of Wessex.

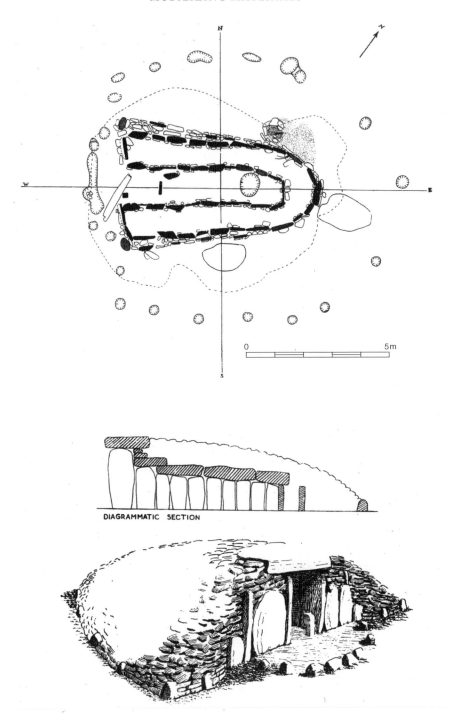

DIAGRAMMATIC SECTION

6.38 Plan and section of a wedge tomb excavated at Island, County Cork

Retrospective

After a period of comparative isolation, Britain and Ireland were suddenly drawn into a new complex of networks linking the islands to the mainland of north-western Europe, initiated by the movement of people from Iberia to southern Armorica and the Loire valley in the period c.2700–c.2500 BC. From there people moved north-wards to western Ireland, introducing the skills of metalworking, and eastwards across Europe to the Rhine and beyond. As mobility escalated, more people crossed to southern and eastern Britain, bringing Beaker ideologies with them. In this highly mobile world, mastery of the sea became an imperative: shipbuilding technologies improved, and power began to be expressed in terms of ability to acquire rare raw materials brought from afar. All this seems to have created a situation in which com-petitive journeying became the favoured activity of a new maritime elite. The cycles of travel seem to have begun around 2000 BC in the western Channel, linking central southern Britain with Armorica, but over the next 500 years they extended to cover the whole Channel and the southern North Sea, incorporating the riverine routes of the North European Plain leading to middle Europe. By the end of this period of maritime connectivity, sea venturing seems to have lost its exclusivity, passing from the realms of elite daring to the more mundane world of the trader.

Over the thousand years from 2500 to 1500 BC the nature of mobility had changed from initial exploration, to population movement and settlement, to elite adven-turing, and finally to trade and settled cultural consolidation. By 1500 BC this ever-increasing mobility had created broad cultural similarities along both sides of the eastern Channel–south North Sea interface.

Over the long-drawn-out period of interaction people needed to communicate one with another to develop relationships, set up complex allegiances, and exchange knowledge about technologies and the subtle values of abstract ideologies. To do this they needed to develop a lingua franca. These are matters we shall explore in the next chapter before resuming the narrative once more.

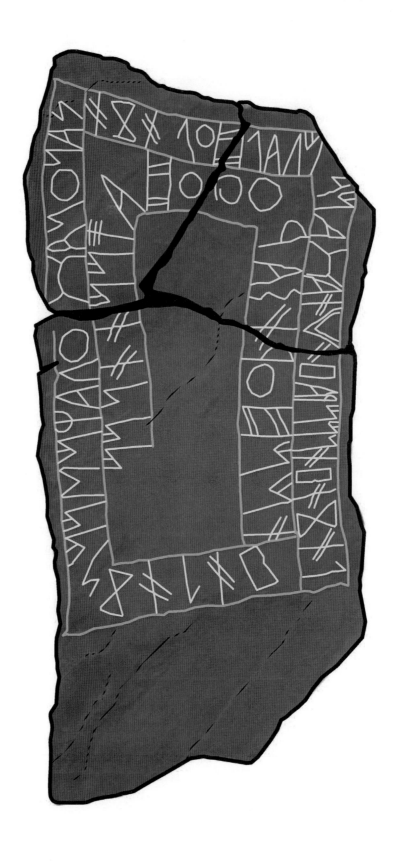

7

Interlude

TALKING TO EACH OTHER

THE middle of the second millennium BC is a convenient point to pause in the narrative, to take stock of where we are and to consider some broader issues. It is, in many ways, the end of the first cycle in the history of Britain and Ireland. Following the cold downturn of the Younger Dryas, the land had been repopulated by hunter-gatherers moving in from continental Europe. Continued incomings bringing the attributes of Neolithization transformed the islands in a remarkably short space of time, creating a distinctively insular Neolithic; and later, in a renewed phase of European-wide mobility, a new set of ideologies accompanied by the 'Beaker package' was introduced, a process that involved an influx of peoples from the Continent. What numbers were involved in this last stage it is impossible to say, but the changes were profound, caused not least by the introduction of metallurgy. Thereafter new social imperatives encouraged continuing mobility, at least at the elite level, and with it the flow of raw materials greatly increased.

By the middle of the second millennium the novelty of travel, and of the visible display of the journey through acquired foreign commodities, had begun to diminish. Seafaring continued, but it was now more the province of the trader than of the hero. Value systems were fast-changing. What the archaeological evidence shows with some vividness is that control of the land and of its productive capacity was now becoming the prime concern of the people: these are issues we shall explore in the next chapter. With this shift of values a new cycle had begun.

The intricate complexity of the social networks—networks of negotiation—that had developed during the first cycle involved human movement ranging in scale from the journeys of individuals to the arrival of migrant communities, their mobility facilitated by increasingly sophisticated sea-craft. The seaways and the navigable rivers provided the arteries of communication. Geography was a determining factor, dividing the islands of Britain and Ireland into the east-facing and west-facing zones that have become familiar in the previous chapters. The Channel sits between the two, offering a link between them and an interface of its own. But in many ways it, too, conformed to the east–west divide: the western Channel, west of the Cherbourg–Solent axis, was part of the western maritime network, while the eastern Channel and southern North Sea belonged to the eastern network. This divide, already inherent in the archaeology of the third and second millennia, becomes even more evident in the first millennium BC and first millennium AD. The east-side and west-side stories are different, contributing significantly to the variation in character of the insular population.

Sharing Ideas

The networks of interaction, of the kind that we have seen binding Britain and Ireland to the Continent, imply that people were able to communicate one with another through a commonly understood language. Simple exchanges could, of course, have taken place without speech. Herodotus describes a system of 'silent' trade between Mediterranean merchants and the natives of the Atlantic coast of North Africa that involved the traders laying out their goods on the shore and going back to their ship to wait until the natives had presented theirs. The traders would then return and, if satisfied with what had been left for exchange, would take it and depart, leaving their own trade goods. If they felt that the offer was insufficient, they would simply return to the ship and wait for the natives to increase their offer by the next time they landed. Such a system depended on mutual trust, but since both parties benefited considerably from successful and sustained trade, there was a strong imperative to abide by the rules.

In silent trade of this kind without face-to-face contact, no implied values and meanings could be exchanged with the commodities: they were simply material. In the systems we have been considering, between Britain and Ireland and the Continent, the amount of information flow was considerable and complex. The passage graves of Ireland, north Wales, and Orkney embodied a mass of interlinked meanings, knowledge, and beliefs, embodied in their architecture, art, and astronomical orientation. Successful communication between communities on this scale could only have been achieved through the use of sophisticated language, allowing people along the entire Atlantic seaways from Iberia to Orkney to communicate one with another—though not necessarily, of course, in the same language throughout. Similarly, the introduction of copper-producing technology from Iberia, perhaps via Armorica, first into south-western Ireland and later into Wales and Cornwall, required the transmission of pyrotechnical skills of some complexity. This could not easily have been achieved without a common language. But perhaps even more impressive was the rapid spread of Beaker ideology and the material package that accompanied it. Originating in the Tagus region, it reached the Rhine valley and Scotland within a few centuries. Although the nature and degree of acceptance varied regionally, the coherence of the package over a considerable area implies that its meaning was communicated and understood. Finally, the 'heroic voyages' of the early second millennium, if we are correct in our interpretation of them, would have required the leaders to bring back new knowledge with them—knowledge acquired through observation and conversation.

In summary, the archaeological evidence demonstrates with great clarity that communities were able to communicate one with another often over huge distances. The pattern of languages and dialects throughout the Atlantic zone was no doubt intricate and at times fast-changing, but that said, there can be little doubt that some kind of lingua franca was already in use by the early second millennium and was, in all probability, emerging a millennium earlier. Of that language and of the other local languages no direct evidence exists, but a convincing case can, I believe, be made that the principal language of intergroup communication was what we now know as Celtic. Since this view runs counter to popularly held beliefs, we need first to understand how the traditional paradigm has arisen before we can explore new perspectives more consistent with the archaeological evidence.

Some Old Myths and Preconceptions

We saw in Chapter 1 how, by the seventeenth century, the view had emerged that a people generally referred to as Celts had originated somewhere in the east and had migrated across Europe, some of them reaching as far west as Brittany, Britain, and Ireland. This myth was largely based on the biblical story of the children of Noah spreading out after the Flood to settle the world, but was given substance by latching onto it stories of the migrations of Celts recorded in the classical texts that at this time were becoming generally available to the scholarly world. The classical sources described warlike Celts from west central Europe moving into the Po valley in the fourth century BC, where they settled and from where they raided deep into the Italian peninsula. A little later others who had settled in the Danube valley were raiding the Balkans and Greece, some eventually crossing to Asia Minor, where they established themselves in central Anatolia and continued to attack the cities of the Aegean coast well into the second century BC.

The fearsome, freedom-loving Celts provided an acceptable role model, and it was comforting to conflate biblical myths with events taken from ancient history to provide worthy ancestors for the French and British. The fact that no classical source recorded a westerly movement of these middle European Celts into Brittany, Britain, and Ireland did not deter the seventeenth-century antiquaries from imagining hordes of Celts sailing to the islands. The Celtic myth reached its most expanded and elaborated form in the writings of the Breton cleric Paul-Yves Pezron in his *L'Antiquité de la nation et de la langue des Celtes*, published in Paris in 1703.

The expanded myth provided a convenient explanatory model for the Welsh scholar Edward Lhuyd when he came to publish his detailed research into the 'original languages' of Britain, Ireland, and Brittany. Recognizing the close similarities between these dialects, he was content to call them all Celtic and to assume that the language was introduced by invaders from the Continent. In the Welsh preface to volume I of his *Archaeologia Britannica* he writes:

> Having now related what none have hitherto made mention of, namely, first that the old inhabitants of Ireland consisted of two nations, Gwydhelians and Scots. Secondly, that the Gwydhelians descended from the ancient Britons, and the Scots from Spain. Thirdly, that the Gwydhelians lived in the most ancient times not only in north Britain ... but also in England and Wales. And fourthly that the said Gwydhelians of England and Wales were the inhabitants of Gaul before they came into this island.

Here Lhuyd was trying to explain the differences he detected in the Celtic languages in terms of a historical model that saw the earliest form of Celtic, Goidelic, or Q-Celtic as it was later called, introduced to the whole of Britain and Ireland from Gaul, later to be replaced in England and Wales by a developed form, also from Gaul, which became known as Brythonic, or P-Celtic. This was the beginning of a hypothesis broadly accepted and much discussed by historical philologists over the last 300 years. Archaeologists were also content to accept the linguist's model and to attempt to fit the material evidence to it.

A major event in the expansion of the hypothesis took place at the International Congress of Prehistoric Anthropology and Archaeology held in Bologna in 1871. Visiting archaeologists from France and Switzerland viewing the finds from a newly discovered cemetery at Marzabotto in the Po valley were surprised to find that the ornamented grave goods buried with the dead were closely similar to those found in their own countries north of the Alps. They immediately realized that they were confronting evidence for the migration of the Celts to Italy as described in the texts of Livy and Polybius. The Celts now at last had a visible archaeological identity. It was a simple step to argue that the particular style of ornamentation adopted—which became known as 'Celtic art'—was representative of the presence of Celts wherever it was found, an assumption that archaeologists today would recognize as grossly oversimplified.

So it was that the Celtic art of the La Tène period (the latter part of the European Iron Age) became a surrogate for the Celts described in the classical texts. The fact that 'Celtic art' was found in Britain and Ireland was seen as 'proof' that Celts migrated to Britain from Gaul in the fifth and fourth centuries BC. This was believed to be the physical evidence for the Brythonic invasions. Since the hypothesis required that Goidelic Celtic had been introduced earlier, archaeologists attempted to find evidence for the invasion of the Goidels in the material culture of the Late Bronze and Early Iron Age in the first half of the first millennium BC.

It has been necessary to lay out the main threads of the Celtic hypothesis to show how the myths that were created in the seventeenth century continued to be elaborated into the first half of the twentieth century, and in some quarters are reiterated even today, long after archaeologists who deal first hand with the evidence have ceased to believe in them.

So, after deconstructing this house of cards, what are we left with? We can accept that the Celtic language in various dialects was spoken over much of western Europe, including probably Ireland and Britain, in the latter centuries of the first millennium BC and has survived today as living languages in parts of Brittany, Wales, Ireland, and Scotland. We can also accept that Celtic-speaking groups from eastern France and southern Germany were involved in migrations between the fourth and second centuries BC south into Italy and east into the Balkans and Asia Minor, probably taking their language with them. Quite separate is the question of La Tène material culture and its associated Celtic art. While this undoubtedly reflects a mobility of ideas and value systems, it need in no way imply ethnic or linguistic identity.

Leaving aside the myths and preconceptions of the past that have so confused the issue, the questions that remain, and on which we must now focus, are, how old is the Celtic language and what can be said of its origin and subsequent spread?

Celtic and the Indo-European Family

It has long been accepted by historical philologists that the majority of the languages spoken in Europe belong to the Indo-European family and that these languages spread throughout the peninsula from a hypothetical 'homeland' in the east at some stage in the prehistoric period. On the European peninsula the Indo-European family can be divided into seven branches: Hellenic, Italic, Illyrian, Slavonic, Baltic, Germanic, and Celtic. Traces of earlier languages remained in small enclaves: Etruscan and Iberian survived until the early first millennium AD and Basque is still very much alive. Much later, in the ninth century AD, movements of people from the east introduced Finno-Ugrian, a branch of the Uralic family that is manifest today in Estonian, Finnish, and Hungarian.

There has been intense debate about the origins and evolution of the Indo-European languages, particularly about the location of the original Indo-European 'homeland', but also about the chronology of the emergence of the different European branches. The question of homeland revolved around whether it lay north of the Black Sea in the steppe region to the west of the Urals (the Kurgan homeland) or south of the Black Sea in Asia Minor (the Anatolian homeland). Both areas have been avidly canvassed by archaeologists, and it may yet prove that a compromise can be reached. Much depends on dating, but philologists have shown a reluctance to engage with these matters since the practice known as glottochronology was discredited some years ago. However, new statistical methods for interrogating wordlists and creating language trees—the phylogenetic approach—are generating interesting patterns that have a promising degree of consistency irrespective of which wordlists are selected or what statistical package is used to interrogate them. The phylogenetic approach can do two things: it can arrange related languages into their order of appearance and can, at least in theory, give some indication of the chronology of the branching. One of the more recent studies, by a New Zealand team, offers a dendrogram of the development of the Indo-European family. In suggesting that the language began to branch around 6500 BC (allowing a large margin of error) it supports the Anatolian hypothesis, which argues that Indo-European was the language of the first farmers who spread to Europe from Asia Minor. However, the very rapid language divergences that occurred about 4500–3000 BC indicate that something significant was happening in the period when supporters of the Kurgan theory believed that Indo-European was spreading westwards at the time of the movement of people from the steppe homeland. It is conceivable that some compromise may be reached that allows that the initial spread was from Anatolia into Greece and the lower Danube region and that interaction here with the steppe population was the creative force that led to the period of rapid language divergence in the fifth and fourth millennia. Since not all scholars will be willing to accept the accuracy of the proposed chronology, the debate is likely to continue for a long time.

But we must now return to the question of Celtic. According to the dating offered in this particular phylogenetic study, Celtic began to separate from Italic some time before 4000 or 3000 BC. Other, differently based, phylogenetic approaches have offered dates for the beginning of Celtic of c. 4100 BC with a wide margin of error,

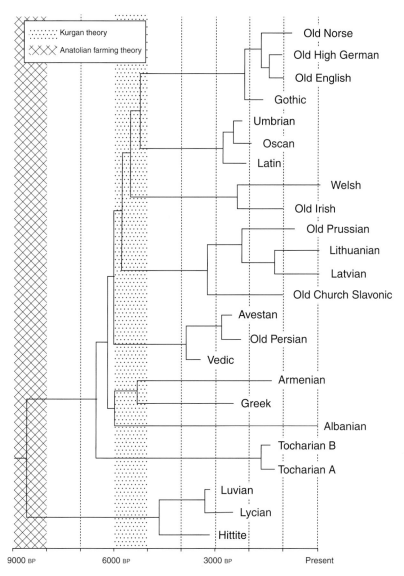

7.1 The diagram, based on the phylogenetic analysis of Indo-European wordlists, suggests the way in which the Indo-European languages may have developed and offers a possible chronology for their development. It suggests an origin around 7000 BC, which supports the theory that the language was introduced into Europe with the Neolithic expansion. The rapid development of language in the fourth millennium suggests a new dynamic, perhaps associated by renewed contacts in the Pontic Steppe region. According to this analysis, Celtic began to evolve as a distinct language around 4000 BC

3200 +/− 1500 BC, and before 2500 BC. If the broad consensus of their estimates is accepted, then the separation of Celtic as a distinct language probably took place sometime in the period between 4000 and 2500 BC. It is highly unlikely that that bracket of probability will ever be narrowed significantly.

It remains now to consider the all-important question, where in Europe did the Celtic language first emerge? All the other Indo-European languages are spoken now in the broad regions where they are thought to have developed (allowing for the distorting influence of Latin and its Romance-language progenies). Is it not possible, therefore, that Celtic emerged in the west to become the language of Atlantic-facing Europe? It is a difficult question to address. An essential starting point must be the map of all recorded

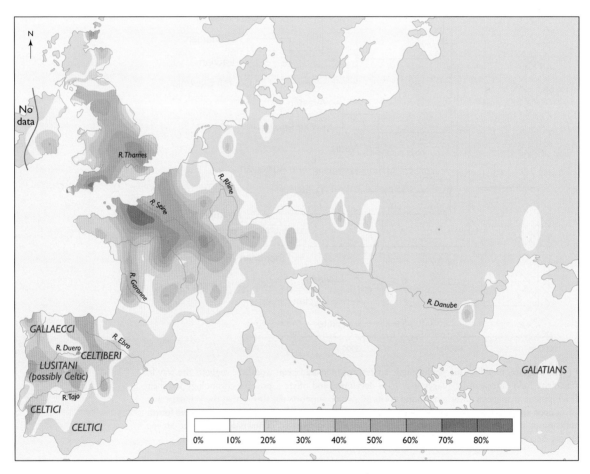

7.2 The distribution of ancient Celtic place names known from a variety of sources shows that the highest frequencies occur in Britain, Gaul, and Iberia; after S. Oppenheimer, *The Origins of the British* (London, 2006), Figure 2.1b, 2007. Based on data from Patrick Sims-Williams, 2006

Celtic place names known up to the Roman period. The map shows high numbers in Britain, Gaul, and western and central Iberia. There are also much smaller concentrations at various points along the Danube and into south Russia and Anatolia, which reflects the historic eastward movements of Celtic bands in the fourth to second century BC. Since many factors will have affected the survival of Celtic place names, it is unwise to rely too much on the map, but, when it is taken at its face value, it is not unreasonable to conclude that Celtic was one of the principal languages spoken along the Atlantic seaboard and into middle Europe in the period before the Roman era. The map in itself, however, offers no clues to the antiquity of the language. To pursue this we have to turn to the few remnants of surviving texts and to the observations of early classical writers.

The Earliest Identifiable Celtic Speakers

The earliest Greek sources to mention the Celts were in no doubt that they were a western people. The geographer Hecataeus of Miletus, writing at the end of the sixth century BC, probably using information gleaned from the Greek traders working out of the colony of Massalia (Marseille), tells us that the colony lay in the land of the Ligurians near to the territory of the Celts and that the settlement of Narbo (Narbonne) was a Celtic town. A little later Herodotus, writing in the fifth century, notes that the Celts lived beyond the Pillars of Hercules (at the entrance to the Strait of Gibraltar) and 'border on the Cynesii, who are the westernmost inhabitants of Europe', thus placing them in south-western Iberia. He also mentions 'the city of Pyrene' as Celtic—possibly to be identified as the Greek colony of Emporion (Ampurias) in the shadow of the Pyrenees on the Mediterranean coast (though he erroneously implied that the Danube rose nearby). A later writer, Ephorus (c.405–330 BC), saw the Celts as the most westerly of the four great barbarian peoples of Europe. Strabo records in his account of Celtica that Ephorus believed the territory to be so large that it included much of Iberia as far west as Gades (Cadiz). Taken together, then, these early texts leave little doubt that the Greeks saw the Celts as a westerly people stretching from the neighbourhood of Massalia to the Atlantic and including much of the Iberian peninsula. It is as well to remember, however, that their cognitive geography was limited by the extent of the information brought back to Massalia by travellers and traders sailing westwards along the Mediterranean shore and out into the Atlantic. The more northerly, inland, extent of Celtica was not mentioned until the explorer Pytheas returned from his expeditions to north-west Europe at the end of the fourth century with the knowledge that Celtica extended westwards to project as a great peninsula (Armorica) into the Atlantic.

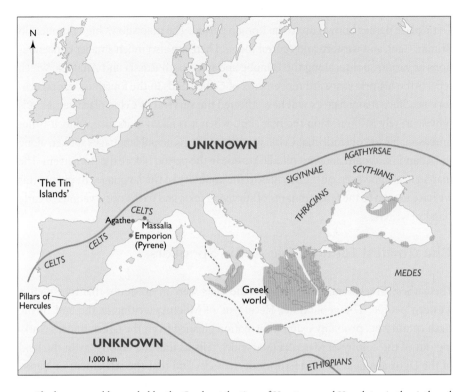

7.3 The known world recorded by the Greeks at the time of Hecataeus and Herodotus in the sixth and fifth century BC. Knowledge of the Celts is likely to have come from traders sailing from the ports such as Emporion, Agathe, and Massalia

The emphasis of the early geographers on the Celtic nature of Iberia is intriguing, the more so in the light of recent work on the early languages of the peninsula. It has long been known, from place name evidence, that Celtic was spoken over much of Iberia, and indeed one of the larger confederations of tribes in the northern Meseta were known to later classical writers as Celtiberians. From time to time philologists working on a scattering of inscriptions as well as place names have raised the possibility that the languages spoken by the tribes in the Tartessian region of the extreme south-west and the Lusitanian region, now central and northern Portugal, may have been Celtic. The evidence from the Tartessian region consists of an increasing number of funerary inscriptions carved on stone stelae in Phoenician script. A recent reconsideration of the entire corpus has shown conclusively that the language used was indeed Celtic and, more to the point, that the earliest examples probably date back to the seventh century BC, making Tartessian the oldest Celtic language so far recorded. If the mature language was being spoken in the seventh century BC, then its advent must have been considerably earlier.

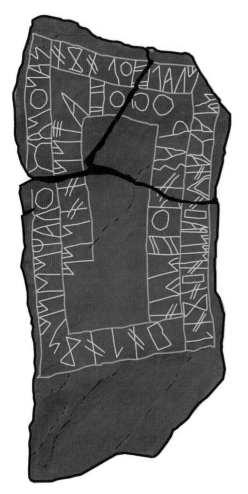

7.4 An inscribed memorial stone from Fonte Velha, Lagos, in southern Portugal, seventh or sixth century BC. The inscription is in the Celtic language but is written in Phoenician script

It is unclear how extensively Celtic was used along the Atlantic seaways at this time, but there is a hint in the late Roman poem the *Ora Maritima* ('Sea-Coasts') that Celtic was also the language of Britain and Ireland in an early period. The names recorded in the poem for the Irish, 'Iverni', and the British, 'Albiones', are both Celtic words. Exact dating is not possible, but the source used may have been a Massaliot periplus of the sixth century BC, though a later source of the fourth century is not impossible. By the end of the fourth century Pytheas was discovering that much of central and western France, including the Armorican peninsula, were part of the Celtic-speaking world.

The Difficult Problem of Origins

Sufficient has been said to show that the hypothesis that Celtic developed in Atlantic Europe has much to commend it. The possible period of origin, suggested by phylogenetics studies to be within the bracket 4000–2500 BC, is not at odds with the fact that Celtic is known to have been a mature language spoken in south-western Iberia by the seventh century BC. All this raises the interesting possibility of being able to bring the archaeological observations into juxtaposition with the philological data.

We know from a substantial body of archaeological evidence that there was considerable mobility along the Atlantic seaways throughout much of prehistory. The origin of the Passage Grave tradition, probably in the Tagus region in the fifth millennium, and its spread, together with the belief systems and skill sets associated with it, as far north as Orkney by around 3000 BC, suggests a high degree of maritime connectivity: some form of lingua franca must surely have been in use to facilitate the communication of such a complex set of ideas. It was from the same region of the Tagus valley that knowledge of metallurgy, together with the ideology of the Beaker package, spread so dramatically around 2500 BC. Again, a commonly understood language would have been a prerequisite for the deep impact made by this phenomenon.

If Celtic had been forming as a lingua franca, called into being by maritime communication in the fourth millennium, then the spread of Beaker ideologies and the accompanying movement of peoples in the period 2700–2400 BC could have been the stimulus that drove the introduction of the Celtic language deep into central Europe along the overland and river routes together with the Bell Beaker package. The restless energies of the time, and the turbulence as disparate cultural groups confronted each other and learnt to coexist, would have created conditions for the development and convergence of language. The interaction, in the fusion zone of the Rhine valley, between the Bell Beaker and Corded Ware–Single Grave communities would have been a time of rapid cultural change, when new vocabularies and new ideas were introduced to the west. The corridor that linked the Rhine valley, the Paris basin, and the Loire valley was, as we have seen, a zone of cultural innovation in the later second millennium: it would also have been a zone in which the pace of language change would have quickened. It was from this broad region that Britain received much of the impetus for its Beaker incursions.

If we were to model a linguistic scenario on the basis of the archaeological evidence, we might suggest that a lingua franca—let us call it 'Atlantian'—grew up along the Atlantic seaways in the period 4500–3000 BC based on the language spoken in the innovative centre of the Tagus estuary and that connectivity over that long period led to the formation of a mature language used for social exchanges and for the communication of complex concepts along the entire length of the Atlantic façade. In the middle of the third millennium new impulses from the Tagus region, reflected in the Beaker package, extended deeply into the continent along the major river highways, taking Atlantian with it. This was a time when Atlantian evolved under the impact of the language spoken by the Corded Ware–Single Grave communities, creating a continental Atlantian closely related to, but distinct from, coastal Atlantian. By c. 2000 BC, while Ireland and the west-facing region of Britain continued to speak coastal Atlantian, much of the rest of Britain, particularly the southern and eastern parts, adopted the continental Atlantian dialect.

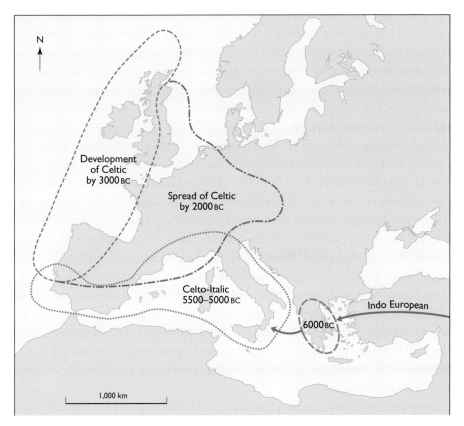

7.5 A model to suggest the stages that may have been involved in the development and spread of the Celtic language following the establishment of Indo-European in south-eastern Europe in the seventh millennium. According to this hypothesis Indo-European was introduced into the central and western Mediterranean with the spread of the Impressed Ware Neolithic and subsequently developed into Celtic as a lingua franca in the Atlantic zone. Later it spread into the rest of western and central Europe with the Beaker phenomenon

Using the term 'Atlantian' is, of course, simply a device for enabling us to think of a likely scenario for language growth in the west freed from the prejudice and pre-conceptions that encumber the word 'Celtic'. But we could simply substitute 'Celtic' for 'Atlantian'. Thus, the languages of Iberia and Ireland represent the early stream of Celtic that developed over the period 4500–2500 BC and which continued little influenced thereafter, while the languages of southern and eastern Britain, and of much of France and Belgium, are the result of changes that took place in and after the mid-third millennium. Could this perhaps explain the difference between Goidelic (Q-Celtic) and Brythonic (P-Celtic)?

If this broad scenario is correct, it would imply that the Celtic language was introduced into central Europe—southern Germany, Switzerland, and the Czech Republic—with Bell Beaker ideology in the latter part of the third millennium, and that it was still spoken in the fourth and third centuries, when migration carried the language to the east. It was entirely reasonable for the Greek and Roman writers who described these unsettling events to refer to the disparate bands of Celtic speakers who descended into the classical world as Celts. While their material culture and social systems were very different from their contemporaries in Iberia, what linked them was a common language.

One more question needs to be explored: how did the branch of Indo-European from which Celtic arose reach Iberia? The most likely context would be with the spread of the Neolithic package from the southern Balkans across the length of the Mediterranean in the sixth millennium BC—a process that can be traced in the distribution of Neolithic material assemblages characterized by pottery decorated with impressions of the cardium shell. Enclaves of Cardial Ware users spread quickly, first to Italy and then to the Mediterranean coast of France and Spain, some sailing onwards through the Strait of Gibraltar to establish themselves in the Atlantic coastal areas of Iberia south of the Mondego estuary around 5000–4800 BC. These settlements were particularly dense in the region of the lower Tagus. It could be argued, then, that the spread of the Indo-European languages, which were to become the Italic languages and into Celtic, accompanied the maritime 'colonization' of the Mediterranean. That Celtic, once it had evolved, spread along the Atlantic sea-routes may be no coincidence.

Attempting to relate archaeology and language is a difficult, and academically dangerous, task, but it is one that we have to face if we are to attempt to write history. The hypothesis of the Atlantic origin of the Celtic languages is more in harmony with the available evidence than the myth of the eastern origin of the Celts, first mooted in the seventeenth century, which formed the basis of the traditional view. It is, I believe, a useful working hypothesis rather than a new myth.

This has been a long interlude—but if the hypothesis offered here is correct, then the inhabitants of Britain and Ireland were speaking Celtic dialects by 2000 BC, and some communities, particularly in the Irish Sea zone, may have been speaking Celtic for a lot longer.

8

The Productive Land
in the Age of Warriors,
1500–800 BC

I N the middle of the second millennium the appearance of Britain and Ireland
began to change as communities started to impose themselves on the landscape, not to create monuments to ancestors or the gods but to take a hold on
the land itself and to tame it once and for all. Man-made boundaries began to proliferate. Regular patterns of fields were laid out: on sloping hillsides the cultivated
areas were shaped by constant ploughing, while on the gravel terraces and claylands
ditches were dug to define and drain the plots. Elsewhere linear earthworks running
for kilometres across the landscape separated vast tracts of territory. The coercive
effort needed for such endeavours implied, at the very least, that communities were
working together to impose a permanent system of management on the land. In the
long history of Britain this was a major revolution. We are seeing here the control of
the productive capacity of the land eclipsing the manipulation of rare raw materials
as the imperative driving society.

Other changes were also in the air. In most regions cremation had become the
most common form of burial rite to survive in the archaeological record, though,
as we shall see, it may only have served a sector of the community, with other means
of deposition, such as excarnation, being the norm. At the beginning of the period
cremations were usually placed singly beneath barrows, but by the end it was more
usual for cremations to be grouped together in flat cemeteries without markers and

without grave goods. The evident implication is that aggrandizement in death was no longer thought necessary, unless, of course, the elite enjoyed a distinctive rite of passage that has left little or no archaeological trace.

That the elite did indeed exist is amply demonstrated by a varied array of bronze weapons, particularly slashing swords and spears, found widely distributed across the landscape of Britain and Ireland. Shields, body armour, and battle horns capable of making a raucous call are more rarely found. Reviewing the panoply of tools, weapons, and other equipment, there can be little doubt that a warrior aristocracy held sway in many, if not most, parts of the country, and that the feast featured large in the social life of the aristocratic class. Whereas, in the preceding period, before c. 1500 BC, status was maintained by control of rare materials and esoteric knowledge and by engaging in distant travels, now it was prowess as a warrior and the ability to uphold the conspicuous consumption of the feast that were the signifiers of society's leaders. Increased agrarian surpluses created by the intensification of production underpinned the fast-growing non-productive class.

Conspicuous consumption is evident throughout the social system, most notably in the deposition of huge quantities of bronze either buried in the earth or thrown into rivers, bogs, or lakes. While archaeologists used to speak of 'hoards', assuming that bronze was buried with the intention that it would be recovered by bronze-founders or by others who had hidden their wealth in times of stress, it is now generally agreed that most, if not all, depositions were made for reasons of ritual. These matters we shall consider later, but what is important here is that over the centuries huge quantities of bronze were taken out of circulation, requiring a constant replenishing of stocks. To meet these needs, trading networks intensified both along the Atlantic seaways and via the east Channel–southern North Sea routes, building on the connections of the earlier period. But whereas previously mobility was probably the sole preserve of the elite, now, it would seem, it was fast becoming the prerogative of traders, who focused their efforts on the shipment of ingots of copper and tin, and scrap bronze for recasting. Gold was also being moved in quantity, and there may also have been other products, now archaeologically invisible, on the move. The intensity of the 'trade' in metals brought the communities on either side of the Channel–North Sea into ever-closer contact, while along the Atlantic seaways a high degree of social interaction among the Atlantic-facing communities is implied by the fact that elite behaviour, manifest in war gear and accoutrements of the feast, was strikingly similar from southern Portugal to northern Scotland. While these broad generalizations apply overall, it would be wrong to give the impression of a uniform culture across Britain and Ireland. There was, as always, much regional variation born of geography and climate, yet the period 1500–800 BC was a time when very similar values and technological skills embraced the islands and the adjacent continent, demonstrating a level of interconnection never before seen.

Climatic Factors

The development of successful agricultural regimes was to some extent dependent on climate. The warm, dry conditions of the second half of the second millennium would certainly have been conducive to the development of stable agricultural regimes, allowing settlement to extend into upland areas up to a height of 400 metres at the peak of the climatic maximum, c.1250–c.1000 BC. But congenial climate was not necessarily the prime cause of the intensification of agriculture in the lowland areas: it will have facilitated it, but the driving forces are more likely to have been social. Sometime around 1000 BC the climate began to change, with the warm, dry conditions of the Sub-boreal period giving way to colder, wetter weather typical of the Subatlantic period. The effect of this on higher upland regions was dramatic. A fall in mean temperature, estimated to be about 2 °C, together with far more stormy conditions, meant that crops could no longer be grown, and there was an overall retreat to below 250 metres. In some regions, like Dartmoor, extensive areas of blanket bog rapidly grew to cover the earlier agro-pastoral landscape. Lowland areas like the chalklands of Wessex were far less affected, if at all, and many of the field systems laid out in the late second millennium simply continued in use, some of them for more than a thousand years.

The effect climatic deterioration will have had on society was dependent on location, but there may have been pressure on land in some areas, which would have led to local tensions. In Ireland the climatic effects appear to have been more widespread. Pollen sequences show that in some regions land went out of cultivation and woodland regenerated, and there may even have been a decline in population by about the middle of the first millennium but the evidence is not entirely convincing. These fluctuations in climate provide an essential backdrop to the regionalism recognized in the different economic strategies developing in the islands.

Enclosing the Land

In the 2,500 years following the arrival of the first farmers in Britain and Ireland around 4000 BC, the wildwoods were cut back to open up the land for cereal growing and animal husbandry. This much is clear from the evidence of pollen sequences, from the survival of charred cereal grains and animal bones, and from the occasional traces of ard marks scored into the subsoil. But surprisingly little evidence exists of how the landscape was organized at this time. The impression gained is that the impact of farming, and indeed of domestic settlement, was slight and perhaps even transient, with cultivated plots being abandoned after a few years and people moving on to more fertile soil, perhaps to return to the old land again a generation or so later. In the century or two after 1500 BC all this changed as across the face of Britain communities began to impose a new structure on the landscape, elements of which are evident in many areas even today.

The impact took on different forms in different geomorphologies. On the chalk downs of southern Britain territories were divided up by ditches running for many kilometres across the countryside, and regular systems of small square fields were laid out, probably in the first instance with timber markers or fences defining individual cultivation plots. Constant ploughing over the years caused soil to move downslope, forming lynchets—negative at the top, positive at the bottom—while the boundaries between grew into hedges and eventually stands of trees, which could be cropped for wood in much the same way as the French *bocage* system. These coaxial field systems, as they are called, are found throughout the chalk downs, and, once established, many of them continued in use for hundreds of years. One example will suffice. At the curiously named site of Windy Dido in Hampshire, close to the border of Wiltshire, it is possible still to trace the linear territorial boundary following the crest of the hills, with up to 90 hectares of coaxial fields systematically laid out on the gentle west-facing slope below, the fields ending on an open area of pasture where the barrow cemetery of the ancestors clustered. The fields seem to have been carefully planned in four blocks of roughly equal size. It is tempting to interpret this as a concerted effort by the larger community to systematize land use and ownership, each block perhaps representing the land of an individual or family. In more low-lying areas, like the Thames valley, a new agro-pastoral landscape was laid out, initially by means of ditches, which would soon have become lined with hedges, the new land division fitting around and respecting the funerary markers of the ancestors. The creation of ponds within the fields suggests multiple use for arable and for pasture. Much the same sort of arrangement can be found around the fen edge in the Peterborough region, but here the boundary ditches defining the plots were carefully designed to facilitate the handling of livestock, suggesting a greater emphasis on pastoralism.

One of the most spectacular examples of organized land apportionment is to be found on the upland massif of Dartmoor, which around 1300 BC seems to have been divided into about ten territorial blocks of roughly equal size by dry-stone walls, known locally as reaves, extending natural boundaries like river valleys. Each territory was contrived to have a range of different ecological zones: river valleys, hill-slopes, and upland moorlands. The open moorland, which was probably the common land

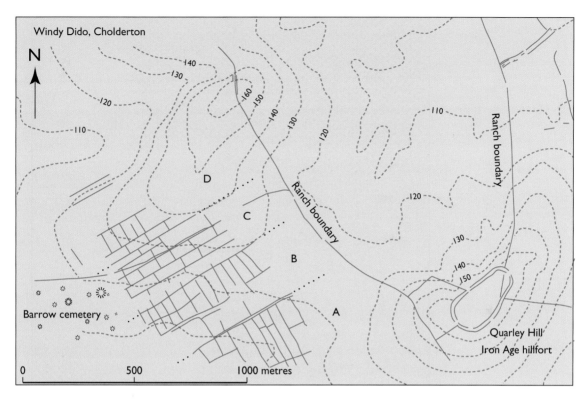

8.1 At Windy Dido, on the chalk downland of western Hampshire, it is possible to trace four blocks of regularly laid-out fields spreading downslope from a ranch boundary ditch which runs along the hill crest. The system is probably late second millennium BC in date. The ranch boundaries continued to function well into the Iron Age, when the hill-fort on Quarley Hill was built

of the larger community, was divided by reaves from the more intensively farmed and settled land, which was subdivided by further reaves into blocks and subdivided again into plots and settlement enclosures. The scale of the scheme of land division was vast: over 10,000 hectares were enclosed, requiring the construction of more than 200 kilometres of reaves. A project of this kind must have involved many separate communities working to an agreed plan under some kind of coercive leadership. In the end it was to no avail because the climatic deterioration that set in around 1000 BC made the moor uninhabitable for the next 2,000 years, driving the population to seek more congenial environments in the heavily wooded lowlands around the upland massif.

The reave system of Dartmoor, the coaxial field system of the chalk downs, and the ditched fields of the midland valleys all imply a high level of social coordination in the appropriation and redistribution of land, but throughout Britain and in parts of Ireland there is ample evidence that communities of much smaller size were beginning to enclose land around their individual homesteads. This is particularly clear

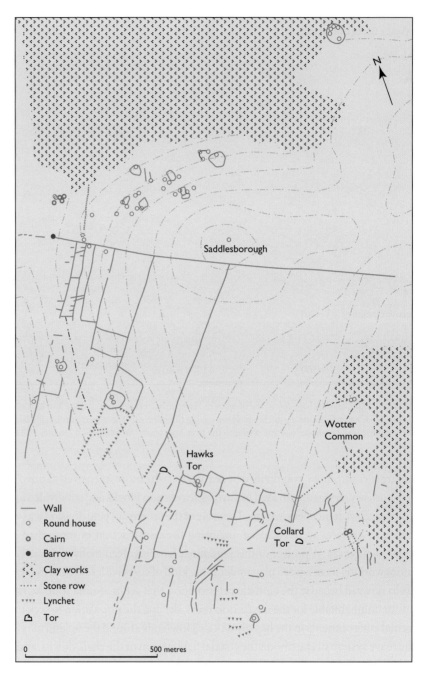

Saddlesborough

Wotter
Common

Hawks
Tor

Collard
Tor

	Wall
○	Round house
◉	Cairn
●	Barrow
	Clay works
	Stone row
	Lynchet
	Tor

0   500 metres

8.2 The system of reaves, paddocks, and settlements on Shaugh Moor and Wotter Common on Dartmoor dates largely to the late second and early first millennium BC

8.3 Part of the system of parallel reaves at Rippon Tor, Horridge Common, Dartmoor

in upland areas in Northumberland and southern Scotland, which were settled for the first time as the climate improved, only to be abandoned during the later decline, leaving the physical remains well preserved. Enclosure would also have been a feature of the lowland settlements, but here subsequent land use has destroyed much of the evidence. In Ireland a marked decrease in tree pollen in bog sequences in the period 1200–1000 BC, and a corresponding rise in grass pollen, suggest a sustained period of land clearance. On the Beara peninsula of the extreme south-west, the well-drained lower slopes of the mountain ridge were cleared for cultivation by small communities enclosing fields and paddocks piecemeal.

Overall the evidence is compelling. Old land was being carefully redivided and new land was being taken as improving climate encouraged expansion into the uplands. Something quite dramatic was happening: the appropriation of land for its productive capacity was now an overriding priority. While this may, in part, have been driven by the pressure of an increasing population, it is difficult to resist the suggestion that the prime cause was the desire to produce agricultural surpluses that could be used in systems of gift exchange, feasting, and the like to maintain and enhance social hierarchies. In other words, society was moving from a sufficer to a maximizer economy. The need to preserve and to store surplus food now led to the building of storage 'barns' and the digging of storage pits within the settlements. With this change would also have come a different attitude to the land. Indeed, it may have been now that the concept of the private ownership of territory first emerged. The drive for agricultural surpluses would also have focused attention on the chthonic deities who controlled fertility and productivity and who needed to be cajoled and placated.

Enclosing the Homestead

At the same time that land was being apportioned and defined by newly constructed boundaries, homesteads were being set up among the fields and often themselves enclosed by banks, ditches, and palisades in various combinations. This, too, was a break from the past, when settlements had been far more diffuse and undefined. Settlement boundaries may have had some protective function, not least in keeping animals away from the living area, but there was probably more to it than that. By enclosing the living area the community was making a visible statement about privacy and ownership. The world was also being divided into 'inside' and 'outside'— zones of different functions where different behaviour sets were appropriate and were expected. Each enclosed homestead, integrated with its fields, was a separate entity defining the family or the kin group: it symbolized the closeness of the human community to its productive land.

The form of the settlements varied from one part of the country to another; there were also variations within regions. On the chalklands of southern Britain fenced enclosures set within low banks were the norm, each enclosure containing on average two circular houses. Sometimes these enclosures were clustered together or were in proximity, joined by trackways creating small hamlets; on other occasions they were isolated among their fields. In Wiltshire and Dorset boundaries were more often defined by ditches. In Essex rectilinear ditched enclosures containing a single centrally placed round house were more frequent. In upland areas like Dartmoor roughly circular stone walled 'rounds' contained stone-built round houses, but similar houses were also found unenclosed among the fields. The same pattern of scattered houses tucked into field edges was also common in Northumberland and other parts of northern Britain. Regional variations must, in part, be a response to different agro-pastoral practices, but they also reflect the regional identities that were beginning to be more clearly defined after the middle of the second millennium.

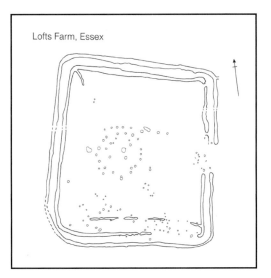

Lofts Farm, Essex

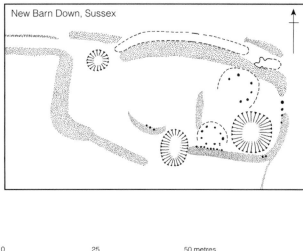

New Barn Down, Sussex

0   25   50 metres

8.4 Two late second- to early first-millennium settlements in the south-east of Britain. *Left*: Lofts Farm in Essex; *right*: New Barn Down in Sussex

8.5 Hut circles and curvilinear enclosures of Bronze Age date on Burton Moor, Wensleydale. The settlement was probably associated with animal husbandry since, at 500 in OD, it is above the level at which crops could be cultivated

Displaying Hierarchies

In some regions disparity in size and form of settlement is suggestive of the appearance of social hierarchies. In central southern Britain a series of larger enclosures of a hectare or more in extent and defined by substantial ditches and banks have been identified in hill-top locations. They stand out in terms of size and grandeur from the normal farmsteads and clearly performed a different function, but insufficient is known of them to be sure what it was. One possibility is that they were the homesteads of a ruling elite, but another is that they were places of assembly for the wider community where they may have congregated at certain times during the year, perhaps for religious ceremonies and to reaffirm social obligations, exchange goods, perhaps enjoy competitions, and generally engage in pursuits that helped to maintain the delicate social network. The two suggestions need not be mutually exclusive since residences of the elite could have provided foci for assembly.

In the east of Britain, in a zone stretching from Kent to Yorkshire, a very distinct type of settlement, the ring fort, has been recognized, dating mainly to the tenth and ninth centuries. As their name suggests, these structures are circular in plan and are defended by one or two concentric ditches backed by palisades or timber-framed earthworks. Some enclose a single large, circular house, while others may contain more than one house. Size and grandeur varies. Thwing in Yorkshire is a double-ditched enclosure over 100 metres in diameter, while Mucking North Ring in Essex is a single-ditched enclosure less than 50 metres across. These sites stand out from unenclosed settlements scattered across the landscape. They were designed to be impressive, and their construction involved considerable effort. It is reasonable to suppose that they represent the homesteads of the elite. Indeed, it may be that, as in other, later societies in Britain and Ireland, social hierarchies were closely defined and the structures reflecting power—defences, gates, towers, etc.—were prescribed according to status. Perhaps the construction of a circular ditched defence marked one status level, while two ditches marked the presence of a lord with a higher status. This highly distinctive structural form was not restricted to Britain.

In Ireland the situation was altogether different. Although small enclosed settlements have been identified in various parts of the country, they are not particularly well known. But what stands out is a series of multivallate forts with widely spaced ramparts occupying prominent positions in the landscape. A number, including Cashel in County Cork, Rathgall in County Wicklow, Mooghaun in County Clare, Dun Aonghasa on Inishmore, Aran, County Galway, and Haughey's Fort in County

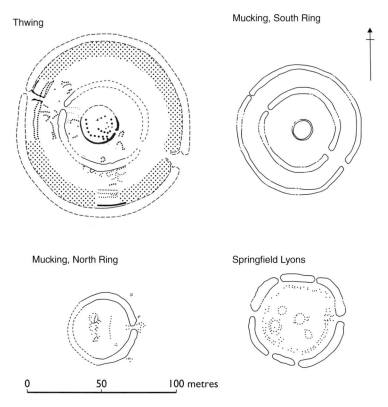

Thwing

Mucking, South Ring

Mucking, North Ring

Springfield Lyons

0   50   100 metres

8.6 A selection of the circular forts of a type found in eastern Britain constructed in the early first millennium BC

Armagh, have now been examined by excavation and all were in use sometime within the period 1200–900 BC. The principal characteristic of these sites is that all had two or three defensive earthwork enclosures arranged roughly concentrically with extensive spaces in between. Where settlement evidence has been found, it was usually within the inner enclosure. At Haughey's Fort two large houses were identified, while Rathgall had one. Excavation within Cashel failed to identify any occupation, but this may well have been because the fort was short-lived and was destroyed by fire in the twelfth century BC.

The huge amount of effort required to build these forts and their commanding positions in the landscape leave little doubt that the construction required the mobilization of the community under the command of a powerful authority, most likely a leader able to make calls on the resources of a considerable region. The multiple lines of enclosure were a mark of status (and may have been added as status increased), but

8.7 The hill-fort at Mooghaun, Clare, Ireland, showing the widely spaced walls of the enclosures

they may also have been functional, providing a place of safety for animals or people brought in from the countryside in times of danger. Forts of this kind are comparatively few in number in Ireland and may well represent the residences of the powerful tribal leaders. Below them would have been men of lesser status about whose settlements we know little.

This brief review has given some idea of the range of settlement within the landscape. Regional variation was considerable, reflecting different economic and social systems and different concentrations of population. Some areas with widely dispersed populations may have been comparatively egalitarian, while in the densely settled areas a more complex social hierarchy seems to have developed. That so much is known about settlement in this period compared to earlier times is mostly due to the fact that more use was being made of enclosing earthworks (making the sites more archaeologically visible), but a contributory factor may

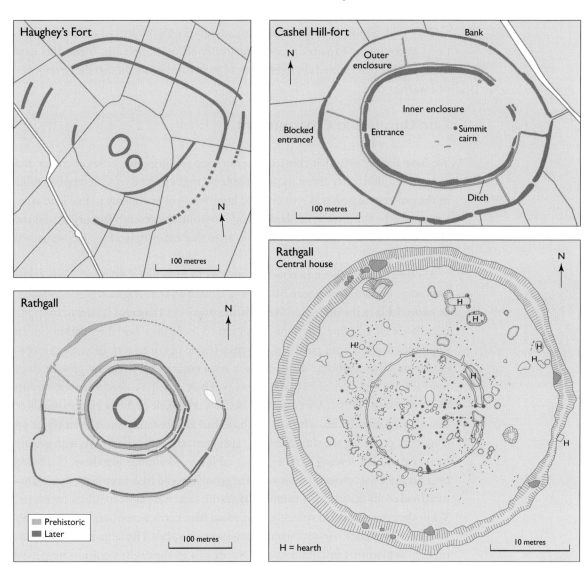

8.8 Three of the large early first-millennium BC hill-forts of Ireland characterized by widely spaced defensive works. Excavations at Rathgall, County Wicklow, showed that the centre of the inner enclosure was occupied by a large circular house

well be that populations were growing rapidly in the improved climatic conditions, encouraging expansion onto previously occupied uplands. It was this new dynamic that determined changes in social structure and facilitated the emergence of a warrior elite.

The Unreliable Environment

We have already seen that climatic deterioration following the onset of colder and wetter conditions after about 1000 BC rendered many upland regions uninhabitable as the growing season was reduced and large tracts of previously usable land were submerged by the growth of blanket bog. Not until the seventh century BC did the climate start to improve again, but even after that many upland regions remained uninhabited.

Another natural phenomenon that appears to have had a dramatic effect on at least some regions in northern Britain and Ireland was the eruption of the Icelandic volcano Hekla in the middle of the twelfth century BC. The event is known from the occurrence of volcanic ash (tephra) preserved as distinct horizons within pollen sequences derived from peatbogs. It is also visible in cross-sections of trees recovered from Irish peatbogs, which show a succession of very narrow growth rings representing a period of extreme stress precisely dated by dendrochronology to the period 1159–1141 BC. A volcano like Hekla was capable of throwing thousands of tons of dust into the air, which could have had a devastating short-term effect on climate by deflecting the sunlight, thus causing much colder conditions with greatly increased rainfall, leading to rising water-tables. In conditions like these, extending over a number of consecutive years, plant growth would have been severely restructured and crops devastated. Communities at this time were close to subsistence level. While they may have had strategies that could have carried them over one crop failure, successive poor harvests would have been a disaster. The large-scale abandonment of settlements in Caithness and North Uist in the twelfth century may have been a direct result of the eruption.

How widespread were the effects of the ash cloud it is not yet possible to say, nor is it easy to distinguish the possible dislocation caused by the eruption from the long-term effects of natural climate change, but one quite sudden change in the economic system can be seen on the chalklands of Wessex at roughly this time. Across the extensive tracts of coaxial fields laid out some centuries before, a new system of linear earthworks, often referred to as 'ranch boundaries', was imposed, redividing the previously farmed land into larger tracts of territory. In many cases it is possible

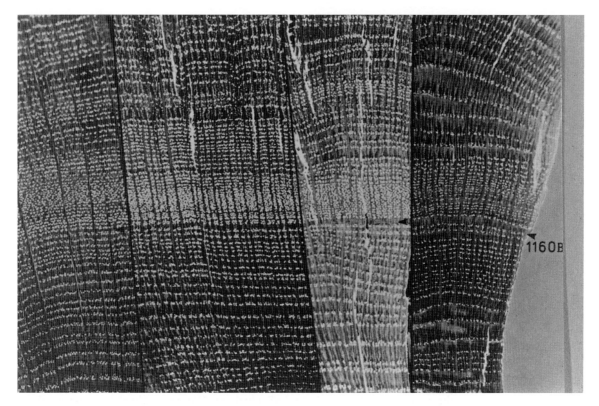

8.9 Section through an ancient oak found preserved in an Irish bog. The tree rings can be accurately dated by dendrochronology. The wide ring from c.1160 BC is followed by a number of extremely narrow rings, implying considerable stress in the growing conditions for a number of years. This was probably caused by ash clouds from the eruption of the Icelandic volcano Hekla temporarily affecting climate

to see with great clarity how the new ditches sliced straight across the small square arable plots, rendering them unusable. It is not easy to say what all this means, but it was clearly a major act of reapportionment and one possibility is that arable down-land was now turned over to raising stock on a large scale. It is even possible that the Hekla effect was the prime cause, with the population turning to animal husbandry in the wake of successive failing harvests. But there are other explanations. Since not all the fields need have been abandoned, it is possible that the ranch boundaries simply reflect the imposition of a communal husbandry strategy running alongside a lineage-based agrarian system, the 'private' fields being given over after harvest to communal use. Another equally plausible explanation is that on the thin chalk soils constant cropping over several centuries depleted the soil of nutrients and destroyed its structure, forcing the change to a more pastoral regime. This gains some support from the fact that it is only on the areas of thin soil that the ranch boundaries focus; on the more clay-rich chalk soils arable farming continues without apparent interruption.

The Dead and the Gods

The way in which communities dispose of their dead reflects their deeply held beliefs and their attitudes to the gods. Until the seventeenth century BC the predominant mode, visible in the archaeological record, was inhumation: cremation was practised, but not widely. This began to change in the early centuries of the second millennium, with cremation becoming the norm. We saw this in the Wessex II burials (Chapter 6), where the ashes of the deceased were usually placed in an urn and buried beneath a barrow, maintaining the tradition of single burial, with the status of the individual, or of the lineage, marked by grave goods. But during the second half of the second millennium symbols of exclusivity died out and instead we find cremation burials clustering together in discrete cemeteries without accompanying grave goods. In Ireland, Wales, and much of northern Britain these small cemeteries were usually set in grave mounds, either earlier burial mounds or, more usually, mounds constructed specifically for the purpose. In the south-east of Britain a rather different tradition, that of the urnfield, developed. Urnfields were flat sites, with no distinguishing mound, with the urned cremations buried in individual pits. Numbers of burials could vary from comparatively few to more than a hundred, and some of the urnfields were in use for several centuries. One of the most comprehensively excavated urnfields, found at Kimpton near Andover in Hampshire, comprised 164 cremations, all but six of these buried in urns. Burial began in a small way in the eighteenth century and continued for a thousand years.

The urnfields of south-eastern Britain belonged to a Europe-wide practice characteristic of the latter part of the Bronze Age. It was one of the traditions that served to bind the communities of the south-east of the island to the Continent, creating a single cultural zone—a theme to which we shall return.

If cemeteries like Kimpton served a local community over many generations, they can only account for a comparatively small percentage of the people who died during the period of use. This implies that the rest of the deceased were disposed of in a way that has left no direct archaeological trace. One possibility is that they were cremated and the cremations scattered or thrown into rivers or other watery places. Another is that bodies were excarnated, perhaps on specially constructed platforms, and left to the elements and the birds. Excarnation was certainly practised widely in the fourth millennium and probably continued throughout the first millennium in most parts of Britain and Ireland, where formal burials of any kind were extremely rare, so the continuation of the practice throughout the third and second millennia alongside cremation is not at all unlikely. A tradition of excarnation could imply a belief in the spirit of the departed entering the realms of the gods of the sky. Much the same concept may lie behind the popularity of cremation, which creates the vision of the spirit rising into the sky with the flames. The practice of consigning what remained of the deceased to the earth or to water may have been bound up with the idea of returning part of the once-living to the chthonic realms to ensure the continued fertility of the land. All speculation of course, but necessary if we are to try to gain insight into the minds of the people.

Watery Places

Another change in behaviour that becomes very evident during this period is a great increase in the practice of depositing bronze-work in rivers, bogs, and lakes, and as 'hoards' buried in the ground. The practice becomes popular from the thirteenth century across the whole of Ireland and Britain, and continues in some areas until the sixth century. In a wider context, it can be seen to be part of a belief system embraced widely across Atlantic-facing Europe.

Bronze finds are particularly prolific in rivers, some, like the Thames and Trent in Britain and the Shannon and Bann in Ireland, producing enormous quantities of material. Discovery, of course, is biased towards rivers that have been extensively dredged, but even allowing for this, some stretches of certain rivers stand out as being exceptionally favoured, an outstanding example being the lower Thames, from which hundreds of items have been recovered. While casual loss and the erosion of riverside settlements may have accounted for a few of these finds, there can be little doubt that a great bulk of the material was deliberately thrown into the flowing water in ceremonies to propitiate the gods. Deposition in lakes and bogs was also widely practised and is particularly evident in Ireland, where watery contexts of this kind are extensive. Indeed, most of the bronze-work found in Ireland had been deposited in water.

Behind the broad picture of watery deposition lies a more nuanced pattern of behaviour. For example, a high percentage of the rapiers and swords recovered are found in rivers rather than bogs or lakes, while metal vessels, shields, and battle horns are more frequently found in still water. A detailed study of the East Anglian fenland added further detail, showing that most of the complete swords and rapiers were found in the channels of the major rivers, while hoards of metalwork tended

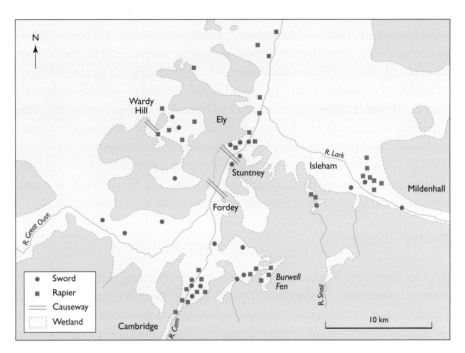

8.10 Part of the fens to the north of Cambridge, showing the distribution of Bronze Age swords and rapiers. All would seem to have been deposited in wetland locations

to be deposited in still water or on dry land nearby. Weapon fragments were invariably found on dry land. Clearly a complex belief system controlled the practice of deposition.

Hoards of bronze-work buried on dry land vary considerably. They may contain complete items, scrap, or ingots, and they may also vary in size from a few pieces to colossal hoards like the 6,500 fragments buried together at Isleham in the Fens. For many years it was conventional to think of hoards of this kind as material buried with the intention that it would be recovered either by itinerant bronze-smiths or by communities in the face of some threat. But more recently hoards are being seen as offerings made to the chthonic deities, a tranche of society's wealth deliberately removed from circulation. Perhaps, since bronze came from rocks, it was believed that some had to be returned to the earth to ensure continuing productivity.

The depositing of weapons and other war paraphernalia in water no doubt represents a different set of beliefs. The simplest explanation would be that the warrior felt a need to dedicate his weapons to a deity presiding in the water as thanks for a successful engagement, perhaps as the result of a vow, or it could be that the weapons were those of defeated enemies. There does seem to be some concentration of weapons in the vicinity of fords, where engagements between opposing forces may well have taken place. Battles at fords and crossing places feature large in the later vernacular literature of Ireland. An alternative explanation would be that the weapons were those of dead warriors whose cremated remains may have been thrown into the water at the same time. The various possible explanations need not be mutually exclusive. Behind the observed behaviour could lie the simple overarching belief that weapons were the property of the gods and had eventually to be returned to them.

Concentrations of bronze objects at certain locations in watery contexts suggest that there may have been specially sacred places for deposition. One such has been excavated at Flag Fen in East Anglia. Here a long timber trackway led out across open water to a large timber platform, which, dendrochronological evidence shows, was being built and repaired between 1365 and 967 BC. Alongside the trackway were found many hundreds of bronze objects—weapons, tools, and ornaments—which had been thrown into the water over a long period of time. Clearly the site had a special significance as a place where the deities could be engaged. Another location was found during dredging operations in the River Trent at Clifton near Nottingham. Here, quantities of bronze swords, rapiers, and spearheads were found together with log boats, in association with an area of piling for a causeway. It may well be that timber causeways of this kind, leading out into rivers or lakes, were the approved places from which to make offerings to the gods. The practice, once established, was long-lived, extending throughout the first millennium BC: indeed, much of the spectacular weaponry of the Iron Age has come from rivers, lakes, and bogs. Deposition on land in the form of hoards, on the other hand, was largely over by the sixth century, by which time other ways were being found to propitiate the gods of fertility, as we shall see in the next chapter.

Following the Seasons

The intensification of agriculture after the middle of the second millennium would have made a careful appreciation of the changing seasons all the more important to the livelihood of the community. Indeed, it may have required an adjustment in time management and the creation of a calendar more designed to meet the demands of the farming year than one relying on the solstices. By the end of the first millennium BC it is known that in Gaul the year was divided into four quarters, Samhain, beginning on 1 November, Imbolc on 1 February, Beltane on 1 May, and Lughnasadh on 1 August, and this same calendar was in operation in Ireland in the first millennium AD. Since it is closely attuned to the farming year, the probability is that the calendar goes back much further and may well have developed at a time when the intensification of agriculture was getting under way in the second millennium. Samhain heralds the quiet winter period when people are at home repairing and making equipment and tending the livestock that are being overwintered. Imbolc marks the time when lambing and calving takes place and the ewes start to lactate, and land has to be prepared for spring sowing. At Beltane cattle are driven through fires to cleanse them of vermin and all the animals are put out to summer pasture. Lughnasadh is the period of harvesting and the preparation of the grain for storage, for turning livestock onto the harvested fields, and for weaning lambs. The culling of the flocks and herds, with the accompanying feasting, probably took place in the days leading up to the beginning of Samhain, when the old year ended and the new year began. This major turning point in the annual cycle was appropriated by the Christians to be the festival of All Saints and is still widely celebrated in its pagan form as Hallow-e'en. The agrarian calendar differs from the solar calendar of the fourth and third millennium, based on the equinoxes and solstices, and is probably to be regarded as part of the great transformation that was taking place in the mid-second millennium.

The Rise of the Warrior Elites

The thirteenth century BC saw the emergence of warrior elites across much of Europe, including Britain and Ireland, made apparent largely through their bronze weaponry and their feasting equipment. In the preceding period elites distinguished themselves in burial with grave goods, including ornate daggers and halberds, symbolic of rank. The development of the short-bladed rapiers might hint at a more aggressive stance, but it was the appearance of heavy slashing swords in the thirteenth century, based on continental types that were beginning to reach Britain through the eastern Channel–southern North Sea networks, that marked the change to a full warrior society.

The warrior panoply included swords, a range of spearheads, and shields, all of bronze. Helmets, cuirasses, and greaves of bronze, known on the Continent, have not yet been found in Britain or Ireland. Another accoutrement of warfare was the horn, for producing a resounding blast to disconcert the enemy. Over 120 bronze horns have been found in Ireland, representing two types: end-blown and side-blown. They were evidently made in Ireland for local use. Elsewhere, where bronze horns are rarer, cows' horns could have been made to serve the same purpose.

The discovery in Ireland of leather shields and of wooden proformers used to mould them on is a reminder that leather would have made effective protective armour, and it may well be that helmets and body armour were made of leather in Britain and Ireland in preference to bronze. Leather would have been far more resilient than bronze and far better able to turn a blow, as experiments have vividly demonstrated. Bronze shields and some of the oversize and unwieldy spearheads that have been found may indeed be little more than flashy parade armour, to be put aside for leather shields and sleeker spearheads when real fighting began. In warrior encounters bombastic display would often have been a prelude to open combat.

No doubt there were regional differences in mode of warfare and changes over time. Spears were far more popular in Britain than in Atlantic France. In north-west France a new sword type, known as the carp's-tongue sword, became popular in the ninth century. These swords combined the heavy slashing blade with a long narrow point effective for thrusting at close quarters. Although carp's-tongue swords are known from south-east Britain, they are usually found only as scrap in hoards, the Britons preferring the heavy slashing swords.

The reality of conflict is vividly displayed by two human burials found at Tormarton in Gloucestershire. Both were of young men about 19 years of age and both had been speared. One had a hole made by a lozenge-sectioned spear in his pelvis; the other had been speared in the pelvis and the lumbar vertebrae and in both wounds the broken tips of the spears remained. The bodies seem to have been

8.11 Two continental swords imported into Britain. *Left*: A Hemigkofen type from the River Thames in London; *right*: an Erbenheim type from the River Lea in London

8.12 *Top*: Leather shield from Cloonbrin, County Longford; *bottom*: bronze shield of Nipperwiese type from Long Wittenham, Oxfordshire. Note the lozenge-shaped perforation on the inner ring (*left*) made by a spear thrust

dumped without ceremony into a ditch or pit. A very similar example was found near Dorchester-on-Thames, again with a broken spear tip wedged in the pelvis. It is, of course, impossible to be certain that these young men were warriors who had died in battle; they could equally well have suffered from a surprise attack or ritual murder. But their mutilated bodies indicate something of the level of violence prevalent in society: evidently spears were used for more than hunting.

The Feast

Another aspect of warrior society was feasting. The feast would have provided the opportunity for those aspiring to high social status to offer lavish hospitality for their peers. By doing so they demonstrated their command of resources and provided a social context in which status could be displayed, debated, and contested. Classical writers describing Gaulish society much later, in the second century BC, give vivid descriptions of feasts in which meat was apportioned according to the perceived status of the recipient. If no one objected to the distribution, then the status quo was regarded as agreed by all, but if someone was not content, they could object, and objection could, in extreme cases, lead to bloodshed and readjustment of the social order. The classical descriptions also emphasize how the warrior elite had to be carefully seated according to status. These were hierarchical occasions vital to maintaining the delicate structure of society in a time of volatility. Although we have no comparable descriptions of British and Irish society at the end of the second millennium, some such system may well have prevailed.

Evidence for the feast comes from the distribution of artefact types essential to a successful gathering: the bronze cauldron for boiling the meat, the flesh-hook for lifting the joint from the cauldron, the roasting spit providing an alternative means of cooking, and the bronze situla (bucket) to contain the drink, probably some kind of mead or beer.

Cauldrons and situlas originated in central Europe, and the forms were avidly adopted in the Atlantic zone, there to be adapted by local craftsmen in the period 1300–1100 BC. The earliest of the locally made cauldrons, known as Class A cauldrons, are found in south-eastern Britain, where foreign swords of European urnfield type are also found. It was probably from here that the idea spread across the British Isles to Ireland. At about the same time cauldrons and buckets began to be made in western France: in Spain the adoption was a century or two later. Flesh-hooks seem to have been introduced in much the same way, beginning in the south-east of Britain, where one has actually been found with a Class A cauldron at Feltwell in Norfolk. The rotary spit for roasting meat was a later introduction, developing in the period

8.13 (*a*) Bronze cauldron from the River Thames at Shipton-on-Cherwell, Oxfordshire. (*b*) Distribution of the two types of cauldron used in feasts in Atlantic Europe in the Late Bronze Age

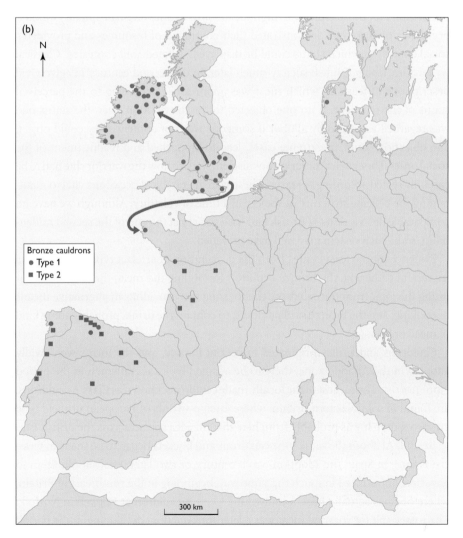

8.14 (*a*) Bronze flesh-hook from Dunaverney, County Antrim, Ireland. (*b*) Distribution of Late Bronze Age feasting equipment in Atlantic Europe. The flesh-hooks were used to lift the boiled meat out of the cauldron, while the spits were for roasting. The different distributions may suggest different culinary preferences

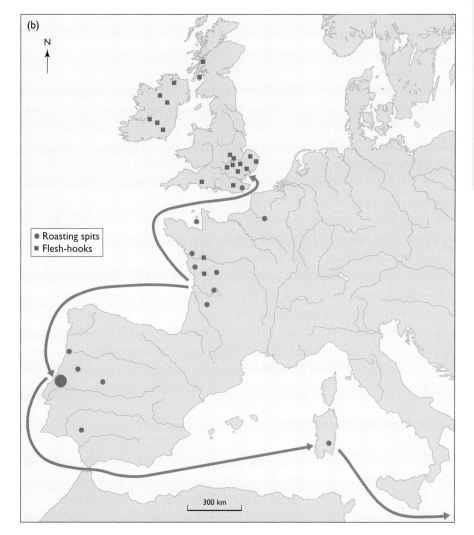

● Roasting spits
■ Flesh-hooks

1100–950 BC. It probably originated in north-central Portugal and spread from there along the Atlantic seaways to western France. Only one example is known in Britain, from Kent, suggesting that in these islands boiled meat remained the traditional fare. The distribution of this assemblage of feasting equipment, stretching along the entire Atlantic seaboard of Europe, reflects not only the adoption of common behaviour systems but also the exchange of elite gear along the seaways. The growth of this Atlantic system will be considered in more detail below.

The feasting probably took place in the residences of the elite, perhaps in the large circular houses found in the ring forts of Ireland and the eastern parts of Britain. One can imagine the cauldron hanging from the roof apex over a centrally placed hearth, with the guests sitting around telling tales of past deeds, drinking, and boasting, the atmosphere becoming increasingly aggressive as the evening progressed.

The existence of a warrior elite in Britain and Ireland raises a number of questions about the working of society. In all probability the elite were non-productive, relying on a peasant class to grow crops and rear the animals. The Irish law tracts of the first millennium AD describe comparable societies in which the 'producers' were dependent on the elite for protection. One method of binding the classes was for the upper class to own cattle, which they 'leased' to their farming clients to look after, requiring a tithe to be paid on a regular basis in terms of food, newborn livestock, and materials. Since the elite 'invested' their wealth (their cattle) in the producing class, it was in their own interest to protect them, thus creating a stable patron–client relationship. Some such system may well have prevailed in some parts of Britain and Ireland in the Bronze Age, though there is likely to have been much regional variation. Given the unstable equilibrium of the times, there may also have been rapid changes in the social system. In this context we might recall how the field systems of the central southern British chalkland were redivided at some stage around 1000 BC into large tracts of land demarcated by ditched ranch boundaries. Is it possible that this major upheaval reflected a change to intensive livestock farming brought about by the emergence of a new elite imposing itself on the peasant community? In the age of the warrior it is not at all unreasonable to suppose that there were periodic upsets in local social systems.

The Channel as a Centre

We saw in the previous chapter how, in the first half of the second millennium, the English Channel became a centre for maritime interaction. To begin with, activity focused on the western part of the Channel, with close links developing between Wessex and Armorica, but from about the seventeenth century BC more easterly networks had begun to develop, extending deep into west central Europe. The nature of the early networks is not entirely clear, but a good case could be made for the suggestion that the maritime journeys were probably undertaken by the elite functioning in a system in which command of exotic materials and esoteric knowledge gained through travel provided the prestige as well as the resources necessary to maintain the system. By the middle of the second millennium all this was beginning to change. The reasons are probably complex and interwoven, lying partly in the social changes brought about by agro-pastural intensification and partly by the fact that the pressure on rare commodities was declining as they became more commonly available.

What we now see is a remarkable degree of cultural similarity developing across the seas on both sides of the eastern Channel–southern North Sea zone, a similarity that can only have come about by social interaction on an entirely unprecedented scale. The cultural convergence, for such it is, is manifest in a number of

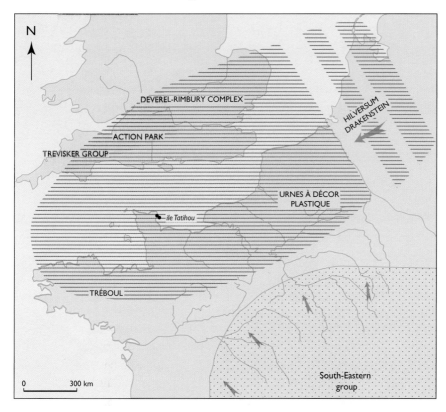

8.15 In the second half of the second millennium BC the communities of south-eastern Britain were in very close contact with those living on the adjacent coasts of northern France, to such an extent that much of the material culture and settlement archaeology on both sides of the Channel developed close similarities. The shaded area shows the extent of the contact zone

ways. Settlements are closely similar on both sides of the Channel, with circular houses and four-post granaries (or hayrick stands) set in enclosures between field systems. The settlement excavated at Île Tatihou, Manche, is almost indistinguishable from contemporary settlements in Wessex in the fifteenth and fourteenth centuries, while later, in the early first millennium, the ring forts of eastern Britain can be paralleled in Normandy at Malleville-sur-le-Bec, Eure, and Cagny, Calvados. The material culture, too, is very similar, most particularly the pottery, which shows a closeness in style on both sides of the Channel developing over the period 1400–800 BC. In the earlier part of the period it is the Deverel–Rimbury complex of south-eastern Britain that compares with the Tréboul wares of Armorica, the *urnes à décor plastique* of Normandy and Pas de Calais, and the Hilversum–Drakenstein wares of Belgium and the Netherlands. Later the facing territories share traditions

8.16 Pottery and a saddle quern from a Bronze Age settlement at Île Tatihou, Manche, in Lower Normandy. The material is closely similar to finds from contemporary sites in central southern Britain

of plainer, more angular pots, and later still, incised and stamped decorated wares. This parallelism in development over many centuries implies continuous and intensive contact spanning the generations. Nothing like it has been seen before.

The explanation of such close similarities must lie in a mobility of population at all levels, not simply on elite contact or periodic trading expeditions. We must envisage people spending time away from their home territories across the seas engaged in gatherings leading to social and political engagement involving intermarriage and the establishment of long-term allegiances. Intensity of contact would have varied over time and from region to region, but it must have remained at a sufficient level to create and maintain the highly distinctive eastern Channel–southern North Sea cultural complex. The sea was now the prime means of communication: it no longer separated communities but bound them tightly together. So, with fluctuations in intensity, it was now to remain throughout the first millennium BC and first millennium AD.

The cultural bridge between south-eastern Britain and the Continent saw the influx into the islands of new types of material culture emanating from central Europe. Cauldrons, buckets, and flesh-hooks have already been mentioned; other important introductions included the heavy slashing swords with blade and hilt cast as one, named after the German site finds from Erbenheim and Hemigkofen. Imported swords of these types are found clustered in the lower Thames valley and in the Seine valley and inspired local developments in both regions. One of the distinctive types to develop in Britain and Ireland is the Ballintober sword, named after a find from County Mayo in Ireland. Ballintober-type swords are found in considerable number in the lower Thames valley and are scattered across southern Britain and the northern part of Ireland. On the Continent they are found concentrated in the Seine and Loire valleys. The type was probably made in the Thames region in the twelfth century and was copied in Ireland, reflecting close contacts between the two islands at the time. Another weapon type commonly found in Ireland and Britain was the basal-looped spearhead, a socketed spearhead with openings in the base of the blade to facilitate attachment. These spears may have developed first in Ireland and spread to Britain and the Continent. The discovery of a mould in Charente region shows that they were also being manufactured in Atlantic France, and Irish examples eventually found their way to southern Iberia.

Other items that demonstrate the connectivity between Ireland, Wales, south-eastern Britain, and north-west continental Europe are gold ornaments—torcs, bracelets, earrings, and hair rings—that span the period from the thirteenth to the seventh centuries. A substantial number of them come from Ireland, where, indeed, the types may have originated and many of the items may have been made, the Irish

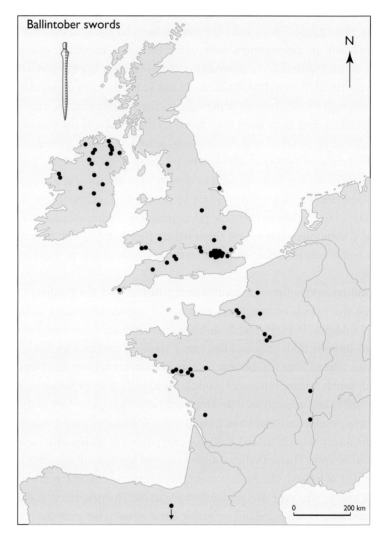

8.17 The distribution of the distinctive Ballintober sword shows the extent to which elite items of metalwork were being exchanged over considerable areas, linking Ireland, southern Britain, and north-western France

goldsmiths being prolific and inventive, particularly in the thirteenth to twelfth centuries and again in the ninth and eighth centuries. The distribution of the different products suggests that two distinct networks were in use, one linking Ireland to the south-east of Britain and the other favouring direct contact with Scotland. The distribution of 'hair rings'—a small penannular ring of lead covered with sheet gold—serves to demonstrate both patterns: a small number are found scattered through Scotland with a rather large concentration in Wessex and Sussex. It was probably

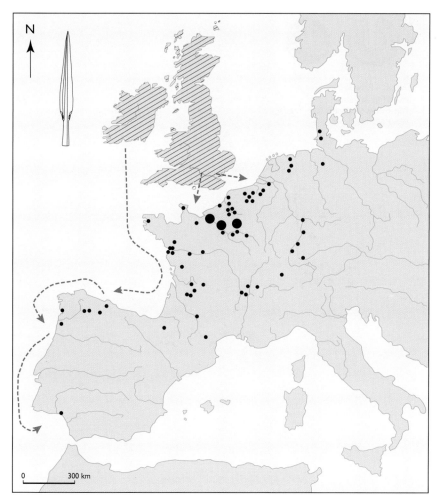

8.18 Basal-looped spearheads, probably made in Ireland, were commonly found in Ireland and Britain and were exported to northern France and along the Atlantic seaways to north-western Iberia

from here that Irish hair rings found their way to the Seine valley and the lower Rhine regions. While it is quite possible that such ornaments were transported as gifts, the possibility remains that some at least may have reached their final destination worn in the hair of travellers. Whatever the explanation, they reflect a pattern of close ties between Ireland, Britain, and the Continent.

The surviving distribution patterns of bronze and gold metalwork are the result of many different social processes. At one level there is simple movement through loose social networks where artefacts are exchanged as gifts, the engaging commu-

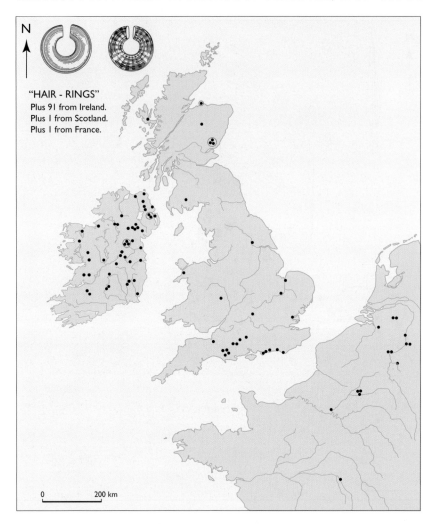

8.19 Gold hair rings of the Late Bronze Age were made in Ireland and exported to central southern Britain and to the Continent between the Seine and the Rhine

nities remaining at arm's length from each other. This was probably the system in use over much of Britain and Ireland. At the other extreme there were the very close social interactions involving the movement of peoples through alliance mechanisms that gave rise over time to cultural convergence of the kind we have seen in the Channel zone. A gold hair ring could have arrived in Wessex from Ireland as the result of successive cycles of gift exchange, but its onward journey to the Paris basin may have been in the hair of a Wessex girl on her way to honour a marriage agreement. Simple distribution maps seldom allow us to distinguish the processes of mobility and the human stories lying behind them.

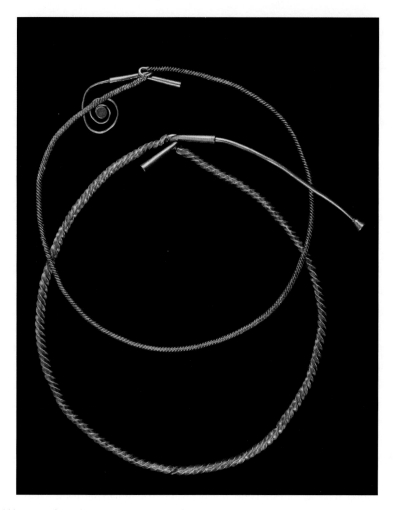

8.20 Gold bar torcs from the Derrinboy hoard, Offaly

The Atlantic Seaways

The networks of interaction along the Atlantic seaway came into their own in the period 1300–800 BC, gaining a new visibility through the distribution of bronze artefacts that visibly allows the changing extent and intensity of the network to be charted in some detail.

During the first half of the second millennium long-distance exchanges along the Atlantic seaboard were few, and for much of the time Britain's principal contacts were with north-western France and the Netherlands. In the fifteenth century Wessex, previously a centre of exchange, seems to have become eclipsed as new networks developed between Ireland, north Wales, and East Anglia and north-west Europe, and by the fourteenth century the distinctive eastern Channel–southern North Sea culture began to develop, linking the whole of southern Britain to north-western France and Belgium. From the Channel core new networks began to develop, extending north to northern Germany and south, first to the Loire valley and later to the Médoc, the systems made visible in the distribution of palstaves, rapiers, and spearheads.

It was during the thirteenth and twelfth centuries, the age of the warrior elite, that the full Atlantic system emerged as ships now crossed the Bay of Biscay, bridging the gap between the Gironde and north-western Iberia. This is the period of the slashing swords, the shields, and the feasting equipment. At first, contacts with western Iberia were tentative, but by the middle of the twelfth century all this had changed and Iberia became a full member of the Atlantic system, contributing the roasting spit to the array of feasting equipment in use throughout much of the zone. It is in this period that the Iberian community began to adopt the practice of depositing bronze-work in hoards, a ritual practice that they may well have learnt from the north.

The movement of materials and ideas along the Atlantic seaways was now on an impressive scale, leading to a great similarity of material culture along the entire zone. This is vividly demonstrated by the grave stelae found in south-western Iberia, which depict the equipment of the warrior, notably his circular shield, sword, and spear—types that can readily be found as far afield as Ireland and Britain. Individual artefacts also travelled considerable distances, like the Irish basal-looped spearheads that ended up in a ritual deposit in the harbour of Huelva in southern Spain.

One of the inventions of Iberian swordsmiths that was to have a considerable influence on the north was the carp's-tongue sword. With its heavy slashing blade and a long, narrow, pointed end, it was probably a hybrid between Atlantic slashing swords and west Mediterranean types of rapier, combining the slashing and thrusting properties of each. The earliest type of carp's-tongue sword (named after the Huelva deposit) probably developed in the early tenth century in southern Iberia, and some varieties found their way northwards through the exchange system to north-western France, where they were eventually copied by local swordsmiths, producing a variant known as the Nantes type, probably in the period 950–875 BC. The Nantes type and its variants were widely circulated in north-western France, their distribution stretching from the Médoc in the south to Pas de Calais, with a few reaching as far north as the lower Rhine. They are also found in the south-east of Britain, particularly in the Thames valley, but here they occur usually broken up or as scrap in hoards, the Britons preferring to use their own type of heavy slashing sword.

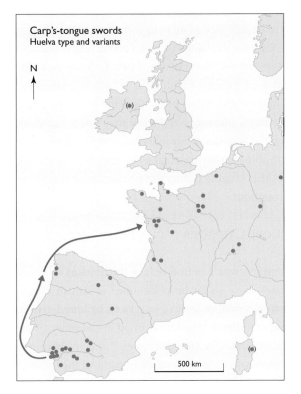
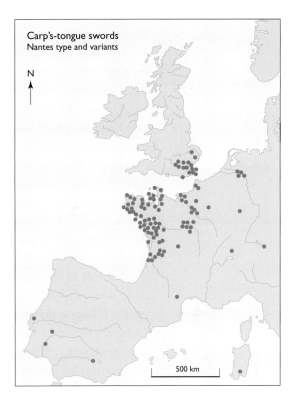

8.21 The carp's-tongue swords of the Late Bronze Atlantic zone probably first developed in south-western Iberia. A later variant that developed in the Nantes region became widespread in north-western France and south-eastern Britain. Together they show the vitality of the Atlantic bronze industry

By the end of the tenth century the role of Iberia in the Atlantic system had much diminished. It was now being drawn into the Mediterranean sphere, and, with the appearance of Phoenician traders along the Atlantic coast in the ninth century, the extended Atlantic networks came to an end. Further north, however, in north-west France, carp's-tongue swords continued to flourish and a lively trade was maintained with south-eastern Britain. Carp's-tongue swords and associated items were carried as scrap to Britain; British slashing swords named after a type found at Ewart Park in Northumberland and British socketed axes were widely circulated in Atlantic France. The *floruit* of this cross-Channel engagement lasted from *c.* 875 to *c.* 800 BC, but some carp's-tongue material was still in circulation in the early eighth century. During this time many hundreds of hoards were consigned to the earth.

Standing back from all the sometimes confusing detail, we can see that the exchange networks, focusing at first on the Channel core, expanded dramatically in the thirteenth century to embrace the whole of the Atlantic seaboard. But in the tenth century the network began to shrink back again to its former size. At its height the Atlantic system involved not only the exchange of metal and artefacts but also the adoption of common value systems and the transfer of new technologies. The sheer quantity of material transported implies a high level of mobility along the coastal route and inland up the major rivers. Much of the time the journeys would have been short-haul, the ship's masters sticking to the water they knew, but some certainly crossed the Bay of Biscay, and occasional intrepid explorers may have made even longer journeys, with Iberian ships venturing as far as Ireland. But against the fluctuating scope and intensity of the Atlantic traffic, the Channel core sea-routes remained alive with sea traffic throughout.

Abandoned Ships and Lost Cargoes

The first half of the second millennium was a period rich in the remains of sewn-plank boats: altogether seven vessels have so far been identified in British estuaries. The following period is less prolific, with only three wrecks so far found: two in the Severn estuary at Goldcliff and at Caldicot, and one at Brigg in the valley of the River Ancholme, a tributary of the Humber. The Goldcliff vessel, dating to about 1170 BC, is represented now by two planks reused in a later trackway, while of the Caldicot boat only three fragmentary timbers survive in a context suggesting a date of about 1000 BC. More of the Brigg vessel has survived, the favoured interpretation being that it was a flat-bottomed raft-like construction suitable for transporting loads by river. Radiocarbon dates of c.825–c.760 BC show it to be the latest of the series. The collection is hardly impressive considering the intensity of maritime activity during the period, but this reflects little more than accidents of survival. All it allows us to say is that the sewn-plank boat-building traditions, already flourishing at the beginning of the second millennium, continued into the first millennium with little noticeable change except that some specialized rivercraft were now being built along with sea-going vessels.

Another source of evidence for sea-going is provided by several offshore finds of metalwork, which are generally interpreted as the remains of wrecks, all boat timbers having rotted or been washed away. The most spectacular was found at Langdon Bay in the shadow of the chalk cliffs of Dover. Here, scattered over a limited area of sea-bed, 360 bronze tools and weapons were found, dating to the period 1300–1150 BC, mostly continental types that could have been assembled along the seaboard of the eastern Channel–south North Sea. The most obvious interpretation of the find is that it was the remains of the wreck of a ship bringing bronze scrap from the Continent to be resmelted by British smiths. However, the possibility that it was a ritual deposit dumped offshore, perhaps to placate the deities of the ocean, cannot be entirely dismissed.

8.22 Bronze Age tools and weapons recovered from the sea-bed at Langdon Bay, Dover. Much of the material is of northern French origin and may well have been brought to Britain on a ship that was wrecked just off the White Cliffs

Another prolific location for underwater finds is the Salcombe estuary in south Devon. Here, three discrete sites have so far been identified. The first, at Moor Sand, produced a hook-tanged sword, six other swords, and two palstaves, all dating to the thirteenth to twelfth centuries but spread over a considerable area of sea-bed. The second site, known as Salcombe, yielded a varied array of material of British and north-west European origins, thirty-one items in all, including rapiers, swords, palstaves, spears, a cauldron ring handle, an agricultural implement from Sicily, a gold torc, and a gold armlet. Again, the material dates to the thirteenth to twelfth centuries, but there is also a fragment of a carp's-tongue sword of the ninth century. Although these two collections are generally considered to be wrecks, it remains a distinct possibility that the finds were lost or thrown overboard from trading ships frequenting the estuary. This could explain the scattered nature of much of the material and the long date range.

The third Salcombe find is more convincing as a wreck. It produced 259 copper ingots and twenty-seven tin ingots together with a leaf-shaped sword and three gold bracelets, all thought to date to *c*. 900 BC. This raises the interesting question whether the cargo was of British material about to set out for the Continent or whether it was an inbound continental cargo.

The Langdon Bay assemblage and the remarkable collection of finds in the Salcombe estuary are probably just the tip of the iceberg, accidents of recovery resulting from the activity of observant underwater explorers. No doubt there is a great deal more to be found along the shores and estuaries of the Channel.

The Middle and Late Bronze Age—the period from *c*. 1500 to *c*. 800 BC—was a time of dramatic change, brought about, at least in part, by a rapid rise in population facilitated by an improved climate which made large tracts of uplands available for colonization. Everywhere throughout the islands communities grew, developing their own distinctive characteristics—settlement types, economic strategies, and material culture—but at the same time they shared in a widely available array of elite metalwork, both bronze and gold, produced by specialists and exchanged over considerable distances. These networks bound Britain and Ireland inextricably to a wide swath of continental Europe stretching from the Rhine to the Algarve. Within this broad zone of interaction lay the Channel core, or, more precisely, the eastern Channel and southern North Sea and the lands on either side, a region which, through constant maritime interchange over the centuries, had developed to become a cultural community with a distinct character of its own. It was to retain its identity throughout the first millennium, providing a theatre for a variety of human interactions, culminating in invasion.

9

Episodes of Conflict,
800–60 BC

I N the terminology of the Three Age System, the Late Bronze Age gives way to
the Iron Age around 800 BC, but the change in technology was far from sudden:
iron was introduced slowly, only replacing bronze as the favoured material
for weapons and tools by around 500 BC in Britain and perhaps a century or two
later in Ireland. But there were other significant changes occurring around 800 BC.
The previous 100 to 150 years or so had been a time when huge quantities of bronze
were consigned to the ground as 'hoards' or were thrown into watery locations, presumably as offerings to the deities—many times more than the quantities disposed
of in this way in previous centuries. It was a spectacular display of society's desire
to 'destroy' its wealth. But after 800 BC in Britain the amount disposed of declined
steadily until, by 600 BC, the practice of deliberately taking bronze out of circulation
was virtually at an end, though weapons, now of iron, continued to be consigned to
rivers throughout the following centuries.

In Britain the period 800–600 BC, most commonly referred to as the Earliest Iron
Age, was a time of readjustment. The hold on the land intensified as more of the landscape was taken into productivity and the eastern Britain–Continental exchange
network remained strong, continuing much as before, with Ireland well integrated
within it. This period is characterized by an assemblage of bronze metalwork named
after a lake deposit found at Llyn Fawr in south Wales.

In the following period, the Early Iron Age (*c.* 600–*c.* 400 BC), the old, long-established exchange networks seem to have disintegrated, and Britain relapsed into relative isolation except for continued close relations between the communities on either side of the eastern Channel narrows. This is a time when regional groups can begin to be recognized, distinguished by their own distinctive pottery styles. Ireland, too, plunged into an unaccountable era of isolation and the Iron Age communities become very difficult to identify. The regeneration of forests, at least in some areas, has suggested that there may even have been a significant decline in population.

From *c.* 400 to *c.* 150 BC, a period commonly called the Middle Iron Age in southern Britain, the island was drawn increasingly into the continental orbit. The introduction of the rite of chariot burial in Yorkshire implies close links with the adjacent continent, even perhaps a limited immigration, while the adoption of European La Tène art styles for decorating elite metalwork may have been initiated by skilled craftsmen coming to Britain to serve local masters. But the islands were now beginning to receive the attention of the Mediterranean world. The historian Herodotus, writing in the fifth century BC, claims to have heard vague rumours of tin-rich islands in the Atlantic, but it was left to Pytheas, an explorer from Massalia (Marseille), to make a first-hand study of Britain about 320 BC. He was probably the first to observe the tin trade between Cornwall and the ports of Atlantic Gaul. He wrote about it and much else in his book *On the Ocean*, a text widely read in the classical world. From this moment Britain enters into written history.

The Middle Iron Age was also the time when the British communities continued to develop very distinctive regional cultures, some of them quite isolated, with each region having its own 'history'. In some areas, notably central southern Britain, extending from the Channel coast, through Wessex and Gloucestershire, to the Welsh Marches, the growth of heavily defended hill-forts is indicative of unsettled conditions. That violence flared up from time to time is clear from episodes of burning at some forts and from bodies scarred with marks of violence. In all probability, in the more densely settled areas, warfare was endemic.

The Late Iron Age, beginning in the middle of the second century, saw a revitalization of the maritime networks owing, at least in part, to the impact of Roman commercial activities in Gaul. New economic imperatives were coming into force, leading to a rapid increase in trade, while uncertainties stirred up by the increasing Roman presence in the south of Gaul caused new confederations to grow in the north of the country. It was in this atmosphere of political self-awareness that social ties on both sides of the Channel were strengthened, new alliances were formed, and mobility became the order of the day. In 58 BC Julius Caesar marched into free Gaul, setting in train a process of conquest and consolidation that was to change the world. His brief forays into Britain in 55 and 54 BC introduced the Britons to the reality of Roman power: they also provide us with first-hand accounts of the people, their leaders, and their political machinations. Although Caesar's armies departed the islands with evident relief, Britain was now, in reality, an adjunct of the empire.

The End of the Old Order, 800–600 BC

The huge quantities of bronze taken out of circulation in Britain and deposited in the ground or in water during the ninth century have intrigued archaeologists for decades. Why would a society feel impelled to do this? Explanations have varied. One view, that it was done under the guise of propitiating the gods to remove surplus metal from circulation in order to increase its rarity and thus to maintain or enhance its value, seems a little over-complex, while to argue that it was a panic reaction to the appearance of iron is unconvincing. Deposition was clearly the direct result of religious or ritual compulsions, but what set it off we can only guess. Perhaps it was a response to a crisis, real or perceived, brought about by successive crop failures or the spread of disease among livestock. This was a period of extreme cold, wet weather, which might have led to failures in the productive systems. In such a situation, the chthonic deity would need propitiating with offerings, and what more appropriate than society's metal wealth? But this is speculation. Whatever the reason, the crisis seems to have passed by about 800 BC, at least in the east of Britain, where the burial of hoards ceased altogether. In central southern Britain and the south-west, the deposition of hoards continued during the Llyn Fawr phase but on a much-reduced scale, ending altogether after the middle of the seventh century. In north-western Gaul, however, particularly in Armorica, the eighth and seventh centuries saw a frantic desire to feed the earth with bronze, so much so that a particular type of socketed axe was made specifically for deposition. They were usually left untrimmed after casting, and many retained the clay core that had formed the central socket. They also had an exceptionally high lead content, rendering them soft and virtually useless. These Armorican axes were buried in huge quantity in Brittany and Lower Normandy in more than 300 hoards containing around 40,000 axes. In Brittany alone it is estimated that, for all the axes produced for deposition, it would have required 7–8 tonnes of copper, 2 tonnes of tin, and 5–6 tonnes of lead. Here was consumption on a conspicuous scale.

South-western Britain and Armorica were clearly in contact during this period, with Armorican axes being imported into Britain to be included in hoards of the Llyn Fawr period. Although the volume of metal depositions in Britain was consistently lower than in north-western Gaul, the continuation of hoarding and the exchange of axes suggest that the two areas enjoyed a close relationship through maritime links

9.1 Hoard of Armorican axes, arranged as originally found, from Langonnet, Morbihan, in Brittany, seventh century BC. The axes, with a high lead content, were not intended for use but may have had a value in exchanges or for ritual

criss-crossing the western Channel throughout the eighth and into the seventh century. Two British ports are known to have been active at this time: Mount Batten in Plymouth Sound and Hengistbury Head, overlooking Christchurch Harbour: it is quite possible that the Isle of Portland and the well-protected Weymouth Harbour offered further landfalls.

Another way in which south-western Britain and western France distinguished themselves as a close-knit system was that they appear to have turned their backs on the new sword type, the Gundlingen sword, which was becoming popular in the more easterly regions in the first half of the eighth century. The Gundlingen sword, with its characteristic chapes (the metal binding at the lower end of the sheath) in bag-shaped and winged form, was adopted throughout central and western Europe, eastern and northern Britain, and Ireland, and was for a long while considered to be a central European invention adopted by the horse-riding elite. Indeed, it was at one time widely believed that these warriors from the Hallstatt cultures of the Continent

9.2 Socketed bronze axes of the seventh century were made in Armorica and were found extensively in the region, shown cross-hatched, usually in large hoards. In Britain and Ireland they are found usually singly or in small hoards with other items. The concentrations in Cornwall and central Wessex suggest the main points of entry

9.3 The promontory of Mount Batten in Plymouth Sound served as a port-of-trade in the Late Bronze Age and Iron Age. It may have been the island of Ictis referred to by classical writers as the place where tin was traded

invaded Britain, bringing a knowledge of iron and, perhaps, the Celtic language with them. Recent detailed study of the typological development of swords, together with a new series of associations, some with precise dendrological dates, has, however, completely changed our understanding. It now appears that the Gundlingen sword developed from the Thames type of sword (which was itself a variant of the popular British Ewart Park sword) around 800 BC, the most likely area of origin being the Thames valley, where large numbers of swords of all these types have been found. From the Thames valley the popularity of the sword spread westwards into north-eastern France and the Low Countries and quite widely beyond, and north-eastwards, across central Britain and into Scotland and Ireland. The distribution map gives a vivid impression of the widely flung networks that must have existed at the time.

In continental Europe the popularity of the bronze Gundlingen sword was comparatively short-lived and it was soon replaced, in the middle of the eighth century, by a larger, heavier iron sword known as the Mindelheim type (after the site in Bavaria where it was first discovered). Since only one Mindelheim sword has been found in Britain—in the deposit at Llyn Fawr—and none at all in Ireland, the implication must be that the islanders were content to continue to use their familiar home-grown products.

That the swords were an attribute of a horse-riding aristocracy is shown by the frequent occurrence of swords together with sets of horse gear in inhumation burials throughout continental Europe. In Britain, where the burial rite probably continued to be excarnation, such associations do not occur, but items of horse gear have been found in eastern Britain, extending into Wales and southern Scotland. They are of continental style and probably reflect the importation of high-quality riding horses complete with their tack. Other items of continental inspiration and production include razors and brooches of various kinds. It is not impossible that the brooches arrived attached to the dresses of incoming brides.

Taken together, then, the evidence for the period from the eighth to the middle of the seventh century suggests that Ireland and much of Britain, except for the central south and south-west, were in contact with north-eastern France and the Low Countries by way of maritime links across the southern North Sea. For the most part, social obligations were maintained by gifts of aristocratic gear appropriate to a horse-riding aristocracy and quite possibly by the exchange of brides. These interactions would have been effected through the coastal communities, and it is no surprise to find considerable similarities in domestic culture, particularly pottery styles, on both sides of the sea from East Sussex to East Anglia and from the Somme to the Rhine. Such similarities speak of frequent interactions between communities sharing familial bonds.

The importance of the sea is further demonstrated by notable similarities in the form and decoration of pottery found in coastal regions of south-east Britain from Dorset to Yorkshire. The implication of this is that the maritime communities retained contact one with another through cabotage along the coastal corridor. This was probably so for much of the British and Irish littoral zone, but only in areas where decorated pottery was in frequent use do the effects become archaeologically visible.

It is difficult to judge the intensity of long-distance exchanges between Britain and Europe after the middle of the eighth century, when the Gundlingen swords went out of fashion on the Continent. The iron

9.4 A Gundlingen sword and its winged chape found, possibly with a burial, at Ebberston, Yorkshire

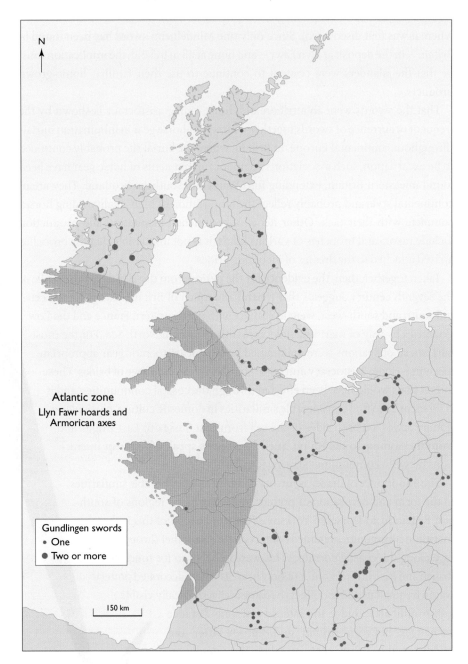

9.5 North-western Europe in the early eighth century, showing the distribution of the Gundlingen sword – a type that may have developed in the Thames valley. In Britain and Ireland, the swords were usually found in watery locations. In southern Ireland, south-western Britain, and north-western France, Gundlingen swords are very rare. It is in just this region that the old Bronze Age tradition of burying bronze hoards still continued. The different patterns of deposition may suggest a cultural divide

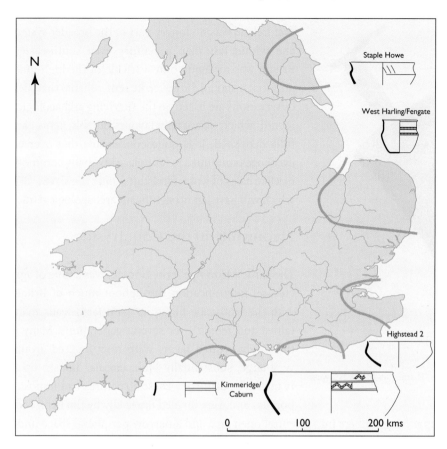

9.6 In the eighth and seventh centuries BC the coastal regions of Britain used a distinctive style of decorated pottery. It is quite possible that this coastal distribution reflects communities that maintained contact through coastal cabotage

Mindelheim sword from Llyn Fawr, dating to around 700 BC, and the scatter of horse gear, including a phalera (decorative disc) of central European type found in a hoard at Sompting, West Sussex, dating to *c.* 650 BC, show that some material was still arriving in Britain. Items continued to drift in throughout the sixth century: an antenna-hilted sword and a simple cauldron found in the Thames, an iron dagger in a bronze sheath also from the Thames at Mortlake (a type that gave rise to a local school of copies), a bronze ribbed pail from Weybridge in Surrey, and the handle of a Rhodian flagon from Minster in Kent. Together they demonstrate an exchange in elite items focused on the Thames valley and its approaches, reflecting the continuance of long-established social networks, but, compared to what had gone before, the scale of activity was much diminished. Indeed, after about 750 BC it would seem

9.7 Hallstatt D dagger from the Thames at Mortlake, west London

that Ireland was no longer part of the broader system, and within less than a century even south-eastern Britain was receiving only a trickle of the high-grade imports. It should, however, be remembered that these observations are based on the surviving archaeological record, which necessarily favours durable items carefully deposited. It is quite conceivable that overseas exchanges continued to take place involving commodities like bales of wool, foodstuffs, and even slaves, all of which will have left no significant archaeological trace.

Meanwhile in the Countryside

The Earliest Iron Age (800–600 BC) was a time of agricultural intensification throughout much of Britain, with the landscape filling up with farmsteads maintained and rebuilt over several generations. Many of the newly created farms were now focused around very large, substantially built, circular houses up to 15 metres in diameter. These structures had imposing porches and were divided internally by the main roof-supporting timbers into a central open area and a narrow peripheral space under the eaves. They were so large that in all probability they had an upper floor, possibly with a roof loft as well. These were not mere huts but grand residences, the Iron Age equivalents of medieval halls, in which all the affairs of the lineage were worked through, where the resident family lived and feasts could be comfortably accommodated. Houses of this kind have been found throughout Britain from the south coast to Scotland. In the south, where agrarian production dominated, they usually stand in their enclosed farmyards amid above-ground granaries and hay-racks and underground silos for storing the seed-corn, their field system spreading out all around.

Another feature of the period is the hill-top enclosure, usually a large area of 15 hectares or more enclosed by a bank and ditch. These structures tend to concentrate in the central swath of Britain from Wessex to the Welsh borderland. They include places like Balksbury hill-fort near Andover in Hampshire, some 18 hectares in extent, and the massive Walbury, high on the Hampshire Downs, where 33 hectares are enclosed. We know comparatively little of these sites, but where magnetometer

9.8 Outline of large Early Iron Age roundhouse excavated at Flint Farm, near Andover, Hampshire, cut into the chalk bedrock. The inner ring of timbers would have supported the roof, while the outer groove took the wattle wall. The massive postholes for the porch lie on either side of the measuring rod

surveys have been undertaken, the interiors appear to be largely empty of major features. This has been confirmed by the almost total excavation of Balksbury, where the interior was found to be open except for a number of hay-racks and a few lightly built circular shelters. The enclosing bank and ditch, however, showed evidence of continuous maintenance. A careful study of the internal soil profile suggested that the enclosure had been used to corral flocks and herds over long periods of time. Taken together the evidence would seem to suggest that these large enclosures were designed to contain animals at certain times of the year when it was necessary to gather them together for castration, culling, redistribution, and other tasks necessary for efficient husbandry. That some of these enclosures are

9.9 The early hill-top enclosure of Walbury, Hampshire. The comparatively slight bank and ditch defines a very large enclosure of 33 hectares

associated with linear ditches suitable for constraining and driving animals gives further support to the argument. The dating of hill-top enclosures still needs to be refined, but what little evidence is currently available suggests that they may have begun in the ninth century and continued to function well into the eighth and possibly seventh century.

In central southern Britain, where most of the enclosures are found, the agricultural regimes would seem to have concentrated around two foci representing different levels of social organization: the farmsteads with their privately owned fields organized at family and lineage level providing the centre for arable operations; and the hill-top enclosures, where the pastoral activities of the broader community were ordered. While it may be that the animals were communally owned, it is more likely that livestock management in these densely farmed landscapes required intercommunity coordination. In any event, the annual round-up would have been an occasion for the population to gather together to celebrate, feast, and give thanks to the gods.

How extensive this southern system was is unclear, but farmsteads with large circular houses extend into northern Britain, and large hill-top enclosures are found in some regions in eastern Scotland. But each ecological zone will have supported its own socio-economic regime. Population densities, climatic conditions, and geomorphology together determined the relative importance of cereal growing and animal husbandry and the systems used to manage them. Britain in the eighth and seventh centuries was a land of micro-regions, each with its own practices and identity. As the population grew, so the expression of that identity came increasingly to the fore.

The Descent into Regionalism, 600–400 BC

The two centuries or so around the middle of the first millennium saw the crystallization of regional cultures across the face of Britain, a process that was to create the structure that framed the next thousand years of development. Standing back from the minutiae of the archaeological data, Britain can be divided into three broad settlement zones: an eastern zone characterized by open villages and enclosed homesteads, a western zone of strongly defended homesteads, and a central hill-fort-dominated zone separating the two. One pleasingly simple way to view this divide would be to see the eastern and western zones as systems in equilibrium while the hill-fort zone represented a liminal space between them, a marcher region of inherent instability.

The eastern zone, stretching from the Thames to the Firth of Forth, presented a varied array of landscapes. Each had its own settlement patterns and economic systems, but a broad divide can be made roughly at the Humber estuary. To the south— an area dominated by the midland river valleys—farmsteads and villages, often unenclosed, prevailed. North of the Humber, in the more broken landscape with areas of upland, small, enclosed farmsteads were the norm.

The western zone, extending from Cornwall to the Northern Isles, is much more varied, not least because of the distance covered and the separation of the different regions by large tracts of sea. The characteristic settlement is the homestead suitable for a single or extended family, often enclosed with earthworks or walls offering a degree of defence. In the latter part of the Iron Age the emphasis on strength

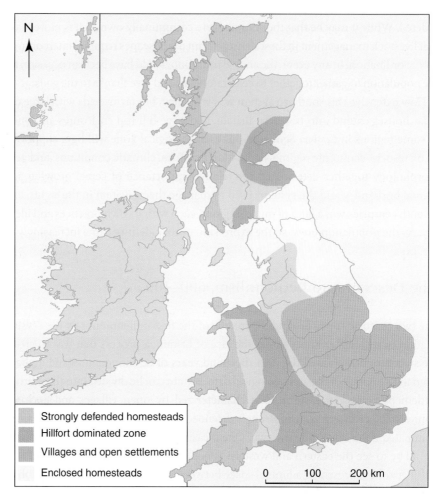

N

Strongly defended homesteads
Hillfort dominated zone
Villages and open settlements
Enclosed homesteads

0   100   200 km

9.10 In Britain in the second half of the first millennium BC it is possible to trace different types of settlement pattern, suggesting broad zones in which the socio-economic systems were much the same. There is a marked contrast between the west of the country and the east

increases, giving rise to a multitude of defended homesteads: the rounds of Cornwall, the raths of western Wales, and the brochs and duns of western Scotland and the Northern and Western Isles: each region has its own readily recognizable vernacular.

The hill-fort-dominated zone stretches from the south coast to north Wales and from the Solway to the Firth of Tay. It is here that hill-forts proliferate in landscapes thickly scattered with smaller settlements. Hill-forts have provided fertile ground for discussion in the past and there is still much to be learnt, but many excavations over the last century or so in the southern region allow certain generalizations to be made. Most of the hill-forts were constructed during the sixth and fifth centuries BC, and all are characterized by a rampart and ditch of defensive proportions and are accessed usually through two gates on opposing sides. The ramparts at this stage were usually vertically fronted, with timber or stone revetments, and were maintained and repaired at intervals throughout their lives. Evidence for use, however, varies considerably. Some, like Maiden Castle in Dorset and Danebury in eastern Hampshire, contained streets with houses, together with storage facilities and evidence of domestic activities suggestive of permanent occupation. Others showed little trace of internal structures or sustained use. Viewed spatially, it is difficult to resist the impression that these early hill-forts were sited to dominate discrete territories, often defined by natural features like river valleys.

So how to explain them? The simplest is to suppose that the hill-fort was the product of the larger community, comprising a group of lineages, designed to express its social cohesion and its ownership of a territory. The very act of building the hill-fort

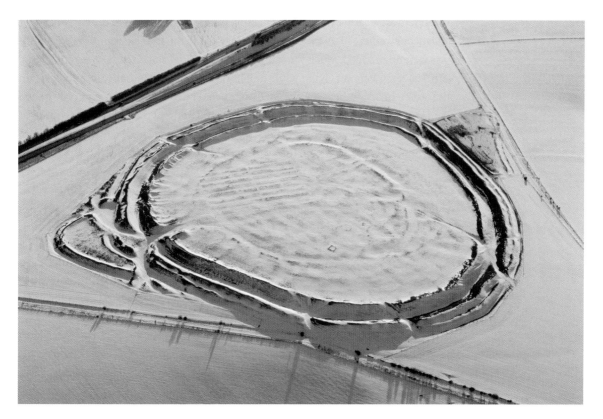

9.11 The hill-fort of Yarnbury, Wiltshire, is typical of a developed hill-fort with massive ramparts and ditches and complex entrance earthworks. The largely levelled defences of the earlier hill-fort can be seen inside

required concerted effort coordinated by an authority: it would have been a process that brought the society together in a common pursuit. It may be seen, therefore, as a defined space proclaiming social unity and set aside for community activities. What these actually were may have varied from place to place and time to time. The opposed entrances suggest some form of procession, one gate for entrance, the other for exit. Such processions would have been appropriate to social gatherings to honour the gods or celebrate seasonal festivals or meetings called to make communal decisions. In times of stress the earthworks could have served as defences against raiders and, in some cases, sectors of the community may have chosen to take up residence for short or extended periods of time.

As time progressed, there seems to have been a coming together of the individual polities to create larger social units. In such a situation once-active hill-forts may have ceased to have meaning and been abandoned while others became central places of enhanced significance serving a larger territory. This can be seen in many parts of the country, most clearly on the eastern Hampshire chalkland, where the early hill-fort of Danebury emerged as the dominant place while the four surrounding early hill-forts were abandoned. Much the same situation can be seen on the Dorset chalkland, with Maiden Castle surviving while neighbouring sites fell into disuse. Why certain sites were chosen to become the focus of an extended territory we can only guess. The site may have been particularly venerated and perhaps the polity whose centre it was exerted leadership over the others: there may even have been coercion. These are issues impossible to decide on the available archaeological evidence.

The increased emphasis on local and regional identity is also evident in the pottery of the period. In the Earliest Iron Age in the south-east of Britain, where pottery was widely used, broad regional groupings can be distinguished in the styles of pottery decoration. After about 600 BC a larger number of discrete styles begin to appear. If we accept the assumption that decorative styles reflect a community's view of its own ethnicity, then, from the sixth century onwards, the populations of the south-east must have been developing, and wishing to display, visible signs of their local identities. Over the whole of Ireland and much of the rest of Britain, except for the Western and Northern Isles, pottery was not used in this way. This does not mean, of course, that other means of visual display were not in use, but simply that we have no archaeological evidence of it. One has only to remember the importance of tartan fabrics as indicators of allegiance among the Scots and the Irish to realize how limited the archaeological record is. Similarly, body decoration and hairstyles have been used to proclaim shared identity among many societies across the world in the more recent past. It is worth remembering that the earliest recorded name for the British, Pretani, noted by Pytheas in the fourth century, means 'the painted ones'.

Meanwhile in Europe

The foundation of the Greek colony of Massalia on the Mediterranean coast of France in about 600 BC was a significant moment in the history of western Europe. Greek and Etruscan traders had been visiting the regions for several decades, building friendly relations with the natives of both the coastal zone and the more inland regions, easing their way with gifts of elaborate metal vessels—what one archaeologist has referred to as 'introductory offers'. But the act of founding a colony, with others following quickly at Agathe (Agde) and Emporion (Ampurias) further to the west, ringing the Gulf of Lion, marked the formal beginning of a long and intensifying interaction between Mediterranean civilization and the elites of west central Europe. The sixth century saw the development of a discrete focus of exchange centring on a broad zone stretching from eastern France to southern Germany, where the local Hallstatt chieftains were able to acquire Mediterranean luxury goods to display and consume in feasts and in elaborate burial rituals.

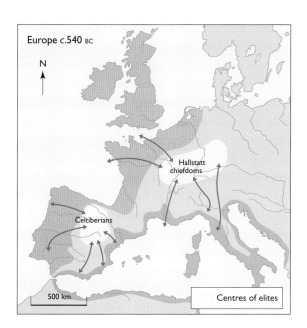
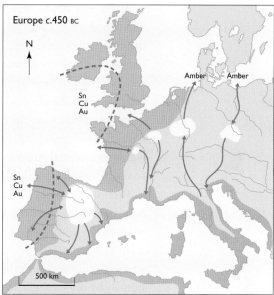

9.12 The acquisition of raw materials such as metals (tin, copper, and gold) and amber from the Atlantic and North Sea zones by the Mediterranean world led to the emergence of communities whose power lay in their ability to control the movement of goods. The two maps illustrate the elite centres in the sixth and fifth century. In the fifth century, while the Celtiberian centre continued to develop in Iberia, in the middle regions of Europe the old Hallstatt culture was replaced by new centres sharing the La Tène culture

By the middle of the fifth century the elite zone had moved outwards to the north and west and had become more dispersed, with the main centres of innovation focusing in the regions of Bourges, the Marne, and the Moselle, and in Bohemia. Each centre commanded a major river route to the Atlantic, the Channel, the North Sea, or the Baltic, strongly suggesting that the new elites based their power on their ability to control access to raw materials from the north-western fringes of Europe—commodities such as tin, gold, and amber, all much in demand in the Mediterranean world to the south.

These La Tène elites had access to luxury goods from the south, but rather than simply copying them, their own inventive craftsmen developed forms and decorative styles of great originality, interpreting the classical ideas until they became abstract and unrecognizable. In this way an entirely new barbarian art style, Celtic art, emerged. Other aspects of Mediterranean culture were also adopted. Etruscan chariots inspired local vehicle makers to create fast battle chariots, which, in many of the La Tène communities, were adopted as an appropriate accessory for a member of the elite.

At the end of the fifth century and beginning of the fourth, the social system, which had maintained the warrior elite for several generations, broke down into a mêlée of folk wanderings, with hordes of people moving out of their native territories to set up new homes in distant lands. There were probably many causes for the movements, among them population growth. Some of these migrations are referred to in the classical sources. Many people moved into the Po valley, while others migrated along the Danube to settle in the Carpathian basin. From these new bases raiders spread still further, deep into Italy, into Greece, and eventually eastwards into central Anatolia. There were the famous Celtic migrations about which so much has been written.

There is no evidence, either textual or archaeological, to suggest that large migrant bands moved northwards or westwards from the original homelands, though this was still a popular belief until comparatively recently. What has confused the situation is that La Tène art, and no doubt the belief system that it represented, was adopted quite widely in the west—in north-western France, Britain, and Ireland—initially by the local elites. There is nothing surprising in this given the networks of connectivity that existed: exotic artefacts of La Tène manufacture could quickly have passed into the peripheral regions as gifts or as traded commodities, and trained craftsmen might follow to serve new masters keen to embrace the exotic art and the intriguing mysteries of magic and belief embedded within it.

The Spread of La Tène Art Styles to Britain and Ireland

The two centres of La Tène aristocratic development nearest to the British Isles were those focused on the Marne and on Bourges, the first linked to the Channel via the Seine and the Somme, the second to the Atlantic via the Loire. It is likely that both routes had a part to play in the transmission of La Tène art styles to Britain. The Seine–Somme routes favoured existing networks that linked to the Thames and to the eastern coasts of Britain. In the sixth and fifth centuries the Thames valley had become a centre for the manufacture of fine daggers, heavily influenced by dagger types developing in eastern France and southern Germany. It is quite possible that these schools of elite weapons manufacturers simply continued in operation, absorbing new styles and fashions and making them their own throughout the succeeding centuries. The two earliest pieces of La Tène art known in Britain, both decorated scabbards for daggers, found at Minster Ditch, North Hinksey, in Oxfordshire and at Wisbech in Cambridgeshire, demonstrate clearly the first faltering attempts of local craftsmen to copy the new art styles. Later, in the fourth and early third centuries, running spiral motifs now popular on the Continent were incorporated into the British repertoire to create splendid items like the highly decorated shield-boss from the River Trent at Ratcliffe-on-Soar, Warwickshire, the sword sheath from Standlake, Oxfordshire, and a pommel fitting found in the Thames at Brentford. In addition to these parade weapons the art style was now beginning to be used on personal items like brooches. Later third-century British products included two swords dredged from the Thames at Hammersmith, their sheaths decorated with 'dragon pairs', a motif popular in Hungary at the time. By the second century local schools were flourishing, producing accomplished work of great originality such as the shield and scabbard from the River Witham near Lincoln, two shield-bosses from the Thames at Wandsworth, and a bronze pony cap from Torrs in Scotland. This British group share sufficient characteristics to suggest that they may have come from the same workshop. Eastern British craftsmen continued to make high-quality products like the famous Battersea Shield and Waterloo Bridge Helmet and the gold torcs of East Anglia, but by now there were craftsmen throughout Britain using La Tène motifs to enhance a range of products besides weapons.

While it must be admitted that the dating of these aristocratic items is open to debate, when considered on stylistic grounds they do seem to represent a long-lived tradition of British craft development extending over centuries, always keeping abreast of continental fashions yet maintaining their own originality.

In parallel with this eastern tradition it is possible to identify a rather different western tradition of transmission, which had more to do with metal vessels than

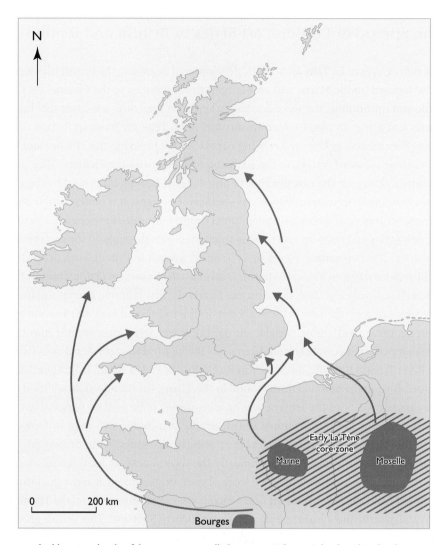

9.13 A highly original style of decoration, generally known as 'Celtic art', developed in the elite centres of Europe in the early La Tène period in the fifth to fourth century BC. Knowledge of the new art style spread to Britain and Ireland along the Atlantic and North Sea routes

with weapons. Armorica was closely linked to the La Tène elite centre of Bourges by means of the Loire valley route, and it was through imported metal items that the Armorican craftsmen learnt La Tène decorative styles, best represented now on pottery. Certain Armorican pots of the fourth century, some bearing La Tène style decoration, clearly copy small bronze bowls that no longer survive in the Breton archaeological record but are known in the south-west of Britain and Ireland, the most notable being the animal-handled bowl from Keshcarrigan, County Leitrim.

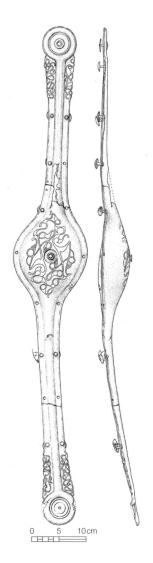

0 5 10cm

9.14 (*far left*) Decorated shield-boss found in the River Trent, near Ratcliffe-on-Soar, Warwickshire. The shield was probably made by a British craftsman well versed in continental styles in the fourth or third century BC

9.15 The decorated top (*above*) and bottom (*left*) plates from a sword sheath found at Standlake, Oxfordshire. The decoration is close in style to continental work of the fourth century BC

The implication of these vessels is that the networks linking Armorica and western Britain were responsible for transmitting craft skills ultimately deriving from the main La Tène centres. The craftsman who made the famous Cerrig-y-drudion 'hanging bowl' (now thought to be an item of ceremonial head-gear), found in a stone cist in north Wales, may have derived his inspiration in this way. There are certain close similarities between the motifs used and those that decorate Armorican pottery of the period.

If we are correct in seeing the western seaways as one of the networks along which La Tène craft styles reached Britain and Ireland, it raises the question of the relative

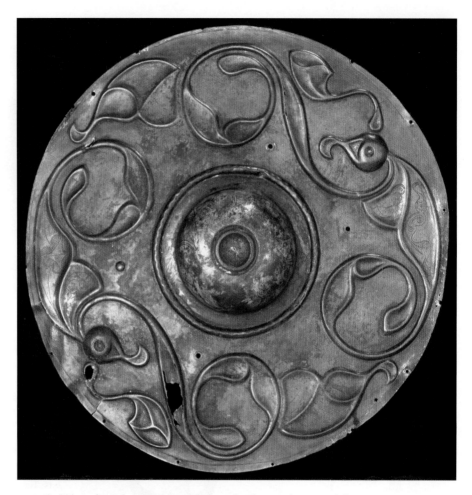

9.16 Shield-boss from the Thames at Wandsworth. The superb repoussé decoration represents two birds with outstretched wings

importance of the eastern and western routes for the development of the insular La Tène art found in the northern part of Ireland. The most coherent, and probably the earliest, style group includes eight sword scabbards from the River Bann and the nearby bog of Lisnacrogher, all of which probably spanned the second to first centuries BC. While there are undoubted similarities between these and contemporary scabbards from Yorkshire, which might have been the prime source of inspiration, some of the motifs used on the Irish pieces hint at direct continental inspiration. It remains a possibility, therefore, that a few swords may have arrived in Ireland along the Atlantic route to contribute to the pool of motifs on which the innovative Irish craftsmen drew.

9.17 One of the classic pieces of 'Celtic', or La Tène, art in Britain is the highly decorated item found in a cist at Cerrig-y-drudion, Clwyd. It used to be thought to be a hanging bowl but the preferred reconstruction now sees it as a helmet

The Eastern Channel–Southern North Sea Axis Again

The narrow seaways to the east and west of the Strait of Dover remained in active use throughout the fifth and fourth centuries, maintaining a tradition of cultural interaction by then almost a thousand years old. This is most clearly demonstrated by the continued parallel development of pottery traditions on both sides of the sea, maintaining the broad cultural zone in Britain stretching from the River Avon to the Wash and on the Continent from the Seine to the mouth of the Rhine. Within this extensive territory, while there were regional differences in the pottery assemblages, there were sufficient similarities to suggest a significant level of social interaction between the insular and the continental communities. The similarities are particularly close between eastern Kent and Pas de Calais and Belgium, where the same kind of rusticated pots and painted wares are found. In Kent the painted wares are known from five sites, but petrographic analysis has not been undertaken so it is not yet possible to say whether the Kent painted pots were actually imports from the Continent or local copies. Either way, they demonstrate the close relationships between communities on the facing sides of the narrow strait.

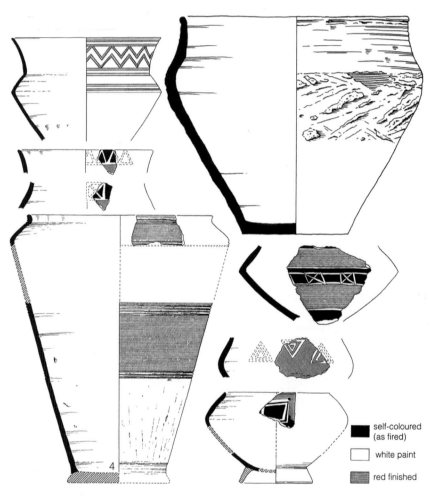

self-coloured (as fired)

white paint

red finished

9.18 A selection of pottery of the fifth and fourth centuries from various sites in Kent. The forms and the styles of decoration, in particular the use of paint, are closely similar to painted wares found in northern France and suggest that the two areas were in close contact

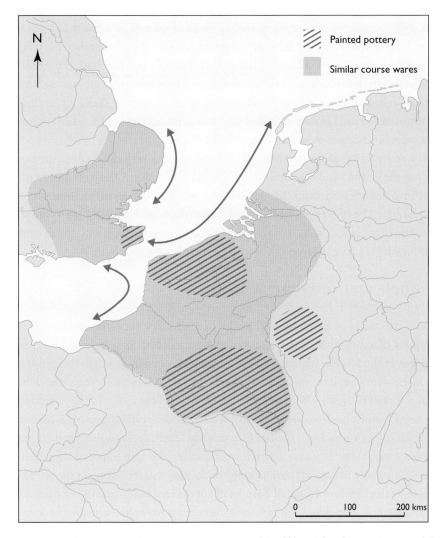

9.19 The map shows the distribution of painted pottery of the fifth and fourth centuries BC and the broad zone, on both sides of the eastern Channel–southern North Sea axis, in which the Coarse Ware pottery shares close similarities

The southern North Sea cultural zone, as we might call it, does not extend very far west along the Channel. In this it mirrors the situation going back to the eighth century, where, as we have seen, a cultural divide existed separating an eastern region where the Gundlingen sword was popular from the western region where the tradition of hoarding bronze continued for another century or more and Armorican axes were traded to Britain.

315

Another similarity, apparently shared by much of the southern North Sea cultural zone, was a disposal rite predicated on exposing dead bodies, rather than burying or cremating them. This is implied by the virtual absence of careful burials over much of south-eastern Britain and the continental zone between the Seine and the Rhine. Instead, in both regions human bones, and sometimes complete skeletons, are found deposited in disused storage pits. It is only towards the edges of this core zone that more regular cremations and inhumations are found.

The relationship of the two littoral communities was very close. Given the *longue durée* of the contact and the similarity of the material culture, the relationship must have involved allegiances, exchange networks, and familial ties maintained over the generations. The exchange of genes throughout the zone must have been considerable, and there is also likely to have been linguistic convergence, with the maritime populations speaking dialects of Celtic or German, or perhaps both.

Chariots and Yorkshiremen

One of the marks of status adopted by the La Tène elites in continental Europe was the burial of a two-wheeled chariot with the deceased. Chariot burials of this kind are frequent in the Moselle region and occur in more limited numbers in the Ardennes, the Marne region, and the middle and lower Seine valley. There is also a cluster of them on the Yorkshire Wolds. Unsurprisingly this group, belonging to what has been called the Arras culture, has been seen by many as direct evidence of a group of La Tène warriors settling in Yorkshire in the late fifth or early fourth century. But the situation is by no means as clear as it may at first seem. Certainly, the appearance of large inhumation cemeteries, the use of chariots in the burial rite, and the setting of the burials in square-ditched enclosures are all features of continental burial practice and are quite alien to the British tradition. But in Britain the vehicles were almost invariably dismantled before burial, unlike the Continent, where they were buried intact and upright, and the inhumed bodies were arranged in a crouched position rather than extended as in the continental manner. Moreover, while the grave goods are of La Tène type and are sometimes decorated with La Tène art, they are of British manufacture. Nor is there anything about the settlement pattern or the material culture that suggests an immigrant community: the houses are all circular and built in the British manner, in contrast to the continental La Tène rectangular house. Given the evidence it is hardly surprising that opinions regarding their origins have varied, some writers denying any significant continental input other than the emulation of a burial rite about which the elite may have heard, others favouring a small incursion of population intermarrying with the indigenous communities and introducing aspects of their own funerary tradition.

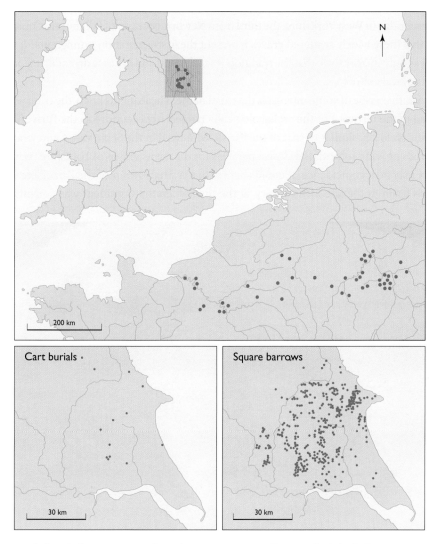

9.20 The burial of prominent members of society accompanied by two-wheeled vehicles was a practice adopted by a number of communities during the La Tène period (*top map*). In Britain vehicle burials cluster in Yorkshire (with a few others beyond). In the same region square barrows, similar to those on the Continent, were also common. The evidence suggests that the Yorkshire communities were in contact with contemporaries in the Seine valley

On balance the latter explanation seems to be the more likely. The differences between the British and continental graves may simply be that the burials so far excavated in Yorkshire belong to second- and third-generation families after changes in burial rite had begun to take place. There are, in fact, three intact vehicles known: one from Pexton Moor in the Arras culture region of North Yorkshire, one from

Ferrybridge in West Yorkshire, the third from Newbridge south of Edinburgh. Could it be that these widely scattered graves represent the first-generation immigrants? If so, it was only in Yorkshire that the tradition was taken up and became an enduring part of the local culture.

Another issue of some interest is the tribal name. The Romans knew the tribe who lived in the territory of the archaeologically named Arras culture as the Parisi. The name is closely similar to that of the Parisii, who lived in the Seine valley and whose burials provide some of the closest parallels for the Arras graves of Yorkshire. While this may be a coincidence, it could suggest that a small group of the Parisii left the Paris basin in the late fifth century, at the time when the Continent was convulsed

9.21 A vehicle burial from Ferrybridge, West Yorkshire, during excavation by Oxford Archaeology North. The vehicle was placed complete in the grave pit with the human body lying within it. The two wheels are represented now by their iron tyres. The pole of the vehicle to which the horses were attached can be seen in the front

with folk movements, and made their way to the tranquillity of Britain, some to settle in the Yorkshire Wolds among the natives. Had this been so, they would have been journeying along the familiar sea-routes that had bound Britain to the Continent for a millennium.

The example of the Arras culture is intriguing, not least because it shows just how difficult it is to interpret the archaeological record. It is also a reminder that there may have been rather more mobility at this time than we can identify in the scraps of evidence that survive. Is it possible, for example, that two centuries or so later a group left Yorkshire to settle in County Antrim and it is the elaborate scabbards of these immigrants and their successors that were found dedicated to the gods in the River Bann and the Lisnacrogher bog?

Tin and Pytheas

The importance of tin in the ancient world cannot be overstressed. As an essential component of the ubiquitous bronze it was constantly in demand, but its compara- tive rarity within Europe meant that knowledge of every source was highly valued and protected. Herodotus, writing in the fifth century BC, had heard that in 'the extreme tracts of Europe towards the west' there were 'islands called Cassiterides whence the tin comes which we use', though he admits to knowing no specific details of them. This information probably came from traders at Massalia who had tapped into the Atlantic tin sources but were probably vague about where exactly the tin was sourced, whether Galicia, Armorica, or south-western Britain. Given the increasing hold that the Phoenicians now had over Iberian metal supply, the tin that made its way to Massalia most likely came from the north-west.

It may have been a desire to gain a more precise knowledge of this rare commodity, so crucial to the consuming society of the Mediterranean, that an entrepreneur and scientist named Pytheas set out from Massalia about 320 BC to explore the north- western extremities of Europe. The easiest way to reach the tin source would have been to follow the tin route through the wilds of western France back to its origin. Piecing together Pytheas' remarkable travels from the surviving fragments of his lost account *On the Ocean* is not easy, but it seems that he probably travelled through Gaul taking a route up the River Aude, through the Carcassonne Gap to the Garonne valley, and on to the Gironde estuary, and then took ship (presumably local) to Armorica; from there he crossed the western end of the Channel to the Land's End peninsula, which he knew as Belerion. Here he observed first hand the processes of extraction and exchange. His description may well survive largely intact in the text of a first-century writer, Diodorus Siculus. Diodorus is known to have relied heavily on the work of Timaeus, another Sicilian writer, for areas about which he had no personal experience, and Timaeus in turn made extensive use of Pytheas' work. The description recorded by Diodorus has the authenticity of an eyewitness account, and Pytheas is the most likely source:

> The inhabitants of Britain who live on the promontory called Belerion are especially friendly to strangers and have adopted a civilized way of life because of their interaction with traders and other people. It is they who work the tin, treating the layer which contains it in an ingenious way. This layer, being like rock, contains earthy seams and in them the workers quarry the ore, which they then melt down to clean of its impurities. Then they work the tin into pieces the size of knuckle-bones and convey it to an island which lies off Britain, called Ictis; for at the ebb-tide the space between this island and the mainland becomes dry and they can take the tin in large quantities over to the island on their wagons. (And a peculiar thing happens in the case of the neighbouring islands which lie between Europe and Britain, for at flood-tide the passage between them and the mainland runs full and they have the appearance of islands, but at ebb-tide the sea recedes and leaves dry a large space and at that time they look like peninsulas.) On the island of Ictis the merchants buy the tin from the natives and carry it from there across the Strait of Galatia [the Channel] and finally, making their way on foot through Gaul for some thirty days, they bring the goods on horseback to the mouth of the Rhône.

> (Diodorus Siculus 5.1–4)

Some further details are offered by Pliny, quoting Timaeus (and thus Pytheas?): 'The Britons', he said, made a six-day journey, carrying tin, to an island called Mictis 'in boats of wicker covered with sewn hides' (*HN* 4.104).

The surviving texts give a remarkably vivid account of the tin trade at the end of the fourth century. There has been much debate about the location of the famous off-shore semi-island of Ictis. St Michael's Mount, near Penzance, is generally favoured, but another possibility might be the promontory of Mount Batten in Plymouth Sound, which the archaeological evidence shows to have been an important port site from the ninth to the first centuries BC. Mount Batten is very conveniently sited on the edge of Dartmoor, an area rich in tin and copper and some gold. It would have been a very convenient assembly point for traders coming from Armorica. It may be, however, that there were a number of ports on the south coast of Cornwall and Devon in active use at the time. The only tangible archaeological evidence of the tin trade is offered by a collection of around fifty small knuckle-bone-shaped tin ingots found by divers at the mouth of the River Erme, where it enters Bigbury Bay, only 16 nautical miles from Mount Batten. The ingots were found scattered along the north face of a reef in some 7–10 metres of water but are tantalizingly undated—it is only their shape that hints of a link with the activities that Pytheas observed.

Scraps of textual evidence allow us to trace Pytheas' journey around Britain. It seems that after Cornwall he sailed northwards through the Irish Sea, stopping at the Isle of Man and probably the Isle of Lewis and Shetland. Whether he then made an open-sea voyage to Iceland (Thule) is debatable, but at the very least he does seem to have talked to people who had. Thereafter he sailed southwards along the east coast of Britain. His knowledge of the sources of amber shows that he was intent on researching the origins of this much-coveted material, either by interviewing locals who had crossed the North Sea to Jutland or by joining one of their expeditions himself. After this he reached Kantion (the Isle of Thanet) before travelling the length of the Channel to Armorica, from where he retraced his outward journey back to Massalia. It was probably in his home port that he composed the epic story of his adventure, *On the Ocean*, which must have been one of the most enthralling books to hit the intellectual world of the day, offering, as it did, startling new information which challenged so many of the old orthodoxies. In spite of its factual accuracy, *On the Ocean* stoked the myth of the mysterious isles lying in the treacherous fog-bound seas beyond Europe.

The description of the tin trade is particularly interesting in that it implies a regular and well-ordered process with the rules known to all. A place of assembly was designated as a free zone where all were given a guarantee of safe conduct. Offshore islands like Ictis were favoured as ports-of-trade in the Mediterranean world. The traders would have timed their visits to the short season, determined by sailing conditions, when the natives knew to expect them. The tin ingots would have been amassed for the occasion, but what products were brought to exchange with the natives is unknown. Exotic foodstuffs, relishes, herbs, and perfumes may have featured, together with fine cloth, and it is not impossible that some of the Mediterranean coins and bronze figurines of Mediterranean deities found scattered across southern Britain may have arrived through Ictis.

The tin trade seems to have been an institutionalized process of exchange. It may be that it was the rarity and desirability of the product that created this particular system, but it remains a distinct possibility that similar systems existed elsewhere linking Britain to the Continent and to Ireland: coastal marts may have been many by the fourth century, but they are difficult to recognize archaeologically. It is a sobering thought that without the description provided by Pytheas we would know very little of the tin trade.

Times of Increasing Tension

There are indications that in various parts of Britain latent aggression was beginning to build into periods of real stress and, from the third century BC, into localized warfare. This is particularly true of the hill-fort zone of central southern Britain, where those hill-forts that continued in use were greatly strengthened. Ditches were redug and ramparts rebuilt, now without a vertical wall but with a continuous slope, or glacis, from the bottom of the ditch to the top of the rampart. There are many examples of forts where one of the gates was blocked while the remaining entrance was provided with forward-projecting hornworks offering greatly enhanced protection. At other forts, of which Maiden Castle in Dorset is a prime example, the defensive circuits were multiplied with additional lines of banks and ditches.

While it could be argued that these changes were designed simply to aggrandize the forts, to emphasize the superiority of the polity who maintained them, it is far

9.22 The massive defensive earthworks of one of the gates of the hill-fort of Maiden Castle, Dorset. Anyone approaching the fort had to weave their way between the ramparts uncertain of their reception from the defenders who commanded the ramparts

more in keeping with the evidence to suppose that the new works were a response to increasing tensions in society, tensions that could at any moment flare up into violent hostility. Several forts bear evidence of devastating fires. At Danebury in Hampshire a fire seems to have damaged large areas of the interior in the late fourth century, and another totally destroyed the gate in the first century BC, after which the site seems to have been largely abandoned. The fires need not, of course, have been the result of enemy action, but the very large numbers of sling-stones found in and around the entrance forecourt suggest that the occupants were intent on defending themselves should the need arise. Add to this the slash and thrust marks of weapons scarring the human bones found within the forts and it is difficult to resist the conclusion that social tensions sometimes boiled over into deadly conflict.

What form the aggression might have taken is open to debate. It is most unlikely that conditions of all-out warfare, with standing armies ravaging the countryside, ever existed. Endemic hostility, much boasting, and occasional border skirmishes involving groups of young men were probably the norm. But occasionally tensions may have escalated, leading to raids on rival hill-forts.

Some indication of competing polities comes from the study of the Danebury region in eastern Hampshire. The hill-fort of Danebury was strongly redefended early in the third century after the first fire and seems to have remained the dominant location for several centuries, but about the beginning of the first century the neighbouring but long-abandoned hill-fort of Bury Hill was suddenly brought back into use, with an entirely new set of defences comprising a ditch with an inner and outer rampart. The most surprising thing about the occupation evidence from within the fort was that horses account for more than a quarter of the animal bones and exceptional quantities of horse gear and chariot fittings were found. The implication would seem to be that activity within Bury Hill now focused on the building of war chariots and the training of teams of horses to power them, reflecting a more excitable and aggressive stance among the elite. While Danebury, only 6 kilometres away, could also boast some chariots at about this time, its basic economy was still focused on the traditional production of sheep and corn. We shall never know the precise relationship between the two sites, but it is tempting to see the inhabitants of Bury Hill as a new polity setting themselves up within what had been Danebury territory, expressing their power with flashy chariots driven by its young men intent on display-

9.23 Decorated horse gear found in a pit in the hill-fort of Danebury, Hampshire

ing their martial prowess. It may even be that it was they who eventually destroyed Danebury.

The chariot, powered by two well-trained horses, had been used in Britain as an item of elite display from at least the fifth century, and, as we have seen, in Yorkshire they were incorporated in the burial ritual to identify people of status. In all probability chariots were used throughout much of southern and eastern Britain from this time, but it is only in the late second and early first centuries that horse harness and chariot fittings become relatively common in the archaeological record. When, in the mid-first century BC, Julius Caesar invaded Britain, the British resistance in the south-east could muster 4,000 chariot teams to oppose him. He was impressed by what he saw and gives a vivid description of the British chariot in action:

> These are the tactics of chariot warfare. First they drive in all directions hurling spears. Generally they succeed in throwing the ranks of their opponents into confusion just with the terror caused by their galloping horses and the din of the wheels. They make their way through the squadrons of their own cavalry, then jump down from their chariots and fight on foot. Meanwhile, the chariot drivers withdraw a little way from the fighting and position the chariots in such a way that if their masters are hard pressed by the enemy's numbers, they have an easy means of retreat to their own lines. Thus, when they fight they have the mobility of cavalry and the staying power of infantry: and with daily training and practice they have become so efficient that even on steep slopes they can control their horses at full gallop, check and turn them in a moment, run along the pole, stand on the yoke, and get back into the chariot with incredible speed.
>
> (B Gall. 4.33)

It is clear from Caesar's account that chariots were now well integrated into the systems of warrior display and prowess that now pervaded society.

Outside the hill-fort-dominated zone of the central south direct evidence of warfare is harder to find, especially in the east of Britain, but warrior burials—male interments accompanied by shields, spears, and weapons—are now frequently found, and from Yorkshire come a series of small chalk carvings of warriors wearing their swords in the middle of their backs so that the sword could be drawn over the shoulder uncluttered by the shield on the left arm. It is in Atlantic Britain that some of the clearest evidence of unsettled times is to be found. Although weapons and horse gear are rarer than in the east, the settlements take on a far more embattled appearance. In Cornwall and west Wales the farmsteads are more heavily enclosed with walls and ditches, while in the Western and Northern Isles and in mainland Scotland broch towers and strongly built duns dominate the landscape, and some settlements are built on crannogs, or small islands set in the safety of lakes. It is an architecture designed to proclaim power and impregnability. This does not, of course, mean that open hostility prevailed, but simply that neighbours could be left in no doubt of one's ability to defend oneself.

If we are correct in interpreting the last few centuries of the first millennium as a time of increasing social strain, we must consider the causes. It could simply be that the warrior ethic, which begins to become evident at the end of the second millennium, continued, exacerbated by tensions caused by a growing population and the desire to acquire and hold onto productive land at a time when fertility may, in some long-utilized landscapes, have begun to fail. While there has been a tendency in the recent past to downplay the signs of aggression and to present the Iron Age as something of a rural idyll, the reality was that warfare remained endemic and social competition could quickly flare up anywhere into hostile and bloody confrontation.

Che Eastern Channel Axis, Second and First Centuries BC

Towards the beginning of the second century BC the tribes of Belgic Gaul—roughly the region between the Seine and the Rhine—began to mint gold coins to use in cycles of gift exchange. Since these communities were in close contact with their British neighbours, it was not long before Gallo-Belgic coins found their way to Britain, their distribution giving a very clear impression of the networks of exchange that were now in operation.

The first issues, known as Gallo-Belgic A, circulated in the region between the Seine and Somme valleys *c.* 175–*c.* 120 BC. In Britain the type shows a distinct preference for the Thames estuary, which must have been the main point of entry, but a few scattered along the south coast point to a secondary network in operation. These distributions echo the contacts that were in operation in the earlier period. A second coin, Gallo-Belgic B, of broadly similar date, reflects even more sharply a Thames valley point of entry. Two later Gallo-Belgic coin types, Gallo-Belgic C and D, in use between *c.* 120 and *c.* 60 BC, are found more widely scattered throughout southern Britain, south-east of a line between the Wash and the Solent, but again with concentrations in the broader Thames estuary region and along the south coast, particularly between Beachy Head and Portsmouth.

Gold coins (staters) minted under the authority of Gallo-Belgic leaders were of considerable value and were not designed for simple commercial transactions. Their primary purpose was for use in the gift exchange systems that facilitated social relations between friends and allies. What the British distributions so vividly reflect are the social networks that existed at the time between the leaders of Belgic Gaul and their British neighbours. This is given further emphasis by a remark recorded by

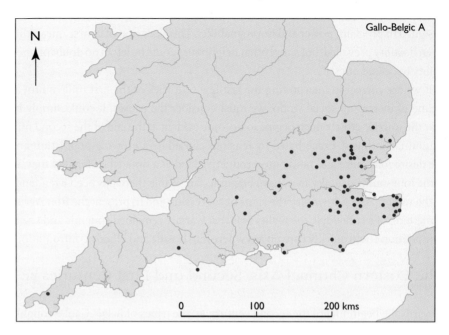

9.24 The distribution of Gallo-Belgic A coins, made in northern France, which reached Britain through systems of gift exchange in the second and early first centuries BC

Julius Caesar in his *Bellum Gallicum* ('The Gallic War'), in which he says that Diviciacus, king of the Suessiones, a tribe centred on modern Soissons in the Marne valley, had dominions in Britain (*B Gall.* 2.4.7), implying that Diviciacus was accepted as a high king by one or more of the British tribes. In such a situation Gallo-Belgic coins may well have been given to British aristocrats to ensure their continued fealty.

Caesar also tells us that the Britons had served in most of the Gallic wars (*B Gall.* 4.20.1), presumably on the side of their Gallo-Belgic confreres against the Romans. To fund the wars the Gauls issued a huge gold coinage, known as Gallo-Belgic E, represented by many hundreds of finds distributed over much of southern Britain. It is tempting to see in this distribution the rewards brought back by successful British war-leaders returning from the battle zone. The involvement of British warriors drawn from across the south-east is not surprising given the long period of close social relations that had existed between the two peoples. By working out the number of dies used to strike the Gallo-Belgic E issue, and estimating the life of a die, it has been suggested that the total minting required 5,000–6,000 kilograms of fine gold, a colossal sum by any standards, particularly compared with the 300–400 kilograms of gold used in the Gallo-Belgic A–C issues. It is a measure both of the intensity of the coordinated native resistance and of the resources available to the war-leaders.

9.25 Gold stater of Gallo-Belgic A type. These coins were minted in Belgic Gaul and brought to Britain probably as gifts for the local elite. Gallo-Belgic coins served as models for British coinage

The Central Channel Axis

Early in the first century BC the coastal port of Hengistbury Head suddenly came into prominence as the prime focus of a reinvigorated trading network linking the south-west of Britain with Armorica and Lower Normandy. Hengistbury Head had many advantages as a port. It was dominated by a prominent headland easy to recognize from far out to sea, and once the headland had been rounded, an incoming ship's master would have found himself in a wide and well-protected lagoon, now Christchurch Harbour, with gently shelving gravel strands on which to beach his ship. The harbour had the added advantage of being served by two rivers, the Avon and the Stour, providing navigable access to the heartlands of Wessex. Hengistbury Head has a long history of use as a sporadic port of call throughout much of the prehistoric period. This culminated in the early first century, when, for a brief period, it became a bustling international port sustaining an extensive trade network that embraced much of the central and western Channel zone.

Well-stratified archaeological horizons on the northern shore of the headland provide a wealth of material reflecting the tentacles of trade. Prominent were the Roman wine amphorae, mostly of a type classified as Dressel 1A used to transport wine from northern and central Italy. Other Mediterranean commodities attested

9.26 The promontory of Hengistbury Head, Dorset, shelters Christchurch Harbour, into which the rivers Stour and Avon flow. The headland was protected by a massive rampart and ditch and served as a port-of-trade during the early first century BC, when regular trade with Armorica was under way

included bronze cups, purple and yellow glass in raw form, and dried figs. These items would have been traded northwards through the ports of Transalpine Gaul, which had recently been taken over by the Roman state. Much of the bulk traffic at this stage probably used the old tin route via the Garonne–Gironde to the Atlantic, and the goods were then carried on native ships northwards to Armorica, where local Armorican merchants took over for the last leg across the Channel, carrying the exotic Mediterranean products along with trade goods of their own to Britain. The excavations at Hengistbury have produced large quantities of Armorican pottery, which arrived probably as the containers of locally produced Armorican foodstuffs.

Other commodities reached Hengistbury from neighbouring ports of Britain. Tin from Cornwall, copper–silver alloy from the fringe of Dartmoor, silver-rich lead from the Mendips, Kimmeridge shale armlet roughouts from the Isle of Purbeck, cattle possibly from Devon, corn from the Hampshire chalklands, and scrap gold from wherever it could be got. All were accumulated at Hengistbury together with iron blooms from the iron-rich sandstones of the headland itself. It was these British products that the Armorican ship's masters transported back to the Continent. A few

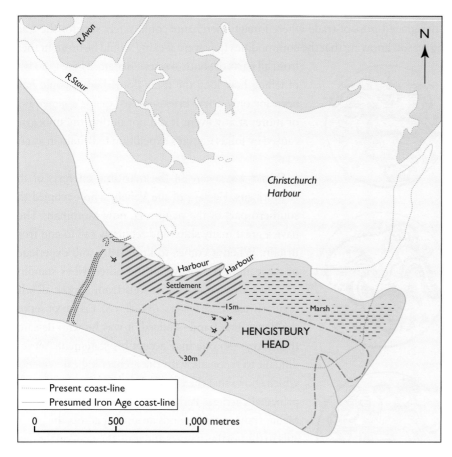

9.27 Hengistbury Head as it would have been in the first century BC, before coastal erosion greatly reduced the width of the headland

decades later the Greek geographer Strabo lists, as the principal exports of Britain, 'grain, cattle, gold, silver and iron . . . also hides and slaves and dogs that are by nature suited to the purposes of the chase' (Strabo 4.5.2). Perhaps slaves and hunting dogs also passed through Hengistbury, but of their passage there is no archaeological trace.

How the trade was actually managed is a matter of speculation. The sheer quantity of Armorican pottery found at Hengistbury suggests that the principal carriers came from the north coast, probably the Baie de Saint-Brieuc, a suggestion supported by the discovery at Hengistbury of a number of coins of the Coriosolites, the tribe who occupied this part of northern Armorica. The journey, sailing almost due north and perhaps stopping at St Peter Port on Guernsey en route, could have been accomplished within two days. Hengistbury, like the tin port of Ictis before it, was probably a designated port-of-trade where foreign merchants could safely stay for the trading season knowing that the commodities they were seeking would be brought there from all parts of south-western Britain. There is no way of telling how long the trade flourished: it could have been for only a few brief seasons, or for a generation or more; at any event it did not outlive the upheavals caused by Julius Caesar's expedition to Britain in 55 and 54 BC.

Caesar was aware of the maritime interests of the Armoricans. He says of the Veneti, who occupied the southern part of the peninsula, now Morbihan: 'They have a great many ships and regularly sail to and from Britain. When it comes to knowledge and experience of navigation, they leave all the other tribes standing . . . They are able to extract tolls from almost all who regularly use these waters' (B Gall. 3.8). Caesar observed the Veneti first hand—indeed, it was he who defeated their navy—so one may accept his statement. Yet it is difficult to reconcile with the archaeological evidence, which shows that the Coriosolites of the north were the principal carriers. Perhaps the Veneti transported the Mediterranean trade goods around or across the peninsula to the northern ports and took their cut on the deal, leaving the northerners to make the onward journey. Alternatively they may, indeed, have traded direct with the British, preferring to take the western route across the wide Channel mouth to reach Cornwall and beyond. There is, however, little positive archaeological evidence of this except for a shard or two of Armorican pottery found at the port of Mount Batten.

The axis between Hengistbury Head and the Baie de Saint-Brieuc seems to have dominated the cross-Channel trade, but there is ample evidence that other routes were also used, if only sporadically. On the French side of the Channel the port at Nacqueville on the northern coast of the Cherbourg peninsula was active at this time, as is shown by a range of exotic material including Armorican coins, Roman Dressel 1A amphorae,

9.28 The different tribes of Armorica produced distinctive coins. These were minted by the Coriosolites, who occupied much of the north coast. Coins of this kind were exported to southern Britain in the first century BC

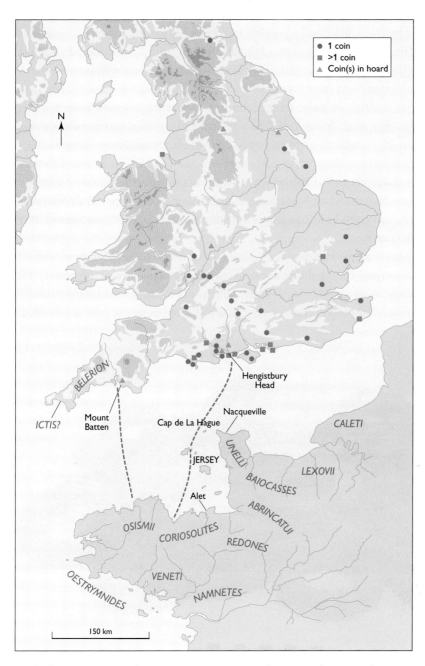

9.29 In the first century BC southern Britain was in contact with Armorica by means of two principal sea-routes serving the ports of Mount Batten and Hengistbury Head. The map shows the distribution of Armorican coins found in Britain. It suggests that the ports of central southern Britain were the main recipients, but the wider distribution hints that the coastal cabotage may have been a factor in their distribution

glass bracelets, gold, and a possible iron currency bar found there. The assemblage also included a quantity of roughout armlets cut from Kimmeridge shale. The shale may have been transported through Hengistbury, but it is equally possible that it was transhipped direct from the Isle of Purbeck by a local entrepreneur. A few shards of Dorset-made pottery also reached the port, probably at the same time. Kimmeridge shale, a fine oil shale that could be easily cut and polished, was popular throughout Armorica for making armlets, beads, and vessels. Its discovery, along with British-made pottery, at the ports of Alet near Saint-Malo and Le Yaudet near Lannion suggests that direct cross-Channel voyages were not infrequent, linking various ports on either side of the water. Nonetheless, the distribution of Dressel 1A amphorae and of Armorican coins in Britain leaves little doubt that Hengistbury remained the main point of entry.

There is ample evidence that cabotage continued to be important. This is well demonstrated by the distribution of highly distinctive decorated pottery known as South Western Decorated Ware, which was made on the Lizard peninsula of Cornwall. The pottery can be recognized by the tempering of grits of gabbro, a rock

9.30 At the site of Nacqueville, on the coast of Normandy just west of Cherbourg, the excavation of a first-century BC settlement brought to light rough-cut rings of shale. These probably came from Kimmeridge on the Dorset coast and were intended to be worked into fine armlets

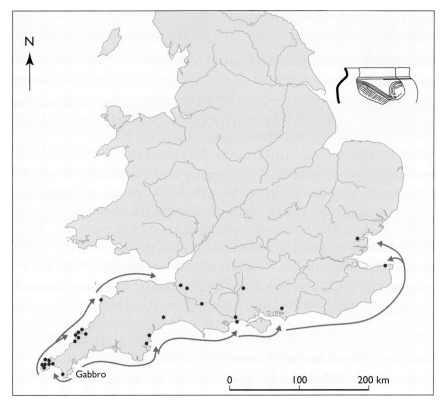

9.31 Decorated pottery made in Cornwall using clay with gabbro grits spread across southern Britain, its distribution pattern suggesting that movement was largely by coastal cabotage

found only on the Lizard. Gabbroic pottery, however, can be found along the south coast as far as the Thames estuary. Another, more tantalizing, hint of cabotage is offered by a different pot type: the large ovoid jars decorated with zones of rouletted arc patterns that are found at coastal localities from Hengistbury to the Humber. The different fabrics suggest that they were locally made, but the forms and decorations clearly belong to the same coastal tradition. Perhaps it is a deliberate statement made by the coastal community of their maritime identity. Another interesting reflection of coastal traffic is the distribution of Armorican coins in Britain. The main concentration lies, as might be expected, close to the Solent and Dorset points of entry, but there is a distinct scatter along the east coast of Britain up to the Humber and also a concentration around the upper Severn estuary. The discovery of an Armorican coin at the port site at Meols on the Wirral peninsula is a hint that some vessels may also have been trafficked along the coasts of the Irish Sea.

The Belgae

There remains the question of the Belgae, a group of immigrants from Belgic Gaul who, Caesar says, 'came to raid and stayed to sow'. He gives no indication of when they arrived or where they settled, thus leaving the subject open to energetic debate. The timing of the event is probably best placed in the late second or early first century BC since the memory was still alive in Caesar's time. As to the location of the incursion, the simplest explanation is that they landed somewhere on the Solent coast and settled in Hampshire, where the Roman geographers later located the Belgae, their capital being Venta Belgarum ('the Market of the Belgae'), modern Winchester. Later Commius, a refugee from Caesar's campaign in Belgic Gaul, fled to Britain to 'join his own people' already here. He probably landed in the Solent and made his way through Hampshire, setting up a new centre, Calleva (Silchester), on the northern extremity of the Belgic enclave. The choice of the Solent region for the settlement of the Belgae may simply have been that it was something of a no-man's-land. To the east the Gallo-Belgic tribes had long-established social ties with the British tribes, while to the west intricate trading networks existed between the Armoricans and the British. The new settlers seem to have deliberately chosen the land in between, where their presence is unlikely to have conflicted with vested interests.

By about 60 BC, then, most of the communities of south-eastern Britain were locked into complex social and economic networks with their Gallic neighbours. People moved with ease between the two regions and commodities flowed, introducing the Britons of the central southern region to the joys of wine and other Mediterranean luxuries. It was the bow-wave: the full force of Romanization was soon to follow.

On the Western Extremity

Away from the core zone of south-eastern Britain communities continued to develop, little influenced by continental events and culture, but local networks ensured that neighbouring polities maintained a level of contact that allowed ideas to flow between them. One example of this is the northern part of Ireland, which probably received its inspiration for La Tène art styles, at least in part, from northern Britain. Another innovation that probably came from much the same area was the beehive rotary quern, which offered a much improved way of grinding grain over the traditional saddle querns. The distribution of both La Tène art styles and rotary querns concentrates in the north part of the island, suggesting a significant cultural divide between north and south, with the south, and particularly the south-west, being largely isolated from European developments.

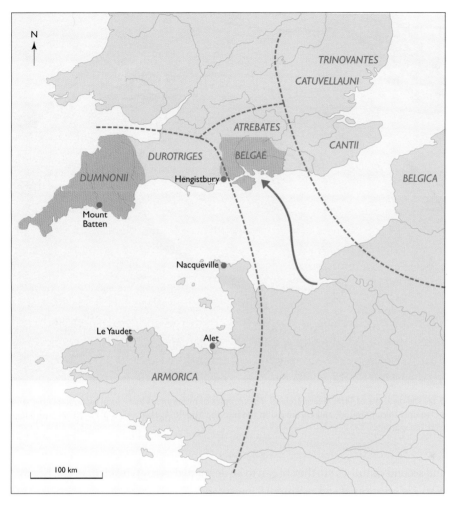

9.32 By the middle of the first century BC the southern part of Britain was closely linked to the Continent. The two main spheres of connectivity linked the south-west with Armorica and the south-east with the Belgic region of Gaul. The central zone, focused on the Solent, seems to have received the Belgic immigrants mentioned by Caesar, who may have come from the Seine valley

One notable development in Ireland was the emergence of 'royal sites', which feature in the vernacular literature of the first millennium AD as the residence of kings and the central foci of the tribes. Four are known: Tara (Temair), County Meath; Navan (Emain Macha), County Armagh; Rathcroghan (Cruachain), County Roscommon; and Knockaulin (Dún Ailinne), County Kildare. All four were sites of great antiquity and must have been central to the tribal memory when, in the third

9.33 The royal site of Tara, Meath, Ireland. The complex of monuments had a long history, starting with a Neolithic burial mound, and continued in use into the Middle Ages. It was a place where Irish kings were inaugurated

and second centuries BC, they began to be developed as royal residences and became places of great ritual and ceremonial importance.

Tara, Navan, and Knockaulin have all undergone limited excavation, and while all display differences, there are some broad similarities that link them. In the latter part of the Iron Age, within the third to first centuries BC, all three were provided with highly distinctive figure-of-eight timber structures comprising a large fenced circular enclosure 30–50 metres in diameter conjoined with a smaller circular structure, probably a house, 15–20 metres in diameter: in all cases the structures were rebuilt on more than one occasion on the same site. At both Navan and Knockaulin the approaches to the entrance of the larger enclosure were bordered by fences.

In the first century BC a new and more varied range of structures was erected. At Knockaulin two concentric timber circles 47 metres in diameter were built around a smaller free-standing timber circle. At Tara an extensive ditched and palisaded enclosure, the Ráith na Rig, was constructed close to the original buildings, enclosing the

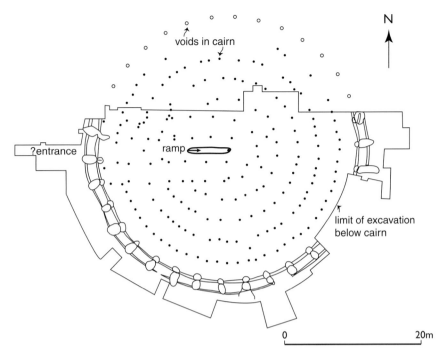

9.34 The great mound of Navan, County Armagh, was built in the early first century BC to cover a huge timber building, which no doubt served a ritual purpose. The construction of the mound would have symbolized the end of one stage in the ceremonial use of the site

hill-top and incorporating a prominent Neolithic tomb: nothing is known of what buildings may lie inside. At Navan the figure-of-eight structure was replaced in the late second century by a circular fenced enclosure, with opposing doorways, rebuilt on two subsequent occasions. Associated finds included status items like shale armlets and glass beads and, more surprisingly, the skull and jaw of a Barbary ape (strictly, a macaque, *Macaca sylvanus*), which had been imported live, stuffed, or as a skeletal trophy from North Africa, presumably along the Atlantic seaways. In whatever state the beast arrived, it must have been an item of wonder, endowing great prestige upon its owner. Its long journey from Africa recalls an event recorded during the Phoenician exploration of the Atlantic coast of Africa a few centuries earlier, when a shore party captured a gorilla thinking it to be a kind of wild human. The creature was killed, stuffed, and brought back to the Mediterranean as a trophy.

At the very beginning of the first century BC the structures at Navan were removed and replaced by a massive timber construction comprising a central timber surrounded by five concentric rings of posts, totalling 208 timbers, the whole enclosed by a double wall built of vertical and horizontal timbers. The central timber, half a metre in diameter, could have stood some 10–15 metres in height, judging from its substantial bedding pit. The felling of the timber was dated dendrochronologically to late 95 or early 94 BC. The building represented a massive input of energy, but even more remarkable was its subsequent history. After only a short period of time, while the timbers were still in place, it was filled with limestone blocks, its outer wall serving as an external revetment for the great cairn which reached a height of 2.8 metres in the centre. The exposed timbers were then burnt and the whole was covered by a mound of turves a further 2.5 metres high at the centre. The structure, and the sequence leading to its abandonment, leave little doubt that the whole was a communal enterprise deeply embedded in ceremony and ritual. It is tempting to believe that it represented a historical act of closure involving the whole tribe: beyond that it is difficult to go.

The four 'royal sites' of Ireland were far more complex in their structures and their histories than the very limited excavations allow us to glimpse. What they show is that by the first century BC social power in Ireland, rooted deeply in the sacred places and traditions of the past, had become consolidated around the four great centres. Britain has nothing to compare.

10

Interlude

APPROACHING THE GODS

JULIUS CAESAR'S campaigns through Gaul and, briefly, into Britain and Germany in the years 58–51 BC brought him into close contact with many barbarian peoples. To enliven his war commentaries, eventually published as *Bellum Gallicum* ('The Gallic War'), he interspersed his narrative of campaigns with discursive accounts of the peoples he encountered and their belief systems. These sections were probably added at a late stage of editing, and, while they will have contained first-hand observations, he probably relied heavily on other published works to provide much of the details. Even so, *Bellum Gallicum* offers an invaluable source for anthropological insights into the Gauls, Britons, and Germans in the middle of the first century BC.

One subject that clearly fascinated Caesar was the Druids. This elite class, he tells us,

are in charge of religion. They have control over public and private sacrifices and give rulings on all religious questions . . . In almost all disputes, between communities or between individuals, the Druids act as judges. If a crime is committed, if there is a murder or if there is a dispute about inheritance or a boundary, they are the ones who give a verdict and decide on the punishment or compensation appropriate in each case. Any individual or community not abiding by their verdict is banned from the sacrifices, and this is regarded among the Gauls as the most severe punishment. Everyone shuns them; no one will go near or speak to them for fear of being contaminated . . .

(*B Gall.* 6.13)

He then goes on to say that in Gaul there is one Druid with authority over the rest and that once a year they all assemble in the territory of the Carnutes (the region around Chartres) to dispense justice to the people. To become a Druid took twenty years' training, but, even so, large numbers of young men flocked to them for instruction.

Caesar's account is, of course, about the Druids of Gaul, but he makes one further tantalizing observation: 'It is thought that the doctrine of the Druids was invented in Britain and was brought from there to Gaul: even today those who want to study the doctrine in greater detail usually go to Britain to learn there.' What can we make of this? Since there is no propaganda benefit for Caesar in this statement, we may accept that he is fairly reporting what he has heard. At the very least, it suggests that druidism was practised in Britain at the time and that it may have been of some antiquity. Britain would have had the reputation of being a mysterious island set in the mists on the edge of the world, and where better, in the minds of the Gauls, for druidism to have originated. They may even have been right.

The presence of Druids in Britain is also attested by Tacitus, writing at the end of the first century AD. He describes the Druids and their wild, screaming female supporters who confronted the Roman army on Anglesey in AD 59 in vivid language, justifying their annihilation with the accusation that they practised human sacrifice: 'it was their religion to drench their altars in the blood of prisoners and consult their gods by means of human entrails'. These practices were carried out in sacred groves 'devoted to Mona's [Anglesey's] barbarous superstitions'. Whatever the truth of these accusations, it suited the Romans to have an excuse to destroy druidism in Gaul and Britain because it was the one power that could organize national opposition to the Roman presence.

The theme of human sacrifice is mentioned by other classical authors. Diodorus Siculus and Strabo both write of ritual killing for the purpose of augury, while Strabo and Caesar mention cages built of branches that were filled with men and animals and set on fire. 'They believe', writes Caesar, 'that the gods prefer it if the people executed have been caught in the act of theft or armed robbery or some other crime, but when the supply of such victims runs out, they even go to the extent of sacrificing innocent men' (B Gall. 6.16). Strabo adds that ritual death may be by archery or crucifixion and that from the death throes of the victims the future can be foretold. Caesar sums it all up by saying that the Gauls 'believe the power of the immortal gods can be appeased only if one human life is exchanged for another, and they have sacrifices of this kind regularly established by the community'. The emphasis on the barbarity of the rites excited the Roman audience and helped to justify the conquest. While there was inevitably some degree of exaggeration, we cannot reasonably doubt that human sacrifice was part of the ritual behaviour of both Gauls and Britons.

Other writers, however, stress different aspects of druidic behaviour. There is a famous account given by Pliny of the herb lore preserved by the Druids. Various plants were collected because of their curative properties. One of the most potent was mistletoe that had grown on an oak tree: 'They call [it] by the name that means all-healing.' It had to be collected at a particular stage of the moon by a white-robed Druid wielding a golden sickle in a ceremony that involved the sacrifice of two white bulls. Anecdotal accounts like these are invaluable in showing just how rich and complex were the religious beliefs of the barbarians of Atlantic Europe.

Caesar is also aware of the philosophical aspect of druidism:

> The Druids attach particular importance to the belief that the soul does not perish but passes after death from one body to another: they think that this belief is the most effective way to encourage bravery because it removes the fear of death. They hold long discussions about the heavenly bodies and their movements, about the size of the universe and the earth, about the nature of the physical world, and about the power and properties of the immortal gods . . .

> (*B Gall.* 6.14)

Our picture of the Druids is, understandably, far from complete since the classical writers selected what interested them and what supported their own arguments and prejudices. Over time it is possible to recognize a subtle change in classical attitudes towards the Druids. The earliest accounts, surviving in the writings of Alexandrian scholars, focus on the more philosophical and scientific aspects of the doctrine. By the late second century BC scholars like Posidonius are taking a more anthropological interest, presenting the Gauls rather in the mode of the 'noble savage', but then, as imperialism takes a hold and the Gauls and Britons are seen as enemies to be conquered and subdued, any religious power that stands in the way has to be demonized and eradicated in the interests of spreading enlightenment.

What emerges from the scraps of text that survive is the picture of a complex religious system of which the Druids were a part. They were the philosophers, the guardians of all knowledge charged with the responsibility of passing it on to future generations. Their wisdom enabled them to intercede between man and the gods and to pass judgement on civil issues. Without their intercession men were cut off from their deities and became outlaws. The power of the Druid was, then, considerable. When sacrifices were needed, they were present, but there was another caste of religious practitioner, called Vates, who were the seers and augurs and may actually have carried out the sacrifices. There were also Bards, highly skilled performers who could recite or sing great epics embodying the tribal histories. They could boost their patrons by singing eulogies or destroy those of whom they disapproved through satire: these too were men with magical powers.

There are evident dangers in building a composite picture of this kind from scraps gleaned from several centuries of observation across extensive territories: there must have been much regional variation and significant change over time. Yet there is a real coherence between what the different classical writers tell us of the Druids which leaves little doubt that druidism flourished throughout Gaul and Britain in the last centuries before the Roman occupation, and in Ireland it continued to be practised well into the first millennium AD.

The Origins of Druidism in Britain

Caesar's account is the earliest direct reference we have to Druids in Britain, but there seems to be an earlier tradition, pre-dating that of Posidonius, which may go back to the journey of Pytheas at the end of the fourth century BC. This is difficult to demonstrate with any degree of certainty, but the Alexandrian writers were evidently reliant on an early source or sources, and would have had access to Pytheas' *On the Ocean*, which may have contained descriptions of the religious practices of Britain and western Gaul. Indeed, Pytheas may even have been the source of the idea that druidism began in Britain. Sadly, we shall never know.

How far back in time the Druids can be traced in Britain is a matter of speculation. It used to be thought that druidism arrived with one of the 'Celtic invasions' from west central Europe in the early or middle first millennium BC, but since we can be reasonably sure that there were no significant incursions, and indeed that 'Celticity' in the form of the Celtic language may well have been an indigenous development in the Atlantic zone of Europe, it remains a distinct possibility that the religious system developed in the west. It may even be that Caesar was correct and that it had originated in Britain. At any event, the practice that became recognized as druidism in the last century of the first millennium BC had its roots deep in prehistory.

One reasonable hypothesis is that the religious system began to evolve in the period after *c.* 1400 BC, when, as we saw, there were significant social and economic changes, notably the development of a warrior society and an increasing emphasis on landholding and on the productivity of the land. This was a time when there was also a much-increased emphasis on the deposition of metalwork in hoards placed in the ground and in watery contexts. Since the social, economic, and religious systems that came into being in the last centuries of the second millennium provided the basis for developments throughout the first millennium, it would not be surprising if the roots of druidism lay in the formative centuries before 1000 BC.

But could they lie even earlier? The impact of Beaker ideology and metallurgy on Britain and Ireland around 2500–2400 BC was profound. The belief systems of the Neolithic period were replaced, or at least significantly modified, by a new set of values and behaviours, with an emphasis now on the celebration of the individual. The social reformation of British society at this time could have provided the context for the genesis of a new set of religious beliefs and ritual practices.

The tantalizing question has to remain unresolved. The emergence of the mature religious system that we glimpse so fleetingly in the comments of the classical writers at the end of the first millennium is unlikely to have happened suddenly: it may have taken hundreds of years to evolve, and it was still evolving when Strabo, Caesar, and the rest recorded their observations. All that can safely be said is that the religious practices of the first century BC came from deep in the prehistoric past and that its practitioners, the Druids, were the inheritors of an ancient religion.

A Brief Archaeology of Religion

Human behaviour, seen through the archaeological record, is seldom easy to interpret with any degree of assurance. A bronze sword dredged from a river could have been a regrettable loss or a deliberate deposition, while a horse leg found in the bottom of a disused storage pit could be an offering to a god or the result of casual disposal of waste. Only when these fossils of action are found time and time again can we consider them to reflect behaviour patterns suggestive of ritual rather than the detritus of mundane life.

The most obvious expression of ritual behaviour lies in the activities associated with the disposal of the dead. We have seen that by the eighth century the procedure of burying the cremated remains of the dead in urnfields was dying out, to be replaced by excarnations as the normative mode of disposal, a procedure that probably continued throughout the first millennium. The beliefs lying behind the exposure of the body probably involved the idea that the spirit of the departed left the body for the sky, there perhaps to join the deities controlling the heavens. Similar beliefs may have lain behind the ritual of cremation, in which the flames consuming the body rise skywards.

By the fourth century BC new disposal rites begin to appear. In Yorkshire inhumation, often in large cemeteries, became the norm, with many of the bodies being accompanied by grave goods, the elite even taking their chariots to these graves. Inhumation cemeteries, with the bodies buried in stone cists, are now found in Cornwall and south Devon; and by the late second and first centuries BC, across southern Britain, certain members of society enjoy well-equipped inhumation and cremation burial, the males usually distinguished by swords, the females by mirrors. During the first century BC the rite of cremation, often in cemeteries, became increasingly popular in the south-east of Britain.

The change from excarnation to burial, at least among certain levels of society, implies a shift in belief systems, with more emphasis now being placed on providing the dead person with grave goods considered appropriate to his or her status. This may imply an increased belief in the afterlife or reincarnation, a belief that Caesar said was prevalent among the Gauls and was part of the druidic teaching. There is noth-

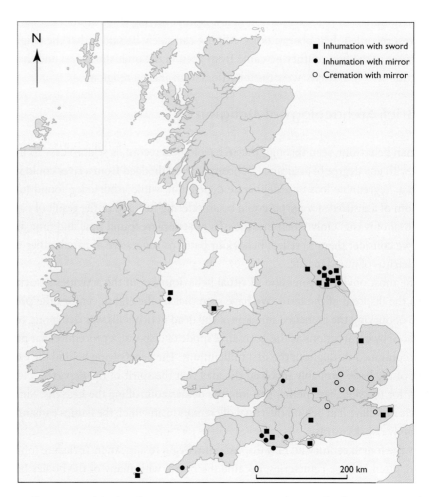

10.1 Different types of elite burial practice were in use in Britain in the second to first century BC. It has been suggested that the mirrors and the swords interred with the dead represented the different genders, but one burial on the Scilly Isles contained both a sword and a mirror, implying that the symbolic meanings of the grave goods may be more complex

ing particularly new in this. The Beaker burials from 2400 BC onwards were usually furnished, and the tradition continued until after the middle of the second millennium. Mode of burial was conditioned by fashion and need not imply deep changes in philosophy.

A belief in the chthonic deities was strong. The gods could be approached either by penetrating the ground, thus breaking through into the underworld, or through liminal places associated with water: rivers, springs, bogs, and, one suspects, coastal waters. 'Hoarding', which became widely prevalent in the ninth century BC, was just one of the ways in which contact could be made with the deities, in this case through the deposition of bronze and occasionally gold. Later in the Iron Age offerings of iron, often in ingot form, were made, while in the first century BC, in the east of Britain, gold torcs were the favoured form of communication. One of the most spectacular depositions was at Snettisham in Norfolk, where a number of substantial gold hoards were found deposited in a circumscribed area. It is tempting to suggest that this may have been a sacred grove of the kind described by the classical sources in southern Gaul, where rich treasures dedicated to the gods were kept entirely safe from theft through fear of the gods' wrath.

Another form of communication was through a pit or shaft deliberately dug deep into the ground. Shafts of this kind were comparatively common in Gaul in the last few centuries before the Romans and frequently contained offerings. In Britain shafts are much less common. One of the most dramatic was discovered at Wilsford, within sight of Stonehenge, dating to about 1400 BC. It was dug into the chalk to a depth of 30 metres, several metres below the contemporary water-table. Finds included wooden objects, amber beads, bone pins, and a shale ring. The presence of a wooden bucket and a length of rope suggested to some a more prosaic explanation, but the shaft is such a remarkable construction that it was surely dug for ritual purposes: water from it would no doubt have been endowed with special properties. There is nothing incongruous in suggesting this: sacred wells presided over by saints are a feature of the medieval landscape. A less ambiguous shaft, dating to around 1000 BC, was found at Stanwick in Hampshire. It was 8 metres deep with an oak trunk,

10.2 One of the hoards of gold and electrum torcs found at the ritual site of Snettisham, Norfolk. A number of precious metal hoards were buried here in the first century BC in a restricted area that was probably sacred to the gods

bark intact, standing at the bottom. The lower part of the pit contained a substance that, on analysis, was claimed to be blood. Standing timber trunks are a recurring feature in some of the continental shafts.

By the middle of the first millennium grain storage pits had become a familiar feature of settlements in central southern Britain. The pits could vary in size but could be up to 2 metres deep, circular in plan, and frequently bell-shaped with a narrow mouth that was easy to seal and make airtight. The generally accepted view is that these pits were dug to store seed-grain to keep it safe in the liminal period between harvest and the next sowing. The grain for consumption was stored in above-ground granaries, but seed-grain was deliberately put underground in the realms of the chthonic deities, where the expectation would have been that the gods would protect it and maintain its fertility. Once the grain had been removed, careful depositions were often made on the pit bottom and a second deposition was sometimes

10.3 Large storage pits, probably for seed grain, dug into the chalk bedrock in the Iron Age hill-fort of Danebury, Hampshire. It is likely that the belief system behind the practice embodied the idea that the vital grain would be protected by the chthonic deities

made later in the year after silting had taken place. A reasonable explanation for these recurring patterns is that the primary deposit was to thank the deity for protecting the seed during the quiescent phase, while the secondary deposit acknowledged successful young growth or a good harvest.

A considerable range of depositions have been identified. Most common were joints of meat, or sometimes whole animals. But pots, quernstones, loom weights, iron implements, or bronze horse gear were incorporated, and there may have been other deposits no longer archaeologically visible, like bales of wool, kegs of butter, or cheeses. Occasionally human skeletons or human body parts were used. It is tempting to suggest that such instances only occurred at times of extreme danger, when the deities need to be appeased with gifts of particular value like the preserved head of a famous enemy, part of a revered ancestor, or even a human sacrifice. The occasion for such extreme deposits might have ranged from a disastrous harvest to failure in a

10.4 Animal offerings were often placed in the Danebury pits after the corn had been removed. Combinations of horse and dog, as in this case, where a complete dog was accompanied by a horse leg, were common, suggesting that these animals in some way were thought to possess special powers

10.5 One of the ways of disposing of the dead in southern Britain in the fourth to second century BC was to place the tightly bound body bundles at the bottom of abandoned storage pits, as here at Danebury

raid or threat of imminent attack. These depositions, in their archaeological sterility, are mute reminders of the traumas of everyday existence and of the dominance of the ever-present gods in the lives of the people.

The deposition of items of value, usually weapons and armour, thrown into watery contexts was a regular practice, becoming increasingly popular after about 1400 BC and continuing throughout the first millennium BC and into the period of Roman occupation. In Britain and Ireland it accounts for most of the elite metalwork recovered during the period, but the practice was also widespread throughout western Europe. It is evident from the distribution of the watery finds that certain rivers were more popular than others and certain stretches of those rivers were particularly favoured, suggesting that the acts of deposition focused on specific locations believed to be especially propitious. In some cases, like Fiskerton on the River Trent and Flag Fen on the fen margin, specially constructed timber walkways provided the platform from which the dedication took place. Elsewhere it might be a conveniently projecting rock, as at Llyn Cerrig Bach in Anglesey, from which large quantities of metalwork were thrown into what was a much larger lake sometime in the first century BC. In the case of Llyn Fawr in south Wales the depositions were made from the sloping side of the corrie overlooking the lake. While some of the depositions may have been one-off events, it remains a strong possibility that people returned to the same spot more than once to placate their deity. This was clearly the case at Flag Fen, where the offerings spanned several centuries.

The deposition of elite gear, usually weapons, in watery contexts is referred to in the classical sources describing sacred locations in Gaul. Strabo specifically mentions lakes in which the natives deposited quantities of gold and silver, and where weapons captured in battle were assembled in piles dedicated to the gods. It may have been in the aftermath of successful military engagements that many of the weapons found in British and Irish rivers and bogs were taken from worldly use and put into the realms of the deities. Many of the items, readily recognizable from the craftsman-

10.6 Part of a timber causeway built out into the River Witham at Fiskerton, Lincolnshire. From the causeway offerings to the gods were thrown into the waters

ship lavished on them, would have been famous in their day, with long histories of engagement in the affairs of man. Their final dedication to the gods would have been events of great moment. Folk memories of such times may underlie the Arthurian story of the famous sword Excalibur rising again from the lake.

Springs, particularly the springs that gave birth to great rivers, were particularly revered as places where the underworld communicated with the world of humans, and each would have been presided over by a specific deity. One of the best known is the source of the Seine in Burgundy, where the river goddess Sequana had a shrine, and where pilgrims flocked in the first century BC and first century AD to benefit from the deity's curative powers. Similar sacred locations must have existed throughout Britain and Ireland. One was the hot spring at Bath presided over by the goddess Sulis. So important was the shrine that it was taken over in the Roman period and developed as a curative establishment dedicated to Sulis Minerva, a conflation of the native and a classical deity.

Classical descriptions of Gaulish religion emphasize the importance of natural places as sacred locations: springs, sacred groves, ancient trees, and prominent rocks— the gods were everywhere within the landscape. But there were also man-made shrines, usually small rectangular buildings sometimes set within a defined temenos (the religious space delineated by a boundary). Examples are known throughout south-eastern Britain, in hill-forts such as Danebury and South Cadbury and in the open countryside at places like Hayling Island in Hampshire and Heathrow. These were probably places of assembly, where the Druids and the ordinary people could meet, contrasting with the great natural sanctuaries where normal mortals feared to go.

Human Sacrifice

That human sacrifice was an ever-present reality in Britain and Ireland we can be reasonably certain. The well-preserved body found in a bog at Lindow in Cheshire, dating to the first century AD, has all the appearance of having been a sacrificial victim. He had been thrice killed: with a violent blow to the head, garrotting, and his throat cut. Such elaboration would have been more appropriate to a ritual death than to mere homicide. In Ireland, too, several bog bodies have been recovered in the course of peat cutting. One found at Clonycavan near Dublin had been struck on the head with a sharp-bladed weapon. Another, found at Croghan, 40 kilometres from Clonycavan, appears to have been tortured before being beheaded and dismembered. It has been suggested that the individuals had been ritually killed and deposited on

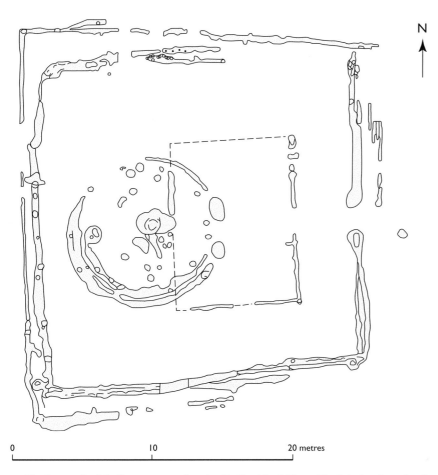

N

0   10   20 metres

10.7 Circular temple of the first century BC found at Hayling Island, Hampshire. It is clear from the plan that there were many phases of reconstruction

boundaries to propitiate the gods and protect territories, but casual violence cannot be entirely ruled out.

In dealing with skeletal material alone it is more difficult to distinguish between simple depositions and ritual killing. But at the hill-fort at Danebury several skeletons have been found, splayed on the bottom of pits with large flints covering them. These are quite different from the more careful tightly crouched burials, also sometimes found in pits, which may be the wrapped bodies of ancestors brought in from the excarnation grounds for special deposition. Another Danebury pit find, the pelvis of a young man sliced from the body and with its legs hacked off at the thighs, is redolent of ritual behaviour, as is the partially dismembered child found in the hill-fort at

Wandlebury in Cambridgeshire. Finds of this kind are not difficult to collate with the classical descriptions of human sacrifice and divination presided over by the Druids.

Who Were the Gods?

Julius Caesar, writing of the Gaulish gods, implies that there were many, all with different powers, that could be broadly correlated with the gods of the Roman pantheon. Indeed, the names of several hundred are recorded on Roman dedicatory inscriptions found throughout Britain, Gaul, and Germany. The plethora of confusing deities falls broadly into two groups: there are the deities of place and the deities of the sky. The first are land-based, often associated with rivers and springs, and are usually female; the second are the tribal gods, who are invariably male. This neat balance is also reflected in the Irish vernacular traditions of the two great gods: the male, Dagda, and the female, Morrigan, who exist in a competitive equilibrium, harmonized once a year when they meet for intercourse. This pleasing structuralism may help us to understand the underlying nature of the religious belief system, but for a Briton living in the Iron Age, the world of the gods would have seemed confusing and dangerous—too dangerous for a mere mortal to navigate without a friendly Druid as an intermediary.

Looking Forward

Caesar makes no mention of British Druids in his account of his brief campaigns in the south-east of the country in 55 and 54 BC, but following the full-scale invasion launched by Claudius in AD 43 the Druids were probably in evidence, stirring up resistance to the Roman advance, and in AD 59 the resistance of the Druids on Anglesey was a matter requiring swift attention. Thereafter the historical record is silent and we can only assume that the native religious elite became integrated into the Roman system. In Gaul we learn from Ausonius of an Armorican Druid who ended his days as a teacher in the University of Bordeaux. But that there may have been dissident voices remaining in the depths of the countryside is suggested by several references to female Druids offering prophecies in third-century AD Gaul. By this stage, however, those few who still clung to the old religion were little more than magicians and fortune-tellers crying in the wilderness.

In Ireland the Druids remained a significant force throughout the first half of the first millennium AD, but with the spread of Christianity in the fifth and sixth centuries the power of the Druids waned. Their function as the learned men of society was assumed by the clergy, and by the eighth century, as the Irish law tracts make clear, they were reduced to the status of casters of spells and makers of love potions. The mood of the time is neatly summed up in an eighth-century hymn which asks for God's protection from the spells of women, blacksmiths, and Druids.

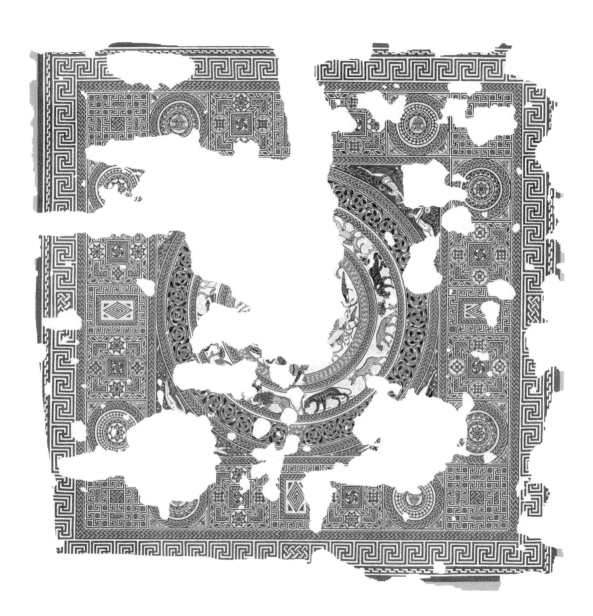

11

Integration

THE ROMAN EPISODE, 60 BC–AD 350

O N 26 August 55 BC Julius Caesar set off from Gaul with two legions and 500 cavalry on what was planned to be a short reconnaissance of the south-east of Britain. His intention had been to launch a major campaign the year before, but a revolt among the tribes of Armorica had distracted him. It may be, as Strabo claimed, that the uprising, organized by the Veneti, was a deliberate attempt by the Armoricans to deflect Caesar from his British exploits, which would have disrupted their lucrative trade with the island. In any event the Armorican insurgents were defeated, and late in 56 BC Caesar turned his attentions to subduing the Morini and Menapii, Belgic tribes who occupied the Gaulish coast flanking the Strait of Dover. The resistance was greater than he had anticipated and he had to return the next year to finish the task, only to be further delayed by an invasion of Germans from across the Rhine. By the time the threat had been dealt with, it was late in the campaigning season, leaving little time for more than a cursory exploration of the tantalizing island glimpsed across the narrow strait.

Caesar was at a crucial stage in his career. In 56 BC he had, somewhat unusually, been granted a second term of office in Cisalpine and Transalpine Gaul, and with Gaul now well on the way to being conquered, he needed to excite the Roman audience with further spectacular deeds. Gaul was bounded by two barriers: the River Rhine and the ocean. It would be an act of great daring to break through these emo-

11.1 Julius Caesar, who commanded expeditions to Britain in 55 and 54 BC

tive limits, and for Caesar the challenge was irresistible. But to campaign outside the territory assigned to him was politically dangerous. The limited expedition to Britain could, however, be presented as a prudent move to teach a lesson to the British, who had been accused of sending troops to fight with the Gauls against the Romans—a version of the modern concept of hot pursuit. In the event, he need not have worried. His audience in Rome was wildly enthusiastic. Caesar had conquered the ocean: it was like putting a man on the moon. The senate voted twenty days of thanksgiving—an unusually long period—thus reassuring Caesar that the way was open for a more extended campaign the next year.

In preparation for the exploratory expedition in 55 BC Caesar had attempted to gather information about the island, with, he claimed, little success. 'In the ordinary way', he wrote, 'no one goes to Britain except traders, and even they are acquainted only with the sea-coast and the areas that are opposite Gaul.' He summoned 'traders from all parts', but they could tell him nothing of value. This is surprising given the extent of trade, and a more likely explanation is that they chose to be highly selective with the intelligence they shared. However, the one positive result was that they warned the British of Caesar's intention, and several of the tribes sent envoys offering hostages and allegiance. To follow up the offers Commius, a chief of the Gaulish Atrebates and confidant of the Romans, was sent back with the ambassadors as a negotiator, but there were misunderstandings and he was immediately imprisoned by the Britons, only to be handed back after the army had successfully landed. Before the expedition left, Caesar sent a tribune on a four-day reconnaissance of the coast to identify suitable places to land.

The expedition was a limited success. The main lesson was that the ocean, with its massive tides, racing currents, and variable winds, was a more formidable opponent than the Britons and it wreaked havoc on the Roman logistics. However, the natives were fierce fighters but were totally unused to facing the serried ranks of the Roman army; more to the point, they were politically fragmented, making careful diplomacy an effective weapon. In his few weeks in Britain, Caesar had learnt much.

The next year, 54 BC, the campaign began in early July and was on an altogether different scale. Five legions and 2,000 cavalry—some 27,000 men—were transported in over 800 vessels, the majority constructed specifically for the purpose. The landing was unopposed. No doubt the preparation of the previous winter had included

11.2 From the description of the Roman landings in Britain in 55 BC it is likely that the legions came ashore somewhere on the shelving beaches in the vicinity of Deal in Kent

political negotiations with British leaders, one of whom was Mandubracius, son of the king of the Trinovantes, a tribe occupying the Essex region. Mandubracius had fled to Gaul to put himself under Caesar's protection after his father had been killed in internecine conflict with his neighbour Cassivellaunus, the king of the Catuvellauni, who, according to Caesar, were in a continual state of war with the other tribes in the area. Mandubracius was invaluable, not least because he was a source of intelligence about the complexities of local politics and the principal centres of power in eastern Britain, and about the terrain through which Caesar must fight. He was also a political pawn that could be played to good effect when the occasion arose.

Armed with this information, Caesar's course was clear. A rapid, though heavily opposed, advance through Kent led him to the Thames, which was crossed, probably at the site of London. The army then made for Cassivellaunus' *oppidum* in the vicinity of St Albans. 'It was protected by forests and marshes, and a great number of men and cattle had been collected in it. I should mention that the Britons give the name *oppidum* to any densely wooded place they have fortified with a rampart and trench and use as a refuge from the attack of invaders' (*B Gall.* 5.21). In the meantime the Trinovantes, whom Caesar describes as the strongest tribe in south-east Britain, sent a deputation to discuss terms. In return for the reinstatement of Mandubracius as king and the promise of Roman protection, they would surrender to Caesar, sending forty hostages as an assurance of their good behaviour and, at the same time, provide grain for the army. This was a turning point and other tribes quickly followed suit: Caesar names five of them. In all probability the outline of the deal had already been negotiated during the winter, when Mandubracius was under Caesar's protection in Gaul. Knowing that he could probably rely on the Trinovantes to come over to Rome would have emboldened Caesar to make his rapid advance into hostile territory across the Thames, dangerously far from his supply base.

But the danger was still there. Cassivellaunus responded to Caesar's successes by instructing the four kings of Kent to attack the Roman base and supply lines. In the event, the attack failed and there was little Cassivellaunus could do but sue for peace. The lateness of the season meant that Caesar was eager to negotiate terms. An annual tribute to be paid by the Britons to Rome was agreed, hostages were handed over, and Cassivellaunus undertook to leave the Trinovantes in peace. Caesar could present this as an honourable deal and, with his aims achieved, leave with evident relief for Gaul, with 'a great many prisoners', to face the threat of new unrest among the Gaulish Belgae, which was soon to flare up into a dangerous rebellion.

Whether these two brief excursions into Britain could be judged a Roman success is debatable since we do not know what Caesar's aspirations really were. Reading between the lines of his carefully edited accounts, it is clear that the perils of the Channel crossing and the ferocity of the British resistance had been grossly underestimated. The expeditions were a considerable risk and Caesar was lucky to escape with his reputation unscathed. For the Romans he had shown that the ocean could be mastered and that the distant island was accessible, if at a price. He could also claim to have taken the first step in bringing it under Roman domination since the Britons were now paying an annual tribute to the Roman state: others could be left to complete the job.

For their part, the Britons of the south-east had gained first-hand experience of Roman military might, but, more to the point, they had learnt just how divisive

Rome could be. Before the invasion tribes engaging in local conflicts could strike up allegiances with each other for mutual benefit. Now a far more powerful force had entered the arena. To be a friend of Rome brought the benefits of protection. By paying a tribute and sending hostages to the Roman world there were real advantages to be had. Lucrative trading monopolies could be negotiated, and the hostages—usually young men from elite families—could be educated in Roman ways. Those who remained abroad would no doubt have maintained filial links with their tribe, while those who chose to return would bring with them new knowledge and a network of contacts that could benefit all. The desire to travel and to explore the world, so deeply embedded in the psyche of the Britons, could now be exercised within an expanded system of patronage linked directly to the Mediterranean elites.

The Proximity of Rome: A New Reality

In less than five years since Caesar first entered Gaul, western Europe had been transformed. The whole of Gaul was now under Roman control. Admittedly Caesar had more battles to fight, but by the time he had finished with the Gauls in the winter of 51–50 BC, the nascent province was beginning to become Roman. War exhaustion slowed progress, and there were occasional local uprisings to be brought under control, but by 27 BC the situation was sufficiently stable for a national census to be instituted, and in 12 BC the culmination of the process of incorporation was marked by the dedication of an altar to Rome and Augustus at Lugdunum (Lyon) in the presence of representatives of the sixty tribes of Gaul.

The integration of Gaul into the political and economic sphere of Rome cannot have failed to have a significant effect on Britain, particularly the south-eastern part of it. After the invasion a marked change in the orientation of trade seems to have taken place. The networks that had linked the north coast of Armorica with the port of Hengistbury Head came to an abrupt end and were replaced by new systems that focused on routes between northern Gaul and the Thames estuary. This is most dramatically shown by the distribution of two types of Italian wine amphora: Dressel 1A, in use between c. 130 and c. 40 BC, which concentrates in central southern Britain and, in particular, the Hengistbury region, and Dressel 1B, which became common in the second half of the first century BC and is found mainly in the east of Britain on either side of the Thames estuary. One plausible explanation for the shift in the trading axis is that Caesar's devastating attack on the rebel Armoricans in 56 BC totally disrupted the traditional networks, while his negotiated settlement with the Trinovantes may have offered them a trading monopoly, or at least preferential treatment in their dealings with the Gallo-Belgic middlemen. This is not to say that trading with Armorica died away altogether. In the last part of the first century BC and early first century AD Poole Harbour seems to have taken over from Hengistbury as a port of entry, but the volume of traded goods was much reduced, and of little significance when compared with the quantity of goods now arriving via the Thames route.

At the time Strabo was writing, late in the first century BC or early in the first century AD, there were four major routes in operation for ships wishing to cross to Britain, starting from the mouths of the four great rivers, the Rhine, the Seine, the Loire, and the Gironde, though he is at pains to make clear that those setting out from the Rhine usually chose to sail down the coast to Gesoriacum (Boulogne) before making the crossing. This does not mean that all trade was confined to these direct routes. A lead anchor-stock of Graeco-Roman type found off the coast of north-west Wales near Porth Felen, and probably lost in the first century BC, sug-

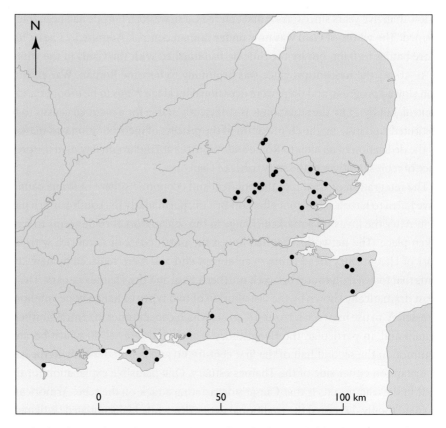

11.3 The distribution of Dressel 1B type amphorae reflects the areas into which wine was imported from Gaul in the second half of the first century BC and the early first century AD

gests a more adventurous exploit. Strabo lists the principal exports of Britain as 'grain, cattle, gold, silver and iron . . . also hides and slaves and dogs that are by nature suited to the purpose of the chase' (Strabo 4.5.2). In return the Britons received 'ivory chains and necklaces and amber gems and glass vessels and other pretty wares of that sort' (Strabo 4.5.3). Thus, Britain provided raw materials and manpower in return for manufactured luxuries.

The development of more regular trading networks with increasingly Romanized Belgic Gaul would have brought about major changes in the native economic system. That there was now a continental market for British-generated surpluses must have encouraged productivity, turning the economy from a sufficer to a maximizer system. One major effect of this can be seen in the slave-trade. In British society there would have been comparably little call for slaves, but the Roman world was an avid consumer, and by the mid-first century BC slaves were in short supply. Caesar's campaigns in Gaul more than met the need, particularly if we believe the exaggerated claim of one writer that he enslaved a third of the Gaulish population. But once Gaul had been transformed from a war zone to a province, the supply rapidly diminished and other sources had to be found. Britain was conveniently close by, and the less developed parts of the west and north would have provided profitable hunting grounds. The demand of the south-eastern elites for marketable slaves is likely to have encouraged the generation of captives in the peripheral regions through the agency of warfare and raiding: thus, conflict became profitable. How extensive was the export of manpower we can only guess. Caesar, as we have seen by his own admission, carried off a great many prisoners. These exotic foreigners from beyond the ocean may have commanded a premium in the slave market. It may have been slaves that Strabo encountered when he described the Britons as taller than the Celti (Gauls) 'and not so yellow-haired, although their bodies are of looser build'. He goes on to say that he himself in Rome 'saw mere lads towering as much as half a foot above the tallest people in the city, although they were bandy-legged and presented no fair lines anywhere else in their figure' (Strabo 4.5.2). Such interesting oddities may well have been in demand.

But it was not only enslaved Britons that were to be seen on the Continent. Caesar took many hostages from the families of the British elite, some of whom might have taken up residence in Rome and there acquired a veneer of Romanization. Of these, a number may have chosen to return to the island to assume leadership roles.

Mobility of people between Britain and the Roman world probably increased over time. There was a tacit acceptance, at least by some of the major tribes of the south-east, that Britain was subservient to Rome. In an ode written about 15 BC the poet Horace could list the Britons among those who 'admired' or 'heard' the emperor

Augustus, and a little later Strabo noted that 'certain of the British dynasts have obtained the friendship of Caesar Augustus by embassies and courtesies and have set up offerings in the Capitol' (Strabo 5.5.3). Acts of this kind helped to maintain the pretence that Britain had been conquered, while in Britain support for Rome was a powerful diplomatic weapon in the constant power struggles that engaged the British elite. For some, Rome provided a safe haven when they were forced to flee. About AD 10 two British leaders, Tincomarus and Dubnovellaunus from the southern kingdoms, evidently on the losing side in some British dispute, put themselves under the emperor's protection in Rome, a fact thought significant enough to be recorded on an imperial monument in Ankara.

The ousting of pro-Roman leaders provided Rome with an opportunity. When, in AD 39, Adminius, a son of the powerful king Cunobelin, fell out with his father and fled the country to seek the emperor's help, Gaius used the event as an excuse to mount an invasion of Britain. The attempt came to nothing, but three years later, when another British dynast, Verica, made a dash for the Continent, the new emperor, Claudius, seized the opportunity. The expulsion of this friend of Rome offered a convenient excuse to mount a full-scale invasion of the island, an adventure that had probably been forming in the emperor's mind for some time. So it was in AD 43 that the Roman armies returned to Britain, this time to stay.

The movement of people between Britain and Gaul was two-way. The best recorded incident was the flight to Britain of the Gaulish Atrebatic leader Commius, who had been employed by Caesar as an ambassador at the time of his British expeditions. In 52 BC Commius suddenly changed sides and threw in his lot with the Gaulish resistance, which later that year failed spectacularly with the capitulation of the rebel leader Vercingetorix. Commius, now an enemy of Rome, was hounded until 50 BC, when he finally escaped with his followers to Britain 'to join his people who had already settled there'. The dynasty he founded was based at Calleva, now Silchester, in the middle Thames valley. How large an influx of people was involved is unknown, but, once established, the new kingdom would have provided a convenient haven for other dissidents fleeing from Gaul.

The ninety years or so between the exploits of Caesar and the invasion of Claudius saw the south-east of Britain drawn ever closer to the neighbouring regions of Gaul. Familial relationships and the intensifying dynamics of trade would have encouraged movement on an unprecedented scale. The major centres of population, the *oppida*, became the main markets where traders assembled. We know little of the arrangements in Britain, but elsewhere in Europe communities of traders from the Roman provinces were regularly found to be living among native communities far beyond the frontiers. So it must have been in Britain.

The effects of these contacts are vividly displayed in the archaeological record. In the second half of the first century BC the material culture of south-eastern Britain, especially Kent, Essex, and Hertfordshire, became almost indistinguishable from that of the southern part of Belgic Gaul north of the Seine. The same types of wheel-turned pottery are used, cremation burial is widely adopted, and luxury goods, including amphorae of wine, fine imported tableware, and bronze and silver wine-serving vessels, were the required accompaniment to an elite burial. The distribution of these luxury burials in Essex and Hertfordshire provides a clear indication of the centres of power: the fiefdoms of the leading men who could control the burgeoning trade and could grow even richer in the process.

Sudden access to the rapidly growing continental markets changed the political geography of Britain. The south-east, roughly bounded by the Jurassic ridge from Dorset to North Yorkshire, became a core zone which rapidly assimilated continental culture. It was divided by the Thames into two broad political powers: the northern polity, dominated by the Catuvellauni and Trinovantes; and the southern polity,

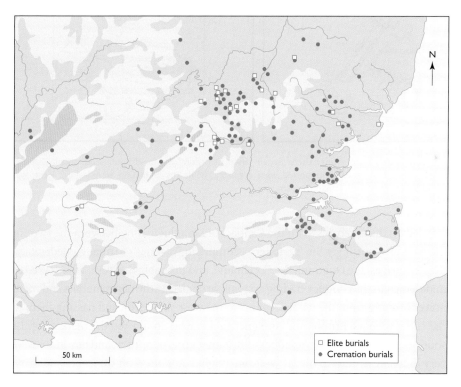

50 km

□ Elite burials
• Cremation burials

II.4 In the first century BC and early first century AD the communities of part of south-eastern Britain opted for the cremation rite that was common on the adjacent continent. Some of the burials of the elite were accompanied by wine-drinking equipment

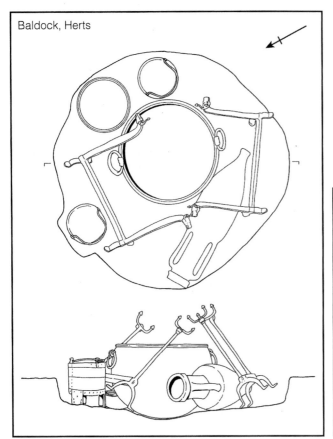

Baldock, Herts

Aylesford, Kent

11.5 Elite burials from south-eastern Britain often incorporated wine-drinking equipment. Baldock, Hertfordshire, contained an imported wine amphora, while the cremation at Aylesford, Kent, was accompanied by a north Italian wine strainer

focused on the Atrebates, with the Cantiaci of Kent fluctuating between the two. To the west and north lay the 'periphery', comprising a series of tribal confederacies, the Durotriges, the Dobunni, the Corieltauvi, and probably the Iceni, who served as middlemen in the complex trading systems, articulating the raw materials and manpower brought from the wilder regions to the west and north, and passing them to the entrepreneurs, Britons and foreigners alike, who dominated the markets of the south-eastern core. The three zones of Britain—core, periphery, and beyond—were very different worlds. In the far west one might eat mutton off trenchers and drink beer from wooden tankards while discussing the impact of the latest slave raids. At the same time, in the south-east choice cuts of pork and figs were eaten from

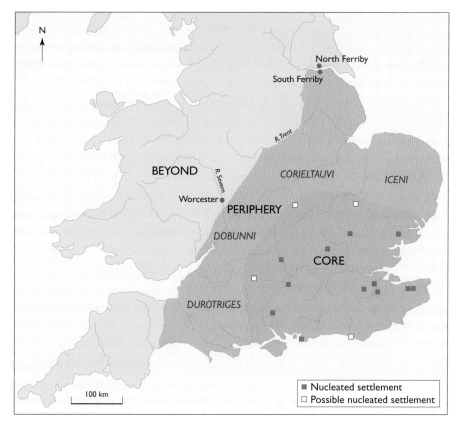

11.6 By the early first century AD three distinct socio-economic zones can be recognized in southern Britain. In the south-east the core zone had developed large settlements that can be regarded as towns and was linked by trade to the Continent, now under Roman control. Beyond the core was a peripheral zone of tribes who traded with the core and through whose territory raw materials and slaves from the north and west of the country passed

imported platters and Mediterranean wines drunk from silver cups newly arrived from northern Italy, while Gaulish merchants negotiated to sell the next ship-load of amphorae. The south-east was now, economically at least, part of the Roman world. To Claudius, eyeing Britain as a potential acquisition, conquest must have seemed an undemanding enterprise.

Conquest and Integration in the Frontier Regions

It was not an auspicious beginning. Four legions and supporting auxiliaries, some 40,000 men in all, had been assembled at Gesoriacum in the spring of AD 43, but superstitions about the ocean and stories of the fearful storms that nearly defeated Caesar played upon men's fears and they refused to embark. The mutiny was eventually defused, but valuable time had been lost. Yet by the end of the campaigning season the native capital at Camulodunum (Colchester) had been taken and most of the south-eastern core was under Roman control. Once the tribes of the peripheral zone had been brought to heel, their territories speared by a military road, the Fosse Way, running from the Devon coast to the Humber, the wilder lands beyond could be tackled. The pace of advance was conditioned by a number of factors: the strength of the resistance, the ability of the commanders, and changes in imperial policy consequent upon events elsewhere in the empire. By AD 51 the south-west peninsula and much of the eastern part of Wales were under Roman control. Further advances into Wales were halted in AD 60 by the rebellion led by Boudicca in the very heart of the nascent province, and it took a decade before the devastating effects of the rebellion, and the Roman reprisals that followed, were overcome and the province was strong enough to bear a renewed period of advance. In the 70s Wales and the north up to the Tyne–Solway line were secured, and by 84 BC the armies had penetrated the far north of Scotland, fighting the last major battle against British resistance at Mons Graupius in the vicinity of Inverness. The commander of the northern campaign, Julius Agricola, could symbolize the end of the conquest by sending a military detachment by ship around the northern extremity of Scotland, visiting Orkney en route, to show that nothing of significance lay beyond. Two years earlier he stood on the west coast of Scotland, looking across the North Channel to Ireland, speculating that the island could be conquered and held by a single legion and a few auxiliaries. His assessment was not, however, to be put to the test.

Within a few years of Agricola's triumphant completion of the conquest, much of Scotland had been abandoned down to the Tyne–Solway line, where, following Hadrian's visit in AD 122, the frontier was now formalized with the linear boundary that bears his name. A generation or so later (AD 139–42) there was an advance into Lowland Scotland, culminating in the marking out of a new frontier line, the Antonine Wall, along the Clyde–Forth line. The new defence was short-lived and by the 160s Hadrian's Wall was again the frontier, though recurrent troubles in the north in AD 181–4, 197–207, and 208–11 demanded new campaigns that reached far into Scotland and involved considerable military commitment.

Britain was not an easy province to keep under control. For much of the first century there were four legions involved in active campaigning, and even after the initial

11.7 (*opposite*) The progress of the Roman army through Britain in the forty years following the invasion of AD 43

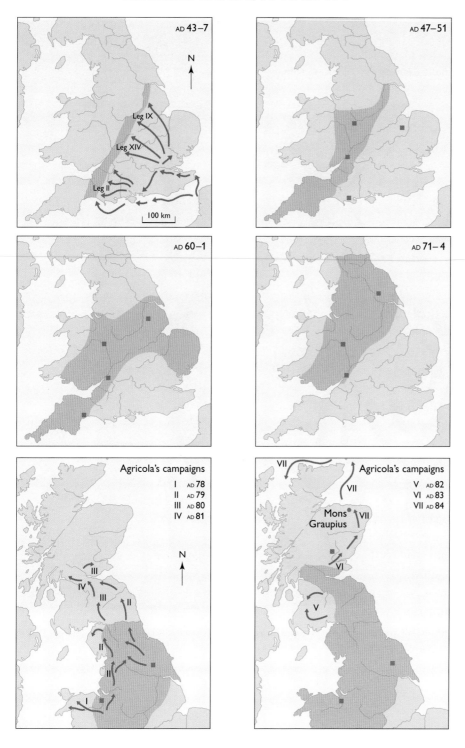

AD 43–7

N

Leg IX

Leg XIV

Leg II

100 km

AD 47–51

AD 60–1

AD 71–4

Agricola's campaigns

I   AD 78
II AD 79
III AD 80
IV AD 81

N

III
IV
III   II
II
II
I

Agricola's campaigns

V   AD 82
VI AD 83
VII AD 84

VII
VII
Mons
Graupius   VII
VI
V

11.8 One of the decorative panels carved on a distance slab found at Bridgeness on the Antonine Wall in Scotland vividly portrays the conquest of the native Britons by the Roman army

conquest was complete it required three legions to maintain order in the military zones of Wales and the north. In addition to the legions, large numbers of auxiliaries were also employed. Indeed, as the occupation continued, it is likely that the actual number of soldiers on active service rose from about 40,000 at the time of the invasion to about 55,000 by the mid-second century. Most of these would have been stationed in the military zones, but probably as many as 2,000 were occupied in various duties in the civilian area, including service in the Governor's Guard, based in London.

In the early years all soldiers, whether legionnaires or auxiliaries, were foreign to Britain. The legionnaires were Roman citizens who were mostly recruited in Italy, while the auxiliaries came from the provinces, quite often the provinces where the legions had been stationed before their move to Britain. This meant that by far the greatest number of auxiliaries came from Gaul, the Rhineland, and Spain, and many would therefore have spoken dialects of the same Celtic language as the Britons. We know that there were four cohorts of Batavians and two of Tungrians (from the Rhine mouth and northern Gaul) in the force commanded by Agricola in the first century, and soldiers from these regions make their appearance on the writing tablets found on the Hadrian's Wall fort of Vindolanda at the end of the century. Far fewer units came from Africa, the Danubian provinces, and the east, but 5,500 Sarmatian cavalry, captured during the Marcomannic Wars in the late second century, were transferred to Britain. The Sarmatians originated in the Pontic Steppe and were descended from horse-riding nomads: as cavalry troops they were renowned. Thracian units, from modern Bulgaria, also served as skilled cavalry in Britain. Other specialist units included Syrian archers, who were stationed on the Antonine Wall. The African provinces also provided troops. One man, attested on a tombstone from Housesteads on Hadrian's Wall, came from Hippo Regius in Tunisia.

The influx of between 40,000 and 50,000 foreign soldiers into Britain in the first century AD made a major addition to the gene pool. Many of these men will have taken wives from among the British population. Though the marriage of serving soldiers was not officially permitted, there is ample evidence of family occupation in well-studied forts like Vindolanda. Many, on discharge, will have chosen to stay in Britain, settling in the *vici* (civilian settlements) around the forts or, in the case of legionnaires, in the veteran colonies at Colchester, Lincoln, and Gloucester. Over time the distinctive ethnic character of the garrisons would have become diluted since from the second century it became the norm to top up existing units with local recruits rather than shipping them in from the country where the unit originated. The pool of recruits, however, would have included the sons of veterans, who may have chosen to serve in their father's regiment. In spite of local recruitment, there

would always have been a constant inflow of men from around the empire eager for an army career. Since the legions were recruited from Roman citizens, it is unlikely that there would have been a sufficient pool available in Britain until the early third century, when the rights of citizenship were greatly extended among the provincials.

Something of the cosmopolitan nature of the military zone is vividly displayed in the late first-century letters preserved at Vindolanda. Of the names recorded, some 200 individuals came from the Rhineland region. Perhaps even more emotive is a tombstone from Hadrian's Wall at South Shields, which records the death of Regina, a freed woman from the tribe of the Catuvellauni who died at the age of 30. This Hertfordshire girl, once a slave, was married to Barates, born in the town of Palmyra on the edge of the Syrian desert. The tombstone he erected for his wife was inscribed in both Latin and Palmyrene. The tombstone of Barates himself was found at Corbridge, 50 kilometres west along the Wall. He is styled 'vexila[rius]' (a dealer in ensigns). What stories lie behind these two stones we can only guess. Was he a dealer or a serving soldier? Was she sold into slavery by poor parents? And how did the couple cope with life on the edge of the civilized world in a landscape alien to them both? There must have been many marriages like this in first- and second-century Britain.

Control of the Land

The conquest of a new territory meant, in theory, the appropriation of its land and resources by the emperor, but in reality there would have been a variety of treatments meted out. Those who supported Rome at the crucial moment of conquest would have been well rewarded. One such was Tiberius Claudius Togidubnus, a client king whose base may have been the palatial building at Fishbourne near Chichester. He seems to have lived well into the 70s and during this time was given extensive territories in the south. To his original kingdom around Chichester were probably added the lands of the Atrebates and the Belgae. His names suggest that he was probably made a Roman citizen by Claudius, but his origins have been much debated. He may have been a member of the local aristocracy in power at the moment of the invasions or a person of royal ancestry, perhaps exiled in Gaul and brought in by the invading forces to be installed to reinforce the flank of the advance party. At any event, he proved his loyalty in the early stages of the conquest and again during the dangerous times of the Boudiccan rebellion and was rewarded accordingly. No doubt he was allowed to retain

11.9 (*opposite*) One of the best-preserved sections of Hadrian's Wall runs along the crest of the Whin Sill. In the foreground (*left*) is the Roman fort of Housesteads, partially excavated, with the earthworks of the civilian settlement (*vicus*) surrounding it

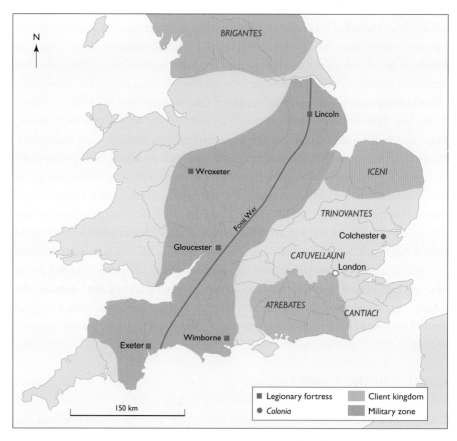

11.10 In the first two decades following the invasion of AD 43 the province of Britannia was under different forms of control. Some tribes were ruled by native kings answerable to the Roman authority, while other parts of the country were under direct military supervision

his rights over his territories, and it may have been under his patronage that his elite supporters were given large estates along the southern slopes of the South Downs, where they emulated their king, building villas in the Roman style.

Another of the Roman client kings was Prasutagus of the Iceni, whose territory lay in Norfolk. On his death in AD 59 the Roman administrators began the process of integrating his lands into the state, thereby sparking the unrest that drove his widow, Boudicca, to rebel. Further north the confederation of tribes collectively known as the Brigantes, who occupied the Pennine region, was left in the hands of Queen Cartimandua until internal dissent led by her husband made it necessary for the Roman army to move in and rescue her. The client kingdoms were a useful expedient in the early stages of conquest, but at best they were a temporary solution to be dispensed with as soon as a suitable occasion arose.

Elsewhere land was variously dealt with. Large tracts of land around the *coloniae*, where veterans were settled, were appropriated by the state and given to the retired soldiers to farm. This must have caused particular hardship to the natives and was a source of considerable resentment. It was one of the reasons why the Trinovantes, whose land around Colchester was confiscated for the settlers, were so ready to join Boudicca's rebellion in AD 60. The arrogant attitude of the time-expired soldiers who had taken part in the initial stages of the conquest, and whose rights as Roman citizens far exceeded those of the natives, must have been intolerable. Imperial control of mineral resources and the creation of vast imperial estates will have caused equal upset, though in much of the countryside local people would have been kept on to do the work, thus maintaining a degree of continuity.

We know little of the rules of landholding under the pre-Roman system, but in all probability most of those farming the land would have been required to pay a tithe or provided labour to an overlord. Under Roman law, landownership rights were redefined. The land was carefully quantified, and those holding title were expected to pay a direct tax or a tribute (*ager stipendiarius*) to the state. This latter would have been in kind in the form of labour services or military levies, but, as time went on, it was increasingly paid in cash. In many ways this was not very different from the situation before the invasion, the principal change being that in the old 'Celtic' system the productive surpluses were essentially redistributed within the community, the patrons providing protection and services to their clients. In the Roman system a significant percentage of the product was taken away from the home domain to support a distant army and to prop up the parasitic Roman state. Yet those who were able to maximize their profits under the new system now had the facility to accumulate wealth as money and to reinvest it. They could also, if they wished, pay for public works, suitably inscribed to proclaim their largess. In the 'Celtic' system a patron would have provided his client with a feast; in the Roman system he might endow the public baths.

In the early years after the initial invasions, new men streamed into the island. We have already mentioned the 40,000 to 50,000 soldiers, but in addition there was the governor and his entourage, including the standard clutter of officials needed to run the new state system (surveyors, tax adjudicators, lawyers, and a huge secretariat), together with those who saw the opening of the new province as a way to turn a quick denarius: moneylenders, property speculators, and merchants. While Richborough on the short Channel crossing from Gaul was the first port of entry, especially for the military, it was not long before the advantages of London, sited at the lowest bridging point of the Thames where the river was still tidal, were recognized and exploited. By AD 60, the year of the Boudiccan rebellion, it was, as Tacitus describes, teeming

11.11 The Iron Age hill-fort of Knook Castle on Salisbury Plain overlooks an area of earthworks that represent the development of a native village from the Iron Age well into the Roman period

with merchants and traders. This was a boom time, with the ever-expanding markets drawing in a constant stream of speculators.

Many, if not most, of the entrepreneurs who moved into the new province will have come from Gaul and the Rhineland, but they may have brought with them slaves from more distant places. Particularly valued were Greek slaves, who served as an educated underclass, providing the skilled and literate underpinning needed in both commercial and administrative undertakings. A few individuals with Greek names are known in Britain, but their total numbers are difficult to guess.

Then there were the specialist craft skills needed to meet the demands of the new province for physical infrastructure. The army will have provided much of this in the early years: surveyors, road engineers, hydraulic specialists, even the masons and brickmakers. But private enterprise would soon have taken over as the demand for skills increased. An interesting example of this is offered by the massive building programme at Fishbourne, which began in the 60s and lasted for more than a decade, during which time increasingly elaborate palatial buildings were erected, quite possibly for the local client king Togidubnus. The project would have required not only architects and engineers schooled in the most up-to-date Roman methods, but a whole range of building specialists: masons, tile-makers, marble workers, sculptors, wall painters, stucco makers, and glaziers, not to mention the horticulturists needed to lay out the extensive formal gardens. This army of skilled practitioners were most likely foreigners from the Gaulish provinces. A remarkable inscription found in nearby Chichester may hint at something of the arrangements at this time. It was a dedicatory inscription from a temple for Neptune and Minerva set up for the welfare of the emperor's household by a guild of craftsmen (*collegium fabrorum*) by the authority of Togidubnus. Since it clearly dates to the time when the great building programme was under way, it is tempting to see it as the work of the craftsmen brought together for the project, who had formed themselves into a trade guild. A temple to Neptune and Minerva, honouring the goddess of craft skills and the god who ensured safe passage across the seas for themselves and their materials, would have been particularly appropriate. It may have been these men and their local apprentices who went on to build the other first-century villas found along the Sussex coast.

A Briton born in the 30s of the first century experienced a lifetime of quite stunning change. The initial turmoil of the invasion gave way to social upheaval on a totally unprecedented scale. Mobility was greatly increased and foreigners flocked in. Some natives opposed the change even to the extent of open rebellion, but many accepted, even embraced, the new world that was opening up. In a famous passage the historian Tacitus offers a somewhat jaundiced view of the Roman impact. He writes of the governor Agricola's encouragement of the natives to build temples and other public buildings as well as private mansions and to compete in their enthusiasm for such things:

> furthermore, he trained the sons of the chiefs in the liberal arts and expressed a preference for British natural ability to the trained skills of the Gauls. The result was that in place of a distaste for the Latin language came a passion to command it. In the same way national dress came into favour and the toga was everywhere to be seen. And so the Britons were gradually led on to the amenities that make vice agreeable: arcades, baths and sumptuous banquets. They spoke of such novelties as 'civilization' when really they were only a feature of enslavement.

> (Tacitus, *Agricola* 21)

New Horizons

After the turmoil of the first century the new province of Britannia settled into a period of comparative stability. The south and east became the civilian zone, the life of which was based on towns that served as the administration centres for the *civitates*, the countryside around. The military zone, embracing Wales and the north, was permanently garrisoned, with auxiliary units supported by three legions usually held in reserve in their bases at Chester, Lincoln, and York. Here the rather more mobile population living in wilder landscapes had to be kept under surveillance, and there was the ever-present threat of raids from Scotland, which, from time to time, called for expeditionary advances to be made into barbarian territory. Beyond the frontier, free Scotland and the whole of Ireland learnt something of Roman culture through trading networks, which showed that entrepreneurs remained active in these difficult but potentially profitable regions.

In both the military and civilian zones, as time went on, the native and the immigrant populations coalesced and the sharp ethnic divides that would have been apparent in the first century became less evident and less significant. Large numbers of the Romano-British population are known to us by name. The 2,400 or so inscriptions on stone mention thousands of individuals by name, while inscriptions on metal curse tablets, the letters recovered from Vindolanda, and graffiti on pots and other artefacts add several thousand more. They give life and reality to the cosmopolitan population, now thought to number between 2 and 5 million.

To take just one example, the inscriptions from the religious spa at Aquae Sulis (Bath) offer a vivid impression of the ethnic mix of those attracted to the healing waters. Lucius Vitellius Tancinus, a Spanish cavalryman, died at Bath having served in the army for twenty-six years. Two soldiers of the Twentieth Legion who were buried there probably came from Gallia Belgica, as did Julius Vitalis, an armourer of the same legion. Another tombstone commemorated Gaius Murrius Modestus of the Second Legion Adiutrix, who gave Forum Julii in southern France as his place of birth. Marcus Aufidus Maximus, probably another Gaul, and a centurion of the Sixth Legion, settled in the Bath region. His memory is honoured on an altar set up by two of his freed slaves. Other residents or visitors from abroad include an unnamed stone-worker (*lapidarius*) from the tribe of the Carnutes (centred on Chartres), Rusonia Aventina of the Mediomatrici (of the region of Metz), and Peregrinus, son of Secundus, a Treveran from the Moselle region. Many other names are recorded without giving their places of origin. Some, from their names, were certainly British, but others might well have come from abroad. One such was a freed woman, Calpurnia Trifosa, who put up a tombstone to her husband, Gaius Calpurnius Receptus, a priest

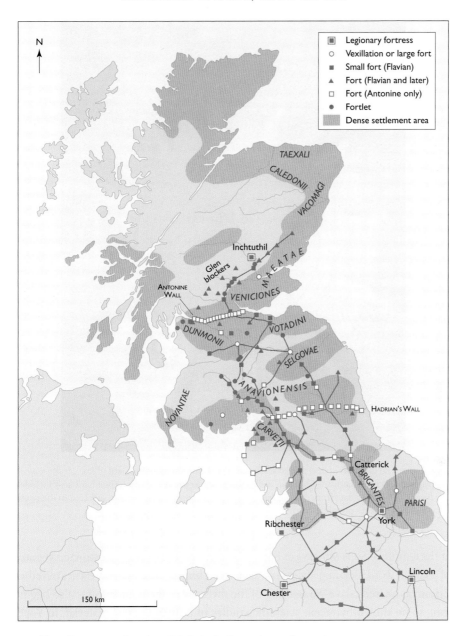

11.12 The military zone of northern Britain in the first and second centuries AD

11.13 The central decorative panel from a scalloped silver bowl found in the hoard of Roman silver work on Traprain Law, East Lothian, Scotland, well beyond the imperial frontiers. The hoard also included five flagons. The items date from the late fourth century and may have been loot gathered in the south during a raid. Another possibility is that the vessels were traded to the barbarians

at the temple of Sulis Minerva at Bath. Her cognomen, Trifosa, is a Latinized version of a Greek word meaning 'dainty' or 'delicious', hinting that she may have arrived in Britain as a Greek slave. Something of the diversity of the population is also beginning to be shown by recent scientific studies of human skeletal material. In York, for example, craniometric analysis of skeletons from one of the Roman cemeteries identified individuals of African origin, while a study of the stable isotopes from the teeth of skeletons buried at Gloucester suggests that as many as 28 per cent of the population may have spent their youth in a warmer climate than prevailed in Britain. Although it is likely that further work will refine our understanding of data of this kind, it is clear that the urban populations were very mixed.

11.14 Excavators at work in the sacred spring in the centre of the sanctuary of Sulis Minerva at Bath. Large numbers of coins and other items were thrown into the spring as offerings to the goddess during the Roman period

The integration of Britain into the empire was an encouragement not only to human mobility but also to trade. The crush of merchants who congregated in London is reflected in the huge quantities of imported pottery recovered from archaeological contexts in the city, some arriving as containers for foodstuffs, some as tableware desirable in its own right, all to satisfy the increasingly Romanized manners of the population. Add to this the metal- and glassware, the spices, the fabrics, and a host of other consumer durables that must have poured into the country, as well as the transport of soldiers, administrators, traders, and slaves, then something of the massive increase in maritime traffic becomes apparent. Shipping movements must have increased exponentially.

The great bulk of trade would have come across the southern North Sea from the Rhine mouth and the coastal ports of northern Gaul to the Thames estuary and in particular to London, where the radiating road system provided the essential distribution network. An illustration of this is the shipwreck located on the Pudding

Pan Rock off the north Kentish coast. The vessel had been carrying a cargo of *terra sigillata*—high-quality red-gloss-coated pottery from Gaul—for the British markets. But even more vivid evidence comes from the North Sea coast close to the estuary of the Rhine, where two temples have been found, at Domburg and Colijnsplaat, both dedicated to the goddess Nehalennia. Here traders and other travellers arriving or setting out across the North Sea made offerings to the goddess, thanking her for a safe passage or in anticipation of one. Over 150 such inscriptions have been recorded. Several traders with Britain (*negotiatores Britanniciani*) are mentioned. One, Placidus, son of Viducus, was a Veliocassian from the district of Rouen. He turns up again on another inscription, this time from York, where he is recorded as a benefactor responsible for sponsoring the building of an arch and a temple in the city in the early third century. Another was Marcus Secund(ius) Silvanus, who specialized in transporting pottery to Britain. Traders in wine and salt are also mentioned. The volume of traffic between the Rhineland and London and York must have been considerable. The Rhineland was a major manufacturing zone, particularly in the second and third centuries. It was also heavily garrisoned and needed supplies. In the fourth century Britain is known to have supplied the Rhine garrison with corn. Other commodities would have included leather (for army tents and other equipment) and the hooded woollen cloak, the *birrus Britannicus*, for which the province became famous. For those prepared to brave the North Sea there were substantial profits to be made.

Merchants based in York were also involved in the Atlantic trade. One Briton, Marcus Aurelius Lunaris, who styles himself a *sevir Augustalis* in the colonies of York and Lincoln, set up an altar to the goddess Tutela Boudig(a) in Bordeaux in AD 237. He tells us that he vowed to do this when he set out from York, a claim supported by the fact that the altar was made of Yorkshire millstone grit. Bordeaux has also produced a tombstone of L. Solimarius Secundinus, a Treveran from the Moselle region, who is credited with being a 'merchant dealing with Britain'. While it is tempting to suppose that the principal attraction of the Bordeaux region for the British was the claret produced there, a range of other commodities may also have been carried. An interesting insight is provided by a third-century wreck found in the harbour of St Peter Port on the island of Guernsey. From the domestic pottery found on board, and presumably used by the crew, the vessel seems to have sailed between western France and the east coast of Britain. The principal cargo of its last journey was large blocks of pine pitch, which, analysis has suggested, came from the pine forests of the Landes in western France. The closest convenient port for loading would have been Bordeaux. The vessel was probably on its way to provide British shipbuilders with an essential raw material when it caught fire and sank in St Peter Port Harbour.

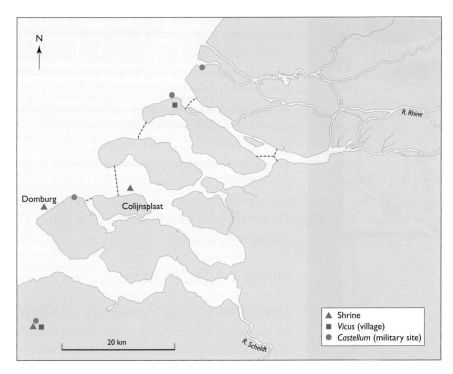

11.15 The mouth of the Scheldt and the Rhine has always been a confusion of river channels and islands changing through time. In the Roman period the main estuary of the Rhine was dominated by two temples, at Domburg and Colijnsplaat, both much used by traders setting out from the Rhine frontier to the ports of eastern Britain

Another direct reminder of Atlantic maritime trade was the detritus from a vessel that had got into trouble off the Sept-Îles near Ploumanac'h on the north coast of Armorica. With the ship driven onto the treacherous islands by north winds, her master had made for a narrow passage between two of the towering rocks, but the vessel foundered and it is unlikely that any of the crew survived. A chance discovery by divers some years ago showed that the ship had been carrying a cargo of lead ingots, of which 271, weighing 22 tonnes, were recovered. Some were stamped with the names of the British tribes the Brigantes and Iceni, the implication being that the lead had come from mines in the Pennines and may have been transhipped through one of the East Anglian ports. Shipwrecks like those from St Peter Port and the Sept-Îles are rare chance discoveries. The sea-lanes and coastal waters must be littered with such disasters: it is little wonder that the shippers relied so heavily on the protection of the deities when trusting themselves to the ocean.

Coastal traffic—cabotage—must also have been intense. Britain was ringed with small harbour settlements. Along the south coast, harbours like Fishbourne,

Clausentum (near Southampton), Hamworthy in Poole Harbour, Weymouth, and Topsham near Exeter probably began as military supply bases in the first year or two of the invasion and continued as civilian ports after the army had moved on. But the other coasts were equally provided for. Every anchorage or beaching point would have been used, but only those with good road or river connections had the potential to develop into major ports. Cabotage was a particularly cost-efficient way of transporting heavy loads like pottery or building stone from one part of the country to another.

Across the Sea to Ireland

Although Agricola cast a conqueror's eye between the narrow seas from the west coast of Scotland and Antrim, there is no evidence that the island was ever invaded, but what we can be sure of is that the seacoasts and harbours of Ireland were very well known to British sailors. This much is clear from the writings of the second-century Roman geographer Ptolemy, whose account of Ireland (Ivernia) is surprisingly full, with a particular emphasis on littoral topography—peninsulas, islands, estuaries—as well as coastal settlements and tribal groupings. That the names are, for the most part, written in P-Celtic spoken in Britain, rather than the Q-Celtic of Ireland, suggests that Ptolemy's informants were probably British sailors who habitually traded with Ireland and were the inheritors of an age-old tradition.

The invasion of Britain would have caused much upset to traditional social systems, and it is quite likely that some refugees fled Britain for the safety of Ireland during the decade of conquest in the first century. One group, who settled on Lambay Island on the east coast just north of the Liffey estuary, burying the dead with artefacts of northern British type, may have been Brigantes displaced by campaigning in the Pennines. There were no doubt others who preferred to settle among their Irish trading partners or distant relatives rather than face life under Roman domination.

11.16 Roman altar erected to the goddess Nehalennia found at the temple of Colijnsplaat in the Rhine estuary. The inscription records that it was set up by Marcus Exgingius Agricola of the Treveri, who was a salt merchant (*negotiator salarius*)

By the second century normal commerce seems to have resumed and is reflected now by a scatter of Roman artefacts found throughout Ireland but with a particular emphasis on the east and north coastal regions. Traditional networks, dating back to pre-Roman times, were being maintained, but there was now a new focus: the promontory of Drumanagh, a 16-hectare headland cut off from the mainland by multival-

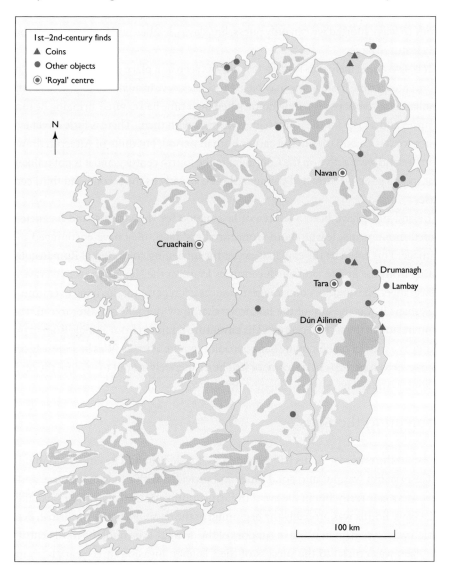

11.17 In the first and second centuries AD Ireland was dominated by four royal centres. Contacts with Roman Britain introduced a few coins and other objects. The main port-of-trade at this time seems to have been Drumanagh

late defences. From the artefacts claimed to have been discovered here, Drumanagh seems to have been a classic port-of-trade, a place where foreign merchants could assemble to engage in peaceful commerce under the protection of the local polity. Among the items brought in by traders were ingots of copper probably from north Wales (Anglesey is only 90 kilometres away). Other imports included pottery and the small consumer durables that usually accompanied trade of this kind. What Irish produce was exported we can only guess, but slaves, leather, and hunting dogs probably featured large.

It is also quite likely that Roman Britain was seen as a place of opportunity by the more enterprising Irish. Some may have chosen to serve in auxiliary regiments in the Roman army, perhaps returning home when their time had expired, bringing Roman luxuries and a taste for the Roman lifestyle back with them. There is little direct evidence for Irish auxiliaries in the earlier Roman period, but units of Attacotti drawn from Ireland were active on the Continent in the fourth century, and it is not unlikely that military service attracted young Irishmen as early as the second and third centuries.

Ireland must have been a source of fascination for the curious, and its ancient sacred monuments, learnt about from travellers' tales, may have encouraged pilgrimage. This could be the explanation for the intriguing collection of Roman coins dating from the first to late fourth centuries found at the Neolithic passage grave at Newgrange. The range of coins suggests a succession of visitors arriving over time.

Perhaps it was the lure of the unknown that drew one ship's master to sail west from Ireland in the second century. His adventure is known from a single Roman pot found by a trawler on Porcupine Bank 250 kilometres out to sea. Was he seriously off-course, driven perhaps by a storm, or had he deliberately set out to explore the open Atlantic? And did he return to tell the tale?

Protecting the Seas

In AD 40 the emperor Gaius had prepared to invade Britain. The embarkation port at Gesoriacum was put into good order and provided with a new lighthouse, and a fleet was made ready, but in the event the army mutinied and the invasion was called off. Gaius' flotilla was probably the beginning of the *classis Britannica*, the British fleet, which was to remain in being in support of the army at least until the third century. The fleet was crucial to the success of the Claudian invasion three years later and provided an essential maritime support arm during the early advances into the west country and the later campaigns into Scotland, ending with the famous sea journey around the north of the island and the visit to the Orkneys.

With the invasion complete, the fleet returned to its Channel posting, to its main base at Gesoriacum and its subsidiary base at Dubris (Dover). Thereafter the marines of the *classis Britannica* ensured the security of the vital sea-lanes, provided transport to the frontiers, took part in occasional building projects, and, in the eastern Weald, oversaw the extraction of iron from the imperial mines.

In the early years the sailors and shipbuilders would have been drawn from the coastal tribes of Belgic Gaul, the Morini and Menapii, and possibly from the Batavi of the Rhine delta, but, as time went on, increasing numbers of Britons would have been recruited, though we know of none by name. In the early second century the prefect of the fleet was an Italian, Aufidius Pantera, from Sassina

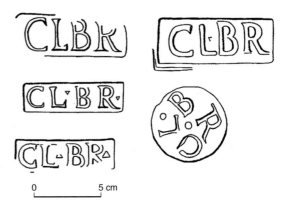

11.18 Stamp marks on bricks made by the *classis Britannica* (British fleet) have been found on a number of sites in Kent. The headquarters of the fleet was at Boulogne

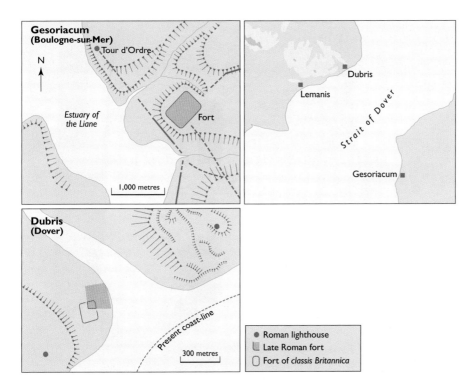

11.19 Throughout the Roman period the most frequented sea-crossing between Gaul and Britain was the Dover–Boulogne route. Both ports were protected by forts and were provided with lighthouses to guide ships into the two harbours

11.20 The Roman lighthouse now within the confines of Dover Castle. The Roman masonry survives to just above the third opening. The top storey is a medieval addition. It was one of a pair of lighthouses flanking Dover Harbour

in Umbria, who had served in Upper Pannonia before coming to Britain. He set up an altar to Neptune at the naval base at Lemanis (Lympne). The first British sailor known by name, a man from Devon called Amelius, son of Saenius, died while serving with the *classis Germanica* on the Rhine and was buried at Cologne.

After the third century the *classis Britannica* disappears from history in the military reorganizations that were taking place at the time. The emphasis now seems to be increasingly on coastal defence, based on a series of massively constructed stone forts built along the south and east coasts from the Solent to the Wash. The earliest of these, at Brancaster and Reculver, were built in the early third century and were garrisoned with cohorts of Aquitanians and Batavians. The rest, Portchester, Lympne, Dover, Richborough, Bradwell, and Burgh, were built in the latter part of the third century, with Pevensey and possibly Clausentum added in the first half of the fourth century. All commanded extensive protected anchorages where naval detachments could be safely anchored, and their size and strength offered

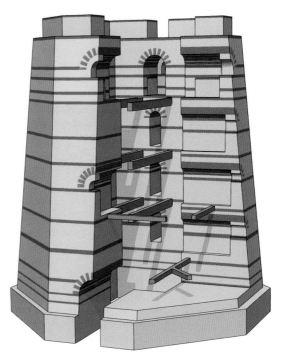

11.21 The Dover lighthouse as it would have looked in the late Roman period after it had been heightened

protection to mariners and to naval stores alike. It is difficult to resist the conclusion that the system came into being in response to the increasing threat of raiding by pirates from the German coastlands.

Matters came to a head in AD 285 when Carausius, a Menapian sailor, was appointed 'to rid the seas of Belgica and Armorica of pirates', implying that his command extended from the Loire estuary to the Rhine mouth. His success in capturing 'barbarians' was soon overshadowed by rumours that he had profited by keeping the confiscated spoils for himself. Whether or not the accusations were correct, he was sentenced to death *in absentia* by the emperor. His response was to assume imperial power and to seize Britain as well as substantial parts of Gaul. At this stage Carausius still commanded the fleet base at Gesoriacum and was able to strengthen his navy by conscripting Gaulish merchantmen. He also enlisted Frankish pirates into his force, providing himself with sufficient resources to withstand Roman counter-moves for seven years, until AD 293, when Constantius Chlorus captured Gesoriacum and with it returned the maritime regions of Gaul to the imperial government. Carausius retreated to Britain, only to be assassinated by one of his officers, Allectus, who assumed the title of emperor of Britain.

11.22 In the late third century the Roman port of Richborough was guarded by a masonry-built Saxon Shore fort. The port had a long history going back to its use as an invasion base at the time of the conquest in AD 43

11.23 The late Roman Saxon Shore fort built at Lympne guarded a major estuary on the northern edge of what is now Romney Marsh. Excavations in 1850 uncovered the east gate

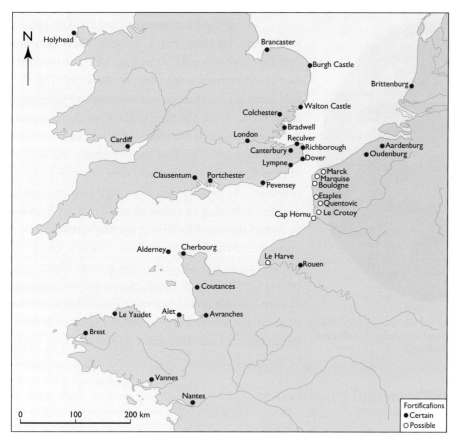

11.24 The late Roman coastal forts and fortified coastal towns in the fourth century AD

Three years later Constantius was strong enough to retake Britain in a carefully planned two-pronged attack. While one force slipped past the waiting British navy under cover of a sea-mist and landed on the Solent shore to seek out Allectus, the other sailed up the Thames and was able to reach London before the remnants of Allectus' army, defeated somewhere in Hampshire, fell back towards the city with the intention of sacking it.

The Carausian interlude tells us much of the state of Britain in the late third century. Two things in particular stand out. Command of the sea had become crucial to Britain's defence and well-being as increasing numbers of Germans and Franks took to the water to prey on merchant shipping and to raid the rich coastal lands. The southern North Sea had become a dangerous place, and the menace was now extending westwards along the Channel. The second point is the growing prominence of mercenaries from the Rhine frontier zone and beyond in the Roman armies and

navies. Not only had Carausius enlisted Frankish pirates to augment his navy, but it is highly likely that the detachments holding the shore forts were also predominantly of Germanic origin. Indeed, we are told that the field army led by Allectus was composed of Germanic mercenaries. From the time of the Claudian conquest there had been large numbers of German conscripts in the auxiliary units. Now, as the old empire was beginning to fragment, the numbers were increasing exponentially. The western seaways were also becoming dangerous, leading to a new phase of military activity in coastal regions. Cardiff was massively refortified to guard the Severn estuary, and there were new forts built at Caernarfon and Lancaster, and a small fortlet was built at Caer Gybi on the western extremity of Anglesey to keep a watch on the seaways. The reason for these preparations was probably to guard against raids from the coast of Ireland. This was a prelude of much worse to come.

11.25 The emperor Carausius (287–93), who set up a breakaway state in Britain, was responsible for strengthening the system of Saxon Shore forts in south-eastern Britain

In Town and Countryside

Tacitus, in an attempt to present his father-in-law, Agricola, as a model governor, stresses, in addition to his military achievements, his encouragement of the natives to embrace the Roman lifestyle and in particular the comforts of towns. This policy, continued by successive governors, led to the rapid growth of urban centres in the south-east of the province in the late first and early second centuries. The four *coloniae*, Colchester, Lincoln, Gloucester, and York, provided the model, but towns, like the burgeoning trading centre of London and the *municipium* established at Verulamium (St Albans), showed something of the vitality of the new province. In spite of their destruction during the Boudiccan rebellion in AD 60, both were soon rebuilt and continued to thrive. Elsewhere in the country each administrative district (*civitas*) was encouraged to develop an urban centre usually sited at, or close to, pre-conquest *oppida*, as at Canterbury, Chichester, Winchester, and Silchester, among others. In all, there were about eighteen *civitas* capitals, with an equivalent number of substantial but smaller towns sited at crucial road junctions in between.

Towns were laid out with enthusiasm, some of them, like Wroxeter and Silchester, on far too ambitious a scale, into which they were never to grow. But by the mid-second century all the major centres could boast a suite of public buildings: forums, basilicas, baths, temples, and sometimes amphitheatres, as well as shops lining the main streets with town-houses built in masonry and adorned with wall paintings and mosaics. By the middle of the second century it would have seemed to any observer that the urban experiment was a success, but thereafter the momentum slackened and in many towns a marked decline set in. At Silchester, by the end of the third century, metalworkers were working within the great basilica. The forum and basilica at Wroxeter was damaged by fire about AD 300 and not repaired, while the basilica at Caerwent had been demolished by the mid-fourth century. Of the fifteen public bath buildings known, six had gone out of use by AD 300. A little after that date the orches-

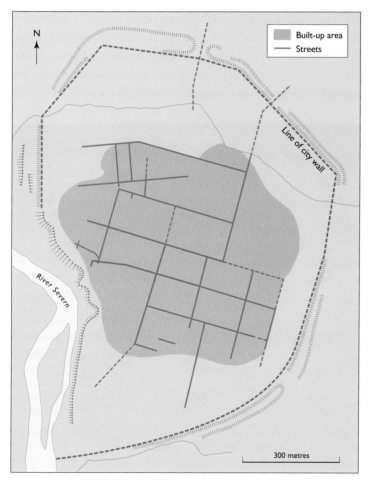

11.26 The Roman city of Viroconium (Wroxeter) was planned on an extensive scale as defined by the city wall, but the town never grew to fill the space

tra area of the theatre in Verulamium was being used as a rubbish dump. Urban life continued, and the fourth century saw a rash of new private housebuilding in many towns, but the aspirations of that first flush of exuberance had faltered.

Why this should have been is difficult to say with any degree of certainty. The simplest explanation would be to suppose that the productivity of the province was insufficient to sustain the large standing army, provide taxes for the imperial coffers, and maintain an urban infrastructure of the elaboration planned in the early decades of the occupation. Another possibility is that urban life was simply not congenial to the British population and after the initial investment, underpinned no doubt by loans and supported by incomers who wanted a stake in the new enterprise, enthusiasm waned and money was no longer forthcoming.

Outside the towns, the countryside presents a kaleidoscope of different settlement patterns reflecting different economic strategies and different systems of landholding. Villas, which can be taken as an indication of the acceptance of Roman values, are unevenly distributed, concentrating in the south-east of the province, where there are significant regional differences to be observed. In the extreme south-east, in Sussex, Kent,

11.27 An exceptionally well-preserved Romano-British settlement at Ewe Close, Crosby Ravensworth, Cumbria, showing the habitation enclosure surrounded by paddocks and garden plots

Essex, and Hertfordshire, villa building was under way in the late first and early second centuries, the patrons, in these areas, favouring the strip house composed of individual rooms arranged side by side providing a series of private spaces, sometimes with a linking corridor. This was the type of building found in Gaul, and its early adoption in the south-east of Britain could represent either the enthusiastic adoption of Roman-style living by the native elites or houses created for incomers from the Continent who were buying up rural estates in the new province. Both explanations were probably true.

Further west, in central southern Britain extending from the south coast northwards to Lincolnshire, masonry buildings were a later development, and when eventually they came, in the late second and early third centuries, they were usually in the form of aisled halls providing a multifunctional communal space where the entire working of the estate could be managed. Although the structure of the building was probably continental in inspiration, the social system that it reflected was native, harking back to that of the pre-conquest period. These estates continued to be centred around their aisled halls throughout the Roman period, but some were later enhanced with strip houses of varying kinds and elaboration, providing the resident owners with private space in which to display their attachment to Roman values. This could simply reflect social 'progress' by the native rural elite, but it could also be interpreted as the arrival of new owners with new money to invest and less attachment to native social practices. In many cases these new buildings appear late in the third and early in the fourth century and might be the result of inward investment by landowners from Gaul fleeing from the barbarian incursions that were disrupting the countryside there to the comparative safety of Britain.

Further west still, in parts of Dorset, Somerset, and Gloucestershire, the villa pattern is different yet again. Early investment followed by progressive elaboration seems to have been the norm, with some of the villas, like Woodchester, becoming particularly sumptuous by the fourth century. The region, with its comfortable market centres at Cirencester and Ilchester, its famous healing sanctuary at Bath, its extensive evidence of literacy in the form of styluses and curse tablets, and the preference of its rural elite for elaborate mosaics depicting scenes from classical mythology, was arguably the most civilized in the country. Why this should be we can only guess. It may have been imperial land taken over by the emperor at the time of the invasion and leased to favoured clients, but it could simply be that the fertility of the land and varied resources available made it particularly productive, to the benefit of those lucky enough to have farms there.

As interest in towns declined, so investment in the countryside increased: the two trends may be linked. It could be that the rural elites, both natives and incomers, were at first drawn to the towns, but a range of factors, among them the financial demands of urban offices which the elite were expected to fill, together with a sluggish econ-

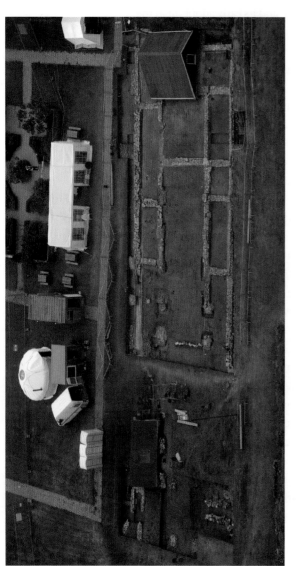

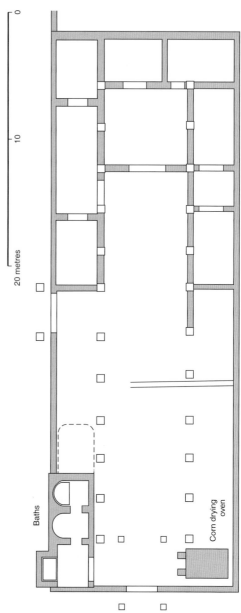

II.28 The late second-century aisled hall excavated at Brading on the Isle of Wight. Halls of this kind formed the focus of Romano-British farming estates in central southern Britain. One end, divided into a series of small rooms, was occupied by the villa owner and his family

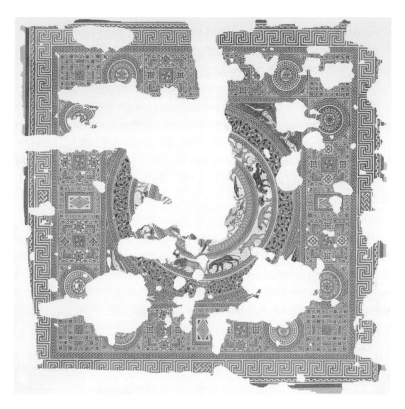

11.29 The mosaic pavement from the principal room of the Roman villa at Woodchester, Gloucestershire (late fourth century), is one of the most elaborate found in Britain. The central panel, now destroyed, once contained a depiction of Orpheus. Painting by David S. Neal

omy, made urban living unattractive, particularly in the third century. Movement back to the countryside may, for many, have seemed the preferable option, leaving the towns to function as market and service centres, now largely bereft of the social and cultural facilities. While some such overarching dynamic may well have been at work, we can be sure that the situation was infinitely more complex, with each community, family, or individual responding in their own way to situations and pressures beyond their control. The slow economic collapse of the empire, accelerating mobility among barbarians beyond the frontiers, and decreasing birth-rate were the principal movers. Against these inexorable forces the individual had but little power.

The Changing British Population

The Roman conquest brought with it a greatly increased mobility of population. The apparatus of empire—armies of conquest and occupation, government officials, administrators and their entourages, and entrepreneurs eager to exploit the opportunities of a new territory—demanded that people moved, often over considerable distances. The map of the Roman world, dominated by its intricate network of roads, says it all. The existence of the empire was predicated on mobility both of commodities and of people.

The three centuries following the invasion of Claudius inevitably saw changes in the British population, but the scale of these changes is difficult to quantify. If we are correct in assuming that the population was in the order of 2 to 4 million (and this is little better than an informed guess), then the influx of 40,000 to 50,000 soldiers and 10,000 to 20,000 administrators and traders in the first century must have had a significant effect on the gene pool. A high percentage of those coming to the island married, stayed, and died here. At first the legions were topped up with citizens born on the Continent, while the auxiliary units were refreshed and extended by new recruits from their home territory. An assessment of the auxiliary recruitment pattern suggests that, of those units sent to Britain in the first and second century, over thirty came from Germany, twenty-five from Gaul, and ten from Spain: the Danubian provinces, Africa, and the east together provided fewer than twenty. But as time went on, Britain could provide more citizens to join the resident legions, while the *vici* that developed around the auxiliary forts would have generated a constant supply of young men for whom military life was a natural career. Indeed, the reforms introduced by Diocletian at the end of the third century *required* young men born of soldiers to join the army. The second and third centuries, then, were a time when the disparate ethnic groups mixed, and, among the army at least, the large-scale mobility so evident in the early years of the conquest decreased. In the civilian part of the province, particularly in the major urban centres, the cosmopolitan nature of the population probably continued to be evident. Inward investment in goods and land would have ensured a constant flow of foreigners, while merchant guilds and religious practices would have provided the contexts in which ethnic identities could be proclaimed and maintained. In Britain before the Roman invasion, identity would have been expressed quite simply in relation to lineage and tribe. The Roman world provided a bewildering variety of new ways in which to define self: the Romano-Briton would have been able to claim many different identities, among which ethnicity may not have been particularly important.

The third century was a time of dramatic change in the Roman world. Much was in flux: it was a time of crisis and uncertainty. Two phenomena in particular contributed to the pace of change: manpower shortage within the empire and rapid increases in population in barbarian lands across the frontiers. It had long been Roman policy to recruit auxiliary troops from among the barbarians living in the frontier regions and to use them in campaigns in other regions. As we have seen, many of the auxiliaries employed in Britain from the time of the Claudian invasion onwards were Germans. This policy continued. In the late third century Carausius' navy was augmented by Frankish sailors, and the field army was largely Germanic. But by now a rather different policy was also being followed: the deliberate settlement of entire Germanic communities on land within the empire, usually not far from frontier regions. These *laeti*, as they were called, were given land in depopulated areas in the expectation that they would hold it with vigour against attack from their fellow countrymen raiding from beyond the frontier. The policy was sound: by taking pressure off the frontier region, where barbarian populations were building to explosive levels, areas dangerously depopulated by manpower shortage and insecurity could be reinvigorated and brought back into productive use. The policy was well under way in Gaul in the late third century and may well have been introduced into Britain at about the same time, but positive evidence is hard to come by.

But still the barbarian population beyond the frontiers continued to build. In AD 260 and 261 the Alamanni broke through and swept across Gaul, and the next year the Franks followed, raiding as far south as Spain. It was the beginning of a phenomenon that was to escalate over the next 150 years, eventually bringing the western Roman world to an end. Britain was not immune as Saxon and Frankish raiders took to the sea to cause chaos in the North Sea and English Channel. Those who were bought off to join Carausius and Allectus may well have been used to help garrison the new coastal forts. This littoral zone from the Wash to the Solent came to be known as the *litus Saxonicum*, which is usually thought to mean the shore attacked by Saxons, but it could equally well mean the shore settled by Saxons.

There had been a constant inflow of people of Germanic origin into Britain over the three centuries following the invasion. In the first and second centuries, as frontier forces and as traders, they had probably integrated with the native population through intermarriage. With Latin as a lingua franca it is unlikely that German speaking became widespread. But in the changed situation in the late third and fourth centuries settlers and mercenaries may well have begun to form enclaves in the eastern and southern coastal zones—the first step in the long process that was to lead to the Germanization of large tracts of lowland Britain.

In this time of renewed mobility other people were beginning to stir. In the far north a new confederation of tribes, now called the Picts, were casting their eyes on the rich lands of the south, while the Irish were beginning to take to the water to explore, raid, and settle the coasts of Britain. For the next century Britain was to face an increasingly mobile foe encroaching from all sides.

12

'Its Red and Savage
Tongue', AD 350–650

S OMETIME around AD 540 the monk Gildas, living in the comparative peace of
western Britain, wrote an impassioned account of the collapse of Roman rule
in Britain and the coming of the Saxons from the east:

> a fire heaped up by the impious easterners spread from sea to sea. It devastated town
> and country round about, and, once it was alight, it did not die down until it had burned
> almost the whole of the island and was licking the western ocean with its red and savage
> tongue . . . All the major towns were laid low by the repeated battering of enemy rams;
> laid low, too, all the inhabitants . . . as the swords glinted all around and the flames crack-
> led. It was a sad sight. In the middle of the squares the foundation stones of high walls
> and towers that had been torn from their lofty base, holy altars, fragments of corpses,
> covered with the purple crust of congealed blood, looked as though they had been mixed
> up in some dreadful wine-press.
>
> (*De Excidio* 24.1–3)

Gildas was writing little more than a hundred years after the tumultuous events in
the first four decades of the fifth century, which saw the inflow of large numbers
of settlers from across the North Sea—people generally referred to as 'Saxons' but
embracing many different groups from the Germanic coast-lands stretching from
the Rhine northwards to Jutland. His great-grandparents will have lived at these

times of devastating change and he may have had access to family traditions. He will certainly have been able to gather folk memories of the fifth century from his contemporaries, and in the monastic libraries there will have been texts referring to the last years of Roman rule to provide the rudiments of a more distant narrative.

Gildas must be taken as a serious, if rather emotional, source for the events of the fifth century even if he glimpsed them only partially and felt the need to simplify to give a greater sharpness to his narrative. There are few other near-contemporary sources. The Greek historian Zosimus, writing at the end of the fourth century, provides some intriguing insights to social upheavals in Britain and Gaul at the time, while the Byzantine historian Procopius and the Gallic Chroniclers, both broadly contemporary with Gildas, add further details. Centuries later writers like Nennius, Bede, and the compilers of the Anglo-Saxon Chronicle take a view of these early times, relying heavily on local chronicles written by the incomers and their descendants. These retrospective compilations provide useful insights but are at best selective and partial, distorted by a confusion of political agendas.

Yet standing back from the often contradictory detail, it is possible to discern the broad narrative, which tells how the prosperous Roman province of the mid-fourth century was transformed into the competing Anglo-Saxon kingdoms of the seventh century. By 409, when Roman rule in Britain was effectively at an end, large tracts of the country had already become Germanized, partly through the increasingly large numbers of Germans who had been recruited into the regular Roman army and partly by communities who had been brought in to settle in depopulated regions. Over the next forty years the inflow of people from the continental coastlands increased dramatically, leading to conflict with the native Britons which did not abate until an equilibrium was reached around AD 500 following the decisive battle of Mons Badonicus (often identified with Badbury Castle in Dorset). Thereafter there was a half-century of comparative peace before the Germanic communities, now well entrenched in the east of the country, began their westward expansion once more into British territory.

But this is only part of the story, for the whole of the British Isles and Ireland seems to have been caught up in this remarkable era of 'folk wanderings'. During the late fourth century the Picts of the far north posed a serious threat to the Romanized south, their periodic raids causing disruption and devastation, on one occasion as far south as the Thames. Meanwhile, the Irish were on the move, first as raiders joining with the Picts and later settling in north-west Britain, Wales, and Cornwall. It may have been the pressure of these raids on the south-western Britons that encouraged communities to emigrate to Armorica (thereafter Brittany), some of them moving even further along the Atlantic seaways, eventually to settle in north-western Iberia.

The extent and intensity of the complex folk wanderings in the period AD 350–600 was on a scale unlike anything we can discern in the earlier history of the islands. That it was a period of massive social and economic transformation most can agree, but what all this means in terms of population replacement remains a matter of energetic debate.

The Age of Usurpers, AD 350–407

'Fertile in usurpers' was how St Jerome described Britain in the late Roman period. Carausius and Allectus had shown the possibilities in the late third century and others were to follow. In 350 Flavius Magnus Magnentius, a man of barbarian origins, deposed the emperor and seized power. One account says that he and his family were *laeti* but there was another tradition that his father was a Briton. Whether or not there was any truth in this, it is clear that Britain offered strong support for his claim, sending troops to join him in Gaul. After his failure to build a power base and his death in 353, extensive reprisals were taken against his British supporters. The episode must have greatly weakened the province. Not only would the elite have suffered in the aftermath, but there would have been an understandable reluctance on the part of the central government to restore the depleted army. The episode in many ways marks the beginning of the end.

A generation later, in 383, another commander in Britain, Magnus Maximus, a Spaniard by birth, made a play for imperial power, again stripping the province of troops. Although he seems to have made local arrangements with the natives for the safety of the northern frontier, the removal of *limitani* (frontier troops) and their promotion to the more prestigious *comitatenses* (field army) meant that few, if any, of the survivors would have chosen to return, leaving the west and north of Britain dangerously exposed.

A few years later, in 401, more troops were withdrawn from Britain by the German general Stilicho to fight on the Continent against the Goths now threatening Rome. And in 407 yet another field army left Britain in support of the last British usurper, Constantine III, a soldier serving in the province who had been chosen by the army to lead them to take control of the western provinces and to drive out the barbarians, now an ever-present threat. In quick succession, in 383, 401, and 407, Britain was deprived of large contingents of fighting men—this following the loss of another army in 350 and the ensuing reprisals. The old province must have been on its knees, with little ability to offer any form of concerted defence: and by now the predators were already moving in.

The Threat from Without: A Brief Narrative

The later Roman historians provide a broad outline of events in Britain in the last decades of the Roman era. The reconquest of Britain by Constantius in 296 seems to have marked the beginning of an interlude that saw the province enjoying a period of comparative peace and prosperity, but in 342 a crisis erupted that required the emperor to make a sudden visit in midwinter. His prime concern seems to have been to strengthen the Roman hold on the broad buffer zone between Hadrian's Wall and the Forth–Clyde axis, where a number of the pro-Roman polities provided *areani* (scouts), whose job it was to warn the frontier garrison of movements among the Picts to the north. At the same time he seems to have reorganized the defences of the Saxon Shore, building a new fort at Pevensey to reinforce the eastern Channel zone. This may suggest that Saxon activity across the North Sea was beginning once more to pose a threat. If so, this operation seems to have met with some success since no raids are recorded for more than twenty years. In 359 a fleet was built to transport British grain to support the army on the Rhine. That regular shipments were made suggests that the sea-lanes were safe, at least for well-protected military convoys.

The first serious trouble to be recorded took place on the northern frontier in 360, when the Picts from north of the Forth–Clyde line and Scots who at this time occupied the north-east of Ireland began to cause trouble among the pro-Roman tribes north of Hadrian's Wall. A general with four detachments of *comitatenses* was sent by the emperor and managed to stabilize the situation, but it was a warning of things to come. In 365 the Picts and Scots, together now with Attacotti (probably from Ireland) and Saxons, all attacked the province. Worse was to come in the summer of 367 when a series of attacks seems to have been orchestrated in what the Roman historian Ammianus refers to as the 'barbarian conspiracy' (*barbarica conspiratio*). Picts, Scots, and Attacotti descended on the north and west of Britain, while Franks and Saxons attacked the frontier of Gaul and the North Sea coasts. It seems that the treachery of the *areani* north of the frontier contributed to the success of the barbarian invasion. It may have been this event that Gildas was recalling when he wrote of the appearance of the old enemy. They were

> like greedy wolves, rabid with extreme hunger, who, dry-mouthed, leap over into the sheepfold when the shepherd is away. They came relying on their oars as wings, on the arms of their oarsmen and on the winds swelling their sails. They broke through the frontiers spreading destruction everywhere.
>
> (*De Excidio* 16)

Hadrian's Wall was overrun and outflanked by sea, the raiders pressing deep into the province, causing chaos as far south as the Thames. The count of the Saxon Shore, Nectaridus, was killed, and the military leader Fullofaudes, the *dux Britanniarum*, was taken prisoner. Military order collapsed and the country was plunged into anarchy.

Imperial response, when it came, was effective. Count Theodosius, with four regiments of *comitatenses* (about 2,000 men), landed at Richborough and made straight for London, where he found scattered bands pillaging the surrounding countryside. How many were barbarians and how many disaffected residents and muti-

12.1 The Roman fort of Birrens, Dumfriesshire, was established by Hadrian as one of the outpost forts protecting the route leading northwards from Carlisle. It guarded the crossing of the River Mean. The outpost forts provided warning of impending attacks from the north. Birrens may also have protected the northern part of the friendly Brigantes cut off from the main tribal area to the south by the construction of Hadrian's Wall

nous soldiers making the most of the opportunity is not clear, but by inducing the scattered units of the provincial garrison to return to order, Theodosius was able to clear the country of dissidents and reinstate the civilian administration. In the north, while the frontier at Hadrian's Wall was restored, the outposts to the north were abandoned, together with the system of *areani*, who had proved to be so unreliable. Instead new agreements seem to have been made with the major polities of the Scottish Lowlands: the Votadini in the east and the kingdom of Strathclyde in the west. These two powerful native peoples provided a solid buffer from sea to sea, protecting the wall garrisons from the Pictish kingdom beyond the Forth–Clyde axis. It was a sound defensive policy and stood the province in good stead for decades to come. Further south the reorganization of the province was equally thorough. A line of signal stations was built along the Yorkshire coast to watch out for Pictish ships trying to outflank the frontier defences, the Saxon Shore forts continued to be garrisoned with a new fort added in Southampton Water at Clausentum, and many of the towns with walls were strengthened with bastions to provide emplacements for defensive ballistae. The lesson had been learnt and the whole province was now on defensive alert.

The Theodosian reorganization, which began in 368, brought the province a brief respite, but the Picts and Scots were again active in 384, causing Maximus to make a hurried return to Britain. He seems to have offered support for the buffer kingdoms of the Votadini and Strathclyde and brought the Novantae, of the south-west of Scotland, into the pro-Roman federation.

In the west the situation was fast deteriorating, with raids from Irish tribes becoming ever more frequent. By the end of the century the Scots from the north of Ireland had begun to settle in north Wales, while Déisi from the south of the island had set up colonies in Pembrokeshire and the Gower and it is possible that Cornwall was now within their reach. In 405 Irish sources record that Niall, high king of Ireland, had now turned his attention to organizing raiding expeditions against the western seaboard of Britain.

By 396 the situation in the province was serious enough for the central government to send an expedition to Britain to counter maritime attacks from Irish, Picts, and Saxons, and it may have been at this time that Attacotti were recruited into the Roman army and sent to serve on the Continent: their presence is recorded in the Roman sources.

The removal of the last troops from Britain by Constantine III in 407, to serve in the field army on the Continent, marked the virtual end of Roman Britain. The Saxons took advantage of the situation and mounted a serious raid in 408. The story is taken up by the historian Zosimus:

The barbarians across the Rhine attacked everywhere with all their power, and brought the inhabitants of Britain and some of the nations of Gaul to the point of revolting from Roman rule and living on their own, no longer obedient to Roman laws. The Britons took up arms and, braving danger for their own independence, freed their cities from the barbarians . . . and all Armorica and the other provinces of Gaul copied the British example and freed themselves in the same way, expelling their Roman governors and establishing their own administration as best they could.

(Zosimus 6.5)

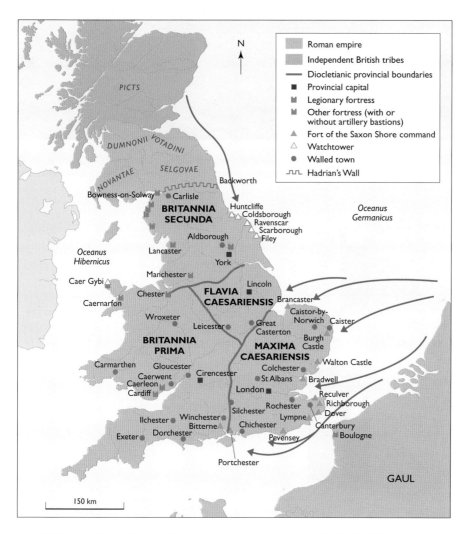

12.2 Britain in the later third and fourth centuries AD became a heavily fortified island. Its eastern coasts, susceptible to raids from the Picts and from the Germanic communities living north of the Rhine mouth, was the first zone to be fortified. Later, raids from Ireland threatened the western coasts

12.3 The late Roman signal station on the promontory now within Scarborough Castle. It was one of several designed to protect the Yorkshire coast from attack by sea. In the centre was a tall watch-tower protected by an outer wall with bastions

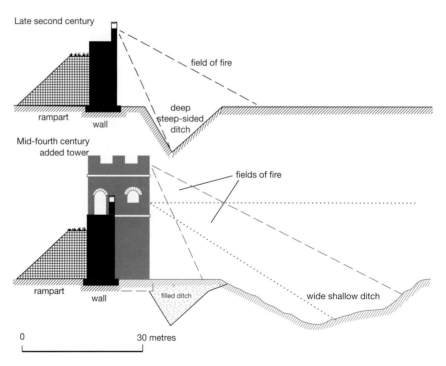

Late second century

field of fire

rampart

wall

deep
steep-sided
ditch

Mid-fourth century
added tower

fields of fire

rampart

wall

filled ditch

wide shallow ditch

0

30 metres

12.4 In the late fourth century the defences of a number of the towns of Britain were strengthened with forward-projecting bastions and wide, shallow ditches to keep would-be attackers within the optimum killing range of defenders manning the walls and towers

12.5 Illustration from the *Notitia Dignitatum* showing the insignia of the count of the Saxon Shore in Britain (*Comes Litoris Saxonici per Britanniam*). The shore forts under his command are individually named and can be identified with structures still extant

The implication is clear enough. The civilian administration left by Constantine III to hold the island after his departure was overthrown by the Britons themselves: no more taxes were paid to the imperial coffers, and centralized government was at an end. Procopius is succinct in his summary of these events. Britain, he said, 'from that time onwards continued to be ruled by tyrants'. The country was fast disintegrating into fiefdoms controlled by rival warlords.

The *Adventus Saxonum*: A Historical View

The coming of the Saxons has long excited historians ever since the Venerable Bede tried to piece together a narrative of the events in his two great works, *Chronica Maiora* (725) and the *Ecclesiastical History of the English People* (731). Among the many sources that Bede used was Gildas' *De Excidio et Conquestu Britanniae* ('On the Ruin and Conquest of Britain'), which, despite its polemic style, had the advantage of being written soon after the events that it described. The story that Gildas tells is simple. After Britain had separated from Rome, there was a long period of prosperity, during which the Picts and Scots were kept at bay. But then raids began again and the country was racked by plague. To help avert the raids one of the British, Vortigern, allowed in certain bands of Saxons, who were settled as *foederati* (fighting troops) in the east of Britain and, in return for monthly rations (*epimenia*) and a supply of corn (*annona*), were expected to protect the east coast from the menace of the Picts. This they did, and after a while more Saxons arrived and negotiated a similar deal. The situation held for some years, but in the end, complaining that the food supplied to them was insufficient, the Saxons rebelled, pillaging the countryside and sacking towns in their way as they thrust west-wards. British resistance was eventually rallied by a war-leader, Ambrosius Aurelianus, after which the two sides fought it out with equal success until, at the battle of Mons Badonicus, the Britons won a resounding victory, heralding a long period of peace.

A separate account, deriving from a Kentish source and recorded by Nennius in his *Historia Brittonum*, offers some corroboration and some further detail. It appears that Vortigern's policy of bringing in Saxon *foederati* was opposed by a pro-Roman faction, who were hopeful of Rome's return. It was they who, by cutting off the supplies and attempting to send the initial settlers home, sparked off the revolt. Vortigern's supporters, who had no desire to see a Roman return, invited in yet more Saxons.

The narrative, as we have it, implies that there were two major stages in the early Saxon settlement of Britain: the initial settlement of the *foederati* and the rebellion. Bede worked out that the initial landings took place in 449, but this is based on mis-understandings and is far too late. An independent document, the Gallic Chronicle, compiled in the mid-fifth century, lists under the year 442 that Britain, 'long trou-bled by various happenings and disaster, passed under the authority of the Saxons'. This would seem to be a reference to the rebellion of the confederates. The revolt was met by an impassioned plea for help from the pro-Roman faction sent by the Roman general Aetius, then campaigning on the Continent, in about 446. Gildas records the 'groans of the Britons' at this time: 'The barbarians drive us to the sea; the sea drives us back on the barbarians: between the two kinds of death we are either slaughtered or drowned.' Aetius was too engaged to respond.

410

The outline chronology, then, is reasonably clear. Soon after the departure of Constantine III in 407 there is a major Saxon incursion. The response of the Britons was to claim independence from Rome and to set about looking after their own defence. By the 420s and 430s more Saxons were settling in the east of the country with the positive encouragement of at least one of the British political factions, but by around 440 the flood of immigrants had so increased that the settlers had to expand out of their proscribed territories, grabbing land as they went. It was not until about 500, at the battle of Mons Badonicus, that the westward advance was, at least temporarily, halted. The broad narrative conforms well with the archaeological evidence: what it means in terms of the changing ethnicity of the country deserves closer attention.

The Germanic East

We have already seen, in the last chapter, how heavily the Roman army relied on troops recruited in the Rhineland and in free Germany to provide for the garrisons in Britain, even during the early stages of the occupation. By the late third century, with pirates from the German coast-lands active in the southern North Sea and eastern Channel, conditions existed for numbers to have been further increased. If the rumours were true, Carausius, himself a native of the Belgian coast, was in league with the pirates: it is inconceivable that he would not have made use of them in his subsequent defence of Britain. And we have already seen that the large field army commanded in Britain by his successor, Allectus, was made up of German mercenaries. Elsewhere in the empire it was policy for barbarians to be brought within the frontier, either as *laeti* or as *foederati*.

By the late third century large tracts of northern Gaul had been settled by Frankish *laeti*. There is no reason to suppose that Britain was immune from these practices. That the Saxon Shore forts were garrisoned with units made up largely of Germans, and that some of the coast-land between was settled by *laeti*, is a real possibility. It has long been known that in the fourth century much of eastern Britain between the Thames and the Humber used a distinctive kind of locally made pottery that has strong stylistic similarities to contemporary German wares. While this cannot reasonably be taken as indisputable evidence of extensive Germanic settlement, it hints at a Germanic component in the urban and rural population from at least the early fourth century.

By the late fourth century Saxons are frequently mentioned among the barbarian bands raiding Britain. The word 'Saxon', a convenient shorthand to Roman historians, probably embraced a multitude of ethnicities. The later English historians like

Bede, more conscious of these matters, made finer distinctions, identifying Frisians, Saxons, Angles, and Jutes. The Jutes occupied the north part of what is now the Danish peninsula with the Angles in the south. Between the Elbe and the Ems lay the homeland of the Saxons, while the coastal regions from the Ems to the Rhine frontier was occupied by Frisians. South of the frontier, in what is now Belgium and northern France, the Franks had settled first as *laeti* within the empire and later as uninvited incomers. Those seeking new lands in Britain set out from scattered home-lands stretching along these 900 kilometres of coast-line.

The reasons behind the folk wanderings were varied and complex, but the princi-pal causes were population pressures and rising sea-levels. The Roman frontier had

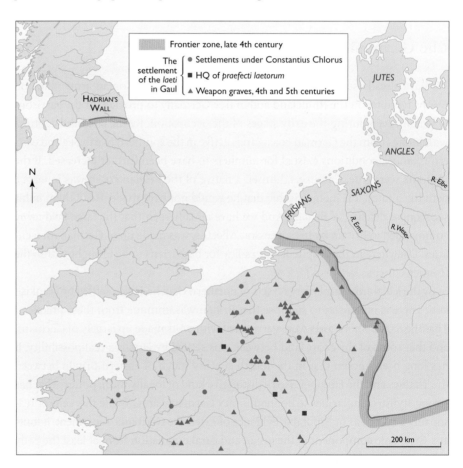

12.6 In the late fourth century the Roman authorities were settling laeti (displaced communities from beyond the frontier) in northern Gaul. It is likely that similar settlements were being made in Britain at the time. The coastal tribes named to the north of the Rhine mouth were those from which settlers came to colonize eastern Britain in the fifth century

for centuries created a barrier to the natural movements that would have eased the pressures caused by steadily rising populations in the North European Plain. As a result the barbarian people bordering the frontier were constantly squeezed by tribes expanding from further north. In the late third century the pressure was so great that the frontiers broke and large numbers of barbarians spread into the Roman world. The situation was restored for a while by Roman military force, but the underlying problem remained and a century later the barrier began its final inevitable disintegration as more and more barbarian communities broke through. The dam had given way, allowing a tidal wave to sweep across what remained of the old Roman provinces.

Those barbarian peoples who lived in the coastal regions of northern Europe faced the sea, which, while a barrier of sorts, encouraged mobility. The population pressure from the north and east was exacerbated by a rise in sea-level during the late third and fourth centuries, resulting in the loss of large tracts of previously inhabitable land. If this was not bad enough, the economy of the coastal zone, which had for centuries benefited from regular trade with the Roman world, suffered from the inexorable breakdown of Roman order. There was little left for the coastal communities but to take to the sea to find new opportunities. Thus, pirate raiding in the late third century gradually gave way to immigration and settlement either by invitation or by force.

The eastern coastal regions of Britain were the obvious areas for the displaced to seek new homes, but some groups sailed through the Strait of Dover to settle on the Channel coasts. By the sixth century settlements had reached as far west as the Solent on the north Channel shore and the Cherbourg peninsula in the south. The discovery of Saxon pottery made from clays from the Cherbourg region at Portchester Castle on the Solent shows that immigrant communities remained in contact with each other across the mid-Channel seaways. The fifth and early sixth century saw a myriad of different movements as gangs of young men, families, and small communities set out from continental Europe by boat to seek new opportunities in the west. Those who were able to gain a foothold pioneered the way for friends and family to follow, and so Germanic communities began to take root in the decay of what had once been Britannia.

The Archaeology of Settlement

The archaeological evidence for the Anglo-Saxon settlement of eastern Britain is stark. The material evidence of the Roman lifestyle disappears. Towns and villas are abandoned, centralized production all but collapses, and coins, once so crucial for taxation and marketing, cease to be minted. Instead, new nucleated settlements of wooden houses appear, usually in previously unoccupied locations, together with an alien material culture clearly derived from the Germanic homelands. The most vivid manifestations of the new people are their cemeteries, cremations at first giving way later to inhumations, in which the symbols of their ethnicity—pottery, jewellery, weapons, and the like—accompany the dead as a material reminder of their heritage. In some places incomers occupied old Roman sites. Saxon houses with floors cut down into the earth have been found in Roman towns like Canterbury and Dorchester-on-Thames, and some Roman villas show continuity of use, but overall the replacement of one culture with another in the east of Britain is stark in its rapidity and thoroughness.

Detailed analysis of the archaeological evidence, exposing changes over time and cultural patterning in its distributions, allows a more nuanced narrative of the Germanic settlement to be sketched. The earliest Germanic settlers in eastern England are represented by large cremation cemeteries found in East Anglia, Lincolnshire, and the east midlands, extending into eastern Yorkshire. The urns that contained the cremations have close parallels both in the Anglian region north of the Elbe and in

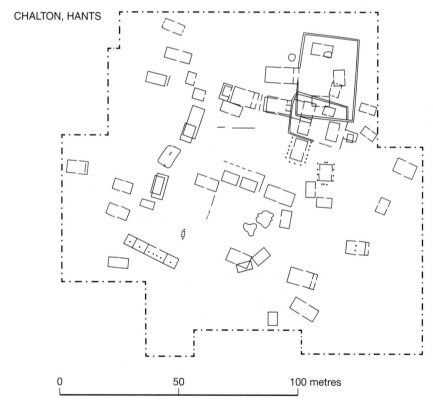

CHALTON, HANTS

0   50   100 metres

12.7 The Saxon settlement on Chalton Down, Hampshire, comprised a series of rectangular timber buildings, some with enclosed yards. The rebuilding shows that the settlement developed over a number of generations

12.8 Part of the Saxon village on Chalton Down, Hampshire, under excavation. The rectangular houses, recognizable from the postholes cut into the chalk, date to the sixth and seventh centuries

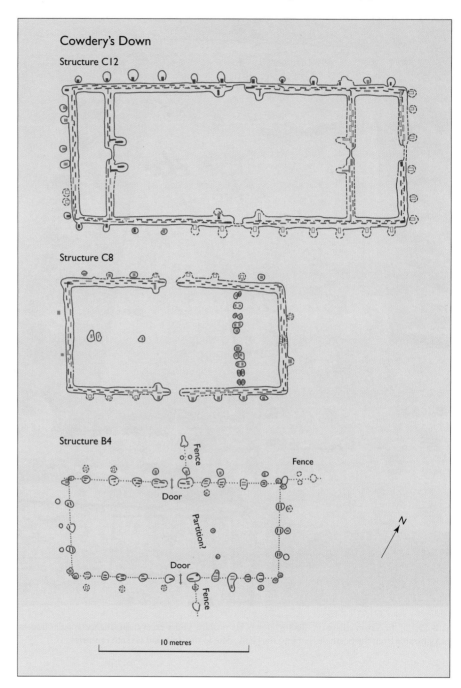

12.9 The Saxon settlement at Cowdery's Down, Hampshire, was like Chalton, composed of a series of well-built timber halls. In some cases the walls were made of overlapping planks set vertically in foundation trenches

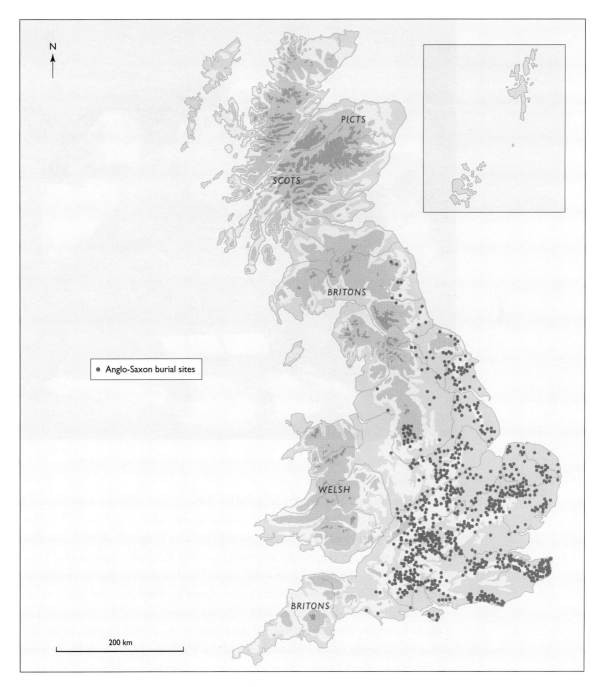

N

PICTS

SCOTS

BRITONS

● Anglo-Saxon burial sites

WELSH

BRITONS

200 km

12.10 The distribution of Saxon settlements of the fifth to seventh centuries reflects the division of Britain into an eastern and western zone

12.11 An early Saxon cremation urn under excavation in the cemetery at Spong Hill, Norfolk

the Saxon homeland between the Elbe and the Weser, clearly showing that the initial immigrants were of mixed origins. In the Saxon homeland urns of the kind found in Britain can be quite closely dated to the period 380–420. The implication, then, is that the earliest cremation cemeteries may well represent the mass movement of families into Britain in the period 408–9 that caused such consternation to the provincial administration and occasioned the plea to Rome for help. Once the pioneers had established themselves, friends and relatives would have followed. By the second half of the fifth century the cultural links of the communities in East Anglia and the east midlands, clustering around the wetlands of the Wash, are firmly with the Anglian and Jutish regions, a fact dramatically demonstrated by the distribution of brooches from female burials. How extensive was the early settlement it is difficult to say. No doubt enclaves of British survived, particularly around Lincoln and Verulamium (St Albans), where the surrounding areas are devoid of early Germanic cemeteries, and there must have been other large tracts of countryside where the descendants of the rural Romano-British population continued to live and farm.

Elsewhere in the country early Germanic settlement seems to have begun in different ways. This is particularly noticeable along the Thames, where, on both sides of the river from its estuary to the Cotswolds, distinctive Germanic inhumation burials have been found, the men buried with weapons and belt fittings derived from late Roman military equipment, the women with a mixture of Romano-British trinkets and Germanic brooches. It is tempting to interpret this group as a deliberate settlement of fighting men recruited from among the Frankish and Saxon *foederati* who had previously served with the Romans in the Rhineland or northern Gaul brought into Britain to protect the approaches to London and the vital Thames route to the productive west. One group based at Mucking on the Essex coast was ideally placed to guard the upper estuary, while others based at Dorchester-on-Thames

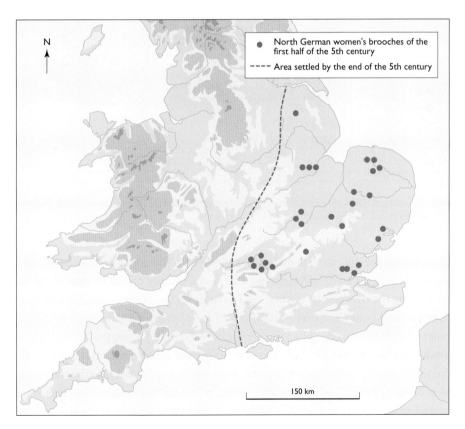

N

●   North German women's brooches of the first half of the 5th century

----   Area settled by the end of the 5th century

150 km

12.12 The distribution of distinctive types of north German brooches of the early fifth century gives an indication of the first areas settled by the 'Anglo-Saxon' incomers

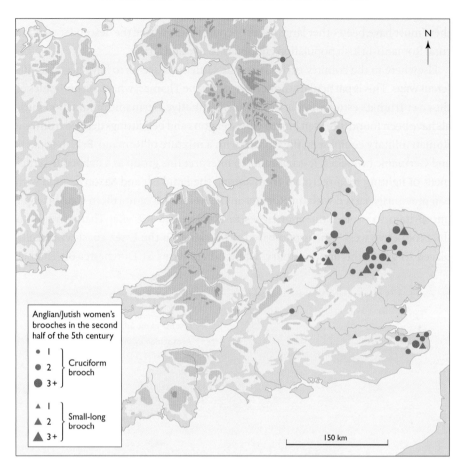

12.13 The constant inflow of settlers from the coastal region north of the Rhine in the second half of the fifth century is indicated by their distinctive brooch types

commanded the major route node at the gateway to the upper Thames valley and the Cotswolds. Other detachments were also strategically placed to control movement along the river and its tributaries. The bringing in of trained militias and their deployment among the native population will have been designed to strengthen the resistance of the Britons against further uncontrolled entry along the Thames, but it would also have served as a buffer to stop the further expansion of Germanic communities, already in the eastern regions, from advancing further into the south and west of the country. These Germanic militia may have been augmented over time by deliberate recruitment of additional forces and by the uninvited arrival of friends and dependants.

A rather different kind of federate settlement took place in Kent. Historical tradition records how three ship-loads of Jutish warriors led by Hengist arrived in the area and were allowed by Vortigern to settle on the Isle of Thanet. They had come from Jutland via the Frisian coast looking for employment. Unlike the federate militias of the Thames zone, they had not served as *foederati* with the late Roman army and were very differently equipped. That the pottery and brooches which they and their dependants brought with them, and which influenced the subsequent culture of the region, was stylistically of Jutish origin gives strong support to the historical tradition. Once settled, the Kentish Jutes forged strong links through trade and intermarriage with the Franks now in control of the adjacent continental regions. The infrastructure of ports and communications inherited from the Romans and the proximity of the two regions facilitated the contact. At about the same time another Jutish enclave settled the Isle of Wight and the neighbouring region of Hampshire.

By the middle of the fifth century, then, a number of disparate Germanic groups had settled in the south-east of Britain, some invited, others not. More were to follow in their wake. A careful study of the pottery used in Britain compared to that of the continental homelands leaves little doubt that the stream of incomers was con-

12.14 Late Roman belt fittings from a cemetery at Mucking, Essex. They may have belonged to a mercenary soldier brought in the late fourth or early fifth century to defend the Thames estuary against Saxon attack

tinuous. Communities of Anglian origin favoured the areas around the wetlands of the Wash, while Saxons were concentrated in the Thames valley, the south midlands, and the Hampshire–Sussex region. In this way the basis of the Anglian and Saxon kingdoms of England was laid.

Once established, the inexorable spread of Anglo-Saxon culture to the west began. But if Gildas is to be believed, it was stalled around the year 500 by British success in the battle of Mons Badonicus. Gildas could write in about 540 of 'our present security', but within a generation the Anglo-Saxons had regained the initiative and the pressure on the west resumed. One can only suppose that growth in population among the pioneering communities and the inflow of new settlers combined to create the conditions for expansion. Advance from the Thames valley was under way in the 570s. The battle of Dyrham in Gloucestershire (traditionally 577) saw the capitulation

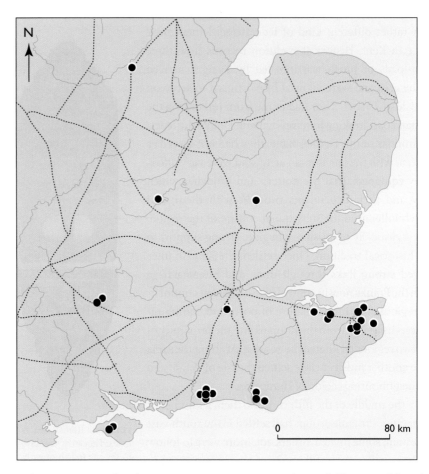

12.15 The concentrations of Anglo-Saxon graves containing Roman glass, probably imported from the Continent in the early Saxon period, indicate that the cross-Channel routes were still in operation

of the old Roman towns of Cirencester, Gloucester, and Bath and with them the prosperous Cotswold region. About 590 the northern Britons were defeated at Catterick in North Yorkshire, and by 650 most of Dorset had been overrun, with Somerset succumbing within the next decade. Of the old province of Britain only Dumnonia in the south-west, Wales, and parts of the Pennines and the north-west remained under the control of British kings.

How Many Were There?

The impact of Germanic culture on the archaeological record of Britain is clear for all to see, but what is far from agreed is what this means in terms of population replacement. On the one hand, it could be argued that the Germanic takeover of the east was total, the Britons being either slaughtered or driven to the west as Gildas so vividly describes; on the other hand, it could be suggested that the number of incomers was comparatively small—as few as 10,000—just sufficient to form a political elite whose culture was avidly embraced by the numerically dominant British population. These are difficult issues, not least because the debate attempting their resolution has relied more on archaeological fashion than on hard facts.

It might be thought that population genetics would provide the key. There have indeed been a number of attempts to approach the question, comparing the Y chromosome variations of sample British populations with samples taken from the supposed continental homelands, but the results are, to say the least, inconsistent. Some researchers have claimed that the male population of eastern Britain was all but wiped out and replaced by Germanic males, while others, using different data sets and analytical approaches, have argued that the Anglo-Saxon male intrusion into eastern England was at most between 9 per cent and 15 per cent and for the British Isles as a whole as little as 4 per cent. Work on mitochondrial DNA has suggested that female immigration is unlikely to have exceeded 20 per cent.

The real problems with the genetic approach lie in characterizing the host populations and taking into account the very difficult issue of chronology. The Germanic settlers arriving in Britain came from a coastal region stretching over 900 kilometres and one where the native population had been mobile over many centuries. This makes identifying the genetic signature of the immigrants very difficult. But a more serious issue is chronology. The east of Britain and the adjacent continent had been exchanging populations, if only on a limited scale, for millennia before the Roman invasion, and the Roman army in Britain included substantial detachments of Germanic troops from the outset. By the fourth century the army in Britain was heavily Germanized and incorporated mercenaries recruited from among the Saxons, and no doubt other tribes, from coastal regions far to the north of the Rhine frontier. It is difficult to see how Y chromosomes introduced into Britain by Germans in the third and fourth centuries can be distinguished from those of the fifth-century settlers. Another problem is that the Angles and Jutes came from modern Denmark, the same territory as the Danes who arrived in eastern England as Vikings several centuries later. Given all these complicating factors it seems unlikely that analysis of modern DNA is ever likely to give reliable figures for Anglo-Saxon immigration. There is no reason, however, why the study of the ancient DNA of the populations buried in the early cemeteries should not, eventually, provide the kind of evidence that will begin to resolve these tantalizing issues.

Attempts to use the archaeological and skeletal data to assess immigration have suggested that, in the Anglo-Saxon cemeteries of the south and east of England, the immigrant–native ratio is between 1:3 and 1:5, while in the areas of later expansion in the west and north, it falls to 1:10. If we assume that the population of Britain had fallen to, say, 2 million by the mid-fifth century, then the total number of immigrants could have been as many as 250,000, but is likely to have been significantly less, around 100,000 to 200,000. Such figures are, of course, beset by uncertainties and at best hint only at an order of magnitude. What is interesting is that both the genetic and archaeological approaches point to a significant level of immigration into south-eastern England during the fifth century in the order of between 10 and 20 per cent.

Mobility in the North Sea

During the fourth and fifth centuries the North Sea would have been alive with shipping. While Roman rule still held, the vessels of traders would have plied to and fro along the southern shipping lanes between the British North Sea ports and the Rhine mouth and northwards along the east coast of Britain, supplying food and materials to the northern garrison. There would also have been freighters and their naval escorts taking British grain, and no doubt other products, to the army on the Rhine. 'Saxon' pirates from the free Germanic coast-lands posed a constant threat. So, too, did the Picts, who took to the sea to outflank the northern frontier and attack the province to the south. By the end of the Roman period the North Sea had become a dangerous place. A vivid glimpse of the situation is provided by the Roman writer Vegetius, who describes the small Roman scout ships called *pictae*, which kept the fleet informed of enemy movements. They were made light for speed and were camouflaged sea-green. Efficient though the system sounds, there is a sense of desperation about it all. With the departure of Constantine III and his army in 407 it is doubtful if the *pictae*, let alone the fleet, were ever seen again.

Within a year or two the first boat-loads of settlers began to arrive in the east coast estuaries, bringing immigrants from the continental coast-lands. The fact that the pottery and jewellery styles of the immigrant communities kept up with fashions in their continental homelands is a clear indication that contacts were maintained, with ships going back and forth on a regular basis. After the initial flood of pioneer settlers was over, maritime links continued, helping to maintain social relationships through marriages and gift exchange, and introducing some level of commercial trade.

The disparate groups of Franks who settled in the Rhineland and northern Gaul in the late fourth century were eventually united early in the sixth century under the leadership of Clovis (481–511). Thereafter, in a new phase of expansionism, the Franks extended their influence through Gaul, reaching the Mediterranean in the 530s–540s. The late fifth and early sixth century also saw the intensification of cross-Channel trade, with Kent receiving an increasing range of luxury goods manufactured in Frankish workshops. These probably arrived largely through systems of elite gift exchange, implying close ties between the two peoples, culminating in the late sixth century with the marriage of the Kentish king Æthelberht to the Frankish princess Bertha. Frankish trading networks also extended along the south coast to include the Saxon enclaves between the rivers Ouse and Cuckmere and the rivers Arun and Adur. It would seem, then, that the establishment of Jutish and Saxon settlements along both sides of the Channel, far from disrupting the maritime networks that had bound the two shores in the Roman period, benefited from their continuation and development under the patronage of the fast-growing state of Frankia.

The British West

The collapse of Roman order and government in the northern and western regions of Britain left the country in a state of near-anarchy, a patchwork of small polities ruled by warlords, or 'tyrants' as Gildas and Procopius chose to call them:

> Britain has Kings, but they are tyrants; she has judges, but they are wicked. They often plunder and terrorize the innocent; they defend and protect the guilty and the thieving; they have many wives, whores and adulteresses; they constantly swear false oaths; they make vows but almost at once tell lies; they wage wars civil and unjust . . . they despise the harmless and humble but exalt . . . their military companies, bloody, proud and murderous men . . .
>
> (*De Excidio* 27)

The stern cleric Gildas was clearly not enamoured of the leaders, but in times of systems' collapse the new men who assume power can seldom afford to abide by the norms of the old order. Two warlords are specifically mentioned by Gildas: Vortigern ('the proud tyrant') and Ambrosius Aurelianus, who, we are told, was descended from Roman aristocracy. It is likely that the towns were rallying centres, and both men may have been members of the urban elite. Another warlord who features large in later romantic tradition is Arthur. He receives no mention by Gildas, though there are a few brief references in later Welsh legend to suggest that a shadowy figure with the late Roman name of Artorius may have played some part in the fifth-century struggles. But, as the scholar Noel Myres has so memorably written, 'no figure on the borderline of history and mythology has wasted more of the historian's time'.

It is a reasonable assumption that the western towns of Roman Britain served as centres of resistance. The specific mention in the Anglo-Saxon Chronicle of the towns of Cirencester, Gloucester, and Bath falling to the Saxons after the battle of

12.16 Wansdyke, snaking across the chalklands of north Wiltshire, was probably constructed in the fifth or sixth century as a territorial boundary in the conflicts between the Anglo-Saxon settlers and the native population

Dyrham (577) is an indication that other towns had survived into the sixth century. Archaeological evidence is sparse, but careful excavation of the baths basilica at Wroxeter has shown continued use well into the fifth century, if not later. Old cities would have provided a degree of protection, but they also conferred a sense of authority, through continuity, on the community and its leaders.

One notable characteristic of the British resistance was the reuse of hill-forts in the west country. The best-known example is South Cadbury in Somerset, where excavations have shown that the inner defensive earth-work of the long-abandoned Iron Age hill-fort was strengthened with a new construction of timber and rubble, representing a massive investment in manpower. Dating evidence is limited but suggests that the reuse took place at the end of the fifth century. Within the defences timber buildings were erected, one of considerable proportions. This, together with the discovery of a range of imported pottery, some from the Mediterranean, points to the presence of a war-leader or some other member of the elite able to exert a significant degree of coercive power. Fifth- and sixth-century occupation associated with imported pottery has also been found at two other Somerset hill-forts: Cadbury near Congresbury and Cannington. Outside Cannington the development of a large sub-Roman cemetery emphasized the importance of the place as a sub-Roman centre. The reuse of hill-forts in the south-west reflects a return to tribalism. It is tempting to suggest that the warlords, by reoccupying them, were making a deliberate reference to a romantic past dimly remembered through oral tradition. But in reality the 500-year-old defences would have provided welcome safe havens for a rural population now constantly under threat.

Scattered among the Heathen

Gildas paints a characteristically vivid picture of the chaos and disruption that engulfed the south-west in the years before the British victory of Mons Badonicus about AD 500 as the Germanic pressure built:

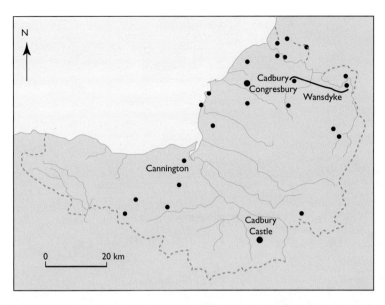

12.17 The map shows the distribution of Iron Age hill-forts and other hill-top locations producing late Roman artefacts, indicating a phase of reuse that may have lasted into the fifth century. Cadbury near Congresbury and South Cadbury Castle produced imported pottery of the fifth century coming from the Mediterranean. Wansdyke was probably built about this time

a number of the wretched survivors were caught in the mountains and butchered whole-sale. Others, their spirits broken by hunger, went to surrender to the enemy; they were fated to be slaves for ever, if indeed they were not killed straight away, the best outcome. Others made for lands beyond the sea; beneath the swelling sails they loudly wailed, sing-ing a psalm, instead of a shanty: 'You have given us like sheep for eating and scattered us among the heathen'. Others held out . . . trusting their lives . . . to the high hills, steep, menacing and fortified, to the densest forests, and to the cliffs of the sea-coasts.

(*De Excidio* 25.1)

Gildas makes no reference to the destinations of those who took to the sea, but Procopius understood that Britons were emigrating to Gaul: by referring to Armorica as 'Britannia' he gives geographical precision to the story. Further support comes from the bishop Apollinaris Sidonius, who mentions the presence of 'Britanni', led by their king Riothamus, on the Loire in the mid-fifth century. A later source stated that 12,000 of them were fighting against the Visigothic invaders. At the Council of Tours in 567 further reference is made to Britanni in Armorica, and from the late sixth century the peninsula is widely referred to as Britannia (hence 'Brittany'). These historical references, together with the fact that the Breton language was closely similar to the Celtic spoken in south-western Britain, inevitably led to the conclusion that there was a mass migration from

12.18 The Iron Age hill-fort of South Cadbury, Somerset, was redefended and occupied in the fifth and sixth centuries by an indigenous community at the time of the Anglo-Saxon advance westwards. It is probably the Camelot made famous in the Arthurian epic

Britain to Armorica in the fifth century. More recent work has questioned the significance of the linguistic evidence, arguing that the native inhabitants of Armorica probably spoke a Gallic dialect closely akin to the Celtic spoken in western Britain throughout the Roman period. This does not diminish the force of the historical evidence but implies that the emerging Breton language, rather than being introduced at this time, was indigenous Gallic strengthened by the British Celtic spoken by the immigrants.

12.19 Reconstruction of the gate and defences at South Cadbury as rebuilt in the fifth or sixth century based on evidence from excavations

While there is no reasonable doubt, then, that communities of Britons did cross the sea to settle in Brittany, and that many of them were making the journey in the fifth century, the duration of the migration and its causes may have been more complex than Gildas would have us believe. The archaeological evidence shows that the ports of northern Armorica like Alet near Saint-Malo and Le Yaudet near Lannion were in direct contact with the ports of the south coast of Britain, at least from the third century, building on a long tradition of maritime interaction going back into prehistory. Such contacts would have involved social exchanges, quite possibly including the movement of people, if only on a small scale. In the growing turmoil of the late third and fourth centuries, with Irish raids on Cornwall and south Wales increasing, more people may have been encouraged to take ship for the comparative calm of Armorica, perhaps to join relatives already there. The late fourth-century movement of armies from Britain to fight on the Continent may also have exacerbated the flow of Britons to Armorica. The ninth-century historian Nennius had access to a source that specifically said that the British in Armorica 'went forth with the tyrant Maximus on his campaign' and were unwilling to return, the reference being to the military deployments of 383. Whether or not this is historically correct, it may embody a tradition that federate troops from Britain were active in Armorica.

Taken together, then, the historical, archaeological, and linguistic evidence suggests that the long-established maritime routes between south-western Britain and Armorica saw an increasing flow of Britons moving to the Continent in the late third and fourth centuries. The exodus referred to by Gildas in the early fifth century will have been a continuation of the process that was still under way, as Procopius reminds us, in the mid-sixth century. The British settlers seem to have concentrated over time in the north and west of the peninsula, creating the kingdoms of Domnonée and Cornouaille, names reflecting the tribal homelands from which they came: Dumnonia (Devon) and Cornwall. This would imply that the number and status of immigrants were sufficient to enable them to enforce political dominance over the native Armoricans.

As part of this Atlantic exodus one enterprising group ended up in Galicia in north-western Iberia, where they and their successors founded the abbey of Santa María de Bretoña near Mondoñedo, a settlement known to have been active in the mid-sixth century. This chance historical survival is a reminder that there may have been other ship-loads of Britons who were prepared to take to the sea to find new homes along the Atlantic seaways in this era of folk wandering.

The Irish Sea and 'the Beat of Hostile Oars'

Knowledge of Ireland among the British, and in particular of its maritime regions, was extensive, as the data recorded by Ptolemy in the second century so vividly show, and there was ample evidence of trading between the two islands throughout the Roman period. But above this low murmur of activity there would have been more significant movements, episodic at first but growing more persistent with time. Ireland, like much northern Europe beyond the frontiers, was probably experiencing a steady population growth, and it was this that would have encouraged the more energetic to seek new opportunities in Britain and the empire beyond. Some young men offered themselves to serve in the Roman armies. Some will have been content to raid the coastal regions of the province, while other communities looked to the westerly parts of Britain as congenial land to settle. These various responses to the desire for mobility begin to be evident in the late third century and intensify dramatically during the fourth and early fifth centuries.

Service in the Roman army would have been a particular attraction to young warriors eager for reward and adventure. Many of those recruited may have started off as raiders, only later to be persuaded to become regular troops. It is hardly surprising, therefore, that the two Irish peoples, the Scotti and the Attacotti, frequently named among the enemies of Britain, also turn up in the units serving on the Continent listed in the *Notitia Dignitatum* at the end of the fourth century. Others may have been recruited to make up numbers in units stationed in Britain. How many returned to Ireland after their service had been completed, it is impossible to say, but those who did would have taken with them knowledge useful to would-be raiders. Many would also have carried home booty acquired during service. The two large hoards of silver found in the north of Ireland, at Coleraine and Ballinrees, and the hoard from Balline in the south-west might have arrived in Ireland with returning soldiers, though it is equally possible that they comprised the loot of raiders or treaty payments by the Roman authorities buying off threatened attack.

12.20 Hoard found at Ballinrees, County Derry, Ireland, consisting of silver of early fifth-century date derived from the Roman world. It may have been loot from raids or payment for mercenary services

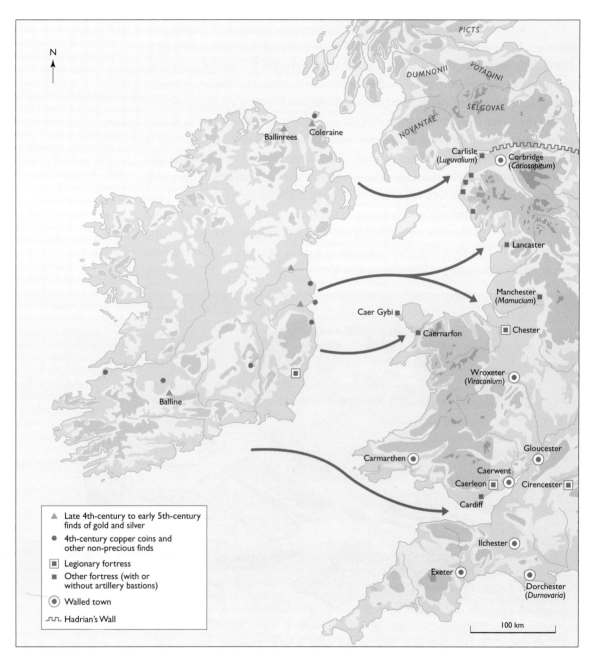

12.21 In the late fourth and early fifth centuries a range of Roman material, especially gold and silver, was found in Ireland, suggesting raiding or payment for mercenary services. Irish raids on the western coasts of Britain led to renewed fortification

Raiding may have begun as early as the third century. The new fort with projecting bastions built at Cardiff in about 260 and the two similar but smaller forts at Caer Gybi on Anglesey and at Lancaster, strategically located on the Lune, probably date to this time. Other forts, like Caernarfon, Chester, Ribchester, Ravenglass, and Maryport, all sited on major rivers or estuaries, were maintained in good order and garrisoned. The evidence is sufficient to show that the more vulnerable coast-lines of western Britain were being kept in defensive readiness. The presence of a fleet based in the Bristol Channel is also suggested by a mosaic found in the sanctuary at Lydney. It was dedicated to the deity by Titus Flavius Senilis, whose rank is abbreviated 'PRREL', interpreted as *praepositus reliquationi classis*, officer in charge of the naval supply depot. The Severn estuary would have been particularly vulnerable to attack, not least because of its rich hinterland. The new fort at Cardiff and fortified towns of Carmarthen, Caerwent, and Gloucester would have provided some security to the surrounding countryside, but the number of coin hoards deposited in the late third century speaks of uncertainty in the region. In the late fourth century evidence of widespread destruction in the countryside shows that fear of raiding had now become a reality.

After the year 360 raiders from Ireland are frequently mentioned by Roman historians, usually in all too brief statements of the fact. Rather more colourful detail is offered by the composer of a panegyric in praise of Stilicho, a German general in charge of western defence at the end of the fourth and beginning of the fifth century. Ireland, we are told, rose up against Britain, and 'the sea foamed to the beat of hostile oars'. Stilicho was so successful in his response that 'ice-bound Hibernia wept for the mounds of slain Scotti'. It was not long after this that an Irish poem credits the high king of Ireland, Niall of the Nine Hostages, with having led seven successful raids against Britain. Clearly he was following in the tradition of his predecessors.

The Irish raiding parties were intent on plundering the wealthy estates of western Britain. The reward for success would have been precious metal, cattle, and slaves. Cairenn, the mother of Niall, was said to have been a British captive. A rather more famous British slave was St Patrick. In his *Confessio* Patrick recounts how, as a boy living in Britain in the early fifth century, where civilized Roman standards were still in force, he was captured by an Irish raiding party and taken to Ireland. There he was sold as a slave and spent six years as a herdsman in remote rural districts before escaping on a trading ship to war-torn Brittany. From there he managed to get back to Britain to rejoin his family, but in a revelatory moment, hearing 'the voice of the Irish', he was drawn back to the island to convert the people to Christianity. There is no reason to doubt the main events of the story: if Patrick is to be believed, thousands of Britons were killed or carried away as slaves when the raiding was at its height, but, as his own experiences showed, the trading ships were still able to maintain their business.

Irish Settlements in Britain

The British west coast, susceptible to Irish raids, was also wide open to settlement. The best attested of the migrations was the movement of the Déisi from Munster and Leinster in southern Ireland to Dyfed in south-west Wales. The story is told in an Irish saga, The Expulsion of the Déisi, and is corroborated in a Welsh manuscript, which confirms the succession of rulers. The archaeological evidence is also impressive. In their Irish homeland the Déisi used ogham, a script derived from Latin but translated into simple incised lines easy to cut along the edges of memorial stones. Ogham inscriptions are found widely distributed in south and south-west Ireland in Waterford, Cork, and Kerry: they are also found in south Wales, concentrated in Dyfed, and in Cornwall, many recording Irish names. Place name evidence also confirms a strong Irish component in south-west Wales in a region stretching along the coast of Cardigan Bay.

The name Déisi originally meant 'payers of tribute' or 'vassals', in other words a class of people who were subservient to overlords, perhaps from a neighbouring conquering tribe. In the fourth century they were not a distinct tribe, but by the eighth century, when The Expulsion of the Déisi was written down, they had assumed tribal status, the text being essentially the formalization of their foundation myth, providing legitimacy in the form of a list of kings. At the time of their migration to Wales, probably at the end of the fourth century, they were still a subservient class looking for new opportunities in a new land. Although the date of the migration has been much debated, some scholars preferring to place it in the third century, it is more generally agreed that the movement began late in the fourth century. Strong contacts were maintained with the homeland for the next two centuries, with additional migrants arriving over time.

The context for the settlement raises many interesting questions, most notably, how was it that a band of second-class citizens from Ireland could settle, apparently unopposed, in south-west Wales during the late Roman period? The simplest explanation would be to suppose that they were invited in by the Roman authority and put in place as federates to help protect the coastal regions from other Irish raiders. Much of western Wales had been stripped of troops by this stage. To establish a strong new settlement here in the extreme south-west would have provided additional protection for the vulnerable Severn estuary and the rich heartlands of the province beyond. The parallels with what was happening on the Saxon Shore at about the same time are striking.

12.22 (*opposite*) The Irish settlement of western Britain in the fifth and sixth centuries is in part indicated by the spread of Ogham inscriptions

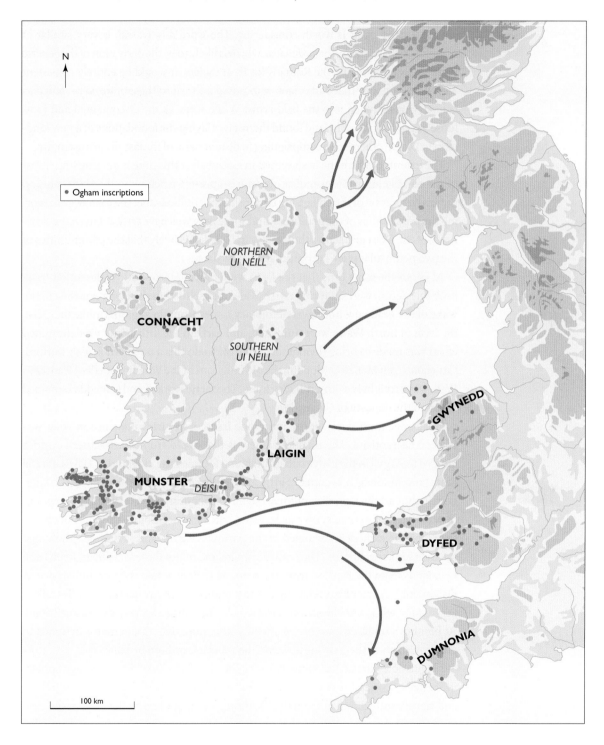

N

- Ogham inscriptions

NORTHERN
UI NÉILL

CONNACHT

SOUTHERN
UI NÉILL

GWYNEDD

LAIGIN

MUNSTER   DÉISI

DYFED

DUMNONIA

100 km

One further point is worth considering. The word *déisi* (vassal) is very similar in meaning to the Irish word *aithechtúatha*, which is likely to be the derivation of the generic name Attacotti, used by the Romans for Irish raiders. It would be entirely consistent with Roman policy that barbarians who posed a threat to the empire were settled as federates or recruited into the field army. While some of the discontented and foot-loose vassal peoples of Ireland found themselves laying the foundations of a new kingdom in Dyfed, others were campaigning in distant parts of the fast-decaying empire.

The extent to which the Irish settled in Cornwall at this time is unclear since most of the datable inscriptions indicating an Irish presence belong to the sixth century. But in the turmoil of the collapsing empire it is not unlikely that the Irish were exploring the possibilities of the peninsula, and some may well have settled. Given the proximity of the Déisi just across the estuary in Dyfed, it is likely that the communities of the two peninsulas were in contact at an early date.

At about the same time that the Déisi were moving into south Wales, other Irish, probably Scotti, were attacking north Wales and settling in the Llyn peninsula in the wake of the gradual withdrawal of military forces from the region. Unlike the Déisi, the Irish in north Wales were uninvited, and early in the fifth century a determined effort was made to bring them under control. To do this a northern British warlord, Cunedda, from Manau Gododdin, the old kingdom of the Votadini north of Hadrian's Wall, was brought in with a military force. The tactic worked and Cunedda remained to found the dynasty of Gwynedd.

Finally, we must consider the intriguing issue of the Irish influence in what was to become Scotland. The traditional view is that Scotti from north-eastern Antrim crossed to Argyll in the early sixth century and founded the kingdom of Dál Riata. Dál Riata grew in strength, eventually, in the mid-ninth century, absorbing the Pictish kingdom in the east through elite intermarriage and conquest to create the united kingdom of Alba, later to become known as Scotland. The historical sources are succinct in the extreme. The earliest is contained in the writings of Bede and says quite simply that the Irish settled in Britain. 'They came from Ireland under the leadership of Reuda and won lands from the Picts . . . from the name of their chieftain they are still known as Dalreudini . . .'. Later texts referring to the founding event five centuries earlier talk of Fergus Mór, who, 'with the nation of Dál Riata', established a Scottish dynasty in Britain. At best both traditions can be regarded as little more than origin myths designed to give legitimacy to the growing power of the Scots in northern Britain.

Linguistic evidence has some relevance to the discussion. The language spoken in western Scotland was Gaelic, the same as the Goidelic Celtic spoken in Ireland and significantly different from the Brythonic Celtic spoken by the Picts in the east. So different were the dialects that in the seventh century St Columba (Columcille) needed translators when he ventured into Pictish territory. The conventional explanation of this is that Gaelic was introduced into the west of Scotland by the Scotti in the sixth century, replacing the indigenous form of Celtic.

The 'historical' and linguistic evidence, however, contrasts with the archaeological, which can identify no significant trace of Irish culture in western Scotland at this time. There are no simple answers to the dilemma. The close proximity of Antrim to western Scotland and the fact that the Scottish west was a disparate maritime community linked by the sea is sufficient to suggest that the two regions must have been as intensively connected in the mid-first millennium as they had been throughout earlier prehistory. Although they might maintain their own distinctive material culture, social intercourse and intermarriage would have created bonds of allegiance, and, given the closeness of the two regions, it would not be surprising if they spoke the same dialect of Celtic. The sea linked them together, while the spine of the Highlands separated them from the Pictish Celtic speakers to the east. In such a situation it is not at all difficult to see how a small elite of Scotti from Antrim could have assumed control of the Atlantic coastal zone of northern Britain. There is no need to argue for a large influx of new settlers.

Contacts between the two regions continued. In 563 Columba, together with twelve followers, sailed from Antrim to Dál Riata and two years later founded the monastery on the island of Iona. The fame of Columba and his new foundation ensured that a record of the event has survived in the historical sources, but it must have been just one of a myriad of movements of people of all kinds across the narrows of the North Channel.

Christians and Mobility

The Christian imperative to proselytize made a significant contribution to human mobility in the fifth, sixth, and seventh centuries. Acceptance of Christianity as a state religion by the Romans in the early fourth century, formalized by the baptism of Constantine the Great, encouraged the spread of the faith throughout the empire. In Britain, that the chi-rho symbol (the first two letters of the name of Christ) has been found painted on walls and displayed on mosaics in Roman villas and inscribed on expensive pewter and silver tableware shows that the elite wished to identify themselves with the new religion. How widespread it was among the poorer classes and in the more remote countryside is less clear. The country dwellers, the *pagani* (those who lived in the *pagi*, the rural districts), may well have adhered to their ancient beliefs, but for those in and around the towns it would have been difficult to avoid the Christian world. The mixing of old and new is nicely demonstrated by one of the curse tab-

12.23 Central roundel from a fourth-century mosaic found at Hinton St Mary, Dorset. The chi-rho symbol behind the figure's head is the Christian insignia (the first two letters of the name of Christ). It may suggest that the depiction is of Christ

lets thrown into the spring sacred to the goddess Sulis Minerva in the centre of the sanctuary at Aquae Sulis (Bath). The curses usually used an all-embracing phrase to ensure that the wrongdoer did not escape the deity's ire. The usual formula said, 'whether he be male or female, freeman or slave'. To be absolutely certain one writer had added 'Christian or pagan'. The implication would seem to be that Christians and pagans were regularly rubbing shoulders in the spa town.

One famous British Christian was Pelagius, who departed Britain for Rome in about 380. His particular interpretation of Christianity was branded as heresy by the Roman Church, but it seems to have become deeply rooted in his native country among the ruling elites—so much so that in 429 Germanus, bishop of Auxerre, was sent, together with the bishop of Troyes, to counter the spread of the heresy and bring the Britons into line with Roman doctrines. According to tradition he confronted

Vortigern, one of the leading Pelagians, and others of the British elite, 'conspicuous for riches, brilliant in dress, and surrounded by a fawning multitude'. The Pelagians were eventually beaten by force of argument, and after visiting the tomb of St Alban near Verulamium, Germanus went on to lead a military expedition against Picts and Saxons, further demonstrating to the Britons his God-given prowess. That he found it necessary to return again to Britain in about 446–7, however, hints that the Pelagians may still have been a force to reckon with.

The visits of Germanus and his entourage, long after Roman government had abandoned the province and during the tumultuous period when Saxons and Angles were beginning to arrive in number, is a revealing reflection of the reach and mobility of the Church. Britain remained in contact with Rome, but after about 460 links seem to have been severed as the east of the country was taken over by pagan Germanic immigrants. It was not until the landing of Augustine in Kent in 597 that Roman Christianity began to be restored.

Meanwhile, in the British west Christianity flourished, and it was probably the increasing mobility of the Irish that brought the spiritual needs of the pagan islanders to the consciousness of the Christian fathers. In the late fourth century Jerome encountered a group of Attacotti in Gaul and reports, with evident distaste, on the habits of these barbarians. They practised polyandry and were not averse to a little cannibalism: 'it is their custom to cut off the buttocks of the herdsmen and their wives, their breasts too, and to judge these alone as culinary delicacies'. While one might be tempted to see this passage as a colourful overstatement pandering to the prejudices of his readers, earlier writers like Strabo had already given hints of such practices. Cannibalism to insult enemies is not unknown among more recent less-developed peoples. To an ardent Christian reading these words, however, Ireland must have presented a worthy challenge.

In 431 Pope Celestine sent Palladius, a Gaulish churchman, to serve as bishop of the Christian Irish, the implication being that some in Ireland had already been converted. On the basis of early church dedications he appears to have been active in County Wicklow and also in south-west Wales, suggesting that he might have begun his mission among the Déisi of Dyfed before setting out for southern Ireland, but little more can be deduced of his activities.

The next year Patrick, having escaped from captivity in Ireland and returned home to north-western Britain, felt a calling to go and minister to the Irish. 'The voice of the Irish' cried out, 'we beseech thee, holy youth, come hither and walk among us'. Patrick would have been familiar with the organization of the Roman Church in Britain, which was based on the urban infrastructure. In Ireland the far more scattered population posed a challenge. This he responded to by building churches set in the open countryside to serve as focal points for large territorial regions, the *paro-chia*, and by appointing bishops to lead the community. In the event his attempt, and that of Palladius, to base the structure of the Irish Church on a version of the Roman urban model failed, and by the end of the fifth century it had all but disappeared, to be replaced by a new system, monasticism, which was being introduced along the Atlantic seaways, ultimately from the eastern Mediterranean.

Monasticism, based ultimately on the beliefs and practices of the Desert Fathers in Egypt, centred around communities of monks who had withdrawn from the secular world to live a life of devotion governed by the rules of their founders. Only in isolation, without the distractions of everyday life, could they serve God and come to understand his will. For this reason the monks chose remote places for their monasteries. As time went on, some communities became more extreme and took to the sea in search of 'desert', settling in great austerity on barren rocks like the spectacular Skellig Michael, 13 kilometres off the south-western tip of County Kerry. Driven on still further, some explored the northern ocean, reaching the Faroes by the year 700 and Iceland by the end of the century: both islands were previously uninhabited. The Irish monk Dicuil, writing about 825, mentions the 'many other islands in the ocean to the north of Britain' where hermits who had set out from Scotland had been living for a century.

While some of these travelling monks, the *peregrini*, sought seclusion in remote places, others saw it as their duty to travel among men to spread their beliefs and their practices. Missionaries from Ireland and from south-west Wales travelled extensively along the Atlantic seaways, establishing churches in south-west Britain and in Brittany, many of them accompanying the folk movements from Britain to the Armorican peninsula in the fifth and sixth centuries. Others took their missionary calling even more seriously, travelling to the centre of Europe and beyond to Italy and the Danube, founding monasteries as they went. The shores of the Irish Sea must at times have been alive with preparations for these journeys, but the actual numbers of people taking part in the missionary exodus can never have been great. What it does indicate, however, is the vitality of Atlantic shipping.

Some insight into shipping movements is provided by anecdotes surviving in the historical record. When Patrick made his escape from slavery in Ireland in the early fifth century, he took ship on a cargo vessel carrying dogs to Gaul. An unlikely cargo perhaps, but then Strabo, four centuries earlier, thought it worth mentioning that hunting dogs were valued exports from Britain. In 610 Columbanus, who was returning from Burgundy to his native Ireland, encountered an Irish cargo ship offloading at Nantes on the Loire estuary. Not long after, the Life of St Philibert mentions Irish traders arriving at the island monastery of Noirmoutier, just south of the Loire, with

12.24 The rock of Skellig Michael, Kerry, lies battered by the ocean off the extreme south-west tip of Ireland. Irish Christian monks chose it as a place removed from the temptations of the world where they could be close to God

quantities of shoes and clothing, reminding us that Ireland was probably an important source of leather. It was on vessels like these that the monks of the Celtic Church would have set out to pursue their missions. The Gauls from the Atlantic region of France were also engaged in shipping ventures. Bede tells the story of a Gaulish bishop, Arculf, who was shipwrecked somewhere off the western coast of Britain and eventually made his way to Iona, while the Life of Columba makes passing reference to Gaulish seamen arriving on Iona from Gaul in a *barca*, presumably a specialized type of merchant ship.

If the historical sources are surprisingly forthcoming about maritime activity along the Atlantic in the fifth to seventh centuries, the archaeological evidence is even more prolific. Most striking is the distribution of pottery of the fifth and sixth centuries emanating from the Mediterranean. The two principal categories found on British and Irish sites are fine red-slip wares made in western Turkey and North Africa (these are known as A Wares) and amphorae from Turkey, Egypt, and North

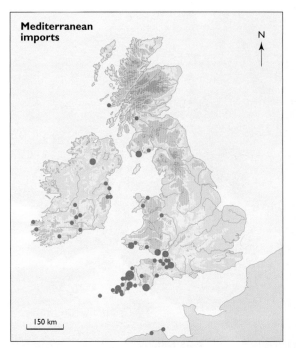
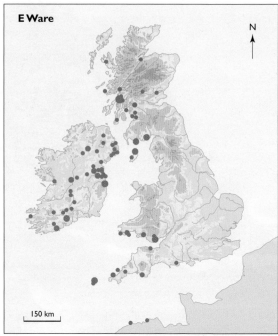

12.25 Imported pottery shows the continued importance of the Atlantic sea-routes from the fifth to the seventh century. The Mediterranean imports are mainly of the fifth and sixth century, while the E Ware from western France is of the seventh century

Africa (B Wares), which were probably used to transport olive oil. These disparate Mediterranean products must have been assembled by traders somewhere in the western Mediterranean and shipped to ports along the Atlantic coast of Iberia. While some of the Byzantine ships involved may have continued their journeys northwards to Britain, it seems more likely that local vessels carried their cargoes forwards to their end users, possibly in a series of short-haul trips. The distribution of these Mediterranean Wares in Britain shows a concentration in the south-west of Britain, but examples are also found around the Irish coasts and as far north as the Clyde estuary. The pottery was, of course, only one of the commodities carried. The possibility of oil carried in amphorae has already been mentioned. To this we might add casks of wine from the Gironde region, glass vessels, fine fabrics, and a whole range of other luxury goods such as spices and pigments of which no archaeological trace survives.

After the middle of the sixth century the supply of Mediterranean products dries up, but the continuation of Atlantic maritime activity is amply demonstrated by the even more widespread distribution of domestic pottery originating in western

France (E Wares), which turn up in quantity in Ireland and western Scotland. These vessels are mainly storage jars, which suggests the importation of foodstuffs, spices, and dyes, but pitchers are present, indicating that casks of wine might have been included in the cargoes. Indeed, it is a distinct possibility that wine was the principal import, the ceramic containers being used to fill the spaces between the casks. Fine tableware, oil, and wine would have been desirable commodities among the secular elite: they were also essential for the rituals of the clergy.

Scraps of archaeological data and historical anecdotes are difficult to quantify, but, standing back from the detail, it would seem that after a period of turbulence involving raiding and large-scale folk movement for a few generations in the late fourth and early fifth centuries, maritime commerce in the Irish Sea and its Atlantic approaches settled down to a period of relative prosperity, inspired largely by the vibrant culture of Celtic monasteries. It was a time of renewal for the Atlantic networks.

The Peoples of the North

The Roman sources are not particularly informative about the Britons living north of Hadrian's Wall. Tacitus mentions a number of tribes by name and Ptolemy adds others. In this divided landscape of mountains, glens, and many islands it is hardly surprising that communities were dispersed and sometimes isolated, giving rise to a confusion of small polities. The Roman presence on the southern borders created a new dynamic among the tribes closest to them, encouraging confederation, the better to oppose the Roman threat. By the end of the second century the historians refer to the Maeatae and the Caledonii as the foremost enemies of the empire, but by the fourth century they have passed from history, the centre stage now being taken by the Picti, the 'painted ones'. While this could reflect a tendency to generalize on the part of historians with no special knowledge of the region, using 'Picti' as a derogatory term, it more likely reflects the emergence of a single large confederation in eastern Scotland similar to those found immediately beyond the frontier elsewhere in Europe at about this time.

For perhaps as much as three generations, from 360 to 430, the Picts took the initiative, joining in successive raids on the Roman south, but the moment passed and the growing strength of the two British kingdoms south of the Clyde–Forth line, the kingdom of Strathclyde in the west and Manau Gododdin in the east, put a stop to further raiding. By the mid-sixth century the Angles had extended their influence up the east coast to the Firth of Forth, creating the powerful kingdom of Northumbria.

The Pictish confederates, bordered by the British kingdoms in the south and the Gaelic-speaking kingdom of Dál Riata in the south-west, stretched across northern

Britain from the North Sea coast to the Outer Hebrides and embraced the Northern Isles of Orkney and Shetland. A broadly similar material culture and a similar language, a dialect of Brythonic Celtic, bound the disparate and scattered entities together, and from the mid-sixth century the first historical high kings begin to appear. Thereafter, for three centuries the Brythonic-speaking Picts existed in a state of unstable equilibrium with the Goidelic-speaking Dalriadans (Scots). Brides were exchanged, treaties agreed, and battles fought until 844, when the Scots finally triumphed and the Islands and Highlands were united under a single king, Kenneth Macalpine. But we have run ahead of the narrative.

In Retrospect

The time from 350 to 650 was, by any standards, a period of dramatic change. A child born in the comparative tranquillity of southern Britain in the 340s, in old age would have looked back on a lifetime of increasing turmoil, culminating in the total collapse of order and government, inextricably bound up with the incursion of aliens on an unprecedented scale. Exponential change of this magnitude was psychologically devastating and few would have been unaffected. The rate of change exacerbated the sense of dislocation, and with it came a resort to mobility. It must have seemed as if all the world was caught up in torment. For the immigrants coming from the Continent, too, this was an extraordinary time. Irresistible population pressures imposed by neighbouring tribes and a declining environment left little choice but to take to the sea and sail west: once under way, the flow continued. In Ireland other pressures, engendered perhaps by an increasingly hierarchical social system, encouraged the young of the underclass to seek a better life through military service, raiding, and settlement abroad. Others, occupying the overcrowded south-western peninsula of Britain, left to seek a new life

12.26 The back of a cross slab from Golspie in northern Scotland profusely decorated with Pictish symbols. Symbols of this type originated in the fourth century and continued to be used until the advance of the Scots in the ninth century. Their meaning is unknown

in Armorica. For someone living through this period of turmoil it must have seemed as if the whole of the world's population was caught up in the madness of mobility.

And yet by the year 500 the momentum had quietened. The Anglo-Saxon front was still pushing against the British west and people were still moving into areas opened up by the pioneer settlers, but the frenetic pace had slackened. It was a time of consolidation, when the individual polities were beginning to redefine themselves and kingdoms were in the making. In the century and a half to follow, new rhythms of trade were coming into being to serve the demands of the emerging elites. The Atlantic seaways continued to bring Mediterranean goods to those living around the Irish Sea, while the growing power of the Frankish kingdom encouraged merchants to engage with communities of the south from Kent to the Solent. The Anglian kings of the east coast looked across the North Sea for trading opportunities, creating extensive new networks that extended into the Baltic, allowing the ruler commemorated in the great ship burial at Sutton Hoo to possess a helmet comparable in style and grandeur to those of the Vendel kings of Sweden. After the storm of migration the seas were calming again.

13

——— ⊶⊶⊶ ———

The Age of the
Northmen, AD 600–1100

To the God-fearing Christians of western Europe the onslaught of the pagan Northmen must have seemed to be the wrath of God let loose. After all, had not the prophet Jeremiah written, 'Out of the north an evil shall break forth upon all the inhabitants of the land'? Through these pagan marauders God was punishing the sinners of Christendom. The first attack fell on the monastery of Lindisfarne in 793 and sent a frisson of horror across the civilized world. The English cleric Alcuin, from the relative safety of Charlemagne's court, summed up the sense of helplessness and disbelief:

> Never before has such terror appeared in Britain as we have now suffered from a pagan race, nor was it thought that such an inroad from the sea could be made. Behold the church of St Cuthbert splattered with the blood of the priests of God, despoiled of all its ornaments; a place more venerable than all in Britain is given as prey to pagan people.
>
> (Letter to Æthelred, king of Northumbria)

It was just the beginning. More raids were to follow for more than half a century, engulfing Britain and Ireland but spreading insidiously along the Atlantic coasts and estuaries of Europe until they reached into the Mediterranean to terrorize the towns

13.1 Commemorative stone from the monastery of Lindisfarne, Northumbria. The scene is thought to depict Doomsday but it may contain a reference to the Viking raid of 793

of northern Italy. Then the pace changed as opportunist raiding gave way to settlement.

Contemporary sources usually refer to the Scandinavian raiders and settlers as Northmen, but they have become more popularly known as Vikings after the Scandinavian word *vik*, which means an inlet from the sea or a trading settlement on the coast. To go *i viking* meant to raid. They are, then, people who have given up farming and have taken to the sea as their main form of livelihood. Norwegians, Danes, and Swedes all embraced the Viking lifestyle. The Norwegians and Danes looked to the Atlantic as their sphere of activity, founding settlements in Britain, France,

13.2 The Viking raids stimulated the imagination. Here a successful raid is lovingly re-created by the nineteenth-century artist Lorenz Frølich

Iceland, and Greenland, and eventually exploring the coast of America, while the Swedes turned east across the Baltic to the great rivers of northern Europe as far as the Black Sea and the Caspian Sea beyond. What they all had in common was an intense desire to be on the move, a reputation as formidable fighters, and an acuity as traders. The breadth and energy of their expansion made a lasting impression on the development of Europe.

Britain and Ireland lay at the centre of the network created by the Norwegians and the Danes. At first the Norwegians focused their activity on northern Britain, Ireland, and the Irish Sea, while the Danes were more interested in the east and south of the island, but with time the spheres overlapped and the Viking communities became more mixed. Once settlement had begun in France and Britain, intermarriage with native people would have become increasingly common. This is convincingly demonstrated by the high percentage of 'Celtic' mitochondrial DNA found among the modern population of Iceland likely to have come from the Irish or Pictish wives and female slaves who accompanied the pioneer settlers. In times of mobility populations can become quickly mixed.

Prelude: Britain, 650–800

By AD 600 the Germanic settlement of eastern Britain had become firmly established and a number of discrete kingdoms had begun to crystallize out of the mêlée of incoming groups. In the north the Anglians had extended up the east coast, after the battle of Catterick in 600 crossing the Tees and moving steadily northwards almost to the Firth of Forth, taking the dominant coastal promontory of Bamburgh as their capital. In the midlands the kingdom of Mercia crept steadily towards the Welsh borderlands, while in the south the West Saxons, having overcome the resistance of Somerset, now confronted the kingdom of Dumnonia, which still retained its freedom in the south-west peninsula. Beyond the loosely drawn border lay the British kingdoms, themselves now consolidated into larger power blocks. Over the next century, as Anglo-Saxon rule extended steadily to the north and to the west, reaching the western ocean, three polities—Northumbria, Mercia, and Wessex—became increasingly more statelike. In the north the Northumbrians reached the Firth of Forth, conquering the Edinburgh Castle rock—the principal centre of the old Gododdin kingdom—in 638, while in the west they engulfed the undefended British kingdoms of Rheged and Elmet and moved into Galloway, taking the famous monastic centre of Whithorn. By 700 Northumbria embraced a huge territory extending from the Irish Sea to the North Sea and from the borders of the kingdom of Strathclyde to the Humber–Mersey axis, which roughly marked their border with the kingdom of Mercia.

Mercia by this time had become the most powerful and fastest-growing kingdom of the south. A rapid westward thrust had brought it to the edge of the Welsh mountains, providing maritime outlets to the west of the Dee estuary and the upper reaches of the Severn. Its border with Wales, defined by the massive linear earthwork known as Offa's Dyke, ensured a degree of stability on the western frontier, with the British allowing the aggressive aspirations of the Mercian kings to focus on gaining ascendancy over their eastern neighbours, Lindsey, East Anglia, and Essex, and the southern kingdoms of Kent, Sussex, and Wessex. Of these only Wessex was a serious rival. The Wessex kingdom had spread westwards to the borders of Cornwall and had gained political power over Sussex and Kent: Wessex was thus well placed to contend with Mercia over control of the growing commercial centre of London. Mercia's expansionist policies were dramatically halted in 825 when King Egbert of Wessex decisively beat the Mercian army at Elendun in north Wiltshire, but by now a third force, the Vikings, had appeared on the stage and were to affect the course of history dramatically.

The seventh and eighth centuries were a time of steady change in the British west and north. In Wales seven kingdoms, based on the earlier sub-Roman divisions, had

13.3 Linear earthworks were a favoured way of defining territorial divisions in the Saxon period. Here Offa's Dyke separates the English from the Welsh

consolidated their power, with Gwynedd and Powys emerging as the most powerful. In the north of Britain the old kingdom of Strathclyde, with its capital on the dominating hill of Dumbarton, remained a major power, while its northern neighbour, the Scottish kingdom of Dál Riata, was expanding inexorably into southern Pictland. In the extreme south-west Dumnonia and Cornwall beyond clung onto their independence.

Ireland, in its relative isolation, developed in its own way, little influenced by what was happening in Britain and on the Continent. On one level its monastic culture rose to great heights of excellence, with craftsmen of all kinds vying with each other to hone their skills and turn them to the service of God. On the social and political level the country was divided into a confusion of small squabbling tribes. Aggression was endemic, but out of the mêlée had emerged seven regional kingdoms to which the smaller groups were bound in intricate and unstable alliances based on kindred and overlordship, constantly upset by issues of succession. Among the kingdoms

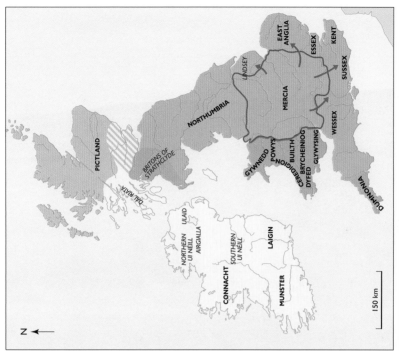
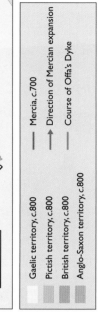

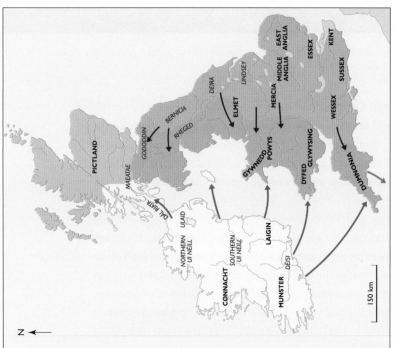
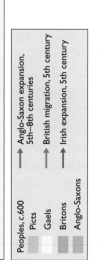

13.4 The two maps of AD 600 and AD 800 show the advance of the Anglo-Saxon kingdoms across Britain and the rise to dominance of Mercia

three were particularly powerful. The midlands and the north were dominated by the northern and southern Uí Néill, while the south of the island, the land of Munster, was ruled by the Eóganachta. The contrast between the tribal nature of Irish society and the emerging state systems in Britain was stark. It goes some way to explaining why the Vikings found it impossible to establish mass settlements in Ireland but were able to achieve considerable land-takes in Britain: people brought up in an atmosphere of internecine conflict made more formidable opponents than those softened by court life and commerce.

The Southern North Sea and the Eastern Channel

While the movement of Germanic communities into south-eastern Britain in the fifth and sixth centuries may have temporarily upset maritime commerce, it soon revived, largely through the entrepreneurial activities of the Franks on the facing continental court. As we have seen, by the middle of the sixth century Frankish luxury goods began to appear in the burials of the Saxon and Jutish enclaves on the south coast from Kent to the Solent, together with more exotic items like Coptic bronze bowls brought in from much further afield. What the Anglo-Saxons had to offer in exchange is less clear, but raw materials like wool and leather probably featured large, and there can be little doubt that slaves were a major export, not least because of the growing demand for them among the Mediterranean merchants dealing with the Islamic world. In the sixth century Pope Gregory noted in passing the fair colouring of the Angli who were sold on in Rome.

The consolidation and extension of the Frankish realm under the Merovingian kings brought most of Gaul under one authority. The entire continental coast-line from the Bay of Mont Saint-Michel to the Rhine mouth was, by 600, stabilized and commerce was flourishing. Northwards from the Rhine mouth the coastal region was still in the hands of the Frisians, but about 680 territorial advances instigated by the Frankish king Pippin brought the crucial lower Rhine under Merovingian control, and less than a century later, in the 770s, the Carolingian armies were pushing northwards again through Saxony to reach the Danish border by 804. By the time Charlemagne was crowned in 800, much of western Europe, apart from Iberia and Brittany, had been drawn into the Carolingian empire.

Increasing political stability on the Continent brought with it a consequential increase in trade, and Britain was to benefit. On the principal continental rivers, usually upstream where the river could be bridged but still within the tidal reach, ports-of-trade were set up: Rouen and Saint-Denis (just outside Paris) on the Seine, Amiens on the Somme, Quentovic on the Canche, and Dorestad on the confluence

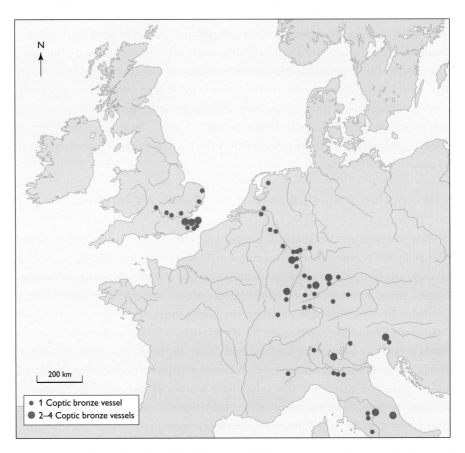

13.5 'Coptic' cast bronze bowls were buried with the dead in many parts of Europe in the sixth and seventh centuries. The distribution map indicates the route by which they were traded from the head of the Adriatic across the Alps to the Rhine valley and thence to eastern England, in particular, Kent

between the Lek and the Rhine. On the British coast equivalent ports came into existence: Hamwic on Southampton Water, Sandwich and Fordwich in east Kent, London (Lundenwic), Ipswich, Norwich, and York (Eoforwic). Significantly, several of these ports developed in close proximity to earlier Roman towns: Hamwic close to Clausentum, Sandwich near Richborough, Fordwich only 4 kilometres down-river from Canterbury, and London and York just outside the defences of their Roman predecessors. While this reflects the beneficial qualities of the location rather than any direct historical continuity, the fact that the Roman infrastructure of roads was still largely intact would have been a great advantage.

The maritime networks binding these ports together were already in place by the early eighth century, but it was in the late eighth and early ninth century, under the patronage of Charlemagne, that trade began to flourish. At Hamwic, where archaeological excavation has been extensive, the coin evidence suggests two peaks of activity. The first, in the second quarter of the eighth century, was at a time when the kingdom of Wessex was subservient to Mercia. The second came late in the eighth and early in the ninth century, when trade was being actively encouraged by Charlemagne and his Mercian competitor, King Offa (d. 796). Relationships were not always entirely amicable. Disagreements between the two kings in 789 led to Charlemagne closing all Frankish ports to British traders, but the power of commerce prevailed and the ports were reopened with a new agreement that protected the rights of traders. The competition between the two powerful states is nicely encapsulated by a gold coin (*mancus*) issued by the Mercian king

13.6 'Coptic' cast bronze bowls, found in burials in Kent and East Anglia, were probably made in northern Italy in the sixth to seventh century. This example is from the ship-burial of Sutton Hoo, Suffolk

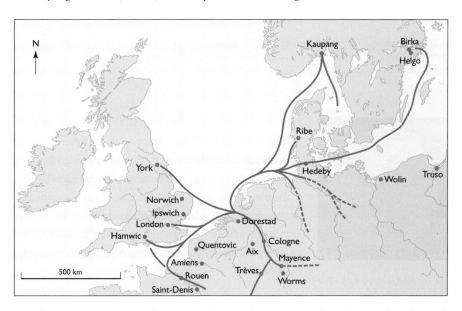

13.7 The major trade routes and ports-of-trade in north-west Europe from the seventh to the ninth century

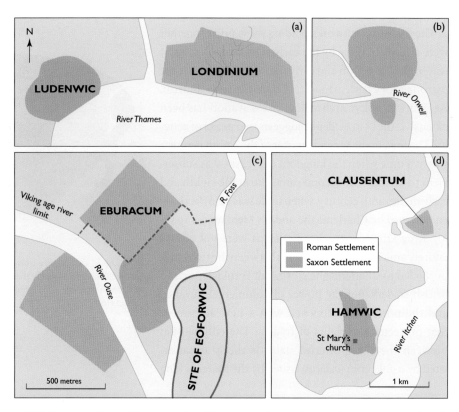

13.8 The location of four of the principal English towns in the eighth to ninth century: (*a*) London, (*b*) Ipswich, (*c*) York, (*d*) Hamwic (later Southampton). All are sited on major rivers and three are located close to earlier Roman towns

13.9 Gold mancus of Coenwulf of Mercia (796–821). The obverse indicates that the coin was minted in London

Coenwulf (796–821). The obverse shows the king with the inscription COENWULFREX M ('Coenwulf, king of the Mercians') while the reverse carries the inscription DE VICO LVNDONIAE ('From the *vicus* of London'). Such a fine piece, issued in almost pure gold, was intended to match the gold solidus of Charlemagne inscribed VICO DORESTAT ('From the *vicus* of Dorestad'). Not only were the kings competing but so, too, were their principal markets.

456

Meanwhile in Scandinavia . . .

The communities of Denmark, Norway, and southern Sweden bordering the fast-expanding Carolingian empire were inevitably drawn into the burgeoning trading networks. The ports of Ribe on the east coast of Jutland near Esbjerg, and Hedeby near the mouth of the Schlei fjord, flowing into the Baltic, served as the major tran-shipment ports between the markets of the Anglo-Saxon and Carolingian world and those of the Baltic and its approaches: Wolin and Truso on the European mainland, Helgö and Birka around Lake Mälar in southern Sweden, and Kaupang on Oslofjord. The Nordic elites, able to control the trade, soon benefited from the power it conferred. For those less privileged and more foot-loose, the prospects of capturing the trading ports in Britain or building new ones to exploit the riches of distant places like Ireland must have seemed particularly attractive. Trade changed people's perspectives. It encouraged them to look outwards beyond their immediate world: it was a stimulus to their innate desire for mobility.

During the seventh and eighth centuries the Nordic countries were in the grip of rapid social and political change. Smaller polities were coalescing into larger entities, and high kings were beginning to emerge, commanding ever-greater territories. In this way Denmark, Norway, and Sweden were each soon to become unified kingdoms. Periods of social upheaval, when competing elites vied for power, were inevitably upsetting. For the young and ambitious they offered huge opportunity, but the process of hierarchization meant that only a few could achieve real success: many aspirants inevitably faced disappointment and disillusionment. For them, adventure and prowess could come from leaving home to raid along foreign shores. Pillaged goods, a copious supply of slaves, and the reputation that comes from having led a successful expedition offered a route to social advancement.

Those who ventured abroad to raid soon became aware of other options. Ireland was largely undeveloped, its tribes locked in interminable bloody wrangles, but with a vibrant artistic heritage harnessed in the service of Christianity. Here was a country where the trading opportunities were endless. But nearer to home, in the Northern and Western Isles, there was rich farmland to be had for the taking, with little challenge from a dispersed and defenceless peasantry. And elsewhere the eastern regions of Britain offered well-farmed estates belonging to Anglo-Saxon lords who, with a little force, could be removed and replaced. To the malcontents of Scandinavia, particularly those who lived in the restricted coastal regions of Norway, where land was scarce, the prospects offered by the islands and coasts of the Atlantic must have been irresistible.

By the end of the eighth century an increase in population, limited land resources, and rapid disruptive social change had combined to drive the Nordic population into an age of intensive mobility. The stimulus was there, the sea offered the way—all that was needed was the means.

The Nordic people were largely a maritime folk, their settlements clustering along the fjords facing the Atlantic or along the less rugged shores and estuaries of the Baltic. Shipbuilding was therefore an essential craft. Already by the fourth century AD sleek clinker-built vessels were being constructed, their overlapping strakes held together with iron rivets. A well-preserved example, dating to the early fourth century, found in 1863 at Nydam in Denmark was 24 metres long with a high prow and stern and a deep keel of T-shaped proportions. The upper strakes had tholes attached to the gunwale to accommodate the oars of fifteen pairs of rowers. Such a vessel would have been well suited to the open seas as well as to coastal shoals: their shallow standing construction would have made them easy to beach on shelving shores and quick to launch again should the need arise.

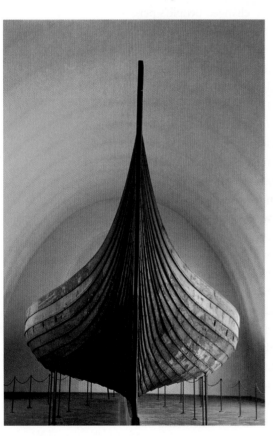

The Viking ships of the eighth century and after developed from the Nydam tradition, but they differed in two principal respects. Instead of oars set on the gunwale, oar ports were now provided lower down the sides of the vessel so that the blade of the oar could strike the water at a low, and thus more efficient, angle. The other difference was the addition of a square sail from a mast set amidships. Although sails were used in the North Sea at the time of the Saxon raids, they do not seem to have come into use in the Baltic until after the seventh century. The earliest extant Nordic vessel with a sail is the Oseberg ship, found in Oslofjord, dating to *c.* 820. Sailing ships are also regularly depicted on coins minted at the Danish port of Hedeby from the early ninth century. It would seem, then, that the sail and the improved oar arrangements may have been innovations introduced in the late eighth century in response to the need for the fast ocean-going ships to transport raiding parties across the North Sea to Britain and Ireland.

13.10 The Gokstad ship from a Viking age burial on Oslofjord, Norway. The vessel was built *c.* 895 and buried *c.* 900–5

The Raiding Begins

The first hint of what was about to burst onto the British Isles came in 789 when three ship-loads of Norwegians landed at Portland on the Dorset coast. Whether they were traders or intent on plunder is unclear. The king's reeve journeyed from Dorchester to meet them, but he and his party were killed. Perhaps there had been a misunderstanding, but in any event, the danger was clear for all to see.

What followed is introduced by the entry for the year 793 in the Anglo-Saxon Chronicle. With a nice sense of drama the chronicler writes:

> In this year dire portents appeared over Northumbria and sorely frightened the people. They consisted of immense whirlwinds and flashes of lightning, and fiery dragons were seen flying in the air. A great famine immediately followed those signs, and a little after that in the same year, on 8 June, the ravages of heathen men . . . destroyed God's church on Lindisfarne, with plunder and slaughter.

In fact the monastic buildings were largely unscathed and by some miracle the Lindisfarne Gospels survived, but the church was sacked and monks were killed or carried off as slaves.

Although the raid on Lindisfarne was traumatic, the threat of Norse attack was not entirely unexpected: after all, the Portland massacre had been the warning. In 792 Offa, king of Mercia, conscious of the growing danger, had spent time improving coastal defences. But even so, little could be done to protect the vulnerable monasteries, and raids from the sea became a fact of life. Other Northumbrian monasteries soon suffered, while in the western seaways Iona was attacked three times in close succession, in 795, 802, and 806. Thereafter the raids became more ambitious in their range as the rich monasteries of Ireland found themselves to be the favoured target. Wexford was raided in 821, Cork in 822 and 824. The remote island monastery of Skellig Michael, in the extreme south-west off the coast of Kerry, succumbed. The Irish annals record that in the period 795–820 there were twenty-six Viking attacks on monasteries. But to put this in perspective, in the same period there were eighty-seven outbreaks of violence resulting from local disputes. More to the point, in the 180 years before the Vikings appeared, thirty monasteries had been burnt down by local warlords. In Ireland, where warfare was a way of life, the Vikings did not get away unopposed. In one famous engagement in 811 a group of raiders were slaughtered by the Ulaid of the north-east, and there are records of other raiding parties being defeated in the south.

For the first thirty years or so the raids were on a small scale, involving only a few ships, seldom more than a dozen, descending on the coastal regions of Britain,

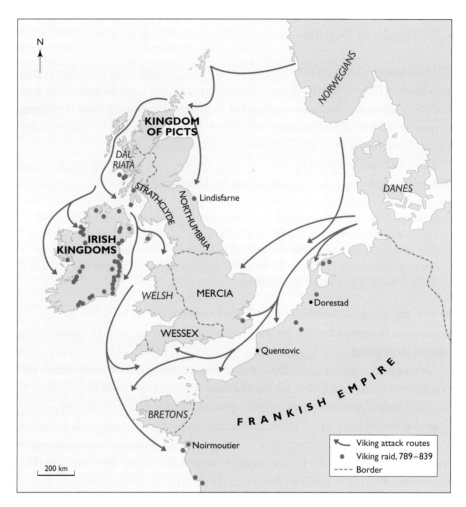

13.11 The Viking attacks of the late eighth and early ninth centuries

Ireland, Frisia, and Frankia. They were uncoordinated hit-and-run affairs carried out by war-leaders and their immediate entourages. Designed for speed, they focused on the coasts and estuaries, never penetrating far inland lest escape to the safety of the open sea should be hindered. But after 830 the scale and nature of the expeditions changed. They became larger and better coordinated, frequently involving thirty to forty ships but with numbers steadily rising over the next twenty years to more than a hundred. Large forces could afford to be more adventurous. Towns were now attacked, and the navigable rivers were penetrated far inland. In Ireland one Viking force sailed up the River Bann to Lough Neah, while another navigated the Shannon to Clonmacnoise and beyond.

13.12 One of the stone corbelled cells in which the monks lived on Skellig Michael, so high that the crashing sea below is only a distant rumble. Next to the cells is a small graveyard

The outbreak of civil wars in the Carolingian empire in 830 provided new opportunities for raiders as the coastal defences of Frankia were weakened. The port of Dorestad was ravaged by a Danish fleet in 834, and the next year Vikings landed on the Isle of Sheppey, from where they proceeded to launch attacks along the Thames estuary. In the same year a raiding party had rounded the Armorican peninsula and was actively pillaging monasteries in the Loire estuary. It may have been this expedition that, on its return in 836, rampaged along the north coast of Somerset and the Severn estuary and attacked the south coast of Cornwall in 838. Thereafter the south coast of Britain suffered ever more frequent devastating attacks, with major battles being fought at Southampton and in Dorset.

Attacks on the Thames estuary intensified, while the Seine also suffered, but events took an entirely new turn in 850 when a large Viking force took the Isle

of Thanet in the Thames estuary and turned it into a winter camp. The great advantage of this was that they were now on hand to start the summer raid considerably earlier than if they had had to set out from Norway or Denmark. The tactic was evidently considered a success, and two years later, in the winter of 852–3, Vikings overwintered on an island in the Seine not far from Rouen. Thereafter, until 865, Viking raiding parties continued to pillage the Atlantic coasts of Europe as far south as Iberia, but it was the major rivers, the Thames, Seine, Loire, and Garonne, and the rich cities they supported that bore the brunt of the attacks. A monk from the monastery of Noirmoutier just south of the Loire estuary, writing in the 860s, sums up the situation in desperation: 'The number of ships increases, the endless flood of Vikings never ceases to grow. Everywhere Christ's people are the victims of massacre, burning and plunder. The Vikings overrun all that lies before them, and no one can withstand them.' The savagery of the Vikings features large in the accounts of those they attacked and may be thought to be something of an overstatement, but we can catch something of the flavour of the times from a poem composed a century later by a Scandinavian in praise of the Norwegian king Erik Bloodaxe: 'The destroyer of the Scots fed the wolves: he trod on the eagle's evening meal [of corpses]. The battle cranes flew over the rows of the slain; the banks of the birds of prey were not free from blood; the wolf tore wounds and waves of blood surged against the ravens' beaks' (trans. A. P. Smyth, *Warlords and Holy Men*).

13.13 Viking battle-axes from London

The Northern Settlement

The proximity of the Northern Isles to the coast of Norway makes it a strong possibility that Shetland and Orkney were the first regions of Britain to be settled by the Norse. In spring with a fair wind a ship leaving Bergen and sailing along the latitude could arrive in Lerwick on the east coast of Shetland within two days. The first settlers

13.14 The extensive Viking settlement on the Brough of Birsay, Orkney, occupies a cliff-edge location high above the sea. The long-houses, some of them excavated, can easily be made out. The site was occupied from the ninth until the twelfth century. Early in the twelfth century the small Romanesque church (in the square enclosure) was built

13.15 One of the excavated long-houses of the Viking settlement at Jarlshof in Shetland. This house formed the nucleus for a community that grew around it

probably began to arrive in the late eighth century, and by 800 the Norse community was well entrenched on the islands. The land was already occupied by Picts and it is highly likely that the initial land-take was aggressive, but no records survive and the archaeological evidence can be variously interpreted. While new settlements and cemeteries were created by the incoming communities, some Pictish settlements, like that at Jarlshof in Shetland, simply continued in existence, with Nordic long-houses replacing the cellular Pictish houses. On the Orkney island of Rousay an existing cemetery continued to be used, the new Viking burials carefully avoiding earlier interments. Such examples could be interpreted as a deliberate taking over of native systems by newcomers claiming legitimacy to the land by its reuse, but they could equally be seen as reflecting a degree of coexistence. That said, the massive change of native place names to Nordic names would suggest a replacement of landowning authority on a large scale even if spread over some generations. Once the land-take had begun, it seems unlikely that it would have ceased until the surviving indigenous population was reduced to serfdom.

The comparatively congenial climate and the fertility of the Orkneys enabled its elites to gain power and to assert political dominance over the Shetlands, leading to the creation of the earldom of Orkney by the end of the ninth century. A century later the earldom had extended its control to the settlements on the northern mainland of Scotland, the Western Isles, and the Isle of Man. The earldom was to remain in Norse hands, albeit gradually reduced, until 1469, when Orkney and Shetland were finally annexed by Scotland.

If, as seems likely, the Northern Isles were being settled in the second half of the eighth century, there is a strong likelihood that they were the home base of at least some of the Norse raiders who sailed down the Atlantic coast to raid the monasteries of the Western Isles and Ireland in the early decades of the ninth century. Some memory of these early times is captured in the twelfth-century Orkneyinga Saga, which reflects on the lifestyle of a local resident, Swein Asleiffson:

13.16 Reconstruction of the first Viking farmhouse at Jarlshof

In the spring he had more than enough to occupy him, with a great deal of seed to sow, which he saw to carefully himself. Then, when the job was done, he would go off plundering in the Hebrides and in Ireland on what he called his 'spring-trip', then back home just after midsummer, where he stayed until the cornfields had been reaped and the grain was safely in. After that he would go off raiding again, and never came back until the first month of winter was ended. This he used to call his 'autumn-trip'.

One cannot help wondering if there was an element of whimsy and caricature in the description, but perhaps it simply looks back with a reluctant nostalgia to an age of ancestors long gone.

The Western Isles and the western coast of Scotland were gradually settled by Norse communities after the initial raids in the first two decades of the ninth century. Fertile land and a maritime environment very much like those of the homeland would have made the region congenial to the early settlers. Place name evidence suggests that Norse settlement may have been intensive. On the island of Lewis, for

13.17 The remains of a small boat, partially eroded by the sea, from a boat-burial at Scar, Sanday, Orkney. The positions of the iron rivets that once held the planks together are shown by the yellow tags. The boat contained three bodies, a man, a woman, and a child, accompanied by a range of rich grave goods

example, of the 126 village names known, ninety-nine are of Scandinavian origin. A further attraction was that the islands lay on the direct route between the Norwegian homeland and the fast-developing markets of Viking Ireland. The number of rich graves and hoards are a clear demonstration that those who sat astride the major trade routes were able to benefit from the proceeds. A reminder of the mercantile activity of the islanders comes from a Viking burial at Kiloran Bay on Colonsay, where the deceased was provided with a beam balance and scale pans together with seven weights, the essential equipment of a man used to measuring carefully the silver bullion used in commercial exchanges.

The Isle of Man and Cumbria were also drawn into the Norse sphere early in the period of colonization. Man was a large, fertile, and easily accessible island, but its main attraction lay in its central position in the Irish Sea. From here the coasts of Ireland and Britain were easily accessible to raiding parties and merchants alike. A study of the cemetery evidence has shown that, while the male graves were clearly Scandinavian, a high percentage of the female graves were of native women. This could be explained by supposing that the island was settled by male warriors coming either directly from Norway or, more likely, setting out as younger sons from Norse homesteads in the Northern or Western Isles.

Place name evidence in Cumbria, along the southern shore of the Solway Firth, and deep inland along the Eden valley is indicative of another zone of Norse settlement. The north coast of the Solway shows much sparser settlement, suggesting that the kings of Strathclyde occupying Galloway were able to hold their own against Scandinavian incursions. But the coastal pilgrimage place of Whithorn, the centre of the cult of St Ninian, appears to have come under increasing Scandinavian influence after about the year 1000, by which time it seems to have taken on the function of a trading mart with close links to Ireland. The Solway settlements and those along the Eden valley route will have gained an enhanced importance in the late ninth century and thereafter as trade between the two great Viking entrepôts of York and Dublin began to develop. While the Western

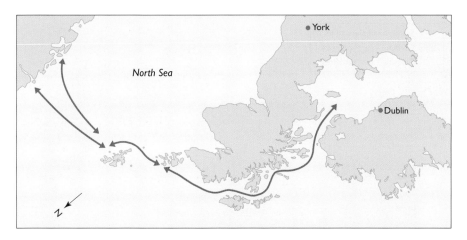

13.18 The sea-routes between Norway and the Irish Sea

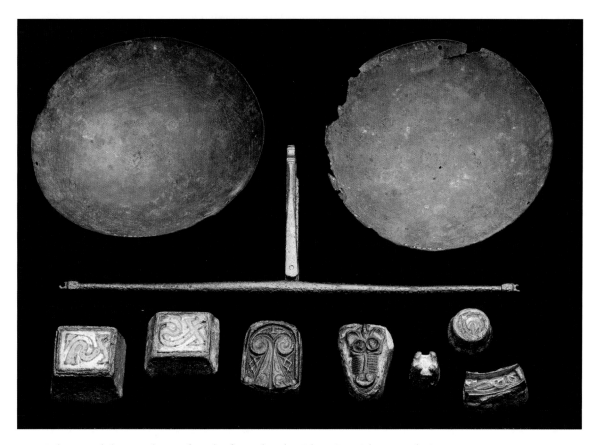

13.19 Scale pans, a balance, and a set of weights from a burial at Kiloran Bay, Colonsay, in the Inner Hebrides. The set is a reminder of the importance of trading

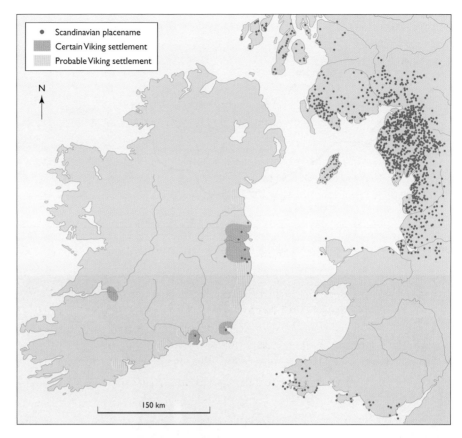

13.20 Scandinavian settlement around the Irish Sea. In Britain the place name concentrations are the best guide to settlement. In Ireland, Scandinavian place names are few, reflecting the fact that here the Vikings set up trading centres rather than taking land

Islanders benefited from the long sea-route from Dublin via the Northern Isles to Norway, these northern British settlers commanded the direct overland route to the Scandinavian settlements of eastern Britain.

The Vikings in Ireland and the Irish Sea

The Norse raids on Ireland followed much the same course as the Scandinavian raids on the rest of the British Isles. Small-scale and opportunist at first, they grew in size and frequency after about 830. In the first four decades of contact the Norse adventurers must have learnt much about the island. It was relatively densely populated by a warlike people whose fighting skills were honed by continuous internal conflicts. High kings could claim the allegiances of their sub-kings, but allegiances could be quickly ended and new ones formed: power broking was an art much relished by the Irish elite. But power lay not only with kings: there was a parallel system residing in the monasteries, some of which had grown to be large institutions commanding the produce of the countryside around and supporting a host of skilled craftsmen. These communities had become virtual towns, owing their authority to the monastic order, not to secular kings. The raiders of the early ninth century soon discovered that, though Ireland was easy to raid, it would be very difficult to settle.

In 841 the Vikings took the first steps towards settlement by setting up *longphuirt*, defended enclosures on navigable waterways designed to protect men and ships over winter. The first *longphuirt* were at Dublin on the River Liffey and probably at Annagassan on Dundalk Bay. Others were soon to follow. But static settlement invited attack and in 847 the Vikings suffered several devastating defeats. In one, led by the Irish high king Mael Seachlainn, 700 Vikings were killed in a single engagement. Two years later the *longphort* of Dublin was sacked by the Irish. The setback was considerable and inspired many of the Vikings previously active in Ireland to turn their attention to the easier pickings in Frankia. The situation was further complicated in 851 when a force of Danish Vikings arrived and took control of Dublin. Although it was regained by the Norwegians two years later, and held with the help of Irish allies, by the 870s the unstable political equilibrium was crumbling and increasingly more Vikings were leaving, some to raid along the Atlantic seaways, others to settle with their Irish wives and slaves in Iceland. For the next forty years or so, apart from another attack by the Danes, led by the Viking king Halfdan in 875, the raids were at an end and Ireland could enjoy an interlude of comparative

13.21 Odd's cross slab from Kirk Braddan, Isle of Man. An example of the Jellinge style of decoration, which originated in Norway

peace. In the early decades of the tenth century the raids began again, many of them instigated by the successful Viking enclaves that had held onto power, but in 962 and 964 Vikings from the Western Isles mounted independent raids of their own on the east and south coasts.

Throughout the long contact with Ireland, the Vikings had made little headway in establishing permanent settlements outside the four towns of Dublin, Wexford, Waterford, and Limerick. It was simply that the Irish resistance was too strong. By the late tenth century Irish Norse power was in sharp decline: the kings of Meath in the east and the kings of Munster in the south were now able to mount an effective opposition to the Viking presence. The conflict culminated in 1014 with the battle of Clontarf, in which the Dublin Vikings in coalition with an Irish army from Leinster was decisively beaten by a force led by Brian Boru, king of Munster. Dublin, however, survived as a prominent, though politically weakened, commercial centre until 1170, when it was finally taken by the Anglo-Norman army.

13.22 One of the exceptionally well-preserved Viking houses found in excavations in Fishamble Street, Dublin

The Norse hold on Ireland had never been strong, and outside the commercial enclaves along the east and south coasts, and at Limerick on the Shannon in the west, there had been little penetration into the interior apart from periodic raids. The strength and belligerence of the Irish kingdoms was one factor, but rivalries, if not outright conflict, between the Vikings themselves also played their part. In 877 Halfdan, who had left York intent on capturing Dublin, was killed by the Norwegians on the east coast of Ulster, while in 937 a force from Dublin led by Óláf Guthfrithson campaigned in the west, destroying the fleet of the Limerick Vikings at Clonmacnoise. The commercial enclaves also vied with each other and in 994 the Vikings from Waterford briefly took control of Dublin. Unlike the north and east of Britain, where the Scandinavians had settled as farmers, the Vikings who managed to gain a precarious foothold in Ireland turned their backs on the land and looked to the sea as their means of livelihood: the Irish Norse enclaves were at best ports-of-trade through which commercial exchanges could be articulated between the rich hinterlands of Ireland and the Atlantic maritime networks.

The Irish Sea formed the heart of the maritime network, with the Isle of Man providing the fulcrum. The place name evidence indicating zones of Norse settlement leaves little doubt that the whole of the west coast of Britain from the Solway Firth to the Dee estuary had been heavily settled, with extensive land-takes in Cumbria, Lancashire, and Cheshire. The coasts of Wales were also well within the Irish Norse sphere of interest. In the early years raids were a frequent occurrence, and particularly vulnerable were the rich monasteries of the south-west: St David's, Caldey Island, Llantwit, and Llancarfan. But in 878 a Viking force spent the winter in Dyfed, and in 914 a massive Viking navy attacked from Brittany. Place name evidence suggests that some Viking communities took land along the south coast, particularly around Milford Haven, where they are likely to have set up a port-of-trade serving the Atlantic network. From here may have come Welsh products like the slaves, horses, honey, and wheat which the Irish annals indicate were in much demand by the Dublin merchants.

Slaves culled from Ireland, England, and Wales were a valuable commodity much sought after by the Irish sea-traders. Together with hides, furs, and wool, slaves would have been taken south to the slave markets in Andalusia to sell to the Arab merchants. The distribution of Arab coins around the Irish Sea is a reflection of this southern trade. Other southern imports would have included the 'saddles beautiful and foreign' and the 'satins and silken clothes, pleasing and variegated' mentioned among the spoils gathered during an Irish attack on the Viking port of Limerick in 968.

The Irish Norse traders who commanded the Irish Sea were fortunate indeed for they sat astride the key route node in the Atlantic system. Southwards they could reach the Mediterranean, and to the north lay Norway and Iceland, while to the east they could use the overland routes to York and the North Sea networks. It is hardly surprising that the communities the Irish Sea so favoured could grow rich and could develop their highly distinctive Hiberno-Norse culture.

Britain: The Arrival of the Great Army

The overwintering of Viking forces on the Isle of Thanet in 850 marked the beginning of a new phase of Viking activity: from now until towards the end of the eleventh century Vikings were never absent from England. Attacks continued, and fifteen years later they were back on Thanet. This time the king of Kent tried to buy peace with Danegeld (protection money), though without success, for the Viking force, having taken the bribe, 'stole away inland by night and ravaged all eastern Kent'. This is the first time that Danegeld is mentioned, but it was to become a regular feature of deals with the Vikings thereafter.

In the year 865, so the Anglo-Saxon Chronicle notes, 'a great heathen army came into England and took up winter quarters in East Anglia and there they were supplied with horses, and the East Angles made peace with them'. The brevity of the record belies its significance, for the arriving Great Army marked an entirely new phase in the Scandinavian onslaught.

'Great Army' is a relative term. There has been much debate about its actual size, but a broad consensus is that it may not have far exceeded 1,000 to 2,000 fighting men. That they could function effectively in England was a reflection both of their military prowess as an experienced and united fighting force and of the political disarray in England and the inability of the English to mount more than peasant militias to oppose them. Some, like the East Angles, were prepared to supply them with horses in return for promises of peace; others paid their Danegeld in kind with supplies of provisions. Support of this kind, acquired through fear, meant that the Great Army could move fast across the face of England, using the still-functioning Roman roads without having to set up a complex supply infrastructure.

In 866 from their base at Thetford the Danes thrust north through Mercia and into Northumbria, taking York without serious opposition. A Northumbrian counterattack the following year was beaten off, bringing Northumbrian resistance effectively to an end. Within ten years the entire region of southern Northumbria from the Humber to the Tees had been brought under Viking control, and in 876 Halfdan set up York as the capital of his Viking kingdom. From its initial capture ten years earlier York had proved to be a convenient base for mounting other campaigns. In 867 the army made a foray from York south into Mercia but was besieged in Nottingham and forced to withdraw back to base. In 869 the army returned to its Thetford camp, from where an autumn campaign into the heart of East Anglia led to the defeat and death of the East Anglian king, Edmund.

With southern Northumbria and East Anglia conquered and Mercia presenting no serious problem, the Great Army now turned its attention to the West Saxons, the only remaining Anglo-Saxon authority able to offer any serious resistance to the invaders. In 870 they marched from Thetford, crossing the Thames near Reading, into West Saxon territory, where they were met by the West Saxon army, led by King Æthelred, his brother Alfred, and Ealdorman Æthelwulf. A long series of confrontations followed, fought out in northern Wessex, with considerable loss of life on both sides. By the end of the year, with the two armies now exhausted, peace terms were hastily agreed and the Danish force retreated to London, making the march back to York in the following year, 872.

Wessex had proved to be unexpectedly resistant, so the Danish army turned its attention to the conquest of Mercia, a task that was completed in the winter of 873–4 with the capture of Repton, which commanded an important crossing of the River Trent. With the loss of Repton the Mercian king Burgred fled to Rome.

It was at this point that the Great Army split. One part, led by Halfdan, turned its attention to the north, marching to the Tyne, where a winter camp was set up, from which the British kingdoms of Strathclyde and southern Pictland were attacked. Thereafter Halfdan decided to consolidate his kingdom of Northumbria. With its usual succinctness the Anglo-Saxon Chronicle records that he 'shared out the land of the Northumbrians, and they proceeded to plough and to support themselves'. The clear implication is that the Great Army, after ten years of campaigning and taking control of large tracts of eastern England, had at last begun the process of permanent settlement. While this no doubt involved the arrival of families and dependants from the Danish homeland, the conquerors would simply have taken over existing estates from the Anglian elite and allowed them to continue to function but under new management. The very large number of Scandinavian place names still surviving in eastern England shows the thoroughness of the land-take. The new landholding elite would have tended to rename the key places in their estates in their own language, and these would soon become formalized in deeds and land transfers. The distribution of the new place names gives an indication of the areas taken and the density of settlement.

The second half of the Great Army, which had split from Halfdan's force at Repton in 874 under the leadership of Guthrum, Oscetel, and Anund, marched south to a military base at Cambridge before setting out in 875 on a second attempt to conquer Wessex. At first it was successful, taking successively Wareham, Exeter, Gloucester,

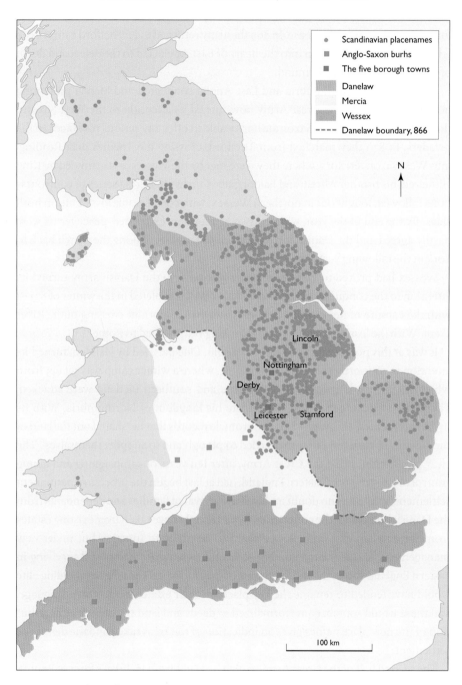

13.23 Britain in the ninth century

and Chippenham. Meanwhile Alfred, now king of the West Saxons, took refuge in the Somerset marshes, where he began to marshal his forces. By 878 he had brought together a large army of men from Somerset, Wiltshire, and western Hampshire and was ready to confront the Danes. The battle, when met, was fought at Edington in Wiltshire and was a resounding success for Alfred. The peace terms negotiated at Wedmore in the aftermath required the Great Army to leave Wessex, but before doing so Guthrum and thirty of his chief followers were to be baptized. With the ceremony completed, the army departed for Cirencester and in 879 returned to East Anglia and 'settled there and shared out the land'. Those who still wished to fight crossed the Channel to Frankia, where there were still plenty of opportunities for the life of a raider bent on plunder.

The events of 865–79 had changed England quite profoundly. A new divide had been created across the country from the Mersey estuary to the Thames at London. To the north as far as the River Tees lay the Danelaw, the old Anglian and Mercian territories now under Danish rule, large tracts of which had been recently settled by Danes. To the south lay the remnants of Mercia, now much weakened, and the kingdom of Wessex, enlarged and strengthened by the military successes of Æthelred and Alfred. Wessex now extended from Cornwall to Kent and from the south coast north to the Thames. Much had been learnt from the fifteen years of confrontation with the Danes, and King Alfred was to use this hard-won experience to good effect. Burhs (strongly defended enclosures) were built throughout the country, particularly around the coasts and border regions. Some protected existing settlements, while, of those newly founded, some became thriving settlements and others remained simply as fortifications: the prime function of all was to provide places of refuge where the population could assemble in times of danger. The maintenance and manning of the burhs was the responsibility of the local population. Alfred also reorganized the army and the process of recruitment to create a standing field force that was mobile and quick to react. The navy, too, received his careful attention: new ships were built and vulnerable coasts were regularly patrolled. The benefit of Alfred's defensive preparations were amply demonstrated when, in 886, Guthrum broke the terms of the treaty and sailed into the Thames estuary. Alfred's rapid response by land and sea managed to contain the threat, and he took the opportunity to wrest the vital port of London from Danish control, but the resulting equilibrium was delicate and was not to last.

The Viking threat had done more than simply sharpen the military response of the English: it had created an enemy who could be characterized as 'other', in contrast to 'we the English'. In other words, it had helped to unite the English, hitherto disparate kingdoms, under the leadership of Wessex and its astute king Alfred. The 'heathen

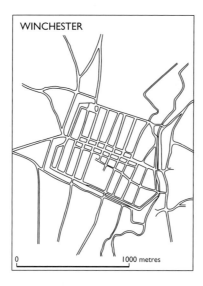
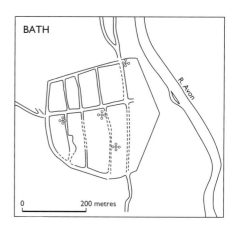
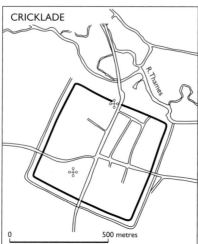
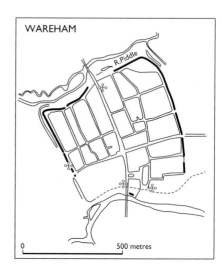

13.24 Four of the Wessex towns listed in the Saxon document the Burghal Hidage. They were laid out with strong defences and regular street grids in the late Saxon period to serve as points of resistance against Viking armies

army' was a neat opposition to 'the Christian English'. As if to intensify the difference, Alfred spent much effort in restoring the Church and the monasteries to power, but more than that, by translating the Christian texts 'most necessary for all men to know' from Latin into English, he made Christianity much more widely available. The founding of schools for the education of the youth of the nobility was another way of instilling Christian learning deep into the consciousness of his people. By

13.25 The town of Wallingford, Berkshire, sited at an important crossing on the Thames, is a good example of one of the burghs established by King Alfred in the 880s to help defend his kingdom from the Vikings. The rectangular plan of the defences can be clearly made out and the streets still follow the late Saxon plan

embracing Christianity with an intense enthusiasm, the sense of English identity was sharpened and encouraged to grow stronger. In the 850s and 860s Wessex and Mercia had formed alliances for the common good. Alfred's success against the Danes at Edington in 878 had given him new authority over the part of Mercia that had not succumbed to the Danes, and by the time he had taken control of London in 886 it could fairly be claimed, as the Anglo-Saxon Chronicle unashamedly did, that 'all the English people not under the subjugation to the Danes submitted to him'. Alfred was now king of the Anglo-Saxons. His authority came from his skill at forging the identity of the English with the hammer of the Danes.

13.26 The Alfred Jewel, so called because the inscription around it reads 'Alfred had me made', was the handle of a pointer (aestel) used to aid the reading of manuscripts. It is symbolic of the revival of religion and learning encouraged during Alfred's reign

13.27 (opposite) The opening of St Matthew's Gospel from the Codex Aureus, produced in southern Britain in the mid-eighth century. An inscription attached to the codex records that the book was bought from a Viking army by Ealdorman Alfred and his wife in the mid-ninth century because they were not prepared to leave holy books in heathen hands

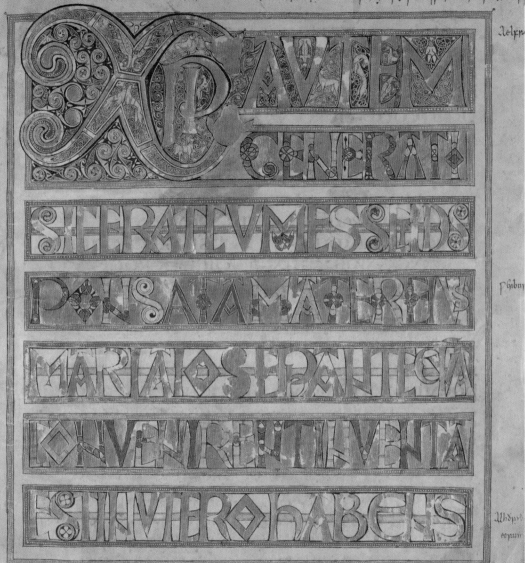

Alfred's military preparations were put to the test in 892 when two Danish armies that had been campaigning on the Continent for a decade descended on Kent. One, carried in 250 ships, landed at Lympne, while the other, comprising eighty ships, sailed into the Thames estuary and took control of the north Kentish coast at Milton. Together they probably numbered between 10,000 and 20,000 men, and their arrival encouraged the Danes of East Anglia and Northumbria to join in with raids along the south coast. In the event, the Anglo-Saxon defences held, and after a series of defeats the Danes dispersed, some retreating to the Danelaw to settle, the others making their escape to the Continent.

The Recovery of the Danelaw, 902–954

The recovery of the Danelaw by the English was a long and somewhat complex process involving the gradual conquest by Wessex-led armies from the south, facilitated by the Norse leaders from Ireland, to take over the kingdom of York. The initial Wessex successes between 912 and 918 brought East Anglia and Danish Mercia under English control as far north as the Humber–Mersey line. Immediately to the north lay the kingdom of York with the earldom of Northumbria beyond, extending between the Tees and the Firth of Forth. In 919 two far-reaching events occurred: Æthelflæd, queen of Mercia, died, opening the way for Wessex and Mercia to be consolidated into one kingdom, and Ragnall, a Norseman from Dublin, captured York, having the previous year defeated the Scots and the Northumbrians near Corbridge. The conquest of York by Dublin created a new power block in the north extending from the Hiberno-Norse settlements of Cumbria to the North Sea, but it was soon challenged by Æthelstan, who, in 927, stormed the city and brought it and much of the north under English control for the first time. The English rule of the north was only possible through careful alliances crafted with the Britons of north Wales and southern Scotland.

In 937 the Dublin Vikings led by Óláf Guthfrithson made a concerted attack, in league with Strathclyde Britons and Scots, to retake York. In the battle that ensued at the unidentified site of Brunanburh, the invading army was roundly beaten. It was a massive confrontation. As the Anglo-Saxon Chronicle put it,

> Never yet in this island before . . . was a greater slaughter of a host made by the edge of the sword, since the Angles and Saxons came hither . . . The Norsemen, the sorry survivors from the spears, put out in their studded ships . . . to make for Dublin across the deep waters, back to Ireland, humbled at heart.

Even the British sources remembered it as the 'Great War'.

Two years later Óláf returned and, making use of the confusion following Æthelstan's death, managed to gain control of Northumbria, York, and Danish Mercia, but it was a brief interlude and in 944 York was returned to the English. The last act in the saga began in 948 when Erik Bloodaxe, the exiled Norwegian king seeking new territories to conquer, took control of the city, but, under constant pressure from the Dublin Vikings, the English, and the Northumbrians, he was finally ousted in 954 and killed in an ambush at Stainmore. So it was in this confusing mêlée of ethnic conflict that the Scandinavian kingdom disintegrated, leaving the way open for the English king Eadred to take over unopposed.

Æthelred the Badly Advised

While England was enjoying almost thirty years of respite from Viking raids, major social changes were under way in Scandinavia as power became ever more centralized. As a result, the cost of maintaining the increasingly complex state escalated, while the number of exiles and people otherwise discontented with their status in society grew. To add to the tensions the supply of silver, so necessary to maintain the Scandinavian economic systems, was drastically diminished as the constant supplies that had come from Russia and the Arab world all but dried up. These factors combined to encourage a new era of raiding, the difference this time being that the Swedes joined in, deflected from their traditional enterprise zone in Russia by the growth of the Russian state.

The raids began in 980 with Norse attacks on the west coast emanating from Ireland and the Isle of Man and Danish attacks from the Scandinavian homeland focusing on the south and east coasts. Thereafter the onslaught intensified as the Norwegians joined in. The expeditions were well organized and generally successful. At first the English put up resistance, but after a disastrous defeat at the hands of the Danes at Maldon in Essex, the old tradition of trying to buy off the attackers with Danegeld resumed. The sums paid were colossal, rising steadily from 10,000 pounds of bullion in 991 to 48,000 pounds in 1012.

By 1002 the drain on the resources of Britain was proving to be unsustainable and the unreliability of the Scandinavians bought off or serving as mercenaries for the English was deeply unnerving for the king and his counsellors. In an ill-advised reaction Æthelred ordered 'to be slain all Danish men who were in England . . . because the King had been informed that they would treacherously deprive him, and then all his counsellors, of life, and possess this Kingdom afterwards'. The massacre was carried out on St Brice's Day (13 November). The scale of the slaughter is unrecorded, but that a Christian king could contemplate ethnic cleansing is a reflection of the stress that English society was now under.

Still the onslaughts continued and Danegeld was paid, financing the Scandinavian warlords in their quests for further power. Óláf Tryggvason was soon able to establish himself as king of Norway, while another warlord, the Dane Swein Forkbeard, spent his time between raiding in England and trying to seize the Norwegian throne. Successful raids in England boosted reputations as well as the coffers, and both were needed to assure success in Scandinavia. Thus it was that England was drained of resource and resolve. The sense of despair is palpable in Archbishop Wulfstan's famous 'Sermon of the Wolf to the English':

> There has been devastation and persecution in every district again and again, and the English have been for a long time now completely defeated and too greatly disheartened through God's anger . . . We pay them continually and they humiliate us daily; they ravage and they burn, plunder and rob and carry on board; and lo, what else is there in all these events except God's anger clear and visible over his people.

These words were written in 1014. A year earlier Swein Forkbeard had returned to England and at Gainsborough in Yorkshire had been recognized by the Northumbrians and the representatives of Danish Mercia as king. On his rapid march south the towns of Oxford, Winchester, and Bath submitted, and London soon followed suit. But early in 1014 Swein died and the English were able to regroup. It was a brief respite, and the next year the Danish army returned, led by Swein's son Cnut, to recover the whole of the original Danelaw, and the rest of Mercia beside, south as far as the Thames. Only the core of Wessex was left in the hands of Æthelred's son Edmund. On Edmund's death in November 1016 Cnut became king of England. Twelve years later he was able to add Norway to his empire, thus fulfilling his father's ambitions.

The Scandinavian Contribution

From the Portland landing in 789 to the unification of England under the rule of the Danish king Cnut in 1016, the British Isles and Ireland had been enmeshed in a maritime network anchored in Scandinavia, most particularly in Norway and Denmark. For the most part the Norwegians focused their interests on the Atlantic coasts while the Danes concerned themselves with the eastern shores facing them across the North Sea: it was all largely a matter of geography. The Swedes, though present towards the end, played little part.

The two and a quarter centuries of ferocious interaction left a lasting impact on the peoples of Britain and Ireland. The cycles of raiding, the trudging of armies back and forth, the set-piece battles, and the bouts of land-take, all succinctly summed up in the Anglo-Saxon Chronicle, are tiring in their detail—even perhaps in the brief summary offered in these pages. The history of events and the actions of the leaders may make the headlines, but this kind of superficial history—the doings of celebrities—often obscures the deep changes that really matter in the *longue durée*. Let us, then, put aside that particular kind of detail to try to discern what was happening to the British and Irish during these crucial centuries.

At its very simplest we can recognize a prelude followed by two cycles with an interlude between. The prelude, *c.* 750–*c.* 800, sees the Norse settlement of the Northern and Western Isles. It is a period of immigration, extensive land-take, and integration, leading to the creation of a cohesive Scandinavian polity that maintained its identity for centuries. The first cycle begins with a phase of raiding, roughly 790–860, which is followed in Ireland by the creation of rather unstable Scandinavian commercial enclaves and in Britain by a large-scale land-take creating the Danelaw. In the interlude, *c.* 880–*c.* 990, a jockeying for political power ensues in Britain at an elite level, with the English royal house emerging triumphant in the south of the island and the Scots in the north. In Ireland, throughout the power struggle and in a turmoil of changing allegiances, the commercial enclaves remain active. The second cycle begins with a renewed phase of raiding, *c.* 990–*c.* 1010, and culminates in 1016 with the takeover of much of Britain by a Danish elite. The overall effect of the external stimuli from Scandinavia was to drive the consolidation of political power among the indigenous populations. In Britain disparate Anglo-Saxon, British, and Danish kingdoms were brought together under a single king. In the north the Scots emerged as the dominant power on the mainland, absorbing the Picts and other Britons. The Northern and Western Isles became a single earldom, while in Ireland the emergence of high kings was a move towards a less fragmented society.

What it all means in terms of the native populations of the islands it is difficult to say with any degree of precision. Raids and battles inevitably brought death and dislocation, sometimes on a very considerable scale, but the greater impact may have been from the removal of captives to be sold abroad as slaves. Rural populations could be devastated to the point of no recovery. That Irish and perhaps Britons were present in some numbers in the communities colonizing Iceland is demonstrated in the genetics of the modern population. While many will have been slaves, some will have been wives accompanying their families as they moved from the troubled commercial colonies to make a new life on the island.

The scale of the Scandinavian immigration into Britain and Ireland will have varied considerably from place to place. In Orkney and Shetland in the late eighth and early ninth centuries immigration was on a large scale, as the archaeological record bears witness. Settlements, burial traditions, and material culture all reflect close links with the Norse homeland maintained over the generations. We may reasonably think in terms of constant interchanges between the islands and Norway, separated as they were by only a two-day sea voyage. On the Western Isles, Norse settlement does not appear to have been quite so intensive, but the constant maritime interchange between Dublin and Norway, using the islands as ports of call, will have enhanced the Scandinavian contribution to the gene pool over time.

The Norse settlements in Ireland were altogether different: they were essentially commercial enclaves with little hinterland, but they were probably all thriving urban centres, Dublin demonstrably so according to evidence gleaned from extensive excavations. These concentrations of population soon became Hiberno-Norse in their ethnicity and developed a distinctive culture that mixed Scandinavian tradition with native Irish. As centres of commerce and industry the influence of the enclaves will have spread widely across Ireland and throughout the Irish Sea region. It is a strong probability that settlers from the Norse enclaves colonized parts of south-west Wales, and interchanges with the Isle of Man will have become a regular part of maritime commerce. The extensive area of Norwegian settlement on the west coast of Britain from Cumbria to the Dee, manifest in the place name evidence, is strongly suggestive of an initial phase of Norse settlement around 900, but this will have been reinforced by constant interaction not only with the homeland but also with other Norse settlements around the Irish Sea. The takeover of York by the Norse kings of Dublin in the first half of the tenth century increased the importance of this western British interface and may well have reinforced the Norse culture of the region with a further influx of settlers.

The Danelaw of eastern Britain was the other area of extensive Scandinavian settlement—but how extensive was it? On three separate occasions the Anglo-Saxon Chronicle refers to land being shared out among the Danish invaders, in 876 in Northumbria, in 877 in Mercia, and in 880 in East Anglia. In each case it was soldiers from the successful Danish armies who had chosen 'to plough the land and support themselves' who were involved, and the numbers cannot have been great, from a few hundred to a few thousand at the most. Later, in 896, when an unsuccessful Danish force of some 10,000 to 20,000 men decided to split up, some went overseas to Frankia while the rest dispersed to settle in East Anglia and Northumbria. New lands would have had to be found for them.

The initial Scandinavian settlers in the Danelaw were, then, soldiers retiring from the fray. As the conquerors they would have expected generous land grants and in all probability took over some of the more profitable estates. No doubt many married local women; others will have brought their families across from Denmark, and, once they were established, dependants and fortune seekers would have begun to arrive. Thus, in the forty years or so following the landing of the Great Army in 865, the eastern part of Britain from the Thames to the Tees began to absorb the Danish language and culture. The impact of the Scandinavian language on place names, as we have seen, was considerable, reflecting the firm hold which the immigrants had on the land and landholding. When, towards the end of the tenth century, the English king Edgar was engaged in drawing up law codes for his now united country, he had to compose a separate code for the Danelaw to accommodate the rights and customs of the inhabitants. The differences between English law and Danish law were further codified in the early eleventh century by Archbishop Wulfstan. The implication is that Danish culture had been firmly and extensively imposed in eastern Britain during the period of settlement in the latter part of the ninth century.

The archaeological evidence goes some way to support the idea that the cultural, and possibly ethnic, import of the Danes was deep. Significant numbers of brooches have been found in the Danelaw representing all the major styles current in Scandinavia in the ninth and tenth centuries. This would suggest constant contact with the homeland throughout, and quite probably an uninterrupted inflow of Scandinavian women arriving to join their menfolk. The discovery of large numbers of hybrid Anglo-Scandinavian disc brooches, however, shows the survival of indigenous traditions, which, in turn, implies that the native population continued to coexist and to integrate with the immigrants. While the place name and archaeological evidence together suggests that the Scandinavian component in the population of the Danelaw was significant, the variables are such that no reliable figures can be offered. Indeed, different communities throughout the Danelaw probably had very different ethnic compositions.

The study of modern DNA does not add much to the debate about the size of the Danish immigration simply because the Danes arriving in the ninth and tenth centuries were coming from much the same homeland as the Jutes and Angles four centuries earlier. Such evidence as there is is consistent with an influx in the Viking period, though any attempt at quantification would be subject to considerable error. The Norse impact on the Northern and Western Isles is, however, much more evident. One detailed study has shown that the modern population of Shetland owes about 44 per cent of its ancestry to an equal male–female Norwegian influx, while in the Western Isles and Skye data suggest a 22.5 per cent male and 11 per cent female

Scandinavian ancestry. This is in broad conformity with both the archaeological and place name data.

The Viking episode undoubtedly had a profound effect on the political structure of the British Isles as well as on its culture, language, and laws: all this was mediated through the impact of Scandinavians coming by sea, often in huge numbers and repeatedly over extended periods of time. The Scandinavian impact on Britain in terms of population change was probably greater than any other incursion at any time in the previous history of the islands and was not matched until the late twentieth century.

The End of the Old Order

Cnut's Britto-Scandinavian empire broke up on his death in 1035 and several years later the kingdom of England was restored to the Saxon royal house when Edward, Æthelred's son, returned to the country from Normandy. Edward's death in 1066 left three claimants to the throne: Harald Hardrada, a scion of the Norwegian royal house, William duke of Normandy, and Harold Godwinson, the earl of Wessex. The English chose Harold Godwinson, leaving Harald and William with no option but to invade in support of their individual claims. Harald set out from Norway with 300 ships and successfully took York on 20 September, but five days later, at Stamford Bridge, he was met by Harold and in the ensuing battle he and the majority of his force were killed. Three days later, on 28 September, William left the port of Saint-Valéry on the mouth of the Somme and landed at Pevensey. At Hastings on 14 October he met Harold and his exhausted army, who had marched south for nineteen days following their hard-won victory at Stamford Bridge. With William's victory that day England passed to Norman overlords.

William's claim to Britain was not unopposed. In 1069 the Danes sent a fleet of 240 ships to join British opposition on the east coast, while the Norse rulers of Ireland supported rebel attacks in the Severn estuary. In 1075 another large Danish–Norwegian fleet was sent and managed to sack York, but by now the resistance to William's authority was all but spent. The attack of 1075 was the last Scandinavian inroad on Britain, almost 300 years after the first ships arrived at Portland in 789.

The Normans—Nor(d)manns—were, as the name by which they were known in France implies, of Scandinavian origin. The original settlers in northern France were Scandinavian soldiers, mainly Danish but under the leadership of a Norwegian, Rollo. After fighting against the Franks at Chartres in 911 they were allowed to settle on land in the lower Seine valley in return for protecting the approaches to Paris from further seaborne attack; Rollo was recognized as count of the region. Rollo and his successors extended their domain gradually westwards until 933, when the Cotentin peninsula was taken into Nor(d)mannia, creating the maritime province that survives today as the French circumscription of Normandy. The original Scandinavian settlement seems to have attracted other Scandinavians to join them, including Norse settlers from the Irish Sea zone, who took over much of the Cotentin, but the overall numbers were small and through intermarriage the immigrants were soon assimilated into Frankish culture, adopting the Frankish language in place of their mother tongue. It was of this hybrid community that Duke William became the leader.

The Norman invasion of Britain was essentially an aristocratic land grab. The Anglo-Saxon and Danish estate owners were almost entirely replaced by Norman lords. What had been 4,000 to 5,000 individual estates was now concentrated in the hands of 144 Norman barons. In the Church, too, the majority of the senior posts were given to Normans. The Norman hierarchy included not only the upper echelons of Normandy but Bretons and Flemish lords who were eager to share the spoils of victory. In the settlement that followed, the Bretons were concentrated in the south-west of England and in Yorkshire, while the Flemings were numerous in south-west Wales, Somerset, and Lincolnshire. The scale of the influx overall is difficult to estimate but it probably numbered in the tens of thousands, amounting to no more than about 2 per cent of the total population.

The low numbers, however, belie the impact. The Norman conquest was an elite takeover. Wealth generation and the organs of the state were now firmly in the hands of the Norman lords. Latin became the language of government, while the aristocracy spoke Norman French: it was a culture of exclusion designed to reinforce the ethnic differences between conqueror and conquered. Although the barriers soon began to break down, they still have their dim reflections in our language and in the more archaic recesses of the class system.

14

Of Myths and Realities

AN EPILOGUE

Around 12,000 years ago, as the ice-sheets receded and temperatures began to rise, bands of hunter-gatherers started to populate the lands later to become the British Isles. Numbers would have been small—a few hundred at the most. Now in Britain and Ireland we are about 68 million, a number that owes its magnitude in part to a gradually increasing rise in birth-rate and in part to inward migration. In the first 11,000 years—the time-span covered in this book—the demographic increase was comparatively slow, by AD 1000 rising to around 2 to 2.3 million. The last thousand years has seen an exponential growth as the holding capacity of the land has been increased, first by gradual improvement in agricultural regimes, culminating, in the eighteenth century, in the introduction of the turnip, which allowed stock to be overwintered on a greatly increased scale; and later by industrialization, which unleashed new energy resources, facilitating further improvements in agricultural production and distribution. Industrialization also allowed some countries to increase the output of commodities and services that could be traded with less developed countries for additional food supplies to support the fast-growing population. As long as technological advance can outstrip demographic growth, populations will continue to rise. When this ceases to be the case, new strategies will need to come into force to reduce the birth-rate and to change lifestyles so that each individual consumes less. In the end we are all governed by simple demographic laws.

The narrative outlined in this book has stressed the innate mobility of human-kind, a mobility that is inherent in our genetic make-up. It is worth stating again the basic truth that the human animal is naturally inquisitive and acquisitive, instincts that provide the impetus for mobility. We are curious about that misty land glimpsed across the sea, or where the whooper swans are making for in their annual northern migrations, and on our journeys we are keen to bring back some novelty—a lump of amber or a finely wrought axe—both as a reminder of the voyage and as a symbol of our prowess in having made it. In the Victorian period it might have been an umbrella stand fashioned from an elephant's foot; nowadays it is more likely to be a collection of digital images.

Mobility may be motivated largely by instinct, but it is controlled within a social structure designed to encourage and reward it. Mobility may also be forced by demographic pressure. A community that has reached the holding capacity of its territory will encourage migration, usually by a section of its young. In more extreme cases populations may be driven from their lands by marauding neighbours or by environmental factors. The Germanic migrants who came to Britain in the fifth century AD were motivated by a combination of reasons: population pressures building up in their homeland, sea-level rise, and the collapse of traditional trading systems. But there will also have been the thrill of the opportunities to be had in a new land. The large numbers of Irish and Scots who left in the wake of the potato famine and the Highland clearances in the early nineteenth century were economic migrants of an extreme kind, but the lure of America and the excitement of change must have been a significant factor drawing them across the ocean. The willingness of *Homo sapiens* to embrace mobility and to adapt to the new is the prime reason for the success of our species.

The narrative outlined in the previous chapters ends in the eleventh century AD with the coming of a new elite from Normandy, Brittany, and Flanders, but it is by no means the end of the story. The arrival of Huguenots and Jews fleeing from persecutions in Europe enlivened the British population in the Middle Ages, while the opening up of global networks in the early modern period brought a trickle of non-Europeans into the islands that increased as Britain's overseas empire developed. In the post-imperial period following the Second World War the influx from Africa, Asia, and the Caribbean has grown dramatically, while the collapse of the Soviet Union in 1991 has seen a new stream of immigrants from Europe, particularly from the Baltic states, Poland, and Romania. And so, as the story goes on, the gene pool of Britain and Ireland continues to be enriched. The islanders have always been a mongrel race and we are the stronger for it.

A Guide to Further
Reading

I N the following pages I have attempted to provide, on a chapter-by-chapter basis,
a guide to general reading to enable the enthusiast to explore the subjects we
have considered, to check the factual basis of the statements made, and, hope-
fully, to be drawn deeper into the intricate and fascinating world of the archaeologist.
What is provided is a brief guide to the first steps in the process of discovery. It is far
from a definitive list, but each of the works included has its own, often extensive,
guide to further reading and will open up new pathways. Once begun, the reader will
find the journey unending.

In compiling this guide I have tried to follow a few general rules. Foremost I have
kept the listings as short as possible consistent with the need to give a fair coverage of
the subject matter, resisting the temptation to claim erudition through length of cita-
tions. I have chosen books in preference to papers in learned journals, but where the
latter are essential they have been included. And I have opted for recently published
works in which the approach is original and the evidence up to date. This constraint
has meant omitting many classic works that, while milestones at the time of their
publication (and still well worth reading), may lead the first-time explorer into redun-
dant byways. They are best visited on the return journey.

The story that we explore spans the long prehistoric period, the brief Roman
interlude, and the earliest centuries of the Middle Ages, in Britain often referred to

as the Saxon period. It has been a tradition for scholars to restrict themselves to one of these periods and often to a limited time-span within. While this is entirely understandable, given the vast amount of data that has to be mastered, it has led to a rather compartmentalized treatment within each specialist area. It has also tended to overemphasize the chronological boundaries, creating unnecessary disjunctions in what is a continuous narrative. The type of literature generated by the research differs in style from period to period. In the prehistoric period—by definition a long span of time without a written historical thread—research is driven by fieldwork and the ancillary skills that support it, and the narratives that can be written are conditioned entirely by archaeological and environmental data. Since the amount of new data generated daily is immense, the narratives are constantly being refined. This means that there are few general works on prehistory, and much of the up-to-date thinking is contained in specialist journals and conference proceedings. With the appearance of historical sources in the Roman and early medieval period, it is much easier to write historically led narratives that can be amplified with archaeological material as it emerges. For this reason there are far more textbooks available on these later periods. This does not mean that the archaeological contribution is less important—far from it since objective archaeology offers a valuable constraint on biased histories—but the accounts that can be written of the first millennium AD have a far richer texture, involving individuals and their motives, than those of prehistory. The bibliographies for Chapters 11–13, therefore, contain more narrative accounts than do those for the earlier chapters.

Some Preliminary Reading on Prehistory

There have been many attempts to write prehistories of Britain. One of the earliest to make a real effort to combine the archaeological and historical evidence together in a coherent narrative of Britain from the earliest times is T. Rice Holmes, *Ancient Britain and the Invasions of Julius Caesar* (Oxford, 1907), which alone served as the textbook throughout the early decades of the twentieth century. Every scrap of textual evidence was eagerly gleaned from the classical sources to provide the framework, with the archaeological details handled, as the author himself makes clear in his preface, 'not for their own sake but only in so far as they illustrate the development of culture'. The 1920s and 1930s saw the rapid development of prehistory as a scientific discipline cut loose from the constraints of classical anecdotes. One of the first attempts of this between-wars generation of professional archaeologists to construct a prehistory of Britain was Cyril Fox's book *The Personality of Britain* (Cardiff, 1932). Its subtitle, 'Its Influence on Inhabitant and Invader in Prehistoric and Early Historic Times', makes clear that the starting point of the work was the geography of the country and the way it affected cultural development. This reflects one of the formative approaches to the early study of prehistory. Soon to follow was a succession of works by the prominent prehistorians of the day: V. G. Childe, *The Prehistory of Scotland* (London, 1935); the same author's *Prehistoric Communities of the British Isles* (London, 1940); G. Clark, *Prehistoric England* (London, 1940); C. and J. Hawkes, *Prehistoric Britain* (Harmondsworth, 1943); and S. Piggott, *British Prehistory* (Oxford, 1949). In Ireland an early start was made with R. A. S. Macalister, *The Archaeology of Ireland* (London, 1928), the new generation of prehistorians being represented by J. Raftery, *Prehistoric Ireland* (London, 1951). Together these volumes represent the first harvest of the new discipline and deserve to be read by those interested in the development of the subject.

Since then there have been many accounts of British and Irish prehistory, some thematic, like Richard Bradley's three books *The Prehistoric Settlement of Britain* (London, 1978), *The Social Foundations of Prehistoric Britain* (London, 1984), and *The Prehistory of Britain and Ireland* (Cambridge, 2007), and G. Cooney and E. Grogan, *Irish Prehistory: A Social Perspective* (Dublin, 1994); others are personal accounts, like Francis Pryor's *Britain BC* (London, 2003) and David Miles's *The Tribes of Britain* (London, 2005), the latter taking the story on into the historic period. Two books also use prehistory and early history to help interpret evidence of population change from the study of modern DNA: B. Sykes, *The Blood of the Isles* (London, 2006), and S. Oppenheimer, *The Origins of the British: The New Prehistory of Britain and Ireland from Ice-Age Hunter to the Vikings as Revealed by DNA Analysis* (London, 2006). We are also well endowed with a batch of excellent textbooks all written by practising archaeologists: J. Waddell, *The Prehistoric Archaeology of Ireland* (4th edn, Galway, 2010); J. P. Mallory and T. E. McNeill, *The Archaeology of Ulster: From Colonization to Plantation* (Belfast, 1991); K. J. Edwards and I. B. M. Ralston (eds.), *Scotland: Environment and Archaeology, 8000 BC–1000 AD* (Chichester, 1997); F. Lynch, S. Aldhouse-Green, and J. L. Davies, *Prehistoric Wales* (Stroud, 2000); and T. Darvill, *Prehistoric Britain* (2nd edn, London, 2010). Together they provide the essential background to this book and should be the constant companions of those who wish to delve into the archaeological detail.

Chapter 1   In the Beginning: Myths and Ancestors

Anyone interested in classical views about the Britons must start with Julius Caesar's *Bellum Gallicum* and Tacitus' *Agricola*, which are widely available in various translations. Of the early English texts dealing with the origins of the British, Gildas and Nennius can be easily accessed through volumes published in the excellent History from the Sources series (Phillimore), both with helpful introductions: *Gildas: The Ruin of Britain and Other Works*, edited and translated by M. Winterbottom (Chichester, 1978), and *Nennius: British History and the Welsh Annals*, edited and translated by J. Morris (Chichester, 1980). For Bede and Geoffrey of Monmouth, the Penguin Classics series offers translations with extensive notes: Bede, *Ecclesiastical History of the English People*, translated and introduced by L. Sherley-Price (Harmondsworth, 1991), and Geoffrey of Monmouth, *The History of the Kings of Britain*, translated and introduced by L. Thorpe (Harmondsworth, 1966).

The classic work on the early British antiquaries and antiquarian thought is T. D. Kendrick, *British Antiquity* (London, 1950), which takes the story up to the Renaissance. The later period, from the Renaissance to the Regency, is stylishly covered in Stuart Piggott's *Ancient Britons and the Antiquarian Imagination* (London, 1989). The same author has also drawn together a number of his papers on antiquarianism in *Ruins in a Landscape* (Edinburgh, 1976). A full treatment of the antiquarian tradition in Britain is offered in S. Smiles, *The Image of Antiquity: Ancient Britain and the Romantic Imagination* (New Haven, 1994). The subject of the Druids features large in early antiquarian debate and is entertainingly presented by Piggott in *The Druids* (London, 1968). A more recent study of the history of thought about the Druids will be found in R. Hutton, *The Druids* (London, 2007). Of the more famous British antiquarians, John Leland's contribution is conveniently summarized in T. D. Kendrick's book *British Antiquity* and is treated in more detail in J. Chandler, *John Leland's Itinerary* (Stroud, 1998). William Camden is considered in a chapter in Piggott's *Ruins in a Landscape*. John Aubrey is given a full treatment in M. Hunter, *John Aubrey and the Realm of Learning* (London, 1975); *John Aubrey's Monumenta Britannica*, ed. J. Fowles and R. Legg (Dorset, 1980); and W. Poole, *John Aubrey and the Advancement of Learning* (Oxford, 2010). William Stukeley's remarkable contribution is examined in Piggott's *William Stukeley: An Eighteenth-Century Antiquary* (2nd edn, London, 1985).

Edward Lhuyd was a towering figure and massively influential in forming ideas about the Celts and their language. His great volume *Archaeologia Britannica*, i: *Glossography* (Oxford, 1707), is well worth looking through if only to gain some understanding of his thoroughness and method. Lhuyd's life and work has been considered by a number of scholars, notably R. T. Gunther, *Life and Letters of Edward Lhuyd* (Oxford, 1945). More succinct summaries of his life are given in G. Daniel, 'Edward Lhuyd: Antiquary and Archaeologist', *Welsh History Review*, 3 (1967), 345–59, and F. Emery, *Edward Lhuyd F.R.S. 1660–1709* (Cardiff, 1971). His Breton contemporary who wrote extensively about Celts was Paul-Yves Pezron, whose book, translated from the French, was published in England as *The Antiquities of Nations; more particularly of the Celtae or Gauls* (London, 1707). A useful introduction to the life and work of Pezron is provided in P. T. J. Morgan's paper 'The Abbé Pezron and the Celts', *Transactions of the Honourable Society of Cymmrodorion* (1965), 286–95.

The exploits of antiquarian excavators in Britain are described in B. Marsden, *The Early Barrow-Diggers* (Princes Risborough, 1974). The quality of some of the best of their work can be appreciated by leafing through Sir Richard Colt Hoare's magnificent monograph *The Ancient History of Wiltshire* (London, 1812; repr. in facsimile, 1975). The Three Age System for dividing prehistory into technological ages is carefully analysed by Glyn Daniel in a small classic, *The Three Ages: An Essay on Archaeological Method* (Cambridge, 1943).

The debate on the antiquity of man focuses around several big men, most notably William Buckland, whose *Reliquiae Diluvianae* (London, 1823) was for long the standard work. Buckland was an engaging character whose creative, if eccentric, life is well captured in E. O. Gordon's book *The Life and Correspondence of William Buckland, D.D., F.R.S.* (London, 1894). For his contribution to the study of early man, see C. Stringer, *Homo Britannicus: The Incredible Story of Human Life in Britain* (London, 2006).

Finally, a reader who wants a short and highly readable account of the origins of archaeology cannot do better than to read *The Idea of Prehistory* (London, 1962) by Glyn Daniel. His later book *The Origins and Growth of Archaeology* (Harmondsworth, 1967) deals in more detail with the theme, quoting extensively from original accounts and reports. A masterly overview of the development of antiquarian and archaeological thought set against the background of European scholarship is to be found in an incomparable volume, *The Discovery of the Past* (London, 1996) by Alain Schnapp.

Chapter 2   Britain Emerges: The Stage Is Set

By far the most lively introduction to early man in Britain is Chris Stringer's *Homo Britannicus* (London, 2006), which presents a wealth of new evidence and thinking, much of it deriving from the recent researches of some thirty archaeologists and other scientists working on the Ancient Human Occupation of Britain project. The bibliography to the book provides an invaluable list of the published sources on which his overview is based. Another invaluable introduction is N. Barton, *Ice Age Britain* (London, 2005). The most comprehensive textbook covering the early part of this period is J. McNabb, *The British Lower Palaeolithic* (London, 2007). Earlier works, D. A. Roe, *The Lower and Middle Palaeolithic Period in Britain* (London, 1981), and J. Wymer, *The Lower Palaeolithic Occupation of Britain* (Salisbury, 1999), also contain much useful detail. The broader European context is given in C. Gamble, *The Palaeolithic Settlement of Europe* (London, 1986). A number of important papers on both British and European themes are to be found in N. Barton, A. J. Roberts, and D. A. Roe (eds.), *The Late Glacial in North-West Europe* (London, 1991).

On specific themes concerning early humans in Britain referred to in the chapter, the following provided useful background: J. Hays, J. Imbrie, and N. Shackleton, 'Variations in the Earth's Orbit: Pacemaker of the Ice Ages', *Science*, 194 (1976), 1121–32; K. Duff (ed.), *The Story of Swanscombe Man* (Canterbury, 1985); N. Ashton and S. Lewis, 'Deserted Britain: Declining Populations in the British Middle Pleistocene', *Antiquity*, 76 (2002), 388–96; P. L. Gibbard and J. P. Lautridou, 'The Quaternary History of the English Channel: An Introduction', *Journal of Quaternary Science*, 18 (2003), 195–9; H. S. Green (ed.), *Pontnewydd Cave: A Lower Palaeolithic Hominid Site in Wales* (Cardiff, 1984); M. J. White and D. C. Schreve, 'Island Britain—Peninsula Britain: Palaeogeography, Colonisation and the Earlier Palaeolithic Settlement of the British Isles', *Proceedings of the Prehistoric Society*, 66 (2000), 1–28; and S. Aldhouse-Green (ed.), *Paviland Cave and the 'Red Lady': A Definitive Report* (Bristol, 2000). For the later Palaeolithic themes and sites mentioned, the following provide much of the background detail: R. N. E. Barton and A. J. Roberts, 'Reviewing the British Late Upper Palaeolithic: New Evidence for Chronological Patterning in the Late Glacial Record', *Oxford Journal of Archaeology*, 15 (1996), 245–66; R. N. E. Barton et al., 'The Late Glacial Reoccupation of the British Isles and the Creswellian', *Journal of Quaternary Science*, 18 (2003), 631–43; P. Bahn and P. Pettitt, *Britain's Oldest Art: The Ice Age Cave Art of Creswell Crags* (London, 2009); A. Currant, R. Jacobi, and C. B. Stringer, 'Excavations at Gough's Cave, Somerset 1986–7', *Antiquity*, 63 (1989), 131–6; and C. Stringer, 'The Gough's Cave Human Fossils: An Introduction', *Bulletin of the Natural History Museum Geology Series*, 56 (2000), 135–9.

The separation of Britain from the Continent is considered in detail in Bryony Cole's seminal paper 'Doggerland: A Speculative Survey', *Proceedings of the Prehistoric Society*, 64 (1998), 45–81. A topographical assessment of the submerged area is offered in V. Gaffney, K. Thomson, and S. Fitch, *Mapping Doggerland: The Mesolithic Landscape of the Southern North Sea* (Oxford, 2007). The fascinating evidence for a tsunami in Scotland in the sixth millennium is discussed in A. G. Dawson, D. E. Smith, and D. Long, 'Evidence for a Tsunami from a Mesolithic Site in Inverness, Scotland', *Journal of Archaeological Science*, 17 (1990), 509–12.

The classical view of Britain as an island is to be found repeated in the writings of Strabo, Caesar, and Pliny, but, as I have argued, the description may well originate in the lost work of Pytheas, *On the Ocean*. An attempt to reconstruct Pytheas' journey is given in B. Cunliffe, *The Extraordinary Voyage of Pytheas the Greek* (London, 2001). A useful source for the geography of Britain seen through Roman eyes is the rather forbiddingly titled *The Place-Names of Roman Britain* (London, 1979) by A. L. F. Rivet and C. Smith. The classical sources for Ireland are conveniently brought together in

P. Freeman, *Ireland and the Classical World* (Austin, 2001). Julius Caesar's descriptions of Britain and the treacherous ocean that protects it, given in his *Bellum Gallicum*, deserve to be read and reread.

The question of sailing in the Atlantic seaways I have dealt with rather more extensively in *Facing the Ocean* (Oxford, 2001) with a supporting bibliography. Early sailing vessels are also considered there. For more technical detail and for the broader context, the most comprehensive source is S. McGrail, *Boats of the World* (Oxford, 2001), where details of the individual British wrecks are given. A fascinating personal account of ancient ships and shipbuilding that offers a brilliant evocation of the maritime world is O. Crumlin-Pedersen, *Archaeology and the Sea in Scandinavia and Britain* (Roskilde, 2010). Log boats are specifically dealt with in S. McGrail, *Logboats of England and Wales* (Oxford, 1978), and R. J. C. Mowat, *The Logboats of Scotland* (Oxford, 1996). The model skin boat from Broighter is discussed by A. W. Farrell and S. Penny, 'The Broighter Boat: A Reassessment', *Irish Archaeological Research Forum*, 2/2 (1975), 15–28. The most recently discovered of the sewn-plank boats, from Dover, is fully detailed in P. Clark (ed.), *The Dover Bronze Age Boat* (London, 2004).

The ancient voyager as a man in search of status was introduced to the archaeological readership in Mary Helms's two very influential works *Ulysses' Sail: An Ethnographic Odyssey of Power, Knowledge and Geographical Distance* (Princeton, 1988) and *Craft and the King Idea: Art, Trade and Power* (Austin, 1993). The concept has since been taken up more widely by archaeologists, most notably by K. Kristiansen and T. B. Larsson in *The Rise of Bronze Age Society* (Cambridge, 2005).

Chapter 3   Interlude: Enter the Actors

The development of the study of ethnology in Britain is helpfully summarized in chapter 4 of M. Morse, *How the Celts Came to Britain* (Stroud, 2005); J. Morrell and A. Thackray, *Gentlemen of Science* (Oxford, 1981); and G. W. Stocking, *Victorian Anthropology* (New York, 1987). A lively treatment of craniology will be found in B. Sykes, *Blood of the Isles* (London, 2006), ch. 4, while chapter 5 in the same book deals with the development of blood group studies.

The growing importance of modern genetics to our understanding of human population in Britain is clearly explained in S. Oppenheimer, *The Origins of the British* (London, 2006), and B. Sykes, *Blood of the Isles* (London, 2006). Sykes's earlier book *The Seven Daughters of Eve* (London, 2001) offers an invaluable and highly readable introduction to the uses of mitochondrial DNA in population studies. For those wishing to understand some of the difficulties raised by attempting to use modern DNA to approach specific archaeological questions—in this case the question of Celtic migration—three papers in B. Cunliffe and J. T. Koch (eds.), *Celtic from the West* (Oxford, 2010), can be recommended: E. C. Røyrvik, 'Western Celts? A Genetic Impression of Britain in Atlantic Europe', 83–106; B. P. McEvoy and D. G. Bradley, 'Irish Genetics and Celts', 107–20; and S. Oppenheimer, 'A Reanalysis of Multiple Prehistoric Immigration to Britain and Ireland Aimed at Identifying the Celtic Contribution', 121–52.

There are as yet no comprehensive accounts of the use of stable isotopes in archaeology so it is necessary to turn to the scientific literature to provide examples. An early paper that sets out to test the parameters of the strontium isotope method is T. D. Price, J. H. Burton, and R. A. Bentley, 'The Characterization of Biologically Available Strontium Isotope Ratios for the Study of Prehistoric Migration', *Archaeometry*, 44 (2002), 117–35. Two papers that show the method in action in prehistoric Europe are T. D. Price et al., 'Prehistoric Human Migration in the *Linearbandkeramik* of Central Europe', *Antiquity*, 75 (2001), 593–603, and R. A. Bentley et al., 'Human Mobility at the Early Neolithic Settlement of Vaihingen, Germany: Evidence from Strontium Isotope Analysis', *Archaeometry*, 45 (2003), 471–86. An interesting example of the use of isotopes to define dietary differences is given in R. Shulting, 'The Marrying Kind: Evidence for a Patrilocal Postmarital Residence Pattern in the Mesolithic of Southern Brittany', in L. Larson (ed.), *Mesolithic on the Move* (Oxford, 2003), 431–41.

To begin to understand the nature of the human species would require massive reading, but two themes in particular should be followed up. The question of innate human aggression and its varied social manifestations is explored by several authors contributing to a book entitled *Conflict* (Cambridge, 2006), edited by M. Jones and A. C. Fabian, while detailed treatments of early warfare will be found in L. H. Keeley, *War before Civilization* (Oxford, 1996), and S. A. LeBlanc, *Constant Battles* (New York, 2003), both drawing extensively on archaeological and anthropological evidence. The other theme of direct relevance to understanding social structures is population dynamics. For this, a good starting point is *A Summary View of the Principle of Population* (London, 1830) by Thomas Malthus, based on his seminal work, his *Essay on the Principle of Population* published in 1798. Two rather more recent helpful reviews are E. Zubrow, *Prehistoric Carrying Capacity: A Model* (Menlo Park, Calif., 1975), and J. W. Wood, 'A Theory of Preindustrial Population Dynamics', *Current Anthropology*, 39 (1998), 99–135.

Chapter 4   Settlement Begins, 10,000–4200 BC

In terms of the old Three Age System this chapter spans the latter part of the Upper Palaeolithic and the whole of the Mesolithic periods. Taking the Upper Palaeolithic first, excellent overviews are offered by Paul Pettitt in his chapter 'The British Upper

Palaeolithic', in J. Pollard (ed.), *Prehistoric Britain* (Oxford, 2008), 18–57, and by Nick Barton in his *Stone Age Britain* (London, 1997). The standard work, now rather out of date, is J. Campbell, *The Upper Palaeolithic of Britain: A Study of Man and Nature in the Late Ice Age* (Oxford, 1977). A number of more detailed papers of direct relevance to Britain are to be found in N. Barton, A. J. Roberts, and D. A. Roe (eds.), *The Late Glacial in North-West Europe* (London, 1991), while chronological matters are carefully considered in N. Barton and A. J. Roberts's paper 'Reviewing the British Late Upper Palaeolithic: New Evidence for Chronological Patterning in the Late Glacial Record', *Oxford Journal of Archaeology*, 15/3 (1996), 245–65. The key site of Launde is fully reported in L. P. Cooper, 'Launde, a Terminal Palaeolithic Camp-Site in the English Midlands and its North European Context', *Proceedings of the Prehistoric Society*, 72 (2006), 53–93. For a broad view of the dynamics of population in western Europe, see C. Gamble et al., 'The Archaeological and Genetic Foundations of European Population during the Late Glacial: Implications for "Agricultural Thinking"', *Cambridge Archaeological Journal*, 15/2 (2005), 193–223.

For the Mesolithic period, three recent works, G. Bailey and P. Spikins (eds.), *Mesolithic Europe* (Cambridge, 2008); S. McCartan et al. (eds.), *Mesolithic Horizons* (Oxford, 2009); and N. Milner and P. Woodman (eds.), *Mesolithic Studies at the Beginning of the 21st Century* (Oxford, 2005), provide broad background studies. More British-focused works include C. Conneller and G. Warren (eds.), *Mesolithic Britain and Ireland: New Approaches* (Stroud, 2006), and R. Young (ed.), *Mesolithic Lifeways: Current Research from Britain and Ireland* (Leicester, 2000). There are a number of important regional studies to be recommended, including A. Saville (ed.), *Mesolithic Scotland and its Neighbours* (Edinburgh, 2004); G. Warren, *Mesolithic Lives in Scotland* (Stroud, 2005); N. Finlay, G. Warren, and C. Wickham-Jones, 'The Mesolithic in Scotland: East Meets West', *Scottish Archaeological Journal*, 24/2 (2002), 101–20; D. Telford, 'The Mesolithic Inheritance: Contrasting Mesolithic Monumentality in Eastern and Western Scotland', *Proceedings of the Prehistoric Society*, 68 (2002), 289–315; A. David, *Palaeolithic and Mesolithic Settlement in Wales with Special Reference to Dyfed* (Oxford, 2007); M. Bell, *Prehistoric Coastal Communities: The Mesolithic in Western Britain* (York, 2007); and three articles by R. Jacobi: 'The Mesolithic of Northern East Anglia and Contemporary Territories', in C. Barringer (ed.), *Aspects of East Anglian Prehistory* (Norwich, 1984), 43–76; 'Population and Landscape in Mesolithic Lowland Britain', in S. Limbrey and J. G. Evans (eds.), *The Effect of Man on the Landscape: The Lowland Zone* (London, 1978), 75–85; and 'Early Flandrian Hunters in the South-West', *Proceedings of the Devon Archaeological Society*, 37 (1979), 48–93. For Ireland, a useful summary is provided by J. Waddell in the first chapter of *The Prehistoric Archaeology of Ireland* (4th edn, Galway, 2010). For a more detailed but earlier assessment of the period, see P. Woodman,

The Mesolithic in Ireland (Oxford, 1978). More recent views are to be found in the same author's 'The Mesolithic of Munster: A Preliminary Assessment', in C. Bonsall (ed.), *The Mesolithic in Europe* (Edinburgh, 1989), 116–24, and P. Woodman and E. Anderson, 'The Irish Later Mesolithic: A Partial Picture', in P. M. Vermeersch and P. van Peer (eds.), *Contributions to the Mesolithic in Europe* (Leuven, 1990), 337–87.

For the environmental background, an essential beginning is B. J. Coles's important paper 'Doggerland: A Speculative Survey', *Proceedings of the Prehistoric Society*, 64 (1998), 45–82. Other important studies include D. Walker and R. West (eds.), *Studies in the Vegetational History of the British Isles: Essays in Honour of Harry Godwin* (Cambridge, 1970), and I. G. Simmons, *The Environmental Impact of Later Mesolithic Culture* (Edinburgh, 1996). The relationship between hunter-gatherers and the environment is thoughtfully considered by Paul Mellars in 'Fire Ecology, Animal Populations and Man: A Study of Some Ecological Relationships in Prehistory', *Proceedings of the Prehistoric Society*, 42 (1976), 15–45.

A number of specific Mesolithic sites are mentioned in this chapter. For the sites in the Kennet valley, see J. J. Wymer and D. M. Churchill, 'Excavations at the Maglemosian Sites at Thatcham, Berkshire, England', *Proceedings of the Prehistoric Society*, 28 (1962), 329–61, and C. J. Ellis et al., 'An Early Mesolithic Seasonal Hunting Site in the Kennet Valley, Southern England', *Proceedings of the Prehistoric Society*, 69 (2003), 107–35. The Oakhanger site in the western Weald has a lengthy bibliography but is usefully summed up in W. F. Rankine and G. W. Dimbleby, 'Further Excavations at a Mesolithic Site at Oakhanger, Selborne, Hants', *Proceedings of the Prehistoric Society*, 27 (1960), 246–62, with a discussion of the revised chronology given in R. M. Jacobi, 'The Last Hunters in Hampshire', in S. J. Shennan and R. T. Schadla-Hall (eds.), *The Archaeology of Hampshire* (Winchester, 1981), 10–25. Star Carr is justly famous, not least for the preservation of organic remains and the quality of the excavation. The original excavation report by J. G. D. Clark was published as *Excavations at Star Carr* (Cambridge, 1954) and was later reviewed by the excavator in his *Star Carr: A Case Study in Bioarchaeology* (Ann Arbor, 1973). The site was again reconsidered by P. Mellars and P. Dark in *Star Carr in Context* (Cambridge, 1998) and was assessed yet again in the light of new fieldwork in the region by C. Conneller and T. Schadla-Hall in 'Beyond Star Carr: The Vale of Pickering in the 10th Millennium BP', *Proceedings of the Prehistoric Society*, 69 (2003), 85–105. Work is continuing. The excavations on Oronsay are fully published in P. Mellars, *Excavations on Oronsay: Prehistoric Human Ecology on a Small Island* (Edinburgh, 1987), and are further considered in a broader context in S. Mithen (ed.), *Hunter-Gatherer Landscape Archaeology: The Southern Hebrides Mesolithic Project 1988–98* (Cambridge, 2000). The work at Mount Sandel in Northern Ireland is published in P. Woodman, *Excavations at Mount Sandel* (Belfast, 1985).

In the section dealing with patterns of connectivity I rely on C. R. Wickham-Jones, *Rhum: Mesolithic and Later Sites at Kinloch, Excavations 1984–86* (Edinburgh, 1990), and R. M. Jacobi, 'The Last Hunters in Hampshire', in S. J. Shennan and R. T. Schadla-Hall (eds.), *The Archaeology of Hampshire* (Winchester, 1981), 10–25. The importance of the sea in encouraging mobility in western Scotland is explored by G. Warren in 'Seascapes: People, Boats and Inhabiting the Late Mesolithic in Western Scotland', in R. Young (ed.), *Mesolithic Lifeways: Current Research from Britain and Ireland* (Leicester, 2000), 94–104.

Mesolithic burials are not well represented in the archaeological record but a few burials and disarticulated human remains have been found. A convenient summary is provided by Chantal Conneller's chapter entitled 'Death', in C. Conneller and G. Warren (eds.), *Mesolithic Britain and Ireland: New Approaches* (Stroud, 2006), 139–46. The human remains from the Cheddar Caves are considered in C. Stringer, *Homo Britannicus* (London, 2006), and by the same author in 'The Gough's Cave Human Fossils: An Introduction', *Bulletin of the Natural History Museum Geology Series*, 56 (2000), 135–9. A detailed study of the Gough's Cave human remains is given in E. Trinkans et al., 'Gough's Cave 1 (Somerset, England): An Assessment of the Sex and Age at Death', *Bulletin of the Natural History Museum Geology Series*, 58 (2003), suppl., 45–50.

Recent work on DNA is conveniently summed up and given a specific interpretation in S. Oppenheimer, *The Origins of the British* (London, 2006). An exploration of some of the problems presented by interpretation are carefully discussed in B. McEvoy et al., 'The *longue durée* of Genetic Ancestry: Multiple Genetic Marker Systems and Celtic Origins on the Atlantic Façade of Europe', *American Journal of Human Genetics*, 75 (2007), 693–702.

Finally, the evidence for the earliest Neolithic introductions along the Atlantic seaways are outlined in two papers: P. Woodman and M. McCarthy, 'Contemplating Some Awful(ly Interesting) Vistas: Importing Cattle and Red Deer into Prehistoric Ireland', and A. Tresset, 'French Connections II: Of Cows and Men', both in I. Armit et al. (eds.), *Neolithic Settlement in Ireland and Western Britain* (Oxford, 2003), 18–30 and 31–9.

Chapter 5   New People, New Ideas, 4200–3000 BC

For many years the classic work on the Neolithic period in Britain and Ireland was Stuart Piggott's *Neolithic Cultures of the British Isles* (Cambridge, 1954). It was published before radiocarbon dating had become the vital tool it now is and adopted the 'short chronology', which, during the 1960s, was revised as radiocarbon dates began to come on stream. That said, the book, elegantly written and well illustrated, is still a useful work of reference, particularly for material culture. The only other attempt to produce an overview of the period is the useful summary by Caroline Malone, *Neolithic Britain and Ireland* (Stroud, 2001). Three other broad-ranging books that can be recommended are M. Edmonds, *Ancestral Geographies of the Neolithic* (London, 1999); G. Cooney, *Landscapes of Neolithic Ireland* (London, 2000); and J. Thomas, *Understanding the Neolithic* (London, 1999). Together they represent the range of thinking current around the turn of the century.

More recently there have been a number of edited volumes, some of them based on conferences, which provide access to a wide range of new research. Among these the more relevant are I. Shepherd and G. Barclay (eds.), *Scotland in Ancient Europe* (Edinburgh, 2004); V. Cummings and C. Fowler (eds.), *The Neolithic of the Irish Sea: Materiality and Traditions of Practice* (Oxford, 2004); I. Armit et al. (eds.), *Neolithic Settlement in Ireland and Western Britain* (Oxford, 2003); R. Cleal and J. Pollard (eds.), *Monuments and Material Culture* (Salisbury, 2004); and A. Whittle and V. Cummings (eds.), *Going Over: The Mesolithic–Neolithic Transition in North-West Europe* (Oxford, 2007).

The questions surrounding the initial 'colonization' of Britain and Ireland have been long debated. One of the most thought-provoking of the early contributions was a paper by Humphrey Case discussing the practicalities of transporting domesticated animals to Britain entitled 'Neolithic Explanations', *Antiquity*, 43 (1969), 176–86. More recently evidence for the movement of peoples from the Continent has been carefully presented and discussed by Alison Sheridan in a series of important papers including 'Neolithic Connections along and across the Irish Sea', in V. Cummings and C. Fowler (eds.), *The Neolithic of the Irish Sea: Materiality and Traditions of Practice* (Oxford, 2004), 9–21; 'From Picardie to Pickering and Pencraig Hill? New Information on the "Carinated Bowl Neolithic" in Northern Britain', in A. Whittle and V. Cummings (eds.), *Going Over: The Mesolithic–Neolithic Transition in North-West Europe* (Oxford, 2007), 441–92; and 'The Neolithization of Britain and Ireland: The "Big Picture"', in B. Finlayson and G. Warren (eds.), *Landscape in Transition* (Oxford, 2010), 89–105. Two detailed contributions directly relevant to the discussion are A. Sheridan et al., 'Revisiting a Small Passage Tomb at Broadsands, Devon', *Proceedings of the Devon Archaeological Society*, 66 (2008), 1–26, and D. Peacock, L. Cutler, and P. Woodward, 'A Neolithic Voyage', *International Journal of Nautical Archaeology*, 39/1 (2009), 116–24, in which questions of maritime transportation are reconsidered. The possibility of a land bridge between Britain and the Continent lasting into the Neolithic period is explored in B. Coles, 'Doggerland's Loss and the Neolithic', in B. Coles, J. Coles, and M. Jørgensen (eds.), *Bog Bodies, Sacred Sites and Wetland Archaeology* (Exeter, 1999), 51–8.

On Neolithic flint mines, see M. Barber, D. Field, and P. Topping, *Neolithic Flint Mines in England* (London, 1999). The discovery of large timber halls of Neolithic date is a comparatively recent development. The halls of Scotland are conveniently discussed in K. Brophy, 'From Big Houses to Cult Houses: Early Neolithic Timber Halls in Scotland', *Proceedings of the Prehistoric Society*, 73 (2007), 75–96, with a full bibliography to earlier publications. For Ireland, the evidence is considered in a number of papers by different authors in I. Armit et al. (eds.), *Neolithic Settlement in Ireland and Western Britain* (Oxford, 2003), 146–87. Evidence for crops is assembled in A. Fairbairn (ed.), *Plants in Neolithic Britain and Beyond* (Oxford, 2000).

The monuments of Neolithic Britain and Ireland have, understandably, generated a considerable literature: here we must be very selective. On causewayed enclosures and related structures there are two publications: T. Darvill and J. Thomas (eds.), *Neolithic Enclosures in Atlantic Northwest Europe* (Oxford, 2001), and A. Oswald, C. Dyer, and M. Barber, *The Creation of Monuments: Neolithic Causewayed Enclosures in the British Isles* (London, 2001). For the chronology of the enclosures using the most up-to-date radiocarbon chronologies, see A. Whittle, F. Healy, and A. Bayliss, *Gathering Time: Dating the Early Neolithic Enclosures of Southern Britain and Ireland* (Oxford, 2011).

The burial monuments of the Neolithic have long been a favourite topic. For the long barrows, a useful compendium is P. Ashbee, *The Earthen Long Barrow in Britain* (2nd edn, Norwich, 1984). Other useful publications are the Royal Commission on Historic Monuments (England), *Long Barrows in Hampshire and the Isle of Wight* (London, 1979), and T. Manby, 'Long Barrows of Northern England: Structural and Dating Evidence', *Scottish Archaeological Forum*, 2 (1970), 1–28. A major contribution to the crucial issue of dating is offered in A. Bayliss and A. Whittle (eds.), *Histories of the Dead: Building Chronologies for Five Southern British Long Barrows, Cambridge Archaeological Journal*, 17/1 (2007), suppl.

On the chambered tombs of Britain, the classic works are G. Daniel, *The Prehistoric Chambered Tombs of England and Wales* (Cambridge, 1950), and A. Henshall, *The Chambered Tombs of Scotland*, 2 vols. (Edinburgh, 1963–72). For Ireland, the basic sources of the tombs are given in R. de Valera and Ó. Nualláin, *Survey of the Megalithic Forts of Ireland*, i–iv (Dublin, 1961–82). The most convenient overview is offered in J. Waddell, *The Prehistoric Archaeology of Ireland* (4th edn, Galway, 2010).

The origin of megalithic tombs in Britain and Ireland is most recently considered in A. Sheridan, 'Ireland's Earliest "Passage" Tombs: A French Connection?', in G. Burenhult (ed.), *Stones and Bones: Formal Disposal of the Dead in Atlantic Europe during the Mesolithic–Neolithic Interface 6000–3000 BC* (Oxford, 2003), 9–25, and in P. Arias et al., 'Megalithic Chronologies', in the same volume, 65–99. An earlier paper by A. Sheridan, 'Megaliths and Megalomania: An Account and Interpretation of the Development of the Irish Passage Grave Tombs', *Journal of Irish Archaeology*, 3 (1986), 17–30, remains a valuable discussion of the evidence for the development of tombs in Ireland. Other volumes of direct relevance to the discussion in this chapter are T. Powell et al., *Megalithic Enquiries in the West of Britain* (Liverpool, 1969); T. Kytmannow, *Portal Tombs in the Landscape: The Chronology, Morphology and Landscape Setting of the Portal Tombs of Ireland, Wales and Cornwall* (Oxford, 2008); and T. Darvill, *Long Barrows of the Cotswolds and Surrounding Areas* (Stroud, 2004). Among the specific sites mentioned, the following are classics: R. Atkinson, S. Piggott, and A. Whittle, 'Wayland's Smithy, Oxfordshire: Excavations at the Neolithic Tomb in 1962–63', *Proceedings of the Prehistoric Society*, 57 (1991), 61–102; S. Piggott, *The West Kennet Long Barrow: Excavations 1955–6* (London, 1962); T. Powell and G. Daniel, *Barclodiad y Gawres: The Excavation of a Megalithic Chambered Tomb in Anglesey* (Liverpool, 1956); M. O'Kelly, *Newgrange* (London, 1982); and G. Eogan, *Knowth and the Passage Tombs of Ireland* (London, 1986).

The still-enigmatic cursus monuments have been considered in a number of publications including A. Barclay and J. Harding, *Pathways and Ceremonies: The Cursus Monuments of Britain and Ireland* (Oxford, 1999), and J. Thomas, 'On the Origins and Development of the Cursus Monument in Britain', *Proceedings of the Prehistoric Society*, 72 (2006), 229–42.

On the question of connectivity, the most dramatic demonstration of artefact mobility in the Neolithic of western Europe is the distribution of jadeite axes, most usefully summed up in P. Pétrequin et al., 'Neolithic Alpine Axeheads, from the Continent to Great Britain, the Isle of Man and Ireland', *Analecta Praehistorica Leidensia*, 40 (2008), special issue: *Between Foraging and Farming*, 261–79. For stone axe distributions in Britain, see T. M. Clough and W. Cummins, *Stone Axe Studies*, i–ii (London, 1979–88). For an introduction to stone axe distribution in Ireland, E. Grogan and G. Cooney, 'A Preliminary Distribution Map of Stone Axes in Ireland', *Antiquity*, 64 (1990), 559–61, and A. Sheridan, G. Cooney, and E. Grogan, 'Stone Axe Studies in Ireland', *Proceedings of the Prehistoric Society*, 58 (1992), 389–416. The axes from Tievebulliagh are discussed in M. Jope, 'Porcellanite Axes from Factories in North-East Ireland: Tievebulliagh and Rathlin', *Ulster Journal of Archaeology*, 15 (1952), 31–60, and A. Sheridan, 'Porcellanite Artefacts: A New Survey', *Ulster Journal of Archaeology*, 49 (1986), 19–32. The distribution of Neolithic gabbroic pottery from Cornwall is explored in D. Peacock, 'Neolithic Pottery Production in Cornwall', *Antiquity*, 43 (1969), 145–9.

The most comprehensive study of the British Neolithic population is D. Brothwell, 'The Human Biology of the Neolithic Population of Britain', in I. Schwidetsky (ed.), *Die Anfänge des Neolithikums vom Orient bis Nordeuropa* (Cologne, 1973), 280–99. Questions of warfare are considered in R. Schulting and M. Wysocki, '"In this chambered tumulus were found cleft skulls": An Assessment of the Evidence for Cranial Trauma in the British Neolithic', *Proceedings of the Prehistoric Society*, 71 (2005), 107–38.

Finally, some views on immigration based on the evidence of modern DNA are outlined in S. Oppenheimer, *The Origin of the British* (London, 2006), ch. 5.

Chapter 6   Mobilizing Materials: A New Connectivity, 3000–1500 BC

This chapter covers the period from *c.*3800 BC to *c.*1500 BC, which in terms of the old Three Age System spans the middle and later Neolithic period, the Chalcolithic, and the Early Bronze Age. Many of the general texts on the Neolithic recommended for Chapter 5 are also relevant to this chapter. There are, however, surprisingly few general works on the latter part of the period. One outstandingly attractive book is the superbly illustrated catalogue published to accompany an exhibition in Edinburgh in 1985: D. Clarke, T. Cowie, and A. Foxton, *Symbols of Power at the Time of Stonehenge* (Edinburgh, 1985). Other books include C. Burgess, *The Age of Stonehenge* (London, 1980), and M. Parker Pearson, *Bronze Age Britain* (2nd edn, London, 2005).

The extensive complexes of ritual monuments have generated a considerable literature. Henge monuments are fully treated in A. Harding and G. Lee, *Henge Monuments and Related Sites of Great Britain* (Oxford, 1987); J. Harding, *Henge Monuments of the British Isles* (Stroud, 2003); and G. Wainwright, *The Henge Monuments: Ceremony and Society in Prehistoric Britain* (London, 1989). The apparently related phenomenon of Grooved Ware has been exhaustively treated in R. Cleal and A. MacSween (eds.), *Grooved Ware in Britain and Ireland* (Oxford, 1999).

Much has been written on Stonehenge. Among the more useful works are R. Cleal, K. Walker, and R. Montague, *Stonehenge in its Landscape: Twentieth Century Excavations* (London, 1995); B. Cunliffe and C. Renfrew (eds.), *Science and Stonehenge* (London, 1997); and T. Darvill, *Stonehenge: The Biography of a Landscape* (Stroud, 2006). More recent excavations hinting at a revised chronology are discussed in M. Parker Pearson et al., 'The Age of Stonehenge', *Antiquity*, 81 (2007), 617–39. The nearby henge of Durrington Walls was extensively excavated in the 1960s and is fully published in G. Wainwright and I. Longworth, *Durrington Walls: Excavations 1966–1968* (London, 1971). More recent excavations at the site are summarized in M. Parker Pearson, 'The Stonehenge Riverside Project: Excavations at the East Entrance to Durrington Walls', in M. Larsson and M. Parker Pearson (eds.), *From Stonehenge to the Baltic* (Oxford, 2007), 125–44. Avebury has also been the centre of much publishing activity. The early excavations are fully presented in I. Smith, *Windmill Hill and Avebury: Excavations by Alexander Keiller 1925–1939* (Oxford, 1965). More recent publications include M. Gillings et al., *Landscape of the Megaliths: Excavation and Fieldwork on the Avebury Monuments, 1997–2003* (Oxford, 2008); M. Gillings and J. Pollard, *Avebury* (London, 2004); and G. Brown, D. Field, and D. McOmish (eds.), *The Avebury Landscape: Aspects of the Field Archaeology of the Marlborough Downs* (Oxford, 2005). Recent work on other monuments in the Avebury region is discussed in A. Whittle, *Sacred Mount, Holy Rings: Silbury Hill and the West Kennet Palisade Enclosures: A Later Neolithic Complex in North Wiltshire* (Oxford, 1997), and J. Leary and D. Field, *The Story of Silbury Hill* (London, 2010). The complex of late Neolithic monuments on Orkney are thoroughly discussed in G. Ritchie, 'The Stones of Stennes, Orkney', *Proceedings of the Society of Antiquaries of Scotland*, 107 (1976), 1–60, and C. Richards, *Dwelling amongst the Monuments: An Examination of the Neolithic Village of Barnhouse, Maeshowe Passage Grave and Surrounding Monuments at Stenness, Orkney* (Cambridge, 2003).

The Beaker period has generated a very considerable literature. A very good general introduction, now understandably somewhat out of date, is R. Harrison, *The Beaker Folk: Copper Age Archaeology in Western Europe* (London, 1980). More recent papers that present aspects of current thinking include M. Linden, 'What Linked the Bell Beakers in Third Millennium BC Europe?', *Antiquity*, 81 (2007), 343–52; V. Heyd, 'Families, Treasures, Warriors and Complex Societies: Beaker Groups and the Third Millennium BC along the Upper and Middle Danube', *Proceedings of the Prehistoric Society*, 73 (2007), 327–79; and F. Nicolis (ed.), *Bell Beakers Today* (Trento, 2001). For Britain and Ireland, the standard corpus of beakers was published and discussed in D. L. Clarke, *Beaker Pottery of Great Britain and Ireland* (Cambridge, 1970). Thereafter, in a series of important papers Humphrey Case has explored aspects of the problem. His most notable contributions are 'Beakers: Deconstruction and After', *Proceedings of the Prehistoric Society*, 59 (1993), 241–68; 'Irish Beakers in their European Context', in J. Waddell and E. Twohig (eds.), *Ireland in the Bronze Age* (Dublin, 1995), 14–19; 'The Beaker Culture in Britain and Ireland: Groups, European Contacts and Chronology', in F. Nicolis (ed.), *Bell Beakers Today* (Trento, 2001), 361–77; and 'Beakers and Beaker Culture', in C. Burgess, P. Topping, and F. Lynch (eds.), *Beyond Stonehenge: Essays on the Bronze Age in Honour of Colin Burgess* (Oxford, 2007), 237–54. Another important paper that considers the spread of Beaker culture to Britain is S. Needham, 'Transforming Beaker Culture in North-West Europe: Processes of Fusion and Fission', *Proceedings of the Prehistoric Society*, 71 (2005), 171–218. For the Amesbury Archer, see A. Fitzpatrick, 'In his Hands and in his Head: The Amesbury Archer as a Metalworker', in P. Clark (ed.), *Bronze Age Connections: Cultural Contact in Prehistoric Europe* (Oxford, 2009), 176–88.

The origins of copper metallurgy in Ireland are fully explored in W. O'Brien, *Ross Island: Mining, Metal and Society in Early Ireland* (Galway, 2004), while for early copper production in Britain, see S. Timberlake, 'Ancient Prospection for Metals and Modern Prospecting for Ancient Mines: The Evidence for Bronze Age Mining within the British Isles', in M. Bartelheim, E. Pernicka, and R. Krause (eds.), *The Beginnings of Metallurgy in the Old World* (Rahden, 2002), 327–57; and by the same author, 'Copper

Mining and Production at the Beginning of the British Bronze Age', in P. Clark (ed.), *Bronze Age Connections: Cultural Contact in Prehistoric Europe* (Oxford, 2009), 94–121; and P. Northover, 'The Earliest Metal Working in Southern Britain', in A. Hauptmann et al. (eds.), *The Beginnings of Metallurgy* (Bochum, 1999), 211–25.

The early gold from Britain and Ireland is fully arrayed in J. Taylor, *Bronze Age Goldwork of the British Isles* (Cambridge, 1980), and G. Eogan, *The Accomplished Art: Gold and Gold-Working in Britain and Ireland during the Bronze Age (c. 2300–650 BC)* (Oxford, 1994). What little is known of tin production is helpfully summarized in R. Penhallurick, *Tin in Antiquity* (London, 1986). The other rare commodities in use in this period are discussed in D. Clarke, T. Cowie, and A. Foxton (eds.), *Symbols of Power at the Time of Stonehenge* (Edinburgh, 1985), and in more detail in A. Harding, 'British Amber Spacer-Plate Necklaces and their Relatives in Gold and Stone', in C. Beck and J. Bouzek (eds.), *Amber in Archaeology* (Prague, 1990), 53–8; A. Sheridan and A. Shortland, '". . . beads which have given rise to so much dogmatism, controversy and rash speculation": Faience in Early Bronze Age Britain and Ireland', in I. A. Shepherd and G. J. Barclay (eds.), *Scotland in Ancient Europe* (Edinburgh, 2004), 263–79; A. Sheridan and M. Davis, 'Investigating Jet and Jet-like Artefacts from Prehistoric Scotland: The National Museums of Scotland Project', *Antiquity*, 76 (2002), 812–24; and S. J. Shennan, 'Exchange and Ranking: The Role of Amber in the Earlier Bronze Age of Europe', in C. Renfrew and S. J. Shennan (eds.), *Ranking, Resource and Exchange* (Cambridge, 1982), 33–45.

The development of centres of power in the early millennium has been widely discussed. Among the more useful papers are M. Braithwaite, 'Ritual and Prestige in the Prehistory of Wessex c.2200–1400 BC: A New Dimension in the Archaeological Evidence', in D. Miller and C. Tilley (eds.), *Ideology, Power and Prehistory* (Cambridge, 1984), 93–110; and a succession of thought-provoking papers by S. Needham, including 'Power Pulses across a Cultural Divide: Cosmologically Driven Exchange between Armorica and Wessex', *Proceedings of the Prehistoric Society*, 66 (2000), 151–207; 'Analytical Implications for Beaker Metallurgy in North-West Europe', in M. Bartelheim, E. Pernicka, and R. Krause (eds.), *The Beginnings of Metallurgy in the Old World* (Rahden, 2002), 99–127; 'Migdale-Marnoch: Sunburst of Scottish Metallurgy', in I. A. Shepherd and G. J. Barclay (eds.), *Scotland in Ancient Europe* (Edinburgh, 2004), 217–45; and 'Encompassing the Sea: "Maritories" and Bronze Age Maritime Interactions', in P. Clark (ed.), *Bronze Age Connections: Cultural Contact in Prehistoric Europe* (Oxford, 2009), 12–37.

Sewn-plank boats, which so effectively increased the possibility of maritime interactions, are discussed in a number of sources, most conveniently S. McGrail, *Boats of the World from the Stone Age to Medieval Times* (Oxford, 2001), 184–91, and R. van de

Noort, 'Argonauts of the North Sea: A Social Maritime Archaeology for the 2nd Millennium BC', *Proceedings of the Prehistoric Society*, 72 (2006), 267–87, and the same author's 'Exploring the Ritual of Travel in Prehistoric Europe: The Bronze Age Sewn-Plank Boats in Context', in P. Clark (ed.), *Bronze Age Connections: Cultural Contact in Prehistoric Europe* (Oxford, 2009), 159–75. On the sea-going capability of the sewn-plank boats, see J. Coates, 'The Bronze Age Ferriby Boat: Seagoing Ships or Estuary Ferry Boats?', *International Journal of Nautical Archaeology*, 34/1 (2005), 38–42. The best-preserved of the sewn-plank boats, from Dover, is fully published in P. Clark (ed.), *The Dover Bronze Age Boat* (London, 2004).

Finally, for remote areas with their own distinct culture, there is much to be read. South-western Ireland provides a well-researched example accessible through two monographs by W. O'Brien: *Sacred Ground: Megalithic Tombs in Coastal South-West Ireland* (Galway, 1999) and *Local Worlds: Early Settlement and Landscapes and Upland Farming in South-West Ireland* (Cork, 2009). The distinctive culture of the north-east of Scotland is considered in R. Bradley, *The Good Stones: A New Investigation of the Clava Cairns* (Edinburgh, 2000); while the entrance graves of the Scilly Isles are presented in P. Ashbee, *Ancient Scilly* (Newton Abbot, 1974). For a recent review of southern entrance graves, see M. Jones and C. Thomas, 'Bosiliack and a Reconsideration of Entrance Graves', *Proceedings of the Prehistoric Society*, 76 (2010), 271–96. These sources are chosen as being directly relevant to what was said in this chapter: needless to say, there is much more besides.

Chapter 7   Interlude: Talking to Each Other

The reader interested in the early history of thought about the Celts could usefully begin with the English translation of Paul-Yves Pezron's book published as *The Antiquities of the Nations; more Particularly of the Celtae or Gauls* (London, 1706) and Edward Lhuyd, *Archaeologia Britannica*, i: *Glossography* (Oxford, 1707). A more developed view, presented by J. Rhys in *Celtic Britain* (London, 1882), formed the basis from which much of the later archaeological interpretation grew.

The debate about Indo-European origins has been long and complex. An excellent introduction favouring the Anatolian origins theory is C. Renfrew, *Archaeology and Language: The Puzzle of Indo-European Origins* (London, 1987). The alternative, Kurgan hypothesis is presented in J. P. Mallory, *In Search of the Indo-European Language, Archaeology and Myth* (London, 1989), providing the clearest exposition of the theory. More recently the topic has been considered in a much broader context in D. W. Anthony, *The Horse, the Wheel and Language* (Princeton, 2007). For a stimulating review paper redolent with good sense, see P. Sims-Williams, 'Genetics, Linguistics and

Prehistory: Thinking Big and Thinking Straight', *Antiquity*, 72 (1998), 505–27. Two useful basic sources are P. Russell, *An Introduction to the Celtic Languages* (London, 1995), and P. Sims-Williams, *Ancient Celtic Place-Names in Europe and Asia Minor* (Oxford, 2006).

The phylogenetic approach to studying the Celtic language has attracted a number of scholars and has generated a fascinating literature, among which the following are of direct interest to our discussions: D. Ringe, T. Warnow, and A. Taylor, 'Indo-Europeans and Computational Cladistics', *Transactions of the Philological Society*, 100 (2002), 50–129; R. D. Gray and Q. D. Atkinson, 'Language-Tree Divergence Times Support the Anatolian Theory of Indo-European Origin', *Nature*, 426 (2003), 435–9; O. Atkinson et al., 'From Words to Dates: Water into Wine, Mathemagic or Phylogenetic Inference?', *Transactions of the Philological Society*, 103 (2008), 193–219. For a critical review of the phylogenetic method, see A. McMahon and R. McMahon, 'Why Linguists Don't Do Dates: Evidence from Indo-European and Australian Languages', in P. Forster and C. Renfrew (eds.), *Phylogenetic Methods and the Prehistory of Language* (Cambridge, 2006), 153–60.

The earliest Greek references to the Celts are conveniently brought together in P. M. Freeman, 'The Earliest Greek Sources on the Celts', *Études Celtiques*, 32 (1996), 11–47. New work on the Tartessian language is presented by J. T. Koch in 'Paradigm Shift? Interpreting Tartessian as Celtic', in B. Cunliffe and J. T. Koch (eds.), *Celtic from the West: Alternative Perspectives in Archaeology, Genetics, Language and Literature* (Oxford, 2010), 185–302. For early Celtic in Britain, see J. T. Koch, ' "Gallo-Brittonic" vs. "Insular Celtic": The Inter-Relationships of the Celtic Languages Reconsidered', in G. Le Menn and J.-Y. Le Moing (eds.), *Bretagne et pays celtiques: Langues, histoire, civilisation: Mélanges offerts à la memoire de Léon Fleuriot* (Saint-Brieuc, 1992), 471–95.

The suggestion that the Celtic languages began in the Atlantic region of Europe is introduced in B. Cunliffe, 'A Race Apart: Insularity and Connectivity', *Proceedings of the Prehistoric Society*, 75 (2009), 55–64, and the same author's 'Celticization from the West: The Contribution of Archaeology', in B. Cunliffe and J. T. Koch (eds.), *Celtic from the West: Alternative Perspectives from Archaeology, Genetics, Language and Literature* (Oxford, 2010), 13–38.

Chapter 8   The Productive Land in the Age of Warriors, 1500–800 BC

The Middle and Late Bronze Age—the subject matter of this chapter—has generated few broad overviews. A. Harding, *European Societies in the Bronze Age* (Cambridge, 2000), offers an invaluable conspectus of the wider European context, while C. Burgess, *The Age of Stonehenge* (London, 1980), and M. Parker Pearson, *Bronze Age Britain* (2nd edn, London, 2005), provide summaries of the British material. Of particular value for understanding the chronology of the period is S. Needham, 'Chronology and Periodization in the British Bronze Age', in K. Randsborg (ed.), *Absolute Chronology: Archaeological Europe 2500–500 BC* (Copenhagen, 1996), 121–40.

Climatic and vegetational changes have been considered in H. H. Lamb, 'Climate from 1000 BC–AD 100', in M. Jones and G. W. Dimbleby (eds.), *The Environment of Man: The Iron Age to the Anglo-Saxon Period* (Oxford, 1981), 53–65; S. Piggott, 'A Note on Climatic Deterioration in the First Millennium BC', *Scottish Archaeological Forum*, 4 (1973), 109–13; and W. Pennington, *The History of British Vegetation* (London, 1974). The possible effects of the eruption of the Hekla volcano are discussed in M. G. L. Baillie, *A Slice through Time: Dendrochronology and Precision Dating* (London, 1995).

Questions of landscape and settlement are summarized in B. Cunliffe, *Iron Age Communities in Britain* (4th edn, London, 2004), ch. 3. Two very useful detailed works are J. Brück (ed.), *Bronze Age Landscapes: Tradition and Transformation* (Oxford, 2001), and D. T. Yates, *Land, Power and Prestige: Bronze Age Field Systems in Southern Britain* (Oxford, 2007). Also to be recommended is a thought-provoking paper, J. Brück, 'Houses, Lifecycles and Deposition on Middle Bronze Age Settlements in Southern England', *Proceedings of the Prehistoric Society*, 65 (1999), 145–66. The thoroughly studied land-scapes of Dartmoor are fully treated in A. Fleming, *The Dartmoor Reaves: Investigating Prehistoric Land Division* (2nd edn, Oxford, 2008), and P. Newman, *The Field Archaeology of Dartmoor* (London, 2011), 60–82, while the extensive programme of work in the fens around Peterborough is conveniently summed up in F. Pryor, *The Flag Fen Basin: Archaeology and Environment of a Fenland Landscape* (London, 2001). Aspects of the Wessex chalkland landscapes are considered in B. Cunliffe, 'Wessex Cowboys', *Oxford Journal of Archaeology*, 23 (2004), 61–8. For Ireland, a good example of a comprehen-sive landscape project is provided by E. Grogan (ed.), *The North Munster Project*, i: *The Later Prehistoric Landscape of South-East Clare*, and ii: *The Prehistoric Landscape of North Munster* (Dublin, 2005). Detailed reports on some of the specific sites mentioned include K. Smith et al., 'The Shaugh Moor Project. Third Report: Settlement and Environmental Investigations', *Proceedings of the Prehistoric Society*, 47 (1981), 205–74; M. V. Jones and D. Bond, 'Late Bronze Age Settlement at Mucking, Essex', in J. Barrett and R. Bradley (eds.), *Settlement and Society in the British Later Bronze Age* (Oxford, 1980), 471–82; T. G. Manby, 'Bronze Age Settlement in Eastern Yorkshire', in the same volume, 307–40; E. Grogan, *The Bronze Age Hillfort at Mooghaun South* (Dublin, 1999); J. P. Mallory, D. G. Moore, and L. J. Canning, 'Excavations at Haughey's Fort, 1991 and 1995', *Emania*, 14 (1996), 5–20.

Comparatively little has recently been written on the tradition of urnfield bur-ials, but one outstanding report that amply demonstrates the nature of these sites is M. Dacre and A. Ellison, 'A Bronze Age Urn Cemetery at Kimpton, Hampshire', *Proceedings of the Prehistoric Society*, 47 (1981), 147–204. The deposition of bronzes and other items of value in watery contexts is thoroughly considered in R. Bradley, *The Passage of Arms: An Archaeological Analysis of Prehistoric Hoards and Votive Deposits* (Cambridge, 1990). More specific studies include M. Ehrenberg, 'The Occurrence of Bronze Age Metalwork in the Thames: An Investigation', *Transactions of the London and Middlesex Archaeological Society*, 31 (1980), 1–15, and D. Yates and R. Bradley, 'Still Waters, Hidden Depths: The Deposition of Bronze Age Metalwork in the English Fenland', *Antiquity*, 84 (2010), 405–15.

Bronze Age arms and armour are discussed in J. Coles, 'European Bronze Age Shields', *Proceedings of the Prehistoric Society*, 28 (1962), 156–90; C. Burgess, 'The Later Bronze Age in the British Isles and North-Western France', *Archaeological Journal*, 125 (1968), 1–45; and M. A. Brown, 'Swords and Sequence in the British Bronze Age', *Archaeologia*, 107 (1982), 1–42. An important and far-reaching reconsideration of carp's-tongue swords is given in D. Brandherm and C. Burgess, 'Carp's-Tongue Problems', in F. Verse et al. (eds.), *Durch die Zeiten: Festschrift für Albrecht Jockenhövel zum 65 Geburtstag* (Rahden, 2008), 133–60. Feasting equipment has been the subject of much detailed study. Important recent publications include S. Gerloff, *Atlantic Cauldrons and Buckets of the Late Bronze and Early Iron Ages in Western Europe* (Stuttgart, 2010); C. Burgess and B. O'Connor, 'Bronze Age Rotary Spits: Finds Old and New, Some False, Some True', in H. Roche et al. (eds.), *From Megaliths to Metals: Essays in Honour of George Eogan* (Oxford, 2004), 184–99; and S. Needham and S. Bowman, 'The Dunaverney and Little Thetford Flesh-Hooks: History, Technology and their Position within the Later Bronze Age Atlantic Zone Feasting Complex', *Antiquaries Journal*, 87 (2007), 53–108. A number of recent papers on the Irish Bronze Age are gathered together in J. Waddell and E. S. Twohig (eds.), *Ireland in the Bronze Age* (Dublin, 1995), and on the British and European Bronze Age in C. Burgess, P. Topping, and F. Lynch (eds.), *Beyond Stonehenge: Essays on the Bronze Age in Honour of Colin Burgess* (Oxford, 2007).

The convergence of culture on both sides of the eastern Channel–southern North Sea zone has generated much debate over the years. Seminal early contributions include J. Butler, 'Bronze Age Connections across the North Sea', *Palaeohistoria*, 9 (1963), 1–286; B. O'Connor, *Cross-Channel Relations in the Later Bronze Age* (Oxford, 1980); and K. Muckleroy, 'Middle Bronze Age Trade between Britain and Europe: A Maritime Perspective', *Proceedings of the Prehistoric Society*, 47 (1981), 275–97. Since then much new work has been done in north-western France and Belgium emphasizing the similarities of culture with Britain across the maritime divide. A convenient and well-illustrated summary is provided in an exhibition catalogue, C. Marcigny et al. (eds.), *La Normandie à l'aube de l'histoire: Les découvertes archéologiques de l'âge du bronze 2300–800 av. JC* (Paris, 2005). More detailed papers include J. Bourgeois and M. Talon, 'From Picardy to Flanders: Transmanche Connections in the Bronze Age', in P. Clark (ed.), *Bronze Age Connections: Cultural Contact in Prehistoric Europe* (Oxford, 2009), 38–59; C. Marcigny, E. Ghesquière, and I. Kinnes, 'Bronze Age Cross-Channel Relations: The Lower-Normandy (France) Example: Ceramic Chronology and First Reflections', in C. Burgess, P. Topping, and F. Lynch (eds.), *Beyond Stonehenge: Essays on the Bronze Age in Honour of Colin Burgess* (Oxford, 2007), 255–67; and C. Marcigny et al., 'Découvertes récentes de l'âge du bronze moyen dans le Département de la Sarthe (Pays-de-la-Loire)', *Revue Archéologique de l'Ouest*, 19 (2002), 7–13. The mechanisms of maritime contact are explored in R. van de Noort, 'Argonauts of the North Sea: A Social Maritime Archaeology for the 2nd Millennium BC', *Proceedings of the Prehistoric Society*, 72 (2006), 267–87.

The position of Ireland in the trading networks is explained in G. Eogan, 'Ideas, People and Things: Ireland and the External World during the Later Bronze Age', in J. Waddell and E. S. Twohig (eds.), *Ireland in the Bronze Age* (Dublin, 1995), 128–35, and in the same author's *The Accomplished Art: Gold and Gold-Working in Britain and Ireland during the Bronze Age (c.2300–650 BC)* (Oxford, 1994).

The Atlantic seaways as a channel of communication are addressed in two collections of edited papers: C. Chevillot and A. Coffyn (eds.), *L'Âge du bronze atlantique* (Beynac, 1991), and S. Oliveira Jorge (ed.), *Existe uma Idade do Bronze Atlantico?* (Lisbon, 1998). The case study of a specific Mediterranean import is presented in S. Needham and C. Giardino, 'From Sicily to Salcombe: A Mediterranean Bronze Age Object from British Coastal Waters', *Antiquity*, 82 (2008), 60–72. For an important review of the changing momentum of Atlantic Bronze Age exchange patterns, see C. Burgess and B. O'Connor, 'Iberia: The Atlantic Bronze Age and the Mediterranean', in S. Celestino, N. Rafel, and X.-L. Armada (eds.), *Contacto cultural entre el Mediterráneo y el Atlántico (siglos XII–VIII ane): La precolonización a debate* (Madrid, 2008), 41–58.

Finally, for the ships and shipwrecks, the evidence for the Salcombe and Langdon Bay 'wrecks' was summarized in K. Muckleroy, 'Middle Bronze Age Trade between Britain and Europe: A Maritime Perspective', *Proceedings of the Prehistoric Society*, 47 (1981), 275–97. More recent finds in the Salcombe estuary have not yet been published but are outlined in a short popular account, D. Parham, S. Needham, and M. Palmer, 'Questioning the Wrecks of Time', *British Archaeology* (Nov.–Dec. 2006), 43–6. The possibility that some of the supposed 'shipwrecks' may be votive deposits is explored in A. V. M. Samson, 'Offshore Finds from the Bronze Age in North-Western Europe: The Shipwreck Scenario Revisited', *Oxford Journal of Archaeology*, 25 (2006), 371–88.

Chapter 9 Episodes of Conflict, 800–60 BC

There are two books devoted to the British Iron Age: B. Cunliffe's *Iron Age Britain* (London, 1995), and a much more detailed book by the same author, *Iron Age Communities in Britain* (4th edn, London, 2005). Recent regional surveys include D. Harding, *The Iron Age in Northern Britain* (London, 2004); J. Henderson, *The Atlantic Iron Age* (London, 2007); B. Raftery, *Pagan Celtic Ireland: The Enigma of the Irish Iron Age* (London, 1994); and N. Sharples, *Social Relations in Later Prehistory: Wessex in the First Millennium BC* (Oxford, 2010). There are also several useful collections of specialist papers that give a flavour of current research, among them C. Haselgrove and R. Pope (eds.), *The Earlier Iron Age in Britain and the Near Continent* (Oxford, 2007); C. Haselgrove and T. Moore (eds.), *The Later Iron Age in Britain and Beyond* (Oxford, 2007); and O. Davis, N. Sharples, and K. Waddington (eds.), *Changing Perspectives on the First Millennium BC* (Oxford, 2008).

The changes in bronze use and deposition in the transition period from the Late Bronze to Early Iron Age have recently been considered in three important papers that render much of the earlier discussion out of date: S. Gerloff, 'Hallstatt Fascination: Hallstatt Buckets, Swords and Chapes from Britain and Ireland', in H. Roche et al. (eds.), *From Megaliths to Metals: Essays in Honour of George Eogan* (Oxford, 2004), 124–54; S. Needham, '800 BC: The Great Divide', in C. Haselgrove and R. Pope (eds.), *The Earlier Iron Age in Britain and the Near Continent* (Oxford, 2007), 39–63; and B. O'Connor, 'Llyn Fawr Metalwork in Britain: A Review', in the same volume, 64–79.

I have said comparatively little in this chapter about the rural economy and the different patterns of land use and settlement across the country. These issues are given extended treatment in B. Cunliffe, *Iron Age Communities in Britain* (4th edn, London, 2005), chs. 12–16, and for central southern Britain are considered in the same author's 'Wessex Cowboys', *Oxford Journal of Archaeology*, 23 (2004), 61–81. Details of Iron Age houses are meticulously presented in D. Harding, *The Iron Age Round-House: Later Prehistoric Building in Britain and Beyond* (Oxford, 2009), while a number of the early hill-top enclosures are described in A. Payne, M. Corney, and B. Cunliffe, *The Wessex Hillforts Project* (London, 2006). The evidence from Balksbury, which is specifically referred to, is published in C. J. Ellis and M. Rawlings, 'Excavations at Balksbury Camp, Andover 1995–97', *Proceedings of the Hampshire Field Club and Archaeological Society*, 56 (2001), 21–94. Regional variety across the British Isles is best appreciated by reference to the general works noted in the first paragraph of this section.

Contemporary events in Europe are summarized in B. Cunliffe, *Europe between the Oceans, 9000 BC–AD 1000* (New Haven, 2008), chs. 9 and 10. La Tène art in Britain is treated in detail in E. M. Jope, *Early Celtic Art in the British Isles* (Oxford, 2000), and is discussed thematically in C. Gosden, D. Garrow, and J. D. Hill (eds.), *Rethinking Celtic Art* (Oxford, 2008).

The significance of the Breton route for the transmission of La Tène art to Britain is considered in B. Cunliffe, 'Social and Economic Contact between Western France and Britain in the Early and Middle La Tène Period', *Revue Archéologique de l'Ouest* (1990), suppl. 2, 245–51. La Tène art in Ireland is presented in B. Raftery, *Pagan Celtic Ireland: The Enigma of the Irish Iron Age* (London, 1994).

The southern North Sea cultural zone is introduced in B. Cunliffe, 'Looking Forward: Maritime Contacts in the First Millennium BC', in P. Clark (ed.), *Bronze Age Connections: Cultural Contact in Prehistoric Europe* (Oxford, 2009), 80–93. The Yorkshire vehicle burials have been frequently considered most thoroughly in I. Stead, *The Arras Culture* (York, 1979); the same author's *Iron Age Cemeteries in East Yorkshire* (London, 1991); and J. S. Dent, 'Three Cart Burials from Wetwang, Yorkshire', *Antiquity*, 59 (1985), 85–92. For a broader assessment of the cultural context, see J. S. Dent, *The Iron Age in East Yorkshire* (Oxford, 2010). The recently discovered vehicle burial from Edinburgh is presented in S. Carter, F. Hunter, and A. Smith, 'A 5th Century BC Iron Age Chariot Burial from Newbridge, Edinburgh', *Proceedings of the Prehistoric Society*, 76 (2010), 31–74.

The journey of Pytheas is reconstructed in B. Cunliffe, *The Extraordinary Voyage of Pytheas the Great* (London, 2001). For the archaeology of Mount Batten, see B. Cunliffe, *Mount Batten, Plymouth: A Prehistoric and Roman Port* (Oxford, 1988), and for tin ingots, A. Fox, 'Tin Ingots from Bigbury Bay, South Devon', *Devon Archaeological Societies Proceedings*, 53 (1997), 11–23.

The question of increasing aggression in the Middle Iron Age has been frequently debated. A selection of the anatomical evidence is examined in R. Craig, C. J. Knüsel, and G. Carr, 'Fragmentation, Mutilation and Dismemberment: An Interpretation of Human Remains on Iron Age Sites', in M. Parker Pearson and N. Thorpe (eds.), *Warfare, Violence and Slavery in Prehistory* (Oxford, 2005), 165–80. The relevance of hill-forts to increased aggression has been doubted by some, for example, M. Bowden and D. McOmish, 'The Required Barrier', *Scottish Archaeological Review*, 4 (1987), 76–84, and the same authors' 'Little Boxes: More about Hillforts', *Scottish Archaeological Review*, 6 (1989), 12–16; but the case for hill-forts as a response to warfare has been convincingly restated in I. Armit, 'Hillforts at War: From Maiden Castle to Taniwaha Pā', *Proceedings of the Prehistoric Society*, 73 (2007), 25–37.

The evidence for social and commercial relations between Britain and the Continent in the second and first centuries BC is extensive. The Gallo-Belgic coinage has been exhaustively studied by J. Sills in *Gaulish and Early British Gold Coinage* (London, 2003). The archaeological evidence from the excavation on Hengistbury

Head is published in detail in B. Cunliffe, *Hengistbury Head, Dorset*, i: *Prehistoric and Roman Settlement, 3500 BC–AD 500* (Oxford, 1987), and its implications are further discussed in B. Cunliffe and P. de Jersey, *Armorica and Britain: Cross-Channel Relationships in the Late First Millennium BC* (Oxford, 1993). The trading port at Nacqueville is described in A. Lefort and C. Marcigny, 'Reprise des études sur le site âge du Fer d'Urville-Nacqueville: Bilan documentaire et perspectives de recherche', in C. Marcigny et al. (eds.), *Archéologie, histoire et anthropologie de la presqu'île de La Hague* (Caen, 2008), 63–123. The distribution of Dressel amphorae was conveniently brought together in A. Fitzpatrick, 'The Distribution of Dressel I Amphorae in North-West Europe', *Oxford Journal of Archaeology*, 4 (1985), 305–40, now updated in M. E. Loughton, 'The Distribution of Republican Amphorae in France', *Oxford Journal of Archaeology*, 22 (2003), 177–207. For the question of the Belgic migration to Britain, see B. Cunliffe, 'Relations between Britain and Gaul in the First Century BC to Early First Century AD', in S. Macready and F. H. Thompson (eds.), *Cross-Channel Trade between Gaul and Britain in the Pre-Roman Iron Age* (London, 1984), 3–23.

For the Irish royal sites, an excellent summary is provided in J. Waddell, *The Prehistoric Archaeology of Ireland* (4th edn, Galway, 2010), 339–74. For reports on the individual sites: C. J. Lynn, *Excavations at Navan Fort 1961–71 by D. M. Waterman* (Belfast, 1997); S. A. Johnson and B. Wailes, *Dún Ailinne: Excavations at an Irish Royal Site, 1968–1975* (Philadelphia, 2007); J. Waddell, J. Fenwick, and K. Barton, *Rathcroghan: Archaeological and Geophysical Survey in a Ritual Landscape* (Dublin, 2009); C. Newman, *Tara: An Archaeological Survey* (Dublin, 1997); H. Roche, 'Excavation at Ráith na Ríg, Tara, Co. Meath, 1997', *Discovery Programme Reports*, 6 (2002), 19–165; and E. Grogan, *The Rath of the Synods, Tara, Co. Meath: Excavations by Seán P. Ó. Ríordáin* (Dublin, 2008).

Chapter 10 Interlude: Approaching the Gods

There is no lack of literature on the ancient Druids. The classic work is S. Piggott, *The Druids* (London, 1968). Among the more recent works are M. Aldhouse-Green, *Caesar's Druids: Story of an Ancient Priesthood* (New Haven, 2010), the same author's more popular illustrated account (under the name of M. J. Green), *Exploring the World of the Druids* (London, 1997); R. Hutton, *The Druids* (London, 2007), which continues the story with a lively consideration of the more recent Druids; and B. Cunliffe, *Druids: A Very Short Introduction* (Oxford, 2010), for those with little time. An excellent summary account of Iron Age religion in Ireland is given by M.-L. Sjoestedt, *Gods and Heroes of the Celts* (Dublin, 1994).

Two useful volumes dealing specifically with the archaeology of religious practices in Britain are G. Wait, *Ritual and Religion in Iron Age Britain* (Oxford, 1985), and

R. Whimster, *Burial Practices in Iron Age Britain* (Britain, 1981). The question of special deposits is discussed in B. Cunliffe, *Fertility, Propitiation and the Gods in the British Iron Age* (Amsterdam, 1993), and J. D. Hill, *Ritual and Rubbish in the Iron Age of Wessex* (Oxford, 1995).

To follow up specific sites and discoveries mentioned in the chapter, see P. Ashbee, M. Bell, and E. Proudfoot, *Wilsford Shaft: Excavations 1960–62* (London, 1989); I. M. Stead, J. B. Bourke, and D. Brothwell, *Lindow Man: The Body in the Bog* (London, 1986); C. F. Fox, *A Find of the Early Iron Age from Llyn Cerrig Bach, Anglesey* (Cardiff, 1946); B. Cunliffe, *Danebury Hillfort* (London, 2003); I. M. Stead, 'The Snettisham Treasure: Excavations in 1991', *Antiquity*, 65 (1991), 447–65; N. Field and M. Parker Pearson, *Fiskerton: An Iron Age Timber Causeway with Iron Age and Roman Votive Offerings* (Oxford, 2003); and F. M. M. Pryor, *Flag Fen: Prehistoric Fenland Centre* (London, 1991).

Chapter 11   Integration: The Roman Episode, 60 BC–AD 350

The literature on Roman Britain is massive, though this is hardly surprising given the amount of energy that has been expended on the subject over the last three hundred years. If only one book is to be chosen, the reader cannot do better than David Mattingley's *An Imperial Possession: Britain in the Roman Empire* (London, 2006), a stimulating, up-to-date, and informative text that challenges many of the old preconceptions; the forty-page bibliographical essay alone is a superb resource. Of the other standard textbooks, S. S. Frere, *Britannia: A History of Roman Britain* (3rd edn, London, 1987), provides an elegantly written narrative. Other volumes offering different perspectives, all of which can be strongly recommended, are P. Salway, *Roman Britain* (Oxford, 1981); the same author's *The Oxford Illustrated History of Roman Britain* (Oxford, 1993); M. Todd, *Roman Britain (55 BC–AD 400)* (2nd edn, Oxford, 1997); M. Todd (ed.), *A Companion to Roman Britain* (Oxford, 2004); M. Millett, *The Romanization of Britain: An Essay in Archaeological Interpretation* (Cambridge, 1990); R. J. A. Wilson, *A Guide to the Roman Remains in Britain* (4th edn, London, 2002); and B. Jones and D. Mattingly, *An Atlas of Roman Britain* (repr. Oxford, 2002).

The campaigns of Julius Caesar are best approached from Caesar's own brilliant account in his *Bellum Gallicum*, supplemented by reading the sensible and balanced assessment by Sheppard Frere in *Britannia: A History of Roman Britain* (3rd edn, London, 1987). The native political scene, in so far as it can be deduced from the texts, coinage, and archaeological data, is explored in J. Creighton, *Britannia: The Creation of a Roman Province* (London, 2006), and the same author's *Coins and Power in Late Iron Age Britain* (Cambridge, 2000). The development of trade between Britain and the Continent is considered in various papers in S. Macready and F. H. Thompson (eds.),

Cross-Channel Trade between Gaul and Britain in the Pre-Roman Iron Age (London, 1984), and B. Cunliffe and P. de Jersey, *Armorica and Britain: Cross-Channel Relationships in the Late First Millennium BC* (Oxford, 1997). A summary of the different tribal configurations in Britain at the time of the invasion will be found in B. Cunliffe, *Iron Age Communities in Britain* (4th edn, London, 2005), 125–219.

The invasion and subsequent campaigning in Britain has been thoroughly treated in the books listed in the first paragraph of this section. A more detailed treatment of the Claudian conquest, the geography of which has recently been much debated, is given in M. Todd, 'The Claudian Conquest and its Consequences', in M. Todd (ed.), *A Companion to Roman Britain* (Oxford, 2004), 42–59. The military campaigns in Wales are conveniently summed up by W. Manning in 'The Conquest of Wales' in the same volume, 60–74, and by J. Davies in 'Soldier and Civilian in Wales', 91–113. For the campaigns in the northern frontier zones: D. J. Breeze, *Roman Scotland* (London, 1996); G. Maxwell, *A Battle Lost: Romans and Caledonians at Mons Graupius* (Edinburgh, 1990); and A. R. Birley, 'Britain 71–105: Advance and Retrenchment', in L. de Ligt et al. (eds.), *Roman Rule and Civic Life: Local and Regional Perspectives* (Amsterdam, 2004), 97–112. Concise and invaluable summaries of the two northern frontiers will be found in D. J. Breeze, *J. Collingwood Bruce's Handbook to the Roman Wall* (4th edn, Newcastle, 2006), and the same author's *The Antonine Wall* (Edinburgh, 2006).

The Roman army in its civilian context is treated in a number of papers in A. Goldsworthy and I. Haynes, *The Roman Army as a Community* (Portsmouth, RI, 1999), and in P. A. Holder, *The Roman Army in Britain* (London, 1982). The remarkable Vindolanda letters are used to enliven Roman frontier life in A. R. Birley, *Garrison Life at Vindolanda: A Band of Brothers* (Stroud, 2003), and A. K. Bowman, *Life and Letters on the Roman Frontier: Vindolanda and its People* (London, 2003). For the *coloniae*, see H. Hurst (ed.), *The Coloniae of Roman Britain: New Studies and a Review* (Portsmouth, RI, 1999). Several papers in S. James and M. Millett (eds.), *Britons and Romans* (York, 2001), deal with matters of social integration.

On the people of Roman Britain glimpsed principally from inscriptions, the most accessible text is A. R. Birley, *The People of Roman Britain* (London, 1979). The same author's *The Roman Government of Britain* (Oxford, 2005) provides the broader context. The community in Bath is described in B. Cunliffe, *Roman Bath Discovered* (4th edn, Stroud, 2000), while the remarkable collection of inscribed curses from the sacred spring is presented in R. S. O. Tomlin, 'The Curse Tablets', in B. Cunliffe (ed.), *The Temple of Sulis Minerva at Bath*, ii: *The Finds from the Sacred Spring* (Oxford, 1988), 59–277.

Of the shipwrecks mentioned, the St Peter Port wreck and its cargo are fully described in M. Rule and J. Monaghan, *A Gallo-Roman Trading Vessel from Guernsey* (St Peter Port, 1993), while the Sept-Îles wreck discovered off the northern coast of

Brittany is published in M. L'Hour, 'Un Site sous-marin sur la côde l'Armorique: L'épave antique de Ploumanac'h', *Revue Archéologique de l'Ouest*, 4 (1987), 113–32. Recent scientific analysis of human skeletal remains with the view to studying population mobility include H. Eckhardt et al., 'Isotope Evidence for Mobility in the Late Roman Cemetery at Lankhills, Winchester', *Journal of Archaeological Science*, 36 (2009), 2816–25; S. M. Leach et al., 'Migration and Diversity in Roman Britain: A Multidisciplinary Approach to Immigrants in Roman York, England', *American Journal of Physical Anthropology*, 140 (2009), 546–61, and C. A. Chenery et al., 'Strontium and Stable Isotope Evidence for Diet and Mobility in Roman Gloucester, UK', *Journal of Archaeological Science*, 37 (2010), 150–63.

For Ireland, P. Freeman, *Ireland and the Classical World* (Austin, 2001), provides an excellent introduction. Roman material found in Ireland was reviewed in J. D. Bateson, 'Roman Material from Ireland: A Re-Examination', *Proceedings of the Royal Irish Academy*, 73C (1973), 21–97, and a number of papers on British–Irish relations in the Roman period were published as *Colloquium on Hiberno-Roman Relations and Material Remains, Proceedings of the Royal Irish Academy*, 76C (1976). The important finds at Drumanagh are still not published, but the site is considered in B. Raftery, 'Drumanagh and Roman Ireland', *Archaeology Ireland*, 35 (1996), 17–19. Roman material found in the elite settlement of Tara is discussed in E. Grogan (ed.), *The Rath of the Synods, Tara, Co. Meath: Excavations by Sean P. Ó'Ríordáin* (Dublin, 2008).

The Carausian episode is fully examined in P. J. Casey, *Carausius and Allectus: The British Usurpers* (London, 1994), and H. P. G. Williams, *Carausius: A Consideration of the Historical, Archaeological and Numismatic Aspects of his Reign* (Oxford, 2003). The Roman coastal defences have been considered on a number of occasions, most usefully in S. Johnson, *The Roman Forts of the Saxon Shore* (London, 1979); V. A. Maxfield (ed.), *The Saxon Shore: A Handbook* (Exeter, 1989); and A. Pearson, *The Roman Shore Forts: Coastal Defences in Southern Britain* (Stroud, 2002).

There is a huge literature on town and countryside. The classic introductory text is A. L. F. Rivet, *Town and Country in Roman Britain* (2nd edn, London, 1995). For towns, the basic work is J. Wacher, *The Towns of Roman Britain* (2nd edn, London, 1995). Recent compilations include S. Greep (ed.), *Roman Towns: The Wheeler Inheritance: A Review of 50 Years' Research* (York, 1993), and P. Wilson (ed.), *The Archaeology of Roman Towns: Studies in Honour of John S. Wacher* (Oxford, 2003). The smaller settlements are conveniently considered in B. C. Burnham and J. S. Wacher, *The Small Towns of Roman Britain* (London, 1990). For the countryside, R. Hingley, *Rural Settlement in Roman Britain* (London, 1989), is essential reading. Roman villas have been considered in general works from time to time, most comprehensively in A. L. F. Rivet (ed.), *The Roman Villa in Britain* (London, 1969); M. Todd (ed.), *Studies in the Romano-British Villa* (Leicester, 1978); and J. T. Smith, *The Roman Villa* (London, 1998).

Chapter 12   'Its Red and Savage Tongue', AD 350–650

Since this chapter covers both the Roman and early Saxon period, the general books on Roman Britain listed at the beginning of the guide to further reading for Chapter 11 are also relevant to Chapter 12. To them we may add three general works specifically covering the late Roman period: S. Johnson, *Later Roman Britain* (St Albans, 1978); S. Esmonde Cleary, *The Ending of Roman Britain* (London, 1989); and N. Faulkner, *The Decline and Fall of Roman Britain* (Stroud, 2000). Also strongly recommended are two thought-provoking chapters in M. Todd (ed.), *A Companion to Roman Britain* (Oxford, 2004): S. Esmond Cleary, 'Britain in the Fourth Century', 409–27, and I. Wood, 'The Final Phase', 428–42. General literature on the early Saxon period is equally extensive. The classic text, now somewhat out of date but still essential reading, is J. N. L. Myres, *The English Settlements* (Oxford, 1986). An up-to-date contemporary view is provided by R. Fleming, *Britain after Rome: The Fall and Rise, 400–1070* (London, 2010), a major text with an extensive and well-structured bibliography. Other general accounts, all offering differing insights, include J. Campbell, E. John, and P. Wormald (eds.), *The Anglo-Saxons* (Harmondsworth, 1991); E. James, *Britain in the First Millennium* (Oxford, 2001); B. York, *Kings and Kingdoms of Early Anglo-Saxon England* (3rd edn, Cambridge, 2003); M. Welch, *Anglo-Saxon England* (London, 1992); L. Alcock, *Arthur's Britain* (London, 1971); and C. A. Snyder, *An Age of Tyrants: Britain and the Britons AD 400–600* (Oxford, 1998). Essential reading for anyone interested in the Anglo-Saxons is the massive compendium, H. Hamerow, D. A. Hinton, and S. Crawford (eds), *The Oxford Handbook of Anglo-Saxon Archaeology* (Oxford, 2011).

The political and military machinations during the last decade of Roman Britain are thoroughly covered in a number of papers, among which the following helpfully discuss the province in its European context: E. A. Thompson, 'Britain AD 406–10', *Britannia*, 8 (1977), 303–18; I. A. Wood, 'The Fall of the Western Empire and the end of Roman Britain', *Britannia*, 18 (1987), 351–62; J. F. Drinkwater, 'The Usurpers Constantine III (407–411) and Jovinus (411–413)', *Britannia*, 29 (1998), 269–9; and M. Kulikowski, 'Barbarians in Gaul, Usurpers in Britain', *Britannia*, 31 (2000), 325–45. The drying up of the money supply has been carefully analysed in P. Guest, *The Late Roman Gold and Silver Coins from the Hoxne Treasure* (London, 2005), while the end of towns is considered in D. A. Brooks, 'A Review of the Evidence for Continuity in British Towns in the Fifth and Sixth Centuries', *Oxford Journal of Archaeology*, 5 (1986), 77–102.

The nature and intensity of the Anglo-Saxon settlement has been, and still is, a much-debated issue and the most convenient place to start is with Noel Myres's seminal account *The English Settlements* (Oxford, 1986). What follows is a selection of more recent works that take the debate forward. The use of *foederati* in Britain is considered in M. Welch, 'The Archaeological Evidence for Federate Settlement in Britain within the Fifth Century', in F. Vallet and M. Kazanski (eds.), *L'Armée romaine et des barbares du IIIe au VIIe siècle* (Paris, 1993), 269–78. The same author tackles the difficult question of chronology in 'Relating Anglo-Saxon Chronology to Continental Chronologies in the Fifth Century AD', in U. von Freeden, U. Koch, and A. Wieczorek (eds.), *Volker an Nord- und Ostsee und die Franken* (Bonn, 1999), 31–8, while the broader issues of chronology are considered by various authors in R. Collins and J. Gerrard (eds.), *Debating Late Antiquity in Britain AD 300–700* (Oxford, 2004). The use of textual evidence, crucial to an understanding of the Germanic settlement, is briefly considered in B. York, 'Fact or Fiction? The Written Evidence for the Fifth and Sixth Centuries AD', *Anglo-Saxon Studies in Archaeology and History*, 6 (1993), 45–50. The all-important question of settlement is discussed in its broader context in H. Hamerow, *Early Medieval Settlements: The Archaeology of Rural Communities in North-West Europe, 400–900* (Oxford, 2002). The nature of the burial evidence is usefully summarized in S. J. Lucy, *The Anglo-Saxon Way of Death: Burial Rites in Early England* (Stroud, 2000). Pottery styles, which have featured so large in discussions of the Anglo-Saxons, can be approached through J. N. L. Myres, *Anglo-Saxon Pottery and the Settlement of England* (Oxford, 1969), though it is as well to remember that pottery studies have developed over the last forty years.

Two interesting papers that demonstrate well how archaeologists attempt to construct history from the archaeological and literary evidence are S. C. Hawkes, 'The South-East after the Romans: The Saxon Settlement', in V. Maxfield (ed.), *The Saxon Shore: A Handbook* (Exeter, 1989), 78–95, and the same author's 'The Early Saxon Period', in G. Briggs, J. Cook, and T. Rowley (eds.), *The Archaeology of the Oxford Region* (Oxford 1986), 64–108. Finally, for an assessment of the Frankish contribution to the early settlement, see V. I. Evison, *The Fifth-Century Invasions South of the Thames* (London, 1965).

The actual numbers involved in the migration have been the subject of lively debate. The subject was briefly reviewed in H. Härke, 'Kings and Warriors: Population and Landscape from Post-Roman to Norman Britain', in P. Slack and R. Ward (eds.), *The Peopling of Britain: The Shaping of a Human Landscape* (Oxford, 2002), 145–75. A rather fuller discussion is given in S. Oppenheimer, *The Origins of the British* (London, 2006), chs. 9–11, using mainly the genetic evidence. For an archaeologist's view of the value of the genetic evidence, see C. Hills, 'Anglo-Saxon DNA', in D. Sayer and H. Williams (eds.), *Mortuary Practices and Social Identities in the Middle Ages: Essays in Burial Archaeology in Honour of Heinrich Härke* (Exeter, 2009), 123–40. The number of immigrants and the degree or otherwise of their integration is being debated in the pages of the *Proceedings of the Royal Society*. Three papers have so far been published: M. G. Thomas, M. P. H. Stumpf, and H. Härke, 'Evidence for an Apartheid-like Social Structure in Early Anglo-Saxon England', *Proceedings of the Royal Society*, B273 (2006), 2651–7; J. E. Pattison, 'Is it Necessary to Assume an Apartheid-like Social Structure in Early Anglo-Saxon England?', *Proceedings of the Royal Society*, B275 (2008), 2412–18; and the original authors' reply, 'Integration versus Apartheid in Post-Roman Britain: A Response to Pattison', in the same journal, 2419–21. A thorough discussion of the size and import of the invasion, balancing a variety of evidence, is given in H. Härke's important paper 'Anglo-Saxon Immigration and Ethnogenesis', *Medieval Archaeology*, 55 (2011), 1–28.

The importance of the North Sea for the movement of people and commodities is thoroughly treated in F. M. Morris, *North Sea and Channel Connectivity during the Late Iron Age and Roman Period (175/150 BC–AD 409)* (Oxford, 2010).

For the British West, Leslie Alcock's *Arthur's Britain* (London, 1971) provides a valuable, if dated, introduction. Gildas as a source is discussed in M. Lapidge and D. N. Dumville, *Gildas: New Approaches* (Woodbridge, 1984), and P. Sims-Williams, 'Gildas and the Anglo-Saxons', *Cambridge Medieval Celtic Studies*, 6 (1983), 1–30. The reuse of hill-forts in the west is reviewed in I. C. G. Burrow, *Hillfort and Hill-Top Settlement in Somerset in the First to the Eighth Centuries AD* (Oxford, 1981). For details of some of the important sites of this period that have been excavated, see P. Barker et al., *The Baths Basilica Wroxeter: Excavations 1966–90* (London, 1997); P. Rahtz, A. Woodward, and I. Burrow, *Cadbury Congresbury 1968–73: A Late/Post-Roman Hilltop Settlement in Somerset* (Oxford, 1992); L. Alcock, *'By South Cadbury, Is that Camelot?': Excavations at Cadbury Castle 1966–70* (London, 1972); and R. C. Barrowman, C. E. Batey, and C. D. Morris, *Excavations at Tintagel Castle, Cornwall, 1990–1999* (London, 2007).

The question of the British migration to Armorica is most clearly summed up in N. K. Chadwick, *Early Brittany* (Cardiff, 1969), and put into a broader context in P. Galliou and M. Jones, *The Bretons* (Oxford, 1991). The most recent and most thorough reconsideration is C. Brett, 'Soldiers, Saints, and States? The Breton Migrations Reunited', *Cambrian Medieval Celtic Studies*, 61 (2011), 1–56. The issues surrounding the origin and development of the Breton language are explained in F. Broudic, *Histoire de la langue bretonne* (Rennes, 1999). The classic text on the subject is L. Fleuriot, *Les Origines de la Bretagne* (Paris, 1982), which is based heavily on the historical and linguistic evidence. The archaeological evidence receives a full treatment in P.-R. Giot, P. Guigon, and B. Merdrignac, *The British Settlement of Brittany: The First Bretons in Armorica* (Stroud, 2003).

The background to Irish history of the period is well presented in D. O'Corráin, *Ireland before the Normans* (Dublin, 1972), while the relevant archaeological evidence is surveyed in H. Mytum, *The Origins of Early Christian Ireland* (London, 1992). The Irish settlements in Wales are discussed in H. Mytum, 'Across the Irish Sea: Romano-British and Irish Settlement in Wales', *Emania*, 13 (1995), 15–22, and R. Rance, 'Attacotti, Déisi and Magnus Maximus: The Case for Irish Federates in Late Roman Britain', *Britannia*, 32 (2001), 243–70. The hoards of late Roman silver-work in Ireland are listed in S. P. Ó'Ríordáin, 'Roman Material in Ireland', *Proceedings of the Royal Irish Academy*, 51C (1947), 35–82, and J. D. Bateson, 'Roman Material from Ireland: A Re-Examination', *Proceedings of the Royal Irish Academy*, 73C (1973), 21–97.

The question of the Scotti and the kingdom of Dál Riata is addressed in E. Campbell, *Saints and Sea-Kings: The First Kingdom of the Scots* (Edinburgh, 1999), and by the same author in 'Were the Scots Irish?', *Antiquity*, 75 (2001), 285–92. Scotland in the post-Roman period has been the subject of a large number of recent works, including B. E. Crawford (ed.), *Scotland in Dark Age Europe* (St Andrews, 1994); S. M. Foster, *Picts, Gaels and Scots: Early Historic Scotland* (London, 1996); and W. A. Cummins, *The Age of the Picts* (Gloucester, 1995); T. Clarkson, *The Picts: A History* (Edinburgh, 2012) and *The Men of the North: The Britons of Southern Scotland* (Edinburgh, 2010); S. McHardy, *A New History of the Picts* (Edinburgh, 2010); and S. Driscoll, J. Geddes, and M. Hall (eds), *Pictish Progress: New Studies on Northern Britain in the Early Middle Ages* (Leiden, 2011). The archaeological evidence, particularly the details of post-Roman age settlements, is reviewed in D. W. Harding, *The Iron Age in Northern Britain: Celts and Romans, Natives and Invaders* (London, 2004).

The Atlantic seaways and the spread of Christianity are given full treatment in E. Bowen, *Saints, Seaways and Settlements* (Cardiff, 1977), and J. Wooding, *Communication and Commerce along the Western Sea Lanes, AD 400–800* (Oxford, 1996). Imported goods travelling along the Atlantic seaways into western Britain are discussed in detail in E. Campbell, *Continental and Mediterranean Imports to Atlantic Britain and Ireland, AD 400–800* (York, 2007). A useful brief introduction to early Irish Christianity remains M. and L. de Paor, *Early Christian Ireland* (London, 1958), but for some more recent debates, see M. Ryan (ed.), *Ireland and Insular Art, AD 500–1200* (Dublin, 1987).

Chapter 13   The Age of the Northmen, AD 600–1100

The reordering of Europe and its systems of connectivity after the fall of the Roman empire has been the subject of a massive literature in recent years. The most comprehensive text dealing with the European-wide issues is the magisterial work by M. McCormick, *Origins of the European Economy: Communications and Commerce, AD*

300–900 (Cambridge, 2001), an essential book of reference. A somewhat easier way into the subject is R. Hodges, *Dark Age Economics: The Origins of Towns and Trade*, AD *600–1000* (London, 1982), and the same author's updating review *Towns and Trade in the Age of Charlemagne* (London, 2000). The archaeology of early marketing, principally in Britain and the near Continent, is discussed in a number of contributions in T. Pestell and K. Ulmschneider (eds.), *Markets in Early Medieval Europe: Trading and 'Productive' Sites, 650–850* (Macclesfield, 2003). More specific works dealing with the near Continent include E. James, *The Franks* (Oxford, 1988), and R. Collins, *Charlemagne* (London, 1998), while for Britain outside the Anglo-Saxon sphere, W. Davies, *Wales in the Middle Ages* (Leicester, 1982), and L. Alcock, *The Neighbours of the Picts: Angles, Britons and Scots at War and at Home* (Rosemarkie, 1993), provide the essential background. For the maritime perspective, J. Haywood, *Dark Age Naval Power* (repr. Hockwold-cum-Wilton, 2006), is invaluable.

The Vikings, who are major players in this chapter, are very well catered for in the extensive literature. Among the most accessible, though still meticulously researched, volumes are J. Graham-Campbell (ed.), *Cultural Atlas of the Viking World* (2nd edn, London, 1989), and P. Sawyer (ed.), *The Oxford Illustrated History of the Vikings* (Oxford, 1997). Also strongly to be recommended, particularly for its superb maps, is J. Haywood, *The Penguin Historical Atlas of the Vikings* (London, 1995), a particularly valuable guide for those wanting to follow the movements of raiding parties and armies. For regional studies, A. Ritchie, *Viking Scotland* (London, 1993); J. Graham-Campbell and C. E. Batey, *Vikings in Scotland: An Archaeological Survey* (Edinburgh, 1998); D. Griffiths, *Vikings of the Irish Sea* (Stroud, 2010); and J. R. Richards, *Viking Age England* (2nd edn, Stroud, 2004), provide full accounts. A collection of congress papers edited by C. Batey, J. Jesch, and C. Morris, *The Viking Age in Caithness, Orkney and the North Atlantic* (Edinburgh, 1993), offers further detail. For Ireland, important contributions are contained in H. Clarke (ed.), *Medieval Dublin: The Making of a Metropolis* (Dublin, 1990). The wonderfully preserved buildings of Viking Dublin are given detailed publication in P. F. Wallace, *The Viking Age Buildings of Dublin* (Dublin, 1992). The fascinating question of the ethnic aspirations of the mixed populations of the Danelaw seen through female dress and brooches is carefully examined in J. F. Kershaw, 'Culture and Gender in the Danelaw: Scandinavian and Anglo-Scandinavian Brooches', *Viking and Medieval Scandinavia*, 5 (2009), 295–325.

Ships of the Viking age have an extensive literature of their own. The classic work is A. Brøgger and H. Shetelig, *The Viking Ships: Their Ancestry and Evolution* (Oslo, 1951), but many new finds have been made over the last sixty years. Two of the more important reviews are O. Crumlin-Pedersen, *Viking-Age Ships and Shipbuilding in Hedeby/Haithabu and Schleswig* (Schleswig, 1997), and the same author's wonderfully comprehensive *Archaeology and the Sea in Scandinavia and Britain* (Roskilde, 2010), especially ch. 4.

The latter part of the chapter deals largely with the Viking settlement of England. One of the principal sources for the historical events of the period is the Anglo-Saxon Chronicle. An excellent translation is to be found in D. Whitlock, *The Anglo-Saxon Chronicle: A Revised Translation* (2nd edn, London, 1965). For the history of the period, there are a number of good books, of which the most recent are W. Davies (ed.), *Short Oxford History of the British Isles: From the Vikings to the Normans* (Oxford, 2003); J. Graham-Campbell et al. (eds.), *Vikings and the Danelaw* (Oxford, 2001); R. P. Abels, *Alfred the Great: War, Kingship and Culture in Anglo-Saxon England* (London, 1998); and D. M. Hadley and J. D. Richards (eds.), *Cultures in Contact: Scandinavian Settlement in England in the Ninth and Tenth Centuries* (Turnhout, 2000). The specific question of the defended burhs is extensively examined in D. Hill and A. R. Rumble (eds.), *The Defence of Wessex: The Burghal Hidage and Anglo-Saxon Fortifications* (Manchester, 1996). For the reigns of the later Saxon kings, see N. J. Higham and D. H. Hill (eds.), *Edward the Elder, 899–924* (London, 2001), and D. Scragg (ed.), *Edgar, King of the English 957–975: New Interpretations* (Woodbridge, 2008). Among the recent overviews of the entire period, R. Fleming, *Britain after Rome: The Fall and Rise, 40–1070* (London, 2010), can be strongly recommended.

ILLUSTRATION SOURCES

The author and publishers wish to thank the following for their kind permission to reproduce the illustrations:

Chapter 1 opener: The Bodleian Libraries, University of Oxford, Vet. AZ c.10 p. 39; **1.1** Bibliothèque Nationale, Paris/ The Bridgeman Art Library; **1.2** © National Portrait Gallery, London; **1.3** © The British Library Board, 577.f.7, p. 69; **1.4** The Bodleian Libraries, University of Oxford, Vet. AZ c.10 p. 39; **1.5** © The British Library Board, C.83.k2; **1.6** The Bodleian Libraries, University of Oxford, Ms Top. Gen.b.52. f.2r; **1.7** The Bodleian Libraries, University of Oxford, Ms Top. Gen c.24 fols 39v–40r; **1.8** The Bodleian Libraries, University of Oxford, Ms Eng Misc. c. 323 fol 1r; **1.9** © The British Library Board, 191.e.10(2), frontispiece; **1.10** The Bodleian Libraries, University of Oxford, Douce H. Subt. 31 frontispiece; **1.11** Wiltshire Heritage Museum, Devizes; **1.12** The Bodleian Libraries, University of Oxford, Douce A. 771, XIII, plts XIV, XV; **1.13** The Geological Society of London; **1.14** Torquay Museum

Chapter 2 opener: © Natural History Museum, London; **2.1** NASA; **2.2** Author; **2.4** After C. Stringer, *Homo Britannicus* (London 2006), 82; **2.5** Various sources; **2.6** Various sources; **2.7** Mike Page; **2.8** Mark Roberts; **2.9** After C. Stringer, *Homo Britannicus*, 122; **2.10** © Natural History Museum, London; **2.11** The Bodleian Libraries, University of Oxford, Vet A6d.1112(3) plt 21; **2.12** After B. J. Coles and S. E. Rouillard, 'Doggerland: a speculative survey', *Proceedings of the Prehistoric Society* (1998), 64, fig. 7; **2.13** After B. J. Coles and S. E. Rouillard, 'Doggerland', fig. 8; **2.14** After B. Cunliffe, *Facing the Ocean: The Atlantic and its Peoples, 8000 BC–1500 AD* (2001), fig. 4.1, by permission of Oxford University Press; and after R. G. West, *Pleistocene Geology and Biology* (London, 1977); **2.15** Alastair Dawson; **2.16** After L. P. Louwe-Kooijmans, 'The Rhine/Meuse delta: Four studies in its Prehistoric Occupation and Holocene Geology', *Analecta*

Praehistorica Leidensia 7 (1974), fig. 14; and after Cunliffe, *Facing the Ocean*, fig. 4.2, by permission of Oxford University Press; **2.17** After B. J. Coles and S. E. Rouillard, 'Doggerland', figs 10 and 11; **2.18** After B. J. Coles and S. E. Rouillard, 'Doggerland', figs 10 and 11; **2.19** Author; **2.20** Author; **2.21** MDA Information Systems/Science Photo Library; **2.22** National Museum of Ireland; **2.23** © Galen Rowell/CORBIS

Chapter 3 opener © The British Library Board, 1704.b.9, Plate 8; **3.1** The Bodleian Libraries, University of Oxford, G. A. Dorset 4°4 pt.11, opp.p.103; **3.2** © The British Library Board, 1704.b.9, Plate 8; **3.3** After J. P. Williams-Freeman, *Field Archaeology as illustrated by Hampshire* (London 1915), 15; **3.4** Royal Anthropological Institute/ RAI 2756–2757 Griffith Llewellyn of Pembrokeshire at 50 years. Photographed by J. Anderson for British Association Racial Committee, vol. 1 © RAI; **3.5** The Bodleian Libraries, University of Oxford, 1902 d.86; **3.6** After E. Røyrvik, 'Western Celts? A genetic impression of Britain in Atlantic Europe' in B. Cunliffe and J. Koch, (eds.) *Celtic from the West* (Oxford, 2010), fig. 4.3; **3.7** After J. Bernard and J. Ruffie, 'Hématologie et Culture', *Annales: Économiques, Sociétés, Civilizations* 31 (1976), editions de l'EHESS; **3.8** After Martin B. Richards redrawn in C. Stringer, *Homo Britannicus*, 231; **3.9** After drawing by Martin Crampin, redrawn after S. Oppenheimer, *The Origins of the British* (London, 2006), fig. 3.6a

Chapter 4 opener: Gordon Roberts; **4.1** After P. Bahn and P. Pettitt, *Britain's Oldest Art* (London, 2009), fig. 2.15; **4.2** © Nick Barton; **4.3** After L. P. Cooper, 'Launde, a terminal Palaeolithic camp-site in the English Midlands and its North European context', *Proceedings of the Prehistoric Society* 72 (2006), fig. 1; **4.4** After J. G. D. Clark, *Excavations at Star Carr* (Cambridge, 1954); **4.5** Modified after L. P. Louise-Kooijmans et al., *The Prehistory of the Netherlands*, vol. 1 (Amsterdam, 2005), fig. B4; **4.6** Modified after C. J. Ellis et al., 'An Early Mesolithic seasonal hunting site in the Kennet Valley, southern England', *Proceedings of the Prehistoric Society* 69 (2003), 108; **4.7** After C. Conneller and T. Schadla-Hall, 'Beyond Star Carr: the Vale of Pickering in the 10th Millennium BP', *Proceedings of the Prehistoric Society* 69 (2003), 86; **4.8** (*left*) Scarborough Archaeological and Historical Society, (*right*) The Star Carr Project; **4.9** After J. G. D. Clark, *Excavations at Star Carr;* **4.10** After J. Mallory and T. McNeill, *The Archaeology of Ulster* (Belfast, 1991), figs 1–24; **4.11** After P. Mellars, *Excavations on Oronsay* (Edinburgh, 1987), figs 2.1 and 2.6; and after B. Cunliffe, *Facing the Ocean*, fig. 4.10; **4.12** After S. Mitham, 'The Mesolithic Age' in *The Oxford Illustrated History of Prehistoric Europe*, edited by B. Cunliffe (1994), illustration 'Distribution of Otoliths of Saithe' p. 114, by permission of Oxford University Press; **4.13** After data provided by Peter Woodman; **4.14** Peter Woodman; **4.15** After J. Mallory and T. McNeill, *The Archaeology of Ulster*, figs 1–14; **4.16** After D. Telford,

'The Mesolithic Inheritance: Contrasting Mesolithic monumentality in Eastern and Western Scotland', *Proceedings of the Prehistoric Society* 68 (2002), fig. 6, based on various sources; after Clarke and Griffiths (1990); after Thorpe and Thorpe (1984); and after Wickham-Jones (1986); **4.17** After B. Cunliffe, *Facing the Ocean*, fig. 4.15, by permission of Oxford University Press; and after B. Cunliffe, *Wessex to AD 1000* (London, 1993), fig. 1.11 with modifications; **4.18 and 4.19** Gordon Roberts; **4.20** (*left*) After S. Oppenheimer, *The Origins of the British*, fig. 3.5; (*right*) after S. Oppenheimer *The Origins of the British*, fig. 3.6b; **4.21** After P. Woodman and M. McCarthy, 'Contemplating some awful(ly interesting) vistas: importing cattle and red deer into prehistoric Ireland' in I. Armit et al. (eds.) *Neolithic Settlement in Ireland and Western Britain* (Oxford, 2003), fig. 4.2

Chapter 5 opener: © National Monuments Service: Dept of Arts, Heritage and the Gaeltacht, Ireland; **5.1** After B. Cunliffe, *Europe between the Oceans, 9000 BC–AD 1000* (New Haven, 2008), fig. 5.10, based on multiple sources; **5.2** © Sean Sexton Collection/CORBIS; **5.3** After E. C. Curwin, various sources; **5.4** By kind permission, Sussex Archaeological Society; **5.5** After A. Sheridan, 'Neolithic connections along and across the Irish Sea', in V. Cummings and C. Fowler (ed.) *The Neolithic of the Irish Sea* (Oxford, 2004), fig. 2.2; and after A. Sheridan, 'French Connections I: spreading the *marmites* thinly' in I. Armit et al. (eds.) *Neolithic Settlement in Ireland and Western Britain* (Oxford, 2003), fig. 2.8; **5.6** (*top*) Robin Redfern/Getty Images; (*bottom*) David Chapman/Photoshot; **5.7** (*far left*) After S. Ó Nualláin, 1972, reproduced by permission of the Royal Society of Antiquaries of Ireland; (*centre left, centre right, and far right*) redrawn from Author, multiple sources, and from Barclay & Russell-White (1993) and Barclay et al (2002); **5.8** Moira Greig, Aberdeenshire Archaeology Service; **5.9** After J. Waddell, *The Prehistoric Archaeology of Ireland* (Dublin, 2010), fig. 2.9 with amendments; **5.10** Author, redrawn after multiple sources; **5.11** © English Heritage Photo Library; **5.12** Getty Images; **5.13** After T. Kytmannow, *Portal tombs in the Landscape* (Oxford, 2008), fig. 1; **5.14** After J. Waddell, *The Prehistoric Archaeology of Ireland*, fig. 3.15; **5.15** Data from Megalithic Survey of Ireland and J. Scott, 'The Clyde cairns of Scotland' in T. G. E. Powell et al. (eds.), *Megalithic Enquiries* (Liverpool, 1969), fig. 61; **5.16** Author: various sources including J. Waddell, *The Prehistoric Archaeology of Ireland*, fig. 3.1; **5.17** After J. Waddell, *The Prehistoric Archaeology of Ireland*, fig. 3.3; **5.18** © National Monuments Service: Dept of Arts, Heritage and the Gaeltacht, Ireland; **5.19** Photograph by Ken Williams for George Eogan, Knowth Publication Project; **5.20** © National Monuments Service: Dept of Arts, Heritage and the Gaeltacht, Ireland; **5.21** (*top*) After Benson and Whittle, *Building Memories: the Neolithic Cotswold Long Barrow at Ascott-under-Wychwood* (Oxford, 2007); (*middle*) © Crown copyright illustration from *The West Kennet Long Barrow Excavations*, Ministry of Works, 196;

(*bottom*) after Alasdair Whittle, *Cambridge Archaeological Journal*, 17(1) 2007; **5.22** After A. Oswald et al., *The Creation of Monuments: Neolithic causewayed enclosures in the British Isles* (London, 2001), xii; **5.23** After B. Cunliffe, *Wessex to AD 1000*, fig. 2.5, based on various sources; **5.24** © English Heritage; **5.25** © English Heritage; **5.26** (i) After J. Waddell, *The Prehistoric Archaeology of Ireland*, fig. 2.15; (ii and iii) after Clough and Cummings, *Stone Axe Studies*, Vol 2 (London, 1988), maps 2 and 6; **5.27** After D. Peacock, 'Neolithic Pottery Production in Cornwall', *Antiquity* 43 (1969), fig. 1

Chapter 6 opener: Joe Cornish/Getty Images; **6.1** Author, multiple sources; **6.2** After B. Cunliffe, *Wessex to AD 1000*, fig. 3.3 with additions; **6.3** After B. Cunliffe, *Wessex to AD 1000*, figs 3–6, based on multiple sources; **6.4** © Crown copyright, English Heritage; **6.5** After B. Cunliffe, *Wessex to AD 1000*, figs 3–11 with additions; **6.6** Last Refuge/Getty Images; **6.7** © English Heritage; **6.8** After B. Cunliffe, *Facing the Ocean*, fig. 5.21, by permission of Oxford University Press; **6.9** Joe Cornish/Getty Images; **6.10** © Skyscan.co.uk; **6.11** After B. Cunliffe, *Wessex to AD 1000*, fig. 3.5, using multiple sources; **6.12** (*left*) After A. Burl, *Rings of Stone* (London, 1979), 13, and B. Cunliffe, *Facing the Ocean*, fig. 5.23; (*right*) after B. Cunliffe, *Facing the Ocean*, fig. 5.23, by permission of Oxford University Press; **6.13** Redrawn after S. Piggott, 'Later Neolithic' in E. Crittall (ed.), *VCH Wiltshire*, vol. 1 (London 1973), fig. 12; **6.14** Author; **6.15** Ashmolean Museum, University of Oxford/The Bridgeman Art Library; **6.16** After B. Cunliffe, *Europe between the Oceans*, fig. 7.22, based on multiple sources; **6.17** William O'Brien; **6.18** William O'Brien, courtesy National Museum of Ireland; **6.19** After William O'Brien, *Ross Island* (Galway, 2004), fig. 252; **6.20** Author: various sources; **6.21 and 6.22** Simon Timberlake, Early Mines Research Group, UK; **6.23** © The Trustees of the British Museum; **6.24** © National Museums Scotland; **6.25** After S. Needham, 'Transforming Beaker Culture in Northwest Europe: processes of fusion and fission', *Proceedings of the Prehistoric Society* 71 (2005), fig. 3; **6.26** After S. Needham, 'Transforming Beaker Culture in Northwest Europe', fig. 12; **6.27** © National Museums Scotland; **6.28** © National Museums Scotland; **6.29** Author: various sources; **6.30** © National Museums Scotland; **6.31** The author: various sources; **6.32** Redrawn from S. Piggott, 'The Wessex Culture' in E. Crittall (ed.), *VCH Wiltshire*, vol. 1 (London 1973), fig. 20; **6.33** After P. Clark (ed.) *The Dover Bronze Age Boat* (London, 2004), 5; © Canterbury Archaeological Trust Ltd; **6.34** © Canterbury Archaeological Trust Ltd; **6.35** (a) © The Trustees of the British Museum; (b) The Royal Pavilion and Museums, Brighton & Hove; (c) Royal Albert Memorial Museum & Art Gallery; **6.36** After S. Needham, 'Encompassing the Sea: "maritories" and Bronze Age maritime interactions' in P. Clark (ed.), *Bronze Age Connections: Cultural Contact in Prehistoric Europe*

(Oxford, 2009), fig. 2.5; (*inset*) Author; **6.37** Author; **6.38** After John Waddell, *The Prehistoric Archaeology of Ireland*, fig. 3.20.

Chapter 7 opener: Collection of Museu Municipal Figueira de Foz; currently in Museu da Escrita do Sudoeste Almodôvar] 136 × 73 × 15cm; Iberian First Iron Age. Drawing by Martin Crampin and John Koch, University of Wales; after J. Koch, 'Paradigm Shift? Interpreting Tartessian as Celtic' in B. Cunliffe and J. Koch, *Celtic from the West*, 210; **7.1** After Q. Atkinson et al. (2005), from 'Words to Dates: Water into wine, mathemagic or phylogenetic inference?', *Transactions of the Philological Society* 103 (2005), fig. 2.15; **7.2** After S. Oppenheimer, *The Origins of the British*, fig. 2.1b, based on data from Patrick Sims-Williams (2006); **7.3** After B. Cunliffe, 'Celticization from the West: the contribution of archaeology' in B. Cunliffe and J. Koch, *Celtic from the West*, fig. 1.3; **7.4** Collection of Museu Municipal Figueira de Foz; currently in Museu da Escrita do Sudoeste Almodôvar] 136 × 73 × 15cm; Iberian First Iron Age. Drawing by Martin Crampin and John Koch, University of Wales; after J. Koch, 'Paradigm Shift? Interpreting Tartessian as Celtic' in B. Cunliffe and J. Koch, *Celtic from the West*, 210; **7.5** Author

Chapter 8 opener: © English Heritage; **8.1** After B. Cunliffe, *Iron Age Communities in Britain* (London, 2004), fig. 3.10; **8.2** After Smith, Coppen, Wainwright, and Beckett, *Proceedings of the Prehistoric Society* (1981); after B. Cunliffe, *Iron Age Communities in Britain* (London, 2004), fig. 3.17; **8.3** © English Heritage; **8.4** After B. Cunliffe, *Iron Age Communities in Britain*, figs 3.2 and 3.7; **8.5** © Crown copyright, English Heritage; **8.6** After B. Cunliffe, *Iron Age Communities in Britain*, fig. 3.6; **8.7** Aoife Daly, from E. Grogan (ed.), *The North Munster Project* (Dublin, 2005); **8.8** (*top left*, *top right*, and *bottom left*) Author: various sources; (*bottom right*) after B. Raftery; **8.9** Mike Baillie in M. Baillie, *A Slice Through Time* (London, 1995), fig. 4.22; **8.10** After D. Yates and R. Bradley, 'Still waters, hidden depths: redeposition of Bronze Age metalwork in the English Fenland', *Antiquity* 84 (2010), fig. 2; **8.11** © The Trustees of the British Museum. All rights reserved; **8.12** (*top*) National Museum of Ireland; (*bottom*) © Ashmolean Museum/Mary Evans; **8.13** (a) © Ashmolean Museum/Mary Evans; (b) after R. Harrison, *Symbols and Warriors* (Bristol, 2004), fig. 8.2 with modifications; **8.14** (a) © The Trustees of the British Museum; (b) After R. Harrison, *Symbols and Warriors*, fig. 8.3 with modifications; **8.15** After C. Marcigny et al., 'Découvertes récentes de l'âge du Bronze moyen dans le Département de la Sarthe (Pays-de-la-Loire)', *Revue archéologique de l'Ouest* 19 (2002), fig. 7; **8.16** Musée Maritime de l'Ile Tatihou, Photo: H.Paitier/Inrap; **8.17** After J. Waddell, 'Celts, Celticization and the Irish Bronze Age' from J. Waddell and E. Twohig (eds.), *Ireland in the Bronze Age*, fig. 60, courtesy of the

Office of Public Works, Ireland; **8.18** After J. Waddell, *The Prehistoric Archaeology of Ireland*; **8.19** hair-rings after J. Waddell, *The Prehistoric Archaeology of Ireland*; map after George Eogan, *The Accomplished Art* (Oxford, 1994), fig. 42; **8.20** National Museum of Ireland; **8.21** After D. Branderm and C. Burgess 'Carps-tongue problems' in *Durch die Zeiten* (Rahden 2008), figs 3 and 5; **8.22** © The Trustees of the British Museum

Chapter 9 opener: © The Trustees of the British Museum; **9.1** Coll. Musée de Vannes, fonds SPM, photo: Musée de Vannes; **9.2** After P. Northover, 'The Late Bronze Age metalwork: general discussion' in B. Cunliffe, *Mount Batten, Plymouth: A Prehistoric and Roman Port* (Oxford, 1988), fig. 40 with modifications; **9.3** Trevor Burrows Photography; **9.4** Museums Sheffield; **9.5** After B. O'Connor, 'Llyn Fawr metalwork in Britain: a review' in C. Haselgrove and R. Pope (eds.), *The Earlier Iron Age in Britain and the Near Continent* (Oxford, 2007), fig. 5; **9.6** After B. Cunliffe, 'Looking forward: maritime contacts in the first millennium BC' in P. Clark (ed.), *Bronze Age Connections* (Oxford 2009), fig. 6.10; **9.7** Museum of London; **9.8** Ian Cartwright/Danebury Trust; **9.9** © Crown copyright, English Heritage; **9.10** After B. Cunliffe, *Iron Age Communities in Britain*, fig. 21.6; **9.11** © Crown copyright, English Heritage; **9.12** After B. Cunliffe, *The Celts: A Very Short Introduction* (Oxford, 2003), figs 3 and 4, by permission of Oxford University Press; **9.13** After B. Cunliffe, *Facing the Ocean*, fig. 8.11, by permission of Oxford University Press; **9.14** drawing by Patricia Mallet © Leamington Spa Art Gallery & Museum (Warwick District Council); **9.15** © Ashmolean Museum/Mary Evans; **9.16** © The Trustees of the British Museum; **9.17** After R. A. Smith 'Two Early British Bronze Bowls', *Antiquaries Journal* 6 (1926) fig. 2, Society of Antiquaries of London; **9.18** After B. Cunliffe, *Iron Age Communities in Britain*, fig. A.14, based on drawings by Nigel Macpherson-Grant; **9.19** After B. Cunliffe, 'Looking forward: maritime contacts in the first millennium BC', fig. 6.4; **9.20** Author: various sources; **9.21** Crown copyright, Highways Agency; **9.22** © Skyscan.co.uk; **9.23** Ian Cartwright/Danebury Trust; **9.24** After B. Cunliffe, *Iron Age Communities in Britain*, fig. 6.2; **9.25** © The Trustees of the British Museum; **9.26** © English Heritage; **9.27** After B. Cunliffe, *Facing the Ocean* (2001), fig. 9.26; **9.28** After N. V. L. Rybot in Bulletin Société Jersiaise, 1937; **9.29** After B. Cunliffe and P. de Jersey, *Armorica and Britain* (Oxford, 1997), figs 35 and 42; **9.30** Research program C. Marcigny; collection Museum E. Liais, Cherbourg; photo: J.-M. Yvon; **9.31** After B. Cunliffe, 'Looking forward: maritime contacts in the first millennium BC', fig. 6.11; **9.32** After B. Cunliffe, *Iron Age Communities in Britain*, fig. 6.1 with modifications; **9.33** © National Monuments Service: Dept of Arts, Heritage and the Gaeltacht, Ireland; **9.34** After J. Waddell, *The Prehistoric Archaeology of Ireland*, fig. 9.14

Chapter 10 opener: © The Trustees of the British Museum; **10.1** After B. Cunliffe, *Iron Age Communities in Britain*, fig. 20.11; **10.2** © The Trustees of the British Museum; **10.3, 10.4, and 10.5** Danebury Trust; **10.6** Photo: Naomi Field; **10.7** After A. C. King and G. Soffe 'Internal Organization and Deposition at the Iron Age Temple on Hayling Island', *Proceedings of Hampshire Field Club and Archaeological Society* 53 (1998), fig. 3

Chapter 11 opener: The Great Pavement, Woodchester, Glos., painting by David S. Neal; **11.1** The Art Archive; **11.2** © Skyscan.co.uk; **11.3** After B. Cunliffe, *Iron Age Communities in Britain*, fig. 17.30; **11.4** After B. Cunliffe, *Iron Age Communities in Britain*, fig. 7.6; **11.5** After B. Cunliffe, *Iron Age Communities in Britain*, fig. 7.4, based on various sources; **11.6** Author; **11.7** After B. Cunliffe, *Iron Age Communities in Britain*, figs 10.3 and 10.4; **11.8** © National Museums Scotland; **11.9** © English Heritage; **11.10** After B. Cunliffe, *Iron Age Communities in Britain*, fig. 10.2; **11.11** © Crown copyright, English Heritage; **11.12** After D. Mattingly, *An Imperial Possession: Britain in the Roman Empire* (London, 2006), fig. 7; **11.13** © National Museums Scotland; **11.14** Bath Archaeological Trust; **11.15** After L. P. Louwe Kooijmans, *De Nehalennia-Tempel te Colijnsplaat* (Leiden, 1971), fig. 5 with modifications; **11.16** © Rijksmuseum van Oudheden, Leiden, The Netherlands; **11.17** Author: various sources; **11.18** After R. Brulet, 'The Continental Litus Saxonicum' in V. A. Maxfield (ed.), *The Saxon Shore: A Handbook* (Exeter, 1989), fig. 20; **11.19** Author: various sources; **11.20** Superstock/Getty Images; **11.21** After K. Booth, 'The Roman Pharos at Dover Castle', *English Heritage Historical Review* 2 (2007), fig. 14 © English Heritage; **11.22** © Crown copyright, English Heritage; **11.23** From C. R. Smith, *Report on excavations made on the site of the Roman Castrum at Lymne in Kent in 1850* (London 1852), 10; **11.24** After B. Cunliffe, *Facing the Ocean*, fig. 10.18, by permission of Oxford University Press; **11.25** © The Trustees of the British Museum; **11.26** After D. Mattingly, *Iron Age Communities in Britain*, 165, with modifications; **11.27** © Crown copyright, English Heritage; **11.28** (*top*) Ian Cartwright; (*bottom*) The Author; **11.29** The Great Pavement, Woodchester, Glos; painting by David S. Neal

Chaper 12 opener: © English Heritage; **12.1** © Crown copyright RCAHMS, Licensor www.rcahms.gov.uk; **12.2** Author: various sources; **12.3** © English Heritage Photo Library; **12.4** After S. Johnson, *Later Roman Britain* (London, 1980), fig. 8; **12.5** The Bodleian Libraries, University of Oxford, Bodl. Ms Canon Misc 378, fol 153; **12.6** Author: various sources; **12.7** After T. Champion, 'Chalton', *Current Archaeology* 59 (1977), 365; **12.8** Dept of Archaeology, University of Southampton; **12.9** After M. Millett and S. James, 'Excavations at Cowdery's Down, Basingstoke, Hampshire, 1978–81', *Archaeological Journal* 104 (1983), figs 37, 39, and 46; **12.10** After H. Härke

'Kings and Warriors' in P. Slack and R. Ward (eds.), *The Peopling of Britain: The Shaping of a Human Landscape* (Oxford, 2002), fig. 5.1, by permission of Oxford University Press; **12.11** © Norfolk County Council; **12.12** After S. C. Hawkes, 'The South-East after the Romans: the Saxon settlement' in Maxfield (ed.), *The Saxon Shore: A Handbook*, fig. 2.8; **12.13** After S. C. Hawkes, 'The South-East after the Romans', fig. 30; **12.14** © The Trustees of the British Museum; **12.15** After V. I. Evison, *The Fifth-century invasions South of the Thames* (London, 1965), map 5; **12.16** © English Heritage; **12.17** Author: various sources; **12.18** © Skyscan.co.uk; **12.19** From L. Alcock, *By South Cadbury, Is that Camelot?* (London, 1972), fig. 29, drawing by Dai Owen; **12.20** © The Trustees of the British Museum; **12.21** and **12.22** Author: multiple sources; **12.23** © The Trustees of the British Museum; **12.24** David Lyons/Getty Images; **12.25** After Ewan Campbell, *Continental and Mediterranean Imports to Atlantic Britain and Ireland*, AD 400–800 (York, 2007), figs 83 and 84; **12.26** © Crown copyright, reproduced courtesy of Historic Scotland www.historicscotlandimages.gov.uk

Chapter 13 opener: Richard T Nowitz/Getty Images; **13.1** © English Heritage Photo Library; **13.2** The Museum of National History in Frederiksborg Castle; **13.3** © English Heritage; **13.4** Author: multiple sources; **13.5** After M. Welch, *Anglo-Saxon England* (London, 1992), fig. 84; **13.6** © The Trustees of the British Museum; **13.7** After B. Cunliffe, *Facing the Ocean*, fig. 11.2; **13.8** Author: multiple sources; **13.9** © The Trustees of the British Museum; **13.10** Richard T. Nowitz/Getty Images; **13.11** Author; **13.12** Author; **13.13** Museum of London/The Art Archive; **13.14** © RCAHMS (John Dewar Collection), Licensor www.rcahms.gov.uk; **13.15** © Crown copyright, reproduced courtesy of Historic Scotland www.historicscotlandimages.gov.uk; **13.16** Alan Braby; **13.17** © Crown copyright, reproduced courtesy of Historic Scotland www.historicscotlandimages.gov.uk; **13.18** Author; **13.19** © National Museums Scotland; **13.20** Author: multiple sources; **13.21** Courtesy of Manx National Heritage; **13.22** National Museum of Ireland; **13.23** After S. Keynes 'The Vikings in England, c. 790–1016' in P. Sawyer (ed.), *The Oxford Illustrated history of the Vikings* (Oxford, 1997), 65, with modifications and additions; **13.24** After B. Cunliffe, *Wessex to AD 1000*, fig. 9.10; **13.25** © English Heritage; **13.26** © Ashmolean Museum/Mary Evans; **13.27** National library of Sweden, MS A135, 11r

The publisher apologizes for any errors or omissions in the above list. If contacted, they will be pleased to rectify these at the earliest opportunity.

INDEX